D1474044

A Reader's Guide
to the Short Stories of

STEPHEN CRANE

A
Reference
Publication
in
Literature

Everett Emerson
Editor

A *Reader's Guide*
to the Short Stories of
STEPHEN CRANE

Michael W. Schaefer

G.K. Hall & Co.
An Imprint of Simon & Schuster Macmillan
New York

Prentice Hall International
London   Mexico City   New Delhi   Singapore   Sydney   Toronto

G.K. Hall & Co.
An Imprint of Simon & Schuster Macmillan
1633 Broadway
New York, NY 10019

Library of Congress Catalog Card Number: 96-10593

Printed in the United States of America

Printing number:
1   2   3   4   5   6   7   8   9   10

Library of Congress Cataloging-in-Publication Data

Schaefer, Michael W., 1951-
   A reader's guide to the short stories of Stephen Crane / Michael W. Schaefer
     p.   cm. — (Reference publication in literature)
     Includes indexes.
     ISBN 0-8161-7285-4 (alk. paper)
     1. Crane, Stephen, 1871-1900—Criticism and interpretation.
   2. Short story.   I. Title.   II. Series.
   PS1449.C85Z824 1996
   813'.4—dc20
                                               96-10593
                                             CIP

This paper meets the requirements of ANSI/NISO Z39.48-1992

Contents

The Author   vii
Preface   ix

"And If He Wills, We Must Die"   1
The Angel-Child   5
The Blue Hotel   10
The Bride Comes to Yellow Sky   60
The Carriage-Lamps   81
The City Urchin and the Chaste Villagers   84
The Clan of No-Name   89
Death and the Child   99
An Episode of War   113
An Experiment in Misery   123
The Fight   138
The Five White Mice   143
Flanagan and His Short Filibustering Adventure   158
"God Rest Ye, Merry Gentlemen"   164
A Grey Sleeve   167
His New Mittens   171
An Indiana Campaign   177
The Kicking Twelfth   181
The Knife   185
A Little Pilgrim   189
The Little Regiment   195
The Lone Charge of William B. Perkins   203
The Lover and the Tell-Tale   207
Lynx-Hunting   211
Making An Orator   216
A Man and Some Others   220
Marines Signaling Under Fire at Guantánamo   230

The Monster   234

Moonlight on the Snow   266

A Mystery of Heroism   274

One Dash—Horses   285

The Open Boat   296

The Pace of Youth   352

The Price of the Harness   361

The Revenge of the *Adolphus*   371

The Second Generation   374

The Serjeant's Private Mad-house   381

Shame   384

"Showin' Off"   388

The Shrapnel of Their Friends   392

The Stove   395

This Majestic Lie   399

Three Miraculous Soldiers   403

The Trial, Execution, and Burial of Homer Phelps   407

Twelve O'Clock   412

The Upturned Face   417

The Veteran   427

Virtue in War   435

War Memories   440

The Wise Men   453

General Index   457

Index of Crane's Works   466

The Author

Michael W. Schaefer is an associate professor of English at the University of Central Arkansas, where he has taught since 1989. He holds an M.A. from North Carolina State University and a Ph.D. from the University of North Carolina at Chapel Hill. He has published articles on John W. De Forest, Ambrose Bierce, and Stephen Crane in various journals. He is currently at work on a book examining American Civil War fiction written by veterans of that conflict.

Preface

This volume offers a distillation of the large body of historical and critical information available as of the end of 1992 on Stephen Crane's short stories. It is intended as both a guide for the general reader and a research source for teachers and scholars with specialized interests. With these ends in view, each of the ensuing fifty-one chapters treats one of the pieces in Crane's *oeuvre* that most readers define as short stories. Deciding which pieces to include in such a book and which to omit is a simple matter in the case of many authors. However, in terms of genre classification and sheer numbers Crane's work poses a good deal of difficulty, and so it seems logical to discuss the principles of selection employed in producing these chapters before going on to a discussion of the material to be found in them.

There is, to begin with, the question of what is and what is not a short story. The case with Crane is similar to the one Lea Bertrani Vozar Newman faced with Nathaniel Hawthorne's work in the first volume of this series, *A Reader's Guide to the Short Stories of Nathaniel Hawthorne.* Like Hawthorne, Crane wrote many different kinds of pieces and tended to apply the terms *story, tale,* and *sketch* to them somewhat indiscriminately, making his own statements of definition inconclusive; and editors and critics since then have found clear-cut classification problematic in many instances. No one disputes, for example, that two of Crane's best-known pieces, "The Open Boat" and "The Bride Comes to Yellow Sky," are short stories, but a number of other works that first appeared in book form with these two in the 1898 William Heinemann volume entitled *"The Open Boat" and Other Stories*—including "An Eloquence of Grief," "The Men in the Storm," and "The Duel That Was Not Fought"—are classified as sketches by Fredson Bowers and Edwin H. Cady in the table of contents of Volume 8 of the University Press of Virginia edition of Crane's collected works. Similarly, most critics offer no objection to the usual classification of the pieces on the Spanish-American War that comprise the 1900 volume *Wounds in the Rain* as stories, but Neville Denny contends that they are sketches and therefore "have no bearing on the nature of [Crane's] creative writing," a view he justifies with the claim that in his short stories "Crane had powerfully felt personal experience to draw on" and that he lacked such felt experience where the *Wounds* tales were concerned (29). This is a questionable premise at best, for while one might legitimately argue that many of these pieces are closely based on Crane's firsthand newspaper reports of events of the war and that the line between journalism and fiction in them is thus somewhat indistinct, this very fact indicates that Crane did indeed have personal experiences to draw on, and no one who has read *Wounds* selections such as "War Memories" and "The Price of the Harness" carefully would be likely to dispute that Crane infuses them with a great deal of feeling related to that personal experience.

Confronted with numerous dilemmas of this type, I have relied on the parameters that Newman establishes in her Hawthorne volume. A piece is a short story for her purposes if it has an "identifiable narrative pattern" or a "viable narrative thread," which she defines as "a series of events that involve fictional characters who participate in and are affected by those events" (xii). The key words *narrative* and *fictional* here eliminate from consideration a number of Crane's disputable pieces, such as the three from *"The Open Boat" and Other Stories* mentioned above, because many are more straightforward descriptions than they are narratives; and because, as Cady points out in his introduction to Volume 8, some others that do exhibit a marked narrative line cannot really be called fiction due to their combination of journalism and invention (handled less expertly in these cases than in most of the *Wounds* volume)—an assessment first advanced by Crane himself (xxiv).

However, even after the application of these criteria there remain over ninety works that pass them. A volume that treated all of these would likely induce in the reader a stronger sense of exhaustion than of exhaustiveness, and so I have decided to consider only those pieces that by general critical accord represent Crane's "major" work in the short-story genre. For instance, I do not cover the Sullivan County sketches featuring "the little man"—which Crane himself regarded as "part fiction, part journalism" (Wolford 5)—or the Bowery sketches centering on Tommie, the younger sibling of Maggie and Jimmie in *Maggie: A Girl of the Streets,* even though they are frequent subjects of books and articles, because most critics treat them as apprentice work, more interesting for the light they shed on the development of Crane's characteristic themes and techniques as those appear in his later stories than for their intrinsic merit. I do thoroughly discuss the connections between all such omitted works and those under consideration in my chapters; readers who are interested in these pieces as freestanding examples of Crane's artistry will find Patrick K. Dooley's 1992 bibliography of Crane scholarship an excellent guide to discussions of them, as it is to every subject relating to Crane studies.

One other problem that presents itself in relation to genre definition in Crane's canon is length. While this problem concerns only one work, "The Monster," rather than the myriad above, it is no less knotty. In the strictest sense, at roughly 21,000 words this piece should be classified as a short novel, since according to C. Hugh Holman and William Harmon in *A*

Handbook to Literature the maximum length of a short story is 15,000 words, with the short novel measuring between 15,000 and 50,000 (442–43). Once again, however, the critics disagree about categorization. Crane himself referred to "The Monster" as a "novelette" (*Correspondence* I, 301); presumably following this lead, James Hafley likewise terms it a novelette (159), while J. C. Levenson calls it Crane's "last great short novel" (xi) and Christopher Benfey labels it a novella (228). On the other side, Robert W. Stallman calls it a story (332), a designation seconded by Marston LaFrance (206). Still another response is not to make a definitive distinction but rather just to acknowledge the complexity of the issue, as Chester L. Wolford does in describing "The Monster" as "the longest of Crane's short stories (or the shortest of his novels)" (44). To reach my own classification, I have applied a further distinction that Holman and Harmon make between the short story and the short novel, one more meaningful than length. A short story, they say, "is usually content to reveal a character through an action," whereas a short novel "is concerned with character development" (442). By this standard, I have classified "The Monster" as a short story and therefore covered it here, on the grounds that, as Donald B. Gibson points out (137–39), neither the protagonist, Dr. Trescott, nor the antagonist, the aggregate of townspeople for which the story is named, actually develops in character over the course of the narrative but rather just reveals the fundamental nature each has held since the outset.

The organization of the stories is alphabetical by title, with each chapter having six divisions. The first section presents the publication history, including where and when the story initially appeared and what Crane and his agents and publishers had to say to one another regarding these matters. The second details what is known or can be hypothesized about when and where Crane composed the story. The third part deals with sources and influences: what works by others—whether authors, painters, journalists, or historians—Crane may have relied on in conceiving and shaping the piece. The fourth section is a discussion of the relationship of the story to Crane's other works, including not only other short stories but also novels, sketches, poems, and journalism.

The fifth division presents all significant critical interpretations of the story and assesses its value for critics. As much as possible, I have organized this discussion into the various categories under which such interpretations can be classified—biographical, historical, philosophical, religious, psychological, formalist, deconstructionist, Marxist, and so on—and have put the interpretations in each category in the order of their original appearance in print.

The sixth section is a list of works cited. My purpose here is to provide a comprehensive bibliography for each story, which means that a number of books and essays must be cited in more than one chapter. To afford maximum convenience to the reader, when such cases arise I give full biblio-graphical information in each citation.

The sources for my texts are four volumes of *The Works of Stephen Crane*, edited by Fredson Bowers and published by the University Press of Virginia: Volume 5, *Tales of Adventure;* Volume 6, *Tales of War;* Volume 7, *Tales of Whilomville;* and Volume 8, *Tales, Sketches, and Reports.* While this edition has provoked a good deal of debate over certain of Bowers's editorial prac-tices, most of this controversy has focused on the novels *Maggie: A Girl of the Streets* and *The Red Badge of Courage;* the majority of critics accept Bowers's texts of the short stories as definitive. Readers who are interested in this argu-ment will find a thorough discussion of the drawbacks to Bowers's approach in David J. Nordloh's essay "On Crane Now Edited: The University of Virginia Edition of *The Works of Stephen Crane.*"

I am of course deeply indebted to the many Crane scholars whose learned, insightful, and humane work is covered in this book. I also owe many more personal thanks. I have often said that the most significant pro-fessional organization to which I belong is my own English department, and never was this fact clearer to me than during my extended work on this pro-ject. The two chairs under which I served during this time, Phillip Anderson and Terrance Kearns, provided invaluable leave time and other forms of administrative support. Raymond-Jean Frontain, Henry N. Rogers III, Conrad Shumaker, and Wayne Stengel offered critical insight and aid on an almost daily basis, which I can never adequately repay. Similar help and wise coun-sel, for which I am similarly grateful, came generously from Linda Arnold, Gary Davenport, Richard Gaughan, Jonathan Glenn, Jefferson D. Henderson, Frances Jeffery, John Lammers, Robert Lowery, Bonnie Melchior, Lou Ann Norman, Ellen Powers Stengel, and Rebecca Williams. Equal measures of thanks are due to Charlene Bland and Barbara Whisnant of the University of Central Arkansas English Department office, to Sandy Breeding of the University of Central Arkansas's Torreyson Library, to Richard C. Noggle, to Ian King and Joseph Lombardi of Hendrix College, to Eric Sterling of Auburn University at Montgomery, to Richard D. Rust and Joseph Viscomi of the University of North Carolina at Chapel Hill, and especially to Lisa L. Nanney of the North Carolina School of Science and Mathematics.

My most personal thanks go to Lynn R. Ramage, whose nurture and understanding are, in the most real sense, responsible for whatever is valu-able in this book.

Finally, I offer my deepest gratitude to Catherine Carter and James Hatch, my editors at G.K. Hall, and to Everett Emerson, editor of the series to which this volume belongs and scholar, mentor, and human being without equal. Their acuity and helpfulness have been exceeded only by their patience and good humor as I have wended my seemingly endless way through this book, and I appreciatively and respectfully dedicate it to them.

Works Cited

Benfey, Christopher. *The Double Life of Stephen Crane.* New York: Knopf, 1992.

Bowers, Fredson, ed. *Tales, Sketches, and Reports.* Vol. 8 of The University Press of Virginia Edition of *The Works of Stephen Crane.* Charlottesville: University Press of Virginia, 1973.

Cady, Edwin H. Introduction. *Tales, Sketches, and Reports* xxi–xli.

Denny, Neville. "Imagination and Experience in Stephen Crane." *English Studies in Africa* 9 (1966): 28–42.

Dooley, Patrick K. *Stephen Crane: An Annotated Bibliography of Secondary Scholarship.* New York: G.K. Hall, 1992.

Gibson, Donald B. *The Fiction of Stephen Crane.* Carbondale: Southern Illinois University Press, 1968.

Hafley, James. "'The Monster' and the Art of Stephen Crane." *Accent* 19 (1959): 159–65.

Holman, C. Hugh, and William Harmon, eds. *A Handbook to Literature.* 6th ed. New York: Macmillan, 1992.

LaFrance, Marston. *A Reading of Stephen Crane.* Oxford: Clarendon, 1971.

Levenson, J. C. Introduction. *Tales of Whilomville.* Vol. 7 of the University of Virginia Edition of *The Works of Stephen Crane.* Ed. Fredson Bowers. Charlottesville: University Press of Virginia, 1968, xi–lx.

Newman, Lea Bertrani Vozar. *A Reader's Guide to the Short Stories of Nathaniel Hawthorne.* Boston: G.K. Hall, 1979.

Nordloh, David J. "On Crane Now Edited: The University of Virginia Edition of *The Works of Stephen Crane.*" *Studies in the Novel* (North Texas State University) 10 (1978):103–19.

Stallman, R. W. *Stephen Crane: A Biography.* New York: George Braziller, 1968.

Wertheim, Stanley, and Paul Sorrentino, eds. *The Correspondence of Stephen Crane.* Vol. 1. New York: Columbia University Press, 1988.

Wolford, Chester L. *Stephen Crane: A Study of the Short Fiction.* Boston: Twayne, 1989.

A Reader's Guide
to the Short Stories of

STEPHEN CRANE

"And If He Wills, We Must Die"

Publication History

This story made its first appearance in the July 28, 1900, issue of the *Illustrated London News* (117:121–22); its initial American publication came in the October 1900, issue of *Frank Leslie's Popular Monthly* (50:533–38). It was first published in book form in 1902 by the English house Digby, Long in the posthumous *Last Words*, a volume of previously uncollected pieces assembled by Crane's common-law wife, Cora (Bowers clxxxviii). In 1926, it appeared in volume 9 of *The Work of Stephen Crane* (12 vols., New York: Knopf, 1925–27), edited by Wilson Follett; and in 1963 Thomas A. Gullason included it in *The Complete Short Stories and Sketches of Stephen Crane* (Garden City, N.Y.: Doubleday).

Circumstances of Composition

As Fredson Bowers has shown, all four of Crane's tales about the Twelfth Regiment of the fictional Spitzbergen army, the series to which this story belongs, were written in England, at Crane's successive homes Ravensbrook, in Surrey, and Brede Place, in Sussex. Crane composed them at some point between January 13, 1899, when Joseph Conrad in a letter to Crane refers to one of them, "The Upturned Face," as an idea that Crane has not yet had time to work on, and early November of that year, when Crane began sending these pieces to his agent, James Pinker (clxxii). "'If He Wills'" was probably written third in this series; Bowers offers evidence that "The Kicking Twelfth" was first and "Face" was last and quotes a letter from Pinker of January 9, 1900, asking for a copy of "the second Spitzbergen story, "The Shrapnel of Their Friends" (clxxx).

Sources and Influences

Very little has been written on either Crane's personal or literary sources for this story. As far as is known, in neither the Greco-Turkish nor the Spanish-American War did he witness or hear of the kind of "defense until the last man" that he depicts here. He probably came close enough, however, and likely encountered the kind of stoic attitude in the face of near-certain death

that he has his soldiers adopt in this story, on June 7–9, 1898, when he participated in the U.S. Marines' defense of Camp McCalla, on a ridge above
Guantánamo Bay, Cuba, against a large Spanish force. Most of Crane's biographers note that the death and burial of a Marine surgeon, John Blair Gibbs,
during this engagement gave Crane the idea for "The Upturned Face"
(Stallman 363), so the possibility of a link between this battle and another of
the Spitzbergen tales is not farfetched. However, as Eric Solomon argues, a
lack of specific sources for this story may have been a conscious artistic
choice on Crane's part, a result of his desire in this and the other Spitzbergen
tales to create "his own picture of war, this time without . . . the restraint of
historical fact"—in other words, to write "war fiction as [he] believed it
should be organized," aimed at emphasizing the universal characteristics of all
wars, of revealing that "[t]he baptism of fire, fear, death, courage, [and] horror are qualities of all war and all war fiction" (79). Two details that can be
specifically identified, however, are the names Crane gives to his mythical
country and its enemy. Spitzbergen and Rostina, as Robert W. Stallman notes,
are Norwegian islands in the Arctic Ocean (605).

In terms of literary influences, the closest analogues of which Crane might
have been aware are Ambrose Bierce's Civil War stories, collected in *Tales of
Soldiers and Civilians*. In several of these, such as "A Son of the Gods," "An
Affair of Outposts," and "One Kind of Officer," soldiers sacrifice themselves for
no higher principle than obedience to orders, just as they do in "'If He Wills.'"
As Solomon points out, though, Bierce's handling of such situations is always
ironic, and Crane's story is not. Crane, unlike Bierce, Solomon says, means for
the reader to see a man such as the sergeant not as a deluded fool who gives
his life and those of his men for no purpose but rather as "a perfect soldier
who obeys his impossible orders in the best tradition of the service. . . . The
sergeant is a good soldier, the orders are clear, the men must die. This is the
way war is" (79).

Relationship to Other Crane Works

"'If He Wills'" is most closely linked to the other three stories devoted to the
Twelfth Regiment of the Spitzbergen Army, "Kicking Twelfth," "Shrapnel of
Their Friends," and "Face." A number of critics have noted that this connec-
tion is based on more than just the same regiment's appearing in all four and
Lieutenant Timothy Lean's being the protagonist in three of them. They read
the stories as stages in a single narrative line that is so clear that Chester L.
Wolford proposes that the four collectively be regarded as forming a "com-
posite novel" that moves from a focus on the whole, fully manned regiment in
"Kicking Twelfth," to the regiment decimated by combat in "Shrapnel," to sixteen men in "'If He Wills,'" to just two men, Lean and the adjutant, in "Face,"

with each stage in this tightening of focus moving the reader closer to "'the real thing'" of combat (77). Milne Holton and Solomon also take this composite view. Holton sees the stories as combining to depict the gradual education of the whole regiment in "the awful reality of war" (268), while Solomon sees them as focused more specifically on Timothy Lean's education. In "Kicking Twelfth," he says, Lean learns about the exhilarating side of combat through his participation in the regiment's first two, successfully concluded, engagements. In "Shrapnel" he begins to discover the illogical side of war when the regiment breaks and runs after being mistakenly shelled by their own artillery. In "'If He Wills'" Crane moves from the illogic of combat to its patent injustice, "in sharp contrast to the earlier tales of the series," in depicting the deaths of sixteen brave men as a result of their courageous adherence to unreasonable orders. Although Lean does not appear in this story, Solomon asserts that "it seems clear that the episode is meant to be part of the lieutenant's military education"; looked at in isolation, it "may seem to lack a point," but as a step in Lean's initiation and "as a part of Crane's final view of war, the tale stands for the ugly side, for the reality of violent painful death." Then in "Face" Lean reappears to confront this reality directly in having to bury a friend under fire (79–80). (Solomon offers the same analysis on pp. 126–27 of his book-length study of Crane's work, published five years after the article quoted here.)

Solomon is also the only critic to address the possibility of connections between "'If He Wills'" and Crane's non-Spitzbergen works. He notes that in this story and the other three in the series Crane turns away from the techniques and the larger historical and social concerns that occupied him in the war stories of *The Little Regiment* and *Wounds in the Rain* and returns to "the approach that produced *The Red Badge of Courage*"—that is, he focuses only on the moment of combat, showing "the Spitzbergen army set apart from history or society. The sole field of endeavor is the battlefield; everything else is extraneous" (78). The point of this full-circle movement in his final war stories, away from "the insensitivity of *Wounds in the Rain*" and back to the "great care for human values" that marks *The Red Badge*, Solomon concludes, is that Crane has discovered "a middle way that conceives of war, like life, as both a glory and an obscenity." Crane himself has learned, as he has Lean discover, that "war is all things to all men—beauty, a test, a muscular way of life, and, finally, a horror" (80).

Critical Studies

Most of what has been written on this story links it with the other three Spitzbergen tales and therefore is covered immediately above in "Relationship to Other Crane Works." Two critics, however, make particular note of elements that distinguish "'If He Wills'" from its companions. Holton asserts that although this story shares with the others a "purified style," marked chiefly by darkened imagery, "bare and functional" language, and a "relentlessly closing" focus (266–67), it has a notably narrower focus and a darker tone than the previous two, and is thereby set apart from them. In both "Kicking Twelfth" and "Shrapnel" Crane's focus is on the regiment as a whole and on two successful attacks; in "'If He Wills'" he narrows to a single squad and depicts its failure in combat, and the circumstances of that combat bring the absurdities of war into higher relief. In this case, in contrast to that of the prior two stories, the enemy is unseen, there is no compelling tactical reason for the squad to defend the house, and many worthy men, including the estimable sergeant, die in this pointless defense. These features lead Holton to conclude that in this third Spitzbergen story "there is everywhere a growing sense of behavioral and environmental disorder" (268). Wolford likewise notes Crane's shift in focus from the aggregate character of the regiment in "Kicking Twelfth" and "Shrapnel" to the more individualized members of the squad in "'If He Wills'"; he says that the final effect is that the reader responds more strongly to the violent absurdity of war in this third story as a result of witnessing the deaths of individuals rather than the seeming loss of mere cogs in a vast demonstration depicted in the previous two stories (78).

Works Cited

Bowers, Fredson. Textual Introduction. *Tales of War*. Vol. 6 of The University of Virginia Edition of *The Works of Stephen Crane*. Ed. Fredson Bowers. Charlottesville: University Press of Virginia, 1970, xxxvii–cxci.

Holton, Milne. *Cylinder of Vision: The Fiction and Journalistic Writings of Stephen Crane*. Baton Rouge: Louisiana State University Press, 1972.

Solomon, Eric. *Stephen Crane: From Parody to Realism*. Cambridge: Harvard University Press, 1966.

———. "Stephen Crane's War Stories." *Texas Studies in Literature and Language* 3 (1961):67–80.

Stallman, R. W. *Stephen Crane: A Biography*. New York: George Braziller, 1968.

Wolford, Chester L. *Stephen Crane: A Study of the Short Fiction*. Boston: Twayne, 1989.

The Angel-Child

Publication History

This story was first published in the August 1899 issue of *Harper's New Monthly Magazine* (99:358–64); it was the initial installment in this periodical's Whilomville series by Crane. Then, like the other twelve pieces in the series, it appeared in a book entitled *Whilomville Stories* that Harper & Brothers published in August 1900 in America and November 1900 in England (Bowers 103). Pioneering Crane editor Wilson Follett placed it in volume 5, issued in 1926, of *The Work of Stephen Crane* (12 vols., New York: Knopf, 1925–27), and it was collected again in 1963 in *The Complete Short Stories and Sketches of Stephen Crane* (Garden City, N.Y.: Doubleday), edited by Thomas A. Gullason.

Circumstances of Composition

Although this story was the first to appear of the series of thirteen tales set in the fictional town of Whilomville that Crane produced for *Harper's New Monthly Magazine*, it was probably the second composed, after "Lynx-Hunting" (Levenson liii), given that Crane sent "Lynx" to his American agent, Paul Revere Reynolds, on January 27, 1899 (*Correspondence* II, 422–23), and then on January 31 sent him "The Angel-Child," calling it "another story . . . which belongs to the Whilomville series" (*Correspondence* II, 424). Since the closest we can come to dating "Lynx-Hunting" is sometime after January 19, 1899 (Levenson xlvi), and since Crane sent "Angel" to Reynolds on January 31, he must have written the latter story in late January, while he was living at his first English home, Ravensbrook, in the town of Oxted, Surrey.

Sources and Influences

Crane's first biographer, Thomas Beer, claims that the climactic episode of this story, the shearing of the Margate twins' long curls, stems from two incidents in Crane's own life. Beer says that when Crane was eight and still being forced by his mother to wear his hair long, his older brother Edmund gave him a quarter to get a barber to cut it for him; the result is alleged to have greatly upset their mother (42). Then, fifteen years later—Beer gives the date as sometime around September 1, 1894, and the place as Albany, New York—Crane is supposed to have followed in Edmund's footsteps, giving money for haircuts to two small boys whose mothers had forced them to wear their hair long in imitation of Little Lord Fauntleroy, a literary character Crane loathed, thereby causing consternation among the local maternal arbiters of juvenile fashion (111).

Various later biographers such as Edwin Cady (46) and Robert W. Stallman (8) have repeated these stories, but because Beer fails to say where he got this information—as is the case with most of his assertions (*Correspondence* I, 6–12)—he is not a totally reliable source. J. C. Levenson points out that Edmund's being the protagonist in one version and Stephen's filling that role in another suggests that these stories may be variants of an apocryphal, free-floating family legend that Crane blended with the memories of another person, his common-law wife, Cora. Levenson sees the story as partly a product of Crane's enjoyment of his new domesticity with Cora and of the intimacy between them that this condition fostered, which led them to share childhood reminiscences and impelled Crane to blend these memories into a new series of tales focused on domesticity and childhood. Evidence for this view in the case of this particular story, Levenson continues, is that the angel-child herself is named Cora, that her parents—an unassertive artist father and a highly assertive and status-conscious mother—are closely modeled on the real Cora's parents, and that the parents' habit of frequently giving the spoiled angel-child money to keep her quiet and out of their hair was a hallmark of Cora's own childhood (xliv–xlv). Corroboration for this view comes from the memoirs of Edith Richie Jones, who was a frequent houseguest of the Cranes' during this period. She recalls Crane saying to her that most of the Whilomville tales were based on stories Cora had told him of her childhood (60). Milne Holton accepts this view and points out that Crane's focus on Cora here and in another Whilomville story, "The Stove," constitutes "a remarkably imaginative departure from the resources of his own experience," although Holton also notes that ultimately Crane's decision to use his live-in paramour's real name for his character may have had some relevance to his own experience, since in both stories, as perhaps in his life during this period, it is Cora's "willfulness" that "upsets the rather rigid and unreasonable pretensions and rituals" of the conventional society into which she is introduced (217).

Literary sources for this story are harder to come by than personal ones. It is likely that Crane was drawing somewhat parodically on recollections of saccharine stories about characters like the angel-child he had read as a boy, since Stallman quotes him as saying that about the time of his Edmund-engineered haircut he became enamored of a little girl character named Little Goldie Brighteyes, "and I wrote a story then which I called after this fascinating person" (8). However, Stallman does not identify his source for this quotation or the provenance of this character.

Relationship to Other Crane Works

All the Whilomville stories are loosely connected in that all focus on Jimmie Trescott and his family and friends, but "Angel-Child" is most closely linked to "The Lover and the Tell-Tale" and "The Stove" because these three work variations on the same subjects: Jimmie's love-hate relationship with Cora, his pretty and spoiled cousin from the city; and the havoc Cora wreaks in both the child and adult worlds of Whilomville—in this case by persuading Jimmie and his playmates, both male and female, to get their hair cut short, to the consternation of their fashion-conscious mothers. Given this particular kind of havoc, Levenson sees this story as the proper introduction to the whole Whilomville series and says that therefore its being the first published although it was the second composed, after "Lynx-Hunting," was the correct aesthetic decision. "Lynx," he explains, constitutes "a farewell to themes of man and nature that run through Crane's [other] work," whereas "Angel-Child" initiates the focus, maintained in the rest of the series, on children in society and on several themes that come into sharp view as a result of that new focus. In this story as in the others,

> the children act spontaneously and see things as they happen; the women, who set the tone of the town, cry after illusion, sentiment, and rank; Dr. Trescott, and by implication a few other men of his sort, stand at the calm center of things and offer a norm of the good and reasonable. (xlv)

Critical Studies

In a letter of February 1, 1899, accompanying his submission of "Angel-Child" to his English agent, James B. Pinker, Crane offers only the tepid comment "We like it a little" (*Correspondence* II, 425). Three days later he promises Pinker that "[t]he next story will be a better one" and tells him that if he too is not impressed with it he should "bury it in the heather i.e. send it to Blackwood" (*Correspondence* II, 428)—in other words, send it to *Blackwood's Edinburgh Magazine*, which Crane regarded as less discriminating and less prestigious than the English periodicals in which his work usually appeared. Plainly, Crane's own opinion of this story was not high, and a number of later critics have concurred. H. E. Bates regards it and the Whilomville series in general as being "as commonplace as calico" and thus an indication of the diminished state of Crane's powers in this late stage of his life. The method of these stories, he says, "is that of any tenth-rate provincial reporter without the wit to determine whether what he is doing is good or bad" (148).

More temperately, James B. Stronks calls "Angel-Child" and the other Whilomville pieces "thin and slight" as a result of their trafficking in mundane situations that do not evoke the "nerveless intensity" of Crane at his best, but goes on to point out that they are still preferable to much of the rest of the literature about children that appeared in this era (343). Ellen A. Brown argues that this preferability is no accident—that in "Angel-Child" and the other Whilomville stories Crane is deliberately countering the thick strain of sentimentality in most contemporary children's literature, particularly the works of Frances Hodgson Burnett, author of *Little Lord Fauntleroy* and many others, and Harriet Lothrop, the perpetrator of the *Five Little Peppers* series. Crane may be occasionally "moved by a sentimental desire to see children in a romantic, soft, and fluffy light," Brown says, "but his compensating practicality always insists as well that he record the realistic, less pleasant aspects of childhood" (105).

Two other critics acknowledge the flaws of "Angel-Child" but find redeeming features. John Berryman calls it "a bore" but sees it as belonging to an interesting triad, the other members being "The Monster" and "The Blue Hotel," in which Crane seeks to work out his guilt regarding his family. Noting the Crane family stories about Edmund's and Stephen's giving little boys money to have their curls trimmed in defiance of their parents' wishes, Berryman says that in "Angel-Child" Crane renders himself similarly—and doubly—guilty by splitting himself between two figures who both suffer persecution at the hands of Whilomville's respectably fashion-conscious citizens. The first of these is Cora's father, who gives her the money, and the second is the barber Neeltje, who carries out her orders (239–40). Gullason places the story in the broader context of a number of familial themes. Neither "Angel-Child" nor any of the other Whilomville stories is individually outstanding, he says, but taken collectively they effectively "illuminate a number of universal truths about children, family life, and one's former home town." This being the case, Gullason proposes that these stories be regarded as a kind of loose novel that presents "a vibrant and full world" and "demonstrates further . . . Crane's range and versatility" (483).

Levenson takes an even more positive view of both this story and the series as a whole, seeing them as offering perhaps the sunniest vision to be found anywhere in Crane's *oeuvre*. Regarding "Angel-Child," he points out that "[t]he world is obviously well ordered in which unwanted haircuts can seem to be 'disasters'" (lvi). In this world of Whilomville, then, in contrast to that depicted in most of Crane's work, "[t]he great evils, whether of character or of the cosmos, never come into question, and the lesser evils of sentimentality and foolishness can be corrected by a simple realism" (lv). Three other critics, however, see the great evils as not absent from this world but rather lurking just below the seemingly sunny surface. Leslie Fiedler reads Crane's handling of little Cora as an early attack on the sentimentally idealized "image of the golden girl child" that is deeply ingrained in the American psyche, in that Crane invites the reader to look beneath her angelic appearance and see her as she really is: "a source of mischief and deceit" (333). Eric Solomon discerns "manifold overtones of serious comment about human behavior in general," including an indictment of pride as manifested in Cora; of the sources of that pride—"the corrupting forces of money, beauty, and the need to be a queen"; and of the mob hysteria that underlies both the children's willingness to follow Cora's dictates and the near maniacal reaction of the adults to the children's haircuts. The similarity between the children's and the adults' hysterical behavior is especially damning, Solomon notes, in that it "heightens the absurdity of the supposedly mature social leaders" (209–10). Chester L. Wolford looks in a somewhat different direction, dismissing the plot focusing on Cora's machinations as "slight" and emphasizing instead one of its consequences, the threatened ostracism of Neeltje by the enraged Margates, as the locus of Crane's real attack on the values of Whilomville and small-town America in general. Neeltje, in Wolford's view, is a more comic but no less pointed version of Henry Johnson in "The Monster," in that Neeltje, like Johnson, disturbs "the complaisant calm of Whilomville"—on the surface by cutting the twins' hair and at a deeper level by being a foreigner with an unpronounceable name—and therefore becomes a source of terror and anger for the town's middle-class mandarins (52–53).

Few readers offer favorable comments on Crane's technique in this story. David Halliburton commends its blend of a "matter-of-fact style" with "authorial self-awareness, a large element of lightness, and sharp-tongued irony," saying that this mixture is highly appropriate to the material. In a more specific vein, James Nagel notes that Crane here consistently employs religious imagery to characterize Cora's parents' attitude toward her, whereas in describing her interaction with the other children he relies heavily on pagan imagery, thus drawing attention to the gap between her parents' "reverential" view of her and the true nature of her behavior. This gamesomely dialectical pattern, according to Nagel "provides the principal source of humor in a story involving only mildly comic events" (137).

Works Cited

Bates, H. E. "H. E. Bates on Stephen Crane." *Stephen Crane's Career: Perspectives and Evaluations*. Ed. Thomas A. Gullason. New York: New York University Press, 1972, 146–50.

Beer, Thomas. *Stephen Crane: A Study in American Letters*. New York: Knopf, 1923.

Berryman, John. *Stephen Crane*. New York: Sloane, 1950.

Bowers, Fredson. Textual Introduction. *Tales of Whilomville*. Vol. 9 of The University of Virginia Edition of *The Works of Stephen Crane*. Ed. Fredson Bowers. Charlottesville: University Press of Virginia, 1968, 103–26.

Brown, Ellen A. "Stephen Crane's *Whilomville Stories*: A Backward Glance." *Markham Review* 3 (1972):105–09.

Cady, Edwin H. *Stephen Crane*. Rev. ed. New York: Twayne, 1982.

Fiedler, Leslie. *Love and Death in the American Novel*. New York: 1960.

Gullason, Thomas A. "Stephen Crane's Short Stories: The True Road." *Stephen Crane's Career: Perspectives and Evaluations*. Ed. Thomas A. Gullason. New York: New York University Press, 1972, 470–86.

Halliburton, David. *The Color of the Sky: A Study of Stephen Crane*. Cambridge: Cambridge University Press, 1989.

Holton, Milne. *Cylinder of Vision: The Fiction and Journalistic Writings of Stephen Crane*. Baton Rouge: Louisiana State University Press, 1972.

Jones, Edith R. "Stephen Crane at Brede." *Atlantic Monthly* 194 (1954):54–61.

Levenson, J. C. Introduction. *Tales of Whilomville* xi–lx.

Nagel, James. *Stephen Crane and Literary Impressionism*. University Park: Pennsylvania State University Press, 1980.

Solomon, Eric. *Stephen Crane: From Parody to Realism*. Cambridge: Harvard University Press, 1966.

Stallman, Robert W. *Stephen Crane: A Biography*. New York: George Braziller, 1968.

Stronks, James B. "Stephen Crane's English Years: The Legend Corrected." *Papers of the Bibliographical Society of America* 57 (1963):340–49.

Wertheim, Stanley, and Paul Sorrentino, eds. *The Correspondence of Stephen Crane*. 2 vols. New York: Columbia University Press, 1988.

Wolford, Chester L. *Stephen Crane: A Study of the Short Fiction*. Boston: Twayne, 1989.

The Blue Hotel

Publication History

This story was first published in America in two parts on November 26 and December 3, 1898, in *Collier's Weekly* (22:14–16; 14–16). That it ran in its full version here was due to an accident; *Collier's* had first agreed, in April 1898, to run only a shortened version, which evidently Crane produced but the magazine's staff mislaid at some point before September 1898, precipitating a decision to run the full text rather than wait for another abridgment (Stronks 346).

However, this chain of events was not the only difficulty Crane experienced in getting this story into print; it was instead just the last in a long series of discouragements. Crane had originally suggested to his American agent, Paul Revere Reynolds, that he sell the story to *Harper's Magazine*, but this periodical rejected it, as did the *Century* and *Scribner's Magazine*. The *Atlantic Monthly* was prepared to publish it if Crane would agree to offer a novel or a volume of Western tales to the publishing house Houghton, Mifflin, but Crane was unwilling or unable to do so (*Correspondence* I, 336–37); and thus "The Blue Hotel," in Robert W. Stallman's words, "ended in a ten-cent weekly, not in a quality magazine" (*Biography* 343). The story next appeared in America in the 1899 collection *"The Monster" and Other Stories*, published by Harper & Brothers, and then in 1901 in the Harpers' English edition of this book (Bowers clxxxv). In 1926, it was included in volume 10 of *The Work of Stephen Crane* (12 vols., New York: Knopf, 1925–27), edited by Wilson Follett. Among the many more recent collections of Crane stories in which it appears, the most notable are *Stephen Crane: An Omnibus* (New York: Knopf, 1952), edited by Stallman, and *The Complete Short Stories and Sketches of Stephen Crane* (Garden City, N.Y.: Doubleday, 1963), edited by Thomas A. Gullason.

Circumstances of Composition

Crane wrote this story during late 1897 and early 1898, while he was living at his first English home, Ravensbrook, in the town of Oxted, Surrey. In a December 20, 1897 letter from that location to Reynolds, Crane says that "The Blue Hotel will come to you in about two weeks" (*Correspondence* I, 318). This promise proved overly optimistic, though, for Crane did not send the story to Reynolds until February 7, 1898, saying in his accompanying letter that "[t]o my mind, it is a daisy" (*Correspondence* I, 336). The delay was evidently time well spent; J. C. Levenson notes a number of changes for the better Crane made from his first to his final draft. The innkeeper's original name, "Renigan," becomes "Scully," a change that deepens the character by virtue of the latter's being a "more neutral, less obviously generic [Irish] name." The son's name shifts from "Jimmie," which Crane frequently uses for characters closely based upon himself, as in the Whilomville stories, to "Johnnie," an indication that Crane is detaching himself from a level of "sympathetic involvement" with this character that would obscure the meaning of the story. The Easterner's last name alters from "Blank" to "Blanc," a shift that produces very little change in significance but that meaningfully emphasizes white, the color of nothingness, "against which the blue of the hotel is Scully's brilliant counter gesture." And finally, Crane methodically pared away "the signs of omniscience and theatrical manipulation" that he permitted in his early drafts, "so that appearances alone might convey all the significant details" (ci).

Sources and Influences

Crane's first biographer, Thomas Beer, asserts that the framework of this story came directly out of Crane's trip to the West as a correspondent for the Bacheller syndicate in the first half of 1895. Sometime in January or February, Beer says, Crane saw an actual blue hotel declaring its position against the winter landscape of the Nebraska plains (113), and he quotes a letter Crane wrote describing his own interposition in a bar fight at the Hotel Lincoln in Lincoln, Nebraska, on February 13. In attempting to break up this contretemps, Crane explains,

> I offended a local custom. These men fought each other every night. Their friends expected it and I was a darned nuisance with my Eastern scruples and all that. So first everybody cursed me fully and then they took me off to a judge who told me that I was an imbecile and let me go; it was very saddening. Whenever I try to do right, it don't [sic]. (113–14)

Most of Crane's later biographers, including Joseph Katz (xiv), Edwin Cady (*Stephen Crane* 48), Robert W. Stallman, and Levenson, agree that these events formed the basis of "The Blue Hotel." Stallman corrects Beer's dating, saying that the bar fight took place on February 12, 1895, rather than February 13 and that the sighting of the actual blue hotel definitely took place after this event, but he concurs that Crane "transposed this experience" into the fight between the Swede and Johnnie that forms the centerpiece of the story (*Biography* 130–32). Levenson extends Stallman's point, noting that Crane not only transposed but transmuted and inverted this experience when he put it into fiction: in his depiction of the Swede "the Eastern scruples were crossed with fear and the ludicrous misreading of local custom turned into a gruesome absurdity" (xxxiv), thus creating a protagonist who is the victim of his own illusions rather than naiveté (xcvi); and in his handling of the Easterner he produces a subplot about nonintervention, in direct opposition to his own real-life Eastern interference (xcvi).

Unfortunately, in following Beer's lead in this matter these worthy critics fall victim to their own form of naiveté—the understandable desire to pin down the sources of an author's artistry in a powerful story—for, as Stanley Wertheim and Paul Sorrentino point out, there is a strong probability that Beer fabricated these biographical details, to the extent of writing "Crane's" letter about the bar fight himself (*Correspondence* I, 6–10; "Thomas Beer" 2–16). (In fairness to these critics, though, it must be borne in mind that the full extent of Beer's mythologizing did not come to light until after they had completed the assessments quoted above.) Absent any verification outside Beer's work for these details, the critic's best course is the one chosen by Bernice Slote, James Colvert, and Edwin Cady (in a later piece than the one mentioned in the previous paragraph): an examination of the journalism Crane produced during his Western trip as a more reliable source of biographical underpinnings. Slote finds no evidence in these writings that Crane did see an actual blue hotel, and so she ascribes this idea to Beer's wishful imagination (198), but she does find considerable similarity between Crane's newspaper account of the town of Kearney, Nebraska, and his later rendition of the setting of "Blue Hotel," Fort Romper, including the fact that Kearney's original name was Fort Childs (197). Colvert notes further similarities between Fort Romper in the blizzard and Crane's description of his arrival in Eddyville, Nebraska; and he and Cady both point to a piece entitled "Nebraska's Bitter Fight for Life," in which Crane details the alternating hardships of drought and blizzard that the state's farmers endured in 1894–95 (Colvert, "Stephen Crane" 114). In his correspondent's persona, Crane questions a Lincoln County farmer, who tells him that he has received neither state nor federal aid for his ruined crops. "'How did you get along?'" Crane asks, to which the farmer replies, "'Don't git along, stranger. Who the hell told you I did get along?'" (*Tales, Sketches* 418). This dialogue, Cady says, is "[a]n obvious part of the unspoken donnée for 'The Blue Hotel,'" an exchange that "provides ironic counterpoint to the activities of every character in this short story" (Introduction xxxix).

Erminio Neglia provides a more general biographical donnée. In his view, the Swede is obsessed with dying, for reasons that the story does not make fully clear. Neglia links this condition to a similar obsession in Crane's own makeup, pointing to his seemingly suicidal daring in several battles during the Spanish-American War. Inevitably, Neglia asserts, "Crane's hallucinatory state of mind during those acts of apparently senseless defiance reminds us of the Swede's mental state in the Nebraska town" (22).

Perhaps the most ingenious tracing of sources is that performed by Jon M. Kinnamon, who contends that the bartender who witnesses the Swede's murder is modeled on Henry James, with whom Crane was friendly during his years in England. The bartender, Kinnamon notes, is named Henry, and he is averse to violence to the point of being sickened by the gambler's stabbing of the Swede yet is too passive to take any physical action of his own to prevent such violence, a combination that in the eyes of the Easterner and the cowboy makes him partly culpable for the Swede's death and that, according to Kinnamon, "characterizes James quite well" (163). When the bartender runs for help after the gambler, who is aware of his passive nature, makes fun of him by ostentatiously wiping his bloody knife on the bartender's own towel, the reader is shown that this bartender "is someone who cannot face up to violence alone; his intestinal fortitude is minimal" (163). These conditions, Kinnamon concludes, indicate that Crane's intention is to ridicule "the Jamesian life-style" of passivity, of observation rather than action (160).

It is possible to pick up stronger overtones of Huck Finn's voice than of Crane's in Beer's apparently ventriloquial account of "a judge who told me that I was an imbecile and let me go" and his lament that "it was very saddening" because "whenever I try to do right, it don't"; and several critics suggest that in his choice of phrasing Beer unwittingly reveals not Crane's biographical sources for "Blue Hotel" but rather his chief literary ones. Jules Chametzky suggests that Tom Sawyer, as Mark Twain depicts him in *Huckleberry Finn*, is one prototype for the Swede, given that both characters insist on making their experience conform to what they have read in meretricious novels rather than attempting to understand their actual circumstances (186). John Berryman (208) and Brenda Murphy both identify Chapter 31 of Twain's *Roughing It* as a source for the Swede's circumstances, for in this chapter the narrator takes shelter in a rural hotel from a flash flood and subsequent blizzard and finds himself stranded there for eight days with the landlord and two unpleasant fellow-guests, an obstreperous Swede and a drunken bully. The landlord attempts to placate the bully with drink, but the bully responds by accusing the landlord of plotting to murder him. When he begins shooting to thwart this supposed plot, the landlord's wife appears and cows him. As Murphy points out, transmutation of source material is once again the hallmark here, for Crane changes the tone of this knockabout comic scene to one of deadly seriousness, merges the Swede and the bully into one figure, and has his landlord's wife appear only after the fight, when she is powerless to do anything to stop the violence that has been set in motion (40–44).

Going farther afield for literary influence, Lars Ahnebrink sees Crane as presenting the Swede's death as the result of a "concurrence of forces which made it impossible for [the Swede] to behave in any other way," a view that Ahnebrink feels Crane may have got from Tolstoy's *War and Peace*. He points specifically to Tolstoy's presentation of the series of chance events that prevent Pierre Bezukhov from carrying out his plan to assassinate Napoleon (358–59). Stallman sees the story as deriving its "germinal conception" from a frequent artistic practice of Robert Louis Stevenson's—the establishing of "a certain scene and atmosphere" to "suggest the correlative actions and persons for that particular locality," followed by the use of those characters and their actions "to express and symbolize" that locality ("Revaluation" 248).

A final literary—or, perhaps more properly, subliterary—influence on this tale is of course the myriad of dime-novel Westerns that were so popular in Crane's day and with which he represents the Swede as having distorted his perceptions. A more detailed discussion of Crane's parody and inversion of the conventions of this genre and how those techniques bear on the significance of this story will be found below, in "Critical Studies."

Relationship to Other Crane Works

Since "The Blue Hotel" has generated an enormous amount of critical commentary that generally agrees in regarding it as among Crane's most significant and most characteristic works, we should not be surprised that it has been linked with almost every other piece in Crane's canon. The most readily perceptible connections of both theme and setting are with several of his other Western tales. Milne Holton asserts that the story is probably Crane's most powerful exploration of a theme that pervades all his Westerns, beginning with "A Man and Some Others": the conflict that inevitably results from Easterners' and Westerners' different ways of seeing and thus responding to their circumstances (128). Ralph Ellison notes much the same point, although, linking "Blue Hotel" most closely to "The Bride Comes to Yellow Sky," he sees this difference and ensuing conflict as resulting more specifically from the characters' failure to understand the speed at which social change occurs in America. Given this speed, he says, the final meaning of both these stories is that "human fate is a creation of human confusion" (74). Frank Bergon notes similarities between these two stories and one of Crane's last Western tales, "Moonlight on the Snow," regarding the theme of social change and its casualties. Crane's point in all three, he says, is that "one mode of creating order in the face of chaos"—the mores of Eastern civilization—has indeed already replaced a prior mode—the gunfight—but neither one is fully efficacious in the realm of human fate. Crane shows, Bergon says, that both codes are necessary in their proper times and places, but "neither is inclusive or powerful enough to enable man to understand or control his essential condition." The behavior of the characters in all three stories demonstrates that "[v]iolence, injustice, and chaos can break through the ways of civilization as easily as they do through the ways of barbarism" (*Artistry* 124).

Many other critics take the view that in terms of theme "Blue Hotel" is most closely related—in dialectical fashion—to the other of Crane's best-known Westerns, "The Bride Comes to Yellow Sky." Maurice Bassan regards these two as "complementary in color and in emotional effect," in that "The Bride" "explodes the myths of the Wild West, [whereas] 'The Blue Hotel' confirms them" (7). Chester L. Wolford likewise sees "The Bride" and "Blue Hotel" as complementary, being "comic and tragic faces of the same misperception": Scratchy is humorously discomfited when he finds the rules of the West changed, while the Swede comes to grief by thinking that these rules have not changed when in fact they have (*Study* 34). Robert Glen Deamer, on the other hand, notes a similarity between these two that sets them apart from Crane's other Westerns. All the other stories in this group, he explains, are about what he calls Crane's "western stance"—that is, the "self-assurance, magnanimity, and unpretentiousness of a true westerner." Instead, "Bride" and "Blue Hotel" are about the encroachment of civilization on that stance; together they reveal that "Crane, like anyone emotionally involved in the myth of the West, was saddened, enraged, and embittered by the advance of modernity" ("Stance" 140–41).

Looking beyond Crane's Westerns for connections, Holton notes that the terrified Swede in "Blue Hotel" seems to have his original in the Swedish farmhand who is equally demented by his fear of the barn fire in "The Veteran," while Levenson sees the story as closely connected in terms of theme and mood to the Greco-Turkish War story "Death and the Child," which Crane wrote at about the same time as "Blue Hotel." Despite their very different settings, Levenson says, Crane's goal in both stories is to make the reader aware that "the world is vast, incomprehensible, and indifferent to the minor conflicts of humankind." Where the stories diverge is that in "Death" there is a single protagonist and a clear point of view, whereas in "Blue Hotel," with its multiple protagonists, Crane does not afford the reader any clear insight into the action, not even in the narrator's statements. Levenson does not regard this failure as a flaw; he sees it instead as the linchpin of Crane's theme of man's epistemological and ontological limitations: in "Blue Hotel," unlike in "Death," Crane presents not "a straightforward plot of discovery" but rather "a narrative in which characters and narrator attain to partial truths about an event, [in which] only the reader is able to comprehend its multiplicity" (xcv-xcvi).

Numerous critics also link "Blue Hotel" to the other story most often classified among Crane's best and best-known, "The Open Boat." Donald Pizer notes that these two may readily be regarded as the complementary poles of Crane's career-long meditation on the idea of human community, since in both cases men threatened by the forces of indifferent nature can only survive by working together, which they do in "Open Boat" and fail to do in "Blue Hotel" (27). Marston LaFrance makes a similar point, noting that despite their physical differences, both the hotel and the dinghy are simply pieces of "the world's external furniture, . . . and whatever each becomes depends upon human actions." Viewed in this light, through the actions of the characters the dinghy becomes a symbol of the accomplishment of human community, while the hotel becomes a concomitant symbol of the failure of community (224). Robert Gleckner takes a slightly different tack, focusing on the "conceit" of the Swede as he walks through the snowstorm, convinced that he can live without the community of the hotel, with which he has just engaged in acts of mutual rejection. Gleckner sees this passage as Crane's most explicit statement of one of his most frequent themes, which is also apparent in "Open Boat" and "The Little Regiment"—the human being's powerful if sometimes misguided will to continue to exist despite his or her utter insignificance in the realm of an indifferent and deadly universe (271).

Colvert regards "Blue Hotel" and "Open Boat" as connected through the perfect harmony between structure and theme that Crane achieves in both. The structure of both stories "is defined by the tension between two ironically divergent points of view: the narrow and deluding point of view of the actors and the enlarging and ruthlessly revealing point of view of the observer-narrator" ("Structure" 200). In "Open Boat" this tension is revealed at the beginning of the story, in the castaways' view of their situation as deadly dangerous, as opposed to the narrator's comment that this situation would look "picturesque" if seen from a balcony. In "Blue Hotel," the same tension is clearest as the Swede walks triumphantly from the hotel to the saloon: he regards the blizzard as a suitable concomitant to the conquering quality of his own will, whereas the narrator takes a distanced view of the Swede and all men as "lice" clinging to a "space-lost bulb." This structural tension derives thematic import, Colvert says, because "the meaning evoked by the ironic projection of the deflated man"—man in the narrator's distanced view—"against the inflated man"—man in the protagonist's view—leads to Crane's essential point: "the consequence of false pride, vanity, and blinding delusion" ("Structure" 200). If the protagonist is able to achieve the narrator's distanced, objective vision of himself, as Colvert argues the correspondent does in "Open Boat," he matures and survives. If he rejects that vision, as the Swede does, he destroys himself ("Structure" 207–08).

Stallman sees this statement of man's conceit as providing an equal link to *The Red Badge of Courage*, for he regards Henry, although he survives while the Swede does not, as remaining in this same condition of conceit at the end of that novel (*Biography* 175). Colvert also makes such a connection, seeing the story as "an ingenious adaptation" of the theme of this novel and also of some of the early Sullivan County sketches: "his radical sense of man's alienation in a problematical universe." Like Fleming and the protagonist of the sketches, who is known only as "the little man," the Swede is in conflict with nature and imagines that he can defeat it; the difference between these characters is that, although Henry and the little man end up looking foolish for this belief, their foolishness does not provoke their death, as is the case for the Swede ("Stephen Crane" 115).

Bergon, Russell Nye, and George Monteiro draw connections to another, earlier novel, *Maggie*. Bergon notes that "Blue Hotel" and *Maggie* are formally and thematically related: in both cases the death of the central character is the result of a collaboration precipitated by and followed by other characters' refusal to accept responsibility for their actions, and in both the main characters also collaborate in their own deaths by refusing to abandon their romantic illusions about life (*Artistry* 74). Nye sees these two stories as paired in their exploration of a twofold concept of evil. *Maggie* principally examines "social evil," which develops from institutions rather than individuals but nonetheless causes individuals to injure one another; and "Blue Hotel" delineates the evil released by the forces of nature. Crane regards these forces as indifferent in themselves, Nye says, but he presents them as obtruding in human relationships and provoking people to treat one another cruelly. In this case, the Swede's death is "the logical result of a series of happenings which were harmless in themselves" but were driven by "fate, the blind force of a naturalistic universe, which . . . has invaded the world of society" (54). Monteiro points out that the role of Scully's whiskey as proximate agent in the Swede's downfall creates a "powerful temperance message" that links "Blue Hotel" to *Maggie* and also to Crane's other Bowery novella, *George's Mother* (6). He also notes that in Crane's era Swedes were reputed to be heavy drinkers and that blue was the color associated with the temperance movement, adding a further layer of irony to a Swede's ending up drunk while seeking relief from the storm in a blue-colored house of refuge (6).

Gerald Warshaver identifies another agent in the Swede's destruction, the misleading representations of the West in popular culture and folklore, which the Swede has allowed to shape his expectations of what he will find in Nebraska. Warshaver notes that this dangerous reliance on popular misconceptions is one of Crane's earliest concerns, first appearing in the sketch "Sullivan County Bears," in which Crane depicts neophyte hunters as holding exaggerated ideas of the belligerence and ferocity of bears due to folktales that veteran hunters have passed along to them (6). Max Westbrook similarly connects "Blue Hotel" to the Sullivan County sketches, seeing them all as studies of "excessive fear and consequent distortion," which lead their protagonists to grief by causing them to react to "a part of existence as if it were the essence of existence" ("Affirmation" 227).

Wolford also links the theme of misperception of reality in "Blue Hotel" to Crane's earliest work, pointing out that it is the central concern in the Sullivan County sketch "The Mesmeric Mountain" and even in Crane's first known work of fiction, "Uncle Jake and the Bell-Handle," which he wrote when he was fourteen. In these early cases, however, these misperceptions are comically "one-dimensional," with the reader in a position of superior understanding and simply enjoying the characters' discomfiture, whereas "Blue Hotel" presents multiple layers of misperception, with the reader being misled along with the characters and at the story's end "offered several ways to perceive the truth" with none being singled out as more likely than the rest (*Study* 31). Perhaps the most ingenious, not to say tortuous, tracing of connections through the theme of agency is Maxwell Geismar's. Geismar, following John Berryman's lead (Berryman 211–14), reads the story as Crane's working out and universalization of his own Oedipal guilt for his rejection of his father's values: in his view, the Swede wills his own death as his punishment for revolting against the hotel's beneficent "father," Scully. This pattern, Geismar says, is the same one in which Henry Johnson and Dr. Trescott engage in "The Monster" (120–23).

Critics have not limited themselves to Crane's stories in identifying thematic connections with "Blue Hotel." Seeing the Swede as responding to the idea of his own death with an inextricable mixture of fear and desire, Stallman (*Biography* 159) and Christopher Benfey (234) both regard the story as more closely linked to poem 56 in Crane's *Black Riders* volume than to any other of his works. This poem reads as follows:

> A man feared that he might find an assassin;
> Another that he might find a victim.
> One was more wise than the other. (10:35)

In addition to such discussions of primarily thematic links, "Blue Hotel" has not lacked for examinations of technical connections to other Crane pieces. Neal Osborn points out that this story and "Moonlight on the Snow" are the two clearest instances of Crane's frequent use of names that carry thematic weight. In "Blue Hotel" the Easterner's name, Blanc, can translate to "blank," an apt description of that character's "civilized ineffectuality," while the town's name, Fort Romper, reflects "the story's paradoxical combination of manly force with childish irresponsibility." Similarly, the surname of the gambler in "Moonlight," Larpent, suggests his nature through its closeness to "serpent," a connection reinforced by his being described as "forked-tongued" and expanded upon by the narrator's occasional use of satanic imagery to characterize him. These "serpentine-satanic associations" further connect the two stories, Osborn concludes, in that the gambler in "Blue Hotel" closely resembles Larpent in terms of "theme, plot, and role"; he argues that this association should prompt the reader of "Blue Hotel" to "vigorously discount the chorus of sympathy" the Easterner and the cowboy express for the gambler at the end of the story and instead assign him a full share of responsibility for the Swede's death (10).

James Nagel links the story to "A Man and Some Others" in terms of point of view, noting that in both stories Crane limits the key fight to the perspective of an Easterner not fully involved in it, with the goal of rendering the action fragmented and confusing in order to create "the dramatic intensity of a person actually on the scene" (51). Nagel also points out that the design Crane employs in this story—opening with a description of sensory details and closing with an ironic comment—is one he uses frequently, beginning with the Sullivan County sketches and *Maggie*. In all these works, but most powerfully in "Blue Hotel," Nagel says,

> [t]he lack of background information, the absence of explanations of the motivation or meaning of the initial scene, has the effect of intensifying interest in sensory details, from which such understandings must be derived. The abrupt introduction of empirical data reflects the fragmentary nature of life with its discontinuous units of experience. The ironic endings often provide a center of meaning for the preceding events. (135)

David Halliburton likewise traces connections to Crane's method of introduction in this story, but he sees the closest parallels in *Red Badge*, "Open Boat," and "The Bride Comes to Yellow Sky." In the openings to all of these stories, he notes, nature is linked to the human characters on the scene and those characters perceive "something foreboding" in nature (206). However, "Blue Hotel" is unique among these pieces because in it a human artifact, the hotel, dominates the natural environment and is the locus of the feeling of threat in the landscape, establishing early on that the danger here proceeds not from nature but from humans' construction of the "social modes of domination and submission" that the Swede will shortly encounter within the hotel (208). Focusing more narrowly, Holton points out that two specific devices Crane uses here, the cash register that carries a good deal of symbolic import and the final sentence in which a character denies his responsibility for the foregoing actions, first occur together, albeit in a lighter vein, in the earlier short story "The Pace of Youth" (24). Sounding one of the very few negative notes to be found in discussions of this story's connections to the rest of Crane's canon, Donald B. Gibson asserts that "Blue Hotel" belongs in a group with the Sullivan County sketches, *Maggie*, and *Red Badge*, the unifying factor being Crane's egregious failure to control his tone in all these cases (xiv).

Critical Studies

Critics have generally been lavish in their praise of this story, regarding it as one of Crane's best and, in many cases, one of the best short stories in the entire American canon. Even the frequently curmudgeonly H. L. Mencken found it a first-rate example of the form, and of Crane's particular adeptness with that form. The Swede's adventure at the hotel and saloon, culminating with his death, Mencken asserts, is "by no means a phenomenon *in vacuo*" but rather "obviously the last scene in a long drama: the life of a nobody"; Crane makes the reader feel that the death "is the fit end to a long series of events, all bound together by chains of occult causation," and the writer's great gift is that he conveys this feeling in an elliptical yet comprehensible manner. "A novelist would have tried to describe those events," Mencken says, "to account for them, to relate them intelligibly," but Crane makes them all readily apparent in the climax: "[h]e depicted that climax with a few strokes of outline and flashes of colour, and at once the whole drama was revealed, its beginning as well as its end, its inner meaning as well as its overt shape" (qtd. in Gullason 96).

Crane specialists are equally laudatory. Gullason calls "Blue Hotel" not only "the darkest of Crane's tragedies" but also one of his best due to its tonal complexity—its embrace of parody, satire, and comedy in addition to tragedy; its "almost Dostoevskyean" psychological insight; and the "inevitable" nature of its action, which links it to Greek tragedy, a connection strengthened by Crane's use of a chorus, consisting of Scully, Johnnie, the cowboy, and the Easterner, to "foreshadow the coming events and help to establish the various moods of the story" (480–81). Cady and Bergon find it especially praiseworthy in the context of its genre. Cady honors "Blue Hotel," and "The Bride" as well, for presenting as no other Western stories do "the reductive sensibility of a realist . . . contemplating the absurdities and indecencies of that neoromantic sensibility which was then busily incubating what would eventually burgeon as Horse Opera in all its glories" (Introduction xxxix). Bergon similarly asserts that Crane's may be the only Westerns that possess high literary value, with "Blue Hotel" at the apex of this group, due to their determination to "make us aware of the tensions and terrors normally obscured by the formulas of popular fiction" (Introduction 1).

Given such assessments, it is not surprising that a number of critics focus their readings of "Blue Hotel" on the ways in which it comments on Westerns and on their role in creating visions of the Wild West that are at odds with the reality of that region. Donald Vanouse sees the story as exemplifying Crane's belief that "popular traditions about the glamorous or monstrous past can limit our awareness" of the unchanging impulses toward violence and wildness that underlie those traditions, particularly those concerning the West. The men in the hotel, Vanouse says, "make the folk historian's mistake" in their failure to see the "gorgeous, terrible violence of the past" as an expression of such impulses, and it is this failure that brings the Swede to grief. In Crane's view, according to Vanouse, these impulses "are the truth of legend," and, properly understood as such, "they are fountains of beauty and strength as well as sources of murderous passion and farcical misfortune"; however, without that clear understanding they lead only to the two latter qualities (425). James L. Dean regards Crane as taking a more wholly negative view of Western traditions than Vanouse does. He argues that Crane intends the town's name, Fort Romper, through its connection to a child's garment, to be a comment on the childishness of his characters, a way of showing them to be "boyish men" who play the games of the West "with all the seriousness and all the improvised rules common to backyard childhood," with the difference that this supposedly grown-up form of seriousness often has fatal consequences (260).

Deamer sees Crane's point as somewhat more complex. The crucial fact with regard to the Western mythical ideal of "courage and nonchalance in the face of death," he asserts, is that the story is expressly *not* a Western. He points out that, "[a]s Johnnie says, Fort Romper simply is not *out West*: it is civilization, the East," and that Crane wishes the reader to recognize this fact and therefore grasp that "the hellishness—the cowardice, the fear, the cheating, the hypocrisy, the greed, the violence—of this story is the product not of the West but of the civilization of which Scully is so enthusiastic a proponent" ("Myth" 122). Jamie Robertson responds to this reading by arguing that the story is not just a condemnation of civilization but is instead "a continuation of Crane's [multistory] examination of the ideal of rugged individualism encouraged by the myth of the West," a myth that the Swede accepts as fact but that the civilized Easterner rejects. Crane's point, Robertson says, is that the Swede needs to move beyond the conventions of this literary myth and forge genuine human relationships, but he refuses to do so. The Easterner, by contrast, has detached himself from this myth, but that stance is not entirely positive either, since the cost of his detachment is his unwillingness to intervene in the fight between Johnnie and the Swede and his concomitant understanding of that unwillingness as one of the causes of the Swede's murder. Nevertheless, Robertson concludes, Crane regards this tragedy as a price that must be paid in order to attain clear vision, for any sort of involvement inevitably produces distortions that may lead to still more dire consequences (255–56). Deamer responds in turn to Robertson with the contention that Crane himself is not to be equated with the Easterner, is not to be seen as accepting this figure's detached, outsider's stance as the only feasible approach to the situation; rather, Crane is critical of this "civilized" attitude as the primary cause of the Swede's death—as is the Easterner himself, in Deamer's reading, in the concluding section ("Stance" 126).

Bergon sees "Blue Hotel" as perhaps the first and certainly the best example of what might be called the nihilist Western, reflecting "a deep cynicism that accompanies the discovery that everything is a game and nothing is certain—even in the supposedly frank and candid West." In support of this view, Bergon points out that in terms of Western codes the Swede can be regarded as "the dude who is to be initiated into the ways of Western life" and who, as such, "does everything right and gets everything wrong." When Scully claps him on the shoulder, for example, the gesture is meant as a ritual welcome to the West, but when the Swede later performs the same ritual on Scully and the gambler its meaning has changed. The result of such shifts, Bergon says, is a "nightmare Western" in which no code can be relied on, with the result that the supposed "values of the Old West collapse, dread is loosed, and all the comforting conventions of the Western get turned inside out." In this "world of shifting meanings," the Swede is a doubly ironic figure, in that he is on the one hand a savage, an outsider who provokes the community's latent violence; while on the other hand, in trying to be a frank, honest Westerner in the heroic cowboy mold, he also "represents noble values." Whereas the actual cowboy cannot see the point of the Swede's fight with Johnnie, the Swede is in fact fighting for the most hallowed of legendary cowboy virtues, honor, and it is through this fight that he achieves a "moment of self-transcendence" as he stands alone in the blizzard. The ironies multiply yet again, however, Bergon continues, when the Swede dies at the hands of the gambler, who is "the town's true hero" in that his action drives home the point, so to speak, that "[t]here is no place in the community for the atavistic values of the Old West as adopted by the Swede. The individualism and self-sufficiency learned from nature," which are the principles the Swede espouses as he walks to the saloon through the blizzard, "destroy social values and breed isolation, narcissism, and violence," and so the gambler assumes the heroic role of the defender of his community from the outside savage. Crane thereby reveals, Bergon contends, not only the drawbacks of the Swede's "Western" stance, but also the horror behind the Western tradition of the quietly effective, nononsense hero; the reality is that this figure is here a cold-blooded murderer. Once again the conventions of the Western are turned inside out, and in "such a world of shifting meanings, there can be no certain understanding or moral judgment" (Introduction 23–27).

Sister Mary Anthony Weinig and Wolford offer analyses of Crane's efforts in this story to link the conventions of the Western to older myths. Weinig notes that Crane uses many of the conventions of epic poetry here, including repeated stock epithets for the characters, frequent military metaphors, a depiction of the Swede as a "grim counterpart of the roistering Herakles" when his fear changes to aggression after his drink with Scully, and a kind of Greek chorus comprised of Scully, the cowboy, and the Easterner. Crane's purpose in these allusions, Weinig explains, is the same as that of later writers who similarly hark back to the epic tradition, such as James Joyce and T. S. Eliot; all seek to "draw into relation the heroic past and the sordid, or at least unheroic present, with implicit commentary on the paltriness of the latter" (7). Building on Weinig's analysis, Wolford says that "Blue Hotel" derives a large part of its "universality and greatness" ("Eagle" 261) from Crane's use of elements drawn from the related genres of epic and classical tragedy. Noting that epics frequently depict the end of a heroic age, he reads the story as an epic depicting the passing away of the values of the American West, and he focuses primarily on the Swede as a classical tragic hero within that epic. Although his vision of the world he has entered is false, the Swede is such a hero, Wolford argues, because he, unlike the rest of the characters, sees that world as "a place that still holds out the possibility for individual heroism, for honesty, for truth" ("Eagle" 262). He manifests this kind of individual heroism in what he sees as his courageous accusation of Johnnie—courageous because he believes that everyone else will oppose him—and in his willingness to stake his life on this demand for honesty, a demand that only fails, finally, because the world of the American West "does not live up to the [heroic] quality of [his] vision" ("Eagle" 262–63).

These conditions, Wolford says, give the Swede a particularly marked resemblance to one specific tragic hero, Bussy D'Ambois, the eponymous protagonist of a Jacobean tragedy by George Chapman. Each of these figures is "willing to act upon his concept of what is true and honest in the world of deceit, . . . willing to dare, even to defy the fates, and consequently as well as paradoxically to rise as he falls." Chapman's and Crane's notion of what constitutes heroic behavior is unconventional, Wolford acknowledges, but their protagonists remain true to that concept and so are "elevated to the highest tragic stature: the giant among men" ("Eagle" 264). This stature is part of what gives this story about the end of the West its epic quality, for within this tragic context the death of the Swede signifies the death of the "childlike but heroic innocence of the West, [the] belief in the dream or myth of an individual-centered world where a man might act and act heroically" ("Eagle" 270–71). What is left when the Swede dies is a more paltry present, "the new world of the group," which Wolford identifies as "Christian-Roman" as opposed to the "Homeric" world of the older West. In this new world there can be neither courage nor hope, because here "no man can assert individuality, break the rules"; the final tragedy of the story is that there can now be no more tragedy, since that condition requires individualism ("Eagle" 273). (Wolford also presents this reading in one of his book-length studies, *The Anger of Stephen Crane,* 100–14).

Several other studies likewise interpret "Blue Hotel" as having epistemological and ontological ramifications well beyond the Western genre, a view predicated on the narrator's assertion that any room anywhere can be the scene of tragedy or comedy, which implies that Crane is more concerned with his characters' minds and the actions they are impelled toward than he is with the specific setting in which these minds and actions are found. In a reading separate from the one discussed above, Wolford says that the story's theme is a series of complex, crucial misperceptions regarding order and chaos. Scully's rules of hospitable conduct in the hotel constitute an effort to establish order as a bulwark against the chaos of the blizzard raging outdoors; the Swede errs by perceiving the hotel as instead a locus of chaos, upon which he imposes his own order, and then he errs again, fatally, by presuming that the saloon is in the same condition and will likewise bend to his rules (*Study* 32–33). Charles Swann also focuses on the story as pondering the dangers of humans' efforts to impose their own ideas of order upon the chaos of experience. The story's main theme, he says, which he considers a frequent one in Crane's canon, is human beings' notion that they can, "as it were, put a frame round their perceptions of the world in order to make some 'sense' of their experience and 'sense' of themselves." Crane's view, Swann explains, is that doing this framing means "they are living a fiction" but that this mode of existence is an attractive alternative to experiencing life directly, without such a frame, since "madness and irrationality are often the result of confronting the chaos" that is unframed, unmediated experience. However, he concludes, the story's ending makes the point that constructing such a frame is equally fraught with danger and offers at best only temporary shelter from chaos, for in this case the Swede's fiction, his "version of the wild, dangerous West," ironically ceases to be a fiction; it "comes to life and kills him" (101).

George W. Johnson offers a similar reading, although his premise is that the story is not so much about a conflict between order and chaos as it is about two incompatible forms of order. Through Scully's code of hospitality, which proceeds from his conception of himself as gentlemanly and respectable, the Swede, who initially is terrified due to his belief that the hotel operates by the Western code of violence, is led to believe that "the social forms of Romper serve rather than threaten him." This code as he understands it then clashes with that of the saloon, which mandates that one not attempt to impose himself upon others and prescribes death as the penalty for violation of this rule. The Swede is thus first discomfited and then destroyed by "the absence of conventions he can count on" (254–55), Johnson concludes—a view not far from Bergon's.

Eric Solomon also focuses on issues of self-conception and social forms. He sees the fundamental themes of the story as "the search for identity and the desire of the outcast to define himself through conflict with a society" (257). The Swede fails in this quest due partly to his own "internal contradictions" (257) and partly to the falsehoods within the society with which he seeks conflict. This shared responsibility is illustrated, Solomon argues, through the fact that in "Blue Hotel" Crane does not follow his usual practice of depicting two worlds, those of illusion and reality, but rather presents three: the Swede's internal world, which is composed wholly of illusions that he likely derived from his reading of dime novels; the world of the hotel, which partakes of both the mythical West and the real version; and the world of the saloon, which is wholly the real West. In the hotel, Solomon says, the men engage in some of the activities of Western myth, such as gambling and fighting, without facing the realities that should underlie those actions, such as paying one's gambling debts and acknowledging that fighting can lead to murder. Thus, despite the surface Western nature of their behavior, these characters are not the "strong, silent men of action" of the conventional Western; when faced with reality they prefer talking to acting (260). The Swede, however, does not realize that the hotel is, in its own way, "as much a parody of reality as are [his own] melodramatic cliches of barroom violence and sudden death" (261), and the denizens of this world fail in their responsibility to help the Swede see their illusions as well as his own. As a result, when he defeats Johnnie he erroneously believes that he has mastered the Wild West, and this belief gets him killed when he seeks further definition of himself through conflict in the truly real West of the saloon, where men act rather than talk, where they do gamble for money and fight to the death.

With the lack of solid shelter or an avenue of escape presented in these readings, a considerable range of critics treat "Blue Hotel" as an espousal of some form of determinism. J. W. Shroeder considers the presence of this philosophy a drawback. He argues that the story is marred by what he sees as Crane's reductive Naturalistic view of man as a thing and the universe as indifferent and his habit of tailoring his writing simply to express that view, which appears in the Easterner's final assessment. This analysis, Shroeder says, falsifies the rest of the story, which does not bear it out but rather depicts the Swede's death as "a remarkable effort of the will-to-destruction" (122). This opinion notwithstanding, most critics who discern elements of determinism offer a positive evaluation of the story. Ahnebrink sees it as a particularly clear example of the mixture of determinism and fatalism that he regards as informing the whole of Crane's canon, in which "the deterministic forces of heredity and environment" are always shown to be operative and yet "the fates of the characters appear to be arbitrarily contrived rather to rise logically" from these forces (193). Charles Child Walcutt discerns a similar mixture, reading the story as "a satire on causation in which the action is the argument," by which he means that the Swede is clearly fated to die due to "his craven and ignorant heart," a fact that would constitute a tragedy were the action not so clear that there is no mystery about this fate. What this action reveals is that the Swede and the other characters have wills and ethics, which they use, but such use scarcely constitutes choice, since their "'choices' entangle them in nets of circumstance from which they cannot be extricated," with the result that the "conventional notion of a moral order presided over by the forms of public morality is made indefensibly ludicrous." This result, Walcutt says, leaves the reader caught between "indignation with conventional morality" and "the pity and terror of tragedy," a combination that is Crane's personal version of naturalism, which does not insist that a particular end is fated to happen but rather simply holds "that men's wills do not control their destinies" (75).

James T. Cox, Richard Keenan, and John Conder all contend that the story reveals Crane to be not a mixer of philosophical positions, as Ahnebrink and Walcutt would have it, but rather a doctrinaire determinist. Basing his reading largely on his discernment of patterns of religious and color imagery, Cox argues that the story's burden of meaning is that once a chain of actions is set in motion no one can stop or alter it, and thus no one is truly responsible for the Swede's death. Keenan likewise derives his position from a close reading of Crane's visual effects. He points out in particular that when the Swede accuses Johnnie of cheating, Crane juxtaposes this "disorganization and loss of control of the men, their speech and actions marked by fragmentation and loss of continuity," with the playing cards lying in disorder on the table. As the "game" now becomes "physical and atavistic rather than mental and rational," the wind from the now-open door blows these cards, an image that to Keenan suggests that the men are no longer in control of the game of their lives. "The violent forces of nature," he says, "clash with the imaginative fantasy of the Palace Hotel, and rational control, like the playing cards, is dashed helplessly by the force . . . of elemental nature"—in the case of the fight, the elemental, ungovernable nature of the men themselves (267).

Conder grounds his deterministic reading on the seeming indeterminacy of the Easterner's final commentary, with its assertion that all the men in the Palace Hotel sinned in not helping to steer the Swede away from his fate. These remarks are open to multiple interpretations, Conder says, because the issue of sin that the Easterner brings up seems to indicate that Crane intends the proceedings to have a moral dimension, and critics have argued endlessly over the nature of that dimension. For Conder, however, the Easterner's also calling the story's events "the apex of a human movement" places them in the realm of determinism and thus renders moral debate moot. Conder supports this contention by noting that Crane gives the reader no means for judging right and wrong; he neither divulges Johnnie's reasons for cheating nor explains why the Easterner refuses to come to the Swede's defense despite his knowledge that the Swede's accusation is warranted (34–36). Crane's ultimate purpose in these withholdings, Conder continues, is to present the characters as types rather than individuals and to show that each man's behavior is dictated by his type: the Swede is the credulous reader of dime novels, the Easterner is a man of rumination rather than action, and so on. And beneath such types, the fight reveals "a common savagery" in all the men. The result, Conder concludes, is that the Easterner is not Crane's spokesman regarding morality but does express the author's own view in his implications of determinism, since prior to this pronouncement Crane has designed the story to lead up to this character's expression of "a classic modern vision," which is "the Hobbesian paradox that undoes liberty with causation. That human movement whose apex is the Swede's death may be the result of characters performing 'freely-willed' actions, but each action is reducible to conditions"—type and innate savagery—"over which the character has no control" (40–42).

In response to such purely deterministic readings, many critics argue that one or more of the characters are in fact the agents of the outcome, are morally culpable. Cady, LaFrance, and Wolford assign the bulk of the blame to the Swede. Cady takes the simple and straightforward view that, regardless of what large forces may be perceived as operating in the story, no "force" dragged the Swede to Fort Romper and compelled him to see it as the Wild West in the first place; these were volitional acts on his part (*Stephen Crane* 155). LaFrance regards the Swede as a variation on the typical Crane protagonist—a man who fears an unknown situation and inflates that fear by his own imaginings of that situation—who follows such a characters' typical curve of action—from fear to confrontation to deflation when he realizes that his fears were out of all proportion to the reality of his situation—with several significant variations. The Swede faces the unknown West, which he has made terrifying by allowing his imagination free rein in the realm of the dime novel, but, unlike most Crane protagonists, he cannot actually confront this unknown quantity—as Henry Fleming is able to confront war in *The Red Badge*, for instance—because in his case that unknown quantity has no real existence; it is entirely a product of his imagination. This circumstance leads to a further significant variation on Crane's usual patterns: "Blue Hotel" is "Crane's only important story in which the fact of experience entirely fulfills both the protagonist's greatest fear and his wildest illusions. Before his death the Swede actually lives, for a brief while, in the wild-West world of his own imagination," a world that he has created himself (222–23).

This creation renders the Swede responsible for his own death, LaFrance continues; his culpability resides in his failure to accept "the prosaic reality surrounding him." When he whips Johnnie he regards himself as "above all fear and thus above the moral reality of humankind: he merges with the pointless violence of the blizzard and lives completely within the world of his own raging illusion," and "[t]he violence of his illusion is to the moral world what the storm's violence is to the physical world" (225–27). This much blame assigned to the Swede, however, LaFrance contends that the rest of the characters must also share in the blame for his death, for it was incumbent upon the denizens of the Palace Hotel to try to help this badly frightened man move out of his illusions, which they failed to do because of their anger at his behavior. LaFrance bases this final moral reading on the difficult passage in which the narrator says, as the Swede struggles through the blizzard from the hotel to the saloon,

> [o]ne viewed the existence of man then as a marvel, and conceded a glamour of wonder to these lice which were caused to cling to a whirling, fire-smote, ice-locked, disease-stricken, space-lost bulb. The conceit of man was explained by this storm to be the very engine of life. One was a coxcomb not to die in it. (*Tales* 165)

Crane's point here, LaFrance says, is that the kind of "human dignity" that impels a man through a blizzard in this fashion can indeed be "an implicit and laughable affront to such overpowering forces," as it is in the case of the Swede. But on the other hand, an individual—unlike the Swede, Johnnie, Scully, the cowboy, and the Easterner—may choose *not* to be a coxcomb and thus not "expose himself through his own failure of responsibility either to a howling tempest, as the Swede does, or to moral domination by the fantasy of an excited imagination, as all five do" (229).

A considerably larger number of critics take LaFrance's apportionment of blame several steps further, arguing that various other characters are at least as responsible for the Swede's death as he himself is, if indeed not more so. Stanley B. Greenfield rejects both of the views of the story presented immediately above—that it is a demonstration that human will lacks efficacy in a deterministic, Naturalistic universe, and that it is a portrait of a man who wills his own destruction—as overly simple. Greenfield argues that the focus of the story is human pretentiousness in all its various manifestations, which blinds the characters to reality, and which leads in turn to a more complex interpretation of the story. Human pretentiousness and illusion are established at the very outset, he says, for the hotel's blue color is said to *seem* to reduce the natural world around it to grey, and this semblance "is symbolic of society's illusions about itself and its place in the universe," illusions that the characters act upon in their individual fashions. Scully, for instance, sees himself in his role of hotelkeeper as "a godlike destroyer and bestower of favors," an image that makes him arrogant and destructive, as when he seeks to maintain his control of the hotel by giving the Swede whiskey and then loses his temper when that gift has the opposite effect, when it places the Swede beyond his control. Similarly, the saloon is "an elaborate moral facade" that breaks down when the gambler stabs the Swede and the others flee, thereby revealing the "precariousness of the sources of man's ethical strength and . . . moral code." These illusions color the characters' attitudes toward external nature as well as internal, particularly when these two areas overlap, Greenfield continues, as is clear when the Swede and Johnnie square off in the blizzard. Confronted with the brutal indifference manifested in the storm, in which "the wind, significantly, swallows up their meaningful words," the men *should* work together, but instead they fight, and the Swede ends up pretentiously asserting that he likes the blizzard rather than aligning himself with his fellow human beings. Such behavior indicates the Swede's role in his own destruction, Greenfield says, but he cannot be seen as solely to blame in light of the complexity introduced by the story's final section. On the one hand, the Easterner's blaming of everyone in this section is another instance of human pretentiousness due to its assumption that human beings control their own and others' fates despite the indifference of the universe and the omnipresence of chance; on the other hand the Easterner's view does possess "some force as a moral injunction" in that the outcome of events *might* have been altered had the other characters intervened. Through this "ambiguity, this refusal to guarantee interpretation" on the side of either determinism or the Swede's or the others' culpability, Greenfield concludes, Crane "balances man's pretensions to moral behavior and interpretative ability with the theme that man must behave morally and try to understand his actions or inactions" (565–68).

Holton also reads the story's outcome as the product of a clash between incompatible illusions—or perhaps more precisely, between incompatible visions, that of the innocent and that of the initiate. The hotel is the locus at which these visions interact, he explains; the innocent Swede sees it as part of the violent West, whereas the initiate Scully sees it as the hub of a "civilized community." Scully's offer of a drink is his effort to initiate the Swede into Scully's vision, but due to the almost insurmountable power of the Swede's vision, which fuels his terror, this initiation fails, and the drunken Swede instead imposes his vision of the Wild West on the others at the hotel and then rejects their community in the fight and its aftermath. Thus far, Holton says, the Swede is a typical Crane protagonist following the typical Crane narrative pattern of flight from community, followed by a change of vision and then a return to community. But like LaFrance, Holton sees "Blue Hotel" as a significant deviation from Crane's usual approach. The Swede does not undergo the customary alteration of his vision as he walks from the hotel to the saloon, where he intends to return to community, and thus upon this return he once more seeks to impose his own erroneous vision of Western clichés, which effort this time costs him his life, his final failure to "see" being symbolized by his seeming to stare, after his death, at the motto on the saloon's cash register, "This registers the amount of your purchase" (*Tales*

169). However, Holton argues that this image is not the end of the story, that the other characters equally fail to "see" reality, in ways that make the story essentially modern, and thus they too are implicated in the Swede's murder. Although the men in the hotel seem to consider themselves a community, Holton explains, they are in fact just a group of individuals living together, "in a state prior to community, and . . . in a state far too modern"—that is, far too alienated from their surroundings—"for any real cohesiveness or sense of brotherhood." This proto-modern condition itself stems, Holton contends, from Crane's equally modern awareness, evident in the story's final section, that "causation is so complex as to be ultimately indecipherable, random, and absurd," an awareness that is set against the Easterner's belief that someone could have done something to prevent the murder, with this juxtaposition creating a vision that moves "beyond simple determinism to a more sophisticated and paradoxical understanding of causation." The final effect of this multiplicity of apprehensions, Holton says, sounding much like Greenfield, is a sense on the reader's part that "the very notion of causation seems man's ultimate conceit," and that what Crane is presenting here is "a vision of man in a universe apprehensionally unavailable to him, a universe in which communities offer little or no comfort, a universe in which the very possibility of the coherence of assumed causation is now seriously in doubt" (234–41).

Like Greenfield and Holton, Bruce Grenberg argues that Crane's presentation of many possible contributing factors in the Swede's demise renders a simple assigning of blame to either the characters or the indifferent fates untenable, although where Greenfield sees Crane as balancing a dark view of humanity and the universe with the possibility of heroism in humans' ongoing attempts to comprehend their circumstances and act morally, Grenberg is more of Holton's mind in regarding the story's complications as leading to a nihilistic stance. Far from misunderstanding the ways of Fort Romper, Grenberg says, the Swede, through his observations of Scully's manipulations and Johnnie's cheating, correctly perceives those ways to be rooted in deceit, a level of understanding that neither the cowboy nor the Easterner ever attains. This circumstance makes the Swede's death as a result of his attempt to resist those ways, along with the survival of the uncomprehending cowboy and Easterner, savagely ironic, and through this irony Crane "reveals the complex fate of man to be that only the foolish survive and only the dead are wise" (212). In response to Grenberg's position, Richard A. Davidson argues for still further complexity in the story; his view is that not merely the response of the other characters to the Swede's accurate perception but rather "a mosaic of several perceptions" is actually to blame for the outcome of the story's events. "The Swede's error of exaggeration in judgment," he contends, "is as much a catalyst to the calamity as the growing hostility of the Nebraskans to this boisterously annoying outsider." It is the Swede's inarguably misplaced terror, Davidson says, that impels Scully to bring out the whiskey to begin with, and it is the Swede's obnoxiously aggressive, board-whacking behavior during the card game that is at least partly responsible for Johnnie's decision to cheat; thus, he seeks to deny or affect their self-determination as much as they do his. To Grenberg's characterization of the Easterner's final analysis as a mistaken rationalization, Davidson replies that this analysis is in fact partly rationalization but partly truth, that Crane's point here is not nihilistic but instead mixed; it is that the "quality of human choice and self-determination is mixed with a moral greyness." As a corollary to this view, Davidson also argues against deterministic interpretations, asserting that the Swede's and the other characters' behavior reveals that Crane "is not illustrating a deterministic universe that precludes man's free will"; rather, he is demonstrating that "[w]illful human ignorance and prejudice reign, not Fate. . . . Crane is attacking human misunderstanding, illusion, prejudice, dishonesty, and stupidity" (537–39).

Another argument for complexity that begins as a response to a deterministic reading, that advanced by Cox, comes from Hugh MacLean. Basing his reading on Crane's comments in a number of letters, the tenor of which is "that man must fight" despite "his weak mental machinery"—that one must "assert [one's] will in the face of a grim universe, . . . and draw satisfaction merely and exclusively from that act"—MacLean says that "Blue Hotel" espouses a similar belief in will over reason. He supports this view by reading the story as occurring in two worlds: the hotel, which is not ideal but at least possesses symbolic resonance as a place where "the actions of men seem to have meaning beyond the immediate environment"; and the saloon, which represents "the heart of society, realistic, all but non-symbolic, and essentially amoral." The Swede, MacLean explains, sets himself apart from the others by acting—by asserting his will—in both of these worlds despite his certain failure. In the hotel, he "overcomes what he conceives to be ignorance and malice by a will prompted by instinct" and is exiled as a result; and in the saloon he "is undone by chance" in unknowingly throttling the wrong man, "but he is not broken." Thus, MacLean concludes, "the Swede's will, futile and even ludicrous as it may be in one sense, continues, by its lonely determination, to draw on the sympathies of the reader," while reason is disposed of in the concluding section, where the Easterner "explicitly and consciously admits its weakness, implicitly and unconsciously suggests its confusion" (262–64).

Westbrook partially disagrees with this reading, finding MacLean's emphasis on the omnipotence of chance and the failure of will more deterministic than the story and Crane's general philosophy will allow. Citing another of Crane's letters, Westbrook argues that Crane holds the individual "responsible for seeing what is in front of him to see" and acting on that vision ("Ethic" 591). In light of this principle, which he calls Crane's "social ethic," Westbrook reads "Blue Hotel" as a study of men's failure to live up to their responsibilities of vision and action. The Easterner, the cowboy, Scully, and Johnnie, he says, all consciously respond to the Swede with "a bad will" in their refusal to help him when they know that he is "not some dark villain" but "merely a frightened human being, a fool certainly, but still a man in need of sympathy" ("Ethic" 594–95). Therefore, Westbrook concludes, the Easterner's final statement does not dispose of reason, as MacLean would have it; instead, it expresses Crane's view that five men are guilty of the Swede's murder due to their refusal to act on their awareness that "man is responsible for doing the best he can with what he has been given" ("Social Ethic" 596).

Joseph Satterwhite takes a similar view, arguing that the Swede is in no way responsible for his own death, that it is Scully and the others who are entirely to blame due to their failure to understand and help him (241). William B. Dillingham also adopts this position, though with a significant modification. He agrees with Satterwhite that Crane's point is the failure of the others to understand the Swede, but he argues that Satterwhite in fact is too gentle in his perception of Crane's attitude toward those others; he believes that Satterwhite falls into Crane's carefully prepared trap of feeling sorry for these men rather than for the Swede. Crane presents the Swede, Dillingham says, as distinctly unlikable due to his alternating fearfulness and bullying, but beneath these features he commits no real crime and is an essentially honest man; it is the failure of the others to see beneath his offensive manner and to act compassionately towards him that brings about his death, a failure that the unwary reader may readily share. With this point in view, Dillingham asserts, the Easterner's remarks in the final section indict not only himself and the others present at the hotel but also the reader. "The complicity the Easterner speaks of," according to Dillingham, "involves not only the characters of the story but also each reader whose sympathies paralleled those of the men who failed to try to understand and to be a little sorry for the waste of human life." Crane's final goal, then, is "to show the reader what he is, no better than the five men of the story, perhaps a little worse" (225–26).

Just as Dillingham modifies Satterwhite's position, Constance Rooke modifies Dillingham's, arguing that Dillingham exaggerates Crane's estimation of the unwariness of his reader. There may be some readers as "gentle"—as unreflective—as Dillingham claims, she says, but Crane aims at a more insightful one. She agrees that Crane does invite easy empathy with the hotel's denizens, but she disagrees that he simultaneously blocks any empathy for the Swede; rather, he challenges the discerning reader by making empathy for this character more difficult. Scully's bonhomie invites the reader to ignore its coercive, overpowering aspects in order to "collaborate in the making of an easy, social world" and to dislike the Swede for disrupting this world with his suspicions (51). The Swede correctly perceives this world to be composed of insiders and outsiders, with himself as one of the latter; his aggression in the card game and the fight with Johnnie is motivated by his desire to be admitted to the inside. This is also his motivation for his assumption of Scully's coercive social role in the saloon, but because he does not concomitantly adopt Scully's graciousness as concealment for his coerciveness, he fails in this role and is killed. "Crane's better reader," Rooke says, is not, as Dillingham argues, repelled by the Swede's conduct as the members of the hotel and saloon communities are; instead, this reader understands the source of this behavior in the Swede's agony of isolation—as does the Easterner, due to his holding a position only at the outer edge of the communal circle. Thus, this reader sees that the Easterner is guilty of moral failure for ignoring his insights into and sympathy for the Swede in order to maintain his own place in the hotel's society. "The sensitive reader," Rooke concludes, "will desire a more consistent and courageous understanding from this character who mediates between Crane, the sensitive reader himself, and the Swede on the one hand, and the company of the blue hotel on the other"; this reader will also grasp the import of the Easterner's final analysis even before that character utters it, and will understand that utterance as "reparation for [his] default" (54–55).

Alan Wycherley proves himself one of Crane's more sensitive readers in his examination of the number of characters who are to blame for the Swede's death. Like Dillingham and Rooke, he believes that Crane expresses his own view when he has the Easterner say that five men—the Easterner himself, the cowboy, Scully, Johnnie, and the gambler—must share the responsibility, but he argues that this tally leaves a sixth guilty man out: the bartender at the saloon. Crane appears to have forgotten, Wycherley notes, that he assigns culpability to this figure for his failure to check the Swede's aggression before it led to violence, most explicitly when he has the cowboy remark that "'If the bartender had been any good . . . he would have gone in and cracked that there Dutchman on the head with a bottle in the beginnin' of it and stopped all this here murderin'"" (qtd. in Wycherley 88).

Levenson espouses a somewhat less sharply defined view of Crane's goals. His interpretation is that multiplicity in and of itself is Crane's point, not an indictment of any particular character or characters or readers. The motto on the cash register upon which the Swede's dead eyes seem to be fixed may be regarded as placing the blame on the Swede, or it may be seen as implying that no one is to blame, since the description of the Swede's murder is phrased such that the knife-blade seems to slice into him of its own volition rather than being thrust by the gambler. Given such matters, Levenson says, "[t]he logic of the narrative is that no particular moral view is exclusively sanctioned by the nature of things, and everything which makes up the action sanctions that argument." As proof of this sanctioning, Levenson identifies three possible lines of thought, all of which lead only to an "equivocal argument." The first of these is that "events are fortuitous except for an occasional feat—like painting the hotel an arresting blue—whereby the assertion of identity seems to bring identity into being." The second is the possibility that "man makes his own destiny, if it is a proof of human agency that Wild West illusions about Nebraska make the Wild West fantasy come true." And the third is that "all men share responsibility even doing nothing—or at least they do if they think they do." Since all of these ideas are advanced but none is either proved or disproved, Levenson concludes, the meaning of the story is that it "constructs a universe which defies every quest for certain meaning" (xcvii–xcviii).

Possibly the most cogent assessment of this issue of multiplicity is Bergon's. He considers Crane's great achievement in "Blue Hotel" to be his success in balancing "all the forces impinging on event so that no single causal development can explain away the Swede's murder without ignoring or seriously distorting other reasons for the death." Such mystery, Bergon continues, is on the one hand "the mystery of experience," but on the other it leads simultaneously to "the illumination offered only by literature of the highest rank, for the reader is made aware of the distinct elements comprising what is ultimately an impenetrable experience" (*Artistry* 125).

Many of the foregoing interpretations take the story's coda-like last section into account, but given the interpretative difficulties that section clearly poses vis-à-vis the rest of the story, it should not be surprising that a significant number of critics devote almost all of their attention to this conclusion. Stallman takes a highly negative view, contending that it is an artistic miscalculation on Crane's part that produces confusion on the reader's part. The story should properly end, he asserts, with the Swede's death in the saloon, at which point it is clear to the reader that the Swede is himself to blame for his fate because of his refusal to alter "his fixed idea of his environment" and leave the gambler alone. The Easterner's ensuing commentary on this death obscures this fact, Stallman says, by raising the possibility that it was not the Swede's idea of his environment but that environment itself that led to the tragedy. Thus, Stallman concludes, Crane in effect provides two endings that "contradict each other in their philosophical import" and thereby sabotage the story's artistic unity (*Biography* 488).

Ray B. West controverts these findings, arguing that the final section is neither tonally nor thematically dissonant. "Blue Hotel," he says, is one of a number of Crane stories that examine the potential for the breakdown of social codes in the face of the indifference of nature. Crane shows the individual, recognizing this indifference, as driven by his conceit to seek some sense of identity within "the protection of the code that binds him to his fellowmen." The Swede's fears, rooted in his ignorance of the particular form of the code that is operative in the West, cause him to disrupt that code, and this disruption, "like a chain reaction, affect[s] all of those social atoms—men—with whom he [comes] into contact." For initiating this reaction the Swede is to blame, West concedes, but he goes on to argue that the others, despite the logic of much of their behavior in reaction to the Swede, are nonetheless also guilty of violating the most basic human code, that of brotherhood—particularly Johnnie, for his gratuitous cheating, the Easterner, for his silence regarding his knowledge of that cheating, and the gambler, for his violent overreaction (226–27).

Bergon likewise disagrees with Stallman's assessment; in line with his interpretation of the whole story, noted above, as "ultimately an impenetrable experience," he argues that the inconclusiveness of the final section is not a failure of technique or of "artistic nerve" but rather an assertion of Crane's willingness here, as in the rest of the story, "to accept the complex irreconcilability of contradictory points of view" (*Artistry* 64). Cady implicitly concurs with much of this judgment, regarding the conflict between the Naturalistic import of the first eight sections and the moral import of the final one as Crane's artistically valid method of creating interpretative tension and ambiguity. Cady discerns specific ideological sources for the final section; he says that "the perspective of the Easterner is that of Christianity as interpreted by Tolstoi and no doubt mediated to Crane through Howells"—"no doubt" because Cady considers the Easterner's assertion that all the men at the hotel are responsible for the Swede's death to be Crane's version of William Dean Howells's doctrine of complicity, the concept that anyone who witnesses a wrongful act and does not attempt to stop it shares responsibility for it with the active perpetrator (*Stephen Crane* 156).

Six other critics are in general accord that communicating this doctrine is Crane's goal in the final section and that this goal does not render this conclusion thematically inappropriate to the story as a whole, but they differ in significant ways in the details of their interpretations. Gullason sees the Easterner's analysis as emphasizing that the story is "a tragedy of inaction" on the part of the Swede's fellows in the hotel, with such emphasis being fitting and necessary because Crane purposefully downplays the tragedy itself in the first eight sections in order to indicate to the alert reader the sources that give rise to such a tragedy in the first place. In these sections, "[n]atural events, such as the snow and the tempest, and the smaller actions, such as the fight between the Swede and Johnnie, cloak the spiritual paucity and terror in life," Gullason explains, "where man's meaning and being can only be found in material objects (playing cards) and physical deeds (the fistfight, the knifing)" (481). Gleckner also argues that the conclusion rightly implicates the spectators at the crime as well as the perpetrators, but in his view the story is a tragedy of action rather than of inaction, even on the part of at least one of those spectators. Crane's central theme in Gleckner's reading, as in Holton's, noted above (Gleckner's is the earlier of these two), is that to attempt to assert control of one's environment is inevitably to demand that others participate in one's own illusions about that environment and thereby to cause harm. Like Holton, Gleckner notes that this theme is illustrated clearly in

Scully's efforts to impose his vision of Fort Romper as a civilized place on the Swede and in the Swede's resulting drunken imposition of his own vision of the Wild West on the others in the hotel and the saloon; what he includes regarding the ending are the points that it is only in this coda that the reader learns that the gambler has been punished for his own imposition of vision upon the Swede and that the Easterner is equally guilty, for his noninterference despite his knowledge of Johnnie's cheating constituted, in its own way, a harmful exertion of control, which is punished by the Easterner's keen sense of this fact (280–81).

James Ellis likewise argues that Crane intends the reader to accept the Easterner's theory of complicity as fact. He predicates this view on his contention that Crane uses the game played by the men in the hotel, High-Five, symbolically to link the "microcosmic" contest in which the men play their cards to "the macrocosmic game of chance in which the players themselves become cards played upon by Fate." Specifically, Ellis says, this linkage takes place when the Swede accuses Johnnie of cheating in the microcosmic game; the Easterner knows that the Swede is right, but he regards himself as "united macrocosmically with Johnnie and the cowboy in a much larger game of High-Five against the Swede," and so he is unwilling to support the Swede, who ironically is his partner in the microcosmic game. When Scully joins in the argument, Ellis continues, the linkage becomes even stronger through nominal similarity, for now there are five players in the macrocosmic game of High-Five. Then, in fitting parallel, the Swede tries to join in a different four-man microcosmic game in the saloon, making it another five-man macrocosmic game in which he becomes a card played by Fate when, "by chance," he manhandles the gambler. Given these connections, Ellis concludes, the only flaw in the Easterner's final analysis is that he misses the Swede's part in the macrocosmic game and so does not assign him his proper share of responsibility (440–42).

Halliburton and LaFrance also argue that the Easterner's evaluation is correct in all ways but one. The Easterner is right to assert that all the characters are to blame, Halliburton says, but he is mistaken in believing that they are all *equally* to blame; he is himself the most culpable due to his silence despite his knowledge of Johnnie's cheating. This circumstance, in Halliburton's view, renders the story not a tragedy of action or inaction but rather "a tragedy of being," in the Existentialist sense of the term *being*. In the Easterner's "moment of crisis," Halliburton says, "knowing and doing and being intersect. Because of what he knows, the Easterner can, by doing what he ought to do, be the man he ought to be. But he does not and so he is not" (227). LaFrance asserts that where Crane purposely has the Easterner go wrong in the conclusion is in his failure to comprehend that the Swede was trapped in his illusions. He is right that all are responsible for the death, but he does not understand—as Crane does and as he intends the reader to—that what he

and the others needed to do was help the Swede out of his illusioned condition. With this argument in view, LaFrance says that the story's two endings
balance one another; the scene of the actual death in the saloon places all the
blame on the Swede, and the aftermath around the campfire exculpates the
Swede and incriminates all the others, with the final point being that together
these two views properly unite *all* of the characters "in an ironic brotherhood
of guilt as the consequence of their failure to manifest real brotherhood when
the situation demanded it of them" (231).

Deamer reads the Easterner's assessment in light of the code of heroism
he believes Crane formulated as a response to his 1895 trip to the West. Prior
to this trip, Deamer says, Crane conceived of life in deterministic terms, but
what he witnessed of human behavior in the West convinced him that people
could shape their fates, at least to some extent, through the "heroic" virtues
of discipline, responsibility, and courage. In the context of this moral vision,
the point of "Blue Hotel" "is not that a seemingly indifferent universe elimi-
nates meaning from human conduct but rather that such a universe makes
responsible, courageous, code-directed conduct unspeakably important" as
the only way to forge any sort of meaning. The events of the story therefore
lead persuasively to the Easterner's evaluation: the Swede is to blame for his
failure to live up to the code, but the men the Easterner accuses are equally
culpable for their own equal failure, their rejection of the code's demand for
"sympathy, honesty, magnanimity, and courage" ("'Code'" 143–45).

Two critics take the opposite view, contending that Crane wishes the
Easterner to be read as not partially but wholly wrong. Viewed from one perspective, Clark Griffith says, the Easterner's comments can be seen as indicating a guardedly positive attitude on Crane's part, at least toward the Easterner
himself. His final comments indicate that from the Swede's death and the
gambler's sentencing he "has wrested a new understanding of what should be
one man's moral involvements with his fellow men." The past may be beyond
remedy, but "with an enlarged comprehension of what it means to be moral
and courageous and human, the Easterner can see to it that the disasters of
the past never recur in the future." However, the problem with this interpretation, Griffith continues, is that Crane makes clear that the Easterner's view
of what has happened is in fact erroneous, that the Swede is the only one
responsible for his fate due to his unconscious death wish. Therefore, Crane's
actual point in the final section is that the Easterner's "great discovery" of
complicity and morality and humanity and courage as a result of the Swede's
death "is, in reality, no discovery at all. . . . Despite the momentous air with
which it is expressed, the sense of guilt he feels is due to nothing more than
his excessive self-esteem" (87–88). Robert Narveson also sees the Easterner's
expression of his own and the others' guilt as a function of pride and thus
likewise "an outrageous distortion" of the reality of the case. Narveson argues
that the narrator's comments on human conceit and coxcombry apropos of

the Swede's trek through the blizzard are crucial to an understanding of the conclusion. During the first eight sections of the story, he says, every character but the Easterner manifests the kind of vanity that Crane sums up in the word *coxcomb*; each of these men is driven by his conceit to act out behaviors that are "caricatures of what is proper for the person he conceives himself to be": in his desire to be the genial host Scully mistakenly terrorizes the Swede and then gets him drunk; in his urgency to prove his manhood the Swede assumes an obnoxiously aggressive manner, and so on. In the last section, Narveson asserts, the Easterner finally gives in to his conceit and becomes a coxcomb as well. "*His* foolish vanity," according to Narveson, "is pride in his superior awareness and understanding," which pride is manifest in the excessive quality of his response, of "[h]is rage, his rhetoric, his sense of guilt." He is partly right that all are to blame for the Swede's death, Narveson concludes, but to "wallow in the costfree luxury of collective guilt" as the Easterner does "is both emotionally cheap and intellectually sloppy." Thus, in Narveson's view not complicity but the inevitability of human conceit is the insight Crane wishes the reader to come away with. "We conclude from the Easterner's pronouncements," Narveson asserts, "not that he has discerned the 'moral' of the whole affair but that his actions here are of a piece with so many others throughout the story" (187–90).

The widest-ranging overview of the problematic nature of the final section comes from Gibson, first in his essay "'The Blue Hotel' and the Ideal of Human Courage" and then in his subsequent book *The Fiction of Stephen Crane*. On the one hand, interpreting the story as an assertion of complicity and a concomitant call for a moral vision based on brotherhood is tenable, Gibson says, on the basis of the last section because the Easterner here does seem to be a spokesman for Crane. On the other hand, however, the chief evidence for the antithetical determinist reading also appears in this section, Gibson points out; in fact, he argues, many critics use the evidence from the final section to read determinism into the rest of the story and then dismiss that final section in order to cancel the competing evidence for a moral interpretation (*Fiction* 108–09). Thus, the moral reading would seem to be more strongly supported, but Gibson identifies problems with it as well. What the Easterner says in the final section about complicity, Gibson says, is not shown to be true in the previous eight sections; in those sections the Swede seems to bear sole responsibility for his death, since "[h]is view of his situation and of other people is completely distorted, his reactions odd and perverse," particularly when Scully makes an honest effort to befriend and reassure him (*Fiction* 111). Given this refusal on Crane's part to develop any sympathy for the Swede, Gibson continues, not only does the Easterner seem wrong about complicity but also critics are wrong when, working chiefly from the "coxcomb" passage, they read the Swede as symbolic of all humanity. According to Gibson, the narrator is justified in this passage in condemning the Swede as a coxcomb for trying to live in isolation from others, but the narrator also emphasizes that the Swede's behavior leading to this attempt is atypical rather than universal, a product not of his fundamental humanity but rather of his tremendously distorted view that, first, those around him plan to murder him, and second, he is "in control of these potential murderers," a view that leads to his accusation of and fight with Johnnie and his assault on the gambler (*Fiction* 113–14).

To resolve these various cruxes and the conflicting interpretations to which they give rise, Gibson proposes that the story's first eight sections be read as revealing the Swede's responsibility for his own death and the last be regarded as presenting the responsibilities of the others. Crane's theme throughout the story, Gibson says, is the necessity of understanding "the magnetic chain of humanity" and the responsibilities that it places upon *all* humans if they are to survive in an indifferent universe, and his point is that all the characters fail in one way or another to live up to those responsibilities. Taking this approach, he asserts, the reader can see the Easterner's view in the final section as not contradicting that of the first eight but rather as being limited in its failure to acknowledge the Swede's neglect of his share of his human responsibilities. Critics have frequently missed this connection between the body and the end of the story, Gibson explains, because of what he regards as Crane's failure to control his tone, a problem noted above, at the end of "Relationship to Other Crane Works." Crane is overly hard on the Swede in the first eight sections, Gibson says, with the result that the reader has no compassion for the Swede and thus rejects the Easterner's final remarks as mistaken rather than seeing their consonance with the rest of the story (115–16).

The above readings do not lack for ideological content in their espousals of determinism or morality, but in these cases this ideology is more or less tacit rather than overtly stated. A considerable number of other critics explicitly read the story as an example of one particular theoretical approach or another, whether psychological, theological, or philosophical. John Berryman, for instance, as noted briefly above in "Relationship to Other Crane Works," reads the story, as he does much of Crane's canon, through the lens of Freudian psychology. Berryman asserts that Crane seeks here to get rid of his guilt regarding his family, chiefly his father, and their putative disapproval of his bohemian life in England, particularly his cohabitation with an ex-madam. Berryman identifies Scully as Crane's father, Johnnie as the side of Crane that seeks to be a "reasonable, decent son," the Swede as his rebellious-son side, and the gambler, with a respectable facade that masks a violent heart, as his image of his own life in England. Initially, in the fight in the blizzard, the rebellious son defeats the dutiful son, but then, in the conflict between the Swede and the gambler, Crane symbolically murders himself, and through this "thrust toward suicide" he seeks to expiate the guilt his rebellion has caused him (212–14). One problem with this reading is that in his cheating and his other provocative actions Johnnie seems to be less than reasonable and decent as a son, and Stallman points out another—that the Swede seems to be not so much Crane's double as his opposite. Stallman argues that Crane shared with Conrad "a fatalistic resignation to what happens," whereas the Swede's actions show that he "distrusts life and runs to meet and shape his own destiny" (*Houses* 108).

Melvin Askew takes a somewhat different approach, though one still rooted in Freudian theory, reading the story not as psychological autobiography on Crane's part but rather as a study of paranoia. The paranoid figure in this reading, obviously enough, is the Swede; his condition is clear in his fear of having to fight and of being murdered at the outset of the story, when there is nothing to warrant such apprehension, a fact that, in Askew's view, reveals that in the action of the rest of the story the Swede actively wills the death he fears. Thus, Askew argues, while deterministic readings of the story carry a degree of validity, the psychological perspective is more fruitful, giving the story "more poignancy, more density, and ultimately more value in human terms" through its revelation that the Swede "is not merely a passive individual to whom things happen, to whom fate comes, or against whom external circumstances direct their malignant influences." Instead, "the external circumstances are shown to be in the positive control of the protagonist and their malignancy a part of his projection, and finally the story both in value and event exudes, as it were, from the motive, the mind, and character of him alone" (48–49). Daniel Weiss offers a similarly Freudian, clinical view, likewise regarding the Swede as being in the grip of a "paranoid delusional system" that leads to his death, with the game of cards and the events that ensue from it not being truly causal but rather simply "the last scrap of reality on which [he] can found his delusions of persecution." Weiss goes further than Askew, however, in analyzing the source of the Swede's paranoia; he speculates that it may spring from repressed homosexuality. "In his relations with other men," Weiss explains, the Swede "denies his love by substituting an equally dynamic attraction—that of hate. He then denies the hate itself, since it lacks any foundation in reality, and puts upon him[self] moreover the guilty burden of aggression and projects his hatred upon the object of his original desire" (149–51).

Charles Proudfit draws on both Freud and another psychiatrist, Harry Stack Sullivan, for his reading, interpreting the story in terms of "an unconscious individual/group process" involving a "misperception of the present in terms of the past"—a process that Freud calls "transference" and Sullivan terms "parataxic distortion" (47). The essence of this condition, Proudfit explains, is that "anticipation and expectation" from the past live on in the unconscious of the adult and cause him or her to interpret people or events in the present in terms of a past traumatic experience, with the result that "in those interpersonal situations where 'parataxic distortion' is in process, unconscious anticipation and expectation can elicit wished-for behavior from the misperceived person by getting in touch with his unconscious" (48). Proudfit sees the Swede as engaged in this process in both the hotel and the saloon; he argues that the Swede's "paranoid behavior, inappropriate laughter, his jumping to conclusions, and his fear that he will be murdered . . . suggest his misperception of the present in terms of something else" and indicate his unconscious desire "to arrange the fulfillment of a deeply buried expectation—annihilation of the self," which he fails to accomplish in the hotel but carries out in the saloon (51). Proudfit says that the nature of this "something else," of the trauma that causes this parataxic distortion and death wish in the Swede, is unclear, open to speculation; he theorizes that Weiss's diagnosis of repressed homosexuality may be correct, since that offers a consonant explanation of his response to the gambler. If the Swede is repressing his homosexuality, Proudfit explains, then he might well unconsciously misinterpret the gambler's initial pleasantness to him "as a loving gesture that [is] both wished for and feared," and that as a result leads to his equally wished-for and feared death in a symbolically appropriate fashion, since "penetration by the gambler's phallic knife" can be regarded as a metaphorical rape (53).

Ronald McFarland and Michael Collins root their analyses in Carl Jung's theories rather than Freud's; specifically, following the lead of many earlier critics, they work with Jung's theories of archetypal characters and situations. McFarland reads the story in the light of hospitality codes that run through many cultures and the literature they produce, from the *Odyssey* onward. Such codes, he says, arose both in culture and in literature because stranger and local are necessary to one another, since the stranger requires shelter from the local and the local regards the stranger as a potential source of information about the outside world, but these codes are simultaneously charged with mutual suspicion because strangers and locals are unknown quantities to one another. McFarland sees "Blue Hotel" as Crane's examination of the degradation of such ancient codes in the modern world. The first section is rife with typical shared ambivalence; in Homer's archetypal versions of such moments, Odysseus is always able to negotiate an understanding, but the Swede cannot, ultimately resorting to the violence that leads to his death. Concomitantly, Scully offers the traditional ritual of welcome but taints it with his desire for profit, from which it largely stems. The Swede's aggression, Johnnie's cheating, and the more passive hostility of the Easterner and the cowboy over the next six sections further violate the ancient code, a process that culminates, McFarland asserts, in the eighth section when the Swede reaches the saloon, for this is a locale in which "even the most elementary rules of hospitality will not be observed"—particularly the rule that a guest's life is sacred. Thus, McFarland concludes, the stranger—the Swede, the two hosts—Scully and the bartender, and the others as well all share responsibility for the Swede's death, a fact that reveals the breakdown in the modern world of the codes that create and sustain community (448–50).

Collins links Crane's work in "Blue Hotel," as well as in "The Bride" and "The Five White Mice," to the genre that preeminent Jungian critic Northrop Frye in *Anatomy of Criticism* calls "ironic myth." In Frye's formulation, this genre is "a parody of romance: the application of romantic mythical forms to a more realistic content which fits them in unexpected ways" (qtd. in Collins 141). Crane "uses the familiar elements of the Western romance in a realistic setting," Collins explains, to create "an ironic world that seems a recognizable representation of the one in which we live," his goal being to reveal for his reader's benefit the disjunction between the world of romance and that of reality. The Swede, Collins says, seeks to live in the Western version of the world of romance by issuing a classic challenge of that world, the accusation that Johnnie is cheating at cards. Then the rest of the characters, rather than counteracting this romantic effort with reality, abide by the conventions of romance as well; although the fight that proceeds from this challenge is patently "the ugly, senseless brawl of two fools," Scully, the cowboy, and the Easterner make sure that it takes place and that it is conducted according to the codes of romance: the antagonists fight one-on-one, even though the others would like to gang up on the Swede, and when the combat is concluded Scully, despite his anger, insists that the Swede be allowed to depart in an atmosphere of "honor, fair play, and hospitality." Outside this simple, clearly governed, romantic Western world of the hotel, however, is the "complex, ironic, ambiguous real world" that does not abide by such conventions— where the Swede is murdered in "an ugly barroom brawl that could have as easily taken place in New York or Boston as in the modern, respectable, law-abiding town of Fort Romper," by a gambler who is a respectable, law-abiding member of this town, in the presence of several other such citizens. In other words, when the Swede leaves the hotel "the code of romance [ceases] to govern, and Fort Romper [becomes] what it always actually was, a law-abiding town in the real world," where, as the Easterner points out in the final section, "human action and inaction have ambiguous, complex, far-reaching, and unforeseen consequences" (145–46).

David S. Gross takes an alternative psychoanalytic interpretive route— one of more recent currency than Freud's or Jung's. He reads the story in terms of Jacques Lacan's description of "the self or ego as a product of insertion (inscription) into the symbolic order" of the perceived outside world. The Swede, he explains, attempts to "inscribe" or "insert" himself into the world of the hotel, which he perceives to be part of "the symbolic order of 'the West,'" through "discursive strategies governed by the generic conventions of the popular Western"—an attempt that is doomed to failure. Thus far, Gross seems merely to be clothing a longstanding idea, that the Swede dies because of his refusal to understand that the actual West is nothing like the one he read about in dime novels—an idea earlier advanced by Cady, Vanouse, Deamer, Robertson, and Bergon, among others—in the raiment of newer theoretical jargon. However, he moves provocatively beyond these discussions in arguing that the Swede is in fact correct about the hotel's being governed by popular Western genre conventions, and that the others therefore reject him not because he is mistaken but rather because he is an unsettling outsider; and he offers further provocative insights in asserting that these circumstances link Crane to Postmodernism. This linkage, Gross says, is discernible in Crane's "profound understanding of 'the problem of the subject' as embodied in the Swede and who he thinks he is and has to be in 'the West'" and, as illustrated in the behavior of the other characters as well as that of the Swede, in Crane's "'nihilistic' deconstruction of the project of philosophy as a whole, his conviction as to the inadequacy of all theoretical attempts to configure reality in a way that does not lie" (19).

William A. Johnsen also applies a relatively recent psychoanalytical theory to "Blue Hotel," one propounded by René Girard. Girard's work is somewhat anfractuous, as is Johnsen's exegesis of it, but in essence Johnsen explains that Girard's analyses of the depictions of ritual sacrifice in ancient texts show that such depictions recreate "the *historically* successful resolution" of conflicts within families, clans, and communities. The victim in such sacrifices in these texts, in Johnsen's presentation of Girard's view, is, "by definition, someone who cannot reply violently," someone who "polarizes everyone against him, unifying the whole [previously disunited] community in opposition to a single antagonist." This victim thereby "gives the community the last word, the decisive violence that cannot be returned, that restores peace." Because of this function, the sacrificial figure is simultaneously, paradoxically, "made to represent all that threatens social stability" and "loved as the instrument of peace" (280).

Girard's identification of an increased level of communal violence since the Enlightenment, Johnsen continues, a function of the "crisis of modernism"—humans' continuing frustration at the failure of "the promethean promise to deliver autonomy from the gods . . . to man himself" (278)—leads to a belief that truly modern literature should manifest a concomitant increase in violence and an equally concomitant heightened awareness of "the sacrificial mechanism" operating in that violence. "Blue Hotel," Johnsen argues, is a perfect example of such modernity, given its violence and its "scandalous, insistent" juxtaposition of that violence with the sacred (281). At the heart of the story, in Johnsen's view, is the Swede's and the Easterner's shared knowledge that the community of the hotel is making the Swede its sacrificial victim; what separates these two men is the fact that the Swede believes he can "forestall violence by unmasking the scapegoat mechanism" while the Easterner "knows better than to quarrel with the town's misunderstanding of their own violence that makes sacrifice possible"—that is, their belief that the Swede's behavior has provoked it. This misunderstanding is particularly clear in Scully's actions in his upstairs interview with the Swede, Johnsen says, for even as the innkeeper calms the Swede's fears he gives him whiskey and encourages him "to assume the scapegoat's momentary privilege of total licence" (283). The action in the saloon and the coda also highlight this necessary misunderstanding. The saloon scene reveals that the gambler is normally the performer of the town's sacrifices, given that a part of his trade is to cheat unwary outsiders—in Johnsen's view, "victims who will not incite illegal violence" in return. With the Swede, however, he does incite such violence, and his fate as recounted in the coda demonstrates that, as the Easterner is well aware, he has himself now become "the scapegoat of the mechanism he administered" (286).

Yet another psychoanalytical approach, perhaps the most arcane, is proposed by Edward J. Stone. Regarding the issue of the influence of French Impressionism on Crane, Berryman argues that Crane in fact derived his theory of color deployment from reading Goethe and "owes nothing whatever, apparently, to painting" (289); Stone moves this idea from the aesthetic-biographical to the psychological realm. According to a friend of Crane's, Frank Noxon, whom Stone quotes, Crane was strongly influenced by Goethe's theory of color psychology, which Goethe outlined in *Zur Farbenlehre*, published in English as *Theory of Color*. Armed with this information, Stone argues that "Blue Hotel," suggestively titled from this perspective, is a study of "morbid human behavior" that is brought on by colors—that the Swede's paranoia and aggression are actually his responses to the red of the stove, which evokes thoughts of blood and death, and the blue of the hotel, which in Goethe's schema produces anxiety. Therefore, Stone claims, it is the colors around him, particularly blue, that are the Swede's true antagonists and determine his fate, a fact that Stone sees as obscured due to Crane's mishandling of the story's ending. Through the first eight sections, Stone says, Crane deploys his colors to create a "strangely compelling mood of impending violent calamity," but he ultimately ends up nullifying the effect of those colors, the actual *raison d'être* of the story, with the Easterner's irrelevant, "appendage-like" disquisition on human responsibility (53).

Four other critics concern themselves with the possibilities of exegesis predicated on Christian rather than psychological patterns. Daniel Knapp sees the story as closely based on the account of Jesus' last days presented in the Gospel of St. John. In this Johannine version, Knapp notes, Christ can be regarded as obsessed with his own death and as, in effect, forcing it to happen, with collaboration from several others—the same tale recounted in "Blue Hotel." However, Knapp asserts, through this parallel Crane is not engaged in "mere narrative paraphrase"; rather, he assigns to each element that he draws from the gospel "a value subtly or grossly different from that of the original," with the goal of providing a deeply unsettling rather than reassuring message. The Swede is a Christ-figure, Knapp says, but with his fear and his braggadocio, he is one lacking "spiritual grandeur," one "from whom all the shreds of myth are coldly blown away," one who undeniably "brings his fate on himself" (273).

A further important inverted parallel proceeding from these conditions, Knapp continues, is that of Scully with the high priest, Caiphas. In his view, Scully like Caiphas decides that the troublesome Christ figure must die so that the nation may live. In the world of the hotel, Scully regards himself as responsible for the comfort and tranquility of his guests regardless of whether the reality of its circumstances—that is, its being a temporary shelter at best in a physically and humanly dangerous world—warrants such feelings, just as Caiphas saw himself as the guardian of his nation despite the corruption of that nation as revealed by Jesus. Thus, both Scully and Caiphas "falsify the nature of the world" without being fully aware of the fact—it is this cheating, not Johnnie's minor violation of the rules of a card game, that is the heart of the story—and when this falsification is pointed out, as when the Swede discerns murderous impulses beneath the surface of Scully's rituals, they seek to kill the truth-teller. To Scully, then, the hotel "is in truth a Palace run by Scullys, not a place of skulls," but "Palace or charnel house, the guests must be comfortable, the nation must not perish." When, "[i]n his insanity, the Swede [sees the] unbearable truth" beneath this facade, he fulfills his role as Christ figure: "Jesus and the Swede sense a spiritual truth of which their fellows are ignorant; both attack the priests for spiritual cheating; both die." However, Knapp concludes, these are the limits of the resemblance between these two, for another inversion of Christ in the figure of the Swede is that the Swede's gospel "is of fear, not of love," with the corollary that "[h]is character is not redeemed by triumph" in dying for the truth but rather is "destroyed by it, and in death he finds no victory"—a bleak message for humankind obsessed by fear of death as the Swede is. In fact, Knapp argues, noting a final inversion, "[i]f there is a hero in 'The Blue Hotel' it is perhaps the gambler, who, recognizing the human condition" of violence and death, "is as moral a man as his own calm recognition of the truth will allow" (273).

Bassan, Nagel, and Benfey all concur, in somewhat briefer analyses, that such parallels are present in the story and that Crane uses them ironically. That Crane would be drawn to use Christian story patterns and character types is not surprising, Bassan says, given his religious upbringing, as a result of which his "model continued to be the minister's vision of primitive Christianity," but, like Faulkner's, "Crane's Christ-figures are all ironically presented and there is little or no possibility of redemption" through them (7–8)—a view that Nagel echoes (143). Benfey focuses on one specific Scriptural analogue to the events transpiring in hotel and saloon, the Last Supper. The Swede's fear correlates to Christ's awareness of his impending martyrdom, Benfey says, and the Swede's drinking with Scully and insistence that the gambler drink with him correlate to Christ's communion with His disciples. These links, according to Benfey, enforce two points. First, they reveal the Swede's unwise emulation of Christ in demanding "certainty in his relations with other people" and refusing to tolerate "any mystery or inscrutability in human appearances," unwise because these attitudes lead to his accusation of Johnnie—which, however correct it may be, results in his expulsion from the community—and his ill-fated harassment of the gambler. Second, in a larger sense these connections suggest the condition of all human beings, entrapped in their particular fantasies; Christ's fantasy, Benfey contends, is His belief that he is fulfilling Old Testament prophecies in undergoing martyrdom, while the Swede suffers a reduced form of martyrdom as a result of the dime-novel scenario that he stubbornly imposes on Fort Romper (237).

Another group of critics sees the Swede in a philosophical rather than theological light; they regard him not as a type of Christ, ironic or otherwise, but rather as a type of twentieth-century humankind. William Bysshe Stein reads the story, as he does most of Crane's canon, as espousing a proto-Existentialist view. The Easterner's concluding remarks on causality and collaboration, Stein says, are essentially Christian in outlook, given their assumption that humans are moral agents due to their possession of free will and the ability to control chaos; these comments are also, Stein continues, self-deception. Far from being capable of controlling chaos, the characters in this story are "hopelessly self-absorbed and . . . lost in contemplation of some private vision of [their] personal role in the universe." Scully's vision is of hospitality, Johnnie's is of cardsharping, the cowboy's is of "bravado," the Easterner's is of "intellectual self-reliance," the bartender's is of indifference, the townsfolk's is of civic pride, and the gambler's is of self-importance. The result is the classic Existential dilemma, Stein contends, in which "[e]ach individual is pathetically estranged from the world in which he seeks to enact a particular role; for his aspirations and desires are completely uncoordinated with any common goal in life," and when the Swede tries to impose his own "distorted fantasies" upon this "existent disorder of reality," he thereby "surrenders his fate to a world rendered irredeemably absurd," a point underlined by the blizzard, which "ignores the absurd prerogatives of honor and pride that [the individual] claims for himself under the authority of his frail ego" (173–74).

While not using the specific term *Existentialist*, Florence Leaver takes a view similar to Stein's; she reads the story as depicting the type of isolation that has come to be regarded as a particular hallmark of the twentieth century—the feeling of terrible aloneness produced by an utter lack of absolutes and a concomitant imprisonment within the self. "Blue Hotel," she contends, is "an outstanding example of men as 'isolatoes.' Not only is the Swede alone, but the others, too, exist each in his own separate little vacuum." And in line with this reading, the story's final section, Leaver asserts, "presents a social aspect which deals with the ever-present question of involvement versus indifference or detachment or isolation in the social community." The characters here choose isolation, a choice that Leaver sees Crane as unironically condemning in the comments of the Easterner (529).

In response to such efforts at doctrinaire philosophical interpretation, particularly Stein's, Marvin Klotz argues that the story is in fact a lampoon of theories in general and "a deliberate burlesque of literary naturalism" in particular. Klotz contends that, far from seriously depicting a man who is fated to die according to some cosmic or universal or natural deterministic theory, Crane shows that it is the Swede himself who determines his end—that the story is in reality a tale of the "absurd" efforts of "a man, determined to die, who surmounts all the obstacles to the achievement of his [own] predetermined end." Therefore, determinism is removed from consideration, as is equally, at the other end of the spectrum, the Easterner's assertion that he and the others share responsibility for the Swede's fate. In the light of the invalidity of both determinism and complicity as explanations of what has happened, Klotz concludes, the reader sees that in these misguided remarks "it is not man who is mocked—it is theory" (171–73).

Three other critics seek to explain Crane's philosophy through an exploration of his aesthetic and technical orientation. Spurred initially by Conrad's remark to Crane that "[y]ou are a complete impressionist" (*Correspondence* I, 315), Ford Madox Ford's more specific comments on the impressionistic character of Crane's technique (25), and Crane's own linkage of his methods to those of the French Impressionists in the short story "War Memories" (*Tales of War* 254), a lengthy and lively debate has raged through the years over Crane's possible incorporation of elements of Impressionist painterly execution into his visual style and the ramifications of such borrowings for an understanding of his philosophical orientation (e.g., Bender 47–55, Kronegger 129–34, Kwiat 331–38). Most of those who touch on this topic in connection with "Blue Hotel" argue that Crane is not borrowing specific techniques from the Impressionists but is heavily influenced by them in his understanding of ontology and epistemology. Rodney O. Rogers asserts that the story shows that Crane shares the Impressionists' views that "[t]he nature of reality, of the physical world, . . . depends primarily upon how it is perceived" and that "[a] corollary to this idea is that a person's psychology affects the way he conceives the world." While the Impressionists convey these ideas purely visually, Rogers says, Crane gets them across in "Blue Hotel" by employing a narrator who "typically registers and simultaneously evaluates the various, frequently contradictory views of the world which define his protagonists' sensibility." The narrator functions most crucially in this respect in the passage describing the Swede's walk from the hotel to the saloon through the blizzard, according to Rogers, for here the narrator's characterization of humans as "lice" that "cling to a whirling, fire-smote, ice-locked, disease-stricken, space-lost bulb" sharply undercuts the Swede's congratulatory view of himself as a powerful, triumphant hero at this point (294–95)—an undercutting that continues when, at the moment of murder, the Swede's body is characterized as "a citadel of virtue" on the one hand—presumably a view the Swede shares—and as a melon, so easily is it penetrated by the gambler's knife, on the other (299). Nagel agrees that the "lice" passage is vital to Crane's point because of its emphasis upon the fact that "people in general delude themselves by seeing their lives and activities as important in a scope far beyond their true status." Such delusion, Nagel reads Crane as saying, is necessary to an extent because it sustains one's will to survive in an indifferent universe, but it can easily be pressed too hard or taken too far and lead to death, as is the case with the Swede. However, Nagel contends, despite its value this passage is in fact the antithesis of Impressionism in a technical sense, for a truly Impressionist prose style eschews the use of authorial comment such as that which Crane relies upon here; literary Impressionism, in Nagel's view, consists of a wholly dramatic presentation of life—that is, a narrative that simply presents what the characters do and say, with no intrusions from a narrator or author (71).

Monteiro is more fully in agreement with Rogers; he regards the story as Crane's "richest" treatment of one of his most frequent themes in connection with Impressionism, the idea that "keeping close to one's personal honesty," as Crane asserted that he sought to do himself, "insures neither the discovery of truth nor the continuance of personal safety," a result of the fact that, in Crane's view, Impressionism entails inevitable, inescapable subjectivity. The Swede's experience bears out this idea, Monteiro says. He is the typical Crane Western protagonist in that he is not the stereotypical cowboy hero but rather a "more interestingly vulnerable, impressionistic outsider who . . . carries around the shining and not-so-shining codes of the West as the intrusive, insistent, potentially implosive baggage of his emotional life," and he hews closely to his personal honesty in refusing to let go of this baggage, in sticking resolutely to his beliefs about the West throughout the story, from his early fears to his later exaggerated sense of his own power in the blizzard and the saloon (1–2). The Easterner also, Monteiro continues, is this sort of figure, for he too keeps close to his personal honesty in his concluding assertion of complicity but nonetheless remains mired in subjectivity and thus does not discover truth any more than the Swede has done. His final speech, Monteiro says, is not Crane's own assessment of what has happened but rather his psychologically accurate observation that human beings "will not, perhaps cannot, readily accept the mystery of things"; instead, they feel impelled to, "ex post facto, feign necessity, forging a link, even if spurious, between collective social behavior and personal fate" (9).

As noted above, these considerations of Crane as an Impressionist of one stripe or another largely eschew examination of his technical methodology. There is no dearth, however, of discussions of Crane's technique in this story based on principles other than those of Impressionism. In the realm of structure, for example, six critics offer analyses. Stallman sees a series of refusals and quarrels, with the second in each group inverting the first in some way, as giving pattern to the narrative: the Swede initially refuses to drink with Scully, who then cajoles him, and then the gambler at first refuses to drink with the Swede, who likewise attempts cajolery, which in this case fails, fatally; the farmer with whom Johnnie initially plays cards twice quarrels with him, with no harmful effect, then the Swede quarrels with him and ends up brutally beating him, then the gambler is said to cheat farmers at cards, once again to no harmful effect (*Biography* 488).

Gleckner discerns a larger number of structuring elements at work. He notes, first, that the story moves in a curve from an initial atmosphere of calm with an undercurrent of potential violence to the overt violence of the blizzard, the fight between Johnnie and the Swede, and the Swede's murder, and then back to calm in the final section; second, that as this curve plays out control of the action shifts from Scully to the Swede to the gambler; and third, that at the center of the story Crane's focus shifts from the cards on the table to the men in the storm. The point of these patterned movements, Gleckner explains, is that any given individual can exert control over his circumstances only briefly and in doing so sets himself up for a potential fall—men like cards are governed by forces beyond their control, so that it is coxcombry to believe, as the Swede does, that one can create and sustain one's own reality by force of will, in the Swede's case that reality being a version of the Wild West in which he triumphs against all comers (271–73).

Richard Van Der Beets sees the story as unified and structured not by parallels in actions but rather by parallels and concomitant reversals between the characters who inhabit the hotel and those found in the saloon. Scully, the extroverted and engaged host at the hotel, has his reverse counterpart in Henry, the bartender at the saloon, who maintains an air of detachment and refuses, unlike Scully, to acknowledge the part he plays in the violence that takes place on his premises by his serving whiskey to the Swede. The Easterner and the cowboy correlate with the two card-playing merchants in the saloon, in that while the Easterner and cowboy clearly play an active role in the bloodshed outside the hotel by their very inaction, their refusal to intervene as a result of their dislike of the Swede, the merchants, while similarly inactive, are "ciphers, blended and localized . . . and faceless." Persecuted Johnnie finds his complementary figure in the district attorney, who winds up prosecuting the gambler, who in Van Der Beets's view is the parallel figure of Johnnie's tormentor, the Swede. It is this last parallel, between the Swede, "cheated and victimized" and completely alienated from his environment, and the gambler, "cheater and victimizer" and "completely integrated with his situation," that Van Der Beets regards as most important; viewed in the light of this connection, he contends, the gambler's murder of the Swede can be seen as "a symbolic purging and strengthening of self—a ritual, Crane is perhaps suggesting, requisite for survival" in a wintry, indifferent universe (294–95).

Tim Pilgrim sees carefully patterned repetitions of dialogue and action as the most meaningful structural elements of the story. In the area of dialogue, he notes three patterns: various characters frequently ask other characters what they mean by a previous statement; characters often repeat statements of their own throughout a scene; characters occasionally repeat a phrase or sentence several times in immediate succession. Collectively, Pilgrim says, these patterns reveal that the characters are largely self-absorbed, are in fact talking more to themselves than to their supposed listeners. This condition in turn evinces a "complexity of alienation" in both the hotel and the saloon, a general "failure in truthful introspection as well as in social interaction" (128). The concomitant repetition of specific actions—card-playing, whiskey-drinking, and fighting—reinforces the sense created by the dialogue repetitions that these characters can find no escape from their internal and external alienation. Therefore, Pilgrim concludes, the story as a whole argues for "a nihilistic pattern in human existence," as stated most explicitly in the narrator's comments on the earth's meaninglessness and man's conceit as the Swede trudges through the blizzard from the hotel to the saloon. This trip is emblematic of life in general—"a trek to nothingness, repetitious of the same journey taken by those gone before" (128–29).

Jürgen Wolter likewise regards structured repetition as the key to interpretation. He notes that four seemingly irreconcilable issues dominate most of the critical discussion of "Blue Hotel"—the role of determinism, the appropriateness of the final section in relation to determinism, the presence of elements of progressive development in the story's structure, and the apparently contradictory presence of parallels in that structure—and he proposes a structural analysis that integrates and resolves these issues. Four basic incidents recur throughout the story, Wolter says: drinking, gambling, fighting, and paying. Gambling, fighting, and paying occur sequentially three times early in the story, in Johnnie's two card games with the farmer and in the game involving Johnnie, the cowboy, the Easterner, and the Swede. This threefold repetition "makes it clear that in the world here described a game of cards is bound to end in violence, and that there will always arise in the end the question of payment, of having to face the consequences of one's behavior." Drinking is then added to the beginning of this sequence on its next repetition, when Scully presses whiskey on the Swede before his second game with Johnnie, the cowboy, and the Easterner. This time, the game ends with the Swede's accusation and subsequent beating of Johnnie, actions indicating that the issue of paying has "now assumed a moral connotation over and above the mere practical one of handing over money" (296). This four-part sequence occurs once more in the saloon, the payment being the Swede's death and thus again assuming moral connotations.

Analyzing the story's structure in this fashion, as five repetitions with additions that create new levels of significance, Wolter asserts, harmonizes the parallel and progressive elements in that structure. It also reconciles the deterministic aspects of the first eight sections with the Easterner's assertion of human responsibility in the last one, for "the fixed sequence of recurring events leads us to the conclusion that the characters . . . possess only a very limited scope in their individual freedom," while the last section sets forth the responsibilities of that scope, however limited it may be. In not standing up for the Swede, Wolter explains, the Easterner adheres to a usual, predictable pattern of passive behavior, but that particular pattern is his own, not a fixed sequence; he is comfortable in it and derives much of his identity from it, but he is nonetheless free to break it and is thus morally culpable for not having done so. The final point conveyed by the story's structure, then, is that in some instances an individual can and should "perform a courageous act of self-negation in order to break out of the damning pattern of predetermined behavior" (297).

Thomas Kent takes a less assured interpretative stance. He discerns a tripartite structure that creates epistemological uncertainty on both the narrative level and what he calls the "extra-textual" level—the level on which the reader rather than the characters themselves interprets the meaning of the action. Each of these three parts, Kent says, concluding with violence of speech or action that results from "the characters' uncertain perceptions about proper codes of behavior" (264). In the story's first five sections, the Swede's ideas about such codes conflict with those of the other denizens of the hotel; in sections six through eight the Swede attempts to impose his code in both hotel and saloon; and in the ninth section the Easterner offers his "naturalistic" explanation that the Swede fell victim to these conflicts in perception, to the differences between his codes and those of the environment of Fort Romper (266). On the extra-textual level, however, in Kent's view, this explanation does not resolve the story for the reader but rather induces further epistemological uncertainty, for the reader must judge the Easterner's assessment as part of the whole story, and in that context it is only one of three possible explanations, the other two being, first, that the Swede was in fact insanely determined to engineer his own death, and second, that Fort Romper was indeed as dangerous as the Swede believed it to be. The narrator, Kent notes, refuses to commit himself to any of these explanations, just as he fails to explain the point of the cash-register legend, and by these refusals Crane communicates that certainty is impossible—at least, it is impossible "for the careful reader" (267).

An equal number of technical studies of "Blue Hotel" focus on Crane's handling of imagery. Hollis Cate points to a widespread pattern of ocular imagery that not only creates structure but also develops theme. Early in the story, he points out, the other occupants of the hotel are described as looking at the

Swede but failing to understand him when he advances his supposition that a good many men have been killed there. Shortly thereafter, the Swede likewise looks but fails to "see" clearly when he asserts that the others are all against him, when he believes that Scully asks him upstairs in order to murder him, and when, after drinking, he decides that he must impose his will upon his fellow card-players. This network of literal and metaphorical failures or refusals to "see" continues throughout the story, Cate says; the others refuse to look at the Swede after the fight with Johnnie, the dead Swede cannot see the legend on the cash register, the Easterner acknowledges that he saw Johnnie cheating but declined to act responsibly, and the cowboy is described as crying out "blindly" when, in reply to the Easterner's assertion of complicity, he contends that he did not do anything. In terms of structure, Cate says, Crane uses these moments focused on "the act of seeing, of taking in the other (or trying to)," to create "[c]rucial incident" and to fashion "pivotal points in his story, one situation naturally leading to another." Regarding theme, Cate like Kent perceives epistemological uncertainty at the heart of the story, for the ocular imagery, he asserts, creates a disjunction between sight and reality: it emphasizes the idea that "[t]he world of 'The Blue Hotel' is in the eyes of the characters as beholders. . . . From the first sight reference to the last, Crane underscores the idea that his participants constantly perceive falsely at the other's expense," and that, in the case of the Easterner in particular, "seeing truly does not necessarily result in . . . acting responsibly" (150–52).

Sue L. Kimball regards another image pattern—of squares, circles, and parallel lines—as providing an oblique commentary on the story. She notes that in the games of High-Five, at the dinner table and in the saloon, the characters sit in square formations, symbolically signifying their refusal "to form a communal circle" with him; at other points, they do sit in literal circles from which the Swede is excluded, particularly around the stove, which imply "a community of interest, but never one that admits the Swede" (426–27). Parallel lines appear, Kimball continues, in Crane's descriptions of railroad tracks, sidewalks, and rows of trees, and all these images suggest the formation of connections that likewise exclude the Swede. Crane's motive in creating these myriad orderly patterns, Kimball argues, is to show that despite his exclusion from the circle of community the Swede is himself responsible for what befalls him. "The irony of the Swede's quest," Kimball says, "is that he is disappointed because he finds order in the West," where he expected to find a chaotic wild frontier. As a result, "[h]is presuppositions and his imagination require that he initiate chaos from the design he discovers," and this compulsion leads to his death (429–30).

Holton's contribution to this area of study is to argue that Crane's handling of imagery in this story, along with several other elements, settles the debate over whether Crane is a Realist or an Impressionist. He is neither, Holton says; his shifts between sharply contrasting scenes, his depiction of "distort-ing" emotions and movements, his "contrived lighting effects," and his "incongruous imagery" make the story "almost purely expressionistic." As such, it is "a climactic demonstration of Crane's development beyond realism" (233–34). Bergon eschews this broad view and impulse toward definition, concentrating instead on one sentence as a paradigm of Crane's accom-plished descriptive technique. As the hotel's occupants move from the dining room to the front room after dinner, the narrator notes the view of the bliz-zard afforded by the two small windows in the latter. In addition to remarking on the profusion of snowflakes to be seen, he says that "A gate-post like a still man with a blanched face stood aghast amid this profligate fury" (*Tales* 144). What this sentence reveals about Crane's craft, Bergon says, is his effective technique of choosing one detail, rather than supplying exhaustive descrip-tion, to carry much of the burden of meaning of a given scene. In this case, he notes, the "fixed position" of the gate-post, coupled with its comparison to a frightened man, conveys the overwhelming power and indifference of the storm; the post "gives meaning and emphasis to the chaotic storm that whirls around it. . . . [T]he inhuman, the indifferent, is given a point of human refer-ence" (*Artistry* 12).

J. F. Peirce offers equal praise but presents it in a more tempered context. The story as a whole has many flaws, Peirce says, including thin characteriza-tions, a lack of sympathy for the Swede, and a confusing and contradictory double ending, but it is redeemed by Crane's expert handling of figurative language. Particularly noteworthy are his descriptions of the mounting vio-lence of the blizzard, which he uses to emphasize the increasing intensity of the quarrels the characters engage in; this "cruel counterpoint . . . gives the story a third dimension beyond the two dimensions of the printed page and stirs and stimulates the imagination." Through such stylistic mastery, Peirce concludes, Crane creates "a multi-colored, three-dimensional Rorschach ink blot in whose symbolic shapes the reader can discern the outlines of his own fears conjured up by his subconscious in nightmare dreams" (160–62).

As the entire previous discussion indicates, "Blue Hotel" is one of the most thoroughly scrutinized stories in the canon of American literature. So heavily studied has it been, in fact, that even such seemingly minor matters as Crane's comparison of the light blue color of the hotel to that of a heron's legs (*Tales* 142) have generated voluminous debate. Robert L. Hough says that Crane is mistaken in making this comparison of the hotel to "a kind of a heron" (*Tales* 142) because, according to Audubon, there is no species of heron in which the adults' legs are light blue. Crane would have been more accurate, Hough contends, to have made his comparison strictly to the young of the species of Little Blue Heron, whose legs are light blue until the birds reach maturity, at which point they turn a dark blue tinged with purple (109). In response, C. T. Peterson contends that Hough is wrong in saying that Crane is mistaken in his implication that a species of heron has light blue legs. The fault, Peterson says, is ultimately Audubon's rather than Hough's, for Audubon errs in saying that the Little Blue Heron has dark blue legs; in certain lights the adult's legs are in fact light blue, while the young do not have light blue legs at all but rather yellowish-green ones (29).

Four other critics devote space to this comparison, but they concern themselves more with its structural and thematic significance than with its indication of Crane's ornithological expertise. Stallman says that the "screaming blue" of the hotel establishes a "psychic quality" of violence at the outset of the story, a quality that foreshadows, perhaps even provokes, the fistfight between the Swede and Johnnie. And, Stallman continues, the mention of the heron as one who, by this screaming color, always "declare[s] its position against any background" (*Tales* 142) links the bird to the Swede, who behaves similarly due to his "fixed idea" that he is going to be killed (*Biography* 486). Bettina Knapp likewise notes the resemblance between the hotel and the heron, with their always-declared positions, and the Swede, who remains "fixed in his ideas, oblivious to his surroundings," lacking insight into himself or anyone else, and thus incapable of seeing either the kindness offered to him at the hotel or the potential for violence that pervades the saloon. Unlike Stallman, however, she then broadens this linkage to include the other characters, saying that they are equally fixed in their own positions, so that they too are incapable of insight and thus share in the responsibility for the Swede's fate (159–61).

Bergon finds particular significance in Crane's use of the verb *declare* in this comparison. It is "a product of that artistic sensibility which can invest the visual with the added power of the aural," and it makes the sentence in which it appears a preparation for the "screaming and howling of the hotel itself." Moreover, this specific word "gives the bird an authority of its own, as if its declaration were an assertion of its will, the same kind of willful assertion that Scully made when he painted the hotel and that Crane himself wills through his art," the final goal of which "seems to be a creation of a similar artistic sensibility in the reader" (*Artistry* 58). Its resemblance to herons aside, Cady says that there is no single satisfactory explanation of what the color of the hotel symbolizes; as possibilities, he suggests "man's 'coxcombry,'" Scully's "assertion of his humanness," or else the Swede's refusal of humanness, or perhaps the other characters' failure of humanness (*Stephen Crane* 155).

Works Cited

Ahnebrink, Lars. *The Beginnings of Naturalism in American Fiction*. Cambridge: Harvard University Press, 1950.

Askew, Melvin. "Psychoanalysis and Literary Criticism." *Psychoanalytic Review* 51 (Summer 1964):43–50.

Bassan, Maurice. Introduction. *Stephen Crane: A Collection of Critical Essays*. Ed. Maurice Bassan. Englewood Cliffs, N.J.: Prentice-Hall, 1967, 1–11.

Beer, Thomas. *Stephen Crane: A Study in American Letters*. New York: Knopf, 1923.

Bender, Bert. "Hanging Stephen Crane in the Impressionist Museum." *Journal of Aesthetics and Art Criticism* 35 (1976):47–55.

Benfey, Christopher. *The Double Life of Stephen Crane*. New York: Knopf, 1992.

Bergon, Frank. Introduction. *The Western Writings of Stephen Crane*. New American Library, 1979, 1–27.

———. *Stephen Crane's Artistry*. New York: Columbia University Press, 1975.

Berryman, John. *Stephen Crane*. New York: Sloane, 1950.

Bowers, Fredson. Textual Introduction. *Tales of Adventure*. Vol. 5 of The University of Virginia Edition of *The Works of Stephen Crane*. Ed. Fredson Bowers. Charlottesville: University Press of Virginia, 1970, cxxxiii–cxcv.

Cady, Edwin H. Introduction. *Tales, Sketches, and Reports*. Vol. 8 of The University of Virginia Edition of *The Works of Stephen Crane*. Ed. Fredson Bowers. Charlottesville: University Press of Virginia, 1970, xxi–xli.

———. *Stephen Crane*. Rev. ed. New York: Twayne, 1982.

Cate, Hollis. "Seeing and Not Seeing in 'The Blue Hotel.'" *College Literature* 9 (1982):150–52.

Chametzky, Jules. "Realism, Cultural Politics, and Language as Meditation in Mark Twain and Others." *Prospects* 8 (1983):183–95.

Collins, Michael J. "Realism and Romance in the Western Stories of Stephen Crane." *Under the Sun: Myth and Realism in Western American Literature*. Ed. Barbara Howard Meldrum. Troy, N.Y.: Whitston, 1985, 139–48.

Colvert, James B. "Stephen Crane." *American Realists and Naturalists*. Volume 12 of *Dictionary of Literary Biography*. Ed. Donald Pizer and Earl N. Harbert. Detroit: Gale Research, 1982, 100–24.

———. "Stephen Crane: Style as Invention." *Stephen Crane in Transition: Centenary Essays*. Ed. Joseph Katz. DeKalb: Northern Illinois University Press, 1972.

———. "Structure and Theme in Stephen Crane's Fiction." *Modern Fiction Studies* 5 (1959):199–208.

Conder, John J. *Naturalism in American Fiction: The Classic Phase*. Lexington: University Press of Kentucky, 1984.

Cox, James Trammell. "Stephen Crane as Symbolic Naturalist: An Analysis of 'The Blue Hotel.'" *Studies in Short Fiction* 1 (1964):224–26.

Crane, Stephen. "The Blue Hotel." *Tales of Adventure* 142–70.

———. "Nebraska's Bitter Fight for Life." *Tales, Sketches, and Reports* 409–20.

———. "War Memories." *Tales of War*. Volume 6 of The University of Virginia Edition of *The Works of Stephen Crane*. Ed. Fredson Bowers. Charlottesville: University Press of Virginia, 1970, 222–263. 10 vols.

Davidson, Richard A. "Crane's 'The Blue Hotel' Revisited: The Illusion of Fate." *Modern Fiction Studies* 15 (1969):537–39.

Deamer, Robert Glen. "Remarks on the Western Stance of Stephen Crane." *Western American Literature* 15 (Summer 1980):122–41.

———. "Stephen Crane and the Western Myth." *Western American Literature* 7 (Summer 1972):111–23.

———. "Stephen Crane's 'Code' and Its Western Connections." *The Importance of Place in the American Literature of Hawthorne, Thoreau, Crane, Adams, and Faulkner*. New York: Edwin Mellen, 1990, 139–52.

Dean, James L. "The Wests of Howells and Crane." *American Literary Realism* 10 (1977):254–66.

Dillingham, William B. "'The Blue Hotel' and the Gentle Reader." *Studies in Short Fiction* 1 (1964):224–26.

Ellis, James. "The Game of High-Five in 'The Blue Hotel.'" *American Literature* 49 (November 1977):440–42.

Ellison, Ralph. "Stephen Crane and the Mainstream of American Fiction." *Shadow and Act*. New York: Random House, 1964, 60–76.

Ford, Ford Madox. "Techniques." *Southern Review* 1 (1935):20–35.

Geismar, Maxwell. *Rebels and Ancestors*. Boston: Houghton Mifflin, 1953.

Gibson, Donald B. "'The Blue Hotel' and the Ideal of Human Courage." *Texas Studies in Literature and Language* 6 (1964):388–97.

———. *The Fiction of Stephen Crane*. Carbondale: Southern Illinois University Press, 1968.

Gleckner, Robert F. "Stephen Crane and the Wonder of Man's Conceit." *Modern Fiction Studies* 5 (1959):271–81.

Greenfield, Stanley B. "The Unmistakable Stephen Crane." *PMLA* 73 (1958):562–72.

Grenberg, Bruce L. "Metaphysic of Despair: Stephen Crane's 'The Blue Hotel.'" *Modern Fiction Studies* 14 (1968):203–13.

Griffith, Clark. "Stephen Crane and the Ironic Last Word." *Philological Quarterly* 47 (1968):83–91.

Gross, David S. "The Western Stories of Stephen Crane." *Journal of American Culture* 11 (1988):15–21.

Gullason, Thomas A. "Stephen Crane's Short Stories: The True Road." *Stephen Crane's Career: Perspectives and Evaluations*. Ed. Thomas A. Gullason. New York: New York University Press, 1972, 470–86.

Halliburton, David. *The Color of the Sky: A Study of Stephen Crane*. Cambridge: Cambridge University Press, 1989.

Holton, Milne. *Cylinder of Vision: The Fiction and Journalistic Writings of Stephen Crane*. Baton Rouge: Louisiana State University Press, 1972.

Hough, Robert L. "Crane on Herons." *Notes and Queries* 9 (1962):108–09.

Johnsen, William A. "René Girard and the Boundaries of Modern Literature." *Boundary 2* 9 (1981):277–90.

Johnson, George W. "Stephen Crane's Metaphor of Decorum." *PMLA* 78 (1963): 250–56.

Katz, Joseph. Introduction. *Stephen Crane in the West and Mexico*. Kent, Ohio: Kent State University Press, 1970, ix–xxv.

Keenan, Richard. "The Sense of an Ending: Jan Kadar's Distortion of Stephen Crane's 'The Blue Hotel.'" *Literature/Film Quarterly* 16 (1988):265–68.

Kent, Thomas L. "The Problem of Knowledge in 'The Open Boat' and 'The Blue Hotel.'" *American Literary Realism* 14 (1981):262–68.

Kimball, Sue L. "Circles and Squares: The Designs of Stephen Crane's 'The Blue Hotel.'" *Studies in Short Fiction* 17 (1980):425–30.

Kinnamon, Jon M. "Henry James, the Bartender in Stephen Crane's 'The Blue Hotel.'" *Arizona Quarterly* 30 (1974):160–63.

Klotz, Marvin. "Stephen Crane: Tragedian or Comedian." *University of Kansas City Review* 27 (1961):170–74.

Knapp, Bettina L. *Stephen Crane*. New York: Ungar, 1987.

Knapp, Daniel. "Son of Thunder: Stephen Crane and the Fourth Evangelist." *Nineteenth-Century Fiction* 24 (1969):253–91.

Kronegger, M. E. "Impressionistic Literature and Narrative Theory: Stephen Crane." *Review* 4 (1982):129–34.

Kwiat, Joseph J. "Stephen Crane and Painting." *American Quarterly* 4 (1952):331–38.

LaFrance, Marston. *A Reading of Stephen Crane*. Oxford: Clarendon, 1971.

Leaver, Florence. "Isolation in the Works of Stephen Crane." *South Atlantic Quarterly* 61 (1962):521–32.

Levenson, J. C. Introduction. *Tales of Adventure* xv–cxxxii.

Maclean, Hugh N. "The Two Worlds of 'The Blue Hotel.'" *Modern Fiction Studies* 5 (1959):260–70.

McFarland, Ronald E. "The Hospitality Code and Crane's 'The Blue Hotel.'" *Studies in Short Fiction* 18 (1981):447–51.

Mencken, H. L. Introduction. *Major Conflicts*. Vol. 10 of *The Work of Stephen Crane*. Ed. Wilson Follett. New York: Knopf, 1926, ix–xiii. Rpt. in *Stephen Crane's Career: Perspectives and Evaluations*. Ed. Thomas A. Gullason. New York: New York University Press, 1972, 94–96.

Monteiro, George. "Crane's Coxcomb." *Modern Fiction Studies* 31 (1985):295–305.

Murphy, Brenda. "'The Blue Hotel': A Source in *Roughing It.*" *Studies in Short Fiction* 20 (1983):39–44.

Nagel, James. *Stephen Crane and Literary Impressionism.* University Park: Pennsylvania State University Press, 1980.

Narveson, Robert. "'Conceit' in 'The Blue Hotel.'" *Prairie Schooner* 43 (1969):187–91.

Neglia, Erminio G. "Fictional Death in Stephen Crane's 'The Blue Hotel' and Jorge Luis Borges's 'El Sur.'" *Chasqui: Revista de Literatura Latinoamericana* 10 (1981): 20–25.

Nye, Russell B. "Stephen Crane as Social Critic." *Modern Quarterly* 11, 6 (Summer 1940):48–54.

Osborn, Neal J. "'The Monster' and 'The Blue Hotel.'" *Explicator* 23 (1964):10.

Peirce, J. F. "Stephen Crane's Use of Figurative Language in 'The Blue Hotel.'" *South Central Bulletin* (Winter 1974).

Peterson, C. T. "Crane on Herons." *Notes and Queries* 10 (1963):29.

Pilgrim, Tim A. "Repetition as a Nihilistic Device in Stephen Crane's 'The Blue Hotel.'" *Studies in Short Fiction* 11 (1974):125–29.

Pizer, Donald. *Realism and Naturalism in Nineteenth-Century American Literature.* Rev. ed. Carbondale: Southern Illinois University Press, 1984.

Proudfit, Charles L. "Parataxic Distortion and Group Process in Stephen Crane's 'The Blue Hotel.'" *University of Hartford Studies in Literature* 15 (1983):47–54.

Robertson, Jamie. "Stephen Crane, Eastern Outsider in the West and Mexico." *Western American Literature* 13 (Nov. 1978):243–57.

Rogers, Rodney O. "Stephen Crane and Impressionism." *Nineteenth-Century Fiction* 24 (1969):292–304.

Rooke, Constance. "Another Visitor to 'The Blue Hotel.'" *South Dakota Review* 14 (1977):50–56.

Satterwhite, Joseph N. "Stephen Crane's 'The Blue Hotel': The Failure of Understanding." *Modern Fiction Studies* 1956–57.

Shroeder, J. W. "Stephen Crane Embattled." *University of Kansas City Review* 17 (1950):119–29.

Slote, Bernice. "Stephen Crane in Nebraska." *Prairie Schooner* 43 (1969):192–99.

Solomon, Eric. *Stephen Crane: From Parody to Realism.* Cambridge: Harvard University Press, 1966.

Stallman, R. W. "Crane's Short Stories." *The Houses That James Built.* East Lansing: Michigan State University Press, 1961, 103–10.

———. "Stephen Crane: A Revaluation." *Critiques and Essays on Modern Fiction*: 1920–1951. Ed. John W. Aldridge. New York: Ronald, 1952, 244–69.

———. *Stephen Crane: A Biography.* New York: George Braziller, 1968.

Stein, William B. "Stephen Crane's *Homo Absurdus*." *Bucknell Review* 8 (1959): 168–88.

Stone, Edward. *A Certain Morbidness: A View of American Literature*. Carbondale: Southern Illinois University Press, 1969.

Stronks, James B. "Stephen Crane's English Years: The Legend Corrected." *Papers of the Bibliographical Society of America* 57 (1963):340–49.

Swann, Charles. "Stephen Crane and a Problem of Interpretation." *Literature and History* 7 (1981):91–123.

Van Der Beets, Richard. "Character as Structure: Ironic Parallel and Transformation in 'The Blue Hotel.'" *Studies in Short Fiction* 5 (1968):294–95.

Vanouse, Donald. "Popular Culture in the Writings of Stephen Crane." *Journal of Popular Culture* 10 (1976):424–30.

Walcutt, Charles Child. *American Literary Naturalism: A Divided Stream*. Minneapolis: University of Minnesota Press, 1956.

Warshaver, Gerald E. "Bushwacked by Reality: The Significance of Stephen Crane's Interest in Rural Folklore." *Journal of the Folklore Institute* 19 (1982):1–15.

Weinig, Sister Mary Anthony. "Heroic Convention in 'The Blue Hotel.'" *Stephen Crane Newsletter* 2 (Spring 1968):6–7.

Weiss, Daniel. "*The Red Badge of Courage*." *Psychoanalytic Review* 52 (Summer 1965):32–52; (Fall 1965):130–54.

Wertheim, Stanley, and Paul Sorrentino. "Thomas Beer: The Clay Feet of Stephen Crane Biography." *American Literary Realism* 22 (Spring 1990):2–16.

———, eds. *The Correspondence of Stephen Crane*. Vol. 1. New York: Columbia University Press, 1988.

West, Ray B. "Stephen Crane: Author in Transition." *American Literature* 34 (1962): 215–28.

Westbrook, Max. "Stephen Crane: The Pattern of Affirmation." *Nineteenth-Century Fiction* 14 (1959):219–29.

———. "Stephen Crane's Social Ethic." *American Quarterly* 14 (1962):587–96.

Wolford, Chester L. *The Anger of Stephen Crane: Fiction and the Epic Tradition*. Lincoln: University of Nebraska Press, 1983.

———. "The Eagle and the Crow: High Tragedy and Epic in 'The Blue Hotel.'" *Prairie Schooner* 51 (1977):260–74.

———. *Stephen Crane: A Study of the Short Fiction*. Boston: Twayne, 1989.

Wolter, Jürgen. "Drinking, Gambling, Fighting, Playing: Structure and Determinism in 'The Blue Hotel.'" *American Literary Realism* 12 (1979):295–98.

Wycherley, Alan H. "Crane's 'The Blue Hotel': How Many Collaborators?" *American Notes & Queries* 4 (1966):88.

The Bride Comes to Yellow Sky

Publication History

This story was first published in America in the February 1898 issue of *McClure's Magazine* (10:377–84); it appeared concurrently in England in *Chapman's Magazine* for February 1898 (9:115–26). It was then collected in the American book *"The Open Boat" and Other Tales of Adventure*, published by Doubleday & McClure in April 1898, and in the English book *"The Open Boat" and Other Stories*, likewise published in April 1898 by William Heinemann (Bowers clxxii). Wilson Follett, the editor of *The Work of Stephen Crane* (12 vols., New York: Knopf, 1925–27), placed the story in volume 12, issued in 1927. It has appeared since that time in almost every anthology of Crane's fiction, including *Stephen Crane: An Omnibus* (New York: Knopf, 1952), edited by Robert W. Stallman, and *The Complete Short Stories and Sketches of Stephen Crane* (Garden City, N.Y.: Doubleday, 1963), edited by Thomas A. Gullason.

Circumstances of Composition

On the basis of statements in several letters, Crane's work on this story can be dated to September and October 1897, during which time he was ensconced in his first home in England, Ravensbrook, in the town of Oxted, Surrey. In a September 9, 1897 letter to his brother Edmund, written from Schull, Ireland, where Crane was recuperating from injuries suffered in a carriage accident, he says that he has just finished "The Monster" (*Correspondence* I, 296). Then, back in England, he writes his brother William on October 29 that "[m]y next short thing after the novelette (The Monster) was The Bride Comes to Yellow Sky" (*Correspondence* I, 301), which he sent to his agent, Paul Revere Reynolds, at some point during that month with the admonition that the story "is a daisy and don't let them talk funny about it" (*Correspondence* I, 305).

Sources and Influences

Crane's biographers are nearly unanimous in locating the primary source of this story in Crane's own life. During his sojourn in Jacksonville, Florida, in late 1896, while he waited for a ship to take him to Cuba so that he could cover the revolt against Spanish rule on that island, Crane became romantically involved with Cora Howorth Stewart, the proprietress of a house of assignation. She nursed him back to a semblance of health following his ordeal in the wake of the sinking of the steamer *Commodore*, and when he left for England and other points east in 1897 she went with him; they established their home in England later that year as Mr. and Mrs. Crane. However, Cora's husband, Donald William Stewart, had refused to divorce her, and so she and Crane had no legal or sacramental sanction for their relationship. In fact, the relatively nonjudgmental atmosphere of England compared to that of America, as well as their own greater anonymity in this foreign land, may have been a key factor in their decision to settle there.

Nevertheless, while many of the friends Crane and Cora made in England knew of and accepted their situation (indeed, several, such as Harold Frederic, were involved in similar arrangements), most of their acquaintances were not aware of it, nor were Crane's strait-laced relatives back in America, and there is evidence that both he and Cora were at pains to conceal it in such quarters. Therefore, most writers on Crane's life find it no accident that in "Bride," composed shortly after he and Cora set up housekeeping, Crane focuses on a man who fears social ostracism as a result of his recent marriage. (Christopher Benfey asserts that in fact not just "The Bride" but all "the great tales of 1897 . . . turn on themes of social ostracism and pretense" [231]). John Berryman points in particular to the end of the story, saying that its anticlimactic character reflects Crane's relief that no hint of scandal about him and Cora had reached his family (195–96). Stallman finds another particular analogue in the "sense of mutual guilt" that settles over the bride and groom as they approach Yellow Sky (*Biography* 326), while J. C. Levenson asserts that the bride is "like Cora in being neither pretty nor very young," although they differ in that the bride is characterized as proletarian and awkward, whereas Cora was neither of those things (lxxiv). Stallman also notes that, as is often the case, Crane seems to split himself between two characters in this story. On the one hand, he puts his fear of conventional morality and scandal into Jack Potter, but on the other, the wildly defiant, gun-toting Scratchy Wilson represents the part of Crane that impelled him to thumb his nose at convention in many ways, including, in the recollection of Ford Madox Ford, sauntering around his English home dressed in Western garb and packing a large Smith and Wesson revolver (*Biography* 327).

With such a rich vein of biographical ore to be mined, few critics have devoted effort to unearthing literary sources for this story. The most obvious ones might perhaps more properly be termed sub-literary—the host of dime-novel Westerns that were so popular in Crane's day, the conventions of which regarding showdowns between bloodthirsty badmen and noble, straight-shooting marshals he deftly subverts here. However, because in most cases consideration of such sources is closely linked to the significance of this story, detailed discussion of Crane's parody and inversion of the conventions of this genre more properly belongs in the section on "Critical Studies," below.

One study that brings together biography and a different genre of sub-literary sources does belong in this section. Samuel Bellman argues that, to quell his distress over his family's likely reaction to his relationship with Cora, Crane in "The Bride" drew heavily from what has been well documented as one of his favorite sources of comic diversion, the vaudeville stage. In support of this view, Bellman points out numerous theatrical references in descriptive passages and asserts that the story's action unfolds as a series of four "skits" that are recognizably vaudevillian in subject matter and presentation. First comes the scene in the parlor car, which, Bellman says, casts Potter and the bride in the customary stage roles of comically victimized innocents. This is followed by a humorous monologue from the traveling salesman, an equally common stage figure, followed in its turn by Scratchy's initial appearance, in which the gunman does a solo turn as the conventional comic drunkard. The final skit is the showdown, which, in its slapstick, deflating form, bears the marks of a "Western follies show." The result of these borrowings, Bellman concludes, is the sense of release from anxiety that Crane sought in his own life at this point; the story "fearfully anticipate[s] dire consequences" and then "dispels [them] with burlesque logic" (19).

Donald Vanouse identifies another, less direct source in the *zeitgeist* in which Crane worked. He "wrote in a period deeply concerned with evolution," Vanouse points out, and this idea affects his work in "The Bride" in that his focus in this story is on "historical process rather than static images," in line with the orientation of most of the best-known writers of popular history in this era. "With the pullman car, a gaudy and meretricious emblem of bourgeois, domestic civilization," Vanouse says, "Crane literalizes the historical transition which was so painful to Francis Parkman" (426–27).

Relationship to Other Crane Works

"The Bride" is one of the few Crane stories in which characters are introduced who reappear in subsequent works. In this case, Jack Potter and Scratchy Wilson play a minor role in a later Western, "Moonlight on the Snow." In this story, gambler Tom Larpent is about to be hanged for murder by the citizens of War Post, a town neighboring Yellow Sky, when Potter and Scratchy, who is now Potter's deputy, arrive and save Larpent by arresting him for an earlier, lesser offense. This reappearance with Scratchy now acting on the side of the law has led a number of critics to consider the possible thematic relationship between the two stories. In James B. Colvert's view, "The Bride" and "Moonlight" are alike in concentrating on the "theme of the conflict between the spirit of anarchy in the legendary West and the constraining influences of commercial and civic ambition" (148), with Potter's and Wilson's appearance in the latter story indicating that the forces of constraint have extended their range of influence since the events of "The Bride." Milne Holton similarly notes that in "The Bride" Scratchy is simply stunned into impotence by the marriage and thus domestication of his old adversary, while as Potter's deputy in "Moonlight" he actively participates in the displacement of "the western way of seeing things" by the "opposed eastern order of apprehension and evaluation" (241–42).

Many other critics take the view that in terms of theme "The Bride" is actually most closely related—in dialectical fashion—to the other of Crane's best-known Westerns, "The Blue Hotel." Maurice Bassan regards these two as "complementary in color and in emotional effect," in that "The Bride" "explodes the myths of the Wild West, [whereas] 'The Blue Hotel' confirms them" (7). Chester L. Wolford likewise sees "The Bride" and "Blue Hotel" as complementary, being "comic and tragic faces of the same misperception": Scratchy is humorously discomfited when he finds the rules of the West changed, while the Swede comes to grief by thinking that these rules have not changed when in fact they have (*Study* 34). Robert Glen Deamer, on the other hand, notes a similarity between these two that sets them apart from Crane's other Westerns. All the other stories in this group, he explains, are about what he calls Crane's "western stance"—that is, the "self-assurance, magnanimity, and unpretentiousness of a true westerner." But "The Bride" and "Blue Hotel" are about the encroachment of civilization on that stance; together they reveal that "Crane, like anyone emotionally involved in the myth of the West, was saddened, enraged, and embittered by the advance of modernity" ("Stance" 140–41).

Jamie Robertson proposes a satiric link between "The Bride" and another of Crane's Westerns, "One Dash—Horses," in which a showdown between a young American and a Mexican bandit twice seems imminent but is deflected. This anticlimactic character, Robertson says, makes both stories parodies of the usual Western conventions, aimed at depicting "a weak imitation of the vital life that had characterized the West" (251). Holton likewise sees "The Bride" as parody, which impels him to regard it as connected to one of the most violent of Crane's Westerns, "A Man and Some Others," in which an Easterner witnesses a showdown that is *not* deflected between an American and a group of Mexicans and that ends with the American and several of the Mexicans dead. This story, Holton says, is the tragic version of the meeting between East and West, and "The Bride" is its comic companion-piece (128). Holton also identifies what may be a forerunner of "The Bride" in a piece Crane wrote in 1896 for the Bacheller, Johnson, and Bacheller newspaper syndicate. Called "A Freight Car Incident" in its American version and "A Texas Legend" when it ran in the June 1896 issue of the *English Illustrated Magazine*, this tale focuses on a gunfighter named Luke Burnham, who is shut into a freight car, assumes that the perpetrator of this action means to kill him, and demands in a very Scratchy-Wilson-like manner—all profanity and waving revolvers—that this person open the car and face him. This story initially seems to end on an anticlimactic note, like "The Bride," when Burnham is let out of the car and rages through the town looking in vain for his supposed enemy; however, the storyteller by way of coda explains that Burnham met his end in a shooting in a saloon that evening (128).

Taking a different approach, James L. Dean links "The Bride" with "Moonlight" and "Horses" in a group that, in juxtaposition with a grouping of "Blue Hotel," "Twelve O'Clock," and "A Man and Some Others," indicates Crane's attitude toward women. In the former group women are the agents of the protagonists' survival; they "keep death at bay and give law a chance to assert its authority." In the latter group the protagonists die due to the lack of such women, thus revealing Crane's belief that "a woman's care for life, with its implications about such facets of civilization as law, marriage, order, and domestic and social ties, is an alternative to lonely courage and annihilation" (261–62).

Ranging beyond the Westerns, David Halliburton connects Jack Potter with Henry Fleming of *The Red Badge of Courage*, Fred Collins of "A Mystery of Heroism," another Civil War tale, and the children of the Whilomville stories in that these are all characters who define themselves by how others see them. Where "The Bride" differs from the rest of these, in Halliburton's view, is that in the others the code is "viable" but some of the characters fail to measure up to it, while Potter does measure up but the code here—that of the Wild West—is depicted as being "dubious" in terms of viability (232). Stallman likewise sees "The Bride" as linked to "Mystery," as well as to two other war stories, "An Episode of War" and "The Upturned Face," in terms of structure as well as theme. All four, Stallman notes, are constructed on a "paradoxical reversal of situation," which yields the insight that "that which is predictable—a code, a theory, or an ideal—is discovered to be unpredictable when faced by the realities" (*Houses* 110).

Stallman's linkage notwithstanding, Levenson and Wolford both point to another story, "The Pace of Youth," as having the strongest structural and thematic affinities with "Bride." Levenson says that "Pace" is as much a source for "The Bride" as is any actual experience Crane underwent during his tour of the West, for in both of these stories "the would-be violent are so caught by convention that the unexpected can undo their purpose, and . . . the triumphant lovers are so colorless that they bleach all the romance out of the happy ending" (xxvii). Wolford notes evidence of Crane's artistic progression between these two: while both utilize the same basic plot—boy meets girl and their love displaces an older order—"The Bride" is a more mature story. "Pace," he says, is "purely archetypal comedy," but in "The Bride" Crane roots his plot in a historically specific situation that is integral to his overall meaning (*Study* 28).

Regarding the use of more specific techniques, Halliburton notes that the train in "The Bride" functions here as it nearly always does in Crane's fiction, particularly in "Blue Hotel" and "The Monster," as an avatar and agent of "challenge and change," and that in "The Bride" as in "Pace," another story centered on change, Crane emphasizes movement at all points—by using racing vehicles and characters constantly in motion, and even, on the level of style, by relying heavily on verbs in the past progressive tense (228–30). James Nagel sees Crane's handling of Potter and Wilson as a typical example of what he terms Crane's development of "Impressionistic protagonists," by which he means "initiates engaged in unfamiliar actions and realizations." Nagel notes that Crane's usual strategy is to measure the "organic change" in such a protagonist "against a fixed point of reference; hence, often the development of an initiate is offset by the stable position of another, as Jack Potter's acceptance of a more 'civilized' West is contrasted to Scratchy Wilson's inability to comprehend 'the new estate'" (117). Levenson also sees this theme of initiation as central to "The Bride"—and in fact to Crane's work in general—but he notes that the conclusion of this story provides a twist on Crane's usual approach to this theme. At the end, he points out, Scratchy is defeated by a "glimpse of another world," which in Crane's work "is usually an initiation into chaos" but in this case the glimpse is of a new order, and so it produces instead "comic affirmation" (lxxvi).

Critical Studies

Maxwell Geismar finds "The Bride" fundamentally flawed by what he calls the "incongruity of the story's emotional action with its outward scene of western antics," by which phrase he means that Potter's emotional distress over what the town will say about his marriage does not ring true to a reader familiar with the standard Western code of discretion regarding a gunfighter's private life. What led Crane to this miscalculation of his materials, Geismar says, is the story's roots in his own situation—his own distress about what people would say if they knew the truth about his relationship with Cora, his projection of "'social hedges' . . . from an abiding fear in himself of social convention and public opinion; or of those spectres and ogres lying in the depths of his own mind, on a still deeper level than that of society" (102). However, Geismar is alone in holding a negative opinion; every other critic regards this story as among the best in Crane's canon, and indeed of the entire canon of the American short story.

This unanimous praise, though, does not mean that all critics agree on the significance of the story; a frequently complex debate about Crane's tone here has raged almost continuously in the interpretive literature, with a number of writers arguing that Crane intends this story as a serious elegy for the passing of the Wild West and an equal number asserting that "The Bride" is actually a parody of this kind of tale—in Edwin Cady's words, a lampoon of "neo-romantic lamentations over 'The Passing of the West'" (103). Robert Barnes takes the serious side, contending that the bride is a symbol of the "Eastern civilization, duplicity, and evil" that are rapidly replacing the heroic code of the old West (39). S. C. Ferguson, on the other hand, argues for comedy, asserting that the larger cultural struggle between East and West is present only as a setting for the events of "The Bride," not as a parallel to them, so that in taking a symbolic, allegorical approach Barnes reads too much into the story. If the bride symbolizes anything, Ferguson says, she represents "adult responsibility," an awareness that, like Scratchy, Yellow Sky as a whole "must put away its toys, its masquerades in the manner of Wild Bill Hickock and his ilk" (59).

A. M. Tibbetts also reads this piece as a comedy, pointing out that, although the reader may be tempted to take the story seriously due to Crane's more usual habit of writing "portentous and symbolic tragedies" such as *Maggie: A Girl of the Streets*, *The Red Badge*, "The Monster," and "Blue Hotel," as well as the subtlety of his comic technique in "The Bride," there is no mistaking the "more than faintly ludicrous" demeanor of Potter and his wife on the train, Scratchy's being described as the "child's idea of a cowboy," Crane's ironic use of epic devices, and his deployment of "a sort of visual comedy that is close to slapstick" (315–16).

In response to Tibbetts, Kenneth Bernard argues that Potter's social distress at the outset is presented as too intense to be regarded as comedy and that he takes his part in the ritual Western showdown with Wilson quite seriously—more seriously, in fact, than the townspeople, who seem to regard it primarily as entertainment. These readings lead Bernard to conclude that "The Bride" is a straightforward lament that the old West and its ideals of honest confrontation and honor are being supplanted by the supposedly civilized East and its baser values. As further support for this view, Bernard says Potter's discomfiture on the train and its provoking the porter to condescend to him and his bride indicate the heroic Western marshal's loss of status in the advent of the East, which is symbolized by the "gaudy, meretricious" character of the train's furnishings (17–20). Shannon Burns and James A. Levernier agree with this assessment, adding to Bernard's evidence by pointing to Crane's frequent employment of funeral imagery, such as Potter's black attire and the associations of his name with "potter's field," the graveyard of the nameless, which they assert is designed to drive home the idea that, although neither Potter nor Scratchy dies in the showdown, the frontier that is their accustomed world does literally and figuratively die to make way for the advance of civilization ("Crane's 'The Bride'" 36–37). Deamer concurs with this elegiac reading, saying that Potter's "pathetic . . . cringing before the subtle, vaguely sinister forces of civilization while he is on the train" indicates that Crane is seriously "sympathizing with the plight of the once-heroic marshal suddenly thrust into a new environment in which he can no longer *be* heroic." This plight is especially clear, Deamer continues, in Crane's presentation of Potter's genuine courage in facing Scratchy unarmed, for the obvious implication is that this is the last time such courage will be necessary now that civilization has arrived. There is no loss of life, but there is nonetheless tragedy present here; "[t]he tragedy . . . is that the train, figuratively speaking, has won" ("Myth" 122–23).

On the other side of the tragedy-satire controversy, Holton argues that the specific circumstances of the showdown, "that event which is climactic and essential to the western romance," make the story unmistakably a parody. As is not the case in the conventional showdown, Holton points out, the conflict here is settled with words rather than guns, and the marshal is focused not on his honor but on his memory of the splendor of the Pullman car, a fact that, in Holton's view, renders this version of the showdown more accurate than the form it parodies, since in reality it was Eastern institutions and comforts, emblematized in this railroad car, that overmatched the supposedly heroic imagination and rituals of the West (226). Frank Bergon likewise looks at the story in light of the differences between the legends and the actuality of the clash of East and West. His view is that Crane is insightfully showing that by the time this story takes place the mythical West, as largely constructed by Eastern writers, is in fact strongly shaping the real West, as evidenced by the fact that, in Bergon's opinion, Wilson and Potter as gunslinger and marshal are both primarily attempting to live out roles they have gleaned from Western myth, a reading reinforced by Colvert's assertion that Scratchy's shirt, made, the narrator says, "by some Jewish women on the east side of New York" (*Tales* 116), is by virtue of that fact a metaphor for the larger reality that Scratchy himself is made in New York—that his gunslinger persona is at its source "a creation of the legend-mongering Eastern imagination" (125). Bergon regards this theme as one of the story's greatest virtues; he asserts that it "would be a denial of historical fact to write realistically of the West without including the Potters or Wilsons or those others who become Westerners by playing the roles of Westerners" (Introduction 11). A still greater indication of Crane's acuity regarding the interplay of myth, history, and popular culture, Bergon says, is that the burlesque of the showdown in "The Bride" appeared four years before such confrontations became firmly fixed as staples of Western literature thanks to Owen Wister's 1902 depiction of one in his best-selling novel *The Virginian*. Crane was thus writing "anti-Westerns even before the Western became a formula," Bergon argues, and he says that in doing so, particularly in including the bride and the townspeople as figures in the conflict, Crane makes clear another historical reality that most formula Westerns ignore, that "the townspeople who advocate a new civil existence for their community" are crucial actors, alongside the lawman and outlaw, in Westerns possessed of any true resonance (Introduction 2).

Wolford also argues for a reading of "The Bride" as meaningfully parodic, pointing out a number of further ways in which Crane systematically reverses his reader's expectations regarding the Western. The marriage of the protagonist and his sweetheart conventionally concludes the story, taking place after the showdown has settled the conflict, he notes, whereas in this case it occurs before the showdown and is in fact the action that decides the outcome of the showdown; and the bride and groom are not the attractive and romantic figures normally to be found in such a story. Wolford also argues that Scratchy is presented as clumsy and a poor marksman, but the text does not entirely bear him out in this claim, since Wilson is depicted at one point as terrorizing a dog by skillfully shooting close to the animal without hitting it and at another as missing a small paper target, which he fires at from a considerable distance while he is moving, by only "a half inch" (*Tales* 117–18). Nevertheless, the rest of Wolford's evidence clearly bears out his thesis, that Crane's intention is to show that "the Old West dies not with a bang, but with a whimper" (*Study* 29). Donald B. Gibson asserts that Crane maintains this parodic, comic attitude in an effective balance with a deeper strain of sympathy for his characters, an accomplishment that in his view often eluded the author. The story's point, Gibson says, is that as marshal and gunfighter Wilson and Potter are both anachronisms in the now-Easternized West, a condition that, in his marriage, Potter has recognized more quickly and fully than Scratchy. (It should be noted, however, that it is possible to see Wilson as understanding the situation more quickly than Potter. As Halliburton observes, at the moment of the showdown Potter seems initially to believe that he too should have a gun rather than a wife, and it is Wilson who says, "'I s'pose it's all off now'" when he learns that Potter is married [Halliburton 229].) When Crane feels sympathy for such figures, as he usually does, Gibson asserts, he tends to intermingle comic and serious tones without tightly controlling them, a problem that results in a somewhat muddled point of view. But in this case, Crane keeps his humor, which arises from his "awareness of the incongruity between the men and their changed environment," separated from his corresponding sense of the pathos of their situation. This detachment, Gibson concludes, makes "The Bride" "one of the few stories seeming to have beneath it a broad, sympathetic understanding of humanity. There is nothing of the desperate fury, the intense anxiety appearing in the fiction where Crane is too personally involved" (125–26).

Overton P. James is another critic who sees the story's success as inhering in a blend of parody and earnestness, in a "fusion of comicality and seriousness that makes it possible for the serious matter to be treated flippantly." Crane achieves this fusion, James says, by presenting the showdown as a game, for games "are based on make-believe and are played for diversion" but are "governed by rules as strict as . . . those that govern the most serious practices"; and by setting the story at the liminal moment between two eras, a moment that enables the reader to "regard the customs of both eras as games and to be amused at those who [take these] games too seriously" (4–5). By these strategies, James argues, Crane demands that his reader walk a line, seeing the customs as games to avoid Potter's and Wilson's error of taking them too seriously, which results in Potter's bumbling in trying to live up to the grandeur of the new customs of the Pullman car and in Wilson's childishness in demanding that the old customs of the gunfight be honored, but at the same time not laughing condescendingly at these men for their excessive devotion to their pursuits. Crane's goal in making this demand, James concludes, is to instill in his reader the sympathetic understanding of humanity with which Gibson credits Crane himself, to make the reader understand that Potter's and Wilson's dilemma is but one variant of "the game of games," life, which is conducted by "a supernatural Master of the Revels" by whose manipulations almost everyone is at some point "tricked into acting unnaturally" (11).

George W. Johnson and Bergon also read "The Bride" as focused on the gamelike, ritualized aspects of the characters' behavior, but they see Crane's aim as less benevolent than James does. In Johnson's view, Crane is presenting a conflict between two equally ritualized and equally meaningless sets of conventions, those of "the Eastern feminized (hence, in the rhetoric of the nineties, civilized) script of the honeymoon . . . [and] the Western, masculine (hence, savage) ceremonies of the gunfight." The fact that nothing results of this conflict but Scratchy's shuffling off dejectedly, Johnson says, reveals "the latent horror of this comic tale"—that "there is no ultimate meaning to either [set of conventions], and that under a yellow sky men and their traditions make but passing indentations in the sands of time" (254). Bergon, as a gloss on this theme of ritual and convention in "The Bride," cites a letter that Crane's first biographer, Thomas Beer, included in his book. Crane here explains to an unknown correspondent that while he toured the West in 1895 he attempted to break up a bar fight in Lincoln, Nebraska. In so doing, he says, "I offended a local custom. These men fought each other every night. Their friends expected it and I was a darned nuisance with my Eastern scruples and all that. So first everybody cursed me fully and then they took me off to a judge who told me that I was an imbecile" (Beer 113–14). Stanley Wertheim and Paul Sorrentino have argued persuasively that a number of letters Beer quotes as Crane's are in fact Beer's own fabrications (*Correspondence* I, 6–10; "Thomas Beer" 2–16), but their findings did not come to light until well after the publication of Bergon's work; Bergon assumes that Crane's account here is genuine and asserts that it recounts his discovery of "[t]he curious ceremonial quality of Western violence," a discovery that he works into "The Bride" to demonstrate that the Western code of confrontation is actually no more "basic and elemental" than the codes of the East, that it is a different but nonetheless equally arbitrary social ritual (Introduction 23).

Marston LaFrance tacitly disagrees with this interpretation, for his thesis implies that the rituals of the East are at least somewhat less arbitrary and more valid than those of the West. The story, he argues, is strictly speaking not about an ideologically equal conflict between East and West but rather about the socially immature West becoming mature as a result of the encroachments of the more adult East. In Holton's formulation, the various manifestations of the West's social immaturity—"Wilson as bad man, the gunfight ritual, Potter's fears and illusions about his position in Yellow Sky"—immediately collapse in the face of his marriage and its attendant responsibilities, "before the mature social reality of his new estate," which is embodied in "the images of the East" such as the splendors of the Pullman car (212–14). Robertson similarly argues that the story is less about a clash of opposed cultures than about a struggle between adolescent image-fulfillment and adult reality. In his view, Scratchy in seeking to be a gunfighter at this moment in history is not only playing an anachronistic role but also attempting to live up to the ritualized, mythical image of such a figure rather than trying to attain the historical reality of the gunfighter; his behavior "is not a reenactment of the days when the West was really West, but a sentimentalized, trivialized experience wrung dry of any human potentiality for growth." When Potter refuses to play out this empty ritual, his marriage indicating his commitment to change, to potential for growth, Scratchy is "shaken from empty image fulfillment to a realization that his gunfighter role has become only a pointless game" (252). Levenson offers a comparable assessment of this moment, asserting that the reason that Scratchy is comically baffled upon meeting Potter and his bride is that here for the first time "he encounters people instead of fixed roles" (lxxv).

A number of other critics, while not disagreeing with the foregoing readings, regard "The Bride" as one of Crane's best stories because of their sense that its significance extends well beyond the historically specific conflict of civilized East and untamed West.

Ben Merchant Vorpahl, for instance, agrees that the story can be read as a parody of the standard Western tale, but he argues that it ultimately transcends this relatively simple level as a result of Crane's "ability to invest the narrative with a chronological urgency by building into its structure a tension between old and new, expressing its theme through image patterns which suggest such a tension on several levels." By this means, Vorpahl says, Crane links the myth of the West that is his immediate subject here with the two other predominant American myths of escape: "a preoccupation with youth, wishfully coupled with the notion that such youth might be discovered or even regained in the 'new' world so often identified with it" (208).

Most of the other critics in this group see Crane engaging not only with larger American levels of meaning but with universal ones. Neville Denny asserts that the train as a whole and the Pullman coach in particular are not just symbols of the advancing East but are as well "images of human order, design, and moral 'glory,'" against which, in Scratchy's obnoxious behavior and the saloon habitués' indifference to it, Crane counterposes "images of moral squalor, of the world of beasts." Crane's goal with this imagery, Denny explains, is a not simply a symbolically shaded depiction of Eastern versus Western codes of conduct but rather a more generally applicable representation of "the conduct which distinguishes us from the animals," conduct that Crane believes is the outcome of "engagement with life, and continual questioning, deliberate or enforced, of the stereotyped patterns conduct is always threatening to freeze into" (35). Stallman offers a similar view, arguing that behind the specific fears of the collapse of the frontier and of the responsibilities imposed by marriage and commitment to civilization that beset Wilson and Potter respectively lies a more universal "fear of changed worlds" (*Biography* 326), in the scheme of which Potter represents "the idealistic world of spiritual values whose force lies in its innocence" and Wilson embodies "the non-imaginative world of crass realities" (*Houses* 109). Bettina Knapp likewise finds universal applicability, asserting that Crane's ultimate goal in his presentation of the showdown is to demonstrate how powerfully a single incident can "point up the meaning of dread, . . . the fear of change and [the] apprehension that comes with the shattering of illusions and preconceived notions" (156).

Wolford offers a more detailed reading of the story's breadth of application. In his view, "The Bride" is "primarily about the fall of America's Old West as it occurs within the structure of a submyth called 'the showdown,'" but he argues that Crane also draws on another, older myth, the story of the fall of Troy, to universalize his tale, to make it "symbolic of all mythical falls" (94–95). Crane's most widespread borrowing from this source, Wolford says, is his use of repeated epithets to identify his characters, but he also builds in more specific links, such as the plot device of having a wayfaring hero return home with an unexpected bride and seek to avoid a confrontation, through which actions Potter brings Paris to mind. The incongruity between these two heroes, Wolford continues, is part of Crane's intention, as is the depiction of Scratchy, allegedly a gunfighter of epic ability, as actually rather clumsy and childish, for Crane's true aim is not just to universalize "The Bride" but also to make it a mock-epic, to call attention to the discrepancy between the idealized behavior presented in the original story and the more mundane reality depicted in his own version, and ultimately by that means to ridicule his ancient sources as well, "to mock the myths that tell the story of all such falls" (100). However, Wolford concludes, Crane does not entirely attain his satiric ends. A problem inherent in any use of classical conventions for mockery is that "something epical may rub off on the thing being mocked," and Crane, unlike Shakespeare in his debunking play about the Trojan War, *Troilus and Cressida*, does not fully overcome this difficulty; the reader of "The Bride" remains at least somewhat susceptible to a "sense of loss and pity over the end of an age and that age's heroes" (100–101).

Gullason, Eric Solomon, Bergon, Burns and Levernier, Michael J. Collins, and William Bysshe Stein present further variations on this theme of wider applicability. Gullason sees the story's immediate setting as pointing to Crane's larger central theme: "the inevitable confrontation between the past, the present, and the future—the tragedy of Time." This broader tragedy, Gullason says, is made clear at the conclusion, as Scratchy shuffles away, for here the reader "senses both the note of expectation for the future, and that of loneliness and resignation for the past" (480). Solomon regards the story as primarily a parody of the classic Western, but beneath the humor he discerns a serious examination of the interdependence of human beings in the creation of identity. In the showdown, both Potter and Scratchy exchange one identity for another: Potter is no longer "the lone marshal, ever ready for a fight," but rather a married man and a responsible official, and Scratchy is no longer the master gunfighter, but rather "the town bum, an aging cowboy who is an anachronism." The difference between these two is that initially Potter recognizes and accepts what has happened while Scratchy does not; the reality of one's dependence on others for identity dawns on both Scratchy and the reader as the erstwhile outlaw gropes his way to the realization that "Potter's shucking off his character as mythic marshal" means that Scratchy "cannot retain his own particular dream role as mythic Western gunfighter" (252–53).

Bergon, building on his argument, noted above, that Crane's point is that the Eastern and Western codes of behavior are both nothing more than arbitrary social rituals (Introduction 23), contends that despite this equality of essential meaninglessness Crane considers such codes necessary to human existence. Despite their unaccustomed divergence in adhering to different codes as a result of the marriage, Bergon says, Scratchy and Potter nevertheless are both still clinging to ritual, to ceremony, and the deeper conflict presented here is not between their different forms of ceremony but rather between the very concept of ceremony itself and its real polar opposite, chaos, which will be the result of the passage of time if one does not insist on some form of ceremony (*Artistry* 124).

Burns and Levernier perceive another sort of deep conflict at work, between male and female principles. They claim that Scratchy embodies the traits traditionally regarded as male, "self-reliance, aggressiveness, and unbridled assertiveness," while Potter exemplifies customarily female ones, "passivity, dependence, and unassuming acceptance," and that Crane underscores this opposition with carefully placed sexual imagery. His motive here, they argue, is to draw the reader's attention to "the androgynous implications of the mating of cultures which occurred on the American frontier" and to make the reader aware thereby that androgyny, "[r]ather than limiting human growth by defining it according to sexual stereotypes, . . . synthesizes male and female attributes into a more integrated, flexible concept of humanity" (237). In aligning himself with his bride, Burns and Levernier explain, Potter chooses social stability, which is desirable but also dull and stultifying, over the values he formerly shared with Scratchy, values that Crane himself "finds both enticing and unsettling" (239). Crane's response to this conflict within himself is to make the showdown provoked by this realignment a test of Potter's and Wilson's "respective masculinities," with Potter's being effectively androgynous, "a new and expanded code of masculinity, one which he need not prove to others because it is based on a realistic appraisal of his own human identity." Viewed from this perspective, they continue, the showdown possesses homoerotic overtones that suggest Freud's three stages of sexual development. Scratchy, roaring and firing his pistols, is at the first of these, the auto-erotic. The showdown itself represents the second stage, the homo-erotic, in that by means of this confrontation Scratchy is attempting to woo Potter away from his bride and back into their former relationship. Potter's refusal of this wooing indicates his progression to the third stage, mature het-erosexual relationships. "Secure in his own identity," Burns and Levernier say, "Potter, like Yellow Sky, has grown up and, from a Freudian point of view, is able to accept the responsibilities which civilization (i.e., the bride) demands of him," a condition that Crane himself, despite a degree of continuing ambivalence, regards as ultimately the best (240–41).

Collins proposes what might be regarded as a Jungian rather than a Freudian interpretation. Specifically, he links "The Bride," as well as two of Crane's other Westerns, "The Blue Hotel" and "The Five White Mice," to the genre that Northrop Frye in *Anatomy of Criticism* calls "ironic myth." In Frye's formulation, this genre is "a parody of romance: the application of romantic mythical forms to a more realistic content which fits them in unexpected ways" (qtd. in Collins 141). Crane uses this mode, "uses the familiar elements of the Western romance in a realistic setting," Collins explains, to create "an ironic world that seems a recognizable representation of the one in which we live," his goal being to reveal the disjunction between the world of romance and that of reality. Although Potter is presented as a comic figure on the train, Collins says, in Yellow Sky he remains essentially the gunfighting marshal of the con-ventional Western romance; and despite Scratchy's humorous aspects he is the villain of this genre, "quick, agile, competent, and dangerous." Thus, the confrontation between these two seems bound to produce the bloody show-down equally typical of the Western romance. But at the climactic moment, Potter suddenly slips out of this realm and into the real world. Like the marshal of romance, he "will still do what has to be done, but now not simply because he must, but because he wants to insure a settled, ordered, civilized life for himself and his wife" (143). In other words, Collins explains, by marrying, Potter metamorphoses from the hero of romance into "a complex human being, a husband as well as a marshal," and he therefore "embodies, as the conventional Western hero never does, the complexities and ironies of life in the real world," a condition that baffles and defeats Scratchy. However, like Burns and Levernier, Collins does not see Crane regarding this conclusion as an unmitigatedly happy one, for Scratchy's forlorn demeanor indicates to the reader that the "complex, ironic, and ambiguous" real world "can never offer anything so pure and heroic as a gunfight" (144).

As he does with many of Crane's stories, Stein reads "The Bride" as a statement of proto-existentialist philosophy, although in this case he sees that statement as comic, whereas he regards it as serious in most of Crane's other works, such as "The Blue Hotel," "The Monster," and "The Five White Mice." Specifically, Stein argues that Potter is depicted in what will later be defined as the existential dilemma over identity and being, for his excessive anxiety over what the citizens of Yellow Sky will say about his marriage shows that, like most modern humans, he lacks any "inward sense of selfhood. He is what people believe him to be, and he has modeled his personality on their expectations" (184). Holton strikes a similar note, asserting that Potter's intense awareness of being seen, of his image, is "a grotesque rendering of the peculiarly reflexive quality of the modern condition," a condition that makes him "curiously unsuited to the role of western marshal" (228–29). However, Holton's point that reflexivity is both modern and unsuitable for this role might require further elucidation to render it fully persuasive, since many of the most famous Western lawmen, with whom Crane would undoubtedly have been familiar, such as Wyatt Earp, James Butler "Wild Bill" Hickock, and William Barclay "Bat" Masterson, certainly exhibited a tremendous concern for their images.

Many critics offer commentaries not only on Crane's themes in "The Bride" but also on his formal skills, which they uniformly rate very highly. In the area of structure, Ralph Ellison sees the story as operating through a series of ironic reversals, the most important being the defeat of the armed Scratchy by the unarmed Potter, followed closely by the juxtaposition of Scratchy's clear recognition of "where he is"—the new West—with Potter's continued failure to recognize that "his new estate has its own complications," such as the condescension he met with from the porter and the waiter on the train. These reversals, Ellison concludes, with their demand for close attention and mental agility from the reader, render "the form of the story . . . one with its meaning: the necessity for vigilance in confronting historical change is unending" (72–74). James concurs that structure and meaning are closely related in this story; he reads it as composed of four sections, each of which presents one aspect of the overall theme of struggle between a passing and a coming era. In the first section, which takes place on the train, Potter awkwardly tries to adapt to the new era. In the second, the scene set in the Weary Gentleman Saloon, Scratchy demands that the passing era not be given up, an action that leads directly to the third section, which chronicles Scratchy's rampage through the town in search of someone to preserve this era with him. Finally, in the fourth section, the showdown, these eras come into direct conflict and that conflict is resolved (7–8).

Robert G. Cook and Holton likewise point out this four-section organization, but they add that Crane reinforces this narrative structure with a related visual schema. Cook says that in terms of narrative structure the story "consists of two converging lines—the one beginning in the train in section one, the other beginning in the Weary Gentleman Saloon in section two," with the lines meeting in section four. This convergence is depicted visually in section one, he continues, in the angle formed by the ribbon of mist rising in one direction and the train approaching from another, with Yellow Sky at the apex; and it reappears in section four when Potter and Wilson meet at right angles rather than head on. This visual representation, Cook says, intensifies "the suggestion of a fateful encounter" impending on the narrative level, and when this encounter dissolves into "embarrassment and awkwardness" Crane once again uses visual imagery to complement his narrative line, for the final description of Scratchy's funnel-shaped tracks suggests "converging elements . . . brought together inconclusively" (369). Holton similarly notes Crane's visual images of convergence that correspond to the plot, pointing out that the river, the gathering place for Wilson's old gang, and the railroad, the symbol of the advancing East, intersect at Yellow Sky; and he points out further that the conclusion is based on shifts of vision. Potter's "new commitment for his eye," the splendor of the Pullman car that he recalls at the moment of the showdown, forces Scratchy to acknowledge "the ritualized artificiality of his vision," and then Potter attains a new vision of himself as well, one that does not include the part of himself that resembled Wilson in its desire for ritualized artifice, a resemblance that Crane suggests by the visual links of black and red in both men's clothing and demeanor. This carefully thought out and meaningful multileveled patterning, Holton concludes, "clearly objectifies Crane's statement" and makes "The Bride" his "most formally correct, perhaps even his finest story" (231–33).

Nagel, linking Crane's visual effects with several other elements, sees "The Bride" as a prime example of Crane's use of an episodic structural approach, a result partly of his artistic roots in sketch journalism and partly of his epistemological orientation, which, in Nagel's view, is a conviction that the nature of experience is an awareness of serial fragments occurring in the individual's consciousness, a belief that places Crane both artistically and philosophically in the Impressionists' camp rather than the Realists' or Naturalists'. What links such fragments together in the case of this story, Nagel says, is Crane's use of them to produce "important juxtapositions of events and ideas." The first two scenes, for instance, of the train and the town respectively, are despite their spatial fragmentation connected by the theme of "cultural displacements," experienced by Potter and his bride on the train and by the drummer in the saloon. The third scene is then linked to these two by its focus on temporal displacement—its presentation of Scratchy as a gunfighter in the right place but the wrong time. The fourth is bound to these three through Crane's emphasis on the naiveté of all the characters suffering these displacements. Thus, Nagel concludes, despite its fragmentation "the story is a model of unity: it combines two antithetical lines of action, focused on a common idea in four episodes, to form a confrontation of great, if comic, intensity" (125–26).

Perhaps the most detailed discussion of Crane's technical achievements in "The Bride" comes from Vorpahl. He locates the story in Crane's sense, brought home to him by his 1895 Western trip, that both his own and the nation's youth were passing; "The Bride" is his linking of "his own intensely individual insights with the larger themes of history," in which he makes "time and its role as killer his theme, expressing it through a remarkably evocative setting and a highly sophisticated structure" (197–98). Crane begins using the setting to establish his theme, Vorpahl explains, in his very first sentence. The idea that the plains of Texas are pouring eastward suggests the civilizing process that Potter has helped by his marriage; Crane uses "optical illusion to identify historical reality," and so his setting "is not merely scenic, but chronological as well." The same is true of the last sentence, Vorpahl continues, for Scratchy's funnel-shaped tracks "signify the retreat of the old order before the new." Thus, "[b]oth first and last sentences designate time as one of the story's central concerns by expressing the landscape as history rather than scenery" (198–99), a fact that renders the landscape a key structural element as well. And Crane further interconnects landscape and structure, Vorpahl asserts, by placing "chronological" elements in tension with "artificial" ones in every setting, with the latter holding out "the brave but delusive hope of escaping history through artifice." In the first scene, for example, the plains are the chronological element, for their seeming to pour eastward indicates the inevitability of time and historical change, and the Pullman car is the artificial one, its decorative interior suggesting stasis in opposition to the seeming movement of the plains (200). This pattern of oppositions ultimately leads the reader in the final scene to perceive Scratchy's retreat as "both historical and emblematic, . . . at once equivalent to the train's actual motion at the outset and identical with the process which sweeps the plains of Texas eastward" (208).

Bergon and John Gerlach tacitly assent to this assessment of Crane's skilled handling of the beginning and ending of this story, for they each provide a similar estimation of one or the other of these elements. Bergon lauds the first sentence as a prime example of its author's talent for dramatic compression, noting that it "fixes the sensation of a train ride through a kinesthetic detail, and that detail also supplies a theme that the rest of the story will develop—that is, the symbolic notion that the plains of Texans are rapidly moving eastward (*Artistry* 94–95). Gerlach is equally complimentary of Crane's talent for thematic compression as evinced in the story's closing sentences. In terms of the immediate level of the action of the story, Gerlach says, "[w]hat triumphs here is common sense; the world of domesticity, of marriage, cancels the games male grownups play with guns." Simultaneously, on a larger level this conclusion serves by virtue of its anticlimactic character as part of what Gerlach terms Crane's thematic architectonics—that is, it "implies something about the relation of endings in fiction to endings in life that [Henry] James would later make more explicit." Crane's characters in general, Gerlach says, "often swell with delusions, some of them never adjusting to an accurate sense of the realities of war or the struggle with nature," and "one way to express this vision is to invert linear narrative . . ., for part of Crane's point is that a mistaken linearity derived from a fictional convention"—the satisfactory resolution of a climactic ending—"which expresses our hopes without reference to our conditions, is what sustains our delusions." In reality, Gerlach concludes, "[l]ife brings down our expectations, and the appropriate vehicle for the discovery of our limitations is the anticlimactic ending" (73).

While many of the above readings incorporate Crane's handling of imagery in this story, Sanford Marovitz's exegesis takes this subject as its primary focus. On the narrative level, he agrees with the consensus that the story is about the victory of civilization over the frontier, which is already gone when the action begins, since trains already run to Yellow Sky on fixed schedules, traveling drummers make regular rounds to the town's merchants, and even the local badman wears a shirt imported from the East. On the level of imagery, however, Marovitz sees "The Bride" as a deterministic version of an archetypal conflict between good and evil, an idea conveyed through the demonic and satanic imagery with which Crane surrounds Scratchy, beginning with the connection of his name to the common diabolic nickname "Old Scratch." In thus depicting Scratchy as "the Devil incarnate" and having him defeated by a marshal who wields not a gun but rather "the irresistible force of the inevitable environmental changes that come with social evolution," Crane implies that

> even the most vicious and malignant evil is in a sense only temporal; for like all earthly goodness, to which it is kin by virtue of its limitations, it is but a moral issue in an amoral world; and it is therefore subject to a changing environment just as the environment itself is paradoxically subject to the ineluctable passage of time. (139)

Alice Hall Petry also concerns herself with Crane's handling of names in "The Bride"; she considers this story one of the best examples of Crane's overlooked technique of giving his characters names that express their personalities and also contribute thematically and tonally. Like Marovitz, she links Scratchy to "Old Scratch," but she argues that the *-y* suffix "deflates Wilson's demonism, his capacity to do real harm," a condition she sees as consonant with her view that Crane's primary purpose here is to deflate and debunk the West. As further proof of this reading, she points out the blandness of the name Jack Potter compared to the names of legendary marshals such as Wyatt Earp and Wild Bill Hickock, as well as its connection to "Potter's Field" as opposed to the more romantic "Boot Hill"; these characteristics imply that Yellow Sky, as Potter's field of action, is anonymous, drained of romance—is "one huge cemetery for the dying Westerners." Equally crucial to this interpretation is the bride's lack of any name, Petry says, for in this story "dramatizing the dying of the sentimentalized West with the encroachment of the lifestyle of the civilized East" the bride is insignificant as an individual; she matters only as a symbolic representative of "this rather abstract cultural and demographic concept" (45–47).

Works Cited

Barnes, Robert. "Crane's 'The Bride Comes to Yellow Sky.'" *Explicator* 16 (1958):39.

Bassan, Maurice. Introduction. *Stephen Crane: A Collection of Critical Essays*. Ed. Maurice Bassan. Englewood Cliffs, N.J.: Prentice-Hall, 1967, 1–11.

Beer, Thomas. *Stephen Crane: A Study in American Letters.* New York: Knopf, 1923.

Bellman, Samuel Irving. "Stephen Crane's Vaudeville Marriage: 'The Bride Comes to Yellow Sky.'" *Selected Essays: International Conference on Wit and Humor 1986.* Ed. Dorothy M. Joiner. Carrollton, GA: West Georgia College International Conference, 1988, 14–19.

Benfey, Christopher. *The Double Life of Stephen Crane*. New York: Knopf, 1992.

Bergon, Frank. Introduction. *The Western Writings of Stephen Crane*. New American Library, 1979, 1–27.

———. *Stephen Crane's Artistry*. New York: Columbia University Press, 1975.

Bernard, Kenneth. "'The Bride Comes to Yellow Sky': History as Elegy." *English Record* 17 (April 1967):17–20.

Berryman, John. *Stephen Crane*. New York: Sloane, 1950.

Bowers, Fredson. Textual Introduction. *Tales of Adventure*. Vol. 5 of The University of Virginia Edition of *The Works of Stephen Crane*. Ed. Fredson Bowers. Charlottesville: University Press of Virginia, 1970, cxxxiii–cxcv.

Burns, Shannon, and James A. Levernier. "Androgyny in Stephen Crane's 'The Bride Comes to Yellow Sky.'" *Research Studies* 45 (1977):236–43.

———. "Crane's 'The Bride Comes to Yellow Sky.'" *Explicator* 37 (1979):36–37.

Cady, Edwin H. *Stephen Crane*. Rev. ed. New York: Twayne, 1982.

Collins, Michael J. "Realism and Romance in the Western Stories of Stephen Crane." *Under the Sun: Myth and Realism in Western American Literature*. Ed. Barbara Howard Meldrum. Troy, N.Y.: Whitston, 1985, 139–48.

Colvert, James B. *Stephen Crane*. New York: Harcourt Brace Jovanovich, 1984.

Cook, Robert G. "Stephen Crane's 'The Bride Comes to Yellow Sky.'" *Studies in Short Fiction* 2 (1965):368–69.

Crane, Stephen. "The Bride Comes to Yellow Sky." *Tales of Adventure* 109–20.

Deamer, Robert Glen. "Remarks on the Western Stance of Stephen Crane." *Western American Literature* 15 (Summer 1980):122–41.

———. "Stephen Crane and the Western Myth." *Western American Literature* 7 (Summer 1972):111–23.

Dean, James L. "The Wests of Howells and Crane." *American Literary Realism* 10 (1977):254–66.

Denny, Neville. "Imagination and Experience in Stephen Crane." *English Studies in Africa* 9 (1966):28–42.

Ellison, Ralph. "Stephen Crane and the Mainstream of American Fiction." *Shadow and Act*. New York: Random House, 1964, 60–76.

Ferguson, S. C. "Crane's 'The Bride Comes to Yellow Sky.'" *Explicator* 21 (1963):59.

Geismar, Maxwell. *Rebels and Ancestors*. Boston: Houghton Mifflin, 1953.

Gerlach, John. "The Bride Comes to Yellow Sky." *Towards the End: Closure and Structure in the American Short Story*. Tuscaloosa: University of Alabama Press, 1985, 71–75.

Gibson, Donald B. *The Fiction of Stephen Crane*. Carbondale: Southern Illinois University Press, 1968.

Gullason, Thomas A. "Stephen Crane's Short Stories: The True Road." *Stephen Crane's Career: Perspectives and Evaluations*. Ed. Thomas A. Gullason. New York: New York University Press, 1972, 470–86.

Halliburton, David. *The Color of the Sky: A Study of Stephen Crane*. Cambridge: Cambridge University Press, 1989.

Holton, Milne. *Cylinder of Vision: The Fiction and Journalistic Writings of Stephen Crane*. Baton Rouge: Louisiana State University Press, 1972.

James, Overton P. "The 'Game' in 'The Bride Comes to Yellow Sky.'" *Xavier University Studies* 4 (1965):3–11.

Johnson, George W. "Stephen Crane's Metaphor of Decorum." *PMLA* 78 (1963): 250–56.

Knapp, Bettina L. *Stephen Crane*. New York: Ungar, 1987.

LaFrance, Marston. *A Reading of Stephen Crane*. Oxford: Clarendon, 1971.

Levenson, J. C. Introduction. *Tales of Adventure* xv–cxxxii.

Marovitz, Sanford E. "Scratchy the Demon in 'The Bride Comes to Yellow Sky.'" *Tennessee Studies in Literature* 16 (1971):137–40.

Nagel, James. *Stephen Crane and Literary Impressionism*. University Park: Pennsylvania State University Press, 1980.

Petry, Alice Hall. "Crane's 'The Bride Comes to Yellow Sky.'" *Explicator* 42 (1983):45–47.

Robertson, Jamie. "Stephen Crane, Eastern Outsider in the West and Mexico." *Western American Literature* 13 (Nov. 1978):243–57.

Solomon, Eric. *Stephen Crane: From Parody to Realism*. Cambridge: Harvard University Press, 1966.

Stallman, R. W. "Crane's Short Stories." *The Houses That James Built*. East Lansing: Michigan State University Press, 1961, 103–10.

———. *Stephen Crane: A Biography*. New York: George Braziller, 1968.

Stein, William B. "Stephen Crane's *Homo Absurdus*." *Bucknell Review* 8 (1959): 168–88.

Tibbetts, A. M. "Stephen Crane's 'The Bride Comes to Yellow Sky.'" *English Journal* 54 (1965):314–16.

Vanouse, Donald. "Popular Culture in the Writings of Stephen Crane." *Journal of Popular Culture* 10 (1976):424–30.

Vorpahl, Ben Merchant. "Murder by the Minute: Old and New in 'The Bride Comes to Yellow Sky.'" *Nineteenth-Century Fiction* 26 (1971):196–218.

Wertheim, Stanley, and Paul Sorrentino. "Thomas Beer: The Clay Feet of Stephen Crane Biography." *American Literary Realism* 22 (Spring 1990): 2–16.

———, eds. *The Correspondence of Stephen Crane*. Vol. 1. New York: Columbia University Press, 1988.

Wolford, Chester L. *The Anger of Stephen Crane: Fiction and the Epic Tradition*. Lincoln: University of Nebraska Press, 1983.

———. *Stephen Crane: A Study of the Short Fiction*. Boston: Twayne, 1989.

The Carriage-Lamps

Publication History

This story made its initial appearance in the February 1900 issue of *Harper's New Monthly Magazine* (100:366–72), number seven in the thirteen-part series—running in every issue from August 1899 through August 1900—of Crane's tales of Whilomville. Like the rest of this series, it was then collected in the volume *Whilomville Stories*, which Harper & Brothers published in August 1900 in America and in November of the same year in England (Bowers 103). In 1926, it appeared in volume 5 of *The Work of Stephen Crane* (12 vols., New York: Knopf, 1925–27), edited by Wilson Follett; and in 1963 Thomas A. Gullason included it in *The Complete Short Stories and Sketches of Stephen Crane* (Garden City, N.Y.: Doubleday).

Circumstances of Composition

"The Carriage-Lamps" was most likely written at Brede Place, Sussex, Crane's last English home, at some point during the summer or early fall of 1899, since it does not appear on two lists of stories that Crane drew up in March of that year but is present on one he compiled sometime that summer (Levenson liii–liv). It was certainly complete and submitted for publication before September 22, 1899, for on that date Crane wrote to his English agent, James Pinker, complaining that the publisher, *Harper's New Monthly Magazine*, had underpaid him for this story and "The Knife," another tale also set in the fictional town of Whilomville (*Correspondence* II, 518). But it is possible to narrow down the time for "The Carriage-Lamps" further—to surmise that Crane had completed and submitted it before August 31, 1899—because a letter of that date from Crane's common-law wife, Cora, to Pinker promises that Crane will shortly finish a Whilomville story that goes unnamed but seems to be "The Knife" (*Correspondence* II, 508–09; Levenson liv), and this story probably postdates "The Carriage-Lamps," given that *Harper's* published this story before it ran "The Knife."

Sources and Influences

Crane's various biographers have shown that many of the Whilomville stories owe at least part of their genesis to events of his own childhood, passed in the

New Jersey towns of Bloomington, Paterson, Jersey City, and Asbury Park, and the New York town of Port Jervis. No one has identified a specific incident of real-life mischief followed by paternal punishment that might have informed "Carriage-Lamps," but it is not difficult to imagine the young Crane, described by a much older sister-in-law as "a lovable boy, full of life and animal spirits" (qtd. in Stallman 7), committing some sort of transgression similar to the one limned in this story; nor is it difficult to imagine his father, allegedly characterized by Crane himself as being "so simple and good that I often think he didn't know much of anything about humanity" (qtd. in Beer 40–41), responding in the benevolently amused manner of Dr. Trescott as he observes the attempted rescue, buccaneer-style, that Jimmie's friends implement.

Milne Holton is on more definite ground in his linking of this story to a literary antecedent. Pointing out the "elaborately literary" nature of Jimmie's friends' pirate plan, followed by Dr. Trescott's "fatuously" forgiving Jimmie, he argues that the story's ending is a deliberate "travesty of what Crane considered the travestied ending of *Huckleberry Finn*" (216).

Relationship to Other Crane Works

All the Whilomville stories are loosely connected in that all focus on Jimmie Trescott and his family and friends, but in two related respects "Carriage-Lamps" is more closely linked to one of the others, "Lynx-Hunting," than to the rest. First of all, in both these stories the same boy, Willie Dalzel, is the instigator of much of the trouble that befalls Jimmie, and this instigation stems in both cases from Willie's overactive, Tom Sawyer-like imagination, conditioned by his reading of adventure novels. In "Lynx-Hunting" it is his grandiloquent insistence that he can bag a lynx with his newly acquired gun that results in Jimmie's inadvertent shooting of Henry Fleming's cow, while in "Carriage-Lamps" it is his trading of presumably this same gun to Jimmie that leads to Jimmie's being punished by Dr. Trescott, with this punishment almost compounded by Willie's desire to rescue Jimmie from confinement in a manner that accords with his recent reading of *The Red Captain: A Tale of the Pirates of the Spanish Main*. (Willie is also presented as the "chieftain" of the boys in Jimmie's circle in three other Whilomville stories, "The Fight," "The City Urchin and the Chaste Villagers," and "The Trial, Execution, and Burial of Homer Phelps"; in the latter two it is once again his insistence that the boys' games conform to the paradigms he has formulated from dime-novels that generates much of the conflict.)

Second, as Chester L. Wolford points out, both "Lynx-Hunting" and "Carriage-Lamps" deal with "boyish crimes left unpunished" due to the relatively minor nature of those crimes and the humor of the exaggerated efforts of the boys involved to evade responsibility. As initiated by Willie, the ridiculous, adventure-novel-derived nature of these efforts leaves the adult male authority figures—in "Lynx" Henry Fleming and in "Lamps" Dr. Trescott—unable to mete out punishment, unable to do anything but laugh, by which response these adults reveal their "natural good sense," residing in their grasp of proportion and keen awareness of absurdity (55–56).

Critical Studies

While not singling "Carriage-Lamps" out for abuse, critics have frequently been unkind to the Whilomville stories. H. E. Bates dismisses them as being "as commonplace as calico" and thus an indication of the diminished state of Crane's powers in this late stage of his life. The method of these stories, he says, "is that of any tenth-rate provincial reporter without the wit to determine whether what he is doing is good or bad" (148). James B. Stronks is a bit less extreme; he regards the Whilomville pieces as "thin and slight" because of their focus on mundane situations that do not evoke the "nerveless intensity" of Crane at his best, but he points out that they are nevertheless preferable to most late-Victorian literature about children (343).

In a more positive vein, Gullason acknowledges that none of the Whilomville stories is individually outstanding but argues that as a group they constitute a kind of loose novel that presents "a vibrant and full world" and in so doing effectively "illuminate[s] a number of universal truths about children, family life, and one's former home town" (483). Gullason does not say what particular truths are revealed in "Carriage-Lamps," but Robert W. Stallman and Eric Solomon do offer specific insights. Stallman says that, with a good deal of humor concerning the melodramatic nature of children's feelings, the story shows Jimmie Trescott learning that "the world is a bitter place where fate conspires to make him the victim of mere chance," since the lamps might just as easily have been placed elsewhere, in which case he would not have broken them in his fury and thus would not have been punished (479). Solomon takes a more serious view. Like Gullason, he regards the Whilomville stories as a loose novel, but he sees the world they depict as grim rather than vibrant; his argument is that the stories track Jimmie's passage from the unthinking and therefore innocent misdeeds of childhood to the hypocritical and thus more odious malfeasances of adulthood (207). "Carriage-Lamps," he says, is a "rather flimsy" chapter in this progression but does contribute to it by partaking of one of Crane's overarching points in the series, that the supposedly mature behavior of adults is in fact as infantile as that of children. Jimmie is plainly childish, Solomon explains, when he blames Peter Washington for his punishment, but his parents are equally childish, albeit in a more subtle fashion, when they blame Jimmie's misconduct on the supposed bad influence of his friends rather than admitting that it stems from his own nature (219).

Works Cited

Bates, H. E. "H. E. Bates on Stephen Crane." *Stephen Crane's Career: Perspectives and Evaluations*. Ed. Thomas A. Gullason. New York: New York University Press, 1972, 146–50.

Beer, Thomas. *Stephen Crane: A Study in American Letters*. New York: Knopf, 1923.

Bowers, Fredson. Textual Introduction. *Tales of Whilomville*. Vol. 7 of The University of Virginia Edition of *The Works of Stephen Crane*. Ed. Fredson Bowers. Charlottesville: University Press of Virginia, 1968, 103–26.

Gullason, Thomas A. "Stephen Crane's Short Stories: The True Road." *Stephen Crane's Career: Perspectives and Evaluations*. Ed. Thomas A. Gullason. New York: New York University Press, 1972, 470–86.

Holton, Milne. *Cylinder of Vision: The Fiction and Journalistic Writings of Stephen Crane*. Baton Rouge: Louisiana State University Press, 1972.

Levenson, J. C. Introduction. *Tales of Whilomville* xi–lx.

Solomon, Eric. *Stephen Crane: From Parody to Realism*. Cambridge: Harvard University Press, 1966.

Stallman, Robert W. *Stephen Crane: A Biography*. New York: George Braziller, 1968.

Stronks, James B. "Stephen Crane's English Years: The Legend Corrected." *Papers of the Bibliographical Society of America* 57 (1963):340–49.

Wertheim, Stanley, and Paul Sorrentino, eds. *The Correspondence of Stephen Crane*. Vol. 1. New York: Columbia University Press, 1988.

Wolford, Chester L. *Stephen Crane: A Study of the Short Fiction*. Boston: Twayne, 1989.

The City Urchin and the Chaste Villagers

Publication History

This story initially ran in the July 1900 issue of *Harper's New Monthly Magazine* (101:216–21). It was the twelfth installment in the series of thirteen Whilomville tales by Crane that appeared in *Harper's* between August 1899 and August 1900. Like the rest of this series, it was then included in the collection *Whilomville Stories*, which Harper & Brothers published in America in August 1900 and in England in November of the same year (Bowers 103).

Editor Wilson Follett placed the story in volume 5, published in 1926, of *The Work of Stephen Crane* (12 vols., New York: Knopf, 1925–27), and Thomas A. Gullason included it in his 1963 collection *The Complete Short Stories and Sketches of Stephen Crane* (Garden City, N.Y.: Doubleday).

Circumstances of Composition

This story appears to have been composed at Crane's last British residence, Brede Place, Sussex, at the end of October 1899, making it the twelfth of the thirteen tales Crane wrote in that year about the fictional village of Whilomville. In a letter of October 26, 1899, to Crane's British agent, James Pinker, Crane's common-law wife, Cora, asks for immediate payment for the eleventh Whilomville story, "The Fight," and promises to send another one the next day (*Correspondence* II, 541). She made good on this pledge on October 30, and in the letter accompanying this new submission she asks £30 for it (*Correspondence* II, 542). Since Crane's usual rate of pay was £10 per thousand words, this amount indicates a story of about three thousand words, a total that, as J. C. Levenson notes, closely matches the length of "The City Urchin" (lv).

Sources and Influences

Crane's biographers have linked many of the Whilomville stories to specific episodes in Crane's own or Cora's childhood, but no such precise connection has been made in the case of this tale. As Robert W. Stallman points out, however, this story and its immediate predecessor, "The Fight," probably had their genesis in Crane's frequent childhood experience of being "the new boy" at school, owing to his family's numerous relocations as his minister father moved from pulpit to pulpit and, after his father's death, as his mother sought a locale in which she could support her children (479). Such conditions would logically have made Crane more than ordinarily sensitive to the subjects he takes up in these two stories: the "tribal" rituals through which members of established groups of children determine their hierarchies and deal with newcomers, and the dynamics of the relationships between "insiders" and "outsiders" that develop as the children enact these rituals.

Relationship to Other Crane Works

All the Whilomville stories are loosely connected in that all focus on Jimmie Trescott and his family and friends, but "The City Urchin" contains a number of specific narrative links with others of the series. Most significantly, as in

"Lynx-Hunting," "The Carriage-Lamps," and "The Trial, Execution, and Burial of Homer Phelps," the principal antagonist in this story is Jimmie's friend Willie Dalzel, who here as usual precipitates trouble by his efforts to maintain his place as "chieftain," as Crane frequently describes him, of the circle of boys to which he and Jimmie belong. In "The City Urchin" these efforts take the form of persecuting Johnnie Hedge, a boy whose family has recently moved to Whilomville from Jersey City, by his Tom Sawyer-like demand that a game of pirates he has devised follow the rules—that is, the narrative line—set forth in "a certain half-dime blood-and-thunder pamphlet" he has read (229), rules mandating that Willie frequently smack Johnnie's younger brother.

This self-aggrandizement through the creation of games based on his own trashy reading is Willie's chief activity in most of the stories in which he appears, including "Lynx-Hunting," "The Carriage-Lamps," and "The Trial," but in this case his goal of getting at Johnnie by this behavior produces a still closer link between "The City Urchin" and another story in the series, "The Fight," for these two both focus on the struggle for dominance between Willie and Johnnie: in "The Fight" Johnnie beats up both Jimmie and Willie; in "The City Urchin" a rematch between Johnnie and Willie, provoked by Willie's mistreatment of Johnnie's little brother, is broken up by Johnnie's mother, upon which the narrator concludes, "[t]he supreme power was Mrs. Hedge" (234).

Given this close narrative link between "The Fight" and "The City Urchin," two critics have proposed a thematic link as well. Chester L. Wolford sees them as combining to create a meditation on the violently primitive way any community responds to an outsider's upsetting of its established order, with the primitiveness emphasized in Crane's frequent use of martial and animal imagery and words such as *chieftain* and *tribe* in both stories to characterize the boys as they maneuver their way into the fights. Johnnie's presence and victory create the upset in "The Fight," and then Willie, as the community's representative, seeks to reimpose its order in "The City Urchin." Even though Mrs. Hedge, ostensibly a civilizing maternal figure, is the victor here, Wolford says, the sense of primitiveness still hangs in the air, for in her boxing of Johnnie's and Willie's ears "the notion remains that power is essentially physical, thus undermining the notion of Whilomville as a rural utopia" (59). Instead, Wolford concludes, in Whilomville "[p]ower resides with the strongest, as it does in the most primitive and savage tribes" (59).

David Halliburton is the other critic who takes this view of these two stories. Additionally, he links their meditation on the connections between savagery and community with two major Crane stories that lie outside the 1899–1900 *Harper's* Whilomville series; he argues that "The Fight" and "The City Urchin" are the comic versions, because the actions are performed by children, of Crane's deadly serious presentations of the savage adult responses to an outsider who supposedly threatens the community in "The Blue Hotel" and "The Monster" (234).

Critical Studies

The Whilomville stories as a group often come in for harsh criticism. In H. E. Bates's view they are "as commonplace as calico" and could be the work of "any tenth-rate provincial reporter without the wit to determine whether what he is doing is good or bad," which renders them nothing more than an indication of the diminished state of Crane's powers in this final period of his life (148). James B. Stronks offers a similar if more qualified assessment, calling the stories "thin and slight" due to their focus on mundane situations that do not evoke the "nerveless intensity" of Crane at his best, but he adds that they are still preferable to much of the rest of the literature about children that appeared in this era (343).

Some other critics take a more favorable view of the series as a whole and of several stories in particular, including "The City Urchin." Neville Denny says that this tale and the best of the other installments in the series effectively combine "lightness and mellow humour" with "a serious reference, an extension into 'adult' life sometimes sombre, sometimes ironic, but invariably penetrating and exact" (32). This combination is clear in "The City Urchin." Regarding a mellow handling of childhood, Stallman notes that along with "The Fight" the story presents one of the primal children's conflicts, that between the insider and the outsider, and humorously dramatizes two points: one of the quickest ways for an outsider to get inside is to defeat a couple of prominent insiders in combat, and, once defeated, those insiders will seek to restore their own standing by whatever means come to hand (281). Levenson likewise regards the story's approach as essentially mellow, but he also says that the younger Hedge boy's racist taunting of Peter Washington produces a sharp break in the story's overall pleasant tone, gives the story's title its meaning, and reveals Crane's lack of sentimentality about his ostensible "middle-class utopia" and what lies outside it. "The new boys from the city test the openness of the old society," Levenson explains, "and, as the victims of exclusion, are pitiable," but in their racism "they also bring intimations of other cruelties and more anarchic realms of being" that exist just beyond the more limited cruelty of Whilomville (lviii).

Denny's "extension into 'adult' life" can clearly be found in Levenson's assessment, but even if one limits such an extension only to the adult world of Whilomville, it is still present, in the common critical view that, despite the humorous elements in the conflict between the outsider and the insiders, Crane intends this conflict as a serious negative commentary on the behavior of supposedly more mature members of the community. In a reading similar to Wolford's argument, noted above in the section on this story's relationship to Crane's other works, that "The City Urchin" is part of a study of a community's reaction to the upsetting of its established order by an outsider, Milne Holton notes that in this story the social order that Johnnie Hedge overthrew in "The Fight" is reasserted by means both primitive and unheroic—nasty bullying and vicious fighting—and is shown to be even more unsavory by Jimmie Trescott's self-interested shifts to whatever party is momentarily winning, the baiting of Peter, and Willie's humiliating punishment by his mother, while Crane's metaphors insistently underscore the universal nature of these circumstances (221–22). Halliburton would seem to concur with this assessment, given his view that all the Whilomville tales deal in a reduced way with the issue of community in crisis (201), for this issue may be regarded as one source of the "universal truths about children, family life, and one's former home town" that Gullason says these stories present. This synthesis of truths leads Gullason to perhaps the most positive critical evaluation of the Whilomville cycle: he argues that their thematic richness and unity give the stories the form of a loose novel that offers "a vibrant and full world" and "demonstrates further . . . Crane's range and versatility" (483).

Works Cited

Bates, H. E. "H. E. Bates on Stephen Crane." *Stephen Crane's Career: Perspectives and Evaluations*. Ed. Thomas A. Gullason. New York: New York University Press, 1972, 146–50.

Bowers, Fredson. Textual Introduction. *Tales of Whilomville*. Vol. 7 of The University of Virginia Edition of *The Works of Stephen Crane*. Ed. Fredson Bowers. Charlottesville: University Press of Virginia, 1968, 103–26.

Denny, Neville. "Imagination and Experience in Stephen Crane." *English Studies in Africa* 9 (1966):28–42.

Gullason, Thomas A. "Stephen Crane's Short Stories: The True Road." *Stephen Crane's Career: Perspectives and Evaluations*. Ed. Thomas A. Gullason. New York: New York University Press, 1972, 470–86.

Halliburton, David. *The Color of the Sky: A Study of Stephen Crane*. Cambridge: Cambridge University Press, 1989.

Holton, Milne. *Cylinder of Vision: The Fiction and Journalistic Writings of Stephen Crane*. Baton Rouge: Louisiana State University Press, 1972.

Levenson, J. C. Introduction. *Tales of Whilomville* xi–lx.

Stallman, Robert W. *Stephen Crane: A Biography*. New York: George Braziller, 1968.

Stronks, James B. "Stephen Crane's English Years: The Legend Corrected." *Papers of the Bibliographical Society of America* 57 (1963):340–49.

Wertheim, Stanley, and Paul Sorrentino, eds. *The Correspondence of Stephen Crane*. Vol. 2. New York: Columbia University Press, 1988.

Wolford, Chester L. *Stephen Crane: A Study of the Short Fiction*. Boston: Twayne, 1989.

The Clan of No-Name

Publication History

This story first appeared in America on March 19, 1899, in a number of news-papers, including the *New York Herald*, the *Chicago Times-Herald*, and the *San Francisco Examiner*. Its first British publication came in the Christmas 1899 number of the magazine *Black and White* (13–16). It was then collected in the book *Wounds in the Rain*, which was published in September, 1900, by Frederick A. Stokes in America and Methuen in England (Bowers cxii–xiv). It was included in volume 2 of *The Work of Stephen Crane* (12 vols., New York: Knopf, 1925–27), edited by Wilson Follett and published in 1925, and it also appeared in *The Complete Short Stories and Sketches of Stephen Crane* (Garden City, N.Y.: Doubleday, 1963), edited by Thomas A. Gullason.

Circumstances of Composition

"The Clan of No-Name" is one of a number of pieces Crane wrote while he was living in Havana, Cuba, after the close of the Spanish-American War, which he covered as a reporter first for Joseph Pulitzer's *New York World* and then William Randolph Hearst's *New York Journal.* Crane was in Puerto Rico when the fighting ended on August 12, 1898, but shortly there-after he returned to Cuba, where he had spent most of his time during the war. He remained in Havana, living first in a hotel and then in a lodging-house, until around December 24 of that year, evidently preferring this mode of life to an immediate return to his home with his common-law wife, Cora, in England, where he faced considerable debts and what he seems to have regarded as excessively burdensome domestic and social obligations. He completed "Clan" by early October of 1898, for at that point he sent the story to his agent, Paul Revere Reynolds, commenting in the accompanying letter that "I am now sending you a *peach*. I love it devoted-ly" (*Correspondence* II, 379).

Sources and Influences

No one has identified any specific incident in Crane's own life as a source for this story. He witnessed a considerable amount of combat in the Cuban theater during the Spanish-American War, and, given the events he reports in many of his newspaper accounts, he evidently saw many men display the demeanor he gives to Manolo Prat here: a willingness to die bravely and quietly not for the sake of any cause but rather simply because such willingness is part of the unspoken code by which professional soldiers expect themselves to abide. One example that may be loosely connected to "The Clan of No-Name" is the behavior of a sergeant that Crane describes in "The Red Badge of Courage Was His Wig-Wag Flag," a newspaper dispatch about an anti-guerrilla operation in the hills above Guantánamo Bay, in which he himself participated, carried out by a mixed force of American Marines and Cuban insurgents of the type that appear in this story. One of the purposes of this action, which Crane also drew on for the story "Marines Signalling Under Fire at Guantánamo," was to indicate to the Navy ships offshore the locations of Spanish positions so that these ships could bombard them. The only way to do so was to turn one's face toward the sea, leaving one's back fully exposed to heavy enemy fire, and make use of signal flags, which rendered one a still more obvious target. Without a word or any indication that he regarded his action as anything other than a routine performance of his duty, Crane says, the "spruce young sergeant" rose and bent himself to this task, "solemnly and intently wigwagging" while twenty Spanish riflemen tried to kill him (*Reports* 138).

Richard Harding Davis, a fellow-correspondent in Cuba, details another wartime episode that may be relevant, an instance in which Crane had the necessarily tacit quality of the code of the professional driven home to him. At one point, Davis says, while the troops to which he and Crane had attached themselves were entrenching under fire, Crane, dressed in a long white raincoat that made him highly visible against the undergrowth, stood up and began walking about with his pipe in his mouth, seemingly oblivious to the storm of enemy bullets he was attracting to himself and those around him. He ignored the orders of officers to get down, but Davis understood him better than they. "I knew," he reports, "that to Crane anything that savored of a pose was hateful, so . . . I called, 'You're not impressing anyone by doing that, Crane.' As I hoped he would, he instantly dropped to his knees" (qtd. in Cady 69). For Crane himself, as for Manolo Prat, coolness in the face of death was to be maintained entirely for its own sake, not to prove anything to anyone else.

Eric Solomon identifies the acknowledged literary influence on Crane that possibly introduced him to or at least reinforced this code of understated professional stoicism. Crane claimed in 1894 to have already outgrown his early "clever Rudyard-Kipling style" (*Correspondence* I, 63), but Solomon points out that the code Prat espouses is straight out of Kipling, that in this and other Spanish-American War stories "Crane's growing admiration for the craft and beauty of war continues to reflect the Englishman's influence" ("Stories" 78). This influence is not only ideological but stylistic as well, in Solomon's view; he asserts that the narrator's paean to Prat's silent, courageous meeting with his death—

[h]e was of a kind . . . and the men of his kind, on peak or plain, from the
dark northern ice-fields to the hot wet jungles, through all wine and want,
through all lies and unfamiliar truth, dark or light, the men of his kind
were governed by their gods, and each man knew the law and yet could
not give tongue to it, but it was the law (*Tales* 131)

—is "a burst of turgid rhetoric that sounds like a bad pastiche of Kipling"
("Stories" 76).

Relationship to Other Crane Works

"Clan" is unique among the stories in *Wounds in the Rain* in its focus on a
Cuban rather than an American protagonist, but the behavior of that protagonist clearly links this story to a number of the others. E. R. Hagemann notes
that Prat's unspoken devotion to duty for its own sake is also the theme of
"The Price of the Harness" and "Virtue in War" (363); Marston LaFrance adds
"The Second Generation" and the earlier Civil War story "The Little Regiment"
to this list (185). LaFrance also points out that this theme ties into the moral
code that pervades Crane's poetry. Following the lead of Daniel Hoffman,
who connects the line "The hard waves see an arm flung high" from the
poem that serves as the story's epigraph with "A weary slow sway of a lost
hand," from the poem "A Man Adrift on a Slim Spar" (Hoffman 153–54),
LaFrance says that in both stories and poems Crane develops this code
through his use of the same classes of characters. There are, first of all, in the
poems "the personally dishonest men who have met their death in the
enchanted forest"; these become the poltroons in the stories, such as Mr.
Smith in "Clan." Then there are "the drones of the huddled procession who
never enter the forest" in the poems, who are transmuted into "the innocent
volunteers" in the stories. And finally, there are "the good men who successfully negotiate the forest" in the poems, who become the Regulars, like
Manolo Prat, in the stories (185).

Donald B. Gibson discerns a similar thematic link between "Clan" and
three of Crane's Civil War stories from the *Little Regiment* collection. Like
Prat, the protagonists of "The Veteran," "A Mystery of Heroism," and "An
Indiana Campaign" all exemplify the belief that "courage is its own justification for being." In Gibson's view, the answer to the riddle-poem that begins
"Clan" is that "[o]ne does what he must do despite the vicissitudes of human
existence" (100).

A number of other critics point out flaws in this code, although they differ
over whether Crane himself was aware of them and thus whether he intended
these stories straightforwardly or ironically. Solomon is condemnatory of
Crane, saying that his treatment of what is in fact Prat's inarticulate foolhardiness is wholly, over-simply admiring, and that this succumbing "to the glamour
of the soldier" in the manner of Kipling reveals Crane's "artistic breakdown" in

terms of complexity of vision, emotion, and characterization in *Wounds in the Rain* in general (74–76). James Nagel, on the other hand, believes that Crane is fully aware of the limitations of Prat and the other protagonists' concept of heroism, that his treatment of it is ironic, especially in "Clan" and "Virtue." In his view, both these stories take not only an "anti-government" but also an "anti-war" stance, leading to the insight that Prat and Major Gates, the protagonist of "Virtue," are not so much truly heroic as "inordinately idealistic and out of tune with reality" and that "idealized human conduct is distortion of realities which leads to disillusionment, destruction, and death." Both men die resolutely adhering to their code of stoically silent professionalism, but in both cases "the code seems out of touch with reality and the story ends ironically," with the lack of appreciation or understanding of this code by others not making the point that such courage is its own reward but rather that it is in fact meaningless ("War" 14–15). Chester L. Wolford, by contrast, takes a medial stance, noting that "Clan" and "Harness" traffic in a *seeming* glorification of the group" [emphasis added] and that "Clan" and "War Memories" both emphasize "the casual way the living respond to the dead" (76).

Nagel notes a formal similarity as well between this story and several others. In its envelope structure (which Hoffman asserts that Crane derived from Walt Whitman's verse [201]), with Mr. Smith's courtship of Margharita in Tampa opening and closing the story and bracketing Prat's exploits and death in Cuba in the story's midsection—and thereby making the point that both courtship and heroism in combat are based on illusions—"Clan" resembles the original newspaper version of "An Experiment in Misery," as well as "The Veteran," and "A Man and Some Others," since these three likewise employ a frame story to enclose and comment on the action of the central section (*Impressionism* 135).

The most wide-ranging link between "Clan" and the rest of Crane's *oeuvre* comes from Neal J. Osborn. Like many other critics, he believes that heeding the injunction that begins and ends the poem that opens the story, "Unwind my riddle" (*Tales* 119), is crucial to an understanding of the story, but he argues further that this unwinding is crucial to a grasp of many of Crane's other major works as well. In Osborn's view, lines 2–5 of the poem,

> Cruel as hawks the hours fly,
> Wounded men seldom come home to die,
> The hard waves see an arm flung high,
> Scorn hits strong because of a lie,

establish "four conditions that support a pessimistic, presumably naturalistic, interpretation of man's situation, motives, and potentiality" (247–48). However, these conditions are counterbalanced by the existence of the "mystic tie" that is affirmed in line 6 of the poem, which for Osborn is "an unknown factor that may transcend Manolo's solitary, cruel, apparently use-less death and the seeming infidelity of human love" (248). What this tie is *not*, Osborn continues, is presented in Margharita's faithlessness, her moth-er's avarice, Mr. Smith's combination of possessiveness and cynicism about love, and the Spanish colonel's devotion to self-advancement at the expense of truth. Moreover, it is not the kind of courage that Prat first displays, courage that stems from a desire for praise by men he considers brave and from a kind of group battle-fever that breaks out in his unit. Instead, this tie inheres in the behavior Prat exhibits just before he is killed, at which point he chooses death knowing that no one will witness or praise his actions, and at which point this choice is a product of his individual will, not a function of group psychosis. Here, Prat "recognizes the existence of a selfless, spiritual tie among men and consequent obligations upon himself," and he recognizes as well that this tie, "[f]ar from holding the promise of satisfying the appetites or personal ambitions of its champions, . . . is more likely to require the quiet and unheralded sacrifice of everything they have" (250–51).

On the basis of Crane's statements in several letters and his admiration for several writers who espouse a similar view, Osborn asserts that Prat's realiza-tion here is "very similar if not identical" to the "struggle, against deterministic influences and toward the possibility of self-determined action for the benefit of one's fellow men," that Crane saw himself as engaged in (251). It is this bio-graphical connection, Osborn continues, that makes unwinding the riddle of "Clan" a key to much of the rest of Crane's best fiction. In these stories as in "Clan," "[g]igantic and at least potentially inimical forces confront man, and the resulting threats to the individual's significance as well as to his survival are all too often complemented by failures within the human community" (256)—failures, that is, to abide by the "mystic tie" of self-sacrifice for the ben-efit of others. Such failures span the entire chronology of Crane's major works, Osborn says, beginning in *Maggie: A Girl of the Streets*, when all those around the protagonist abandon her to her fate for the sake of their own self-aggrandizement (256). In *The Red Badge of Courage*, Henry Fleming similarly rejects this tie when he deserts the mortally wounded tattered soldier, but by the end of the story, in Osborn's view, he has come to understand this failure and will live up to the tie in the future (256). In "The Blue Hotel," it is the refusal of the other men to extend to the Swede the compassion that is his due according to this tie that leads to his death, while in "The Monster" Henry Johnson sacrifices himself in rescuing Jimmie Trescott from the fire, and Dr. Trescott recognizes this fact and abides by the tie in return in caring for the maimed Henry, although the rest of the townspeople regard such an obliga-tion as at best burdensome and at worst a threat to their society—a grim irony, since these obligations are in fact the essence of any viable human com-munity (256–57). And it is precisely the centrality of such obligations that is the point of "The Open Boat," in which the correspondent "discovers that the cynical view [of men] is negated by a unifying and selfless relationship among men that can be intuited though it is not directly expressed," just as in the later story the clan of self-sacrifice can be given no name (257).

Critical Studies

As might be inferred from the foregoing discussion, one of the major bones of contention in the criticism devoted to this story is whether Crane's view of Prat's stoic death is straightforward or ironic, with the writer's answer to this question often strongly influencing his or her judgment of the story's merits. In amplifying his negative comments quoted above in the "Relationship to Other Crane Works" section, Solomon says that Crane is wholly unironic in his narrator's admiration for Prat's quiet, workmanlike courage, and that the detached perspective Crane takes as a result has disastrous consequences for the story. Whereas in *The Red Badge*, "A Mystery of Heroism," and "Death and the Child" Crane evinces a tremendous "power of sympathetic projection" into the minds of his inexperienced and mentally tormented protagonists and produces brilliantly insightful psychological portraits as a result, in "Clan" Crane does not probe the veteran Prat's consciousness in the same depth, presenting Prat's acceptance of death as "irrational and instinctive, the deed of a mechanical man" ("Stories" 75–76). Although Crane himself is moved by this kind of "professional" demeanor, lauding it with Kipling-derived rhetoric, he blocks any meaningful response on the reader's part, since "there can be no emotional impact in a work of fiction that recounts the death of a hero who, as far as the reader is concerned, was never alive in the first place" ("Stories" 76). (All of Solomon's comments on "Clan" in this essay may also be found in his book *Stephen Crane: From Parody to Realism*, pp. 118–19.) Edwin Cady likewise sees Crane as wholly approving of Prat and the story as "embarrassingly Kiplingesque" in its hero-worship and lack of ambiguity (149).

Several other critics agree that Crane's attitude toward Prat is straightforward, but they differ from Solomon and Cady in believing that his admiring tone makes the story a success rather than a failure. Hoffman argues that Prat's way of meeting death is a movingly rendered assertion that courage for its own sake is the only viable value in an absurd universe. Prat's dying is clearly futile from a purely practical standpoint, Hoffman notes, since it accomplishes no military objective; "[i]ts only significance is in the testing of his spirit," but there is no irony in this circumstance, because this is the sole significance that matters to Crane, since for him "fidelity to courage as a code of life," which Prat maintains to the end, "is all that gives meaning to . . . death" (152). Similarly, Robert W. Stallman says that the unwinding of the riddle posed by the poem that begins the story is the realization that the law in both love and war is fidelity. Prat's behavior demonstrates his understanding of and adherence to this law, despite the infidelity of his lover and the practical irrelevance of his death, and his conduct obviates the need for any other meaningful source of identity (386–87).

LaFrance and Lillian Gilkes are in accord with this reading as well. LaFrance says that Prat earns membership in the clan that abides by the unspoken code of the Regulars, as that code is presented in a number of the Spanish-American War stories, of which "Clan" is the best, through choosing to sacrifice himself to live up to the ideal of courage. The point of the final passage exalting this behavior, in LaFrance's view, is that nothing in the "pragmatic world"—not Margharita's faithlessness, nor her mother's venality, nor Smith's "victory" over Prat in the contest for Margharita—in any way diminishes Prat's "moral princeliness or the code of conduct he dies to uphold" (183–84). Gilkes similarly argues that Crane does not intend for these pragmatic concerns to detract from Prat's heroism. "Although he [Crane] appears to have arrived at the conviction of war's futility" at the story's end, she says, careful analysis reveals his belief that "exposure under conditions of actual combat called forth the individual's highest potential for action in a supreme test of courage, endurance, [and] sacrifice for an existentialist ideal of duty, loyalty, honor" (442).

Warren Anderson takes a related but more fully intertextual view of the story, considering it as part of Crane's career-long meditation on the nature and meaning of courage. Noting Henry Fleming's and thus Crane's own evident familiarity with the *Iliad* and the *Odyssey*, Anderson argues that in both *The Red Badge* and "The Veteran," the short story that depicts the aged Fleming's death, Crane sorrowfully asserts that courage in the Homeric sense of *areti*—that is, consciously willed excellence on the part of the individual— is no longer possible in the modern world, since he presents Henry's bravery in both cases as stemming from "a madness like the delirium of a sick man" (84). In "Clan," on the other hand, "thought and style alike have changed" (85): Crane eschews the irony and ambiguity of the earlier works, indicating that he has recovered his belief in the viability of *areti* in the contemporary realm. In his panegyric on Prat's death in particular, Anderson concludes, Crane triumphantly "speaks for himself, and thereby becomes the spokesman of all that company whose traditions go back to Hector and Achilles" (85).

Robert Glen Deamer also sees "Clan" as representing the last stage in the development of Crane's concept of heroism. Prior to his 1895 Western trip as a correspondent for the Bacheller syndicate, Deamer says, Crane conceived of life in deterministic terms, as evinced by many of his early works, particularly the novels *Maggie: A Girl of the Streets* and *George's Mother*. However, what he witnessed of human behavior in the West convinced him that people could in fact shape their fates, at least to some extent, through the "heroic" virtues of discipline, responsibility, and courage—a shift in viewpoint borne out by the changed tone of many of his post-1895 stories (143). These tend to be studies of men who either attain these virtues and thus merit Crane's admiration or else reject them and therefore warrant his censure. Prat belongs to the former group, Deamer concludes; in his view, this officer is presented as unambiguously displaying "the wordless, inborn understanding of man's obligation to courage that, above all else, defines the hero" (147).

Taking the other interpretive side, Milne Holton and Wolford both discern irony and ambiguity in Crane's handling of Prat, which they consider crucial to the story's success by making it more than a simplistic celebration of a warrior ethos, whether that ethos is seen as Homeric or merely Kiplingesque. Ignoring the structure of the earlier "Experiment in Misery," "The Veteran," and "A Man and Some Others," discussed above in "Relationship to Other Crane Works," Holton calls "Clan" the "most ambitious" story in *Wounds in the Rain* because of Crane's personally innovative use of an "envelope structure" of two plots—Mr. Smith's courtship of Margharita and Prat's experiences of combat—to "articulate an ethic for the individual confronting such an absurd reality as war" (262). The two plots produce this articulation, Holton explains, in that Crane focuses on the code of proper conduct in both: Smith performs the correct social rituals by which to woo a woman, while Prat behaves as a true professional in facing death silently and courageously. Through the implicit contrast between Smith's hollow, self-aggrandizing, and manipulative forms and Prat's selfless bravery, the reader comes to understand that only Prat's code is meaningful, enabling him to develop the ability to love truly—that is, without the desire for any reward in return—an ability that Smith and Margharita patently lack. However, Holton says, this envelope structure raises the irresolvable possibility that this insight is suffused with irony, for by returning at the end of the story, after Prat's death, to Smith's success with Margharita and her consequent burning of the photograph that memorializes her relationship with Prat, Crane leaves the reader with "an uneasy doubt as to whether Manolo Prat was an absurd saint or simply a fool of his own illusions" (265).

Wolford notes a different sort of envelope structure operating to produce ambiguity. Just as the story opens with a riddle, he says, it closes with one in Crane's refusal to offer a precise meaning in the final paragraph. Echoing the language of his earlier description of Prat's decision to sacrifice himself, quoted above in "Sources and Influences," Crane follows Margharita's burning of the photograph with the comment that

> the word is clear only to the kind who on peak or plain, from dark northern ice-fields to the hot wet jungles, through all wine and want, through lies and unfamiliar truth, dark or light, are governed by the unknown gods, and though each man knows the law no man may give tongue to it. (*Tales* 136)

This would seem to be final praise for Prat, but, Wolford points out, Crane does not expressly state what "the word" is, thus leaving the reader in doubt. Wolford speculates that the word may be *love*, of the selfless variety that Prat evinces for Margharita, or it may be *treachery*, which Margharita has engaged in, or it may even be both of these, since Smith's love for Margharita includes a belief in her capacity for faithlessness. The most likely possibilities, in Wolford's view, are *absurdity* or *meaninglessness* or *pathos* or *death*, since the one point that *is* clear in this uncertain conclusion is that "death is final, ending everything—even love" (77).

Perhaps the most tenuous interpretation is John Berryman's Freudian reading. Focusing on the physical circumstances of Prat's death rather than on Crane's comments on it, Berryman argues that Crane has a black man kill Prat because he links blacks with sex and sin—an insight he derives from Thomas Beer's uncorroborated claim that at the age of twelve Crane saw a white girl stabbed by her black lover and was traumatized by the incident. Therefore, in Berryman's view, the story is more than anything else one of many expressions of Crane's Oedipal guilt (308).

Regardless of their varying interpretation of the story's significance, many critics agree in praising Crane's technical skill in "Clan." In addition to the "enclosing structure" that creates a form of shaped irony in the contrast between Smith and Prat, Berryman lauds a deep interest in the details of "prose-movement and syntax" in this story that is new to Crane (255). Gibson says that "Clan" is distinguished by the most complex, sophisticated handling of a frame story to be found in Crane's canon, and by equally complex work with shifting perspectives, which enable the reader "to see the action from the points of view of all the groups involved and finally from the point of view of one character" (98–99). Holton discerns a purposeful evolution in Crane's imagistic approach here. Whereas in his earlier work Crane relies primarily on visual imagery, in "Clan" and many of his other late stories he largely shifts to auditory images, a change that Holton speculates stems from Crane's acceptance of the absurdity of the universe as a given at that point in his life: if whatever one sees is inevitably absurd, then attaining clear vision is less important than courageous action in the face of that absurdity. Thus, the relative paucity of visual images in "Clan" conveys the idea that "the real subject is Manolo's conduct, not his vision" (262).

Nagel provides the most thorough and perhaps the most appreciative discussion of Crane's technique in "Clan." He regards it as one of Crane's "most artistically complex and thematically sophisticated" war stories ("War" 13), largely because Crane's envelope structure is not limited to the enclosure of Prat's story by Smith's. The opening poem contains within itself an envelope of refrain—"Unwind my riddle"; and the central sections devoted to Prat, III through VII, are framed in sections II and VIII by scenes focused on the behavior and attitudes of the Spanish soldiers before and after the attack in which Prat is killed. All these enclosures, Nagel says, combine powerfully to make the point that both courtship and war "are conducted according to ritualized codes of behavior that are essentially false" (*Impressionism* 132–34).

Works Cited

Anderson, Warren D. "Homer and Stephen Crane." *Nineteenth-Century Fiction* 19 (1964):77–86.

Berryman, John. *Stephen Crane*. New York: Sloane, 1950.

Bowers, Fredson. Textual Introduction. *Tales of War*. Vol. 6 of The University of Virginia Edition of *The Works of Stephen Crane*. Ed. Fredson Bowers. Charlottesville: University Press of Virginia, 1970, xxxvii–cxci.

Cady, Edwin H. *Stephen Crane*. Rev. ed. New York: Twayne, 1982.

Crane, Stephen. "The Clan of No-Name." *Tales of War* 119–36.

———. "The Red Badge of Courage Was His Wig-wag Flag." *Reports of War*. Vol. 9 of The University of Virginia Edition of *The Works of Stephen Crane*. Ed. Fredson Bowers. Charlottesville: University Press of Virginia, 1971, 134–42.

Deamer, Robert Glen. "Stephen Crane's 'Code' and Its Western Connections." *The Importance of Place in the American Literature of Hawthorne, Thoreau, Crane, Adams, and Faulkner*. New York: Edwin Mellen, 1990, 139–52.

Gibson, Donald B. *The Fiction of Stephen Crane*. Carbondale: Southern Illinois University Press, 1968.

Gilkes, Lillian. "Stephen Crane and the Biographical Fallacy: The Cora Influence." *Modern Fiction Studies* 16 (1970–71):441–46.

Hagemann, E. R. "Crane's 'Real' War in His Short Stories." *American Quarterly* 8 (1956):356–67.

Hoffman, Daniel G. *The Poetry of Stephen Crane*. New York: Columbia University Press, 1957.

Holton, Milne. *Cylinder of Vision: The Fiction and Journalistic Writings of Stephen Crane*. Baton Rouge: Louisiana State University Press, 1972.

LaFrance, Marston. *A Reading of Stephen Crane*. Oxford: Clarendon, 1971.

Nagel, James. *Stephen Crane and Literary Impressionism*. University Park: Pennsylvania State University Press, 1980.

———. "Stephen Crane's Stories of War: A Study of Art and Theme." *North Dakota Quarterly* 43 (1975):5–19.

Osborn, Neal J. "The Riddle in 'The Clan': A Key to Crane's Major Fiction?" *Bulletin of the New York Public Library* 69 (1965):247–58.

Solomon, Eric. *Stephen Crane: From Parody to Realism*. Cambridge: Harvard University Press, 1966.

————. "Stephen Crane's War Stories." *Texas Studies in Literature and Language* 3 (1961):67–80.

Stallman, R. W. *Stephen Crane: A Biography*. New York: George Braziller, 1968.

Wertheim, Stanley, and Paul Sorrentino, eds. *The Correspondence of Stephen Crane*. 2 vols. New York: Columbia University Press, 1988.

Wolford, Chester L. *Stephen Crane: A Study of the Short Fiction*. Boston: Twayne, 1989.

Death and the Child

Publication History

This story first appeared in two parts in England in the March 5 and 12, 1898, issues of *Black and White* (15:332–34; 368–70) and in America in the March 19 and 26, 1898, issues of *Harper's Weekly* (42:281–82; 297–98). It was then published in America in April 1898 in the Doubleday & McClure book *"The Open Boat" and Other Tales of Adventure* and in England in the Heinemann *"The Open Boat" and Other Stories*, also in April 1898 (Bowers clxxvi). Wilson Follett, editor of *The Work of Stephen Crane* (12 vols., New York: Knopf, 1925–27), placed it in volume 12 of this collection, published in 1927; and in 1963 Thomas A. Gullason included it in his compendium *The Complete Short Stories and Sketches of Stephen Crane* (Garden City, N.Y.: Doubleday).

Circumstances of Composition

Crane evidently wrote "Death and the Child" sometime in late 1897, while he was living in his first home in England—Ravensbrook, in the town of Oxted, Surrey—since his initial mention of it comes in a letter from that locale, dated December 20, 1897, to his agent, Paul Revere Reynolds. Crane tells Reynolds that he has not yet offered this story for sale in England, explaining that "I am holding it in order to give you a chance with the big fellows"—the prestigious and high-paying American magazines (*Correspondence* I, 337). John Berryman offers further information, but it is somewhat shaky, being based on the evidence of a letter that has no source outside Thomas Beer's biography and thus may be Beer's fabrication, as Stanley Wertheim and Paul Sorrentino explain (6–10). Beer has Crane writing to an unnamed recipient from Brown's Hotel, Dover Street, London, on December 3, 1897, explaining that he has fled to this locale from Ravensbrook because he had so many guests there that he could not get any work done (166). Berryman identifies "Death" as Crane's project of that moment, completed at the hotel (203).

More substantial is J. C. Levenson's assertion, on the basis of a surviving draft page in the hand of Crane's common-law wife, Cora, that this is one of the first stories Crane dictated rather than wrote out himself. This point is worth noting because Levenson goes on to show that comparison of this draft with the final story reveals that Crane added much to the original text, particularly in the way of description, whereas in revisions of earlier stories he had been much more prone to cut than to add. This evolution in Crane's writing process, Levenson concludes, demonstrates that "Crane's conscious art, like his intuitive imagination, led him to put his inward dramas into an increasingly complex outer world" (*Adventure* lxxviii).

Sources and Influences

Crane's principal source for this story was his own experience at the Second Battle of Velestino, fought in Greece on May 5, 1897, which he witnessed as a correspondent covering the Greco-Turkish War for William Randolph Hearst's *New York Journal*. This was the first full-scale combat Crane had ever seen, and he drew heavily on his own situation, as that is recorded in his newspaper accounts—"Crane at Velestino" (*Reports* 18–23), "Stephen Crane at Velestino" (*Reports* 23–27), "A Fragment of Velestino" (*Reports* 27–44), "A Battle in Greece" (*Uncollected* 274–83), and "The Dogs of War" (*Reports* 49–53)—for details of setting and action. Most significantly, Peza, the protagonist of "Death and the Child," is a noncombatant, like Crane, who comes upon the battle already in progress after walking twelve miles up the road from the town of Volo, as Crane reports himself doing in "Stephen Crane at Velestino" (24). J. C. Levenson adds that a Greek soldier shot through the jaw and bearing his wound with dignity, like the one whom Peza encounters at one point, appears in "A Battle in Greece," as does an encounter between a no-nonsense young Greek lieutenant and an excitable observer upon which Crane evidently drew for a similar scene in "Death and the Child"; he also notes that the original of the child in the story, who plays in blissful ignorance of the battle going on around him, is an equally oblivious puppy that Crane describes himself as encountering in "The Dogs of War" (*Adventure* lxxxiv–lxxxv). (Crane christened this dog "Velestino" and took him back to England when his reporting stint was ended.)

However, in limning Peza's mental collapse in the face of the horrors of a battle conducted against the backdrop of uncaring nature, Crane drew less on his own responses than on what he had already imagined in *The Red*

Badge of Courage, before he had ever heard a shot fired in anger, because he felt that what he witnessed at Velestino corroborated what he had put Henry Fleming through. Thomas Beer has Crane just prior to his departure for the war writing to an unidentified friend, "I am going to Greece for the *Journal*, and if the Red Badge is not all right I shall sell out my claim on literature and take up orange growing" (qtd. in *Correspondence* II, 672). Given Beer's unreliability regarding sources (*Correspondence* I, 6–10), Crane likely never wrote such a letter, but he evidently felt something akin to its sentiment, for a more credible reporter, Joseph Conrad, recalled Crane's expressing relief to him because his Greek adventure had proved that *The Red Badge* was "all right" (qtd. in *Correspondence* I, 283). Robert W. Stallman explains that what Crane evidently meant by this statement was that at Velestino and other engagements he witnessed "the very same kind of bathos—the collapse of grandiose illusions" regarding war that he had had Fleming undergo (282), a view particularly borne out by his ironic tone in his coverage of the battle in "Stephen Crane at Velestino" and in his making Peza like Fleming a neophyte whose "theory of war gets exploded by realities" and who flees as a result (289).

There is, of course, the danger that someone who has read and thought and written as much about war as Crane did before witnessing it will not have his theory exploded by reality but rather will warp the reality to fit his theory. Crane's friend Harold Frederic once complained of most writing in their era about battle that "at best [the author] gives us a conventional account of what happened, but on analysis you find that this is not what he really saw but what all his reading has taught him he must have seen" (22). However, since Frederic made this statement in a laudatory review of *The Red Badge*, he evidently believed that Crane avoids this pitfall in this novel, and a number of more recent critics concur that he likewise avoids it in "Death," owing partly to his determination to "keep close to my honesty" (*Correspondence* I, 196) and partly to the fact that the one literary source upon which he may have drawn for this story, Tolstoy's *War and Peace*, is generally acclaimed to be highly accurate regarding the nature of battle. As Lars Ahnebrink (357) and J. C. Levenson both note, Peza's response to combat is similar to that of another first-time eyewitness, Tolstoy's protagonist, Pierre Bezukhov. Like Peza at Velestino, Bezukhov at Borodino is "to his supreme surprise . . . caught up by pity and national feeling and a desire to get to the meaning of war," but what he first discovers instead are "the patternless cross-purposes of battle." And like Crane, Tolstoy places this battle into "its larger social context and the war itself into an overarching natural scene that [makes] human catastrophe seem inconsequent" (Levenson *Adventure* lxxxiii). Whether Crane had in fact read *War and Peace* is uncertain; the parallels may be even more striking if he had not, for they then reveal him working independently toward the same vision as the masterly Tolstoy.

Another possible influence on this story is Impressionist painting. Numerous critics have seen Crane as trying to find a verbal analogue for this visual style, largely on the strength of his saying of a horrifying scene in his story "War Memories" that

> I bring this to you merely as an effect . . . of mental light and shade, if you like; something done in thought similar to that which the French Impressionists do in color; something meaningless and at the same time overwhelming, crushing, monstrous. (254)

In "Death and the Child," as Peza approaches the battlefield he encounters a number of wounded men, as well as some "gunless and jaded" ones, heading away from it, and he is surprised to note that none of them seems at all frightened. He theorizes that "during the fight they had reached the limit of their mental storage, their capacity for excitement, for tragedy, and had then simply come away" (129); Peza bases this idea on his own response at an art gallery, which he had to leave due to the overwhelming, crushing, monstrous effect of its works. He saw there

> the sunshine beating upon red desert sands, nude bodies flung to the shore in the green moon-glow, ghastly and starving men clawing at a wall in darkness, a girl at her bath with screened rays falling upon her pearly shoulders, a dance, a funeral, a review, an execution, all the strength of argus-eyed art. . . . (129)

As James Nagel points out, these descriptions are too brief for positive identifications of all of them with specific paintings, but those for which educated guesses are possible derive from Impressionism: he hypothesizes that Peza's memories of the dance and the bathing girl may be derived from works by Edgar Degas, and that the execution may be a reference to Edouard Manet's 1867 *Execution of the Emperor Maximilian* (18).

Relationship to Other Crane Works

Given the discussion in "Influences" of Crane's evident belief that what he witnessed in Greece confirmed the accuracy of what he had imagined in *The Red Badge*, it is not surprising that there is a good deal of critical commentary on connections between "Death" and this novel. Much of this commentary is the work of James B. Colvert, who notes resemblances "in the incident of the cowardly desertion, in [the] involvement of nature in the drama of self-discovery, and in [the] attribution of motive and conduct to faulty perception in the hero" (*Crane* 115). However, Colvert regards these links not as proof that what Crane had imagined in *The Red Badge* turned out to be the truth but rather that, as in Frederic's formulation of what usually happens in war writing, he allowed his preconceptions to color his experience—that what he saw in actual war was "what his literary sense of war compelled him to see" (*War* xxxi). In this story, Colvert explains, Velestino "is rendered not as history but as history transmuted by the resources of [Crane's] imagination[:] the images, themes, motifs, and descriptive patterns he had already worked out by the time he came to see the real thing." "Death," therefore, can be regarded as an example of "the powerful control his purely literary resources could exercise over his observation—a remarkable variation on the themes and imagery of *The Red Badge of Courage*" (*War* xvi). (The same analysis can also be found in another of Colvert's essays, "Stephen Crane: Style as Invention," p. 131.)

David Halliburton concentrates on one such theme as it is reflected in the similarity between the protagonists of these two works: Peza like Fleming is a novice soldier for whom "the basic ontological question . . . of what one amounts to as a man is posed by battle" (160). Levenson, on the other hand, identifies a number of differences between these two characters that may be used as an index to Crane's artistic growth. Although neither character can exert much control over "the flux of sensation and will" that Crane presents as the composition of consciousness, Peza is older and more self-aware than Fleming, as well as having patriotism for his initial motivation rather than Fleming's more adolescent thirst for personal glory. Peza is thus more complex than Fleming, indicating that by the time of "Death" Crane's "conception of character was no longer summed up in the categories of innocence and experience," as it had been in *The Red Badge* (*Adventure* lxxxii).

Christopher Benfey likewise notes the connection between Peza and Fleming; but he also identifies analogues to the other main character in this story, the nameless child who appears most prominently near the beginning and at the end. Benfey points out that Crane's "baby sketches" of 1893—"An Ominous Baby" (*Tales, Sketches* 47–50), "A Great Mistake," (*Tales, Sketches* 50–52), and "A Dark Brown Dog" (*Tales, Sketches* 52–58)—are his first explorations of a small child's "capacity for intense absorption" in its own desires and its play of the moment, which is brought to its fullest realization in "Death," in which the toddler remains focused on his own game as the war rages all around him (213). Other stories containing possible links to "Death" are "The Open Boat" and "The Blue Hotel." Nagel points out that Peza's movement from detachment to compassion as a result of his discovery of his own insignificance is very like the intellectual and emotional journey the correspondent in "Open Boat" makes in conjunction with his physical one (104). Levenson discerns not only connections of theme but also of mood between "Death" and "Blue Hotel," perhaps a function of their proximity in order of composition, both being written in late 1897. Although their settings are quite different, they make the same point: "the world is vast, incomprehensible, and indifferent to the minor conflicts of humankind" (*Adventure* xcv).

Critical Studies

Like many of Crane's stories, "Death and the Child" has elicited widely divergent assessments of its merits and interpretations of its significance. Some idea of the range of these responses can perhaps be inferred from the fact that critics do not even agree on the concluding action of the story: some argue that the "[p]alsied, windless, and abject" Peza dies when the child asks him, "'Are you a man?'" (141), while others assert that he lives—that he is merely exhausted, not mortally stricken, by his flight from the battlefield. One negative judgment of its aesthetic success appeared only a few years after its publication, from the pen of H. G. Wells. Wells notes that "Death" takes up the same theme as *The Red Badge*—the initiation of an innocent idealist into the realities of war—but he says that the story is inferior to the novel due to the "encroachment of journalism" that he regards as marring much of Crane's later work. The primary characteristic of this encroachment in "Death," he says, is that "[t]he generalized application is, to my taste, a little too evidently underlined; there is just that touch of insistence . . . as of a writer not sure of his reader, not happy in his reader, and seeking to drive his implication (of which he is not quite sure) home." The most glaring example of this insistence, in Wells's view, is that "[t]he child is not a natural child; there is no happy touch to make it personally alive; it is THE CHILD, something unfalteringly big; a large, pink, generalized thing . . . after the fashion of a Vatican cherub" (128).

Donald B. Gibson agrees that the child is the primary source of artistic weakness, although his reason for this judgment differs from Wells's. In Gibson's view, Crane sets up Peza as a negative force due to his fear and consequent flight from battle, and he counterposes the soldiers and the child as positive forces because of their separate kinds of courage, the soldiers displaying coolness and concentration on their tasks despite their awareness of their perilous condition, and the child maintaining an equal concentration as a result of his obliviousness to danger. The problem with this ideational structure, Gibson argues, is that to say that the child's "unconsciousness" is in fact courage and therefore worthy of emulation by an adult "is merely to be sentimental" (a charge also levelled by Stallman [283]); thus, the meaningful link that Crane wishes to establish between the soldiers and the child as complementary "centers of value" is nonexistent, resulting in a blurring of the significance of the story (Gibson 100–101).

Gullason faults Crane's handling of the other major character. At the outset, he says, the story "recalls the finest kind of Biercean allegory" about war, epistemology, and ontology. However, it ultimately falls short of this mark because Peza is not fully convincing as a character and because he fails to recognize the reality of his condition at the conclusion, preventing the full catharsis of tragedy at which Crane seems to have aimed (478).

Balanced against these adverse comments is a considerable body of praise, which begins with the judgment of one of Wells's contemporaries, Edward Garnett. He lauds "Death and the Child" as a "haunting masterpiece," primarily due to "the calm detachment of the little child playing, by which the artist secures his poetic background; man, pigmy man, watched impassively by the Fates. The irony of life is here implicit" (144). Maxwell Geismar is equally complimentary, although his remarks run in another vein. He considers the story one of Crane's best treatments of war, along with the Civil War tale "A Mystery of Heroism," because here Crane does not celebrate the essentially mindless professionalism of the veteran that is the focal point of most of his battle pieces; instead, in a far more complex treatment, he confronts his own deepest feelings about battle. Taking a Freudian approach, Geismar argues that Crane's fascination with war stems from his compulsion for mutilation and castration, a function of his desire to suffer in atonement for his sexual guilt, and that it is precisely these urges that Crane dramatizes in Peza, particularly when the latter picks up a rifle and is immediately struck by its resemblance to a snake, and when in several scenes the author develops "the weird fascination—and odd communion—of Peza-Crane with the wounded and dying men who [are] trying to claim him for their own" (105).

While not explicitly presenting his reading of "Death" as a rejoinder to Geismar's comments, Eric Solomon takes a sharply opposed view, arguing that the story, which he too rates as one of Crane's best on war, does in fact celebrate the veteran's professionalism. *The Red Badge* and "Mystery of Heroism," Solomon says, offer sympathetic portraits of sensitive novice soldiers, men who "falter because they think" (107). Peza is another, if better-educated, member of this group; his life of "intellect, emotion, and culture" (109) has not prepared him for the trauma of war, and so he too falters in his first test on the battlefield: when he decides to join the fight, he is given a bandolier taken from a dead man, and when the sensitive youth puts it on he imagines it to be the man's arms wrapping around him, a sensation that unmans him and impels him to flee. The difference between Peza and the protagonists of *The Red Badge* and "Mystery," Solomon continues, is that in this case Crane offers "no trace of the sympathy that marked his treatment of contemplative men like the sensitive dreamer, Fleming, or the thoughtful fool, Collins [the protagonist of 'Mystery']." Instead, Solomon argues, Crane extends his sympathy to the young but battle-hardened and stoic lieutenant Peza encounters early into the story and to the uneducated peasant-soldier posted next to Peza on the battle line, who, at the moment of that youth's breakdown, calmly eats while he waits for the next enemy attack. According to Solomon, this juxtaposition shows Peza to be "an intellectual perverted by animal fear" and the peasant to be "a simple soul whose innocence has turned into a brutal—and to the author *acceptable*—phlegmatic attitude of calm" (113). Thus, Solomon concludes, "Death" marks a major shift in Crane's thinking about men in battle, constituting his "final rejection of the sensitive hero who in the world of war searches for the life of reason" (107). Henceforth, as exemplified in his stories of the Spanish-American War, Crane's combat heroes are not sensitive neophytes but stoic veterans.

Milne Holton likewise sees the story as crucial to an understanding of a shift in Crane's thinking about men in war, but in his view that shift—a result of Crane's own first experience under fire—is somewhat more complex. Holton emphasizes the many similarities between Henry Fleming's initiation into war in *The Red Badge* and Peza's in "Death." Both characters begin with romantic illusions about war that are shattered by its reality; in both cases, Crane juxtaposes human emotions with the indifference of nature, thereby forcing his protagonist to confront the "absurd dichotomy between the human creature and the natural universe, . . . which, if it is to be bridged, must be bridged by means of individual human understanding" (185); and in both works, it is this confrontation that provokes the protagonist's flight from the battlefield. However, there is one key difference between the two characters: Henry finally returns to his community—his regiment—and from there to the battlefield, with new knowledge, whereas Peza remains isolated (a divergence that Halliburton also notes, pointing out the lack of formation of a beneficial community here, in contrast to "The Open Boat" and "The Price of the Harness" as well as to *The Red Badge* [161]).

Holton identifies this difference as the key to the change in Crane's thinking—a change in his understanding of the nature of consciousness. Peza attempts to bridge the gap between human and nature, Holton says, by maintaining an objective apprehension of battle, and the story is Crane's test—for himself as well as Peza—of the possibility of such an apprehension. As usual in Crane's mature corpus, vision is the paramount metaphor for such objectivity, and war poses many obstacles to Peza's clear sight: the "visual satiation" produced by combat (186), concern for personal safety, and the "rituals of military conduct" that impose an "artificial order . . . upon the natural chaos of battle" (187). But the most important impediment to objective apprehension for Peza, as for Henry, is "animal fear." While Crane depicts Henry as able ultimately to overcome this feeling, attain such apprehension, and become one of the calm, comradely community of veteran soldiers, Peza fails permanently in "the attempt to participate and to objectify"; he tries to join the community of soldiers, but when he dons the bandolier and hallucinates the dead man's grasp he irrevocably "withdraws from participation and apprehension, away from present actuality and into the isolation of his terrifying fantasy . . ., [which,] in all its synaesthetic horror, . . . obliterates his sense of reality"

(189). Although Holton regards the conclusion of the story as clumsy, he argues that in his reading it is tonally consonant with what precedes it, free of the sentimentality with which Gibson and Stallman charge it, because Peza's inability to answer the child's question reveals that the objective stance toward war that Peza and, by extension, Crane himself seek is impossible. Peza is forced to confront "the fact of his own dehumanization"—the loss of any ability to apprehend reality (191)—and Crane dramatizes thereby his discovery in his own case of the results when "sensitive men" try to "tolerate even the apprehension of the reality of battle" (194).

Chester L. Wolford is another critic who sees a change in Crane's conception of consciousness as the central theme in "Death." He places it in a long-standing literary genre that he terms the "epic of consciousness," in which the hero is embarked on a quest for transcendence of the self, the capacity to be both conscious and unconscious, simultaneously aware of his own individuality and subsumed into a larger awareness (130). Peza does not complete this quest, Wolford says, for in his flight from his discovery of his own death, brought on by his glimpse of the face of a corpse and his imagining of the dead man's grasp, he fails in "the final confrontation which must be overcome before transcendence is possible" (138–39). Wolford agrees with Holton that Peza is defeated here, but he rejects Holton's claim that this defeat dehumanizes him, arguing that it is actually the very thing that makes him fully human. In his earlier works, Wolford contends, Crane does identify this failure of the quest with dehumanization, but "Death" marks an alteration in his thinking. In Wolford's view, Peza's final encounter with the child makes the point that the child himself—representing "all children in any age"—is "probably doomed to repeat" Peza's experience; the act of "confronting reality and then running from it in horror" is the essence of the human condition (139).

Bettina Knapp also sees the child as a figure representative of humankind, but she argues that in this role the child provides Peza with qualified success in his quest for insight rather than emblematizing his failure. Peza "comes to understand his foibles and fears by projecting them on the child," Knapp says. In his eyes, the child "is *everyman* at the beginning and the end of the ordeal that is life. Preoccupied by his own imaginary wars, . . . unaware of reality, . . . [n]either naive nor innocent, he is potential man" (158).

Marston LaFrance tenders more qualified praise than that offered by Geismar, Solomon, Holton, and Knapp. His opinion is that "Death" is "probably the least satisfying of Crane's major works" because the author embodies too many ideas in Peza, because the reality that Peza must see is "comparatively abstract" alongside that presented in other stories, because the panoramic scenes that this tale requires are not Crane's artistic strong suit, because the ending is contrived, and because the child's concluding question seems "unnatural" and "overemphasized" (215). Nonetheless, LaFrance does regard this as a major story, for reasons that differ sharply from Geismar's and Holton's. LaFrance's central premise is that Peza is *not* an autobiographical mask for Crane himself. Peza and Henry Fleming are related, LaFrance says, in their common illusion that nature is sympathetic to human suffering, but both are thus also different from Crane, who in LaFrance's estimation never regards nature as anything other than utterly detached from human concerns. Those who are more closely identified with Crane's own viewpoint in this story are the young lieutenant, who devotes himself to his business without concerning himself with the sympathies of nature, and the child, who is "explicitly identified with [the] mindless indifference of nature . . . because of his complete ignorance of the moral reality in which he has been abandoned" (216). He is therefore the opposite of Wordsworth's intuitively moral child, LaFrance says, and when he asks Peza the final question "he merely voices the implicit question that Crane's universe puts to all men." For LaFrance, this question carries primarily proto-existential significance: "born into an amoral world where chance may maim or kill, where the good are often unrewarded and the evil unpunished, man is duty-bound to act morally merely because he is a man, and each man's conduct implicitly answers the child's question" (217).

However, LaFrance does not regard this philosophical dimension as the most significant aspect of the story. He points out that Crane offers this proto-existential view in many stories, whereas only in this one does he take up the relationship of patriotism to courage and manhood. Unlike Henry Fleming and all of Crane's other war-story protagonists, Peza is moved by the ideal of service to his country; he wishes to fight for Greece, the land of his father. What the story reveals about this attitude, LaFrance says, is that Greece, "as the *land* of his father, is just so much insensate dirt. Man's fighting a war, like any other human action, is meaningful in moral terms only as it affects the lives of other men"; and in his terror-stricken flight from the battlefield, his refusal to help a wounded man because of his terror, his sentimental pitying of the soldiers at one moment and his contempt for them as ignorant peasants the next, "Peza fails miserably in his relationship with the men of his fatherland" (218). Thus, Peza's romantic notions about patriotism prevent him from taking a more efficacious practical view of himself and others. He is "never able to consider the men simply as human beings working at an unpleasant task," and therefore he never reaches Crane's highest ideal of behavior, "the stoic acceptance of practical responsibility" (218–19)—the "mystique of the veteran" that, as Maurice Bassan points out, first emerges clearly in this story and permeates much of Crane's subsequent war writing (8). But, LaFrance concludes, Peza *will* eventually attain this standard, for in his recognition of the insignificance of his own misery in response to the child's asking him if he is a man, he begins to shed his self-absorption, an action that is the first step toward sympathy for others, and thus toward actually becoming a man (220–21).

Levenson takes a similar view of the conclusion. In his reading, to become a man by Crane's definition, Peza must rid himself of egotism, which he begins to do when he joins the military community and starts following the orders of its officers. However, this larger vision of war and life "still must be made actual and particular, and this can only occur with his experience of death and the child" (*Adventure* lxxxiii). Through this experience, in which he undergoes "the collapse of his own personality as well as of the common-place world around him, he touches bottom," thereby earning the chance of "reviving as a new man" (*Active Service* xlii).

Frank Bergon takes another approach, identifying the true protagonist as a figure outside the story. In his view, Peza's heightened perception of battle and the matter-of-fact demeanor of the soldiers around him are "two modes of perception [that] are equally valid, [but] one of them"—Peza's—"cannot survive in the world." The story itself, Bergon says, in its encompassing of both of these modes, is Crane's solution to this dilemma: both *can* survive in the realm of art, which is thus the only realm in which one can present "the truthful complexity of experience" that evokes both these modes as responses. Therefore, neither Peza nor the soldiers are finally the heroes of this story; it is the artist himself who takes that role in creating the story in the first place (60).

Several other critics, while not going so far as to assert that the artist is the hero of "Death," also concern themselves primarily with the artistic aspects of the story—with Crane's technical skills—and their relevance to an understanding of themes. J. W. Shroeder concentrates on figurative language. Shroeder's view is that "Death" is one of a number of stories in which Crane espouses a limited Naturalistic philosophy of man as "part of the mechanism" of neutral nature, and that as a rule these stories are among Crane's weakest, since his philosophical agenda weighs down his creative faculties. However, Shroeder continues, "Death" is the exception to this rule, for Crane's expert deployment of arresting images, similes, and metaphors—particularly in characterizing his antagonists, alternately aggressive and fearful man on the one hand and indifferent nature on the other—contributes powerfully to "an indwelling and animating excellence" that makes this story Crane's "one real Naturalistic triumph" (120–21).

Rodney O. Rogers sees the story as embodying Crane's final epistemological stance, a belief that the meaning of experience is forever indeterminate due to relativity of perception, an idea that Crane conveys by his use of a third-person narrator who "exists primarily to evaluate the two antithetical definitions of man suggested by . . . Peza's war experience" (301). More specifically, Rogers says that Crane uses his flexible third-person point of view to modulate between close-up and distant views of his characters and their actions, two views that "correspond to the two disparate attitudes between which Peza wavers," the first of these being the belief that the individual is important and heroic with respect to the cosmos, and the second being the sense that the individual is utterly insignificant within a completely indifferent universe (302). At the conclusion of the story, Rogers says, in a reading similar to Bergon's view of the artist as holding complex, antithetical ideas in tension, "the child's question implicitly asks for an unequivocal definition of man, which the narrator is patently unwilling to supply." Rather, "[t]he story's relentless irony ultimately intends not to deny but only to qualify Peza's romantic view that man is an heroic individual who ought to be supported by the world" (303).

Nagel also praises Crane's skillful handling of modulations of point of view in this story, but he regards these modulations as even more intricate than Rogers does. Nagel identifies three separate points of view: Peza's and the child's, both of which come through the third-person narrator; and that of the narrator himself, who, particularly at the outset of the story, offers his own descriptions and perceptions, independent of Peza's and the child's eyes. Through shifts among these perspectives, Nagel says, Crane creates a meaningful "Impressionist parallax" (72). The narrator takes a distant, bird's-eye view that, as in "The Open Boat" and "The Blue Hotel," "serves to diminish the intensity of activity as perceived by those more directly involved" (72). At first, Peza also holds this view, but when he begins to involve himself in what he witnesses, empathizing with the soldiers, he experiences an epiphany like those of Henry Fleming and the correspondent in "The Open Boat": he arrives at "a realistic sense of his [own unimportant] position in the universe" (74). Meanwhile, the child's point of view functions contrapuntally; while Peza moves from "detachment to involvement to abstraction," the child distorts "sensory details into new patterns commensurate with his play" (74). As the story progresses and Peza's perceptions become completely subjective when he is gripped by fear, as when he imagines that the straps of the bandolier are the arms of its dead owner embracing him, Crane switches to stream-of-consciousness narration to convey this alteration in awareness, while at the same time the child's point of view remains detached almost until the end of the story, when he begins to cry without comprehending why he does so, an action that contrasts with Peza's knowing distress at his own situation, his own insignificance, into which he gets his final insight through the child's closing question. Thus, Nagel says, "[t]he narrative method of the story, with its modifications of perspective, not only traces the progression of Peza's conceptual development but contrasts it with superior views"—those of the bird's-eye narrator—"and an inferior one"—that of the child (76). The result is that the powerful final effect of the story "is the product of a dramatic plot, the theme of insignificance, and especially the intensity of the contrast of perspectives in its narrative counterpoint" (76).

Michael Fried also focuses on the story's shifting perspectives, arguing that Crane thereby demonstrates the epistemological inadequacy of both an engaged point of view, represented by Peza, and a detached one, represented by the child. Peza's engagement entails constant movement over the landscape and thus equally constant change in his angle of vision, which "prevents the reader from regarding any single perspective that Peza happens to occupy as definitive," while the child's recreation in his play of what he sees of the battle "involves a necessarily narcissistic misreading of the visual data." This epistemological quandary, Fried says, reflects Crane's doubts concerning the efficacy of "his own extreme version of the 'impressionist' enterprise"—that is, his effort in his writing to make the reader see, both literally and figuratively, what he himself saw (115).

Still another examination of Crane's handling of point of view in this story comes from Benfey. Like Rogers and Fried, he sees two perspectives operating, which for him are Peza's "psychic overload" in response to the battle, and the child's "active play [that] incorporates and reproduces aspects of the fighting, thus mastering it" (217). Through this split, Benfey argues, Crane is "mapping out two possible responses to overwhelming experience" (217), and he links these to Freud's identification of "two phenomena in which people repeat, in dreams and in waking fantasy, the unpleasant events to which they have been exposed: soldiers after the trauma of war and children in their play" (218). This connection leads Benfey to a despairing interpretation, for he says that it renders "all but explicit" in the story Freud's implicit theory of creativity—that it merely repeats trauma rather than providing catharsis. Viewed in terms of this theory, Crane's child "is the artist, repeating in different terms the horror of war, while Peza is the helpless victim" of that horror (218).

Works Cited

Ahnebrink, Lars. *The Beginnings of Naturalism in American Fiction*. Cambridge: Harvard University Press, 1950.

Bassan, Maurice. Introduction. *Stephen Crane: A Collection of Critical Essays*. Ed. Maurice Bassan. Englewood Cliffs, N.J.: Prentice-Hall, 1967, 1–11.

Beer, Thomas. *Stephen Crane: A Study in American Letters*. New York: Knopf, 1923.

Benfey, Christopher. *The Double Life of Stephen Crane*. New York: Knopf, 1992.

Bergon, Frank. *Stephen Crane's Artistry*. New York: Columbia University Press, 1975.

Berryman, John. *Stephen Crane*. New York: Sloane, 1950.

Bowers, Fredson. Textual Introduction. *Tales of Adventure*. Vol. 5 of The University of Virginia Edition of *The Works of Stephen Crane*. Ed. Fredson Bowers. Charlottesville: University Press of Virginia, 1970, cxxxiii–cxcv.

Colvert, James B. Introduction. *Tales of War*. Vol. 6 of The University of Virginia Edition of *The Works of Stephen Crane*. Ed. Fredson Bowers. Charlottesville: University Press of Virginia, 1970, xi–xxxvi.

———. *Stephen Crane*. New York: Harcourt Brace Jovanovich, 1984.

———. "Stephen Crane: Style as Invention." *Stephen Crane in Transition: Centenary Essays*. Ed. Joseph Katz. DeKalb: Northern Illinois University Press, 1972.

Crane, Stephen. "A Battle in Greece." *Stephen Crane: Uncollected Writings*. Ed. Olov Fryckstedt. Uppsala, Sweden: Uppsala University Press, 1963, 274–83.

———. "Crane at Velestino." *Reports of War*. Vol. 9 of The University of Virginia Edition of *The Works of Stephen Crane*. Ed. Fredson Bowers. Charlottesville: University Press of Virginia, 1971, 18–23.

———. "A Dark Brown Dog." *Tales, Sketches, and Reports*. Vol. 8 of The University of Virginia Edition of *The Works of Stephen Crane*. Ed. Fredson Bowers. Charlottesville: University Press of Virginia, 1973, 52–58.

———. "Death and the Child." *Tales of Adventure* 121–41.

———. "The Dogs of War." *Reports of War* 49–53.

———. "A Fragment of Velestino." *Reports of War* 27–44.

———. "A Great Mistake." *Tales, Sketches, and Reports* 50–52.

———. "An Ominous Baby." *Tales, Sketches, and Reports* 47–50.

———. "Stephen Crane at Velestino." *Reports of War* 23–27.

———. "War Memories." *Tales of War* 222–263.

Frederic, Harold. Review of *The Red Badge of Courage*. *New York Times,* Jan. 29, 1896:32.

Fried, Michael. *Realism, Writing, Disfiguration: On Thomas Eakins and Stephen Crane*. Chicago: University of Chicago Press, 1987.

Garnett, Edward. "Stephen Crane and His Work." *Friday Nights: Literary Criticisms and Appreciations*. First Series. New York: Knopf, 1922, 201–17. Rpt. in *Stephen Crane's Career: Perspectives and Evaluations*. Ed. Thomas A. Gullason. New York: New York University Press, 1972, 137–38.

Geismar, Maxwell. *Rebels and Ancestors*. Boston: Houghton Mifflin, 1953.

Gibson, Donald B. *The Fiction of Stephen Crane*. Carbondale: Southern Illinois University Press, 1968.

Gullason, Thomas A. "Stephen Crane's Short Stories: The True Road." *Stephen Crane's Career*, 470–86.

Halliburton, David. *The Color of the Sky: A Study of Stephen Crane*. Cambridge: Cambridge University Press, 1989.

Holton, Milne. *Cylinder of Vision: The Fiction and Journalistic Writings of Stephen Crane*. Baton Rouge: Louisiana State University Press, 1972.

Knapp, Bettina L. *Stephen Crane*. New York: Ungar, 1987.

LaFrance, Marston. *A Reading of Stephen Crane*. Oxford: Clarendon, 1971.

Levenson, J. C. Introduction. *Tales of Adventure* xv–cxxxii.

Nagel, James. *Stephen Crane and Literary Impressionism*. University Park: Pennsylvania State University Press, 1980.

Rogers, Rodney O. "Stephen Crane and Impressionism." *Nineteenth-Century Fiction* 24 (1969):292–304.

Shroeder, J. W. "Stephen Crane Embattled." *University of Kansas City Review* 17 (1950):119–29.

Solomon, Eric. *Stephen Crane: From Parody to Realism*. Cambridge: Harvard University Press, 1966.

Stallman, R. W. *Stephen Crane: A Biography*. New York: George Braziller, 1968.

Wells, H. G. "Stephen Crane from an English Standpoint." *North American Review* 171 (August 1900):233–42. Rpt. in *Stephen Crane's Career* 126–34.

Wertheim, Stanley, and Paul Sorrentino. "Thomas Beer: The Clay Feet of Stephen Crane Biography." *American Literary Realism* 22 (Spring 1990):2–16.

———, eds. *The Correspondence of Stephen Crane*. 2 vols. New York: Columbia University Press, 1988.

Wolford, Chester L. *The Anger of Stephen Crane: Fiction and the Epic Tradition*. Lincoln: University of Nebraska Press, 1983.

An Episode of War

Publication History

In an inventory of his published stories that he drew up in the spring or summer of 1897, Crane listed "An Episode of War" as having appeared in the American magazine *The Youth's Companion*. In fact, however, it was not published until 1899, in the December issue of the English periodical *The Gentlewoman*. This discrepancy, as Fredson Bowers noted in 1970 his textual introduction to the story for the Virginia edition of Crane's works, constituted one of the many minor mysteries of Crane bibliography (lxxx–lxxxi), until a 1984 article by Paul Sorrentino presented the solution, which is also given in the footnotes to the relevant correspondence in the 1988 two-volume edition of Crane's letters that Sorrentino co-edited with Stanley Wertheim.

In a letter dated October 31, 1895, the editor of *Youth's Companion* (who signed him- or herself only "L. B.," probably either L. J. Bridgman or Louise Baker) compliments Crane on *The Red Badge* and invites him to contribute to this periodical, offering to send him "a few hints as to the kind of stories we want and don't want" (*Correspondence* I, 129–30). Crane responded on November 5 that at the moment he was busy working on "a small novel," *The Third Violet*, but would consider this request in the future if the editor would inform him of the magazine's "literary platform" (*Correspondence* I, 133). The editor evidently complied with this request, for at the top of this letter is the notation "Ans./Nov 9." In March 1896 Crane submitted "Episode" to *Youth's Companion*, perhaps at that point entitling it "The Loss of an Arm," since this is how he designated it in the 1897 inventory (Bowers lxxx–lxxxi), or even, as Sorrentino suggests, "The Loss of an Arm: An Episode of War," thus bringing it into uniformity with the full titles of his two Civil War volumes, *The Red Badge of Courage: An Episode of the American Civil War*, and *"The Little Regiment" and Other Episodes of the American Civil War* ("Sale" 247). In the letter accompanying the typescript, Crane tells the editor that this "small sketch . . . was written for you," asks for the editor's opinion of it, and raises the possibility—never realized—of adding a "Part II," although he assures the editor that the piece is "of course complete" as it is (*Correspondence* I, 220). However, the story did not run, probably, as Sorrentino hypothesizes, because Crane did not follow whatever guidelines he received closely enough and had produced a "sardonic treatment of war [that] was . . . too harsh for a family magazine" ("Sale" 244). Sorrentino bases this theory on his discovery of the appearance of "Episode" in the March 16, 1916 issue of *Youth's Companion*, where it is introduced with the explanation that it "was written for *The Companion* just twenty years ago this month" and that "[w]hen it is read in the light of the news of to-day [i.e., reports of World War I], this story has, we believe, an unusual interest" ("Sale" 245).

Despite their failure to use the story in 1896, the publishers of *Youth's Companion*, Perry Mason & Co., paid Crane for it at that time, which accounts for his marking it in his inventory as appearing in this magazine, and then to recoup their costs sold the English rights and placed the story with *The Gentlewoman* ("Sale" 245). One ramification of this discovery, Sorrentino points out, is that the text that finally ran in *Youth's Companion* is likely closer to Crane's original manuscript than that used by *The Gentlewoman*. The latter was the best available at the time the Virginia edition was assembled, but the *Youth's Companion* version should probably now be regarded as authoritative ("Sale" 425–48).

"Episode" was not included in any of the books published during Crane's lifetime. It made its first appearance between hard covers in *Last Words*, a variegated volume that Crane's common-law wife, Cora, assembled after his death, published in England in 1902 by Digby, Long. Pioneering Crane editor

Wilson Follett included it in volume 9, published in 1926, of *The Work of Stephen Crane* (12 vols., New York: Knopf, 1925–27); since then it has appeared in many collections of Crane's work, including *Stephen Crane: An Omnibus* (New York: Knopf, 1952), edited by Robert W. Stallman, and *The Complete Short Stories and Sketches of Stephen Crane* (Garden City, N.Y.: Doubleday, 1963), edited by Thomas A. Gullason.

Circumstances of Composition

Following the great success of *The Red Badge of Courage* in 1895, publishers and syndicates besieged Crane with requests for more Civil War material. As James B. Colvert points out, he was not eager to write further on this subject at this time, since he had not yet witnessed combat and was thus uncertain about the truthfulness of his pictures of war (xi–xv). Nevertheless, he composed five stories with Civil War settings between October 1895 and February 1896, including "Episode," while he was living at his brother Edmund's house in Hartwood, New York. The other four were produced for the Bacheller and McClure syndicates and eventually included in the volume *"The Little Regiment" and Other Episodes of the American Civil War*, which was published by D. Appleton in October 1896; "Episode," as noted above, had a different genesis and destiny.

Crane's correspondence with the editor of *Youth's Companion* places the story specifically between mid-November 1895 and early March 1896, but its place in the sequence of the Civil War stories he produced during this time is uncertain. Because it is the only one of this group not to appear in *"The Little Regiment*," Maxwell Geismar and Chester L. Wolford both assume that Crane wrote it too late for inclusion—in February or March of 1896—and thus regard it as his final writing on the Civil War (131; 61). However, this theory is complicated by the fact that when Crane finished the story "The Little Regiment" in mid-February 1896, he called *this* piece "positively my last thing dealing with battle" (*Correspondence* I, 205). Perhaps Crane, only now remembering the *Youth's Companion* offer, geared himself up for one more story after this exasperated statement, or perhaps he had actually written "Episode" prior to "The Little Regiment" and chose not to include it in the book of that title for reasons that are now lost.

Sources and Influences

Crane himself asserted that "Episode" was drawn directly from life: he concludes the March 1896, letter to the editor of *Youth's Companion* that accompanied the typescript with the request that "[a]s for the title—make it, perhaps, [something] which labels them [sic] as *real accounts*" because "[t]his lieutenant is an actual person" (*Correspondence* I, 221). No biographer or critic has attempted to identify this lieutenant; instead, those who have taken up the hunt for specific sources have focused upon Crane's own illnesses. John Berryman says that the central question posed by the story—which he regards as one of a handful that establish Crane as a "master" of the short-story form—is "[h]ow to act, wounded," and that therefore it is one of Crane's meditations upon his own case as he wasted away at his final English home, Brede Place, Sussex, in 1899 (256). This is an interesting theory, but it ignores the inconvenient fact that the story was written three years earlier. Somewhat more persuasive is Nicholas Delbanco's point that from the beginning of Crane's career some of his contemporaries regarded him as a genius doomed to die young, like Edgar Allan Poe, so that even in 1896 Crane would have found personal resonance in a story about a man upon whom a wound "confers a kind of dignity in apartness, the mark of one about to die and whom the survivors revere" (49).

There is even less discussion of the story's possible literary antecedents. Although critics have proposed a number of sources Crane may have used in composing *The Red Badge* and his other Civil War stories, including John William De Forest's *Miss Ravenel's Conversion From Secession to Loyalty* (O'Donnell 579) and Tolstoy's *War and Peace* and *Sebastopol* (Beer 54, Stallman 26, Levenson xl), all of which prominently feature the physical and psychological effects of wounds, only Lars Ahnebrink has made an explicit connection between any of these works and "Episode," noting that in terms of visual detail the lieutenant's arrival at the field hospital may owe something to Pierre Bezukhov's first sight of the surgeons' tents at the battle of Borodino in *War and Peace* (346). Further links might well be drawn to *Sebastopol*, for in the opening section of this work a wounded soldier inspires in the narrator a mixture of sympathy and deference quite similar to that which the lieutenant evokes from his men in "Episode," and Tolstoy's soldier responds to the amputation of his leg with the same kind of low-key fatalism that Crane's lieutenant expresses to his female relatives about the loss of his arm at the end of the story. "'First of all things, . . . we mustn't think,'" Tolstoy has his soldier explain to the narrator when asked if the operation hurt. "'When we don't think we don't feel'" (11). This is not a far cry from the lieutenant's deflection of his family's tears with "'Oh, well, . . . I don't suppose it matters so much as all that'" (93).

More generally, it is also instructive to note Crane's reaction to the *Century* magazine series of articles on the war, collectively entitled *Battles and Leaders of the Civil War*. According to his artist friend C. K. Linson, Crane spent a great deal of time in Linson's studio reading these pieces in early 1893, finding them absorbing but simultaneously frustrating due to their focus on the impersonal aspects of combat. Finally, Crane remarked impatiently, "'I wonder that *some* of these fellows don't tell how they *felt* in those scraps! They spout eternally of what they *did*, but they are as emotionless as rocks'" (37). "Episode" can be regarded as one more of his attempts, along with *The Red Badge* and the stories in "*The Little Regiment*," to work out for himself how those fellows *did* feel.

Relationship to Other Crane Works

Wounded men feature prominently in a number of Crane's war stories besides "Episode," most notably *The Red Badge*, but the story's closest connection in terms of plot, as Stallman points out, is to the Spanish-American War story "The Price of the Harness." In both of these pieces a character is wounded in the arm, feels disoriented as a result, moves away from the battle line in an increasingly confused state, and winds up being intimidated by a surgeon whose crushing workload causes him to react to the wounded man with exasperation rather than compassion (*Stephen Crane* 396). More broadly, in terms of theme, several critics have included this story in groupings of Crane's works in which suffering leads to increased insight. Stallman sees "Episode" as one of three war stories, the other two being *The Red Badge* and "A Mystery of Heroism," in which the protagonist has his vision of battle altered by his painful experiences with it. He also notes structural parallels between "Episode" and *The Red Badge*, pointing out that despite their differences in length both are composed of "alternations of moods: perspectives of motion and change shifting into picture-postcard impressions where everything is felt as fixed and static" (*Houses* 106). Marston LaFrance implicitly agrees but does not limit this theme of altered vision to Crane's war stories; he says that the lieutenant belongs to a small cadre of Crane protagonists of various stripes—the others being Henry Fleming, the correspondent in "The Open Boat," Manolo Prat in "The Clan of No-Name," and Dr. Trescott in "The Monster"—who possess both imagination and conscience. Taken together, these qualities can lead to self-knowledge and a concomitant understanding of one's small place in the universe, which is "the only 'salvation' that Crane ever offers" (103). Similarly, Wolford says that "Episode" is one of a group of stories in which the main character "discovers a small measure of reality relating to the unknown—specifically death," but he notes further that these pieces are also linked by their protagonists' "corresponding inability to make [their discovery] known." He identifies the others in this group as *The Red Badge*, "A Mystery of Heroism," and "The Monster" (41).

Wertheim groups "Episode" with "The Open Boat" and "The Monster" as Crane's most potent meditations on "the pervasive theme of American literature[:] . . . Human isolation in its physical, emotional, or ideological manifestations"—a theme Crane was drawn to because of his own revolt against and subsequent feelings of isolation from his respectable, religious family. When the lieutenant finds himself estranged from his men because his wound puts them too much in mind of their own mortality, Wertheim says, he becomes, like the correspondent and Dr. Trescott, one of Crane's "autobiographical . . . isolatoes," men locked in "an unsuccessful struggle to integrate their lives with that of society and yet preserve separate identities" ("Wrath" 499).

Milne Holton sees "Episode" as belonging to several groups with different characteristics. Like Stallman, LaFrance, and Wolford, he points out its close connection to *The Red Badge* through the emphasis in both on "the process of gaining an apprehension," of seeing the nature of the universe and one's place in it more clearly as a result of hardship (144). He also links it to the Spitzbergen tales in that these, like "Episode," deal with "the paradox of apprehension and love"—that is, with the tension between forming a meaningful relationship with another person and the terrifying awareness of death which that person's being killed or wounded produces (266). And finally, he views it as one of a set of stories, also including "The Five White Mice," "Flanagan and His Short Filibustering Adventure," and "War Memories," which have ironic endings that "deny the very [stories] they conclude" (83–84).

Critical Studies

As Stallman's mention of the fact that the lieutenant has his arm amputated in a schoolhouse—the place "where one learns" (*Biography* 396)—might suggest, nearly all the critics who discuss "Episode" locate the key to interpreting the story in the insight regarding this amputation that the lieutenant expresses in the final line. Predictably, however, they differ as to the nature of that insight. Stallman asserts that it inverts Crane's usual theme, that "no man can interpret life without first experiencing it," since the lieutenant arrives at it through being removed from experience by his wound, through being forcibly made into an observer ("Reevaluation" 262). Donald B. Gibson says that what the lieutenant learns is that "man is able to adjust with stoical resignation to the undeserved and uncontrollable adversity befalling him by seeing himself and his world in undistorted perspective" (94). What this perspective comes down to is a rejection of the simultaneous sensations of dependency and separateness that the lieutenant feels early in the story due to the deference and fear with which his men treat him as a result of his wound's adumbration of death for them. He is able to accomplish this rejection when he reaches the field hospital, through the impersonality of the surgeon and the serenity of the dying man whom he encounters there; they show him that in a universe where such brutal things as amputation and death happen without discernible cause "nothing 'matters so much as all that'" (96).

Bettina Knapp focuses on the man dying outside the field hospital to reach much the same conclusion. In her reading, the tranquility with which this man smokes his pipe, she says, inspires the lieutenant to reconcile himself to his condition on the spot; she argues that he only imagines the scene with the women lamenting over his sleeve and his response to them. This development of courage and stoicism, she concludes, reflects "Crane's belief that one learns to conform to new situations" (169–70).

In LaFrance's view the lieutenant's final attitude is not so much a matter of stoicism as of deflation. LaFrance sees "Episode" as operating according to the pattern that he discerns in most of Crane's best stories: the protagonist faces a significant experience that his imagination distorts to still more momentous and terrifying proportions, a process that produces a profound sense of disillusionment when the actual experience falls short of his anticipation. For LaFrance, then, the lieutenant is not truly isolated because of the fear his wound induces in others but rather because of his own unarticulated and unconscious fear of losing his arm, a fear that he only becomes fully aware of when he tells the surgeon that he will not have the arm amputated. (Since the surgeon has not raised this possibility, LaFrance says, the lieutenant's statement proves that he is himself the cause of his psychological isolation.) That his fear is out of proportion to the actuality of amputation is then proven by the end of the story, in which the lieutenant's dismissal of the sorrows of his female relatives shows that the loss of the arm did not afford him the great insight that his fear led him to anticipate. "He stands shamefaced before these feminine tears," LaFrance concludes, "because the reality of his experience has fallen far short of what his imagination conceived it would be, and his fears and illusions before the fact have now deflated to a memory of which he is somewhat ashamed" (239).

Holton, on the other hand, says that the "diminishing intensity" (144) that the lieutenant expresses in the final line is not a result of deflation but rather of either ineffability or the resistance necessary to continued existence. What the lieutenant has discovered, Holton asserts, is his own "ultimate insignificance," but the low key of his last statement indicates either that this insight cannot be shared or that "it is the fading of that apprehension, as the maimed lieutenant . . . rejoins his family, that makes the apprehension at all humanly bearable" (144). Charles Swann's view accords with Holton's idea of ineffability, while Wolford's agrees with Holton's hypothesis that the lieutenant's ultimate response is an effort to refuse the knowledge of his own insignificance. Swann says that the crucial point of the story is the narrator's comment that "[a] wound gives strange dignity to him who bears it"; this is a statement that "[t]he only certain reality—though itself beyond meaning—is death, which is at once satisfying and horrifying in its finality. It means everything and nothing" (100). Wolford argues that as a result of being isolated from other soldiers and from war itself by the wound, the lieutenant discovers "the indifference of war" (68) and, by extension, the indifference of the universe. As the lieutenant walks from the battle line to the field hospital, he learns that "[t]he war represents a universe that has little to do with [him] except that it can, quite by chance, annihilate him"; his final utterance reveals that "[m]aintaining a casual or indifferent stance is a way to shy away from being reminded that men are 'little' and mortal" (68–69).

George W. Johnson also says that the lieutenant's final statement constitutes a way of avoiding being crushed. In observing the actions of others on and behind the battle line, the lieutenant has learned that the human condition is "an untenable position between an unknowable world and incongruous ceremonies" (251). His ritual self-abnegation is such a ceremony, Johnson explains; it shows that in the lieutenant's and Crane's view "the decorum of the veteran [is] no more meaningful than the rituals of tea" (251). However, despite its essential meaninglessness it and other such rituals are the appropriate response, in that they permit the survivor of war "to accept incongruities which would otherwise overwhelm his imagination" (253).

A somewhat different response to the lieutenant's stance comes from James Nagel. Like Gibson and Knapp, Nagel regards the lieutenant's last pronouncement as a stoic's recognition of ultimate truth rather than a refusal to confront that truth, but he says that what this statement reveals is not only the "necessity for . . . objectivity in war" but also its "inappropriateness" ("Stories" 11). Throughout the story, he notes, men detach themselves from the lieutenant when they discover he is wounded and thus stands poised to pull the curtain from before the fact of death; they must do so to enable themselves to continue functioning, and the lieutenant himself does much the same thing for the same reason in his concluding remark. However, the reader is not intended to regard this behavior as normative but rather to regard it negatively in comparison to that of the lieutenant's family. These women, "like the reader, cannot and need not withhold emotion at the sight of the tragedy," with the result that "the story becomes a condemnation of war through a dramatic portrayal of its effects" ("Stories" 13).

In another study, however, Nagel takes a different tack. Like LaFrance, he here sees this story as employing Crane's typical narrative pattern, which in Nagel's view consists of the protagonist's beginning in circumstances that literally and metaphorically restrict his sight and then gradually moving toward an epiphany. Sounding a bit like Stallman in his "Reevaluation" essay, Nagel points out that in this case the lieutenant is able literally to see and thus comprehend the nature of war only when he is disengaged from it, when he is forced into the literal and metaphorical stance of observer. Like Maggie Johnson encountering men of progressively lower social rank as she makes her final walk, the lieutenant on his way to the rear meets men who are sequentially lower in military rank but inversely higher in terms of their insight into the meaning of battle. The end of this progress is, in Nagel's view, the typical Crane discovery of one's own insignificance in the larger scheme of things (*Impressionism* 100–01), but in calling this discovery typical he has in mind a sort of typicality at odds with the frequent critical view of Crane as a Naturalist. In works of authentic Naturalism, Nagel says, the central characters "are portrayed as being insignificant without cognition of that fact, without realizing anything beyond the pathetic misery of their lives imposed upon them without justification or meaning"; he regards Crane as taking his protagonists at least one step further and thus being more susceptible of identification as an Impressionist. "Ordinarily," Nagel explains,

> Impressionistic protagonists experience the feeling of insignificance as a stage in their growth. They customarily go on to a moment of reflection of such depth and sensitivity that these moments alone imply a refutation of their lack of importance. (*Impressionism* 102)

In Nagel's view, the lieutenant's final pronouncement to his female kin is the epitome of such a moment.

In contrast to these generally approving assessments of the lieutenant's valedictory, Arno Karlen argues that Crane intends it to create a negative impression in the reader. By design, it makes the lieutenant seem "a little ridiculous," as well as "not very bright or especially brave." Nevertheless, Karlen says, Crane stops short of vindictiveness in this portrait, making it clear that the lieutenant's essential flaw is that he is merely human. "Crane is not willing to forgive him his weakness nor the world its random cruelties," Karlen concludes, "[b]ut he seems ready to settle for indictment rather than revenge" (482).

Eric Solomon and Knapp offer praise for Crane's style in this story. Solomon notes the lyricism of many of the descriptions of the battle scenes the lieutenant witnesses as he walks to the rear. At this point in his life "[t]he sheer beauty of war moves Crane," Solomon says, arguing that this fact, this ability to see the grace as well as the ugliness of the battlefield—the latter reflected in the lieutenant's wound—illustrates that Crane's judgment regarding war has matured, has moved beyond the wholly negative view expressed in *The Red Badge* (124). Similarly, Knapp notes "the melodic and visual beauty" of Crane's prose here, through which war is presented "in all its dazzling violence as a glorious but viciously cruel experience" (169).

Works Cited

Berryman, John. *Stephen Crane*. New York: Sloane, 1950.

Bowers, Fredson. Textual Introduction. *Tales of War*. Vol. 6 of The University of Virginia Edition of *The Works of Stephen Crane*. Ed. Fredson Bowers. Charlottesville: University Press of Virginia, 1970, xxxvii–cxci.

Colvert, James B. Introduction. *Tales of War*. xi–xxxvi.

Crane, Stephen. "An Episode of War." *Tales of War* 89–93.

Delbanco, Nicholas. *Group Portrait: A Biographical Study of Writers in Community*. New York: William Morrow, 1982.

Geismar, Maxwell. *Rebels and Ancestors: The American Novel, 1890–1915*. Boston: Houghton Mifflin, 1953.

Gibson, Donald B. *The Fiction of Stephen Crane*. Carbondale: Southern Illinois University Press, 1968.

Holton, Milne. *Cylinder of Vision: The Fiction and Journalistic Writings of Stephen Crane*. Baton Rouge: Louisiana State University Press, 1972.

Johnson, George W. "Stephen Crane's Metaphor of Decorum." *PMLA* 78 (1963): 250–56.

Karlen, Arno. "The Craft of Stephen Crane." *Georgia Review* 28 (1974):470–97.

Knapp, Bettina L. *Stephen Crane*. New York: Ungar, 1987.

LaFrance, Marston. *A Reading of Stephen Crane*. Oxford: Clarendon, 1971.

Levenson, J. C. Introduction. *The Red Badge of Courage*. Vol. 2 of The University of Virginia Edition of *The Works of Stephen Crane*. Ed. Fredson Bowers. Charlottesville: University Press of Virginia, 1975, xiii–xcii.

Linson, Corwin K. *My Stephen Crane*. Syracuse: Syracuse University Press, 1958.

Nagel, James. *Stephen Crane and Literary Impressionism*. University Park: Pennsylvania State University Press, 1980.

———. "Stephen Crane's Stories of War: A Study of Art and Theme." *North Dakota Quarterly* 45 (1975):5–19.

O'Donnell, Thomas F. "De Forest, Van Petten, and Stephen Crane." *American Literature* 27 (1956):578–80.

Solomon, Eric. *Stephen Crane: From Parody to Realism*. Cambridge: Harvard University Press, 1966.

Sorrentino, Paul. "Stephen Crane's Sale of 'An Episode of War' to *The Youth's Companion*." *Studies in Bibliography: Papers of the Bibliographical Society of the University of Virginia* 37 (1984):243–48.

Stallman, Robert W. *Stephen Crane: A Biography*. New York: George Braziller, 1968.

———. "Stephen Crane: A Revaluation." In *Critiques and Essays on Modern Fiction: 1920–1951*. Ed. John W. Aldridge. New York: Ronald, 1952, 244–69.

Swann, Charles. "Stephen Crane and a Problem of Interpretation." *Literature and History* 7 (1981):91–123.

Tolstoy, Leo. *Sebastopol*. Trans. Frank D. Millet. Ann Arbor: University of Michigan Press, 1961.

Wertheim, Stanley. "Stephen Crane and the Wrath of Jehovah." *Literary Review* 7 (1963):499–508.

Wertheim, Stanley, and Paul Sorrentino, eds. *The Correspondence of Stephen Crane.* Vol. 1. New York: Columbia University Press, 1988.

Wolford, Chester L. *Stephen Crane: A Study of the Short Fiction.* Boston: Twayne, 1989.

An Experiment in Misery

Publication History

This story was first published in the *New York Press* on Sunday, April 22, 1894 (pt. III:2). As Fredson Bowers notes, in this incarnation it included opening and closing sections that make clear the meaning of the word *experiment* in the title (862). In the opening section the youth who is the protagonist and an older friend debate the possibility of knowing the feelings of a tramp they are observing. The friend asserts that this kind of knowledge can come only from firsthand experience, an admonition that impels the youth to don battered clothing and gain such experience, leading to "the veracious narrative of an experiment in misery" that follows (qtd. in Bowers 862). In the conclusion the friend asks the youth if he has in fact come to understand the tramp's point of view. The youth responds, "'I don't know that I did . . . but at any rate I think mine own has undergone a considerable alteration'" (qtd. in Bowers 863).

The story was subsequently collected as one of the "Midnight Sketches" in the English book *"The Open Boat" and Other Stories*, published by Heinemann in 1898. In this version Crane excised the introductory and concluding sections, possibly because he felt they gave the piece a journalistic air inappropriate in what he intended to be a volume of short stories (Bowers 863). It subsequently appeared, in its cut Heinemann form, in volume 11, published in 1926, of *The Work of Stephen Crane* (12 vols., New York: Knopf, 1925–27), edited by Wilson Follett; and in 1963 in *The Complete Short Stories and Sketches of Stephen Crane* (Garden City, N.Y.: Doubleday), edited by Thomas A. Gullason. Robert W. Stallman used the original *New York Press* version, with the opening and closing framework, in his *Stephen Crane: An Omnibus* (New York: Knopf, 1952).

Circumstances of Composition

Émile Stangé and Corwin Knapp Linson, two of the artists with whom Crane was friendly during the years he lived in New York City, 1891–1896, left reminiscences of how "An Experiment in Misery" came to be written. Stangé recounts that on a morning just after a blizzard in late February 1894 he went to the studio of another artist, Frederic Gordon, and discovered that Crane and an unnamed illustrator friend had just arrived there. These two were

> both in rags, no overcoat, clothes all holes, toes out of their shoes, no umbrellas (of course not), and soaked to the skin, water dripping pools about them. I noticed Crane's rather flat chest was shaking every little while with spasms of a very hollow cough. His blond hair was matted over his eyes. A great wave of pity swept over me; I thought, "My Lord! has it come to this?" (qtd. in Stallman, *Biography* 94)

Crane's response to Stangé's solicitude was to grin and explain that he and the illustrator had spent the previous night in the Bowery, first standing in a breadline and then sleeping in a flophouse, as a way of discovering the feelings of the men who were compelled to do these things every night.

Linson picks up the story at this point, explaining that he and his brother visited Gordon's studio later that same morning to find Crane alone there, lying on a cot and looking sick but nevertheless having already completed a draft of the first piece to come out of this experience, the sketch "The Men in the Storm." When the Linsons berated Crane for not having dressed more warmly for his expedition, he replied, "'How would I know how those poor devils felt if I was warm myself?'" He then said that he now had enough ideas for stories to keep him busy for the next two years (24), an assertion he bore out at least in the short run by getting almost immediately to work on "Experiment in Misery," which he finished by mid-April 1894.

Sources and Influences

Crane's principal source for this story was, of course, his own experiment as recounted above. However, David Weimer notes that this experience would seem to have been too brief and limited to produce the "marvelously certain feelings of disorientation men have . . . in the face of . . . vast social instruments of unseen powers" that the story imparts (57). Weimer says that such certainty proves that Crane was also deeply indebted to the "existing body of notions and impressions" of slum life that could be found in the journalism and fiction of his era (57), treatments that, like "Experiment in Misery," functioned simultaneously, in the words of Maurice Bassan, as "realistic description, psychological analysis, and social indictment" ("Misery and Society" 107).

Chief among such works were the reformist exposés of Jacob Riis, whose *How the Other Half Lives* (1890), as Bassan points out, locates the roots of Bowery life in the same kind of "moral cowardice" as Crane is alleged to have said that he identifies in his story—in a kind of tramp mindset that the world owes one a living ("Misery and Society" 108–09), although Riis is careful where Crane is not to distinguish between incorrigible vagrants and those willing to work but unable to find employment ("Misery and Society" 110). (See the "Critical Studies" section of this chapter for a discussion of the problems involved in attributing the "moral cowardice" statement to Crane.)

Bassan further notes that Crane may have derived his "experimental" approach from the works of Josiah Willard, who wrote a number of articles on tramps during the 1890s. In one of these, "Life Among German Tramps," published in *Century Magazine* in October 1893, Willard adopts the guise and manners of such a figure in order to gain a clearer understanding of the tramps' psychology and, as part of this experiment, spends a night in a horrifying flophouse. In another piece, published in *Century* in February 1894, Willard recounts his performance of the same experiment in Albany, New York, and reaches the same conclusion as Riis and Crane about moral cowardice as the source of congenital tramping ("Misery and Society" 112–14). Bassan also identifies Thomas Flynt as a possible source; in one essay, "The City Tramp," published in *Century* in March, 1894, Flynt categorizes flophouses according to their prices, which ranged from seven to twenty-five cents per night. Crane in "Experiment," Bassan says, seems largely to be describing Flynt's "seven-center," although the beds and lockers with which Crane furnishes his version were usually only found in "fifteen-centers" and up; the "seven-centers" ordinarily offered only hammocks and lacked any provision for the storage of their tenants' belongings ("Misery and Society" 117).

Bassan also says that in addition to the works of these writers, who devoted themselves chiefly to analyzing slum life, Crane may have drawn—particularly for his detailed descriptions—on articles and books by William Dean Howells, Julian Ralph, H. C. Bunner, and Brander Matthews, who were less concerned with analysis and more interested in presenting "the picturesque aspects of slum and Bowery life," though often a condemnatory tone similar to the one Crane is frequently cited as using finds its way into their work, particularly their descriptions of conditions in flophouses ("Misery and Society" 115–16). A more general possible source, first identified by Crane's contemporary Frank Norris, is Emile Zola's novel *L'Assomoir*, a naturalistic portrayal of the effects of slum conditions on human character and fate. Both Lars Ahnebrink and James B. Colvert (*Crane* 40) suggest that Crane drew on this book for much of his Bowery writing; Ahnebrink details similarities in theme and method between *L'Assomoir* and Crane's Bowery novels *Maggie: A Girl of the Streets* and *George's Mother* (250), and he asserts that "in the choice of milieu and sordid detail" "Experiment" owes an equal debt to Zola (276). It should be noted, however, that Colvert argues convincingly against Zola's influence on *Maggie* in terms of technique, pointing out that Zola achieves his effects through massive inclusions of particulars whereas Crane works by selecting only the most telling details (*Bowery Tales* xliv–xlvi), an argument that would seem also to apply to "Experiment."

As is the case for many of his works, suggestions have also been made that Crane was influenced in "Experiment" not only by literary precursors but also by antecedents in the visual arts. Alice Hall Petry sees Crane's pairing of this story with another piece, "An Experiment in Luxury," as deriving from the work of the eighteenth-century engraver William Hogarth, who was given to companion pieces and frequently used them to depict the degradation of slum dwellers, as in his linked pictures *Gin Lane* and *Beer Street* (425). Another possible influence is Impressionist painting, with which critics such as Joseph Kwiat ("Painting") and James Nagel (*Impressionism*) have frequently linked various of Crane's works. Certainly a connection might well be drawn between visual Impressionism and the opening sentence of "Experiment": "It was late at night, and a fine rain was swirling softly down, causing the pavements to glisten with hue of steel and blue and yellow in the rays of innumerable lights" (*Tales, Sketches* 283).

Relationship to Other Crane Works

This story is most closely related to what Crane seems to have intended as a companion piece, "An Experiment in Luxury," which appeared in the same newspaper, the *New York Press,* on Sunday, April 29, 1894—one week after "Misery." Here, as in the newspaper version of "Misery," a young man begins by talking to a friend about discovering how another class of people live through the "experiment" of becoming a member of that class for a brief time; in this case the class is the very wealthy rather than the indigent. Despite this parallelism, most critics find "Luxury" distinctly inferior to "Misery," largely because Crane seems to find the rich family with whom the protagonist associates extremely insipid, probably as a function of their well-cushioned lives. Marston LaFrance's comment on this matter is perhaps the most pithy; he asserts that reading these two stories side by side reveals that Crane "was immensely interested in the professional tramp's point of view and as immensely bored with the millionaire and his family" (78).

Bassan concurs with this assessment of the stories' relative merits but offers a view that slightly dissents from the position of most critics regarding their narrative connections. The customary critical assumption is that, given the many parallels between the stories, the same young man is the protagonist of both; Bassan argues that this is not the case. He notes that in both stories the protagonist begins in a state of naiveté and measures his illusions against reality, thereby bringing his understanding of his environment into closer alignment with Crane's own. If these two protagonists were the same person it would be logical to expect the protagonist of "Luxury" to begin from a point of greater insight as a result of having carried out the experiment of "Misery." However, Bassan points out,

> the young man of "Luxury," does not seem to have profited at all from the experience of the "youth" in the first story, whose point of view had undergone "considerable alteration" in the direction of perceiving the shaping power of environment and the essentially brutalizing nature of the class struggle. ("Eternal Mystery" 389)

Whether or not they agree that "Misery" and "Luxury" are as disjunctive in terms of character as Bassan argues, many critics believe that where artistry and depth of insight are concerned "Misery" has stronger connections to some of Crane's other Bowery works than to "Luxury." Pointing to these particular areas, LaFrance sees another contemporaneous sketch of the lives of tramps on the lower East Side, "The Men in the Storm," as the true "artistic companion piece" to "Misery" (83). He also links it specifically to *Maggie*, saying that the story and Crane's putative description of it as an exemplification of "moral cowardice" can shed light on his frequent references to *Maggie* as a study of environment: what he meant in these references, in LaFrance's view, was not physical environment but rather the mental environment of moral cowardice on the part of those around her—her mother, Jimmie, and Pete—in which Maggie, like the youth in "Misery," finds herself trapped. Regarded from this perspective, LaFrance concludes, neither work posits a theory of determinism, since the characters have free will to choose between moral bravery and cowardice and opt for the latter (42). LaFrance further links the story to one of Crane's Spanish-American War stories, "War Memories," in that both are framed by comments from the protagonist about the difficulties involved in communicating "'the real thing'"—experience—to anyone else, with the difference that in the more mature "Memories" these remarks are more subtle and more self-reflexively ironic (232–33).

Several writers also trace connections between "Misery" and Crane's corpus as a whole. Bassan says that in this story as everywhere Crane relies heavily on his favorite metaphor, war, to externalize "that interior conflict of the tormented psyche and of the degraded self" that is always his primary interest; in this case the war is between classes, whereas in other works it is between family members, as in *Maggie*, or actual armies, as in *The Red Badge of Courage* ("Misery" 104). Nagel notes that the wail of protest that the youth hears coming from the sleeping tramps is the most striking example of one of Crane's most common motifs, a howling sound used to express characters' internal "anguish of alienation and hopelessness." This aural motif begins in some of Crane's earliest works, the Sullivan County sketches "The Cry of a Huckleberry Pudding" and "The Black Dog," and continues to appear at least as late as "The Price of the Harness," one of the Spanish-American war stories (*Impressionism* 107).

Milne Holton focuses on visual rather than aural motifs. He argues that although Crane depicts the youth's experience as involving all his senses, the most important is sight, especially in his late-night and early-morning encounters with the sleepers in the flophouse; and he asserts that this emphasis is consonant with Crane's work as a whole. In Holton's view sight is Crane's central trope for comprehension, an idea Holton bases on Crane's frequent presentation of innocent characters whose initiation into under-standing is accomplished by their literally seeing their situations clearly for the first time (68).

In perhaps the most comprehensive study of the thematic and technical connections between "Misery" and the rest of Crane's canon, Robert Shulman asserts that the potential for the formation and breakdown of community that is central to this story is in fact central to most of Crane's work, and he notes as well the occurrence here of a number of Crane's frequently employed artis-tic devices: the blurring of clear outlines between the protagonist and his environment at the outset of the story, the vividly rendered "descent into the depths of the self and existence," the use of third-person point of view to cre-ate the "formal distancing" necessary to achieve "immersion in experience," and the deployment of hellish imagery to convey the "threat of death, misery, and loss of self in a universe where traditional religious assurances are nonex-istent" (442–44).

Critical Studies

Crane himself may have provided the earliest interpretation of this story. His first biographer, Thomas Beer, quotes a letter of November 12, 1896, from Crane to a woman named Catherine Harris, in which he says, "[i]n a story of mine called 'An Experiment in Misery' I tried to make plain that the root of Bowery life is a sort of cowardice. Perhaps I mean a lack of ambition or to willingly be knocked flat and accept the licking" (140). Beer is the only source for this letter, and in recent years Stanley Wertheim and Paul Sorrentino and others have demonstrated that Beer appears to have fabricat-ed a good deal of what he presents as Crane's correspondence, so that any letter in Beer that cannot be authenticated from another source must be regarded with skepticism (*Correspondence* II, 671; "Thomas Beer" 7); how-ever, prior to the publication of the discoveries of these astute literary sleuths, most critics quite reasonably accepted Beer's "Crane" letters at face value, so that many of those who comment on "Misery" base their analyses on Crane's remarks on the story as reported by Beer. Daniel Hoffman adverts to this letter as the premise for his assertion that Crane wishes his reader to see the real conflict in this story as taking place not between the individual and society but rather between the individual and his or her own "inner forces, inherent indolence and cowardice." As proof of this thesis, he says that from the beginning to the end of "Misery" Crane "simply presents what he sees" rather than explicitly blaming society; "there is no alternative offered" to the sufferings of the tramps, "no plea for any ameliorative measures" (176–77). In an assessment similarly linked to Crane's putative letter, Edwin Cady judges "Misery" and "Luxury" together as revealing Crane's fundamental conviction "that the trouble with the poor was finally cowardice"— and as demonstrating, coincidentally, that Crane "could both think and write rings around Theodore Dreiser" (xxxv).

LaFrance and Yoshie Itabashi also take their cues from the letter. LaFrance argues against the usual editorial practice of printing the story without its framing conversations between the curious youth and his compatriot, because in his view these are what make clear that the youth's experiences in the Bowery are indeed an "experiment" that moves him from his "conventional feeling of mere pity without any understanding of the outcast" (43) to the greater awareness that the tramps' own moral cowardice is to blame for their condition, an awareness that Crane seeks also to instill in his reader. The story's movement from night to morning, from darkness to light, LaFrance says, enacts this progression on the structural level, and the sequence of the plot's events enacts it on the experiential level. The protagonist's vision of society as having discarded the Bowery denizens, LaFrance asserts, is a misguided product of his innocence, as shown by the fact that the tramp known as "the assassin" with whom the youth passes the night is actually a willing dropout from society rather than its reject, given that his reminiscences about his life reveal that he is shiftless rather than persecuted. Likewise, the young man's vision of the sleepers in the flophouse as victims of the pitiless granite wheels of society is innocent, LaFrance argues; it is shown to be false by the greater complexity of the appearance of these sleepers in the light of day, at which point many of them look healthy and robust, not victimized. And the youth's final sense that the city is not hostile but rather merely indifferent to the fate of individuals demonstrates, according to LaFrance, his mature awareness that being a "professional bum" as opposed to an "honest man temporarily reduced to suffering in Bowery flophouses" stems from a conscious act of will, a capitulation to one's moral cowardice, rather than from external persecution (48). Itabashi likewise cites both Crane's alleged letter and the newspaper version of the story—particularly the conclusion, in which the youth confesses that he is still not sure that he understands the tramp's point of view but says that his own has certainly changed—to argue much the same point. When the protagonist takes his morning view of the notably hale sleepers and ends up feeling guilty for being an outcast himself as he contemplates the bustling, unconcerned city, Itabashi says, Crane reveals that despite his frequently proclaimed repudiation of the Christian ideology of his upbringing he is still operating from a "distinctly Puritanical frame of mind—one which formulates that an idler, or a failure, is a spiritual criminal and one of God's rejected," and which therefore formulates as well that poverty is a "purely personal, mental problem" (246).

An equal number of critics, while not doubting the authenticity of Crane's letter, refuse to take the author completely at his word. Ahnebrink argues that the import of the story runs directly counter to the idea of "cowardice" proposed in the letter. In his view, the story is evidence that Crane was in fact a thoroughgoing determinist who held an unchanging belief that "man's will was enslaved" (189). The characters, he says, are depicted as unalterably temperamentally out of place in society, and society is presented as equally unalterably disposed to discard such people. Crane shows the Bowery's denizens, Ahnebrink concludes, to be simply "the unfit, unable to assert themselves. There [is] no room, no foothold for them, only despair and frustration in a world where the battle [is] to the strong, and the weak and humble [are] trampled down" (194).

Most of the other critics who dissent from the "cowardice" argument take a more mediate position, one less diametrically opposed to it than Ahnebrink's. Russell B. Nye is the earliest to argue that Crane is presenting a complex, pluralistic vision rather than a doctrinaire determinist or Puritanical doctrine. In Nye's reading, the protagonist's nocturnal encounters with the tramps and his matitudinal view of the city combine to show that both individuals and society must bear a share of the blame for the misery he has witnessed. Crane seeks to communicate the idea, Nye says, that, confronted with the dynamism of the city, "weak men quail, and this lack of courage, this giving up of personal aim, is . . . one great cause of social illness" but not the only one; the city itself, with its primary characteristic of "terrible and impersonal cruelty," must also be assigned a measure of culpability (50–51). Max Westbrook likewise argues that Crane is consciously depicting large social forces that are out of the tramps' control as one cause of their condition and their own failure of will in the realms in which they could exercise control as another (221–22). Weimer is of the same general opinion, but he regards these two causes as more intricately linked than Nye and Westbrook do. "It is not so much character or environment . . . to which Crane addresses himself" in "Misery" and in all his writings about cities, Weimer asserts, "as it is a relationship between a particular sort of character and a particular sort of environment, a peculiar emotionalism in certain egos and a singular disorder in the . . . urban worlds to which those egos submit" (60).

A number of other critics who discern such complexity in Crane's attitude explain it in terms of a conflict between his emotional and his more causally oriented responses to the vagrants and their world. Stallman sees Crane as feeling pity for his socially outcast characters but also recognizing "the irony of their plight"—that is, its roots in their own indolence, epitomized in the behavior of the assassin. And this composite viewpoint, with "the ironic voice undercutting the sentiment" in the narrator's speech, Stallman argues, is a highly innovative handling of point of view in American fiction, well ahead of its time (*Biography* 102). Donald B. Gibson also regards Crane as an innovator here; in his view, Crane is indeed contending that the root of his characters' degradation is their own moral cowardice, as he is warranted to assert in the letter in Beer and as most of the other writers upon whom he draws insist, but Crane—perhaps recognizing in his Bowery denizens something he himself might easily become, given his experimenting protagonist's close resemblance to him—also shows more sympathy for his characters and concomitantly takes society more strongly to task for its failings than any of these other authors do (53–54). Colvert and Chester L. Wolford offer similar interpretations. Colvert says that Crane's depiction of the assassin as "a drunkard and shirker exemplifies an incorrigible personal irresponsibility" but that this behavior is balanced against "evidences of cruel and invincible social forces" that arouse pity, if not for the assassin himself, then at least for other, less inveterately idle, members of his class (*Crane* 61). Wolford likewise points to the assassin as proof that Crane does see the tramps as largely responsible for their circumstances, but he also similarly asserts that Crane does not withhold his sympathy from such characters because of their culpability (23).

Bassan, on the other hand, regards the story as neither apportioning blame nor offering pity to the characters. The expressionistic imagery through which Crane renders the saloons and flophouses as devourers of men and the flophouse residents as speared fish and corpses, Bassan says, makes the point that it is not the tramps themselves but rather their deracinating environment that is responsible for their condition. However, Bassan further asserts, Crane does not sympathize with these men, whom he presents as "despicable"; rather, in the narrator's comments that the youth sees them as the representatives of "a whole section, a class, a people" (*Tales, Sketches* 289), he separates himself from individual contact with them, choosing instead to regard them impersonally but not negatively, making clear that his "indictment is not of [this] class, but of the society which produces it and tortures it" ("Misery" 119).

Shulman also focuses on the protagonist's comprehension of the flophouse sleepers as symbolic of a class, although he derives a different conclusion from it. In his view, this understanding instills in the youth a sense of connectedness, of community, that, when coupled with his awareness that this community is based on a "protest against death and inexorable misery," constitutes "one of the most profound of Crane's social insights." And, from this perspective, what gives the ending its force is the sense that in the impersonal world of the city such misery is the only basis for community. As the youth despairs on the park bench, Shulman says, Crane's point is "not the conventional indictment of an indifferent, money-grubbing society but the youth's feeling that he is 'an outcast,' . . . a characteristic Crane response but one that at the center of the story the youth [had] momentarily transcended" in his perception of community expressed in the "nightmare voice" of the flophouse (445–47).

Gullason takes a less favorable view of "Misery," judging it "solid" in its study of social problems but flawed technically by a "heavy-handed" approach (477). Stallman as well faults it on technical grounds, claiming that "Crane has not patterned the imagery or made it consistently metaphorical" (*Bowery Tales* Introduction 11). However, most critics have offered nothing but praise for Crane's craftsmanship here, beginning with his contemporary Edward Garnett, who lauds the story for "the nervous audacity" of its phrasing, "which reveals the quality of chiaroscuro of a master's etching" (qtd. in Gullason 144). Directly responding to Stallman, Bassan points out a pattern of geographical circularity in the story's imagery, moving from park to restaurant/saloon to flophouse to restaurant/saloon to park, which "reinforces the rhythm of monotony, of hopeless repetition" in the tramps' lives ("Design" 130). Moreover, he continues, the central image in the flophouse, which itself lies at the center of the story, is "the imperturbable granite wheels" (*Tales, Sketches* 289) of society, an image that "generates precisely that aura of pathos that arises from the tale's circular structure" as a whole ("Design" 130). "Metaphor and structure thus join," Bassan concludes, proving that "[t]he imagery . . . is, in short, patterned, and tightly welded to the structure," and it thereby "initiates the reader, like the latter-day Goodman Brown who is its hero, into the reality of evil, and into what Crane was to call, in 'The Open Boat,' the 'pathos' of man's condition" ("Design" 132).

Nagel also discusses links between imagery and structure. He sees the story as comprised of five units, each having its own theme and imagery, which combine to trace the alteration in the protagonist's perspective and emotions. The first section is the introductory paragraphs, which establish that "the youth has entered a world of depravity, identified with its inhabitants, and has felt the oppressive power around him which threatens him in his new and assumed impotence" ("Structure" 170). The second part reveals the predatory nature of the Bowery environment and introduces the assassin, with an emphasis on the fact that his guilty, criminal aspect is a reflection of this predatory atmosphere rather than an emanation of his fundamental nature. With this fact in view, he functions as the youth's physical and moral guide to this new world, leading him to "an understanding of the degradation and pathos of the lives of the poor" ("Structure" 170). This moral insight develops in the third section via Crane's imagistic depiction of Bowery existence as a living death, with men forced to be passive and receptive to "the destructive will of external forces" ("Structure" 171)—a depiction that climaxes with the wails of the men sleeping in the flophouse, which "transcend immediate depravity to become emblems of a universal anguish" and provide the crucial step in the youth's "psychological growth toward compassion and a mature grasp of the conditions of life for these men" ("Structure" 172). The fourth part then "extend[s] the implications of the flophouse in both temporal and spatial dimensions," showing that poverty and degradation are eternal and widespread through imagistic references to ancient Egyptians and through the assassin's recitation of his travails in various regions of the country. Finally, the fifth section brings the youth back to his physical starting point, City Hall Park, and thus highlights by contrast the distance he has traveled from his initial psychological state. Whereas at the beginning of his quest he chiefly felt curiosity, he now feels guilty, both for having been "an objective 'experimenter' amid social conditions that demand the utmost compassion" and for his current "association with a class looked down upon with suspicion by the social norm" ("Structure" 174). (Nagel gives much the same analysis in his book *Stephen Crane and Literary Impressionism*, the only real difference being that in the book he more explicitly raises the possibility that, given their capacity for "individual moral choice," the Bowery denizens bear some responsibility for their condition [112, see also 139–40].)

Bergon makes much the same point as Bassan and Nagel regarding the effect of Crane's imagery. Specifically, he regards "Misery" as a prime example of Crane's effective and innovative use of metaphors to transform observed reality into subjective interpretation. As soon as the youth takes on the condition of a tramp, Bergon points out, "references to objective facts give way to interpretations by a predisposed imagination" and thus "[c]ommon objects suddenly become threatening" (32), as when the saloon is imaged as eating the men who pass through its doors "like sacrifices to a heathenish superstition" and the elevated train station is described as resembling "some monstrous kind of crab squatting over the street" (*Tales, Sketches* 284). By means of such metaphors, Bergon says, "all details are unified by a hallucinatory apprehension of scenes, in which objects are threatening, devouring, malignant, and finally demonic," and Crane thereby conveys the sense that "[l]ife in this world is a form of living death" (32).

Colvert's discussion of technique in this story is more general; he calls attention to what he calls Crane's "quasi-surrealistic style," his method of "describing scenes from odd angles of vision, deliberately distorting the conventional realistic treatment of space and time and thus intensifying the sense of a threateningly incoherent order of reality" (135). In a similar vein, Sergio Perosa notes that throughout the story "the impression of life that is conveyed is always filtered through the writer's subjectivity. Any discursive of purely narrative possibility is sacrificed to immediacy," with the effect that the "vividness of details leads thus to sudden 'epiphanies' of reality." And this method of subjective rendition, he argues, controverts the frequent proposal that Crane be classified as a Naturalist, since Naturalism as a style mandates the painstaking accumulation of photographically detailed descriptions, whereas Crane here aims at "the apprehension of life through the play of perceptions, the significant montage of sense impressions, the reproduction of chromatic touches by colorful and precise notations, the reduction of elaborate syntax to the correlation of sentences," all of which conduces to "a sketchy, and at the same time evocative, kind of writing" that is better termed Impressionistic than Naturalistic (85–86). Bettina Knapp likewise praises Crane's technique in this story for its creation of an emotionally charged effect, but she concentrates on his use of even more abstract means. Noting Crane's handling of color as almost purely itself, almost devoid of representationality, in passages such as the early "a fine rain was swirling softly down, causing the pavements to glisten with hue of steel and blue and yellow in the rays of innumerable lights," she says that such "interweaving of soft and harsh tonalities points up the stressful suffering and pain of the characters, whose dismal lives Crane is about to depict" (17).

Perhaps the most wide-ranging and insightful discussion of Crane's technical/stylistic evocation of subjectivity in "Misery" comes from Alan Trachtenberg. In his view, Crane's goal here, as in much of his writing about the city, is to transform the conventional genre of the newspaper slum sketch by cultivating within its confines "an authentic style as a vehicle of personal vision" (141)—in other words, to shake this form out of cliché by developing "techniques for rendering events on city streets as unique and complex experiences" rather than as the generic events of a thousand other articles and tales (143). One such technique is subjectivity within the third-person-limited point of view: Crane "projects the youth's consciousness; he is made into a register of the world-as-it-is-felt of the particular setting. In this way Crane transmutes social fact into felt experience," not only for the youth, but also, by extension, for the reader, who is unaccustomed to the communication of such fact in such a manner of felt immediacy (150). Along this line, the story's framing conversation in the newspaper edition, Trachtenberg explains, with its emphasis on what follows as an experiment in the underclass by one who is not a member of that class, was a conventional distancing device in slum sketches, but Crane uses this very device to subvert such distancing when in the morning the youth truly feels himself to be one of that underclass and directly partakes of its estrangement. His "experiment" thus reveals to him, Trachtenberg says, that "the homeless poor are victims whose inner acquiescence is a form of cowardice." But, more crucial than this insight, "[m]ore important than such 'meanings,' are the strategies compressed in the word 'experiment,'" for in Trachtenberg's formulation this word

> denotes the subject as well as the method; the sketch is 'about' the youth's experiment. . . . Crane is concerned with the investigator, with the

exercise of the logic of investigation upon his subjectivity. The experiment transforms the youth, and it is [only] through that transformation that the life of the city's strangers becomes manifest. (153)

In this strategy of transformation—of the protagonist, and thus of the form, and thus in turn of the reader of this form—Trachtenberg says, "lie[s] the specifically urban character of Crane's writings, a character that is his calculated invention out of the materials of newspaper culture" (153). Thus, Crane can be seen to have "accepted the condition of newspaper production"—that it was a marketplace of conventionalities to be consumed—"and produced work within it that, with the complicity of his careful reader, converts the data of street life into memorable experience" (149).

In response to Trachtenberg's focus on "the narrative progress of the sketch as it changes social fact into personal experience" for both the protagonist and the reader, Alan R. Slotkin offers still further insights into Crane's technical methodology here, examining modifications in the youth's speech system as a key to this narrative progress. According to Slotkin, "Crane's clearest statement of his correspondent-persona's increasing involvement with the life of the poor he wants to understand, not merely observe, resides in clearly manipulative changes in the youth's idiolect." The framing device of the youth's pre- and post-experimental conversations with his friend is crucial to an understanding of the role of these changes, Slotkin explains, because in these exchanges the reader hears "the dictional patterns of the reporter within his accustomed environment," which "provide a functional norm of speech representative of a class demonstrably above that of the Bowery." With this norm established at the story's outset, the youth's idiolect moves in perceptible stages toward the divergent norms of the Bowery, thereby indicating his altered perceptions of and concomitantly greater involvement with the practitioners of these norms. The first of these stages is prompted by "the realization that the external world perceives his altered status" when he dons clothing appropriate to the Bowery "and expects him to be and to behave as what he appears"—an expectation that includes and thus affects his manner of speaking. The second is a product of his "increasingly intimate and lasting contacts with members of the new class," especially the assassin, "that allow the testing and ultimate adoption of dictional forms that reflect altered status." The third and ultimate stage is reached in his next-morning conversation with the assassin, in which the youth's speech is completely harmonized with his interlocutor's in terms of idiolect and thus constitutes "a verbal display of his understanding of the values of the Bowery hobo" (274).

The most focused discussion of Crane's technique in "Misery" is an exchange between Thomas Bonner and Clarence Johnson. Bonner says that in identifying the youth's companion as "the assassin" Crane links this character to the assassin bug, a blood-sucking member of the Reduvidae family; in thus connecting human and animal predators he "underscores the naturalism of life in the Bowery" (56). Johnson replies that, while Crane does give the assassin "bestial characteristics" as part of his depiction of a naturalistic world, the epithet is not part of that effort, for he did not possess the entomological expertise to make so precise a human-insect link (21).

Works Cited

Ahnebrink, Lars. *The Beginnings of Naturalism in American Fiction*. Cambridge: Harvard University Press, 1950.

Bassan, Maurice. "The Design of Stephen Crane's Bowery Experiment." *Studies in Short Fiction* 1 (1964):129–32.

———. "Misery and Society: Some New Perspectives in Stephen Crane's Fiction." *Studia Neophilologica* 35 (1963):104–20.

———. "Stephen Crane and the Eternal Mystery of Social Condition." *Nineteenth-Century Fiction* 19 (1965):387–94.

Beer, Thomas. *Stephen Crane: A Study in American Letters*. New York: Knopf, 1923.

Bergon, Frank. *Stephen Crane's Artistry*. New York: Columbia University Press, 1975.

Bonner, Thomas, Jr. "Crane's 'An Experiment in Misery.'" *Explicator* 34 (1976):Item 56.

Bowers, Fredson. "The Text: History and Analysis." *Tales, Sketches, and Reports*. Vol. 8 of The University of Virginia Edition of *The Works of Stephen Crane*. Ed. Fredson Bowers. Charlottesville: University Press of Virginia, 1973, 769–969.

Cady, Edwin H. Introduction. *Tales, Sketches, and Reports* xxi–xli.

Colvert, James B. Introduction. *Maggie: A Girl of the Streets*. In *Bowery Tales*. Vol. 1 of The University of Virginia Edition of *The Works of Stephen Crane*. Ed. Fredson Bowers. Charlottesville: University Press of Virginia, 1969, xxxiii–lii.

———. *Stephen Crane*. New York: Harcourt Brace Jovanovich, 1984.

———. "Stephen Crane: Style as Invention." *Stephen Crane in Transition: Centenary Essays*. Ed. Joseph Katz. DeKalb: Northern Illinois University Press, 1972.

Crane, Stephen. "An Experiment in Misery." *Tales, Sketches, and Reports* 283–93.

Garnett, Edward. "Stephen Crane and His Work." *Friday Nights: Literary Criticisms and Appreciations* (First Series). New York: Knopf, 1922, 201–17. Rpt. in *Stephen Crane's Career: Perspectives and Evaluations*. Ed. Thomas A. Gullason. New York: New York University Press, 1972, 137–38.

Gibson, Donald B. *The Fiction of Stephen Crane*. Carbondale: Southern Illinois University Press, 1968.

Gullason, Thomas A. "Stephen Crane's Short Stories: The True Road." *Stephen Crane's Career* 470–86.

Hoffman, Daniel G. *The Poetry of Stephen Crane*. New York: Columbia University Press, 1957.

Holton, Milne. *Cylinder of Vision: The Fiction and Journalistic Writings of Stephen Crane*. Baton Rouge: Louisiana State University Press, 1972.

Itabashi, Yoshie. "New York Sketches: Crane's Creed and Art." *Studies in English Literature* 48 (Mar. 1972):243–58.

Johnson, Clarence O. "Crane's 'Experiment in Misery.'" *Explicator* 35 (1976): 20–21.

Knapp, Bettina L. *Stephen Crane*. New York: Ungar, 1987.

Kwiat, Joseph J. "Stephen Crane and Painting." *American Quarterly* 4 (1952):331–38.

LaFrance, Marston. *A Reading of Stephen Crane*. Oxford: Clarendon, 1971.

Linson, Corwin K. *My Stephen Crane*. Syracuse: Syracuse University Press, 1958.

Nagel, James. *Stephen Crane and Literary Impressionism*. University Park: Pennsylvania State University Press, 1980.

———. "Structure and Theme in Crane's 'An Experiment in Misery.'" *Studies in Short Fiction* 10 (1973):169–74.

Nye, Russell B. "Stephen Crane as Social Critic." *Modern Quarterly* 11, 6 (Summer 1940):48–54.

Perosa, Sergio. "Naturalism and Impressionism in Stephen Crane's Fiction." *Stephen Crane: A Collection of Critical Essays*. Ed. Maurice Bassan. Englewood Cliffs, N.J.: Prentice-Hall, 1967, 80–94.

Petry, Alice Hall. "Gin Lane in the Bowery: Crane's *Maggie* and William Hogarth." *American Literature* 56 (1984):417–26.

Shulman, Robert. "Community, Perception, and the Development of Stephen Crane: From *The Red Badge* to 'The Open Boat'." *American Literature* 50 (1978):441–60.

Slotkin, Alan R. "Dialect Manipulation in 'An Experiment in Misery.'" *American Literary Realism* 14 (1981):273–76.

Stallman, R. W. *Bowery Tales* Introduction. *Stephen Crane: An Omnibus*. Ed. R. W. Stallman. New York: Knopf, 1952, 3–22.

———. *Stephen Crane: A Biography*. New York: George Braziller, 1968.

Trachtenberg, Alan. "Experiments in Another Country: Stephen Crane's City Sketches." *Southern Review* 10 (1974):265–86. Rpt. in *American Realism: New Essays*. Ed. Eric J. Sundquist. Baltimore: Johns Hopkins University Press, 1982, 138–54.

Weimer, David. *The City as Metaphor*. New York: Random House, 1966.

Wertheim, Stanley, and Paul Sorrentino. "Thomas Beer: The Clay Feet of Stephen Crane Biography." *American Literary Realism* 22 (Spring 1990):2–16.

———, eds. *The Correspondence of Stephen Crane*. Vol. 2. New York: Columbia University Press, 1988.

Westbrook, Max. "Stephen Crane: The Pattern of Affirmation." *Nineteenth-Century Fiction* 14 (1959):219–29.

Wolford, Chester L. *Stephen Crane: A Study of the Short Fiction*. Boston: Twayne, 1989.

The Fight

Publication History

This story made its first appearance in the June 1900 issue of *Harper's New Monthly Magazine* (101:56–63). It was the eleventh to be published in Crane's series of thirteen Whilomville tales that *Harper's* ran between August 1899 and August 1900. Along with the other installments in this cycle, it was then collected in the volume *Whilomville Stories*, which Harper & Brothers published in August 1900 in America and in November of the same year in England (Bowers 103). Editor Wilson Follett placed it in volume 5, published in 1926, of *The Work of Stephen Crane* (12 vols., New York: Knopf, 1925–27), and Thomas A. Gullason included it in his 1963 *Complete Short Stories and Sketches of Stephen Crane* (Garden City, N.Y.: Doubleday).

Circumstances of Composition

The time and place of the composition of this story can be identified more easily than those of many of the other tales in the Whilomville series. In a letter that the editors of Crane's correspondence date October 26, 1899, Crane's common-law wife, Cora, reminds Crane's British agent, James Pinker, of the ever-precarious state of Crane's finances and asks Pinker to send immediate payment for "The Fight," which story she says he received the day before (*Correspondence* II, 541). Since Crane evidently completed the previous Whilomville story, "The Trial, Execution, and Burial of Homer Phelps," around September 28 (*Correspondence* II, 525), he must have written this piece at Brede Place, Sussex, his last English residence, between that date and October 23 or 24, when he would have had to post it for Pinker to receive it by October 25.

Sources and Influences

Although Crane's biographers have connected a number of the Whilomville stories to specific episodes in Crane's own or Cora's childhood, no such precise identification has been made for this tale. However, as Robert W. Stallman points out, this story and its immediate sequel, "The City Urchin and the Chaste Villagers," likely stem from Crane's frequent childhood experience of being "the new boy" at school, a result of his family's numerous relocations as his minister father moved from church to church and as his mother sought a locale in which she could support her brood after his father's death (479). Such conditions would logically have made Crane more than ordinarily sensitive to the subjects he takes up in these two stories: the "tribal" rituals through which members of established groups of children determine their hierarchies and deal with newcomers, and the dynamics of the relationships between "insiders" and "outsiders" that develop as these rituals are played out.

Relationship to Other Crane Works

All the Whilomville stories are loosely connected in that all focus on Jimmie Trescott and his family and friends, but "The Fight" also contains a number of particular narrative links with others of the series. Most significantly, as in "Lynx-Hunting," "The Carriage-Lamps," and "The Trial, Execution, and Burial of Homer Phelps," the principal antagonist in this story is Jimmie's friend Willie Dalzel, who here as usual precipitates trouble by his efforts to maintain his place as "chieftain," as Crane frequently describes him, of the circle of boys to which he and Jimmie belong. In "The Fight," these efforts take the form of persecuting Johnnie Hedge, a boy whose family has recently moved to Whilomville from Jersey City. This persecution creates the strongest connection between this story and another in the series, "The City Urchin and the Chaste Villagers," for these two both focus on the struggle for dominance between Willie and Johnnie. In "The Fight," Johnnie beats up both Jimmie and Willie; in "The City Urchin," a rematch between Johnnie and Willie is broken up by Johnnie's mother, upon which the narrator concludes, "[t]he supreme power was Mrs. Hedge" (7:234).

Given this close narrative link, two critics have proposed a thematic link as well between these two stories. Chester Wolford sees them as combining to create a meditation on the violently primitive way any community responds to an outsider's upsetting of its established order, with the primitiveness emphasized in Crane's frequent use of martial and animal imagery and words such as *chieftain* and *tribe* to characterize the boys as they maneuver their way into the fights. Johnnie's presence and victory create the upset in "The Fight," and then Willie, as the community's representative, seeks to reimpose its order in "The City Urchin." Even though Mrs. Hedge, ostensibly a civilizing maternal figure, is the victor here, Wolford says, the sense of primitiveness still hangs in the air, for in her boxing of Johnnie's and Willie's ears "the notion remains that power is essentially physical, thus undermining the notion of Whilomville as a rural utopia" (59). Instead, Wolford concludes, in Whilomville "[p]ower resides with the strongest, as it does in the most primitive and savage tribes" (59).

David Halliburton takes much the same position regarding "The Fight" and "The City Urchin" and then links their meditation on community and violence with two stories outside the Whilomville series; he argues that "The Fight" and "The City Urchin" are the comic versions, because the actions are performed by children, of Crane's deadly serious presentations of the savage adult responses to an outsider who supposedly threatens the community in "The Blue Hotel" and "The Monster" (234). John C. Martin views the juvenile violence in "The Fight" in a less comic light, asserting that it links the story to a grim picture of childhood, marked by group cruelty to individual outsiders and by desperate efforts by individuals to join or stay within groups, that Crane presents in various works throughout his career, beginning with his first novel, *Maggie: A Girl of the Streets*, continuing through the middle-period pieces "The Monster" and "His New Mittens," and concluding in the Whilomville series (40).

Critical Studies

Critics have often been dismissive of the Whilomville stories. H. E. Bates says they are "as commonplace as calico" and that they could have been written by "any tenth-rate provincial reporter without the wit to determine whether what he is doing is good or bad." More than anything else, he concludes, they are an index of the diminished state of Crane's powers in the last phase of his life (148). James B. Stronks essentially agrees, rating the Whilomville pieces "thin and slight" as a result of their trafficking in mundane situations that do not evoke the "nerveless intensity" of Crane at his best, but he also asserts that they are still preferable to much of the rest of the literature about children that appeared in this era (343).

With all due respect to such opinions, a number of critics are more complimentary of the series as a whole and of several stories in particular, including "The Fight." Neville Denny says that this and the best of the other Whilomville stories effectively combine "lightness and mellow humour" with "a serious reference, an extension into 'adult' life sometimes sombre, sometimes ironic, but invariably penetrating and exact" (32). This combination is clear in "The Fight," as favorably delineated by several other writers. In terms of a mellow handling of childhood, Stallman notes that the story presents one of the primal children's conflicts, that between the insider and the outsider, and humorously dramatizes the point that one of the quickest ways for an outsider to get inside is to defeat a couple of prominent insiders in combat (281). Despite the violence inherent in this point, J. C. Levenson likewise regards the story's overall approach as mellow: given the narrator's assertion that "the long-drawn animosities of men have no place in the life of a boy," Levenson says the reader is prompted to understand that ultimately "the boy's world will work out its problems perfectly happily" (lvii).

Denny's "extension into 'adult' life" can be found in the view that, the humorous elements in the conflict between the outsider and the insiders notwithstanding, Crane intends this conflict as a serious commentary on the behavior of supposedly more mature members of the community. Eric Solomon argues that the purpose of Crane's seemingly "overblown" diction in this story, such as his characterization of various boys as "chieftains" and "sub-chieftains," is to link the children's behavior to that of the adult societies that would more usually be described in these terms, thereby making the point that, in aggrandizing themselves at the expense of others by fighting, the boys are acting out an only slightly cruder version of adult behavior (225). In line with Solomon's point, Milne Holton says that the combats in "The Fight" show "how [simultaneously] threatening and vulnerable is the outsider" and "how complex the ritual of initiation is," while Crane's metaphors emphasize both the primitive and the universal nature of these circumstances (221–22). Halliburton tacitly concurs with this assessment, given his view that all the Whilomville tales deal in a reduced way with the issue of community in crisis (201), which can be regarded as one source of the "universal truths about children, family life, and one's former home town" that Gullason says these stories present. This interpretation leads Gullason to perhaps the most positive critical assessment of the Whilomville cycle: he proposes that this thematic richness and unity renders the stories a kind of loose novel that offers "a vibrant and full world" and "demonstrates further . . . Crane's range and versatility" (483).

Like Denny, Ellen A. Brown sees Crane working with an effective combination in "The Fight," although she focuses more precisely on point of view than Denny does. She asserts that this story is a prime example of Crane's working with a dual point of view, a characteristic as well not only of the other Whilomville tales but of all of Crane's best fiction. On one hand in "The Fight," she explains, "Crane presents the dialogue and action of the children dramatically, and sometimes goes into their minds to reveal their reactions to situations"; on the other hand, he "filters [the children's] action and thought through an adult narrator." The result, Brown says, is a more complex response on the reader's part: "the reader knows how the children feel, . . . as well as what they do, and the objective adult point of view pushes the action to an ironic level, attacking the pseudo-heroics of the boys" (105).

Works Cited

Bates, H. E. "H. E. Bates on Stephen Crane." *Stephen Crane's Career: Perspectives and Evaluations*. Ed. Thomas A. Gullason. New York: New York University Press, 1972, 146–50.

Bowers, Fredson. Textual Introduction. *Tales of Whilomville*. Vol. 7 of The University of Virginia Edition of *The Works of Stephen Crane*. Ed. Fredson Bowers. Charlottesville: University Press of Virginia, 1968, 103–26.

Brown, Ellen A. "Stephen Crane's *Whilomville Stories*: A Backward Glance." *Markham Review* 3 (1972):105–09.

Denny, Neville. "Imagination and Experience in Stephen Crane." *English Studies in Africa* 9 (1966):28–42.

Gullason, Thomas A. "Stephen Crane's Short Stories: The True Road." *Stephen Crane's Career: Perspectives and Evaluations*. Ed. Thomas A. Gullason. New York: New York University Press, 1972, 470–86.

Halliburton, David. *The Color of the Sky: A Study of Stephen Crane*. Cambridge: Cambridge University Press, 1989.

Holton, Milne. *Cylinder of Vision: The Fiction and Journalistic Writings of Stephen Crane*. Baton Rouge: Louisiana State University Press, 1972.

Levenson, J. C. Introduction. *Tales of Whilomville* xi–lx.

Martin, John C. "Childhood in Crane's *Maggie*, 'The Monster,' and Whilomville Stories." *Midwestern University Quarterly* 2 (1967):40–46.

Solomon, Eric. *Stephen Crane: From Parody to Realism*. Cambridge: Harvard University Press, 1966.

Stallman, Robert W. *Stephen Crane: A Biography*. New York: George Braziller, 1968.

Stronks, James B. "Stephen Crane's English Years: The Legend Corrected." *Papers of the Bibliographical Society of America* 57 (1963):340–49.

Wertheim, Stanley, and Paul Sorrentino, eds. *The Correspondence of Stephen Crane*. Vol. 2. New York: Columbia University Press, 1988.

Wolford, Chester L. *Stephen Crane: A Study of the Short Fiction*. Boston: Twayne, 1989.

The Five White Mice

Publication History

This story was first published in an abridged version in the Sunday supplement of the *New York World* for April 10, 1898. It appeared in its complete form when it was included in the American book *"The Open Boat" and Other Tales of Adventure*, published by Doubleday & McClure in April 1898, and in the English collection *"The Open Boat" and Other Stories*, published in April 1898 by Heinemann (Bowers clix–clx). The complete form was likewise used by Wilson Follett in volume 12, published in 1927, of *The Work of Stephen Crane* (12 vols., New York: Knopf, 1925–27), and by Thomas A. Gullason in *The Complete Short Stories and Sketches of Stephen Crane* (Garden City, N.Y.: Doubleday, 1963).

Circumstances of Composition

In a letter from England dated June 1897, Crane asks his brother Edmund to search for the manuscripts of two stories, "The Five White Mice" and "The Wise Men," among the possessions Crane left at Edmund's house in the village of Hartwood, New York, and to send them to him as soon as possible, presumably so that he could prepare them for sale (*Correspondence* I, 292). On the basis of this request and several other circumstances, J. C. Levenson persuasively deduces that Crane wrote "Mice" while he was staying with Edmund and his family in Hartwood during the spring and summer of 1896. Levenson points out that Crane could not have written the story earlier than this period, because after the trip in early 1895 to the West and Mexico as a correspondent for the Bacheller syndicate that gave him the basis for it, he was occupied first with completing the novel *George's Mother* and then with writing and publishing journalistic accounts of his trip, as well as with other matters that kept him busy until his 1896 retreat from New York City to Hartwood. After his return to the city following this period of rustication, Levenson continues, Crane was equally busy, first defending himself against the harassments of the metropolitan police resulting from his allegations that the arrest of an acquaintance of his, Dora Clark, for prostitution was groundless, and then attempting to deal with the accusations of an actress and theater critic, Amy Leslie, that he had jilted and defrauded her (xli–xlii). These problems, along with other circumstances, led Crane to quit the city and state of New York permanently, aside from a few brief visits, in November of 1896. Therefore, Levenson concludes, he would have had no chance to leave manuscripts at Edmund's house after his 1896 sojourn there—a fact that, in connection with the others described above, leaves this sojourn as the only logical period in which Crane could have composed those manuscripts (xli).

Sources and Influences

For some of Crane's Western stories, such as "One Dash—Horses" and "A Man and Some Others," specific episodes in his Western tour can be identified as sources. Such is not the case, however, with "The Five White Mice." The only incident in Crane's biography that critics note as possibly relevant to this story came earlier, in the fall of 1890, during his brief tenure as a student at Lafayette College in Easton, Pennsylvania. As recounted separately by Lyndon Upson Pratt and Robert W. Stallman, Crane had pledged Delta Upsilon fraternity on September 18 and then spent two or three weeks in mortal fear of receiving a middle-of-the-night visit from upper-class brothers bent on hazing him. When such a visit did come, one of the participants later recalled,

> Steve tried to play possum by not answering a loud summons, and the usual practice followed by battering in the door. The sophomores crowded in, lighted a lamp. . . . Steve was petrified with fear and stood in a grotesque nightgown in one corner of the room with a revolver in his hand. . . . There was no time to escape what might have proved a real tragedy until Crane unexpectedly seemed to wilt limply in place, and the loaded revolver dropped harmlessly to the floor. (Qtd. in Stallman 24)

As Robert Glen Deamer points out, this episode of potential violence derailed into anticlimax as a result of a drawn revolver bears a considerable resemblance to the situation the New York Kid finds himself in at the end of "Mice," with the significant difference that the Kid does not lose his nerve as Crane himself appears to have done; instead, it is the Mexican grandee who lacks the stomach for a counter to the explicit threat of the Kid's pistol ("Stance" 138).

Discussions of literary antecedents for "Mice" are similarly few in number. Only Lars Ahnebrink has proposed one, Tolstoy's *War and Peace*, in that both works identify moments of great stress—and, indeed, life in general—as products of "a series of irrational circumstances" (359). However, whether Crane ever read this novel is by no means certain. Stallman has him putting it down unfinished, declaring that it "'goes on and on like Texas'" (179), but this critique, in its pithiness and diction sounding more like Mark Twain than Crane, may be one of the many fabrications Thomas Beer perpetrated in his pioneering biography of Crane (*Correspondence* I, 6–10). There is substantial evidence that Crane did read Tolstoy's *Sebastopol*, but such solid indications are lacking for *War and Peace*. It may well be that a vision of life as just one irrational thing after another is something Crane worked out on his own during his progress through the streets of New York City, given his presentation of an incident similar to the one recounted in "Mice" in a Bowery sketch that predates the Western trip, "The Duel That Was Not Fought," discussed below.

Relationship to Other Crane Works

This story is one of three—the others being "The Wise Men" and the "feeble, probably very late" (Berryman 301) "A Man by the Name of Mud"—that feature the adventures of the New York and San Francisco Kids, characters probably based respectively on Crane himself and Charles Gardner, a young engineer from Chicago with whom Crane traveled from San Antonio to Mexico City and who also appears as the "Chicago capitalist" in several of the newspaper sketches Crane wrote about the trip (Levenson xxxvi–xxxvii; Stallman 147; Holton 122). Stallman notes further that the unnamed bartender who appears in "Mice" is likely Freddie, the bartender who runs the foot race in "Wise Men" (147).

In terms of plot and theme, Milne Holton points out that "Mice" is related to two of Crane's early pieces of journalism. The Bowery sketch "The Duel That Was Not Fought" concerns a similar incident of potential violence that never comes to pass, although in this case the protagonists seem more fully cognizant of the nature of their situation. Here two blowhards, Patsey Tulligan and a nameless Cuban, ferociously threaten one another in a barroom but at the same time tacitly collaborate to avoid coming to blows until a policeman arrives on the scene and hustles the Cuban out, thus precluding any actual mayhem while averting a loss of honor by either party (130). The kind of lack of understanding that pervades "Mice," Holton says, is to be found in an earlier form in Crane's coverage for the August 21, 1892, *New York Tribune* of the Asbury Park, New Jersey, parade of the Junior Order of United American Mechanics. Crane depicts the Asbury Park residents as misunderstanding the Mechanics because the locals are accustomed to evaluating others solely by how much money they have to spend in the resort town, whereas the Mechanics are impoverished and unsophisticated but principled workingmen. Here, as in the encounter between The Kids and the Mexican grandees in "Mice," Holton explains, Crane focuses on a confrontation "between two uncomprehending groups of people whose failure to understand one another is the result of their social conditioning" (22).

In the view of James L. Dean, the sudden emergence of danger and the potential for death from encounters rooted in such mutual incomprehension links "Mice" to nearly all of Crane's Western fiction. Dean sees this theme as omnipresent beneath the various levels of adventure, comedy, and parody upon which these stories operate, and he ascribes this underlying darkness to Crane's recognition that his own life would be brief; here, as in his war stories, he is "examining the ways in which death might come" ("Wests" 261). Marston LaFrance identifies more specific thematic and structural links to one of the other Western tales, "One Dash—Horses." Both stories "concern merely the appearance of a moral reality, courage, a pretence which saves the protagonists from death." Also, both are "structurally broken in the middle: 'Horses' ends in an artistically inconsequential chase, and the sluggish first part of 'Mice' entails an awkward shift in tone to the tense confrontation in the second part" (180). (It should be noted, however, that many critics do not regard the tonal disjunction between the two parts of "Mice" as awkward. Drewery Wayne Gunn, for example, argues that the two parts are effectively linked in terms of plot, theme, and dramatic progression in that both present situations in which the New York Kid "is called upon to show his composure"—the dice game in the first half and the confrontation with the Mexicans in the second—with the second being logically, with regard to structure and developing intensity, more serious than the first (47).)

Levenson considers "Mice" a sort of complement to another of the Western stories, "A Man and Some Others": in "Mice" the reader gets an intimate look at a sudden encounter with death that fills the protagonist with fear and self-pity, whereas in "Man" the focus is on a "sustained encounter against fearful odds, which evokes the calm of certainty" in the protagonist, a condition that in this case gives the Easterner, unlike the New York Kid in "Mice," the chance to learn "to look steadily at what is, to see it whole" (xlviii). Levenson takes a larger thematic view as well, pointing out that "Mice" is a component in Crane's sequential development of one theme through a number of stories, not all Westerns—the threat of violence in a realm other than war. A revolver is "wildly brandished" in "The Pace of Youth," it is "seriously drawn and pointed" in "Mice" and "Horses," and at last fired in "Man" (xlix).

Several other critics also note connections between "Mice" and Crane's non-Western fiction. Levenson sees this story as an example of Crane's "great invention," first developed in *The Red Badge*, "for putting together his psychological insights with his moral concerns." The thrust of this invention in both cases is the realization that

> the will is not enough to enact the event without the intervention of chance, a term which refers equally to Crane's dynamic psychology and his empiricist sense of the nature of things. In this respect the intervention of chance is comparable to the intervention of grace in a theological view; in secular terms, it teaches the distrust of egotism. (Introduction, *Red Badge*, lxviii)

Daniel Hoffman perceives another ramification of the distrust of egotism that connects "Mice" to two other stories, "The Open Boat" and "The Price of the

Harness." Through different means—mutual suffering in "Boat," mutual courage in "Harness," and mutual fear in "Mice"—all three of these stories hold out the possibility that "at the moment when the individual is most alone with fear and insufficiency, there is still the possibility of finding the comradeship that releases man from isolation" (269). LaFrance looks all the way back to some of Crane's earliest fiction, the Sullivan County sketches, and finds in one, "The Cry of a Huckleberry Pudding," an ending quite similar to that of "Mice" (31). Here three campers are awakened in the middle of the night by bloodcurdling screams. Terrified, they gather all their nerve and set out to face the monster, only to discover that the source of their terror is the fourth member of their party, identified only as "the little man," who is suffering from stomach cramps as a result of overindulgence in huckleberry pudding. As is the case with the New York Kid at the end of "Mice," their relief that their fear has been out of proportion to the actuality of their situation quickly turns to anger. Coming upon the agony-wracked little man, the narrator says, "[t]he three men contemplating him suddenly felt themselves swell with wrath. They had been terrorized to no purpose. They had expected to be eaten. They were not. The fact maddened them" (*Tales, Sketches* 258).

Critical Studies

Several critics have found this story wanting in various respects. Like LaFrance, whose objections are noted above, Donald B. Gibson faults the first half, devoted to the gambling in the barroom, for being too long and too diffuse in its handling of detail. While Crane frequently uses the strategy of beginning with a general description and then narrowing to specific details quite effectively, Gibson says, in this story he remains too general and does not focus his descriptions to contribute to plot or theme. As an example, Gibson notes that Crane informs the reader that the four men playing seven-up by the window are a professional gambler, a millionaire, a train conductor, and an American syndicate agent, but these men and their occupations are never made relevant to the story in any way (120). Gibson also finds the second half weak, due to irresolvable problems in Crane's insights concerning the nature of chance and its role in human affairs. At the end of the story, Benson and the New York Kid agree that a fight with the Mexican grandees did not occur because the Kid had earlier lost the dice game and was therefore sober rather than drunk, like Benson and the other Kid. However, Gibson points out, had the New York Kid won at dice and gone drinking with his friends, the three of them might never have encountered the Mexicans in the first place, a possibility that is lost not only on Benson and the Kid but on Crane as well; all three assume that the only variable in the situation was the Kid's being drunk or sober, an assumption that, Gibson notes, is in fact "antithetical to the logic of chance" that Crane purports to be exploring (121).

Gibson's assessment is not wholly negative, though; he praises Crane's intensity and simultaneous compression and expansion of time in the story's second half as "an outstanding artistic achievement" (122).

Raymund Paredes, on the other hand, *does* take a wholly negative view, condemning "Mice," as well as "Man" and "Horses," for what he regards as Crane's racist attitude toward Mexicans. In all three stories, he says, Crane takes the view that "when Yankee confronted Mexican, mortal danger was the usual concomitant," and that this is the case because of the Mexican's "savage appetite . . . beyond all reason," which Crane always presents as accompanied by a large streak of cowardice, a combination that causes the Anglo to react with a mixture of fear and contempt. At the moment of confrontation, the Mexican crumbles, "totally bereft of dignity and nobility," while the Anglo responds to his own fear "with courage, reacting coolly and weighing his options, reacting quickly to stay alive." And Crane depicts the Anglo's subsequent contempt as warranted because the Mexican hides his cowardice "behind a colossal pretentiousness"; he seeks to bluff the Anglo but ultimately fails "because he has no bravery to fall back on," thus making "a mockery of an honest emotion." With these notions in view, Paredes offers perhaps the strongest denunciation to be found anywhere in the corpus of Crane criticism. In his Westerns, Crane constructs "a Darwinian world of constant and bitter struggle" in which the Mexican—sinister, treacherous, mysterious, and murderous—"is clearly the lowest form of humanity" and is thus destined to lose to the Anglo. And "the virulence of Crane's attitude toward the Mexican," Paredes concludes, "is even more meaningful and disturbing when viewed in the light of his own personal experience." In America, Crane "championed the destitute and disfranchised" and routinely "associated amicably with gamblers, dopeheads, and prostitutes." He was able to discern "virtue and dignity in some of the most unsavory characters of New York's Bowery," and yet, "with all his artistic sensibility," he failed ever to locate a single redeeming characteristic in any Mexican (31–38).

A well-reasoned response to these charges comes from Jamie Robertson. He begins by arguing that Crane arrived in the West at a date late enough to enable him to realize that the Western myth, "that individual courage gives meaning to life," which was still being fostered in Western fiction by Eastern writers for Eastern readers, was in fact defunct. (Although Deamer argues that Crane sets "Mice" and "Horses" in Mexico because he believed that one could still live by the Western "code of self-reliant courage" there, if not in the completely co-opted American West ["Myth" 118], Robertson points out that the Mexico City setting of "Mice" scarcely partakes of the Wild West; it is presented as quite cosmopolitan—perfectly capable, for instance, of attracting and sustaining a world-class circus.) Thus, Crane creates protagonists much like himself in "Mice," "Man," and "Horses": they "participate in the convention of popular Western fiction" but they take an ironic view of that convention.

Crane's goal in using this ironic stance toward the Western myth is to show that courage in confronting the unknown, which in these stories is the possibility of death in conflicts with Mexicans, does not in itself give meaning to life but rather leads to a larger insight into what for Crane is the desideratum of any person's individual development: "a humble awareness of one's own insignificance," like that which the correspondent in "The Open Boat" discovers in his contemplation of nature's indifference to his fate. And this fact absolves Crane from Paredes's charge of racism, Robertson concludes, because in all three of the stories in question, Anglos and Mexicans are not placed in hierarchy but rather united in their mutual recognition of their individual insignificance. Specifically in "Mice," Robertson says, the Kid at first sees his encounter with the Mexicans as romantic and then as imagistic, but it quickly escalates "beyond such rather foolish literary conventions to become a serious confrontation with death, an experience that makes him aware of his own insignificance" and also of the Mexican grandees' similar feelings, so that his new perception "affirms the humanity of New Yorker and Mexican" alike (244–49).

A number of equally divergent interpretations can be found in the work of critics who take a wholly favorable view of "Mice." One locus of disagreement is whether Crane intends the story to be read as an ironic/absurdist commentary on the Western myth and human life in general or as a straightforward assertion that significance of some sort inheres in the exertion of courage. The earliest absurdist reading comes from Beer, who asserts that what the New York Kid realizes at the end of the story, when, as the narrator says, "Nothing had happened" (*Tales of Adventure* 52), is that his "emotion [of fear and courage] has projected its intensity against nonsense, against a posture of some loungers. It is the last point in futility, the hurtle of mighty chords on an unhearing ear" (118). While not taking quite so extreme a point of view, Edwin Cady and Michael J. Collins both regard the story as ironic in intent. Cady says that "Mice" is one of three Westerns, along with "Horses" and "The Bride Comes to Yellow Sky," which Crane concludes with the sudden deflation of what seems to be an inevitable outburst of mayhem, and in so doing he ironically undercuts the Western code of violence, since it is only from the perspective of one who regards violence as the sole viable resolution that it can be said of these endings that "Nothing had happened" (175).

Collins offers a view similar to Robertson's idea, outlined above, that Crane is purposefully taking an ironic approach to the Western myth of self-reliant bravery. Specifically, Collins links Crane's work in "Mice," as well as in "Bride" and "The Blue Hotel," to the genre that Northrop Frye in *Anatomy of Criticism* calls "ironic myth." In Frye's formulation, this genre is "a parody of romance: the application of romantic mythical forms to a more realistic content which fits them in unexpected ways" (qtd. in Collins 141). Crane uses this mode, "uses the familiar elements of the Western romance in a realistic setting," Collins explains, to create "an ironic world that seems a recognizable representation of the one in which we live," his goal being to reveal the disjunction between the world of romance and that of reality. In "Mice," Crane sets up one of the key elements of Western romance, the showdown, when the two Kids and Benson jostle the three Mexicans; but then, with the Mexicans' more perverse than heroic sensitivity regarding their own honor, Benson's and the San Francisco Kid's ineffectuality due to their drunkenness, and the New York Kid's nearly paralyzing fear, "almost at once we are taken out of the Western and back to the real world and to what is actually only an ugly street fight." And, most crucially, we are forced out of romance and into the real world because the focus of the narrative at this point "is not on the external drama of the confrontation," as it would be in a straightforward Western myth, but rather on "the complex, internal experience of the New York Kid, who seems, as a result, to lack the style, the requisite restraint and control of the Western hero." Therefore, in saving himself and his friends by the seemingly Western mythical gesture of drawing his revolver, the Kid actually behaves "like an Easterner (afraid he will fail, unsure of the effect), and thus in what seems a recognizably human way"; Crane emphasizes thereby that this story "is set not in a simple world of romance, but in a complex, ironic world that seems close to the world in which we live" (141–42).

John Berryman provides the first refutation of this ironic/absurdist approach. In direct response to Beer, he argues that at the end of the story the Kid does not discover his own futility but rather that he is not alone in feeling fear and that, concomitantly, "his fear need not prevent his controlling his own fate," a realization that Berryman applies to Crane himself as well. The implicit point of the story, he asserts, "is that the five mice are blind, that is to say indifferent." As such, they supply the elements of the individual's fate, but "they interfere no further; what happens to him is up to himself." Thus, what the Kid ultimately discovers is that courage is a source of personal autonomy; his "faith, in substance—Crane's new faith—is in circumstances as *not* making impossible the individual's determination of his destiny" (109–10).

Eric Solomon likewise sees "Mice" as depicting the Kid's discovery of self-reliance, although he stops short of Berryman's assertion that it charts a concomitant new realization on Crane's own part. At the beginning of the story, Solomon says, the Kid believes that "the five white mice are as good as anything else to believe in." At the end, having discovered his antagonist's fear and his own capacity for action despite such fear, he has learned that "some gambles are worthwhile because all men are not as strong as they appear"— he has learned, in essence, "to believe in himself" (250–51).

Deamer explicitly agrees with Berryman's view that "Mice" marks the development of a new faith in its author as well as its protagonist. Crane began, he says, with a deeply skeptical attitude toward individual bravery, as evinced in his ironic handling of this subject in *The Red Badge of Courage*. When he made his Western trip, however, he encountered the genuine article, as in the undaunted demeanor of the Nebraska farmers whose battles with the elements he described in several newspaper pieces. As a result, he shifted to the "sympathetic, nonskeptical, essentially nonironic" conception of courage that Deamer sees exemplified in "Mice," which he reads as straightforwardly encouraging the reader to "identify with the Kid and participate in his change in consciousness" as he discovers and adopts the "code of self-reliant courage" ("Myth" 118–19).

In a similar vein, Frank Bergon argues that the valediction "Nothing had happened" is not meant to resonate with irony regarding the Kid's action but rather is designed as a provocatively false summary of the situation, one "intended to begin disintegrating as soon as [its] immediate formal purpose is achieved" (*Artistry* 97). In other words, in the Kid's reaction to the moment of showdown and its anticlimactic aftermath Crane's primary goal is not an ironic commentary upon the myth of the fearless Western hero but rather an exploration of the psychology of a man under the stress of a life-or-death moment (*Artistry* 114). Thus, Bergon argues, "Mice," like "The Wise Men" and "A Man and Some Others," is more a story of comprehension than of action: the Kid's initiation is largely into a new way of seeing, accomplished when his preconception of Mexicans as fearless villains dissolves and he and his primary antagonist "merge in their mutual fear and vulnerability" (Introduction 15–16). And in this moment of merging the psychology of comprehension is further anatomized, for the Kid and the reader both realize that "[w]hile many preconceived moments may not be supreme, the opposite may occur; a trivial or unheroic moment may blaze with sublimity, as the Kid . . . discovers when, faced with death, he experiences the 'unreal real'" (*Artistry* 43). Thus, Bergon concludes, to read this story—and indeed much of Crane's other work—as simply an undercutting of illusions is too limited; for Crane, "truth was pluralistic, and he depended upon multiple points of view and paradoxical configurations to present its complexity" (*Artistry* 43).

Crane as pluralist is likewise the burden of Levenson's reading of "Mice." Levenson is in accord with Bergon that "Nothing had happened" is neither irony or understatement; instead, he regards it as "a comment on the equivocal way in which the incident may be regarded." What he means by this assertion is that it is possible to see nothing having happened here not merely on the level of action but, depending on a particular reader's orientation, on the levels of ontology, epistemology, and morality. "Has anything happened," Levenson asks, "if the witnesses are unaware? Is there value to the moral effort which prevents violence rather than performing it?" And, equally crucial, what is the most powerful determining factor in the outcome of the story—chance, in that the Kid happens to be sober and thus able to conceive of the stratagem of drawing his revolver; will, in that once he has conceived this stratagem he is able to execute it successfully; or some larger general law regarding the psychology of men involved in moments of life-or-death confrontation? With such questions left unresolved at the story's end, Levenson says, Crane can be seen as moving toward a vision that is more complex than that of his previous fiction, a movement accomplished by a new approach to "the concentration of the short-story form," in which, "[i]nstead of elaborating plot or character in the traditional sense, the tale exposes more facets of the single intensely rendered episode" (xliii–xliv).

With these various facets in view, Levenson argues, in a vein similar to that of Robertson's discussion of the individual's discovery of his own insignificance, that, although Crane makes "no overt metaphysical statement" to this effect, the point of the story is that the Kid attains "grace under pressure" and in doing so recognizes that his own will was only partially responsible for his success, that the fear his antagonists felt, and several other factors as well, played equal roles. He now realizes, therefore, that he himself "does not make the circumstances in which action is possible, and he does not even understand how he happens to generate the will to act." As a result, a key element of his attaining the state of grace under pressure is that "he learns so much about the pressures on the mind," and about the external forces that interact with those pressures, that "he is truly humble about making any claim to grace." And applied to Crane himself and his artistic/philosophical vision, Levenson concludes, this point indicates that the increasing complexity of his outlook was tending in a specific, recognizable philosophical direction: "the world of his fiction was becoming a pluralistic universe in which chance, will, and general laws all had room to exist" (xliv–xlv).

A number of other critics as well either implicitly or explicitly interpret "Mice" as evidence of Crane's intellectual evolution toward pluralism. Holton says that the story "reflects Crane's growing awareness of the randomness of events and his interest in patterns of causation and the lack of them." He asserts that two separate sets of causes produce and resolve the confrontation, and that while the first of these—the Kid's losing dice throw—is essentially random, the second—"the capacity for clear apprehension" of the circumstances of the confrontation itself that the Kid ultimately demonstrates—is susceptible of human control. At the moment of greatest tension, it is largely the Kid's ability to size up "the raw facts of his situation" and to face "one more gratuitous fact," that he either will or will not be able to draw his revolver without a hitch, that saves him and his friends. Thus, Holton concludes, Crane here creates a universe in which randomness is a major force but the individual's capacity for comprehending his circumstances and acting on that comprehension can also play a role in determining his fate (129–31).

David Halliburton sees Crane examining two other sets of interrelated forces and ultimately expressing frustration at the tacit pluralism of their interactions. Rather than randomness and apprehension, the first pair of discrete but related forces Crane focuses on here, Halliburton says, are randomness and fortune. He differentiates between these two by identifying the former as *chance*, "all that is random and beyond control," and the latter as *luck*, "a mysterious attraction [or lack thereof] between an individual and a sudden outcome in a game" (255). Although the Kid's decision to draw his revolver does have an effect, Halliburton says, his succeeding in doing so is more due to luck than to apprehension. This view clearly reduces the role that Holton's principle of comprehension and will plays, and that role is further diminished by Halliburton's second pair of forces, concreteness and abstraction, the presence of which he deduces from Crane's use of the word *equality* (*Tales of Adventure* 50) to characterize the fear that both the Kid and his principal Mexican antagonist experience. Like Robertson, Halliburton interprets the Kid's sudden understanding of this mutuality of emotion as a "recognition of common humanity" (267), but in his view it makes the Kid not humble but furious, not connected with others but still fiercely alone, because for him such commonality is an abstract principle but "down there on the [concrete] level of particularity and practice is the reality of discrete entities [such as himself and the Mexican], rattling against each other like shaken dice, each wanting to go its own way but balked by the presence of the others." Given this set of circumstances, what "Mice" ultimately reveals, Halliburton argues, is

> a split between the abstract and the concrete that is itself the reflection of an individualist orientation . . . that can never seize upon the possibility of solidarity simply because the latter never looks real enough to make the effort seem worthwhile. A world unto himself, the solitary person possesses a reality that is never quite that of anyone else—that certainly never matches perfectly the reality of that realm of otherness called the "world"—and that therefore makes the very idea of reality contingent and problematic, even at times unreal. (267)

Charles W. Mayer's reading is equally elaborate but more conventionally and expressly pluralistic. He points to "Mice" as a refutation of critical efforts to classify Crane as a naturalist or determinist, for in his view, as in Levenson's and Holton's, this story presents human life as "a mixture of necessity, freewill, and chance" and therefore unmistakably pluralistic. Chance operates in the Kid's loss of the dice game, which causes him to be sober and therefore possessed of the capacity for effective action, and free will enters in when he overcomes his fear and actually takes effective action. However, Mayer says, Crane's point is that this taking of action does not result from egotism regarding the power of free will on the Kid's part, but rather from his understanding of the relationship between that will and chance. The Kid's invocation to the "five white mice of chance" (*Tales of Adventure* 50) in the instant before he attempts his draw, Mayer argues, is "an admission of uncertainty in a universe whose laws are incomprehensible, unpredictable, and subject to incalculable operations of chance." The Kid's attitude here, Mayer continues, "amounts to a kind of self-reliance in reverse: instead of power being gained from confidence in oneself, it is gained from awareness that confidence is probably not justified." More specifically, the "mice take the Kid out of his sickly state of subjectivity and allow him to act" because his surrender to them constitutes an acceptance of the fact that "the outcome of any course of action or inaction is uncertain in the face of haphazard circumstances." With these ideas in view, Mayer concludes that the Kid's trust in the mice "suggests a correct interpretation, from Crane's point of view, of a world in which the vaunted power of the individual counts for little." And Crane's implied larger principle here is that those individuals who follow the Kid's example in recognizing the sharp limits of their own power are "more likely to master their passions and escape the prison of their egos, more likely to calculate their chances and make meaningful choices in the uncertain game of life" (52–55).

In addition to evoking these pluralistic readings, "Mice" has also impelled two critics to characterize Crane as a proto-existentialist. William Bysshe Stein reads nearly all of Crane's fiction as tending in the direction of existentialism, but he considers this story a particularly clear instance of that tendency because of the especially sharp anticlimax with which Crane "deliberately and treacherously" concludes. This ending, Stein argues, "may excite immediate laughter" at the Kid's discomfiture, but, given its expression of Crane's belief in "the unpredictability of fate," the reader should turn that laughter upon him- or herself, because at a deeper level its anticlimactic character "challenges the pompous self-importance of the ego, simply designating a mode of ludicrous self-deception"—that is, the belief that one can control one's own fate. Viewing the entire story in the light of this conclusion, Stein says that "with all the conscious purpose of a doctrinaire existentialist, [Crane] traces the cause of this consternating incident to a hidden law of chaos, 'the five white mice,' a gambling term for incalculable chance" (186–87). Michael D. Warner sees the story as dramatizing a central existentialist dilemma: on the one hand, an awareness that moral judgments are pointless due to a disjunction between individuals and their actions, and on the other hand an equal awareness that humans find living without such judgments nearly impossible. The Kid's confrontation with the Mexican grandee "foregrounds the category of valor by drawing on the narrative conventions of agonistic conflict, as well as by suggesting that valor is all that protects the social from the valueless condition of the outlaw," but balanced against such foregrounding is the narrator's final report that nothing has happened, which Warner asserts is "representative of the Cranian uncanny, the 'mystery of heroism,' the condition in which human action bears no relation to the absolute values without which it remains unthinkable" (91).

Daniel Weiss reads the story through the lens of psychology rather than philosophy. For him, its crucial event is the Kid's thinking of his father at the moment of confrontation with the Mexican; Weiss argues that this conjunction indicates that the Kid associates the two figures and thereby evinces that, from a psychoanalytical point of view, the more important confrontation takes place on the Freudian level of "the relationship between fraternal competition and paternal omnipotence." Weiss says that the Kid's impulse to draw his gun and thus vanquish the Mexican—"a flight to activity . . . out of character with the gambling man Crane has described"—is initially "inhibited by his recognizing in 'the Spanish grandee' the authoritarian figure of his 'unyielding and millioned' father." When the Kid does will himself to draw despite the taint of parricide in that action, he releases this inhibition, realizing that, instead of his seemingly omnipotent father, "he has only to deal with a vulnerable sibling like himself" (146–47).

In addition to such discussions of themes and insights, a number of critics offer analyses of Crane's style in "Mice" and its implications for the story's significance. The earliest such comments come from Ford Madox Ford, who uses "Mice" as an example of what he means by the term *impressionism*. To be an impressionist, he admonishes his reader, "[y]ou must render: never report." To illustrate this concept, he says that

> You must never write: "He saw a man aim a gat at him"; you must put it: "He saw a steel ring directed at him." Later, you must get in that, in his subconsciousness, he recognized that the steel ring was the polished muzzle of a revolver. So Crane rendered it in *The Three White Mice*. (25)

Fortunately, Ford's own impression of Crane's technique is clearer than his memory of Crane's title.

Focusing on Crane's interest in a slightly different property of human consciousness, Bergon argues that "the seeming incoherence of the images" that run through the Kid's mind in the instant before he draws—his visions of his father's response to his death, his recollection of the scene carved on the handle of his revolver, and so on—is not technical maladroitness. Instead, this incoherence is Crane's effort to depict the workings of the mind, particularly the mind under stress, its capacity to move simultaneously at a number of different levels (*Artistry* 15). In a similar vein, Levenson asserts that this use of rapidly shifting images to convey the Kid's state of mind under stress constitutes a significant technical innovation on Crane's part. Through this "rendering [of] the psychological narrative with sharp intensity," Levenson says, Crane "broke through the melodramatic convention of the Wild West plot and made the usual gun-drawing scene into a horrifying absurdity." And this creation of absurdity makes this approach not merely a matter of practical craftsmanship but a method of effectively marrying form and meaning. The "imaged style" of this story, Levenson says, "was more than a rhetorical technique; it was Crane's medium for expressing his grasp of the inner life" (xlvii).

James Nagel places this imaged style in a historical/philosophical context, noting that the swift succession of images in which the Kid envisions the aftermath of his own death, being "presumably an instantaneous flash of scene" in the Kid's mind, is a prime example of Crane's efforts to depict the kind of "mental flow" that William James called "the stream of consciousness" in his 1890 treatise *The Principles of Psychology* (79). Halliburton concerns himself with "Mice" as a locus of confluence between philosophical and literary contexts. He regards the story's two sections as presenting "two durations, each with its own pace," pace being for Crane a measure of competitive status. In the first section the Kid wins this competition by slowing down his roll of the dice in order to master the frenetic pace of the betting on that roll. In the second section, the physical pace of the confrontation is likewise frenetic, but this is counterweighted by the slower pace of the Kid's consciousness, which is that of "one who sees himself somehow apart from the situation even as he is caught in it." This second pace, with its expansion of physical time within the individual consciousness, Halliburton asserts, constitutes what Crane terms "the unreal real," which Halliburton, drawing on Heidegger's concept of "contemporaneity," defines as a simultaneous awareness of the past, present, and future—the Kid's memories of his family, his immediate condition, and his projection of his family's reaction to his death—overladen with what Halliburton calls the "transcendental vision" of new-mown hay that obtrudes itself into the Kid's mind at this instant as well. Crane's multilayered dramatization of such a multilayered moment in the Kid's consciousness, Halliburton concludes, "amounts to a modern topos": the desire "to render the wonder of things as they are both in their familiarity and in the strangeness with which that familiarity is interpenetrated" (257–64).

Works Cited

Ahnebrink, Lars. *The Beginnings of Naturalism in American Fiction*. Cambridge: Harvard University Press, 1950.

Beer, Thomas. *Stephen Crane: A Study in American Letters*. New York: Knopf, 1923.

Bergon, Frank. Introduction. *The Western Writings of Stephen Crane*. New American Library, 1979, 1–27.

———. *Stephen Crane's Artistry*. New York: Columbia University Press, 1975.

Berryman, John. *Stephen Crane*. New York: Sloane, 1950.

Bowers, Fredson. Textual Introduction. *Tales of Adventure*. Vol. 5 of The University of Virginia Edition of *The Works of Stephen Crane*. Ed. Fredson Bowers. Charlottesville: University Press of Virginia, 1970, cxxxiii–cxcv.

Cady, Edwin H. *The Light of Common Day: Realism in American Fiction*. Bloomington: Indiana University Press, 1971.

Collins, Michael J. "Realism and Romance in the Western Stories of Stephen Crane." *Under the Sun: Myth and Realism in Western American Literature*. Ed. Barbara Howard Meldrum. Troy, N.Y.: Whitston, 1985, 139–48.

Crane, Stephen. "The Cry of a Huckleberry Pudding." *Tales, Sketches, and Reports.* Vol. 8 of The University of Virginia Edition of *The Works of Stephen Crane.* Ed. Fredson Bowers. Charlottesville: University Press of Virginia, 1973, 254–59.

———. "The Five White Mice." *Tales of Adventure* 39–52.

Deamer, Robert Glen. "Remarks on the Western Stance of Stephen Crane." *Western American Literature* 15 (Summer 1980):122–41.

———. "Stephen Crane and the Western Myth." *Western American Literature* 7 (Summer 1972):111–23.

Dean, James L. "The Wests of Howells and Crane." *American Literary Realism* 10 (1977):254–66.

Ford, Ford Madox. "Techniques." *Southern Review* 1 (1935):20–35.

Gibson, Donald B. *The Fiction of Stephen Crane*. Carbondale: Southern Illinois University Press, 1968.

Gunn, Drewery Wayne. *American and British Writers in the West and Mexico, 1556–1973.* Austin: University of Texas Press, 1979.

Halliburton, David. *The Color of the Sky: A Study of Stephen Crane*. Cambridge: Cambridge University Press, 1989.

Hoffman, Daniel G. *The Poetry of Stephen Crane*. New York: Columbia University Press, 1957.

Holton, Milne. *Cylinder of Vision: The Fiction and Journalistic Writings of Stephen Crane*. Baton Rouge: Louisiana State University Press, 1972.

LaFrance, Marston. *A Reading of Stephen Crane*. Oxford: Clarendon, 1971.

Levenson, J. C. Introduction. *The Red Badge of Courage*. Vol. 2 of The University of Virginia Edition of *The Works of Stephen Crane.* Ed. Fredson Bowers. Charlottesville: University Press of Virginia, 1975, xiii–xcii.

———. Introduction. *Tales of Adventure* xv–cxxxii.

Mayer, Charles W. "Two Kids in the House of Chance: Crane's 'The Five White Mice.'" *Research Studies* 44 (1976):52–57.

Nagel, James. *Stephen Crane and Literary Impressionism*. University Park: Pennsylvania State University Press, 1980.

Paredes, Raymund A. "Stephen Crane and the Mexican." *Western American Literature* 6 (Spring 1971):31–38.

Pratt, Lyndon Upson. "The Formal Education of Stephen Crane." American Literature 10 (1939):460–71.

Robertson, Jamie. "Stephen Crane, Eastern Outsider in the West and Mexico." *Western American Literature* 13 (Nov. 1978):243–57.

Solomon, Eric. *Stephen Crane: From Parody to Realism*. Cambridge: Harvard University Press, 1966.

Stallman, R. W. *Stephen Crane: A Biography*. New York: George Braziller, 1968.

Stein, William B. "Stephen Crane's *Homo Absurdus*." *Bucknell Review* 8 (1959): 168–88.

Warner, Michael D. "Value, Agency, and Stephen Crane's 'The Monster.'" *Nineteenth-Century Literature* 40 (1985):76–93.

Weiss, Daniel. "*The Red Badge of Courage*." *Psychoanalytic Review* 52 (Summer 1965):32–52; (Fall 1965):130–54.

Wertheim, Stanley, and Paul Sorrentino, eds. *The Correspondence of Stephen Crane*. Vol. 1. New York: Columbia University Press, 1988.

Flanagan and His Short Filibustering Adventure

Publication History

This story made its first appearance in England in the August 28, 1897, number of the *Illustrated London News* (111:279–82); in America it ran in the October 1897 issue of *McClure's Magazine* (9:1045–52). It was then collected in the American volume *"The Open Boat" and Other Tales of Adventure*, published in April 1898 by Doubleday & McClure, and in the English book *"The Open Boat" and Other Stories*, also published in April 1898 by Heinemann (Bowers clxvii–viii). Pioneering Crane editor Wilson Follett placed it in volume 12, published in 1927, of *The Work of Stephen Crane* (12 vols., New York: Knopf, 1925–27), and in 1963 Thomas A. Gullason included it in his *Complete Short Stories and Sketches of Stephen Crane* (Garden City, N.Y.: Doubleday, 1963).

Circumstances of Composition

John Berryman quotes Crane telling H. G. Wells that "The Open Boat" and "Flanagan and His Short Filibustering Adventure" were "all I got out of Cuba"

(166). On the basis of this remark, Berryman asserts that Crane must have begun this story sometime in February 1897, just after completing "The Open Boat," while he was still in Florida after the ordeal of the January sinking of the *Commodore*, a small ship Crane had boarded in Jacksonville in an effort to get to Cuba to cover the revolution there for the Bacheller newspaper syndicate. He was at this time either still in Jacksonville, where he had returned after coming ashore in the *Commodore*'s dinghy, or in the swamp country around the Indian River, where he went, according to a letter of March 11, 1897 to his brother William, in a second, fruitless attempt to get to Cuba (*Correspondence* I, 281). James B. Colvert agrees with Berryman's hypothesis, noting that Crane likely wished to get an immediate second story out of his shipwreck experience, following "The Open Boat," because he was short of money; during the *Commodore* disaster he had lost seven hundred dollars in gold that Bacheller had advanced him, and once ashore he had had to borrow from the McClure syndicate to cover his immediate expenses. "Flanagan" would have constituted a quick way of beginning to repay this loan (108).

Regardless of exactly when Crane began this story, he was evidently hard at work on it by mid-March 1897, for in a letter from New York City dated the sixteenth of that month Crane tells William that he will be able to visit the latter at his home in Port Jervis, New York, for only "about two hours," because he is embarking for France in a few days and is "in the middle of a story which I am bound to finish before I leave" (*Correspondence* I, 281), a story that the editors of Crane's letters identify as "Flanagan" (282). At the cost of not going to Port Jervis at all, Crane evidently succeeded in meeting this deadline—although, as J. C. Levenson notes, this urgency probably stemmed from the McClure syndicate's desire to have a piece that they had in effect already paid for in hand as soon as possible rather than from an immediate need for material *per se*, since the syndicate did not run the story until eight months later (lxx–lxxi).

Sources and Influences

As Robert W. Stallman has noted, "Flanagan and His Short Filibustering Adventure" is a companion-piece to "The Open Boat" (598): in "The Open Boat" Crane draws on his own experience of being adrift in a ten-foot dinghy for thirty hours after the *Commodore* sank, while in "Flanagan" he draws on what befell him on this ship prior to and during its foundering, focusing in this case, however, not on himself in the role of correspondent but on the captain of the ill-fated vessel. This character, Flanagan, is based on the *Commodore*'s actual captain, Edward Murphy; he apparently served as Crane's technical advisor on "Boat," assuring Crane that his rendition of the actual events was accurate (Stallman 257), but he seems not to have been consulted for "Flanagan" despite his role as prototype, for in this case Crane deviates in several important respects from the facts of the *Commodore* disaster, as a comparison of the story with Crane's nonfiction account of the sinking, "Stephen Crane's Own Story," reveals.

Crane is true to the facts as recorded in "Story" in making faulty engines the reason for the ship's sinking in "Flanagan," in having nearly all of the Cuban insurgents on board suffer spectacularly from seasickness, in mentioning fears and mishaps that many crewmen regarded as evil omens concerning the voyage, and in making Flanagan himself a calm and capable handler of his ship. However, he fleshes out this character considerably compared to his treatment of Captain Murphy, making him a newcomer to filibustering who has volunteered for it not out of a desire for pay or glory but rather simply because he is a ship's captain by trade and by nature and evidently can find no other command (94–95). The story thus becomes to an extent an account of Flanagan's initiation into the life of a filibuster, as is evident in his refrain-like repetition of statements such as "'By the piper, . . . this filibustering is no trick with cards'" (97) in the moments of stress that close the first and second of the story's four sections.

With this theme of initiation in view, Crane fleshes out not only the captain but also the events as compared to his presentation of them in "Story." First, he offers some background in a section on the efforts of Pinkerton detectives to thwart expeditions such as Flanagan's, which may derive from a similar discussion in another piece of Florida reportage, "The Filibustering Industry" (94–99). Second, whereas the *Commodore* steamed out of Jacksonville already loaded with its cargo of contraband munitions and never reached Cuba to unload them, Crane in "Flanagan" gives a fuller picture of the process of filibustering by having the *Foundling* rendezvous with the arms suppliers in the middle of the night on a deserted stretch of Florida coast and by providing a parallel scene of midnight unloading off the Cuban coast while a Spanish gunboat looms on the horizon. Third, Crane has Flanagan pass his initiation by meeting the threat of this gunboat with an attempt to ram it with his own ship, which sends the Spaniard steaming off as Flanagan, at the end of the third section, says triumphantly to himself, "'There, by God. . . . There, now!'" (104). And finally, Crane has Flanagan get all of his crewmen off the foundering ship, which Murphy was unable to do; give way to his emotions and sob and swear as the *Foundling* goes down (107), in contrast to Murphy's stoicism; and ultimately drown, evidently satisfied with the performance of his duty, judging by the calm expression on his face when his body is washed ashore under the indifferent eyes of a group of hotel guests who, unlike the actively solicitous figures who actually met the castaways according to "Story," have come down to the water solely to be entertained by the spectacle of the lifeboats landing (108).

Joseph T. Skerrett proposes another source for "Flanagan," one less immediately apparent than Crane's voyage on the *Commodore* and his acquaintance with Edward Murphy: Crane's childhood. In his lack of experience with filibustering Flanagan resembles Crane himself more closely than he does Murphy, Skerrett points out, asserting that this identification makes the story a tonal counterpoint to "Open Boat." Whereas the Crane character in "Open Boat," the correspondent, survives and learns about the value of human brotherhood from his experience, Skerrett says, Crane has himself as Flanagan drown with no such insight attained; thus, the two stories "respectively include and exclude, affirm and negate Crane's heroism, self-control, and acceptance at the time of the disaster" (25). In Skerrett's view, Crane returned to that disaster to send up the "second, weaker, and above all contradictory signal" (25) that is "Flanagan" because, owing to his childhood experiences of his father's and best-loved sister's deaths, his mother's neglect, and his isolation from his much older surviving siblings, the feelings of "doubt, mistrust, inadequacy, and imminent failure" that he expresses in this story were the ones that predominated in his nature. The hopefulness regarding human community that pervades "Open Boat," Skerrett concludes, was for Crane "an insubstantial reality which faded away in time" as the experience receded in his memory; "Flanagan" marks his return to his normal mode of despair (27).

Relationship to Other Crane Works

As much of the foregoing discussion makes obvious, the Crane work to which "Flanagan" is most closely linked is "Open Boat"; Stallman goes so far as to call the two companion-pieces, as noted above. However, there is general critical agreement that these two are comparable only in subject matter, not in level of achievement: Stallman's complete view is that "Flanagan" is an *inferior* companion piece to "Open Boat," and no one has offered reasons to dispute this judgment. Levenson is persuasively specific about the causes of this disparity, explaining that whereas Crane allowed himself a good deal of time to work through "Open Boat," "Flanagan" demonstrates "what could happen when he worked hurriedly under pressure" (lxxi). The result of these conditions is that "Flanagan" is simply a tale of adventure, not the fusion of adventure with interpretation by a thoughtful consciousness that Crane accomplished in "The Open Boat." "Flanagan," Levenson concludes, effectively presents "acid ironies" in the fate of the sailors juxtaposed to the attitude of the hotel guests, who in their safe position refuse to consider that men may drown, and it is marked by "the colorful Crane style," but it ultimately lacks the symbolic resonance that produces the depth and universality of "The Open Boat"; instead, its events "define a world no bigger than the scene in which they take place" (lxxi–lxxii).

In terms of connections of technique, only Milne Holton says anything regarding "Flanagan." While not denying that it is one of Crane's weaker stories, he sees it as one of a generally distinguished group, including "The Five White Mice," "An Episode of War," and "War Memories," which deploy ironic endings that "deny the very [stories] they conclude" (83–84). In this case, Flanagan's initiation into filibustering, his discovery that he can be a man in the realm of this activity, is ultimately denied, rendered meaningless by his drowning, since neither he nor any of the hotel guests who watch his body wash up onto the beach gain any insight from this experience; unlike the ending of "Open Boat" here no one feels that this death has enabled him or her to become an interpreter (84). Holton's final judgment of this story is that it is of light weight compared to "The Open Boat," but he also points out that, given Crane's ironic temperament, after the "qualified and tragic affirmation" of "The Open Boat," such a "darkly comic negation," a "death-wish fantasy . . . [that] recounts imaginatively the darker side of Crane's experience" with the *Commodore*, was perhaps inevitable (158–59).

Critical Studies

John Berryman compares "Flanagan" favorably to "Stephen Crane's Own Story," noting in particular that the description of the engine-room in "Flanagan" is much more artistically effective than the version in "Story" (157). However, as noted in the "Relationship to Other Crane Works" section, most critics consider "Flanagan" alongside "The Open Boat" and find the former distinctly inferior. Eric Solomon takes this position, rating the story "not one of Crane's finest" due to its lack of depth, particularly considered alongside "Open Boat" (153). However, he does find it interesting as a broader version of Crane's *Commodore* experience, as his rendition of "the eternal triangle made up of a man, his ship, and the sea—three parts of an impossible affair," impossible because of the indifference of the third-named participant (154). Flanagan loves his ship, Solomon explains, and thus possesses the will and the skill to bring her safely through the man-made obstacles of Spanish gunboats and shore batteries despite the incompetence of his crew, but he cannot defeat or even survive the natural forces of the sea. However, Solomon does not share Skerrett's and Holton's belief that Flanagan's fate renders his experience meaningless; he argues that in emphasizing in the story's final section the "vapid stupidity of those on the shore, those untempered by a sea journey," Crane throws Flanagan's experience, failure notwithstanding, into favorable relief (157).

Rodney O. Rogers is the only one who takes a wholly positive view of this story, praising it as a significant example of Crane's espousal of the Impressionist epistemology of relativity of perception. When at the end of the story the narrative focus shifts from the shipwrecked sailors to the dancers at the hotel, Crane, in Rogers's view, is emphasizing "irony growing out of . . .

disparate impressions of the same moment." Crane's skill at pointing out these disparate impressions is most clearly discernible in his diction, as when he uses the word *floated* to describe first the wafting of a woman's perfume through the air and then the motion through the surf of the body that washes up on the beach. Through such sharply pointed juxtapositions, Rogers says, Crane powerfully reminds his reader that "man's experience of the world is multifaceted," is inevitably dependent on his position within that world (296).

Works Cited

Berryman, John. *Stephen Crane*. New York: Sloane, 1950.

Bowers, Fredson. Textual Introduction. *Tales of Adventure*. Vol. 5 of The University of Virginia Edition of *The Works of Stephen Crane*. Ed. Fredson Bowers. Charlottesville: University Press of Virginia, 1970, cxxxiii–cxcv.

Colvert, James B. *Stephen Crane*. New York: Harcourt Brace Jovanovich, 1984.

Crane, Stephen. "Flanagan and His Short Filibustering Adventure." *Tales of Adventure* 93–108.

———. "The Filibustering Industry." *Reports of War*. Vol. 9 of The University of Virginia Edition of *The Works of Stephen Crane*. Ed. Fredson Bowers. Charlottesville: University Press of Virginia, 1971, 94–99.

———. "Stephen Crane's Own Story." *Reports of War* 85–94.

Holton, Milne. *Cylinder of Vision: The Fiction and Journalistic Writings of Stephen Crane*. Baton Rouge: Louisiana State University Press, 1972.

Levenson, J. C. Introduction. *Tales of Adventure*. Vol. 5 of The University of Virginia Edition of *The Works of Stephen Crane*. Ed. Fredson Bowers. Charlottesville: University Press of Virginia, 1970, xv–cxxxii.

Rogers, Rodney O. "Stephen Crane and Impressionism." *Nineteenth-Century Fiction* 24 (1969):292–304.

Skerrett, Joseph T., Jr. "Changing Seats in the Open Boat: Alternative Attitudes in Two Stories by Stephen Crane." *Studies in the Humanities* 4 (1982):22–27.

Solomon, Eric. *Stephen Crane: From Parody to Realism*. Cambridge: Harvard University Press, 1966.

Stallman, R. W. *Stephen Crane: A Biography*. New York: George Braziller, 1968.

Wertheim, Stanley, and Paul Sorrentino, eds. *The Correspondence of Stephen Crane*. Vol. 1. New York: Columbia University Press, 1988.

"God Rest Ye, Merry Gentlemen"

Publication History

This story was first published in America in the May 6, 1899, issue of the *Saturday Evening Post* (171:705–07); its initial English publication came in the May 1899 number of *Cornhill Magazine* (n. s. 6:577–92). It then appeared in book form in *Wounds in the Rain*, published in America by Frederick A. Stokes and in England by Methuen in September 1899 (Bowers cxxvi–xxvii). Wilson Follett, editor of *The Work of Stephen Crane* (12 vols., New York: Knopf, 1925–27), placed it in volume 9, published in 1926; and in 1963 Thomas A. Gullason included it in his *Complete Short Stories and Sketches of Stephen Crane* (Garden City, N.Y.: Doubleday).

Circumstances of Composition

The time and place of composition of "'God Rest Ye, Merry Gentlemen'" are easy to pinpoint thanks to three letters Crane sent to James Pinker and Paul Revere Reynolds, his literary agents in England and America, respectively. In a February 1, 1899, letter to Pinker from his first English domicile, Ravensbrook, in Oxted, Surrey, Crane says that he is enclosing the Whilomville tale "The Angel Child" and then continues, "You will be glad to know that I am now writing a story with which you can have good game: 'God Rest ye, Merry Gentlemen.'[sic] We are sure that you will like it" (*Correspondence* II, 425). In a letter of February 4, likewise from Ravensbrook, he tells Pinker that "'God Rest Ye, Merry gentlemen' [sic] is coming on finely" (*Correspondence* II, 428). And finally, on February 13, now ensconced at Brede Place, Sussex, the crumbling baronial manor in which he spent most of the rest of his brief life, Crane sent the completed story to Reynolds to sell in America; he notes in an accompanying letter that he has already submitted it to Pinker for English sale (*Correspondence* II, 435).

Sources and Influences

This story is based closely on some of Crane's experiences during the Spanish-American War. At the outset of the war, Crane, who was then a correspondent for Joseph Pulitzer's *New York World*, was forced to cool his heels in Key West, Florida, along with the rest of the press corps, waiting for the American Navy to locate and blockade the Spanish fleet of Admiral Pascual

Cervera so that the American invasion force could safely land in Cuba. Bored and seeking a story, Crane, along with Sylvester Scovel, the chief *World* correspondent, and James Hare, a photographer for *Collier's* magazine, chartered the harbor tug *Somers N. Smith*, a name changed to *Jefferson G. Johnson* in the story, and set out for the Windward Islands to find Cervera's fleet themselves. The first part of the story recounts their failure to do so; the rest of it describes the landing of the first American troops in Cuba, hewing tightly to Crane's own observations of and actions during this event (Stallman 359). Robert W. Stallman identifies the actual figures behind many of the characters: Little Nell is Crane himself; Walkley is Edward Marshall, correspondent for the *New York Journal*; Shackles is Ernest W. McCready, correspondent for the *New York Herald*; Point is Burr McIntosh, photographer for *Leslie's Weekly*; and the unnamed, grizzled old captain is Captain Bucky O'Neill of the Tenth U.S. Cavalry, who also appears in another story, "The Second Generation," this time as General Reilly (378–80).

Relationship to Other Crane Works

This story is linked to another Spanish-American War tale, "The Revenge of the *Adolphus*," by some narrative details: the same group of correspondents appears in both—although only one, Shackles, is mentioned by name in "*Adolphus*"; both are set on the ships of the squadron blockading Cuba, with the *Adolphus* figuring by name in both; and the action of both takes place during the early stages of the war. However, the principal connection critics note between "'God Rest Ye'" and any of the rest of Crane's stories is a perceived lack of merit it shares with several other pieces in *Wounds in the Rain*, particularly "*Adolphus*" and "Marines Signaling Under Fire at Guantánamo." Milne Holton lumps these pieces together as "inferior work written in a time of illness and need, . . . framed out of Crane's reportage by means of a weak plot, with hardly any discernible form or theme and with only occasional sparks of good writing" (257).

E. R. Hagemann notes a somewhat more positive connection between "'God Rest Ye'" and two other *Wounds in the Rain* stories, "The Price of the Harness" and "The Lone Charge of William B. Perkins," possibly the result of Crane's having observed combat for himself before he wrote them: an awareness of the attraction violence holds for many soldiers. Calling this attraction "the common and all-important . . . concomitant of war," Hagemann asserts that these stories constitute

> a signal act of recognition on [Crane's] part that the simple brutal act of killing, the manipulation of the weapons of destruction, the sense of being in the presence of death—all of these and more—bring a terrifying feeling of joy, nay elation, to a man at war. (359)

Critical Studies

In her introduction to volume 9 of *The Work of Stephen Crane*, Willa Cather sharply criticizes this story for being nothing more than a hackneyed product of its times and circumstances. It is executed, she says, "in an outworn manner that was considered smart in the days when Richard Harding Davis was young, and the war correspondent . . . was a romantic figure"—Davis being one of Crane's fellow-war correspondents in Cuba, whose flamboyant personal style and racy prose were much admired by the public. "This sketch indulges in a curiously pompous kind of humour which seemed very swagger then" (xi). Subsequent Crane scholars seem to express their agreement with this assessment by their silence, since almost no one outside of Holton, as noted above, offers any comment on this story. The only favorable critique comes from Gullason, who sees it not as a straight imitation of the swaggering Davis style but as a subtle satire of it, as a clever debunking of "the demands of yellow journalism." Gullason points out that the essential conflict in the story is between Nell and his editor: the editor continually demands sensational reports of the war to excite the reading public, while Nell ignores these demands to spend his time at the more important task of caring for the sick and wounded, a course of behavior that finally gets him fired for what the editor calls his "'inaction'" (240).

Works Cited

Bowers, Fredson. Textual Introduction. *Tales of War*. Vol. 6 of The University of Virginia Edition of *The Works of Stephen Crane*. Ed. Fredson Bowers. Charlottesville: University Press of Virginia, 1970, xxxvii–cxci.

Cather, Willa. Introduction. *"Wounds in the Rain" and Other Impressions of War*. Vol. 9 of *The Work of Stephen Crane*. Ed. Wilson Follett. New York: Knopf, 1926, ix–xiv.

Gullason, Thomas A. "The Significance of *Wounds in the Rain*." *Modern Fiction Studies* 5 (1959):235–42.

Hagemann, E. R. "Crane's 'Real' War in His Short Stories." *American Quarterly* 8 (1956):356–67.

Holton, Milne. *Cylinder of Vision: The Fiction and Journalistic Writings of Stephen Crane*. Baton Rouge: Louisiana State University Press, 1972.

Stallman, R. W. *Stephen Crane: A Biography*. New York: George Braziller, 1968.

Wertheim, Stanley, and Paul Sorrentino, eds. *The Correspondence of Stephen Crane*. Vol. 2. New York: Columbia University Press, 1988.

A Grey Sleeve

Publication History

This story was first syndicated by Irving Bacheller to a number of American newspapers—including the *Kansas City Star*, the *Minneapolis Tribune*, the *San Francisco Chronicle*, and the *Chicago Times-Herald*—in October 1895. Bacheller then published it in the May 1896 issue of his *Pocket Magazine* (2:69–103). In between these appearances, the story ran in Britain in the *English Illustrated Magazine* for January 1896 (14:437–47). It first came out in book form in *"The Little Regiment" and Other Episodes of the American Civil War*, which was published in America by D. Appleton in October 1896 and in England by Heinemann in February 1897 (Bowers lxxv–lxxvii). Wilson Follett, editor of the twelve-volume *The Work of Stephen Crane* (New York: Knopf, 1925–27), included it in volume 2, published in 1925, and it appeared again in 1963 in Thomas A. Gullason's *Complete Short Stories and Sketches of Stephen Crane* (Garden City, N.Y.: Doubleday).

Circumstances of Composition

Most information about Crane's writing of this story comes from a reminiscence by Nelson Greene entitled "I Knew Stephen Crane." Greene was one of the young artists with whom Crane lived at intervals from the fall of 1893 through the fall of 1895 in the Needham building on East Twenty-third Street in Manhattan; in 1944, he wrote down his recollections of the author at the request of the then-president of the Stephen Crane Association of Newark, Max Herzberg (Wertheim 46). One of Greene's memories is of Crane working on "A Grey Sleeve" while he lived in Greene's studio in the summer of 1895. Greene recalls that Crane complained that writing this story was difficult and lamented that his "producing power" had deserted him. Crane struggled until he reached roughly the midpoint of the piece, "fussed some and then quit. He said he couldn't get anything out of himself for it." Greene says he read what Crane had produced thus far, liked it, and told his friend "to lay off for awhile and his kick would come back to him," but he notes that Crane did not finish the story until some time after they had gone their separate ways late that summer (qtd. in Wertheim 52). In any case, Crane must have completed it early that fall, since it was in syndication by October 1895, a circumstance that indicates it was the second Civil War story Crane wrote after *The Red*

Badge, "A Mystery of Heroism" being the first and all the others not begun until November 1895, when the McClure syndicate asked Crane for more Civil War material to follow up on the success of *The Red Badge* (Colvert xiii).

Sources and Influences

Although Nelson Greene provides a clear picture of Crane at work on this story, neither he nor Crane himself nor anyone else offers any explicit insights into the personal or literary background that Crane may have drawn on for it. One possibility is that, like "The Pace of Youth," one of Crane's few other love stories, it constitutes a kind of wish-fulfillment regarding an unrequited passion on Crane's part. In January 1895, in New York, Crane met a young woman named Nellie Crouse, a visitor from Ohio, at a tea party. Despite the brevity of this encounter, he was apparently deeply infatuated, but he waited until December of that year, after the publication and great success of *The Red Badge of Courage*, to declare himself, by letter, presumably because, as Paul Sorrentino and Stanley Wertheim say, he did not wish to court her until "his fame as an author had been secured" and he would cut an impressive figure as a suitor (*Correspondence* I, 163). His courtship over a span of seven letters did not succeed, however, for Crouse responded in a friendly way but kept him at arm's length where romance was concerned until he lost heart. Since "A Grey Sleeve" was composed between Crane's meeting with Crouse and the start of this courtship, it may be that the story's depiction of a shy young man and woman who fall into immediate but unarticulated love and indirectly promise to meet again later is what Crane hoped—in vain, as it turned out—had happened between himself and her in January of 1895.

Evidence for this view is that on January 6, 1896, Crane made a particular effort to send Crouse a newspaper clipping of "A Grey Sleeve." Although in the accompanying letter he described it as "not in any sense a good story" (*Correspondence* I, 171), when she responded a week later that she liked it he wrote back, "[o]f course [the young lovers] are a pair of idiots. But yet there is something charming in their childish faith in each other. That is all I intended to say" (*Correspondence* I, 180). Since it seems that the childish faith of a lover was something Crouse conspicuously lacked where Crane was concerned, perhaps he actually intended the story to say much more, at least to her.

Relationship to Other Crane Works

In terms of plot, theme, and style, this story is most closely connected to Crane's two other works that focus on young love and courtship—the short story "The Pace of Youth" and the novel *The Third Violet*. That an author as prolific as Crane should have essayed this subject so rarely may seem surprising, but a reading of these three works and some of the criticism on them provides a clear explanation: Crane had very little skill with this subject. Noting Crane's conventionally sentimental tone and the stilted dialogue of the lovers in *Violet*, John Berryman says Crane "stammers on this theme" (122), while Chester Wolford notes the equal lameness of tone and conversation in "Sleeve" (64). These critics, along with most others who have addressed these works, agree that "Pace" is Crane's only successful love story (Berryman 123; Holton 132; Colvert 91).

On the basis of theme and tone, two critics have also linked this story to other pieces in *"The Little Regiment."* Wolford sees it as connected to the story that gives this volume its title because both examine "the parallel between private attachments and public" ones in a wartime environment (63). Gullason notes that "Sleeve" resembles "Three Miraculous Soldiers" not only in the above respect but also in that both focus on young Southern women confronted by only slightly older Yankee officers, although the romantic dimension receives much greater highlighting in "Sleeve," and in that Crane's treatment of this relationship in both stories is sentimental, melodramatic, and cliché, which results in artistic failure in both cases ("True Road" 475).

Critical Studies

Very few critics have seen any reason to controvert Crane's own judgment of "Sleeve" as "not in any sense a good story." James Nagel says that it begins promisingly enough, "with much of the artistry of *The Red Badge*" apparent in Crane's skillful deployment of imagery involving flags and animals, his depictions of soldiers as nearly blinded by smoke, and his emphasis on the mindlessness of the charge; subsequently, however, "the action deteriorates into romance, the images lose referential significance, and the theme collapses into a simple love motif" (7). Gullason's view accords with this assessment, but he extends his criticism, seeing this story as of a piece with all those in the *"Little Regiment"* collection in that they all "clearly demonstrate the themes, the conflicts, the irony and imagery of *The Red Badge* reduced to a series of fragile, synthetic miniatures" ("Wounds" 235). Wolford likewise gives the story low marks for being silly and overdone, but he seeks partially to exonerate Crane for these flaws by offering the possibility that the story was intended as a lampoon of the kind of "high-flown Romantic war fiction" that its author detested (63).

Marston LaFrance offers the most ingenious explanation for the artistic weakness of this story. He asserts that one reason Crane dealt with romantic love so infrequently is that he himself was aware that this theme was poorly suited to the narrative pattern of ironic deflation that LaFrance sees as structuring almost all of Crane's work. He points to "Sleeve" as a prime example of this mismatch of structure and theme: if Crane's artistic predilection is to create a situation in which the protagonist faces a significant experience that his imagination distorts to still more momentous proportions, followed by a profound sense of disillusionment when the actual experience falls short of his anticipation, then he can do little more with his love story than have the captain make "rather an ass of himself before experience deflates his swelling illusions [of romance] to an unpleasant recollection" (247). Faced with this limitation, LaFrance argues, Crane tries the solution of using a love theme to write something other than a love story—what he ends up producing is "a suspense story masquerading as a romantic meeting." When one views "Sleeve" from this perspective, LaFrance concludes, it is not a failure, since in his opinion Crane's carefully calibrated gradual revelation of information—what is in the house, what the girl is holding behind her back, who is upstairs, whether the corporal actually spots the sleeve, how the captain will deal with the situation—effectively creates the ongoing suspense that is his goal (180).

Works Cited

Berryman, John. *Stephen Crane*. New York: Sloane, 1950.

Bowers, Fredson. Textual Introduction. *Tales of War*. Vol. 6 of The University of Virginia Edition of *The Works of Stephen Crane*. Ed. Fredson Bowers. Charlottesville: University Press of Virginia, 1970, xxxvii–cxci.

Colvert, James B. Introduction. *Tales of War* xi–xxxvi.

———. *Stephen Crane*. New York: Harcourt Brace Jovanovich, 1984.

Gullason, Thomas A. "The Significance of *Wounds in the Rain*." *Modern Fiction Studies* 5 (1959):235–42.

———. "Stephen Crane's Short Stories: The True Road." *Stephen Crane's Career: Perspectives and Evaluations*. Ed. Thomas A. Gullason. New York: New York University Press, 1972, 470–86.

Holton, Milne. *Cylinder of Vision: The Fiction and Journalistic Writings of Stephen Crane*. Baton Rouge: Louisiana State University Press, 1972.

LaFrance, Marston. *A Reading of Stephen Crane*. Oxford: Clarendon, 1971.

Nagel, James. "Stephen Crane's Stories of War: A Study of Art and Theme." *North Dakota Quarterly* 43 (1975):5–19.

Wertheim, Stanley. "Stephen Crane Remembered." *Studies in American Fiction* 4 (1976):46–64.

Wertheim, Stanley, and Paul Sorrentino, eds. *The Correspondence of Stephen Crane*. Vol. 1. New York: Columbia University Press, 1988.

Wolford, Chester L. *Stephen Crane: A Study of the Short Fiction*. Boston: Twayne, 1989.

His New Mittens

Publication History

This story first ran in America in the November 1898 number of *McClure's Magazine* (12:54–61); it was published the same month in England in *Cornhill Magazine* (n. s. 29:630–39). Its initial book appearance came in *"The Monster" and Other Stories*, which Harper & Brothers published in America in 1899 and in England in 1901 (Bowers 75). Editor Wilson Follett included it in volume 5, published in 1926, of *The Work of Stephen Crane* (12 vols., New York: Knopf, 1925–27); it also appeared in *Stephen Crane: An Omnibus* (New York: Knopf, 1952), edited by Robert W. Stallman, and *The Complete Short Stories and Sketches of Stephen Crane* (Garden City, N.Y.: Doubleday, 1963), edited by Thomas A. Gullason.

Circumstances of Composition

Crane wrote this story set in the fictional village of Whilomville—a locale he had used before in "The Monster" and would use again later in thirteen stories for *Harper's New Monthly Magazine*—at some point in April and May of 1898. During this time he traveled from England to New York to enlist in the American Navy so that he could fight in the Spanish-American War and then, when he failed to meet the Navy's physical standards, accepted a job covering the war for Joseph Pulitzer's *New York World*, which took him first to Florida and then to the press dispatch boats accompanying the American fleet blockading Cuba (*Correspondence* I, 291). It was from one of these boats, probably the *Three Friends*, that on May 30 he sent "His New Mittens" to his American agent, Paul Revere Reynolds, describing it as "a short story of boy life in Whilomville—the town of The Monster" (*Correspondence* II, 360). This message establishes the time the story was completed, but when it was begun is open to some dispute: Stallman asserts that Crane started working on it on the ocean liner *Germanic*, upon which he made the crossing from Queenstown, Ireland, to New York between April 14 and 21 (350), while Stanley Wertheim and Paul Sorrentino maintain that he did not begin it until after he reached Florida on April 26 (*Correspondence* II, 361).

Sources and Influences

As he does for many stories, Crane's first biographer, Thomas Beer, links the plot of "Mittens" to an event in the author's own life, asserting that Crane's mother made him a pair of bright red mittens when he was about eight (42). As is also frequently the case, later biographers accept and embellish Beer's claim: Stallman repeats the story of the mittens and says they were intended to match a pair of boots with red tops (8). And as is further usually the case, the likelihood is that Beer invented his biographical source, as Christopher Benfey points out (42).

A more reliable possibility, assuming that Crane did not begin the story until he arrived in Florida, is John Berryman's assertion that this tale of a boy goaded to action by merciless teasing arose partly from the ridicule Crane endured from many of the other war correspondents on the *Three Friends* as a result of his slovenly dress and habit of keeping to himself (218–20). J. C. Levenson agrees with this idea but adds that the story also stems from Crane's biography in a more general sense, in that "[i]t is the story of a boy who runs away, written by a man who had put three thousand miles between himself and his urgent responsibilities"—that is, his common-law wife, Cora, whom he left in England to deal alone with their mounting debts (xxxiii–xxxiv). Given Crane's ambivalent picture of female-dominated domestic life in "Mittens," showing it to be both emasculatingly smothering and tenderly welcoming, this is probably the most tenable hypothesis.

Relationship to Other Crane Works

Milne Holton links this story to one of Crane's earliest-developed and most pervasive themes, originally articulated in his comments to Hamlin Garland and others regarding his first novel, *Maggie: A Girl of the Streets*: "environment is a tremendous thing in the world and frequently shapes lives regardless" (*Correspondence* I, 53). "Mittens," Holton says, reveals specifically "how the Whilomville of the child shapes the apprehension of the man" (213); with his mother's strictures on one side and his peers' demands on the other, Horace, like Jimmie Trescott in the later Whilomville stories, is trapped in a situation in which "everything seems to turn upon individual acceptability to the group and individual status within it" (215), with the added problem that whatever he does to preserve his status in one group will cause him to be punished by the other. The effect of such pressure, Holton concludes, is the stunting not only of Horace's behavior but of his imagination, for "[n]o one in Whilomville asserts original fantasies or experiments with direct confrontations with reality or with new ways of seeing," a condition Holton identifies as operating in much of Crane's work (215–16).

Holton also links "Mittens" to one of Crane's war stories, "A Mystery of Heroism," and one of his Westerns, "The Five White Mice," through the concept of environment as the primary shaper of lives. "Mystery" and "Mice," Holton believes, are Crane's meditations on adults' willingness to accept dares and do foolhardy things to maintain their standing in their communities; "Mittens" constitutes an assertion that such behavior is formed by one's childhood relationships (219).

Like Holton, Levenson links "Mittens" to *Maggie*, noting that Horace's engaging in the snowball fight to preserve his honor is similar to Jimmie Johnson's involvement in a rock fight "for the honor of Rum Alley" (1:7), although he acknowledges a "fall in intensity" in the shift from stones to snowballs (xxxiv). He further connects both these works to *The Red Badge of Courage* through similarities in the behavior of Horace, Jimmie, and Henry Fleming in their respective combats, noting that the three stories collectively reveal that "men who were reduced by extraordinary stress to their natural state, and boys in their normal circumstances, were [alike] subject to the capricious flux of consciousness." With this fact in view, "Mittens" can be seen as part of a trilogy recognizing the fact that "the emotions of the playing field and the emotions of red battle could be mutually enlightening" (xxxiv).

John C. Martin looks only at the playing field, but he finds it as full of red emotion as the battlefield. Throughout Crane's canon, Martin says, from the early *Maggie* to the late *Harper's* Whilomville series, childhood is depicted as grim at best, marked by group cruelty to individual outsiders and ruthless efforts by individuals to join or stay within groups. "Mittens," in Martin's view, is a prime middle-period example of this gloomy vision, given the crowd's vicious taunting of Horace and his desperate responses (40–42).

Gullason takes up more directly than these other critics the question of the relationship of "Mittens" to the later Whilomville series. He argues that, taken collectively, these subsequent stories effectively "illuminate a number of universal truths about children, family life, and one's former home town" (483) and therefore constitute "a 'novel' of episodes" (471), and that from a thematic viewpoint "Mittens" is part of this "novel." As much as the other Whilomville tales, he says, "Mittens" is about children but is aimed at the adult reader; Crane's purpose in all is to show such a reader—a male one, in Gullason's formulation—scenes from childhood that give that reader "repeated shocks of recognition" in the depiction of "the dares and threats, the boredom, the bragging, the sarcasm, the follies and 'wisdoms' of his youth" (483).

A more specific narrative as well as thematic connection to one of the later Whilomville stories, "'Showin' Off,'" is also possible. One of the two main characters here is named Horace Glenn, and his principal action is to ride his velocipede down a sheer bank, which results in his hurting himself and shattering his vehicle, to prove to a taunting Jimmie Trescott that he is not afraid (7:156–57). Although Crane gives Horace no last name in "Mittens," he may well have regarded these two Horaces as the same person, particularly since in both cases the story's conflict arises from the Horace character's determination to defy the immutable laws of his world—in "Mittens" maternal ones and in "'Showin' Off'" physical ones—to prove to his peers that he is not afraid and thus maintain his place in their community.

Critical Studies

Like Martin and Gullason, Maxwell Geismar regards "Mittens" as thematically related to the other Whilomville stories, and in fact to Crane's work in general, in its focus on the "instinctive cruelty" of society. In this particular case, the children, as society's representatives and raw material, act out "all the intimations and echoes . . . of Jung's Archaic Man," against which the individual, Horace, can counterpose only "desperate and often just as ruthless dignity" (126). However, Geismar is also of the opinion that Crane's handling of these ideas here and in the other Whilomville tales suffers by comparison with what he does in this line in other works, a result of the author's being too conscious of writing for a popular audience and thus failing to make the children's actions "quite primitive and savage enough" (127).

Other critics have expressed similarly mixed judgments of "Mittens" and the rest of the Whilomville cycle since their first appearance. Crane's contemporary Edward Garnett calls "Mittens" a "delightful graphic study of boy morals" but also says that here, as elsewhere, "when Crane breathes an everyday atmosphere his aesthetic power . . . weakens" (144–45). Stallman tacitly assents, noting that this piece partakes of the sentimentality that mars all the Whilomville tales; however, he says that the final scene, in which Aunt Martha offers home-brewed root beer to the butcher Stickney, is saved from bathos by Crane's employment of a double viewpoint. While Horace sees himself, melodramatically, as being at the mercy of his mother, his aunt, and the rest of his environment, an alternative understanding, stemming from the viewpoint of the women, is that "people [brew] their own drink and their own fate" (476).

Levenson makes a more wholly positive assessment of the story, crediting Crane with innovation in the sphere of domestic fiction by shifting the focus in "the war between the sexes" from husband and wife or courting lovers to mother and son and by having Horace perceive thereby that "in a maternally centered family, nurture is transformed into an instrument of domination." With this shift in place, Levenson says, "[t]he comedy ends with the sound, not of wedding bells as under the older convention, but of suppressed maternal sobs." And that it is a comedy is unquestionable for Levenson. "The tears signify a kind of pleasure," he explains, "and the ending—so ambiguous as to be win, lose, and draw all at once—is doubtless to be taken as happy" (xxxv–xxxvi).

Several other critics, while in accord with Levenson's sense of the ambiguity of the story's ending, see this circumstance as less indicative of an entirely happy conclusion. Neville Denny says that through the imagery of the butcher-shop as the locus of shelter from the storm, in which the butcher himself embodies "a healthy vigor, a robust masculine quality" missing from Horace's feminine household, Crane makes the story not only a perceptive depiction of "the inarticulate intensity of feeling of childhood, the tensions and yearnings and keenly felt injustices of Horace's world" in opposition to the "inbred, restricted quality of the women's lives," but also a tale of larger application. In this condition Horace subtly represents "Everyman, inarticulate, buffeted by storms, cruelly used by thoughtless and selfish others, and needing to find a balance between masculine and feminine values," a balance still in doubt at the story's end, if he is "to assert any meaningful independence in a rough, intractable world" (30–31). Similarly, Bettina Knapp argues that the aunt's final statement concerning the root beer, "we make it ourselves," applies more largely to the matriarchy that enfolds Horace and to the suffering that this matriarchy causes him. As a counterbalance he needs but seems unlikely to be granted the "patriarchal power" embodied in the "warm and understanding" butcher (177).

Holton also takes a negative view of the conclusion; he regards "Mittens" as, like "The Monster," a meaningful variation on Crane's usual narrative pattern of escape from and return to community, a variation in that in these two cases, unlike the others, this pattern does not lead the protagonist to a greater degree of insight. Horace escapes and returns, Holton says, but he has learned nothing because he faced no confrontation during that escape, a function of the fact his flight is not from community to freedom, as is usually the case in Crane stories, but rather from one repressive authority to another. On the one hand, Horace faces "the hierarchial community of children, which demands participation in fantasy games and enforces these demands with ridicule and a threat of ostracism"; on the other he faces his mother, "whose demands have moral authority, and who uses love and its deprivation (in the form of food) to achieve her ends." In this dilemma, punished by one authority or the other no matter what he does, Horace cannot win (a point also made by Ellen A. Brown [107]); as a result, he cannot attain the freedom of action and thus of imagination that is necessary for deeper understanding in Crane's cosmos. His return to the maternal bosom seems to make everything all right, but, Holton concludes, he has been unable to develop the crucial, for Crane, "capacity for autonomous apprehension of reality" (30–31).

Chester L. Wolford takes a similar view of Crane's use of food imagery and of the story's concomitantly epiphany-less ending. Food is the story's main motif, Wolford contends, and the point is that the adult characters consistently use it "to corrupt the natural tendency of children to rebel, to move outside the family and community, and, perhaps, even to confront chaos."

Horace's rebellion is scotched by the hunger that leads him to the butcher-shop and thus back home, where the butcher is welcomed with the social ritual of a food offering, the root beer. The upshot of these circumstances for Horace, Wolford says, is that he "cannot escape; he cannot even learn anything about escaping from Whilomville. Chaos is too frightening and communal ties too strong to admit of learning" (51).

Perhaps the most in-depth commentary on "Mittens" comes from Max Westbrook, who focuses on it and several of Crane's other stories to refute the claim advanced by various critics, especially Warner Berthoff and Jay Martin, that Crane's art is incoherent due to a perceived lack of unity between the action of his stories and his narrators' language—a sense that in many cases "the language invokes meanings the story cannot accommodate" (86). As an example of this putative problem in "Mittens" Westbrook points to the imagery Crane uses in describing the snowball fight, such as his characterization of the boys as "soldiers" and "Indians" and his reference to Horace's family's overprotectiveness as "a public scandal." These images seem overscaled, conjuring up ideas well beyond the reality of the action and thereby making the story incoherent, Westbrook says, until one learns to read Crane dualistically—that is, to recognize that such figures do not express either the actual thoughts of the characters or the narrator's straight view of them, but rather constitute "an ironic expression of the further implications of the characters' reactions." In other words, the characters' exaggerated, self-dramatizing behavior puts the reader in mind of the ideas expressed in the figures and thus the figures sardonically emphasize the exaggeration and self-dramatization to which humans are prone. When one learns to read "Mittens" dualistically, Westbrook concludes, "[e]vent and language interweave" to produce "a critique of a small boy's pride" that expands to indict the whole community, for "it is pride which is the subject of the story" (101).

Works Cited

Beer, Thomas. *Stephen Crane: A Study in American Letters*. New York: Knopf, 1923.

Benfey, Christopher. *The Double Life of Stephen Crane*. New York: Knopf, 1992.

Berryman, John. *Stephen Crane*. New York: Sloane, 1950.

Bowers, Fredson. Textual Introduction. Tales of Whilomville. Vol. 7 of The University of Virginia Edition of *The Works of Stephen Crane*. Ed. Fredson Bowers. Charlottesville: University Press of Virginia, 1968. 75–79.

Brown, Ellen A. "Stephen Crane's *Whilomville Stories*: A Backward Glance." *Markham Review* 3 (1972):105–09.

Denny, Neville. "Imagination and Experience in Stephen Crane." *English Studies in Africa* 9 (1966):28–42.

Garnett, Edward. "Edward Garnett on Stephen Crane." *Stephen Crane's Career: Perspectives and Evaluations*. Ed. Thomas A. Gullason. New York: New York University Press, 1972, 137–45.

Geismar, Maxwell. *Rebels and Ancestors*. Boston: Houghton Mifflin, 1953.

Gullason, Thomas A. "Stephen Crane's Short Stories: The True Road." *Stephen Crane's Career: Perspectives and Evaluations*. Ed. Thomas A. Gullason. New York: New York University Press, 1972, 470–86.

Holton, Milne. *Cylinder of Vision: The Fiction and Journalistic Writings of Stephen Crane*. Baton Rouge: Louisiana State University Press, 1972.

Knapp, Bettina L. *Stephen Crane*. New York: Ungar, 1987.

Levenson, J. C. Introduction. *Tales of Whilomville* xi–lx.

Martin, John C. "Childhood in Crane's *Maggie*, 'The Monster,' and Whilomville Stories." *Midwestern University Quarterly* 2 (1967):40–46.

Stallman, Robert W. *Stephen Crane: A Biography*. New York: George Braziller, 1968.

Wertheim, Stanley, and Paul Sorrentino, eds. *The Correspondence of Stephen Crane*. 2 vols. New York: Columbia University Press, 1988.

Westbrook, Max. "Whilomville: The Coherence of Radical Language." *Stephen Crane in Transition: Centenary Essays*. Ed. Joseph Katz. DeKalb: Northern Illinois University Press, 1972. 86–105.

Wolford, Chester L. *Stephen Crane: A Study of the Short Fiction*. Boston: Twayne, 1989.

An Indiana Campaign

Publication History

This story initially appeared in a two-part form syndicated by Bacheller, Johnson, and Bacheller to a number of newspapers—including the *Minneapolis Tribune*, the *Buffalo Commercial*, the *Nebraska State Journal*, and the *Kansas City Star*—on May 23 and 25, 1896. Bacheller then placed it, in toto, in the company's September 1896 issue of *Pocket Magazine* (2:92–114). It was next included in the book *"The Little Regiment" and Other Episodes of the American Civil War*, published by D. Appleton in October 1896. In Britain, it first ran in the *English Illustrated Magazine* for December 1896 (16:320–26) and then appeared in the English version of *"The Little*

Regiment," which Heinemann published in February of 1897 (Bowers lxix–lxx). Pioneering Crane editor Wilson Follett included it in volume 2, published in 1925, of *The Work of Stephen Crane* (12 vols., New York: Knopf, 1925–27), and Thomas A. Gullason also collected it in 1963 in *The Complete Short Stories and Sketches of Stephen Crane* (Garden City, N.Y.: Doubleday).

Circumstances of Composition

Crane wrote "An Indiana Campaign" while he was living at his brother Edmund's house in the rural community of Hartwood, New York, between October 1895 and February 1896. It was probably composed as one of a number of stories with Civil War settings that Crane produced during this period in response to a request from the McClure newspaper syndicate for more such material to capitalize on the current success of *The Red Badge of Courage* (Colvert xiii–xiv), but Crane first submitted it to the *Atlantic Monthly* when the editor of that prestigious journal, Walter Hines Page, also solicited material from him, in a letter dated March 2, 1896 (*Correspondence* I, 210). However, Page ultimately passed on this story for the *Atlantic*, explaining in a letter of April 7, 1896, that although he found it "vividly and excellently" written, "in substance it is somewhat too slight for our more or less serious pages" (*Correspondence I*, 226). Satisfying the McClure request with several other stories, Crane then successfully placed "Indiana" with the Bacheller syndicate.

Sources and Influences

No one has identified any specific sources for this story in either Crane's life or his reading. As Chester L. Wolford suggests (66), it is likely that, given its focus on the posturings, rumor-mongering, and ultimate timidity of the inhabitants of a rural town, the story is a reflection of Crane's general experience of growing up in several such communities, particularly Port Jervis, New York, which is only a few miles distant from Hartwood, his residence while he was writing it. As Robert W. Stallman points out, this story "has the same mellow humor" as some of the tales set in Whilomville, Crane's fictionalized version of Port Jervis, and in fact it "might just as well be located in Whilomville as in the village called Wigglesville" (477). This mellow humor regarding the generally self-aggrandizing pretenses and foibles of country villagers who believe they face war in their vicinity also suggests a possible literary source, Mark Twain's "The Private History of a Campaign That Failed," which appeared in the *Century* magazine series *Battles and Leaders of the Civil War*, with which Crane was familiar (Dolmetsch 42–49).

Relationship to Other Crane Works

Wolford sees "Indiana" as closely linked to one of the other stories in *"Little Regiment,"* "A Mystery of Heroism," in that both focus on a character who performs a seemingly foolhardy gesture in order to save face before his peers (66). Donald B. Gibson likewise links these two stories on this basis, but he perceives as well a considerable difference between Fred Collins, the protagonist of "Mystery," and Major Tom Boldin in "Indiana," one that also links the latter story to another *"Little Regiment"* piece, "The Veteran." Like the aged Henry Fleming in this tale, Gibson says, Boldin "is an old soldier" and thus has already resolved the issue of his own courage that Collins is just confronting. As a result, unlike Collins, "[n]either of the old soldiers has the least hesitation about doing what he does. Neither has the same tenacious hold on life [as Collins], though at the same time neither of the old men is simply foolhardy" (93). Beyond these differences, however, Gibson sees all three of these stories as carrying the same final meaning: "courageous action in the face of adversity is necessary and desirable despite the fact that it might or might not have some intimate relationship with the nature of things, that it might not accomplish what it was intended to accomplish" (94).

Milne Holton sees "Indiana" as harking back to some of Crane's earliest work, the sketches he wrote about rural Sullivan County in 1892. In most of these sketches, Holton notes, Crane employs the same basic plot pattern he uses in the later story: the protagonist faces an unknown entity—a cave in one sketch, a mountain in another, a howling emanating from an unseen source in a third, a supposed invading Confederate in "Indiana"—and allows his imagination to run nearly wild with fear as he prepares to face it, only to be deflated and perhaps humiliated when he does confront it and realizes that such fear was unwarranted. And in its treatment of this pattern, Holton continues, "Indiana" not only looks back to the Sullivan County material but also shows Crane moving toward the Whilomville stories, for in "Indiana" he deals not just with the delusions of an individual, his subject in the Sullivan County sketches, but also with the kind of "communal misapprehension" that becomes one of his primary targets in the Whilomville tales (143).

Marston LaFrance similarly regards "Indiana" as related to the Sullivan County sketches in their common use of this plot movement from inflation to deflation, a movement he sees as underlying nearly all of Crane's work (179–80). He also views this story as predictive of Whilomville in its emphasis on communal misapprehension, but he singles out the first tale Crane wrote with a Whilomville setting, "The Monster," as particularly closely related in this respect. In the scene in "Indiana" in which the crowd stands at the edge of the cornfield waiting for Boldin and Peter Witheby to emerge with the supposed invader in tow, LaFrance says, Crane is for the first time making not an individual but rather an entire town his protagonist, which he would do to much greater effect a year later in "The Monster" (180).

James B. Colvert also singles out this crowd scene as worthy of note, but for a less significant reason. In his view, it simply reveals "Crane's method of adapting the portentous imagery of the Sullivan County sketches and *The Red Badge of Courage* to a comedy of manners" (xxvi).

Critical Studies

Very few critics have discussed "Indiana" on its own, without reference to its connections to other pieces by Crane, a circumstance suggesting that most critics share Page's view of it as slight. Gullason certainly takes this view, judging the story a near-total failure due to Crane's alleged inability to maintain "control and balance between comic and serious themes" and his flatly moralistic conclusion (475). Wolford, on the other hand, praises certain aspects of Crane's technique here, noting in particular the pointed but subtle parallelism between the flock of chickens panicked by a boy at the outset of the story and the townspeople frightened nearly to hysteria by the reports of a rebel in the woods (66). Bettina Knapp also offers a measure of praise, asserting that "Indiana" is better than most of the other "*Little Regiment*" pieces due to its skillful, powerful depiction of a "crescendo of collective fear, anger, and hatred and the dangers involved in such irrational outbreaks" (167).

Works Cited

Bowers, Fredson. Textual Introduction. *Tales of War*. Vol. 6 of The University of Virginia Edition of *The Works of Stephen Crane*. Ed. Fredson Bowers. Charlottesville: University Press of Virginia, 1970, xxxvii–cxci.

Colvert, James B. Introduction. *Tales of War* xi–xxxvi.

Dolmetsch, Carl. "Cowardice and Courage: Mark Twain, Stephen Crane, and the Civil War." *Profils Americains: Les Ecrivains Americains Face à la Guerre de Secession* 3 (1992):39–50.

Gibson, Donald B. *The Fiction of Stephen Crane*. Carbondale: Southern Illinois University Press, 1968.

Gullason, Thomas A. "Stephen Crane's Short Stories: The True Road." *Stephen Crane's Career: Perspectives and Evaluations*. Ed. Thomas A. Gullason. New York: New York University Press, 1972, 470–86.

Holton, Milne. *Cylinder of Vision: The Fiction and Journalistic Writings of Stephen Crane*. Baton Rouge: Louisiana State University Press, 1972.

Knapp, Bettina L. *Stephen Crane. New York: Ungar, 1987.*

LaFrance, Marston. *A Reading of Stephen Crane*. Oxford: Clarendon, 1971.

Stallman, R. W. *Stephen Crane: A Biography*. New York: George Braziller, 1968.

Wertheim, Stanley, and Paul Sorrentino, eds. *The Correspondence of Stephen Crane*. Vol. 1. New York: Columbia University Press, 1988.

Wolford, Chester L. *Stephen Crane: A Study of the Short Fiction*. Boston: Twayne, 1989.

The Kicking Twelfth

Publication History

This story was first published in England in the February 1900 issue of *Pall Mall Magazine* (20:173–79); in America, it first ran in *Ainslee's Magazine* for August 1900 (6:46–51). It did not appear in book form during Crane's lifetime, only being collected in *Last Words*, the posthumous volume Crane's common-law wife, Cora, compiled and had published by the London house Digby, Long in 1902 (Bowers clxxii–clxxiii). It was collected again in 1926 in volume 9 of *The Work of Stephen Crane* (12 vols., New York: Knopf, 1925–27), edited by Wilson Follett, and it also appeared in Thomas A. Gullason's 1963 *Complete Short Stories and Sketches of Stephen Crane* (Garden City, N.Y.: Doubleday).

Circumstances of Composition

Crane wrote "The Kicking Twelfth" at some point between January 1899 and probably November of that same year, while he was living at his final English home, Brede Place, in Sussex. It appears to have been the first composed as well as the first in narrative order of four tales about the Twelfth Regiment of the army of the fictional nation of Spitzbergen. Fredson Bowers establishes this dating and sequence: he notes that the first reference to any of these stories comes in a letter of January 13, 1899, from Joseph Conrad to Crane that mentions an apparently embryonic version of the final one, "The Upturned Face"; and he asserts that the series was finished, in order, by November 4, when Crane sent an unidentified story "that must be 'The Upturned Face'" to his British agent, James Pinker (clxxii). In any case, "The Kicking Twelfth" was definitely completed before January 1900, for on January 8 of that year, in a letter to Cora, Pinker says that he has recently sold the British serial rights for it (*Correspondence* II, 580).

Crane originally dictated this story to Edith Richie (later Edith Richie Jones). A niece of Harold Frederic's common-law wife, Kate Lyon, Richie was a house guest at Brede Place from the summer of 1899 through January 1900. She was invited as a companion for Crane's niece Helen, visiting from America during this period, but she also served as Crane's occasional amanuensis. She saved her manuscript, and in 1942 she sent it to her brother-in-law, Mark Barr, also a friend of Crane's, accompanied by a letter that illuminates the author's writing habits during his final year. "As far as I can remember," Richie says,

> S. Crane dictated it to me as he sprawled on the couch with the dogs in the big hall. . . . Sometimes in a train or out-doors or in a room he'd say: "Anyone got a pencil & paper? I've just thought of something." Then Cora or I wd [sic] write it down & afterwards type it. He rarely altered any of it but seemed to have it all straight in his mind when he began. . . . Note the General Richie (after me) & Colonel Sponge (after the [Cranes'] dog). (Qtd. in Bowers clxxiii)

Sources and Influences

No one has identified any specific sources for this story in Crane's experiences in the Greco-Turkish or Spanish-American War, but Eric Solomon notes that these experiences underlie it in a general way, pointing out that the story "is underwritten in Crane's antiheroic style and filled with realistic touches drawn from his own combat observations" (79). In fact, as Solomon argues persuasively, this lack of specific sources may have been a conscious artistic choice: it may indicate Crane's desire in this and the other Spitzbergen tales to create "his own picture of war, this time without . . . the restraint of historical fact"—in other words, to write "war fiction as [he] believed it should be organized," with the goal of emphasizing the universal characteristics of all wars, of revealing that "[t]he baptism of fire, fear, death, courage, [and] horror are qualities of all war and all war fiction" (79). Two details that *can* be specifically identified, however, are the names Crane gives his mythical country and its enemy. Spitzbergen and Rostina, as Robert W. Stallman points out, are the names of two Norwegian islands in the Arctic Ocean (605).

Relationship to Other Crane Works

"Kicking Twelfth" is most closely linked to the other three stories devoted to the Twelfth Regiment of the Spitzbergen Army, "The Shrapnel of Their

Friends," "'And If He Wills, We Must Die'" and "Face." A number of critics have noted that this connection is based on more than just the same regiment's appearing in all four and Lieutenant Timothy Lean's being the protagonist in three of them; they read the stories as stages in a single narrative line that is so clear that Chester L. Wolford proposes that they collectively be regarded as forming a "composite novel" that moves from a focus on the whole regiment, fully manned, in "Kicking Twelfth," to the regiment decimated by combat in "Shrapnel," to sixteen men in "'If He Wills,'" to just two men, Lean and the adjutant, in "Face," with each stage in this tightening of focus moving the reader closer to "'the real thing'" of combat (77–78). Milne Holton and Eric Solomon also take this composite view. Holton sees the stories as combining to depict the gradual education of the whole regiment in "the awful reality of war" (268), while Solomon sees them as centered more specifically on Timothy Lean's education. In "Kicking Twelfth," he says, Lean learns about the exhilarating side of combat through his participation in the regiment's first two, successfully concluded, engagements. At the end of this story, he notes, although Crane points out "the unromantic aspect of the charge" in that the men are winded after their exertions, nonetheless "[e]veryone is happy; the general congratulates the colonel who, in turn, congratulates Lean, the first man in the attack." For Lean, "this is the way war should be, the hero brave, the charge a success, the enemy defeated." However, "Kicking Twelfth" is only the first stage in Lean's education. In "Shrapnel" he discovers the illogical side of war when the regiment breaks and runs after being mistakenly shelled by their own artillery. In "'If He Wills,'" Solomon continues, Crane moves from the illogic of combat to its patent injustice, "in sharp contrast to the earlier tales of the series," in depicting the deaths of fifteen brave men and a sergeant who is "a perfect soldier who obeys his impossible orders in the best tradition of the service." Although Lean does not appear in this story, Solomon asserts that "it seems clear that the episode is meant to be part of the lieutenant's military education," revealing "the ugly side" of war, "the reality of violent painful death." Then in "Face" Lean reappears to confront this reality directly in having to bury a friend under fire (79–80).

Solomon is also the only critic to address the possibility of connections between "Kicking Twelfth" and Crane's non-Spitzbergen works. He notes that in this story and the other three in the series Crane turns away from the techniques and concerns that occupied him in the war stories of *The Little Regiment* and *Wounds in the Rain* and instead returns to "the approach that produced *The Red Badge of Courage*—that is, he focuses only on the moment of combat, showing "the Spitzbergen army set apart from history or society. The sole field of endeavor is the battlefield; everything else is extraneous" (78). The point of this full-circle movement in his final war stories, away from "the insensitivity of *Wounds in the Rain*" and back to the "great care for human values" that marks *The Red Badge*, Solomon concludes, is that Crane has discovered "a middle way that conceives of war, like life, as both a glory and an obscenity." Crane himself has learned, as he has Lean find out, that "war is all things to all men—beauty, a test, a muscular way of life, and, finally, a horror" (80). (Solomon repeats this assessment of the Spitzbergen cycle on pp. 125–28 of his book-length study *Stephen Crane: From Parody to Realism*.)

Critical Studies

Most of what has been written on this story links it with the other three Spitzbergen tales and therefore is covered immediately above in "Relationship to Other Crane Works." Only two critics have anything to say about this story in isolation, and even in these cases they make a connection with the rest of the series. Holton points out that in "Kicking Twelfth" Crane inaugurates the "purified style"—marked by darkened imagery, "bare and functional" language, and a "relentlessly closing" focus—that he uses throughout the four Spitzbergen stories (266–67). Wolford notes that this tale differs from the others in the comparatively greater authorial distance Crane maintains in this story: rather than focusing on a single character, as he comes to do in "Face," Crane here, according to Wolford, uses the regiment as a whole as his protagonist, with the result that the reader "seem[s] to be lulled into the story by [this] fairly generalized, long-distance view of war," just as the regiment itself is lulled into a sanguine and therefore incomplete view of war as result of the favorable outcome of this, their first battle (78).

Works Cited

Bowers, Fredson. Textual Introduction. *Tales of War*. Vol. 6 of The University of Virginia Edition of *The Works of Stephen Crane*. Ed. Fredson Bowers. Charlottesville: University Press of Virginia, 1970, xxxvii–cxci.

Holton, Milne. *Cylinder of Vision: The Fiction and Journalistic Writings of Stephen Crane*. Baton Rouge: Louisiana State University Press, 1972.

Solomon, Eric. *Stephen Crane: From Parody to Realism*. Cambridge: Harvard University Press, 1966.

———. "Stephen Crane's War Stories." *Texas Studies in Literature and Language* 3 (1961):67–80.

Stallman, R. W. *Stephen Crane: A Biography*. New York: George Braziller, 1968.

Wertheim, Stanley, and Paul Sorrentino, eds. *The Correspondence of Stephen Crane*. Vol. 2. New York: Columbia University Press, 1988.

Wolford, Chester L. *Stephen Crane: A Study of the Short Fiction*. Boston: Twayne, 1989.

The Knife

Publication History

This story first ran in *Harper's New Monthly Magazine* for March 1900 (100:591–98), the eighth in the thirteen-part series of Crane's Whilomville tales published in this magazine between August 1899 and August 1900. Like the others in this series, it was then included in the collection *Whilomville Stories*, which Harper & Brothers published in America in August 1900 and in England in November of the same year (Bowers 103). Editor Wilson Follett placed it in volume 5, published in 1926, of *The Work of Stephen Crane* (12 vols., New York: Knopf, 1925–27); it appeared again in *Stephen Crane: An Omnibus* (New York: Knopf, 1952), edited by Robert W. Stallman, and *The Complete Short Stories and Sketches of Stephen Crane* (Garden City, N.Y.: Doubleday, 1963), edited by Thomas A. Gullason.

Circumstances of Composition

There is strong evidence that "The Knife" was written around August 31, 1899, at Crane's last home in England, Brede Place, Sussex. On that date Crane's common-law wife, Cora, sent a letter to his agent, James Pinker, informing him that within three or four days Crane will send the next tale in his series set in the fictional village of Whilomville. Cora does not give the name of this story, but she says it will be four thousand words (*Correspondence* II, 508); as J. C. Levenson notes, "The Knife" is the most likely candidate, since it runs 4095 words and is the only one of the Whilomville stories known to be finished by this date—owing to its presence on a list Crane compiled at some point that summer—that cannot be accounted for by some other evidence (liv). It was certainly complete and submitted for publication before September 22, 1899, for on that date Crane wrote to Pinker complaining that the publisher, *Harper's New Monthly Magazine*, had underpaid him for this story and "The Carriage-Lamps," another Whilomville tale (*Correspondence* II, 518).

Sources and Influences

All of the other Whilomville tales have as their protagonist young Jimmie Trescott, whom most critics view as largely modeled on Crane himself, a fact that generally makes linking those stories to his own life a relatively easy and fruitful line of study. However, "The Knife" focuses on two African-American men, Peter Washington and Alek Williams, with Jimmie and his family relegated to the background as Peter's employers. Perhaps as a consequence of this shift in focus, no biographer or critic has suggested any source for this story in Crane's life. Crane certainly had some familiarity with African-Americans, drawing on his memories of their community in Port Jervis, New York, for his first Whilomville piece, "The Monster" (Levenson xiii, Stallman 333), but given his use of broad dialect and a somewhat condescending tone toward his characters in "The Knife," his principal inspiration here seems more likely to have been some reading in racist "humor" pieces written by whites about blacks, or perhaps simply the generally racist attitude of the white society of which he was a member. As Lyle Linder points out, aside from his sympathetic portrait of Henry Johnson in "The Monster" Crane's depictions were "not far ahead of the worst contemporary stereotypes of blacks and other ethnics in his fiction" (2), an assessment further borne out by "The Ideal and the Real" and "Brer Washington's Conversion," two other Crane stories, never published, that likewise focus on African-Americans but employ even more offensive stereotyping than that found in "The Knife" (Linder 1–2).

Relationship to Other Crane Works

In some ways "The Knife" links clearly to the rest of the Whilomville stories, but in others it stands apart. Although Crane here concentrates on members of the town's African-American community rather than the white middle-class children and adults who take center stage in the others, this community is connected narratively and thematically to the white world through Crane's use of Peter Washington and Alek Williams as his main characters. In terms of narrative connections, both of these men are sometime employees of the principal family in the series, the Trescotts. Peter is their coachman, successor in that capacity to Henry Johnson, who figures centrally in Crane's first story set in Whilomville, "The Monster," and who is mentioned in "The Knife" as "the late gallant Henry Johnson," (7:185); and Alek is the man whom Doctor Trescott hires in "The Monster" to shelter Henry after the latter is physically and mentally impaired during his rescue of Jimmie Trescott from a fire.

On the thematic level, "The Knife" is linked to the other Whilomville stories through Crane's showing, in Peter's and Alek's attempts to one-up each other in terms of respectability in relation to watermelon theft, that the African-American community is just like the white adult and child communities: in all three, as Milne Holton notes, "everything seems to turn upon individual acceptability to the group and individual status within it" (215). In a similar vein, David Halliburton sees Crane's anomalous focus on African-American men rather than white boys as intended to reveal "the relation of the child to the adult as mediated by the black"—in other words, Crane like the majority of his culture sees the black adult characters as essentially child-ish, as humorously aping adult white society's mores and behavior just as the white children do in the rest of the series (205).

Gullason and Eric Solomon see this underlying theme of imitation as making the Whilomville series in effect a kind of loose novel that, in Gullason's words, "illuminate[s] a number of universal truths about children, family life, and one's former home town" (483). For Solomon the most significant of these truths is that the white adult society that the blacks and children so eagerly emulate is in fact the worst of the three due to its basis in a conscious hypocrisy that the other two groups, as chiefly represented by Jimmie Trescott, initially lack but are gradually educated into as the series unfolds (207).

The difference between "The Knife" and the rest of the Whilomville tales grows out of this thematic link, for although many critics, as noted above, fault Crane for racism in this story, others judge that in thematically equating the African-American community with the white ones Crane gives his African-American characters a dimension of complexity that they lack in the others of the *Harper's* series. Peter appears in several other stories—"Shame," "The Carriage-Lamps," "The Stove," and "The City Urchin and the Chaste Villagers"—but in these, as Levenson points out, he is limited to "the stereo-type of the simple, jocular Negro servant" (lviii), whereas in "The Knife" both he and Alek are fully as complicated and intelligent as the white townsfolk, even though they use these assets to attain the same shallow ends that the whites are after. Levenson also notes that in its depiction of a web of rela-tionships between members of the African-American society and between them and whites, "The Knife" uses the most sophisticated "social and narra-tive conventions" to be found in the Whilomville tales, which Levenson finds appropriate for the only *Harper's* story that mentions the heroic Henry Johnson (lvii).

Critical Studies

Critics have often denigrated the Whilomville stories as a group. H. E. Bates says they are "as commonplace as calico" and regards them as doing little more than revealing the diminished state of Crane's powers in his final illness. The method of these stories, he says, "is that of any tenth-rate provincial reporter without the wit to determine whether what he is doing is good or bad" (148). Taking a more moderate view, James B. Stronks rates the Whilomville pieces as "thin and slight" because of their focus on mundane sit-uations that do not evoke the "nerveless intensity" of Crane at his best, but he points out that they are nevertheless preferable to most late-Victorian litera-ture about children (343). However, as is indicated by Levenson's comments about Crane's endowing his African-American characters in "The Knife" with a degree of complexity rare in his work, noted above in the "Relationship" section, a few critics single this story out for distinctly favorable commentary, for higher praise than they accord to the rest of the series. In addition to Levenson, Stallman believes this is the best of the Whilomville cycle due to Alek Williams's refusal to tell Si Bryant that the knife Bryant has found belongs to Peter Washington. By this gesture, Stallman says, Crane shows that he understands the dynamics of race relations; in Stallman's view, Crane is here making the point that in the struggle of white against black, "the Negro's salvation . . . lies in the fidelity of Negroes to one another, and so [Williams] saves Peter Washington by telling a 'white lie'" (478).

Solomon also praises Crane for his depiction of solidarity between Alek and Peter. Although these characters are handled somewhat stereotypically, Solomon says, when Bryant confronts them their ability to put aside their argument and work together enables them to "make the white owner of the watermelons appear as foolish as most adults do in Whilomville." Solomon concludes that "[t]he authority may belong to the white farmer, but the imaginative audacity belongs to the childish Negro; Crane has the ironic grace to make both worlds equally absurd" and thus create one of the better tales in the Whilomville series (220).

On the other hand, as is equally indicated by the comments of Linder, Holton, and Halliburton in the "Sources and Influences" and "Relationship" sections, a number of critics see "The Knife" as clearly of a piece with the rest of the series and thus not particularly worthy. Halliburton, for instance, agrees with Stallman that in saving Peter, Alek sides with his fellow African-American, but he also notes that this solidarity is undercut by the fact that prior to Bryant's arrival Peter had "assumed the role of moral enforcer" and thus had Alek under his thumb, so that part of Alek's reason for lying is to regain the advantage over Peter by maintaining a threat of blackmail. With these points in mind, Halliburton concludes, the African-American community in fact fails to cohere, for "in the crisis Peter spontaneously takes on the part, not of his counterpart in race, but of the white owner" (206).

Works Cited

Bates, H. E. "H. E. Bates on Stephen Crane." *Stephen Crane's Career: Perspectives and Evaluations*. Ed. Thomas A. Gullason. New York: New York University Press, 1972, 146–50.

Bowers, Fredson. Textual Introduction. *Tales of Whilomville*. Vol. 7 of The University of Virginia Edition of *The Works of Stephen Crane*. Ed. Fredson Bowers. Charlottesville: University Press of Virginia, 1968, 103–26.

Gullason, Thomas A. "Stephen Crane's Short Stories: The True Road." *Stephen Crane's Career: Perspectives and Evaluations*. Ed. Thomas A. Gullason. New York: New York University Press, 1972, 470–86.

Halliburton, David. *The Color of the Sky: A Study of Stephen Crane*. Cambridge: Cambridge University Press, 1989.

Holton, Milne. *Cylinder of Vision: The Fiction and Journalistic Writings of Stephen Crane*. Baton Rouge: Louisiana State University Press, 1972.

Levenson, J. C. Introduction. *Tales of Whilomville* xi–lx.

Linder, Lyle. "'The Ideal and the Real' and 'Brer Washington's Consolation': Two Little-Known Stories by Stephen Crane." *American Literary Realism* 11 (1978):1–33.

Solomon, Eric. *Stephen Crane: From Parody to Realism*. Cambridge: Harvard University Press, 1966.

Stallman, R. W. *Stephen Crane: A Biography*. New York: George Braziller, 1968.

Stronks, James B. "Stephen Crane's English Years: The Legend Corrected." *Papers of the Bibliographical Society of America* 57 (1963):340–49.

Wertheim, Stanley, and Paul Sorrentino, eds. *The Correspondence of Stephen Crane*. Vol. 2. New York: Columbia University Press, 1988.

A Little Pilgrim

Publication History

This story first appeared in the July 1900 issue of *Harper's New Monthly Magazine* (101:216–21). It was the final entry in Crane's series of thirteen Whilomville tales that this magazine ran between August 1899 and August 1900. Along with the others in the series, it was then collected in the book *Whilomville Stories*, which Harper & Brothers published in America in August 1900 and in England in November of the same year (Bowers 103). It was placed in volume 5, published in 1926, of *The Work of Stephen Crane* (12 vols., New York: Knopf, 1925–27), edited by Wilson Follett, and it was included as well in *The Complete Short Stories and Sketches of Stephen Crane* (Garden City, N.Y.: Doubleday, 1963), edited by Thomas A. Gullason.

Circumstances of Composition

"A Little Pilgrim" was likely the last written of Crane's tales about various residents of the fictional town of Whilomville. Crane composed it at his final English home, Brede Place, Sussex, evidently in early November 1899. In a letter from that location posted on October 30 of that year, Crane's common-law wife, Cora, sent to his British agent, James Pinker, what is probably the twelfth piece in the series, "The City Urchin and the Chaste Villagers," and in the accompanying letter tells him that "[t]here will be another Whilomville Story for you in four days" (*Correspondence* II, 543). Since all the other Whilomville tales can be accounted for in some fashion, J. C. Levenson and the editors of Crane's correspondence concur that "A Little Pilgrim" is the story promised here (Levenson lv; *Correspondence* II, 543).

Sources and Influences

Crane in his surviving correspondence offers no clue regarding either experiential or literary sources for this story. Nevertheless, it is not difficult to conceive of Crane, a minister's son who seems to have developed an ironic cast of mind almost as soon as he could talk, coming to an early awareness that he was being manipulated by hypocritically pious Sunday-School teachers like the ones who appear in this tale, and likewise recognizing and later parodying the coercion behind the morally pointed stories of children performing self-sacrificing deeds that he would have encountered in such schools and even at home, since his mother was herself a writer of stories of this ilk, with titles on the order of "How Jonathan Saved the Ash Barrel" and "Thanksgiving or Christmas. Which?" ("Cache" 72).

Even though there is no precise source for this tale, Ellen A. Brown and Patricia Hernlund have identified the probable provenance of the name Crane chose for the town in which religious-minded adults practice their not-so-subtle wiles on children. As J. C. Levenson has noted, Crane is likely exploiting the meaning of *whilom*, "once upon a time," to create a sense that the town "exists outside of time, exempt from progress" (xiii); Brown and Hernlund agree with this assessment, but they note in addition that Crane's maternal grandfather, George Peck, and his four brothers had when children formed a family fife-and-drum band that they called "the Whilom Drum Corps." In adulthood these five, all ministers, re-formed this group for family reunions in the 1850s, -60s, and -70s. The young Stephen Crane may have been present at one of these concerts, but even if he was not he certainly had heard about this aggregation from relatives and from an 1897 book, *Luther Peck and His Five Sons*, by his cousin Jonathan Kenyon Peck. It would be logical, Brown and Hernlund conclude, that when Crane turned to writing stories of childhood he would fix on a word that carried familial childhood associations for him (116–18).

Relationship to Other Crane Works

All the Whilomville stories are loosely connected in that all focus on Jimmie Trescott and his family and friends, and in most, as Milne Holton observes, "the pain of . . . experience in Whilomville is remembered pain, [and] the lessons which are intended are never the lessons learned" (223). Certainly these general links are present in "Pilgrim," for the central characters here are Jimmie Trescott and his friend Homer Phelps, who also figures prominently in "The Trial, Execution, and Burial of Homer Phelps," and at the end of the story, when Jimmie finds himself coerced into giving up a Christmas tree and party at two different Sunday-Schools, ostensibly for the sake of the poor but in fact mainly to increase the superintendents' and teachers' smug sense of their own charitable impulses, the narrator says that, "[i]f he remembered Sunday-School at all, it was to remember that he did not like it" (239). The dominance of superintendents and teachers here also creates a more specific connection to one other of the Whilomville stories, "Making an Orator." In the rest of the series, the emphasis is on what children and other groups that lack the power of the white adults who govern Whilomville do among themselves, when those white adults are not around, to create their own hierarchical structure within the larger system. In "Pilgrim" and "Orator," on the other hand, Crane focuses on the tortures that white adults actively put children through in school while misguidedly or hypocritically believing that they are educating their young charges.

Beyond these connections, however, "Pilgrim," with its focus on hypocritical manipulations of God and religion for the sake of self-aggrandizement, seems more closely related to some of the pieces in Crane's first volume of poetry, *The Black Riders*, published in May 1895, than to the other Whilomville stories. Poem 16, for instance, appears to be a less comical handling of the kind of hypocrisy practiced by the superintendents and teachers, particularly in its first three lines:

> Charity, thou art a lie,
> A toy of women,
> A pleasure of certain men. (10)

Similarly, the conclusion of poem 18 seems to be an implicit rebuke to the adults in charge of the school who take great pleasure in contemplating their own charity, for when God in this poem asks some blades of grass what they did, all but one begin to describe their merits. When God asks "'what did you do?'" of this one, it replies,

> "Oh, my lord,
> "Memory is bitter to me
> "For if I did good deeds
> "I know not of them."
> Then God in all His splendor
> Arose from His throne.
> "Oh, best little blade of grass," He said. (11)

Given God's response here, it is no stretch to link the story to poem 32 as well. As Jimmie's Sunday-School teacher expostulates on the difficulties of being good, "the angels, the Sunday-School superintendent, and the teacher" all swim together in the little boys' eyes as beings "so good that if a boy scratched his shin in the same room, he was a profane and sentenced devil" (238). Yet in poem 32 a considerable gulf opens between angels and these earthly paragons holding forth within their church:

> Two or three angels
> Came near to the earth.
> They saw a fat church.
> Little black streams of people
> Came and went in continually.
> And the angels were puzzled
> To know why the people went thus,
> And why they stayed so long within. (19)

At the end of the story, Jimmie, although he is no angel, is evidently puzzled by the same thing.

Critical Studies

Levenson observes that the Whilomville stories collectively present the sunniest vision to be found anywhere in Crane's *oeuvre*, largely because Crane's focus here is on a comfortably middle-class culture as opposed to the more extreme realms that usually occupy his attention. In Whilomville, in contrast to the worlds depicted in most of Crane's work, "[t]he great evils, whether of character or of the cosmos, never come into question, and the lesser evils of sentimentality and foolishness can be corrected by a simple realism" (lv). However, Levenson regards "Pilgrim" as something of a special case, in that in this story Crane is looking beyond his focus on this particular setting and does have some of the larger evils of the cosmos in view. Given that Jimmie's change of churches does not get him the Christmas celebration that he desires, that he finds both churches essentially the same, Levenson sees the point of the story as a lack of differentiation in the spiritual lives of Whilomville's citizens, and he sees this sameness as stemming from a sameness in their middle-class condition. Like the superintendent, Levenson says, no one in this middle-class utopia has ever suffered firsthand from the hunger, thirst, or threat of dishonor that the congregations seek to remedy in far-off locales. By contrast, by the time he wrote this story Crane had himself known ample portions of all three and thus sees Whilomville's comfortable altruism somewhat ambivalently; the story reflects Crane's discovery that "[t]he changelessness of Whilomville, which in moments of reminiscence seemed the very essence of security, was equivocal when looked at from the outside" (lviii–ix).

Most critics concur that at bottom "Pilgrim" is not particularly sunny, but many also see this fact as making the story of a piece with the rest of the series rather than something of an anomaly. Gullason proposes that as a group the Whilomville stories comprise a kind of loose novel that presents "a vibrant and full world" and in so doing effectively "illuminate[s] a number of universal truths about children, family life, and one's former home town" ("True Road" 483); following this line of thought, George Monteiro says that two such truths, the disappointments of childhood and the concomitant hypocrisies of adulthood, run throughout the series and come into particularly sharp focus in "Pilgrim." He notes that the boys' own gestures of charity are hollow but these gestures "have their source in, and are sustained by, adult platitudes of a spuriously religious and pseudo-ethical nature." Thus, Jimmie's involvement with Whilomville's Sunday schools "introduces him to adult hypocrisy, to specious values and disingenuous charity—all of which effectively deny the most salutary meaning of the saw that charity begins at home" (185). Monteiro points to a number of elements that develop these themes: the superintendent's emotional blackmail of the children before he asks for their supposedly free and democratic decision on what to do about Christmas; Crane's reference to Jeremiah 7:14, in which the prophet scorns establishment churches of the sort that dominate Whilomville; and the link of the teacher's pet, Clarence, with whom the other boys plan to settle as soon as school is over, to the lithograph of the martyr St. Stephen that hangs behind the superintendent's desk (188–89).

Gregory Sojka agrees with Monteiro that the theme of this story, as is the case for all the Whilomville tales, is Jimmie's introduction to the hypocrisy of adult society, but he proposes a different interpretation of the lithograph of St. Stephen. Rather than linking this picture to Clarence, whom the class will martyr for his self-satisfiedly correct answers to the teacher's questions, Sojka argues that it is more thematically appropriate to see St. Stephen's martyrdom as a commentary on Jimmie's situation. Sojka points out that this saint was martyred for speaking out against the corrupt forms of worship practiced by the established church, and Jimmie is likewise "martyred" for his resistance to a form of corrupt worship. In support of this view that Crane here intends to keep the reader focused on Jimmie, he notes Crane's alteration of his working title for this story, "A Little Pilgrimage," to one that more strongly emphasizes the protagonist, "A Little Pilgrim" (3).

Eric Solomon, Holton, and Chester L. Wolford likewise identify the child's initiation into adult hypocrisy as the theme of the Whilomville stories in general and "Pilgrim" in particular, but they see additionally in this story a kind of synoptic quality regarding this theme, which they account for by its being the final story of the series. And unlike Sojka, all three regard Jimmie not as a martyr to religious corruption but rather as a willing acolyte. Solomon argues that the stories chronologically delineate Jimmie's growth from an innocent imitator of adult hypocrisies to a full-fledged adult hypocrite in his own right; "Pilgrim" provides the capstone to this movement, for in shifting churches Jimmie shows himself "now able to carry out the kind of conscious deception that his parents use." His disappointment when his "conversion" does not bring the result he desires reveals that he "dislikes the adult world of hypocrisy, gossip and false pride," but his behavior also demonstrates that he is nevertheless now "admirably prepared to enter it" (226–27).

In much the same vein, Holton asserts that here, as in all the Whilomville stories, Jimmie is learning "how to lie—how to misrepresent his intentions—to others and even to himself," with the learning coming more directly in this story than in the others, since here, as part of a class, Jimmie is being directly taught these values rather than simply imitating what he sees adults doing. And it is this directness and Jimmie's response to it that is in Holton's view significant in light of the story's position in the series. Crane's typical narrative pattern, Holton argues, begins with the protagonist's rejecting the values of community and concludes with his return to this community as a more insightful and sympathetic individual, as in "The Open Boat." According to Holton, Jimmie does indeed engage in the typical Crane rejection of his community in the early stories of the Whilomville cycle and in the later ones returns to it, but in this case he has not learned lessons of understanding and sympathy but rather has learned how to rejoin society simply by adopting the duplicities the members of this society practice on others and on themselves. In this final story, Holton says, with its concentration on religious indoctrination underlain by hypocrisy and Jimmie's own self-deceiving reaction to this teaching, Jimmie has learned all the lessons his community has to teach: he has surrendered his intellectual and spiritual autonomy and become a confirmed citizen of Whilomville (223). Similarly, Wolford says that, because this story concerns adults making themselves happy by coercing children to sacrifice their treat, it encompasses "all the meanness, the tribalism, the communal degradation of individuality, and the brainwashing cruelty of society" presented in the rest of the stories and "casts a religious light" on these things. Crane's focus on the Sunday school moves this last story, in Wolford's view, "from a depiction of child-like discomfort to communal repression, and perhaps contains a metaphor for the oppression humanity forces on itself" (60).

Works Cited

Bowers, Fredson. Textual Introduction. *Tales of Whilomville*. Vol. 7 of The University of Virginia Edition of *The Works of Stephen Crane*. Ed. Fredson Bowers. Charlottesville: University Press of Virginia, 1968, 103–26.

Brown, Ellen A., and Patricia Hernlund. "The Source of the Title of Stephen Crane's *Whilomville Stories*." *American Literature* 50:116–18.

Gullason, Thomas A. "A Cache of Short Stories by Stephen Crane's Family." *Studies in Short Fiction* 23:71–106.

———. "Stephen Crane's Short Stories: The True Road." *Stephen Crane's Career: Perspectives and Evaluations*. Ed. Thomas A. Gullason. New York: New York University Press, 1972. 470–86.

Holton, Milne. *Cylinder of Vision: The Fiction and Journalistic Writings of Stephen Crane*. Baton Rouge: Louisiana State University Press, 1972.

Levenson, J. C. Introduction. *Tales of Whilomville* xi–lx.

Monteiro, George. "Whilomville as Judah: Crane's 'A Little Pilgrimage.'" *Renascence* 19 (1967):184–89.

Sojka, Gregory S. "Stephen Crane's 'A Little Pilgrim': Whilomville's Young Martyr." *Notes on Modern American Literature* 3 (1977):3.

Solomon, Eric. *Stephen Crane: From Parody to Realism*. Cambridge: Harvard University Press, 1966.

Wertheim, Stanley, and Paul Sorrentino, eds. *The Correspondence of Stephen Crane*. Vol. 2. New York: Columbia University Press, 1988.

Wolford, Chester L. *Stephen Crane: A Study of the Short Fiction*. Boston: Twayne, 1989.

The Little Regiment

Publication History

This story was first published in America in the June 1896 issue of *McClure's Magazine* (7:12–22); it ran in England in the *Chapman's Magazine* number for that same month (4:214–32). It then became the title story of the book *"The Little Regiment" and Other Episodes of the American Civil War*, published in America by D. Appleton in October 1896 and in England by Heinemann in February 1897 (Bowers xliv). Pioneering Crane editor Wilson Follett included it in volume 2, published in 1925, of *The Work of Stephen Crane* (12 vols., New York: Knopf, 1925–27), and it appeared as well in *The Complete Short Stories and Sketches of Stephen Crane* (Garden City, N.Y.: Doubleday, 1963), edited by Thomas A. Gullason.

Circumstances of Composition

In October 1895, Crane left New York City for his brother Edmund's home in the rural town of Hartwood, where he remained, for the most part, through February 1896. His primary purpose in making this move was to find enough peaceful time to finish his novel *The Third Violet*, but the McClure newspaper syndicate had asked him for more Civil War material to follow up on the current success of *The Red Badge of Courage*, and so he also turned out five such stories, including "The Little Regiment," during this sojourn (Colvert xiii–xiv). James B. Colvert says Crane began this particular story in November and finished it in February (xiv–xv); in any case, he was verifiably at work on it in January, for in a letter of January 7 from Hartwood to a New York City friend, Willis Brooks Hawkins, Crane complains, "I am writing a story—'The Little Regiment'—for McClure. It is awfully hard. I have invented the sum of my invention in regard to war and this story keeps me in internal despair. However I am coming on with it very comfortably after all" (*Correspondence* I, 175). And on January 27 he tells S. S. McClure, the head of the syndicate, "I am getting the Fredericksburg row [by which he means 'Little Regiment'] into shape" (*Correspondence* I, 192). The February completion date is bolstered by another letter, this one dated February 15, 1896, in which Crane, in response to a request for information from the periodical *The Critic*, says that he is now finishing "a novelette for S. S. McClure called The Little Regiment," though the use of the term *novelette* makes it uncertain whether Crane is here referring to the story or the collection to which the story ultimately gave its name. Be this as it may, Crane's opinion of his work seems here to have altered from that expressed to Hawkins in January, for he goes on to say that this "novelette" is "my work at it's [sic] best I think and is positively my last thing dealing with battle" (*Correspondence* I, 205).

Sources and Influences

As Crane's letter to McClure quoted above makes clear, the battle in "The Little Regiment" is based on Fredericksburg, a Union defeat fought on December 13, 1862. John Phillips of the Phillips and McClure syndicate had suggested in the fall of 1895 that Crane, now an acclaimed Civil War writer thanks to *Red Badge*, might produce a series of nonfiction pieces about various Civil War battlefields. Crane replied on December 30 that he felt this project would be too great an undertaking, requiring visits to the battlefields during the season in which the battles took place, a good deal of research, and a strong will to brace up against the accusations of inaccuracy that he envisioned coming from every general upon whose head he "did not place the only original crown of pure gold" (*Correspondence* I, 161).

Nevertheless, because the season was right Crane did journey to Virginia in January to study the Fredericksburg and Chancellorsville fields and interview some Confederate veterans (Stallman 194, Katz in Lawrence 26), an expedition that only convinced him he was correct in his judgment that the sketches would entail more research than he was willing to undertake at that point, given his desire to finish *The Third Violet* as soon as possible. He therefore chose to write Civil War stories instead, which, being "invented things," in Robert W. Stallman's words (194), required far less in the way of background study. But he made such research as he had done pay off by using it in "The Little Regiment" to frame the conflict between the Dempster brothers; C. B. Ives notes that the setting and troop movements Crane describes correspond closely to the circumstances of Fredericksburg (249–55) and that a number of specific references make clear that the Dempsters' regiment is modeled on the 69th New York, the famed "Fighting 69th," even though Crane does not name the battle and the regiment because he wishes to universalize the situation, to convey the sense that "in praising these good soldiers he [is] praising all good soldiers" (259).

As Ives points out, however, Crane did not accrue all this information simply by walking around the battlefield and talking to some veterans; a good deal of reading in both history and fiction probably lay behind it as well. Ives notes Crane's well-documented reading of *Century* magazine's four-volume *Battles and Leaders of the Civil War*, and he suggests that for specific details about Fredericksburg Crane may also have consulted the U. S. government's official report, *The War of the Rebellion: A Compilation of the Official Records of the Union and Confederate Armies* (247–48). Also worthy of consideration are the various novels and memoirs that have been suggested as possible sources for *Red Badge* and thus for Crane's Civil War writings as a whole: John W. DeForest's *Miss Ravenel's Conversion From Secession to Loyalty* (O'Donnell 578), Frank Wilkeson's *Recollections of a Private Soldier in the Army of the Potomac*, Warren Goss's *Recollections of a Private*, Wilbur F. Hinman's *The Adventures of Corporal Si Klegg and His Pard*, the frequent Civil War articles that ran in *Harper's Weekly* in the 1880s and -90s, and Ambrose Bierce's *Tales of Soldiers and Civilians* (Ahnebrink 97).

Of this group, Bierce's work is most likely as a specific source for "Little Regiment," since, as Lars Ahnebrink points out, like Bierce, Crane here focuses on the ugly aspects of war; both authors employ a style that works by giving "a few vivid impressions" rather than "elaborate and exact details"; and both are chiefly concerned with "the impact of war on the individual consciousness" (351). A further point of resemblance is that like Crane in this story Bierce sometimes concentrates not on a single protagonist but on a pair of estranged relatives or friends whose conflict is set in the larger context of the war, although in most cases Bierce does not provide the kind of reconciliation that concludes "Little Regiment." Such stories in Bierce's volume include "A Horseman in the Sky," "The Coup de Grâce," and "An Affair of Outposts."

Relationship to Other Crane Works

As Gullason notes, all the stories in the volume to which "The Little Regiment" gives title are related by virtue of their varied subject matter within the overall framework of the Civil War. In their disparate focuses on soldiers in battle, young and old civilians behind the lines, potential lovers on opposite sides, and veterans in the postwar era, Gullason says, these stories approximate "the life and scope of a novel," revealing Crane's "growing awareness of larger possibilities for the single story, as well as for a collection of stories" (474). Regarding more specific relationships between "Little Regiment" and the other pieces in this volume, Chester L. Wolford sees this story as most closely connected to "A Grey Sleeve," in that both examine "the parallel between private attachments and public" ones in a wartime environment (63). Donald B. Gibson agrees with this view and adds a third story, "Three Miraculous Soldiers," to this group, but he does not regard this connection as positive. In their examination of private and public attachments, he says, all three of these stories remain superficial, giving little attention to plot or character development and aiming only at evoking a "stock response" of sentimentality from readers (97).

Three other critics regard "Little Regiment" more favorably in examining its relationship to *Red Badge*. Stallman links Dan Dempster to Henry Fleming, asserting that Dan's "fervid insubordination, an almost religious reluctance to obey the new corporal's orders," resembles Henry's "religious reluctance to follow the example of Jim Conklin—Christ in the Army of the Lord," a reluctance that in both cases the protagonist finally overcomes (175). James Nagel sees the story's "impressionistic style" as deriving from Crane's approach in *Red Badge*; he also says that the relationship between the Dempster brothers is another example of the "theme of psychological growth toward confidence and compassion" that Crane first examined in this novel through Henry and Wilson ("Stories of War" 7). Conversely, Ives sees Dan not as a continuation of Henry but rather as a break from him; he regards the story as marking a significant shift from *Red Badge* in Crane's understanding of the nature of courage. Crane, he says, is deeply denigratory toward Henry's acts of supposed courage in the second half of the novel owing to his own imperfect grasp of the close relationship between fear and bravery, but in "The Little Regiment" Crane diffidently atoned for his previous cynicism by linking the "self-mockery" of the men in this regiment to their "acts of extraordinary bravery . . . to show . . . that fear and courage are inseparable" (259).

Rather than looking to earlier works, Marston LaFrance examines the relationship between this story and Crane's later war writings. In his formulation, "The Little Regiment" is the first in a group of stories concentrating on the brotherhood of men in war, the others being "The Price of the Harness," "Virtue in War," "The Second Generation," and "The Clan of No-Name." All of these fall short of Crane's best work, LaFrance says, "because Crane has too much to say in them; he becomes so emotionally aroused by his subject that he loses his artistic detachment, and the prose becomes implicit propaganda seasoned with explicit preaching" (181). And within this group, he concludes, "The Little Regiment" is the weakest due to its having been written, unlike the others, before Crane saw combat for himself, a circumstance that produces two negative effects. First, his view of men in battle is even more sentimental here than in the other pieces. Second, and perhaps more significant, this story lacks the leavening of realism in the later stories that resulted from his discovery in the Spanish-American War that regulars in battle must contend not only with the enemy but also with the well-meaning but incompetent volunteer troops in their own army and, worse, with the "moral foe of infamy in those personally dishonest people on their own side who, both at the front and at home, have wormed themselves into responsible positions" (182).

E. R. Hagemann, on the other hand, sees "The Little Regiment" as showing in two respects the continuity between the war fiction Crane wrote before seeing battle firsthand and that which came after this experience. Citing "A Mystery of Heroism" as another pre-observation example and "Harness" as a post-observation case, Hagemann says that in his depiction of the destruction of the trees by the Union artillery in "The Little Regiment" Crane develops his frequent theme of men's ability to ravage nature with their machines of war (356). And in line with this idea of war as a matter of machines, Hagemann sees this story as partaking of Crane's pervasive view of the individual in battle as simply a dehumanized cog in the largest war machine of all, the army, an idea first brought up in *The Red Badge* and carried all the way into one of his last war stories, "The Kicking Twelfth" (358).

Critical Studies

Colvert emphasizes Crane's difficulties with writing this story, well documented in the letters cited above in the "Circumstances of Composition" section, and speculates that these problems may partly have stemmed from Crane's belief that *Red Badge*, with its impressionistic characteristics, violated what he regarded as his literary theory of documentary realism, derived from two of his early mentors, Hamlin Garland and William Dean Howells. Their ideas were in fact "largely irrelevant to his vision and aims as a writer," but Crane failed to realize that this was the case and so felt that writing more Civil War stories simply compounded "the literary error to which *The Red Badge* already stood as a conspicuous monument" (xiv). Colvert couples this possibility with another source, also linked to *Red Badge*, for Crane's reluctance: his difficulty in "Little Regiment" in "adapting his rhetorical materials to a situation intended to reveal character." The focus of the story, Colvert says, is the Dempster brothers' true affection for another beneath their incessant sniping, with the war setting entering in only to afford "the crisis of danger" that forces them to reveal their true feelings. However, Colvert argues, Crane is unable to describe this setting in the muted, backdrop way appropriate to his needs; instead, despite its essential irrelevance to his plot he attempts "to impose his reflexive style on an ineffectively conceived subject": he makes the war his "familiar symbol of a radical violence in nature, fulsomely described in Crane's characteristic imagery and rhetoric of the haunted landscape," a technique that blurs his focus on the brothers (xxviii). (Colvert also offers this assessment on p. 142 of a slightly later essay, "Stephen Crane: Style as Invention.")

Most other critics are in accord with Colvert's judgment of the story as a failure, some offering evidence very similar to his and others proffering a variety of other explanations for this state of affairs. Gullason like Colvert sees rhetorical problems as the cause, citing Crane's overwriting, editorializing, lack of movement in describing the action of the story, failure to develop the brothers' relationship fully enough, and, closest to Colvert's view, his "faulty counterpointing between the men [i.e., the Dempsters] and the regiment" (475). In the same vein, Gibson cites Crane's lack of clear focus, his failure to develop an intrinsic connection between the sections of the story that deal with the Dempster brothers and those that deal with the regiment as a whole (97).

Taking a somewhat different approach, Maxwell Geismar calls attention to what he regards as evidence in "Little Regiment" of an unwholesome evolution in Crane's ideology; he asserts that Crane's celebration of the machine-like professionalism of veteran soldiers here is a step down from his exploration of the more human Henry Fleming in *Red Badge*. "Little Regiment" reveals, he says, a "hardening and stratification of an attitude toward war (and toward the fresh and original amateur soldiers in Crane's own work) that one notices also in Kipling. . . . Here Crane descended to the rhetoric of heroism or the fervor almost of the dime novel" (90–91). Wolford also identifies Crane's ideology as a source of artistic problems, but he focuses on a literary rather than a military form. He sees "Little Regiment" as one of Crane's experiments in Naturalism (most of the others being Bowery sketches), in that the protagonists here are not portrayed as "isolated individuals," as Henry Fleming is, but rather as members of a group, with Crane's goal being to present "a variation on the theme of the egotism necessary for living" that he delineates most clearly in "The Blue Hotel." Billie and Dan Dempster reconcile, Wolford argues, as a result of realizing their own insignificance in the massive chaos of war—something the Swede in "Blue Hotel" is never able to do with anyone—and Crane intends the aggregate character of the regiment as a larger example of the same impulse, stemming from humans' need to "attach themselves to something outside themselves in order to create order and a sense of importance" (62–63). However, Wolford concludes, Crane fails to accomplish these aims because his "talent and vision were not amenable to naturalistic methods"—because he does not create memorable characters undergoing this process of recognition and reconciliation but rather only "undifferentiated naturalistic types" (62). Milne Holton sees the story as more of a piece with Crane's mainstream *oeuvre* than Geismar and Wolford do, pointing out that it can be read as one of many examples of Crane's continuing interest in duality of vision, in this case with the duality between "the private sensibility and the public assertions about war" and that between "the self as it apprehends reality and the self as it presents itself to be apprehended," but he also rates the story as one of Crane's less successful explorations of this subject (141).

Dissenting views concerning the merits of "Little Regiment" come from Daniel Aaron, Nagel, and Bettina Knapp. In contrast to Geismar, Aaron praises Crane's ideology here, seeing maturity rather than stratification in Crane's tribute to the "chastened and seasoned brotherhood" of veterans, men who, admirably unlike Henry Fleming, "have no illusions about their importance to the universe" and see themselves as integral parts of the regiment, which they venerate above their individualities and which is a machine in a positive sense, "welded . . . by the flame of discipline, loyalty, and experience" (218). Nagel lauds the story as a prime example of Crane's frequent use of patterns of animal imagery in his war stories to characterize "behavior lacking compassion" (*Impressionism* 138), and, responding explicitly to Gibson's assessment of the story as lacking in plot and character, he notes that the story unfolds in eight episodes that have their own themes and techniques but also effectively integrate and counterpoint the conflict between the Dempster brothers and the larger fratricidal conflict of the Civil War. The first episode links these conflicts by demonstrating that both take place in "an insensitive and indifferent universe"; the second and third delineate the brothers' separate concerns for one another; the fourth through seventh initiate the brothers into the ferocity of battle and the concomitant insignificance of the individual, realizations that lead them to recognize their concern for one another; and the eighth depicts their understated reunion in a scene "enriched by duality: joy submerged in indifference, near-hate fused to brotherly love, joy of survival set amid mass destruction, and psychological conflict imbedded in a vast physical struggle" ("Stories of War" 7). Knapp focuses her praise more narrowly, on Crane's effective use of fog on the battlefield to symbolize "the sense of mystery surrounding the brothers' relationship." Just as the soldiers' vision of the world in which they move is veiled by the fog, the brothers fail to see the reality of their fraternity; each "lives blanketed in his own repressed world, ashamed of revealing his true feelings to the other for fear of being accused of weakness" (164).

Works Cited

Aaron, Daniel. *The Unwritten War*. New York: Alfred A. Knopf, 1973.

Ahnebrink, Lars. *The Beginnings of Naturalism in American Fiction*. Cambridge: Harvard University Press, 1950.

Bowers, Fredson. Textual Introduction. *Tales of War*. Vol. 6 of The University of Virginia Edition of *The Works of Stephen Crane*. Ed. Fredson Bowers. Charlottesville: University Press of Virginia, 1970, xxxvii–cxci.

Colvert, James B. Introduction. *Tales of War* xi–xxxvi.

———. "Stephen Crane: Style as Invention." *Stephen Crane in Transition: Centenary Essays*. Ed. Joseph Katz. DeKalb: Northern Illinois University Press, 1972. 127–52.

Geismar, Maxwell. *Rebels and Ancestors*. Boston: Houghton Mifflin, 1953.

Gibson, Donald B. *The Fiction of Stephen Crane*. Carbondale: Southern Illinois University Press, 1968.

Gullason, Thomas A. "Stephen Crane's Short Stories: The True Road." *Stephen Crane's Career: Perspectives and Evaluations*. Ed. Thomas A. Gullason. New York: New York University Press, 1972, 470–86.

Hagemann, E. R. "Crane's 'Real' War in His Short Stories." *American Quarterly* 8 (1956):356–67.

Holton, Milne. *Cylinder of Vision: The Fiction and Journalistic Writings of Stephen Crane*. Baton Rouge: Louisiana State University Press, 1972.

Ives, C. B. "'The Little Regiment' of Stephen Crane at the Battle of Fredericksburg." *Midwest Quarterly* 8 (1967):247–60.

Katz, Joseph. Introduction and Notes. *The Real Stephen Crane*. By Frederic M. Lawrence. Newark: Newark Public Library, 1980.

Knapp, Bettina L. *Stephen Crane*. New York: Ungar, 1987.

LaFrance, Marston. *A Reading of Stephen Crane*. Oxford: Clarendon, 1971.

Nagel, James. *Stephen Crane and Literary Impressionism*. University Park: Pennsylvania State University Press, 1980.

———. "Stephen Crane's Stories of War: A Study of Art and Theme." *North Dakota Quarterly* 43 (1975):5–19.

O'Donnell, Thomas F. "De Forest, Van Petten, and Stephen Crane." *American Literature* 27 (1956):578–80.

Stallman, R. W. *Stephen Crane: A Biography*. New York: George Braziller, 1968.

Wertheim, Stanley, and Paul Sorrentino, eds. *The Correspondence of Stephen Crane*. Vol. 1. New York: Columbia University Press, 1988.

Wolford, Chester L. *Stephen Crane: A Study of the Short Fiction*. Boston: Twayne, 1989.

The Lone Charge of William B. Perkins

Publication History

This story made its first appearance in England, in the January 2, 1899, edition of the *Westminster Gazette* (13.1819:1–2). It first ran in America seven months later, in the issue of *McClure's Magazine* for July 1899 (13:279–82). It was then included in the book *Wounds in the Rain*, published in America in September 1900 by Frederick A. Stokes and in England that same month by Methuen (Bowers cix). Wilson Follett placed it in volume 9, which he edited and published in 1926, of *The Work of Stephen Crane* (12 vols., New York: Knopf, 1925–27), and it appeared again in 1963 in *The Complete Short Stories and Sketches of Stephen Crane* (Garden City, N.Y.: Doubleday), edited by Thomas A. Gullason.

Circumstances of Composition

"The Lone Charge of William B. Perkins" was one of a number of pieces Crane composed while he lived in Havana, Cuba, after the close of the Spanish-American War, which he had covered as a reporter first for Joseph Pulitzer's *New York World* and then William Randolph Hearst's *New York Journal*. Crane was in Puerto Rico when the fighting ended on August 12, 1898; he then went to Havana as soon as possible. He remained there, living quietly, first in a hotel and then in a lodging-house, writing steadily all the while, until around December 24 of that year. He apparently preferred this mode of life to an immediate resumption of his existence with his common-law wife, Cora, in England, where he faced considerable debts and what he seems to have regarded as burdensome domestic and social obligations. He did not return to face these difficulties until January 11, 1899 (Stallman 413–42).

In a letter from Havana dated September 14, 1898, Crane tells his agent, Paul Revere Reynolds, that he is sending "The Lone Charge" in a separate envelope and recommends that Reynolds try to sell it in America to the McClure syndicate, which did buy it, and in England to *Blackwood's Magazine*, which turned it down (*Correspondence* II, 369). On the basis of this letter and the lack of mention of any stories predating this one in Crane's correspondence from Havana, Fredson Bowers and the editors of Crane's letters agree that this was the first story about the Spanish-American War he wrote during his sojourn in Cuba (Bowers cviii; *Correspondence* II, 369).

Sources and Influences

Stanley Wertheim and Paul Sorrentino note that Crane based "The Lone Charge" on the experience of a fellow-correspondent in the Spanish-American War, Ralph D. Paine (*Correspondence* II, 369). As Paine later recounted this event in his 1922 memoir, *Roads of Adventure*, which he dedicated to Crane's memory, it occurred in June 1898, during the skirmishing following the landing of the U. S. Marines at Guantánamo Bay. At one point Paine borrowed a rifle and went after what he thought was a Spanish sniper in the bushes at the perimeter of an American encampment. He found no sniper, but he did find himself, with an empty rifle, caught in a murderous crossfire when Spanish troops suddenly attacked the camp. The nearest cover he could find was a discarded sugar boiler; he crawled into it and stayed there until the attack was repulsed (251–56).

Crane altered this incident only slightly in turning it into "The Lone Charge," making Perkins somewhat more naive about military operations and the nature of heroism than Paine himself actually was. Gullason suggests that this modification reflects Crane's disgust with his wartime employers, Joseph Pulitzer and William Randolph Hearst, for demanding that their correspondents emphasize sensationalism over accuracy in their reportage, since the former sold more newspapers than the latter. Perkins's ignorance, Gullason says, is a slap at newspaper editors' habit of worrying more about a correspondent's ability to write inspiringly purple prose than about his ability to understand and intelligently describe the military operations he was to cover (206).

Relationship to Other Crane Works

James B. Colvert cites "The Lone Charge" as a prime example of Crane's tendency when writing war stories based on actual experience to focus on things he had already imagined in his earlier, pre-eyewitness war fiction, since this story is in many respects an adaptation of some of the elements of *The Red Badge of Courage* to comic effect. Both stories, Colvert notes, give us

[t]he vainglorious hero, the wild assault upon the concealed enemy, the mystical aspect of the adversary, the sudden panic, the yearning vision of a reassuring, idyllic nature, the retreat to the degraded temple, [and] the reconstruction of pride to humility. (xxxiv–xxxv)

(Colvert makes the same point in a slightly later essay, "Stephen Crane: Style as Invention"; he also notes here that in his boastfulness and the subsequent deflation of his ego Perkins harks back to the prideful, hapless character known only as "the little man," the protagonist of some of Crane's earliest fiction, the Sullivan County sketches [150].)

Chester L. Wolford links this story to another of Crane's Civil War pieces written before he had acquired any firsthand knowledge of combat, "A Mystery of Heroism," in that in both cases the protagonist makes a foolhardy gesture under enemy fire but manages to return safely to his own lines, with the narrator commenting more or less directly on the absurdity of a concept of heroism that drives men to such behavior. A major difference between the two, however, is that while the comrades of Fred Collins, the protagonist of "Mystery," cheer his return and acclaim him a hero even if the narrator does not, no one cheers Perkins; the marines with whom he is associated would not have noticed had he been killed in his wild charge, and they call him "'that crazy man'" when he makes his way back. The result of this change—possibly a function of Crane's having seen between the composition of these two stories how men under fire actually regard foolhardy gestures—is that the absurdity is presented more emphatically in "The Lone Charge" than in "Mystery" (70).

E. R. Hagemann notes another change possibly explicable by Crane's having observed combat for himself: the awareness manifested in this story—and also in two other pieces in *Wounds in the Rain*, "The Price of the Harness" and "'God Rest Ye, Merry Gentlemen'"—of the attraction violence holds for many soldiers. Calling this attraction "the common and all-important . . . concomitant of war," Hagemann asserts that these stories constitute

a signal act of recognition on [Crane's] part that the simple brutal act of killing, the manipulation of the weapons of destruction, the sense of being in the presence of death—all of these and more—bring a terrifying feeling of joy, nay elation, to a man at war. (359)

Critical Studies

Only two critics have considered the merits of this story apart from its links to other Crane works. Milne Holton rates it one of the least successful of Crane's many depictions of "the gratuitousness of the events of war," owing to its lack of clarity about the significance of these events. The reader sees Perkins's experience clearly enough, Holton says, but Crane offers no clues as to what he makes of that experience (257). James Nagel is more positive, regarding this lack of clues as itself the significance of the story. Pointing to Perkins's seemingly ludicrous mistaking of a palm branch for a Spaniard, a mistake resulting from his agitated state of mind, Nagel says that this error is emblematic of "the unreliability of empirical data" in the world as a whole, a problem that besets almost all of Crane's protagonists in their efforts to make sense of their experience. The reader is not given an understanding of what sense Perkins makes of events because ethics is not Crane's concern; his focus is on epistemology. This orientation, Nagel argues, makes Crane an Impressionist rather than a Realist, for Realists assume that objective truth can be apprehended, whereas Impressionists reject that assumption, as Crane does here (93).

Works Cited

Bowers, Fredson. Textual Introduction. *Tales of War*. Vol. 8 of The University of Virginia Edition of *The Works of Stephen Crane*. Ed. Fredson Bowers. Charlottesville: University Press of Virginia, 1970, xxxvii–cxci.

Colvert, James B. Introduction. *Tales of War* xi–xxxvi.

———. "Stephen Crane: Style as Invention." *Stephen Crane in Transition: Centenary Essays*. Ed. Joseph Katz. DeKalb: Northern Illinois University Press, 1972, 127–52.

Crane, Stephen. "The Lone Charge of William B. Perkins." *Tales of War* 114–18.

Gullason, Thomas A. "Stephen Crane's Private War on Yellow Journalism." *Huntington Library Quarterly* 22 (1958):201–08.

Hagemann, E. R. "Crane's 'Real' War in his Short Stories." *American Quarterly* 8 (1956):356–67.

Holton, Milne. *Cylinder of Vision: The Fiction and Journalistic Writings of Stephen Crane*. Baton Rouge: Louisiana State University Press, 1972.

Nagel, James. *Stephen Crane and Literary Impressionism*. University Park: Pennsylvania State University Press, 1980.

Paine, Ralph D. *Roads of Adventure*. Boston: Houghton, 1922.

Stallman, R. W. *Stephen Crane: A Biography*. New York: George Braziller, 1968.

Wertheim, Stanley, and Paul Sorrentino, eds. *The Correspondence of Stephen Crane*. Vol. 2. New York: Columbia University Press, 1988.

Wolford, Chester L. *Stephen Crane: A Study of the Short Fiction*. Boston: Twayne, 1989.

The Lover and the Tell-Tale

Publication History

This story was initially published in the October 1899 issue of *Harper's New Monthly Magazine* (99:759–63), the third installment of the thirteen-part series of Crane tales set in the fictional town of Whilomville that this magazine ran between August 1899 and August 1900. Like all the pieces in this series, the story was then collected in the book *Whilomville Stories*, which Harper & Brothers published in America in August 1900 and in England in November of the same year (Bowers 103). It appeared in volume 5, published in 1926, of *The Work of Stephen Crane* (12 vols., New York: Knopf, 1925–27), edited by William Follett; and Thomas A. Gullason included it in his 1963 *Complete Short Stories and Sketches of Stephen Crane* (Garden City, N.Y.: Doubleday).

Circumstances of Composition

"The Lover and the Tell-Tale" was the third to be written in the Whilomville series; Crane identifies it as such in two letters announcing its completion, one to his brother William and the other to his American agent, Paul Revere Reynolds (*Correspondence* II, 446–47). Since Crane wrote these letters from his final English home, Brede Place, in Sussex, he evidently composed the story there—at some point, as J. C. Levenson notes, between January 31, 1899, the date on which he submitted the second tale, "The Angel-Child," to Reynolds, and March 2 of that year, the date of the letters (xlvii). He may, however, have finished it as early as February 7, since he gave the original manuscript of it to friends, the Pease family, around that date (*Correspondence* II, 431).

Sources and Influences

The genesis of this story appears to have been a real-life crush that developed in the household that Crane and his common-law wife, Cora, established in England in 1898–99. While Crane himself was away covering the Spanish-American War, Michael Pease, the eleven-year-old son of friends of the Cranes, fell in love with seven-year-old Helen Frederic, a Crane houseguest because of the recent death of her father, the writer Harold Frederic, another friend of the Cranes. Upon his return, Crane heard about this turn of events and fairly quickly worked them into a story. The evidence for this source is a letter of February 7, 1899, from Cora to Michael Pease's mother, Margery, which accompanied the manuscript of another Whilomville story, "The Angel-Child," sent as a gift from the Cranes to the Pease family. Cora notes that the Peases have already been presented with the manuscript of "The Lover and the Tell-Tale" and explains that the enclosed manuscript of "Angel" is "a little story that comes before Michael's 'story.' I thought you would like them both. You can see that Michael for the moment is 'Jimmie' and he writes to 'The Angel Child'" (*Correspondence* II, 431).

In a letter of November 11, 1948, to Crane scholar Melvin H. Schoberlin, Michael Pease himself confirms Cora's identifications; he notes that Jimmie Trescott's letter declaring his love to Cora may be a verbatim transcript of the one he wrote to Helen Frederic (Levenson xlv–xlvi). However, he seems to reverse himself in subsequent remarks to Robert W. Stallman: "I'm afraid the story of the Tell Tale, the fight, and the School Mistress was Stephen Crane's romance—or rather, I should say the hero was not me" (qtd. in Stallman 449). On the basis of Crane's own identification with Jimmie and Cora's with the angel-child in other stories, Stallman agrees, asserting that "Jimmie Trescott was Stephen Crane in his Port Jervis [New York] boyhood, and little Cora was Cora Crane" (449).

However, Pease's statements are not as self-contradictory as they initially sound if we bear in mind Crane's usual practice of weaving together strands of his own and other people's experiences and memories in his Whilomville pieces. Crane may well have drawn the basic situation of this story from the Pease-Frederic liaison and then amplified it with incidents out of his own past or imagination, such as those Michael Pease mentions to Stallman as not having befallen him: Rose Goldege's tattling, Jimmie's assault upon his male classmates, and his teacher's forcing him to stay after school for refusing to tattle himself on those with whom he fought. It seems certain at least that Rose Goldege came out of Crane's personal experience, for this child is, as Levenson notes, a junior version of the "backbiting female gossip who occupied so special a place among Crane's dislikes" (xlvi) and who appears in many acid-drenched incarnations in Crane's various works, the most notable being the saber-tongued Martha Goodwin in "The Monster."

Only one critic, Eric Solomon, raises the possibility of literary antecedents for "Tell-Tale," noting that a boy's writing a love letter to his sweetheart and being forced to endure ridicule as a result was a common plot in the juvenile fiction of Crane's period. However, Solomon continues, Crane places his own stamp on this situation by refusing to take the conventional approach of presenting it comically and sentimentally. Instead, he uses it "to comment on the savage behavior of society . . . toward one who goes his own way" (213).

Relationship to Other Crane Works

All the Whilomville stories are loosely connected in that all focus on Jimmie Trescott and his family and friends, but "Tell-Tale" is more closely linked to two others in particular, "The Angel-Child" and "The Stove," because these three work variations on the same subjects: Jimmie's love-hate relationship with Cora, his pretty and spoiled cousin from the city, and the havoc Cora wreaks in both the child and adult worlds of Whilomville. "Tell-Tale" differs from those other two, however, since in this story unlike the others Cora is not the direct cause of the trouble; in fact, she does not even appear. Here, rather, it is another little girl, Rose Goldege, who brings suffering and adult punishment on Jimmie by ridiculing him for writing a love letter to Cora, which leads to general mockery, Jimmie's resorting to physical violence to recover his reputation, and his being kept after school for fighting.

The centrality in this story of the behavior of Rose and the other children and Jimmie's desperate response to it prompts Chester L. Wolford to link "Tell-Tale" thematically to another Whilomville story, "'Showin' Off,'" wherein Jimmie and another boy, Horace Glenn, compete for social standing and the affections of a little girl by boasting about their ability to perform progressively more dangerous stunts on their velocipedes. In both these cases, Wolford says, Crane shows "the power of communal standards over individual behavior." The main difference between the two, he continues, resides in the fact that in "Tell-Tale" the punishment comes actively and directly from the girl herself, whereas in "'Showin' Off'" the loser, Horace, brings his punishment on himself through his efforts to impress the disdainful girl (56).

The character of Rose also ties "Tell-Tale" to "The Monster," as briefly noted above. This girl is, in Wolford's words, "a miniature bastion of Whilomville's morality" (56), a morality that the narrator of "Tell-Tale" points out reposes in the bosoms of a group of widows and spinsters and takes the form of smug self-satisfaction regarding their own sins coupled with eagerness to gossip about the supposed sins of others, such backbiting being "the principal and solitary joy which enter[s] their lonely lives" (145). As a child of this group, Rose is a junior version of fractious, sharp-tongued Martha Goodwin in "Monster," although Crane seems to see Martha as at least possessing the redeeming trait of refusing to go along with most of the townspeople's hysterical fear of Henry Johnson, whereas Rose has no admirable qualities at all.

Critical Studies

As the foregoing discussion of children's aping adults' conformist, communal mentality suggests, many critics agree that this is the central theme of "Tell-

Tale," as it is in most of the stories in this series. Indeed, the prevalence of this theme in most of the stories is one of the strongest pieces of evidence for Gullason's argument that as a group the Whilomville stories constitute a kind of loose novel that presents "a vibrant and full world" and in so doing effectively "illuminate[s] a number of universal truths about children, family life, and one's former home town" (483). For Stallman, the particular variation that "Tell-Tale" works on the theme of children's cruelty to one another as a parallel to the behavior of adults is a presentation of a microcosm of mob mentality, in that when Jimmie's enemies make fun of him for writing the note his supposed friends get caught up in this action and turn on him as well (481). Milne Holton sees the children's response here as more deliberately motivated, regarding it as an example of the ways in which the children's community of Whilomville, like its adult model, "imposes rigid demands upon the behavior and imaginations of its members." The children should be using their imagination to develop their own code of conduct, but instead they surrender their imaginative faculties and devote most of their time and energy to learning how to imitate the adults' code and to punishing those who refuse to accede to this code, just as their parents do. Jimmie's treatment illustrates "how ridicule is used to inhibit the expression of feelings and to enforce conformity," while Rose Goldege exemplifies the community's conditioning of the individual's imagination, since in being a tell-tale she is simply acting out what she has learned from her gossiping, financially embarrassed but socially proud female relations (218). Solomon in effect synthesizes Stallman's and Holton's views; he notes that Crane's presentation of Rose's behavior as an imitation of that of her relatives indicts the adult society of Whilomville and in so doing reveals "a world where children repeat the age-old unpleasant roles of mob and victim" (216).

Levenson argues that this presentation of Rose as just doing what she has been conditioned to do indicates sympathy for her on Crane's part (xlvi), a view that is not surprising given Levenson's opinion that the Whilomville stories as a group offer the sunniest vision of all Crane's works due to their focus on a comfortably middle-class culture, in which "[t]he great evils, whether of character or of the cosmos, never come into question, and the lesser evils of sentimentality and foolishness can be corrected by a simple realism" (lv). However, Wolford, like Stallman, Holton, and Solomon, rejects any such intimation that these stories are in any sense an idealization of small-town life. The community of Whilomville, in his view, is presented as inherently paradoxical: its supposed goal is to ameliorate the barbarism and chaos manifested in the children's behavior, yet this behavior is in fact an imitation of the adult community's own barbarism, which differs from the children's only in being somewhat more covert. In this light, Wolford says, the seemingly trivial events of a story such as "Tell-Tale" "partake of the tragic sense of a remote and indefinite past, and because the events they depict belong to the past, they cannot be undone" (49–50).

Works Cited

Bowers, Fredson. Textual Introduction. *Tales of Whilomville*. Vol. 7 of The University of Virginia Edition of *The Works of Stephen Crane*. Ed. Fredson Bowers. Charlottesville: University Press of Virginia, 1968, 103–26.

Crane, Stephen. "The Lover and the Tell-Tale." *Tales of Whilomville* 144–49.

Gullason, Thomas A. "Stephen Crane's Short Stories: The True Road." *Stephen Crane's Career: Perspectives and Evaluations*. Ed. Thomas A. Gullason. New York: New York University Press, 1972, 470–86.

Holton, Milne. *Cylinder of Vision: The Fiction and Journalistic Writings of Stephen Crane*. Baton Rouge: Louisiana State University Press, 1972.

Levenson, J. C. Introduction. *Tales of Whilomville* xi–lx.

Solomon, Eric. *Stephen Crane: From Parody to Realism*. Cambridge: Harvard University Press, 1966.

Stallman, R. W. *Stephen Crane: A Biography*. New York: George Braziller, 1968.

Wertheim, Stanley, and Paul Sorrentino, eds. *The Correspondence of Stephen Crane*. Vol. 2. New York: Columbia University Press, 1988.

Wolford, Chester L. *Stephen Crane: A Study of the Short Fiction*. Boston: Twayne, 1989.

Lynx-Hunting

Publication History

This story first appeared in the September 1899 issue of *Harper's New Monthly Magazine* (99:552–57), the second in that magazine's thirteen-part series—running in every issue from August 1899 through August 1900—of Crane tales set in the fictional town of Whilomville. Like the rest of this series, it was then included in the collection *Whilomville Stories*, which Harper & Brothers published in America in August 1900 and in England in November of the same year (Bowers 103). Editor Wilson Follett included it in volume 5, published in 1926, of *The Work of Stephen Crane* (12 vols., New York: Knopf, 1925–27), and it also appeared in 1963 in *The Complete Short Stories and Sketches of Stephen Crane* (Garden City, N.Y.: Doubleday), which Thomas A. Gullason edited.

Circumstances of Composition

Although "Lynx-Hunting" was the second to be published, after "The Angel-Child," of the Whilomville stories that Crane produced for *Harper's*, it was probably the first composed, since Crane sent it to his American agent, Paul Revere Reynolds, on January 27, 1899 (*Correspondence* II, 422–23), and then on January 31 sent him "The Angel-Child," calling it "another story . . . which belongs to the Whilomville series" (*Correspondence* II, 424). Crane evidently wrote "Lynx" at his first English home, Ravensbrook, in the town of Oxted, Surrey, between January 19 and 27, 1899. J. C. Levenson notes that January 19 is likely the earliest possible starting point because Crane makes no mention of this story in a letter of that date to Reynolds; given his chronic need for money, he probably would have told Reynolds about the story and suggested periodicals to which it could be sold, as he often did, if he had had it in mind then (xlvi). The terminal date of January 27 is certain, for, as noted above, on that day Crane sent the story to Reynolds, telling him in an accompanying letter that "I would like to have you use [it] as a boost for a loan which I am trying to get out of [syndicator and publisher S. S.] McClure" (*Correspondence* II, 422–23).

Sources and Influences

Crane's first biographer, Thomas Beer, quotes a letter from Crane to an unidentified recipient, possibly earlier would-be biographer Willis B. Clarke (Levenson xliii), that seems to locate the genesis of this story in Crane's own childhood. "Will, one of my brothers," Beer has Crane saying, "gave me a toy gun and I tried to shoot a cow with it over at Middletown [New York] when father was preaching there and that upset him wonderfully" (40). Later biographers such as Robert W. Stallman (477) repeat this story, but because there is strong evidence that Beer fabricated a number of letters that he claims Crane wrote (*Correspondence* I, 6–10; Wertheim and Sorrentino 2–16) one must be wary of his assertions regarding Crane's sources. Since no original of this letter has ever been located, there is a strong chance that it is Beer's invention.

The wisest course, perhaps, is to remain open to the possibility that this cow-hunting incident did actually occur but place it within the larger context of Crane's memories and literary aims, as Levenson and Neville Denny do. Levenson reports the incident but emphasizes that "Lynx" and the other Whilomville stories that follow it stem more generally from Crane's naturally turning toward recollections of his own and meditations upon others' childhoods in the year of their composition, since at this point Crane was enjoying a new-found domesticity with his common-law wife, Cora, and two small children, Héloise and Barry Frederic, whom the Cranes had taken in after the untimely death of their father, the writer Harold Frederic (xlii–xliii). Denny points out that the question of sources for the story in Crane's own life is less important than what he does in the story itself. Crane may well be drawing on his own past in "Lynx" and other Whilomville tales, Denny says, but he does not precisely reproduce that past in adherence to "any mechanical theory that literature should describe experience exactly" (31). Rather, he uses his past loosely, perhaps following Mark Twain's lead, to capture the "imaginative 'feel' of childhood; the vitality, the directness, the absolutism—the terrible innocence of childhood; and the pain and helplessness and inarticulateness—the terrible vulnerability" (31). In other words, Crane here takes the usual approach of the literary artist, transmuting something of his own experience into "new shapes and relations through which experience generally is appraised" (32).

Relationship to Other Crane Works

All the Whilomville stories in the *Harper's* series are loosely connected in that all focus on Jimmie Trescott and his family and friends, but "Lynx-Hunting" differs somewhat from the others in two respects. First, although the main characters here, Jimmie Trescott and his domineering, troublemaking friend Willie Dalzel, feature in most of the Whilomville tales, in "Lynx" Crane also brings in characters from outside his usual Whilomville cast: Henry Fleming, the protagonist of *The Red Badge of Courage*, now an aging farmer, and his Swedish hired hand, presumably the same Swede whose hysterical reaction to the barn fire costs old Fleming his life in "The Veteran." However, these two characters do not bring any of the seriousness of tone of those other stories into this one; they simply laugh until they are "helpless" (143) at the cornered Jimmie's desperate explanation that he shot Fleming's cow because he mistook her for a lynx. Second, in this first composed of the Whilomville stories, as Levenson points out, Crane does not focus on children in society and concomitant themes of sentimental illusion-spinning and competition in the realms of fashion and social rank, as he does in the rest of the series. Instead, "Lynx" seems to mark a transition from his hitherto customary subjects of man and nature to this new Whilomville material, a transition effected by his setting the scene in nature but using children rather than men as his central characters. With this fact in view, Levenson concludes, the second story composed, "Angel-Child," set in the social sphere of the town, is the proper beginning of the Whilomville series (xlv).

These differences notwithstanding, Chester L. Wolford sees one of the central themes of "Lynx" as closely related to that of one other Whilomville tale, "The Carriage-Lamps." Both of these are stories of "boyish crimes left unpunished" due to the relatively minor nature of those crimes and the exaggerated efforts of the boys involved to evade responsibility, efforts that leave the adult male authority-figures—Henry Fleming in "Lynx" and Jimmie's father, Dr. Trescott, in "Lamps"—laughing, by which response these adults reveal their "natural good sense," their grasp of proportion and keen awareness of absurdity (55–56).

Critical Studies

Levenson says that as a group Crane's Whilomville stories offer the sunniest vision to be found in his *oeuvre*, chiefly due to Crane's focus in them on a comfortably middle-class culture as opposed to the more extreme realms that usually occupy his attention. By way of fuller explanation of the precise nature of this vision, he notes that in "Lynx" Crane does not sentimentalize childhood, since he presents the boys as avid hunters, ready to kill anything that moves—whether bird, lynx, or cow—and as natural liars, anxious to escape the fear, guilt, and punishment attendant upon their actions; and yet "the leap of childlike fancy" that Crane finds necessary to project himself into this Whilomville milieu cuts him off from some of his darker themes. As evidence for this view, Levenson points out that the main characters in this story, Jimmie Trescott and Henry Fleming, seem unmarked by their respective previous ordeals in "The Monster" and *The Red Badge of Courage*, a fact that suggests, as does Fleming's failure to punish Jimmie for shooting the cow, that "the truthfulness of the child's world in this story seems less than the whole truth of human experience that Crane had once insisted on" (xliv).

Wolford sees a somewhat more meaningful implication in the confrontation between old Fleming and young Jimmie: not a refusal on Crane's part of the darker truths of life but rather a coming to grips with them. He says that "[t]he criminal act that had forced young Henry . . . in *The Red Badge of Courage* to lie to his fellow soldiers," and which had caused Henry himself "excruciating pain, is here transferred to a little boy. That the result is laughter seems to absolve not only Jimmie Trescott, but Henry Fleming as well" (55).

Eric Solomon likewise discerns serious import in the meeting of Fleming and Jimmie, but he regards the old man as the boy's mentor rather than his partner in absolution. He argues that through figurative language that characterizes the boys' behavior in adult terms, as when Jimmie is described as "pompous" and the others are called "distinguished," Crane universalizes the story. The boys' lies about their hunting skills become paradigms of adults' pretenses to knowledge and expertise, and the story thus becomes "a tense précis of man's corruptibility in society" (210), a study of humans' readiness to prevaricate to others about their misdeeds. The appearance of Fleming is particularly significant to this study, Solomon says, because in *The Red Badge* he, like the boys here, "started his battle of life as both a coward and a liar" but then rose above the general, corrupt level of adult society by acknowledging and remedying his failings. Now he insists that Jimmie and the other boys follow his example by telling the truth; he demands, albeit unsuccessfully, that they too "pierce through their illusions and accept the responsibility for their actions" (212).

Gullason argues that collectively the Whilomville stories form a loosely constructed novel that presents "a vibrant and full world" and in so doing effectively "illuminate[s] a number of universal truths about children, family life, and one's former home town" (483). In line with this view, Milne Holton sees this story as focusing, like a number of the others, on the detrimental effects that the community, with its powerful demands for conformity, works on the individual's imagination and ability to arrive at his or her own understanding of experience. Specifically, "Lynx" reveals that in Whilomville "even apprehensional experience in nature is blunted by communal pressure," for the conclusion of the story shows that Jimmie and Willie "live in such an atmosphere of lies and derived fantasy"—the handiwork of their small-town world—that for them "the truth is strange and difficult to arrive at, and, once it is confronted, it is recognized neither by the boys who are too afraid to see, nor by the adults, who no longer care" (216).

Despite frequent critical attacks on the Whilomville stories as subpar not only thematically but technically, such as H. E. Bates's estimation of Crane's method in them as "that of any tenth-rate provincial reporter without the wit to determine whether what he is doing is good or bad" (148), James Nagel singles out "Lynx" as a highly praiseworthy technical achievement. He sees the story as hewing to Ezra Pound's dictum that an image should present "an intellectual and emotional complex in an instant of time" (Nagel 151), in that it contains numerous instances of Crane's use of "imagery rather than exposition to reveal the mental life of his characters." For example, the story takes place on a sunny day, but when Jimmie shoots the cow the landscape instantly turns black, "'as if it had been overshadowed suddenly with thick storm-clouds.'" In this case as in many others, Nagel explains, Crane is presenting "not a meteorological condition but an image revealing Jimmie's anxiety and trepidation" (151).

Works Cited

Bates, H. E. "H. E. Bates on Stephen Crane." *Stephen Crane's Career: Perspectives and Evaluations*. Ed. Thomas A. Gullason. New York: New York University Press, 1972, 146–50.

Bowers, Fredson. Textual Introduction. *Tales of Whilomville*. Vol. 7 of The University of Virginia Edition of *The Works of Stephen Crane*. Ed. Fredson Bowers. Charlottesville: University Press of Virginia, 1968, 103–26.

Crane, Stephen. "Lynx Hunting." *Tales of Whilomville* 138–43.

Denny, Neville. "Imagination and Experience in Stephen Crane." *English Studies in Africa* 9 (1966):28–42.

Gullason, Thomas A. "Stephen Crane's Short Stories: The True Road." *Stephen Crane's Career: Perspectives and Evaluations*. Ed. Thomas A. Gullason. New York: New York University Press, 1972, 470–86.

Holton, Milne. *Cylinder of Vision: The Fiction and Journalistic Writings of Stephen Crane*. Baton Rouge: Louisiana State University Press, 1972.

Levenson, J. C. Introduction. *Tales of Whilomville* xi–lx.

Nagel, James. *Stephen Crane and Literary Impressionism*. University Park: Pennsylvania State University Press, 1980.

Solomon, Eric. *Stephen Crane: From Parody to Realism*. Cambridge: Harvard University Press, 1966.

Stallman, R. W. *Stephen Crane: A Biography*. New York: George Braziller, 1968.

Wertheim, Stanley, and Paul Sorrentino. "Thomas Beer: The Clay Feet of Stephen Crane Biography." *American Literary Realism* 22 (Spring 1990):2–16.

———, eds. *The Correspondence of Stephen Crane*. 2 vols. New York: Columbia University Press, 1988.

Wolford, Chester L. *Stephen Crane: A Study of the Short Fiction*. Boston: Twayne, 1989.

Making an Orator

Publication History

This story first ran in the December 1899 number of *Harper's New Monthly Magazine* (100:25–28), the fifth in the thirteen-part series of Crane tales set in the fictional town of Whilomville that appeared in *Harper's* from August 1899 through August 1900. Like the rest of the series, it was next published in the book *Whilomville Stories*, which Harper & Brothers put out in America in August 1900 and in England in November of the same year (Bowers 103). Wilson Follett, editor of *The Work of Stephen Crane* (12 vols., New York: Knopf, 1925–27), placed the story, along with the rest of the Whilomville tales, in volume 5, published in 1926; it was collected again by Thomas A. Gullason in his 1963 *Complete Short Stories and Sketches of Stephen Crane* (Garden City, N.Y.: Doubleday).

Circumstances of Composition

The evidence regarding the composition of "Making an Orator" is slim; the best surmise is J. C. Levenson's hypothesis that it was written at Brede Place, Sussex, Crane's final home in England, sometime in April or May of 1899, based on the fact that the story does not appear in two inventories of material that Crane drew up in March of 1899 but does show up in a list compiled that summer (liii–liv). This circumstance would make it the fifth composed in addition to being the fifth published of the Whilomville tales.

Sources and Influences

John Berryman and Robert W. Stallman both identify the source of this story as Crane's recollection of his own boyhood distress at being made to memorize and recite Alfred, Lord Tennyson's "Charge of the Light Brigade," probably at some point between 1888 and 1890, while he attended Claverack College, just as Jimmie Trescott is forced to do (Berryman 15, Stallman 19). While not arguing that Crane did not undergo this ordeal, George Monteiro points out a likely literary antecedent as well: Chapter 4 of Mark Twain's *The Adventures of Tom Sawyer*. In this chapter, entitled "Showing Off in Sunday School," Tom must memorize and recite five Bible verses. Like Jimmie, he experiences acute discomfort in carrying out this assignment and gets through his recitation only haltingly (67). Another point of connection is Tom's classmate Tanner, for in "Orator" a boy named Johnnie Tanner gives the first speech (68). Ultimately, though, Monteiro concludes that these two works diverge in their effects, for in focusing on Tom's misery Mark Twain seeks "to set his hero off from [the] other children," whereas Crane's goal, as is the case in most of the Whilomville stories, is to make Jimmie representative of *all* tortured schoolchildren (68).

Relationship to Other Crane Works

All the Whilomville stories are loosely connected in that all focus on Jimmie Trescott and his family and friends, and in so doing, in Gullason's words, they present "a vibrant and full world" and effectively "illuminate a number of universal truths about children, family life, and one's former home town," which impels Gullason to argue that they be regarded as a kind of episodic novel (483). However, "Orator" differs somewhat from most of the others, with the exception of "A Little Pilgrim," in concentrating on Jimmie's agonies within the schoolroom rather than on the playground or sidewalks. In the other stories, the emphasis is on what children and other groups that lack the power of the white adults who dominate Whilomville do among themselves, when the white adults are not around, to create their own hierarchical structure within this larger system. In "Orator" and "Pilgrim," on the other hand, Crane focuses on the tortures that white adults actively put children through in school while misguidedly and sometimes hypocritically believing that they are educating their young charges. This difference in focus aside, "Orator" does resemble all the Whilomville stories in terms of theme, for in it as in the rest, as Milne Holton points out, what is ultimately revealed is that "the pain of . . . experience in Whilomville is remembered pain, that the lessons which are intended are never the lessons learned" (223).

Critical Studies

Gullason's praise notwithstanding, critics have frequently denigrated the Whilomville stories in general as subpar for Crane. James B. Stronks rates them as "thin and slight" because of their focus on mundane situations that do not evoke the "nerveless intensity" of Crane at his best (343), while H. E. Bates says that they could have been written by "any tenth-rate provincial reporter without the wit to determine whether what he is doing is good or bad" and thus regards them as nothing more than an indication of the diminished state of Crane's powers in this late stage of his life (148). However, Monteiro regards "Orator" as one of the best of the Whilomville group, and in fact one of Crane's better stories overall, due to Crane's intelligent grasp and exploitation of literary precedent in it. In line with his linkage of "Orator" to *Tom Sawyer*, Monteiro notes that the humorously handled "theme of the victimized child" was common in nineteenth-century literature (64), which leads him to argue that in this story Crane is less concerned with recollecting his own childhood than with using this situation "as a literary motif" through which to depict one of his favorite satiric targets, "the individual enmeshed in the institution" (65). Monteiro finds this particular depiction effective due to Crane's frequent use of images of torture and death, which create the impression that Jimmie's recitation is "a botched initiation" of a tribal sort, a "barbarous" ritual, which in turn produces the story's sharp satire in that this barbarism takes place within the educational system. Crane's point, Monteiro asserts, is that the classroom is precisely the place to find such primitive rituals in the modern world (66).

Monteiro does acknowledge one flaw in the story, the fact that Crane does not use the speeches that the other children must give to emblematize their feelings in this situation; these are irrelevant to their condition. He notes on the other hand, however, that Jimmie's recitation *is* skillfully selected for its relevance to his condition. In fact, in Monteiro's view Jimmie's relationship to the Light Brigade whose praises he must declaim is crucial to understanding his reaction to his initiation. Jimmie, Monteiro says, suffers quite as much "sheer pain and brute fear" at the front of the classroom as the Light Brigade did in charging the Russian artillery at Balaclava, but the outcome is that he fails to rise—or, perhaps more properly, sink—to their example: he rejects "mindless admiration for the disastrous heroics" of the Light Brigade's charge by immediately forgetting the poem when his recitation is over. Thus, "the forces of mis-education are defeated, at least temporarily" (71).

James Nagel similarly praises Crane for his humorous linking of Jimmie's agonies to those of the Light Brigade (137), while Chester L. Wolford is less wholly positive, seeing the story as funny but flawed by Crane's frequent editorializing on the action. Nevertheless, in the same vein as Monteiro and Nagel, he regards it as a persuasive attack on social institutions—first on schools for the cruel demands they place on children and then, when one links Tennyson's poem to Jimmie's situation, on society as a whole for its "amazing power to make people do incomprehensible things," such as reciting a poem or charging into a cannon's mouth (57). The linkage between Jimmie and the Light Brigade, Wolford says, constitutes one of Crane's most effective uses of one of his most frequently employed techniques: "universalizing a situation by creating a metaphor from the particular" (58).

Works Cited

Bates, H. E. "H. E. Bates on Stephen Crane." *Stephen Crane's Career: Perspectives and Evaluations*. Ed. Thomas A. Gullason. New York: New York University Press, 1972, 146–50.

Berryman, John. *Stephen Crane*. New York: Sloane, 1950.

Bowers, Fredson. Textual Introduction. *Tales of Whilomville*. Vol. 7 of The University of Virginia Edition of *The Works of Stephen Crane*. Ed. Fredson Bowers. Charlottesville: University Press of Virginia, 1968, 103–26.

Gullason, Thomas A. "Stephen Crane's Short Stories: The True Road." *Stephen Crane's Career: Perspectives and Evaluations*. Ed. Thomas A. Gullason. New York: New York University Press, 1972, 470–86.

Holton, Milne. *Cylinder of Vision: The Fiction and Journalistic Writings of Stephen Crane*. Baton Rouge: Louisiana State University Press, 1972.

Levenson, J. C. Introduction. *Tales of Whilomville* xi–lx.

Monteiro, George. "With Proper Words (or Without Them) the Soldier Dies: Stephen Crane's 'Making an Orator.'" *Cithara* 9 (1970):64–72.

Nagel, James. *Stephen Crane and Literary Impressionism*. University Park: Pennsylvania State University Press, 1980.

Stallman, R. W. *Stephen Crane: A Biography*. New York: George Braziller, 1968.

Stronks, James B. "Stephen Crane's English Years: The Legend Corrected." *Papers of the Bibliographical Society of America* 57 (1963):340–49.

Wolford, Chester L. *Stephen Crane: A Study of the Short Fiction*. Boston: Twayne, 1989.

A Man and Some Others

Publication History

This story was first published in the February 1897 issue of *Century* (53:601–07) (Bowers clxiv), but only after a good deal of hesitation on the part of the magazine's editor, Richard Watson Gilder. According to Joseph Kwiat, Gilder may have been somewhat concerned about rumors of unsavory behavior on Crane's part—a theory that J. C. Levenson discounts (lii)—but he was verifiably and deeply perturbed about Crane's having his character Bill utter "B'Gawd" at one point in the story. On October 24, 1896, Gilder wrote to Crane's agent, Paul Revere Reynolds, requesting that the word be changed and lamenting that

> [i]t is difficult to know what to do with swearing in fiction. When it appears in print it has an offensiveness beyond that of the actual word; and it is never 'realistic' because, if the actual oaths were printed just as the swearer swears, it would be unendurable among men as among gods. (qtd. in Kwiat, "Magazine," 314–15)

Whether or not Crane agreed to make the change himself is unknown, but the word was finally emended for *Century*, appearing as "B'G___" (Bowers clxv).

The story next appeared in America in the book *"The Open Boat" and Other Tales of Adventure*, published by Doubleday and McClure in April 1898. It came out the same month in England in the similar volume *"The Open Boat" and Other Stories*, published by Heinemann (Bowers clxv). Crane's early editor Wilson Follett placed it in volume 12, published in 1927, of *The Work of Stephen Crane* (12 vols., New York: Knopf, 1925–27), and it appeared again in 1963 in *The Complete Short Stories and Sketches of Stephen Crane* (Garden City, N.Y.: Doubleday), edited by Thomas A. Gullason.

Circumstances of Composition

Crane wrote "A Man and Some Others" along with two other Western tales, "The Five White Mice" and "The Wise Men," in the spring and summer of 1896, while he was living at his brother Edmund's house in what Levenson calls "the easy atmosphere of Hartwood," a rural town in New York State (xli). He finished it before August 18, 1896, for on that date Theodore Roosevelt, then the president of the Board of Police Commissioners of New York City, sent a letter thanking Crane for letting him read the story in manuscript (*Correspondence* I, 249).

Sources and Influences

According to Crane's first biographer, Thomas Beer, Crane based this story on a conversation that took place during his 1895 Western trip as a correspondent for the Bacheller syndicate. In a San Antonio rooming house he met a tough ex-Bowery boy and former saloon bouncer, going by the name of Keenan, who described himself as having a checkered, violent past. As one instance, he explained that he had shot several members of a group of Mexicans who had tried to drive his sheep away from a waterhole and he had then sold the sheep to the survivors. According to Beer, in 1897 Crane sent Keenan a copy of the issue of the *Century* with "Man" in it, but the prototype was not pleased that Crane had killed Bill off in the end; allegedly, he "hated Crane ever after for spoiling the point of the story" (116), which was that he had not only survived but prevailed.

Robert W. Stallman repeats this information, dating Crane's conversation with Keenan more specifically to April 1895; however, as is frequently the case with claims that cannot be verified by sources outside Beer's account, it is possible that Beer made up this story (*Correspondence* I, 6–10). In this case more than most, though, we might hope that Beer was accurate, since, as Neville Denny points out, the changes Crane makes in Keenan's supposed story are an excellent illustration of an artist's transmutation of actual events into an expression of his or her own vision. "What is imitated and put to artistic use," Denny says, is not necessarily every fact of the original but rather "the tone and flavour of a way of life, realized with arresting actuality and charged with metaphorical significance" (35)—precisely the qualities, one suspects, that would have been lacking in Keenan's self-congratulatory recounting.

Robert Glen Deamer takes a different tack, arguing that the story is derived not from a specific episode in Crane's Western journey but rather from a change in his mindset provoked by the aggregate of his experiences on this trip. Prior to this adventure, Deamer says, Crane conceived of life in deterministic terms, as is evident in many of his early works, particularly the novels *Maggie: A Girl of the Streets* and *George's Mother*. However, what he witnessed of human behavior in the West convinced him that people could shape their own fates to some extent by exercising the "heroic" virtues of discipline, responsibility, and courage ("'Code'" 143). As a result, many of his post-1895 stories are studies of men who either attain these virtues and thus merit Crane's admiration or else reject them and therefore warrant his censure. "Man" is such a study, and Bill is one of the men who lives up to the heroic code: he "fronts a desperate situation with independence and pride and will," and he "goes down on his own terms" ("'Code'" 147).

Relationship to Other Crane Works

Various critics have noted a myriad of thematic links between this Western story and many of Crane's others, Westerns and non-Westerns alike. Where the Westerns are concerned, Deamer sees "Man" as closely related to "The Five White Mice" and "One Dash—Horses" in that all three affirm the Western "code of self-reliant courage" that Crane found highly admirable. Deamer also points out that in some respects "Man" differs from the other two, since in those the "Crane-surrogate" who discovers this code is the protagonist, whereas here the protagonist is Bill, who already embodies this code in his willingness "to die alone and unknown for his rights" while not seeing his circumstances as tragic or even serious, and who does not wish an innocent outsider, the Easterner who is the Crane-surrogate here, to be drawn into the conflict ("Myth" 118–20).

Levenson and Chester L. Wolford also make connections between "Man" and these two stories. Levenson considers it a sort of complement to "Mice," for in "Mice" the reader gets an intimate look at a sudden encounter with death that fills the protagonist with fear and self-pity, whereas in "Man" the focus is on a "sustained encounter against fearful odds, which evokes the calm of certainty" in the protagonist, a condition that in this case gives the Easterner the chance to learn "to look steadily at what is, to see it whole" (xlviii). Wolford sees "Man" as linked very closely to "Horses" in terms of shared themes, including "sheer chance, the apprehension of reality in danger and death, the cowardly bravado of groups, and the tenacity with which some people do what they do, all the while knowing the dire consequences" (41). From a broader perspective, Wolford also links this story to the non-Westerns *The Red Badge of Courage*, "A Mystery of Heroism," "An Episode of War," and "The Monster"; in all these stories, he says, the protagonist "discovers a small measure of reality relating to the unknown—specifically death—and a corresponding inability to make it known" (41).

Levenson likewise takes a larger thematic view in addition to his strictly Western focus, pointing out that "Man" is the logical culmination of one theme developed sequentially in certain of Crane's stories: the threat of violence in a realm other than war. A revolver is "wildly brandished" in "The Pace of Youth," it is "seriously drawn and pointed" in "Mice" and "Horses," and at last fired in "Man," thereby yielding the moment to which Crane has built up in this group, the moment "when the horror of killing and the absoluteness of death are more important than the fear of dying, when the intensity of self-regard has given way to the perception of truths." Those truths, Levenson explains, are "the forms that live out from the incoherence, . . . the fragility of life, . . . [and] the dignity of death." And in creating this moment of insight under fire, Levenson concludes, Crane not only reaches the end of this sequence but also the limit of his ability to imagine the significances revealed by the imminent presence of death; "[i]n experience and in art he would hereafter build on what he had done in his early Western tales" (xlix).

Deamer and James Nagel also link "Man" to another story in which death seems not only imminent but immanent, "The Open Boat." Deamer notes that Joseph Conrad early on saw a connection between these two; he believes that Conrad was implicitly aware that they are thematically convergent, their point being that only experience yields the true understanding that "reality, [which encompasses] both nature's indifference and the brotherhood of the men, is felt rather than intellectualized or romanticized." Deamer considers these two stories Crane's most successful depictions—"Mice" and "Horses" being lesser ones—of this necessity of experience to the attainment of felt and therefore genuine comprehension, and of the fact that only such comprehension truly affords "the possibility of human dignity, courage, heroism" ("Stance" 135–37).

Nagel sees "Man" as anticipating "Open Boat" not just thematically but in many technical respects: an opening paragraph that emphasizes the limitations of the individual's vision; the use of more than one protagonist and thus the employment of shifting narrative perspectives; a double plot of "physical adventure and psychological growth" that leads to the "related themes of nature's indifference to man and . . . the development of compassion in a moment of stress"; and the deployment of a repeated refrain to chart the protagonists' growing awareness of nature's indifference ("Impressionism" 30). In a separate study, Nagel also links "Man" to "The Blue Hotel" in terms of technique, noting that in both stories Crane limits the key fight to the perspective of an Easterner not fully involved in it, with the goal of rendering the action fragmented and confusing in order to create "the dramatic intensity of a person actually on the scene" (*Stephen Crane* 51).

Critical Studies

Joseph Conrad not only discerned similarities between "Man" and "Boat" but also regarded both very highly. In a letter dated December 1, 1897, he tells Crane that "The boat thing is immensely interesting" and that "'A Man and Some Others' is immense. . . . I admire it without reserve" (*Correspondence* I, 315). However, several other critics have expressed a good deal of reserve about "Man." Stallman says that it is immense only in length, with a "false" middle and a "melodramatic" ending (327–28). Gullason agrees that the story is too long and concludes weakly; he adds that it is further marred by Crane's related failures to focus the plot effectively and provide his characters with convincing motivations. "Man" would be highly valued in the canons of most short-story writers, he says, but it falls far short of the almost impossible standards Crane sets in his best works in this genre (478). Perhaps the most dismaying criticism comes from Theodore Roosevelt, who, in his letter of thanks to Crane for the opportunity to read the story in manuscript, faults him for having the Mexicans kill Bill in the end. "Some day," he admonishes Crane, "I want you to write another story of the frontiersman and the Mexican Greaser in which the frontiersman shall come out on top; it is more normal that way!" (*Correspondence* I, 249).

Raymund Paredes also criticizes Crane's handling of his characters, but rather than seeing Crane as being too generous to the Mexicans, as Roosevelt does, he argues that Crane's attitude toward them is in fact the same as Roosevelt's. In "Man," and in "Mice" and "Horses" as well, Paredes says, Crane takes the view that "when Yankee confronted Mexican, mortal danger was the usual concomitant," and that this is the case because of the Mexican's putative "savage appetite . . . beyond all reason." However, Paredes continues, Crane always presents this appetite as accompanied by a large streak of cowardice, a combination that causes the Anglo to react with a mixture of fear and contempt. At the moment of confrontation, the Mexican crumbles, "totally bereft of dignity and nobility," while the Anglo responds to his own fear "with courage, reacting coolly and weighing his options, reacting quickly to stay alive." Crane depicts the Anglo's subsequent contempt as warranted because the Mexican hides his cowardice "behind a colossal pretentiousness"; he seeks to bluff the Anglo but ultimately fails "because he has no bravery to fall back on," thus making "a mockery of an honest emotion." With these notions in view, Paredes offers perhaps the strongest denunciation to be found anywhere in the corpus of Crane criticism, asserting that in his Westerns Crane constructs "a Darwinian world of constant and bitter struggle" in which the Mexican—sinister, treacherous, mysterious, and murderous—"is clearly the lowest form of humanity" and is thus destined to lose to the Anglo. And "the virulence of Crane's attitude toward the Mexican," Paredes concludes, "is even more meaningful and disturbing when viewed in the light of his own personal experience." In America, Crane "championed the destitute and disfranchised" and routinely "associated amicably with gamblers, dopeheads, and prostitutes." He was able to discern "virtue and dignity in some of the most unsavory characters of New York's Bowery," and yet, "with all his artistic sensibility," he failed ever to locate a single redeeming characteristic in any Mexican (31–38).

A well-reasoned response to these charges comes from Jamie Robertson. He begins by arguing that Crane arrived in the West at a date late enough to enable him to realize that the Western myth, "that individual courage gives meaning to life," which was still being fostered in Western fiction by Eastern writers for Eastern readers, was in fact defunct. This realization was curative for Crane himself, and he therefore offers a similar cure for his readers in his Westerns. Thus Crane, aware of his Eastern outsider status in the West, creates protagonists much like himself in "Man," "Mice," and "Horses": they "participate in the convention of popular Western fiction" but they take an ironic view of that convention. Crane's goal in using this ironic stance toward the Western myth, in Robertson's view, is to show that courage in confronting the unknown, which in these stories is the possibility of death in conflicts with Mexicans, does not in itself give meaning to life but rather leads to a larger insight into what for Crane is the desideratum of any person's individual development: "a humble awareness of one's own insignificance," like that which the correspondent in "The Open Boat" discovers in his contemplation of nature's indifference to his fate. And this fact absolves Crane from Paredes's charge of racism, Robertson concludes, because in all three of the stories in question, Anglos and Mexicans are not placed in hierarchy but rather united in their mutual recognition of their individual insignificance. In "Man," specifically, according to Robertson, Crane creates in the Easterner the character who out of all those in his Westerns is most like himself at the outset of his own encounter with the West, one who, "as tourist, looks at the myth of the West with . . . impassioned detachment"; and through this particular contemplative condition, Robertson sees Crane as in fact deflating rather than celebrating the Western myth of individualistic moral courage and its concomitant racism in the encounter between Bill and the Easterner. Crane presents Bill, Robertson says, as having confronted the unknown of death many times but as not having attained the desirable result of a meek awareness of his own unimportance. Rather, all he has achieved is a sense of pride in his ability to murder others. On the other hand, when the Easterner has his first encounter with the possibility of death, and when he in his turn kills a man and finds the act easy, he does not swell with pride. Instead, "the act strips his romantic vision of the West from him and makes him face the fact of the insignificance of human life, an insignificance that he shares with Bill and with the Mexicans he has just battled" (244–51).

While not accusing Crane of ethnocentrism, Ben Merchant Vorpahl implicitly disagrees with Robertson's reading, for he argues that Bill is presented as superior to the Mexicans, at least in terms of his understanding of the relationship between chronology and ontology. Vorpahl sees "Man" as the second piece in a triad of stories, "Horses" being the first and "The Bride Comes to Yellow Sky" the third, in which Crane focuses on a conflict between an awareness of chronology—of the passage of time—and a desire to escape this awareness by the only means available, illusion and artifice. Through his choice to fight the Mexicans despite his understanding that he will be killed, Vorpahl says, Bill accepts the passage of time as embodied in its central fact, the inevitability of death, and he is therefore the "Man" of the story's title.

José, the leader of the Mexicans, on the other hand, fails to accept "death as a central fact of experience," clings to an artificial configuration that rejects the meaning of death, and he is therefore one of the "Others." And within this schema the Easterner is likewise among the "Others." Impelled by his desire and "ability to ignore the facts of experience"—the fragility of life that is revealed in Bill's death and his own easily accomplished killing of one of the Mexicans—the Easterner exercises "the mythologizing faculty of his romantic fancy" in his continued reverence for Bill. "In other words," Vorpahl concludes, "the American responds to chronological actuality by transforming it into myth"—specifically, the myth of the self-reliant Western hero who escapes the ravages of time precisely because of his artificial, illusory mythical status (210–13).

Bettina Knapp and Marston LaFrance likewise regard Bill, not the Easterner, as the hero of the story, arguing, in contrast to Robertson, that Bill *has* changed, has abandoned his pride for new insight, by the time of his death. Knapp says that the description of Bill's background and his remarks to the Easterner are designed to "let the reader understand the dignity of a man who was once a killer . . . and the serenity that follows the acceptance of one's mortality" (150–51). Similarly, LaFrance contends that the point of the narrator's summation of Bill's previous life is to reveal that in the past he was indeed a proud, "swaggering bully," a very familiar type in Crane's fiction, so that the reader will contrast that behavior with his present decision to die honorably, resisting overwhelming odds in a fight that he did not seek but rather had forced upon him. And unlike Vorpahl, LaFrance discerns nothing indelibly characteristic of the Western mythos in Crane's handling of this anagnorisis; he points out that Crane's fundamental interest is always character, not setting— that the West here is essentially the same as the city or the battlefield or the sea in Crane's other stories: all simply provide "the setting in which men have to be aware or unaware, personally honest or dishonest" (188).

Frank Bergon likewise notes that Crane's compelling interest in all his work is character, specifically that of the "isolated, unaccommodated man," but he points out as well that Crane's choice of setting does play a role in his pursuit of this interest—in particular, he says that the Western landscape, with its resemblance to the barren wastelands of his bleakest poems, is the ideal setting for Crane, and that it reaches its highest, most sharply defined form in "Man," in which it sets off probably the most unaccommodated of Crane's many *isolatoe* protagonists (*Artistry* 110). By stripping life to its bleakest essentials in the figure of Bill viewed against the stark backdrop of the Western void, Bergon says, Crane seeks to make the proto-existentialist point, found in all his Westerns, that at bottom courage "consists of nothing more than a realistic knowledge and technique," such as Bill exhibits when he is able initially to get the drop on the Mexicans by placing a dummy in his sleeping bag and then waiting at the edge of his camp for the Mexicans to reveal their positions by shooting at what they take to be his slumbering form (*Artistry* 115). And as further proof of Crane's complex outlook and skill at conveying that outlook, Bergon points out that, in addition to recounting this seemingly totally elemental story, Crane manages to comment as well on the historical truth about this Western landscape and the West in general—that it was never completely "wild" but rather always composed of inextricably "wild" and "industrialized" elements—through his detailing of the past life that has led Bill to his currently unaccommodated state. Prior to being a sheepherder, Bill was a mine owner and thus "part of the corporate, industrial West," a cowboy who was "not a free spirit but a hired hand," and a "hired goon" for the most powerful emblem of the advancing industrialized East, the railroad. And even as a sheepherder far from civilization, Bergon concludes, Bill meets not only the expected Wild West gang of thieves, but also a tourist from back East (Introduction 5).

Eric Solomon also praises the congruence of setting and character in "Man." He regards this story as one of Crane's most successful, infused with "a terrible beauty," due to its "comprehending the paradoxes inherent in the Western setting"—that is, Crane presents that setting as simultaneously "heroic and anti-heroic, funny and terrible, absurd and inevitable" (243), seemingly discrepant qualities also manifested by Bill, who is an "uneasy combination of strength, amorality, vulnerability, and shame" (246). The recitation of this character's past establishes his terrible, anti-heroic side (and reveals on Crane's own part "an understanding of the decadent influence of violence" that is purposefully ignored in his war fiction [244]), while, paradoxically, his final spasm of violence brings him close to heroism, as close as he has ever come to "self-realization and integrity" (247). And despite his failure totally to achieve these ends, Bill's death carries significance, Solomon says, for through his observation of Bill and his own participation in the climactic shootout, leading to his discovery of the ease with which he can kill another man, the Easterner edges still closer than Bill to self-realization. This complex story's final paradox is, once again, the link between violence and insight, the fact that in "that moment when a panther is born in [the Easterner's] heart, understanding and perhaps manhood are also born" (248).

Milne Holton and Donald B. Gibson similarly see Crane operating at a high level of complexity, deftly juggling a number of themes, in this story. In Holton's view, Crane produces a unified artistic whole that nevertheless proffers insights on such diverse matters as the differences in the viewpoints of Easterners and Westerners, Americans and Mexicans; the idea that fear of the unknown "can perhaps sometimes be overcome by a momentary detachment, an awareness of human inconsequence, which can come from the unblinking apprehension of what is"; and, most significantly, the initiation of the innocent Easterner into an understanding of how quickly and easily violence can blunt a man's higher sensibilities and convert him into an eager killer (126–27).

Gibson also focuses on the Easterner, regarding him as a close relative of Henry Fleming in that the tourist like the neophyte soldier is "an innocent who has yet to be tempered in the fire of experience" and thus has yet to acquire "the psychic freedom necessary to establish his identity." Because of this condition, Gibson argues, like Robertson and Solomon and unlike Vorpahl and LaFrance, that it is the Easterner rather than Bill who is most changed by the events of the story and who is therefore the protagonist; he asserts as well that Crane traces the intricacies of this change quite sophisticatedly. At the end of the story, for instance, he points out that Crane does not simplify the Easterner's state of mind but rather insists on its complexity. Although he has learned from Bill how to face unblinkingly his aloneness in the indifferent universe and how to meet danger bravely and skillfully, as a new initiate to violence he is nevertheless still somewhat frightened and "not comfortable in the midst of the carnage wrought partly by himself." In other words, Crane is aware, and makes his reader aware, that Henry Fleming cannot metamorphose into Tom Larpent, the philosophical, whimsically fatalistic gambler-gunfighter protagonist of "Moonlight on the Snow," overnight (118–19).

David S. Gross tacitly concurs with this appraisal of Crane's complexity of mind and technical skill; in his view, these traits make this story a significant forerunner of some trends in modern and postmodern thought. Crane's phrasing of his narrator's thoughts on "the inconsequence of human tragedy" before and after the Mexicans' attack on Bill's camp, Gross says, is related in terms of tone and point of view to existentialism and to "all those varieties of modern thought in which the power of language, of discourse, is emphasized." Crane is always concerned, according to Gross, with "the shaping power of language, especially the language and belief system of the popular Western and the Horatio Alger self-help literature of the time," and it is this type of inflated language he employs to make the tonally contradictory point of nature's indifference to human suffering. For example, just after Bill has killed one of the Mexicans, the narrator offers this burst of rhetoric:

> The silence returned to the wilderness. The tired flames faintly illuminated the blanketed thing and the flung corse of the marauder, and sang the fire chorus, the ancient melody which bears the message of the inconsequence of human tragedy. (*Tales* 62)

By creating this disjunction between the expected uplifting meaning of such pseudo-poetic language and its actual grim import here, Gross says, "Crane derides the false simplicities and easy assurances of such forms of discourse even as he emphasizes their shaping power—the action and interaction, mutual influence and interpenetration of texts and textualities." However, lest Crane be blamed for what in many quarters are condemned as the excesses of those modern and postmodern considerations that he seems to anticipate here, Gross concludes by asserting that Crane's position "is not an idealist view which would assert that there is nothing but texts, no reality outside of thought and its formations, but rather a powerful awareness that all our notions of truth and meaning are always textual" (19).

Works Cited

Beer, Thomas. *Stephen Crane: A Study in American Letters*. New York: Knopf, 1923.

Bergon, Frank. Introduction. *The Western Writings of Stephen Crane*. New American Library, 1979, 1–27.

———. *Stephen Crane's Artistry*. New York: Columbia University Press, 1975.

Bowers, Fredson. Textual Introduction. *Tales of Adventure*. Vol. 5 of The University of Virginia Edition of *The Works of Stephen Crane*. Ed. Fredson Bowers. Charlottesville: University Press of Virginia, 1970. cxxxiii–cxcv.

Deamer, Robert Glen. "Remarks on the Western Stance of Stephen Crane." *Western American Literature* 15 (Summer 1980):122–41.

———. "Stephen Crane and the Western Myth." *Western American Literature* 7 (Summer 1972):111–23.

———. "Stephen Crane's 'Code' and Its Western Connections." *The Importance of Place in the American Literature of Hawthorne, Thoreau, Crane, Adams, and Faulkner*. New York: Edwin Mellen, 1990. 139–52.

Denny, Neville. "Imagination and Experience in Stephen Crane." *English Studies in Africa* 9 (1966):28–42.

Gibson, Donald B. *The Fiction of Stephen Crane*. Carbondale: Southern Illinois University Press, 1968.

Gross, David S. "The Western Stories of Stephen Crane." *Journal of American Culture* 11 (1988):15–21.

Gullason, Thomas A. "Stephen Crane's Short Stories: The True Road." *Stephen Crane's Career: Perspectives and Evaluations*. Ed. Thomas A. Gullason. New York: New York University Press, 1972. 470–86.

Holton, Milne. *Cylinder of Vision: The Fiction and Journalistic Writings of Stephen Crane*. Baton Rouge: Louisiana State University Press, 1972.

Knapp, Bettina L. *Stephen Crane*. New York: Ungar, 1987.

Kwiat, Joseph J. "Stephen Crane and Frank Norris: The Magazine and the 'Revolt' in American Literature in the 1890s." *Western Humanities Review* 30 (Autumn 1976):309–22.

LaFrance, Marston. *A Reading of Stephen Crane*. Oxford: Clarendon, 1971.

Levenson, J. C. Introduction. *Tales of Adventure* xv–cxxxii.

Nagel, James. "Impressionism in 'The Open Boat' and 'A Man and Some Others.'" *Research Studies* 43 (1975):27–37.

———. *Stephen Crane and Literary Impressionism*. University Park: Pennsylvania State University Press, 1980.

Paredes, Raymund A. "Stephen Crane and the Mexican." *Western American Literature* 6 (Spring 1971):31–38.

Robertson, Jamie. "Stephen Crane, Eastern Outsider in the West and Mexico." *Western American Literature* 13 (Nov. 1978):243–57.

Solomon, Eric. *Stephen Crane: From Parody to Realism*. Cambridge: Harvard University Press, 1966.

Stallman, R. W. *Stephen Crane: A Biography*. New York: George Braziller, 1968.

Vorpahl, Ben Merchant. "Murder by the Minute: Old and New in 'The Bride Comes to Yellow Sky.'" *Nineteenth-Century Fiction* 26 (1971):196–218.

Wertheim, Stanley, and Paul Sorrentino, eds. *The Correspondence of Stephen Crane*. Vol. 1. New York: Columbia University Press, 1988.

Wolford, Chester L. *Stephen Crane: A Study of the Short Fiction*. Boston: Twayne, 1989.

Marines Signaling Under Fire at Guantánamo

Publication History

This story was first published in America in *McClure's Magazine* for February 1899 (12:332–36). It then appeared in the collection *Wounds in the Rain*, published in September 1900 by Frederick A. Stokes in America and Methuen in England (Bowers cl–cli). Editor Wilson Follett assigned it to volume 9, published in 1926, of *The Work of Stephen Crane* (12 vols., New York: Knopf, 1925–27).

Circumstances of Composition

"Marines Signaling Under Fire at Guantánamo" is one of the numerous pieces Crane wrote while living in Havana, Cuba, after the end of the Spanish-American War. Crane covered the war as a reporter, first for Joseph Pulitzer's

New York World and then for William Randolph Hearst's *New York Journal*; he was in Puerto Rico when the peace treaty was signed on August 12, 1898, but he then went to Havana rather than returning to his common-law wife, Cora, who awaited him at their home in England. Crane evidently chose this course, not returning to England until January 11, 1899, because he and Cora had amassed considerable debt there and he wished to delay facing this problem (Stallman 413–42). In Havana he lived quietly, first in a hotel and then in a lodging-house, writing steadily and posting the results to his agent in New York, Paul Revere Reynolds. He sent "Marines" on October 20, 1898, calling it "a 'personal anecdote' thing" and recommending that Reynolds sell it—which he did—to the syndicator S. S. McClure, imploring the agent to "[h]it him [McClure] beastly hard. I have got to have at least fifteen hundred dollars this month, sooner the better" (*Correspondence* II, 380).

Sources and Influences

As Crane's reference to this story as "a 'personal anecdote' thing" indicates, it is based on some of his own experiences during the Spanish-American War—specifically, on two engagements in which he took part. The first of these was an attack on the night of June 11, 1898, that Spanish guerillas mounted against Camp McCalla, a position that U.S. Marines had established after coming ashore at Guantánamo Bay. Crane wrote up this attack for the *World* in an article dated June 12 and headlined "In the First Land Fight Four of Our Men Are Killed" (*Reports of War* 128–30), but he does not mention there the incident on which he focuses in the story, the action of four Marine signalmen who fearlessly stood up and turned their backs to the quick-firing Spanish attackers in order to transmit messages to the Navy ships anchored in the bay. The first section of "Marines" is given over to a paean to the courage of these men, with Crane depicting himself as simply lying in their trench and admiring their behavior; in reality, as Robert W. Stallman notes, citing official Marine dispatches, Crane participated in the signaling, taking his fair share of turns with the four Marines (364).

Crane likewise downplays his own active and courageous role in his treatment of similar incidents in the second engagement, the battle of Cuzco (Stallman 371), which was a sortie out of Camp McCalla by two companies of Marines and some Cuban insurgents to dislodge a Spanish guerilla force threatening the camp. And again as well, he covers the heroic behavior of the signalmen more thoroughly—and in fact more accurately—in the story than in his reportage of this engagement for the *World*, which was dated June 22 and headlined "The Red Badge of Courage Was His Wig-Wag Flag" (*Reports of War*, 134–42). In the newspaper article, Crane conflates two separate episodes of signaling into one, describing how, at the beginning of the attack, "a spruce young sergeant" stood with his back to the enemy to direct the fire of the ship *Dolphin*, which supported the attack from offshore (138). In reality, as Crane makes clear in "Marines," this transmitting was performed by a private, whom Crane describes as a "red-headed 'mick'—I think his name was Clancy" (198), but whose true name was probably John Fitzgerald (Stallman 371). The "spruce young sergeant" actually performed his mission later in the battle, signaling the *Dolphin* to stop shelling the shore because some Marines had moved into her line of fire. Again, Crane makes this fact clear in the story, and in this case he correctly identifies the man involved as Sergeant John Quick, who, along with Fitzgerald, was awarded the Congressional Medal of Honor for his actions (Stallman 371).

Relationship to Other Crane Works

Crane covers the same events depicted in "Marines," the attack on Camp McCalla and the battle of Cuzco, in another of his *Wounds in the Rain* stories, "War Memories," but he does not mention the signalmen in that version. The only connection any critic notes between this work and the other pieces in *Wounds in the Rain* is a perceived lack of merit that it shares with "'God Rest Ye, Merry Gentlemen'" and "The Revenge of the *Adolphus*." Milne Holton lumps these stories together as "inferior work written in a time of illness and need, . . . framed out of Crane's reportage by means of a weak plot, with hardly any discernible form or theme and with only occasional sparks of good writing" (257).

Discussions of technical connections between this story and others of Crane's works are equally few. In fact, the only link any critic has drawn is a very general one noted by James B. Colvert. Crane witnessed firsthand the fall of night and the coming of dawn at Guantánamo, but his descriptions of these events, Colvert points out, are variations on one of his most frequently used patterns of imagery, a pattern incorporating in most cases, as here, "the grass-green valley, the terrible monsters of prey [in the imagery], the blasted vegetation, the blighted atmosphere, the cloud-muffled mountains in the middle distance, and over all the serene and poignantly remote sky." Colvert says that Crane formulated this pattern in some of his earliest writings, the Sullivan County sketches, and used versions of it in many of his nonfiction pieces, poems, and prose fictions, most notably *The Red Badge of Courage*, "The Open Boat," and "The Blue Hotel" (xix).

Critical Studies

Praise for "Marines" came almost immediately upon its publication. In a letter to Crane from Washington, D.C., dated February 17, 1899, Marine Captain (later Major General) G. F. Elliott, who had commanded a company in the battle at Cuzco and had cited Crane for bravery in his official report of that engagement, tells him, "You did just right, in bringing forward the enlisted men, with all their faults, their rough and sometimes ugly corners (usually from early rearing)." These men, Elliott continues, "are as a rule loyal and true at heart . . . and to see that a brave act becomes known out of their own little community, one of their own, stimulates the whole company" (*Correspondence* II, 438). Subsequent critics have generally been less enthusiastic, when they bother to mention the story at all, and tend to limit themselves to autobiographical readings. Edwin Cady, for instance, faults it for its repeated, jarring shifts between a "dry, rather deprecating" tone and a "lush, heroic" one, a flaw he ascribes to Crane's own philosophical vacillation at this point, his being "torn between the loyalties both natural and preferential to the emotions and modes of the realists"—loyalties that produce the deprecating sections—and an attraction to the "Rooseveltian, 'strenuous life' [of the] neoromantics," which accounts for the heroic sections (87). Similarly, Christopher Benfey sees the story as notable only to the extent that it is revelatory of Crane himself, indicating his own desire to be, as both warrior and writer, like the signalman: "[c]onspicuously calm, a cool messenger of feverish events, a trafficker in codes and signals" (247–48). And Holton, despite his low opinion of this story, noted above in "Relationship to Other Crane Works," regards it as a significant indicator of the change that took place in Crane's philosophy as a result of his observation of combat in Cuba. Whereas in earlier stories Crane was mostly concerned with the state of awareness which his protagonists exhibited, here, as in the Spanish-American War stories in general, he focuses on "the stoic virtues, not the keen awarenesses," of the "ordinary soldier, fighting steadily and without fanfare, doing his job," which results in a writing style with less fanfare as well, one that is "barer," "drier," and "more resigned" in its tone (245). Regarding Crane's handling of the signalman, Holton says, "[i]t is his courage and not his apprehension which is important, a courage which is the one unyielding fact in an event which is too absurd even to yield to apprehension" (247). Holton asserts that "[t]his courage, the stoic virtue, is all that is left for Crane to celebrate" (247) at this point in his life, and his doing so here and in the rest of *Wounds in the Rain* renders these stories a "halting beginning toward the transformation of his disillusionments and his admirations in the Spanish American War into a formulated ethic for man in an absurd universe" (256).

Works Cited

Benfey, Christopher. *The Double Life of Stephen Crane*. New York: Knopf, 1992.

Bowers, Fredson. Textual Introduction. *Tales of War*. Vol. 6 of The University of Virginia Edition of *The Works of Stephen Crane*. Ed. Fredson Bowers. Charlottesville: University Press of Virginia, 1970, xxxvii–cxci.

Cady, Edwin H. *Stephen Crane*. Rev. ed. New York: Twayne, 1982.

Colvert, James B. Introduction. *Tales of War* xi–xxxvi.

Crane, Stephen. "In the First Land Fight Four of Our Men Are Killed." *Reports of War*. Vol. 9 of The University of Virginia Edition of *The Works of Stephen Crane*. Ed. Fredson Bowers. Charlottesville: University Press of Virginia, 1971. 128–30.

———. "Marines Signaling Under Fire at Guantánamo." *Tales of War* 194–200.

———. "The Red Badge of Courage Was His Wig-wag Flag." *Reports of War* 134–42.

Holton, Milne. *Cylinder of Vision: The Fiction and Journalistic Writings of Stephen Crane*. Baton Rouge: Louisiana State University Press, 1972.

Stallman, R. W. *Stephen Crane: A Biography*. New York: George Braziller, 1968.

Wertheim, Stanley, and Paul Sorrentino, eds. *The Correspondence of Stephen Crane*. Vol. 2. New York: Columbia University Press, 1988.

The Monster

Publication History

This story was first published in America in the August 1898 issue of *Harper's New Monthly Magazine* (97:343–76) (Bowers 3), after having been rejected by the editor of *Century*, Richard Watson Gilder, allegedly with the comment that "We couldn't publish that thing with half the expectant mothers in America on our subscription list" (qtd. in Beer 164). It then appeared in America in the collection *"The Monster" and Other Stories*, published by Harper & Brothers in 1899; it first came out in England in 1901, when Harper released a British edition of this book, increased by several stories over the American version (Bowers 3). Wilson Follett placed it in volume 3, which he edited and published in 1926, of *The Work of Stephen Crane* (12 vols., New York: Knopf, 1925–27), and it also appeared in *The Complete Short Stories and Sketches of Stephen Crane* (Garden City, N.Y.: Doubleday, 1963), edited by Thomas A. Gullason.

Circumstances of Composition

On August 19, 1897, Crane and his common-law wife, Cora Stewart, were injured in a carriage accident while they were traveling from their first English home, in Oxted, to the nearby town of Kenley, intending to visit there Harold

Frederic, another expatriate American writer, and *his* common-law wife, Kate. The Cranes convalesced at the Frederics' home for about a week and then both families removed to Dunmanus Bay, Ireland, for three further weeks of recuperation and recreation (Stallman 310–11). From here—specifically, Attridge's Hotel, Schull, County Cork—Crane wrote his brother Edmund on September 9 that "I have just finished a novelette of 20000 words—'The Monster'" (*Correspondence* I, 296).

Despite its having been composed under his aegis, so to speak, Frederic found this story offensive. At a luncheon in early December 1897, at Crane's home in Oxted, he urged Crane to destroy it. According to Sanford Bennett, another guest who was also a writer, Crane's response was to pound the furniture with the butt of a revolver he had acquired in Mexico and demand to know why Frederic thought people would be put off by a story that had "some sense in it" (qtd. in Weintraub 149). Crane was moved to still greater demonstrativeness a moment later when Frederic shifted to criticizing *The Nigger of the "Narcissus,"* a recent book by Crane's good friend Joseph Conrad. This time he smashed a dessert plate with his pistol and shouted at Frederic, "You and I and [Rudyard] Kipling couldn't have written The Nigger!" (qtd. in Stallman 332).

Sources and Influences

Crane's first biographer, Thomas Beer, theorizes that Crane derived the outlines of "The Monster" from his youthful memories of the case of Levi Hume, a black teamster disfigured by facial cancer who lived in the town of Port Jervis, New York, where Crane passed much of his childhood and where a sizable contingent of his family still resided (13). Robert W. Stallman concurs with this hypothesis (333), but the fact is that Beer could not find anyone to verify this possibility (Levenson xiii). The nearest thing to a positive identification is the statement of Crane's niece, Edna Crane Sidbury, who said that her father, Crane's brother William, told her that he thought the story was based on "a local carter, 'his face eaten by cancer,'" whose name she could not recall (qtd. in Levenson xiii). Whether or not William's identification is correct is unknowable, but apparently at the time the story was published many people in Port Jervis, which Crane had changed to Whilomville (his setting for an additional fourteen stories in the years to come), made some identification of their own between events in their town and the Whilomville citizens' cruel treatment of Henry Johnson, for on March 3, 1899, Crane wrote to William,

> I forgot to reply to you [in several previous letters] about the gossip in Port Jervis over "The Monster." I suppose that Port Jervis entered my head while I was writing it but I particularly dont [sic] wish them [the

townspeople] to think so because people get very sensitive and I would not scold away freely if I thought the eye of your glorious public was upon me. (*Correspondence* II, 446)

Crane's sarcasm here about the gossip of the glorious public suggests his considerable familiarity with the receiving end of such talk, a fact that has led many critics to regard this letter as evidence that Crane actually used himself as the chief model for Henry Johnson and for Dr. Trescott as well. Sy Kahn notes that like Johnson and Trescott, by 1897 Crane had encountered a good deal of public opprobrium as a result of his well-intentioned efforts to help others and to remain true to his own conscience. He had been persecuted by the New York City police and vilified by much of the press for his defense of a prostitute, Dora Clark, against what he regarded as an unjust arrest by a corrupt officer; he had borne countless accusations of drug addiction, alcoholism, and various other forms of debauchery; and he had been harshly attacked by many reviewers for the seeming blasphemies of his first volume of poems, *The Black Riders*, published in May 1895 (37–38).

This theory of the story's origin is also variously voiced by James B. Colvert (124), J. C. Levenson, who adds Crane's honesty in writing about the Bowery and his non-matrimonial relationship with Cora as possible sources of persecution (xv–xix), and John Berryman, who casts his analysis in Freudian terms. Behind Jimmie Trescott's attempted "rescue" of the broken flower at the outset of the story, Henry Johnson's rescue of Jimmie from the fire, and Dr. Trescott's rescue of Henry from the enraged townspeople, Berryman sees Crane's own impulse to rescue such "broken flowers" as Dora Clark and Cora Stewart, and he reads the story as Crane's effort to work out with his long-dead minister father this attraction to those condemned by conventional society (192–94). Berryman supports this contention by pointing out that Henry Johnson's name is an amalgam of Henry Fleming, in his view another stand-in for Crane, and Johnson Smith, which Crane intended to be his pseudonym— but which the printer altered to John*st*on Smith—as author of the novel that was his first literary effort at rescuing a broken flower, *Maggie: A Girl of the Streets*. He also notes that at the end of "The Monster," when Dr. Trescott shelters Henry, Crane presents the father as "imperturbably protective of the criminal, in spite of the community's terror, disapproval, and power. Crane has his father in effect say: 'I am with you; go ahead'" (193).

Stanley Wertheim takes a similar view, seeing Crane in "The Monster"—as well as in "An Episode of War" and "The Open Boat"—as engaged with "the pervasive theme of American literature, . . . [h]uman isolation in its physical, emotional, or ideological manifestations," as a result of his own revolt against his respectable, religious family. Trescott is one of Crane's "autobiographical protagonists," one of his "isolatoes engaged in an unsuccessful struggle to integrate their lives with that of society and yet preserve separate identities"

(499). Specifically, Trescott, like Crane in his defense of Dora Clark, "is baffled when he finds himself ostracized for a charitable act in a community which professes to a Christian view of human affairs" (503).

Looking in a cultural rather than psychobiographical direction, Alice Hall Petry theorizes that Crane's contemporary John Merrick, the severely disfigured Englishman widely known as "the Elephant Man," might have served, along with Levi Hume, as a source for Henry Johnson. Petry bases this suggestion on Merrick's notoriety in England in the 1890s, which means that Crane could scarcely have been unaware of his case, and a number of parallels between Merrick's and Johnson's situations: both men are essentially faceless, both have only one functioning eye, both wear veil-like coverings to conceal their deformity, both regard themselves as gentlemen and practice good manners that accord with that image, and both are conscientiously tended by concerned physicians—Dr. Trescott in Henry's case and Dr. Frederick Treves in Merrick's (348–52). Perhaps, Petry speculates, discovering Merrick's "appearance, personality, and situation both resurrected Crane's memories of Hume and enabled him to flesh Hume into one of the most pathetic characters in American literature" (347). If so, she concludes, Crane's ever-present irony clearly comes into play, for the glaring difference between Merrick and Johnson is that Merrick, with Treves's help, became widely appreciated and respected despite his appearance, and Treves's career was enhanced as well, whereas Henry and Trescott are both persecuted (352).

Several critics have identified the prototype of another character in "The Monster," the gossip-prone Martha Goodwin, in a letter Crane is alleged to have written from Port Jervis in 1894 complaining about an old female busybody there who chastised him for taking an innocent buggy ride with a thirteen-year-old girl. The "big joke in all this," he says, is that

> [t]his lady in her righteousness is just the grave of a stale lust and every boy in town knows it. She accepted ruin at the hands of a farmer when we were all 10 or 11. But she is a nice woman and all her views of all things belong on the tables of Moses. (*Correspondence* II, 667)

Both Stallman (114) and Kahn link this woman to Martha Goodwin; Kahn notes similarities in phrasing between Crane's letter and his description of Martha, such as his calling the Port Jervis woman "the grave of a stale lust" and Martha "the mausoleum of a dead passion," and his presentation of both women as deriving their avidity for social propriety and cutting conversation from their youthful romantic disappointments (41–43). The only problem with this reading is that the letter in question first appears in Thomas Beer's 1923 biography and, as is the case with many such letters, no original has ever come to light, which means there is a strong possibility that Beer fabricated it (*Correspondence* I, 6–10; "Thomas Beer" 2–16).

In response to much of this biographical detective work, Milne Holton asserts that it is in general "unsupported and conjectural" (204) and ultimately less important for its own sake than as part of an examination of what Crane does in the story to transform portions of his own experience into an aesthetically effective expression of his artistic vision. In line with this belief, Holton sees Crane responding to his experiences of public disapprobation over his relationships with Dora Clark and Cora Stewart by creating in "The Monster" a vision of the human community that is "considerably darkened and inward-turned" compared to his depiction of it in *The Red Badge of Courage* and "The Open Boat" (204). In those works, Holton points out, the protagonists' confrontations with the terrors of the unknown lead them to a new appreciation of the positive aspects of community, whereas in "The Monster" such confrontations lead the protagonist precisely in the opposite direction, to a discovery that the community is in fact not worth being a part of (205).

Robert Glen Deamer likewise sees this story as indicative of a change in Crane's vision rooted in his personal experience; he argues, however, that this change is in the direction of a guarded optimism rather than a deeper pessimism. Early in his career, Deamer says, Crane conceived of life in deterministic terms, as evinced by many of his early works, particularly the novels *Maggie: A Girl of the Streets* and *George's Mother*. However, what he witnessed of courageous and effective human behavior during a trip through the American West and Mexico in 1895 as a correspondent for the Bacheller syndicate in the West convinced him that people could in fact shape their own fates, at least to some extent, through the "heroic" virtues of discipline, responsibility, and courage—a shift in viewpoint borne out by the changed tone of many of his post-1895 stories (143). These, Deamer explains, tend to be studies of men, whether in the West, on the battlefield, or in the seemingly placid environs of a small town, who either attain these virtues and thus merit Crane's admiration or else reject them and therefore warrant his censure. Trescott belongs to the former group, owing to the "independence, courage, and magnanimity" he displays in his treatment of Henry in defiance of the wishes of his fellow-citizens (147).

Seekers of literary sources for this story have been fully as active as the biographical trackers. Lars Ahnebrink proposes Henrik Ibsen's 1882 play *An Enemy of the People*. Ibsen's protagonist, like Trescott, is a doctor in a largely middle-class community who finds himself ostracized as a result of his taking an ethically worthy but socially unpopular stand. Like Trescott, he loses much of his practice, sees his family suffer, and endures a visit from a group of sympathetic but thoroughly conventional leading citizens who urge him to give up his position—a group led by a man who, like Crane's Judge Hagenthorpe, is an "egoistic bachelor" and a "smug and mighty" community arbiter. Moreover, Crane's technique in "The Monster" of working toward "objectivity by presenting both sides of a problem" is similar to Ibsen's method in this play (378–81). Holton agrees with all these connections and adds some stylistic links as well, pointing out that Crane's prose style here is, like Ibsen's, considerably toned down in comparison to his previous work, and that "The Monster" largely employs the dramatic point of view—that is, the characters are presented as they would be on the stage, with the reader/spectator having access to their actions and speech but not to their thoughts (205). However, despite this lengthy list of correspondences Colvert remains unconvinced, asserting that there "is no external—and no convincing internal—evidence" that Crane ever read Ibsen (181).

Another possible source, this one identified by Donald Pizer, is Leo Tolstoy's *What To Do?*, which was translated into English in 1887. Pizer notes that the title of this work seems to echo in Dr. Trescott's speech in Chapter 11 when Judge Hagenthorpe suggests that Henry be euthanized. "'And what am I to do?'" Trescott shouts. "'What am I to do? He gave himself for—for Jimmie. What am I to do for him?'" (*Tales* 32). Tolstoy himself, Pizer says, drew this question from the New Testament, Luke 3.10–11, where it is asked of John the Baptist, who replies that one must share all one has with the needy. This, Pizer continues, is likewise Christ's, Tolstoy's, and Crane's answer—an answer that Trescott knows is correct but that Hagenthorpe willfully ignores in concluding, "'It is hard for a man to know what to do'" (*Tales* 32; Pizer 127–28).

Margaret Anderson raises a second possible Biblical connection through the unusual name of John Twelve, a member of the group of leading citizens who counsel Trescott to abandon Henry. This name, Anderson says, may be a reference to the twelfth book of the Gospel of St. John, which recounts Jesus' raising of Lazarus from the dead and the subsequent desire of the chief priests to put Lazarus to death because this miracle drew many converts to Jesus. Anderson theorizes that by this parallel Crane intends a "general association" rather than a precise correspondence between Trescott and Jesus, making the point that by their total unselfishness these two reveal the utter selfishness and hypocrisy of the leaders of their communities, reveal that "altruism can result in just as much hostility from society as malevolence" (23–24).

Looking to a very different source, Robert Morace says that the injured Henry's single unwinking eye that so disconcerts Hagenthorpe may stem from the similar organ and its effect in Edgar Allan Poe's "The Tell-Tale Heart" (72), with the point here as in Poe's story being that the malevolence perceived in that eye is not really there but rather manufactured in the eye of the perceiver. Taking a more general view, David Halliburton reads the town's behavior as perhaps deriving from Crane's awareness of the widespread "crises of identity and self-confidence" afflicting American communities in the 1890s. As they confronted the changes wrought by the rise of big business and successive waves of immigrants, Halliburton says, such communities frequently responded with the kind of hostility toward difference as is shown Henry, in the form of campaigns for temperance and patriotism that thinly disguised xenophobia—such campaigns being acceptable ways of reasserting their traditional Anglo-Saxon "unity and purity" (198).

Relationship to Other Crane Works

"The Monster" is closely related in terms of characters, if not of tone, to the later series of short stories Crane also set in Whilomville. Jimmie Trescott and his parents, who figure so prominently in "The Monster," play roles in most of these short stories, including "The Angel Child," "Lynx-Hunting," "The Lover and the Tell-Tale," "'Showin' Off'" "Making An Orator," "Shame," "The Carriage-Lamps," "The Stove," "The Trial, Execution, and Burial of Homer Phelps," "The Fight," "The City Urchin and the Chaste Villagers," and "A Little Pilgrim." The only story the Trescotts do not appear in is "The Knife," which focuses on two of their sometime employees, Peter Washington, who has succeeded "the late gallant Henry Johnson" (*Tales* 185) as their coachman, and Alek Williams, the man whom Doctor Trescott hires in "The Monster" to shelter Henry after the latter is physically and mentally impaired during his attempted rescue of Jimmie from the fire. However, despite these connections, Daniel Hoffman maintains that "The Monster" is most closely related to *Maggie*, in that these two stories are the only ones in which Crane engages with the conflicts created or complicated by the hierarchical orders of society—with the "presence of society as a complex interrelationship of persons and classes" (5).

Hoffman may be correct insofar as these two works are perhaps Crane's most sustained investigations of social orders, but they are not the only such investigations. Certainly the other Whilomville stories, particularly "The Stove," "Shame," "The Fight," and "The City Urchin," deal, albeit more lightheartedly, with levels of society in one sort of conflict or another, while several critics note a close relationship between "The Monster" and "The Blue Hotel" in terms of social themes. Morace points out that Crane himself seems to have been aware of this link, since in a letter of March 16, 1898, to his American agent, Paul Revere Reynolds, Crane argues against putting both "Monster" and "Death and the Child" in the same book, saying that he prefers instead to have "Monster" and "Blue Hotel" between the same covers. Morace's view is that this preference stems from Crane's understanding that these two stories share two elements: the theme of human beings' failure to create the "quasi-Christian community" that Crane regards as the only hope of survival in an indifferent universe, and the metaphor of the game as their central structural element (66). Ralph Ellison takes a very similar stance regarding the theme of community in these two stories, saying that they are linked together by the "failure of social charity" at the center of each (75). Chester L. Wolford notes the same link, expressing it in terms of "humanity's elemental fear of facing elemental chaos," but he sees the stories as complementary rather than identical. Both are tragedies, he says, but "Blue Hotel" is a "heroic" one as a result of its implications that truth and justice do have some place in the world even if they are "unsustainable," whereas "The Monster" is a "nihilistic" one in that here wrong totally and unambiguously triumphs over right (*Study* 44).

Looking at the story in terms of one of its protagonists rather than of society as a whole, Stallman and Holton both draw parallels between "The Monster" and "The Veteran," Crane's tale of the aged Henry Fleming's fatal attempt to rescue some colts from a fire. Holton notes that both Henry Fleming and Henry Johnson come to grief as a result of "an absurd and destructive fire" and that in both cases the narrator says that the hero's face stopped being a face in this moment of crisis (116), a point that Stallman says Crane uses purposely to dehumanize each man (335). Kahn places this fire in a more general context, asserting that it is but one variation on Crane's "central situation" in nearly all of his work—"man under attack by irrational forces." In many stories, Kahn says, Crane uses war to create this situation; in those set in civilian locales he uses elements such as fire, which he renders, especially in "Monster," as the equivalent of war through "patterns of sound and . . . images" that cause the fire to "symbolize threatening, evil human forces" (37).

Several other critics also link "Monster" to other works through Crane's seemingly career-long fascination with fire as both literal event and source of symbolism. Levenson points out that as early as November 25, 1894, Crane was working out the ideas surrounding fire that come to fruition in "Monster." On that date, the *New York Press* ran Crane's report of a fire—an event he may well have made up—in which are to be found clear prefigurements of the "serpentine flames" of "Monster" and of this story's presentation of "the horror of nature gone wild" that is "matched by a horror of human helplessness that is scarcely distinguished from indifference" (xxi). Marston LaFrance agrees that through his handling of fire Crane links cosmic and human indifference, pointing out that in both the newspaper report and the story the mob's behavior is closely associated with the action of the fire (208). Holton also notes the motif of fire running from the *New York Press* account through "The Veteran" and on to "Monster"; he hypothesizes that "fire was associated in Crane's mind with some threatening and chaotic principle of the universe" that, like war or the sea, humans must confront (207).

John C. Martin notes the presence in "Monster" of another subject that similarly preoccupied Crane throughout his career, the behavior of children. Beginning with the early *Maggie*, continuing through the middle-period "Monster" and "His New Mittens," and concluding in the late Whilomville series, Martin says, Crane consistently depicts children as marked by three dominant traits: "innocent curiosity," a desire to remain acceptable to one's social group, and group cruelty toward those individuals who are unacceptable (40). In "Monster" Crane illustrates how the first of these can easily metamorphose into the other two. Following Henry's accident, Jimmie and his friends are at first innocuously inquisitive about the hooded figure sitting in isolation outside the Trescott home. This inquisitiveness quickly turns malign, however, when the boys begin challenging one another to touch the fearsome creature and, to maintain their standing in the group and enable themselves to lord it over the others, Jimmie and another boy take up this challenge, heedless of the ugliness of their conduct toward the uncomprehending Henry (42).

James Nagel makes note of two further connections in the area of technique, between "Monster" and other Crane works. First, he argues that this story's twenty-four sections break down into twelve that show how Henry becomes a monster and twelve that depict how the community becomes monstrous in response to him, which makes it "structurally identical" to *Red Badge* and also links it to *Maggie* and Crane's other Bowery novella, *George's Mother*, since although the precise number of chapters in these varies, both are similarly broken in half, with the first half devoted to setting up causes and the second to exploring effects (132). And second, Nagel says that in both "Monster" and "The Bride Comes to Yellow Sky" Crane concludes by using an "imagistic correlative"—by which he means an image that "focuses the meaning of the preceding action on a vivid, sensory figure." In "Monster" this figure is that of the dying fire in the stove faintly illuminating the fifteen empty teacups, while in "Bride" it is the funnel-shaped tracks that Scratchy Wilson makes as he leaves the scene of his thwarted showdown with Jack Potter (151).

In another interpretation of symbolism, Michael Fried notes that "The Monster" and one of Crane's last stories, "The Upturned Face," are connected in that both focus on an upward-staring face—Henry's in "The Monster," a corpse's in "Face"—which is disfigured—Henry's by burning chemicals, the corpse's by dirt as it is buried. In Fried's view, Crane's ultimate goal in this focus is an allegory of the act of writing and the inevitable disfiguring of reality involved in that act. These faces, he says, "are at once synecdoches for the bodies of those characters and singularly concentrated metaphors for the sheets of writing paper that the author had before him." With this possibility in mind, Fried continues, "one way of accounting for the peculiar horror of the violence that befalls the faces . . . is as the writer's response *as reader* to the deathliness of the blank upward-staring page," which the writer is intuiting as "a sign that the natural world has died and cannot be resuscitated . . . though by the force of art—of literary writing—it can at least be consumed or buried (his solution to Romanticism)" (*"Gross Clinic"* 94–95; restated in expanded form in Fried's book *Realism, Writing, Disfiguration* 94–96, 132–36).

Critical Studies

Harold Frederic's adverse judgment, quoted above in "Circumstances of Composition," notwithstanding, "Monster" began eliciting critical praise even before Crane had published it. In a letter of January 1, 1898, Joseph Conrad, evidently responding to an outline or a partial draft, tells Crane that "[t]he damned story has been haunting me. . . . I think it must be fine. It's a subject for you" (*Correspondence* I, 328). And almost every critic who has read it in its finished form concurs. Howells considered it one of the greatest American short stories (Stallman 334), and Rupert Hughes, writing as "Chelifer" for *The Criterion* in 1900, says that "'The Monster' is an incursion into the realms of the horrible without once losing sight of realism or plausibility. There is no strain on credulity, no mysticism of any sort." To those who might agree with Richard Watson Gilder's alleged accusations of nauseating characteristics, Hughes responds that "its sickening qualities are mitigated by the indirectness of their suggestion, its trivialities redeemed by the psychological dignity of the physician's problem" (qtd. in *Stephen Crane's Career* 71).

Many others tacitly concur with Conrad's assessment of the subject of small-town life as an especially apt one for Crane, since they regard this subject as evidence of his taking a number of important intellectual and artistic steps forward. Donald B. Gibson asserts that in several respects "Monster" is Crane's most ambitious work, for here he does not focus solely on his accustomed protagonist, the isolated individual possessed of "only his own internal strength to rely on" but rather looks beyond this single figure to examine and critique a carefully detailed social fabric (136). Levenson, Alfred Kazin, and Edwin Cady likewise praise Crane's newly enlarged vision in this story. Levenson sees it as a major achievement in that here "Crane present[s] with considerable sympathy that common life" that William Dean Howells, one of his early mentors, argued was the American writer's proper subject, while "at the same time he show[s] the world beyond the safe bounds of comfort and routine where chance and violence are as natural as life itself." Thus, Levenson concludes, Crane proves that "he [does] not need a battlefield or an open boat for subject in order to imagine a state of warfare or a game against fearful odds" (lxxiii). Kazin points out that in returning in imagination to the small town of his own youth as his sense of mortality bore in on him in his premature last years, Crane is to be praised for going back to where his heart lies and yet refusing to succumb to sentimentality, for seeing that the tranquility of such a town is only a mask covering a number of highly unpleasant features (259). Cady regards this broad, penetrating vision as evidence of Crane's artistic maturity, of his movement "toward a dense, adult, demonstratedly complicit society" in which "the monster" potentially lives in everyone, both individually and collectively (157).

This issue of the culpability of both individuals and societies is one of the key interpretative matrices in the story. No one disputes Nagel's point that the story's central conflict is between "individual moral responsibility and an unassailable human will" (132); however, much of the criticism divides over the question of whether Crane is more interested in the behavior of the community as a whole or that of the few individuals who defy the community's mores. Taking the former view, LaFrance argues that the townsfolk as a group function as the protagonist of the story, not Henry Johnson or Dr. Trescott, as the reader might conventionally assume. In LaFrance's formulation, the community undergoes a pointedly truncated version of the pattern of initiation to which Crane usually subjects his individual protagonists in his stories. Typically, LaFrance says, the Crane protagonist begins by facing an experience of the unknown; he then develops a near-paralyzing fear because his illusions about this experience take over, but this fear is deflated when the experience actually occurs and the protagonist realizes that it did not match his inflated fears, at which point he feels ashamed of his earlier illusions, an emotion that is the beginning of wisdom, of an ability to see the world in a more realistic, unillusioned fashion. In "The Monster," LaFrance says, the townspeople of Whilomville as a group undergo only the first two of these stages: they face the unknown quantity of the physically and mentally disfigured Henry Johnson and work themselves into a state of hysteria about him as a result of the wild imaginings they foster in one another. Crane's halting his usual pattern at this juncture, LaFrance argues, is precisely the point—the community never learns to get beyond their illusions and acquire the wisdom to look at Johnson realistically (206–07). Thus, the true "monster" of the title is not Henry but the town in which he lives. For LaFrance, this tactic powerfully conveys Crane's general precept that individual values are finally superior to those of the group, that "[l]ife is meaningful, morally significant, because every individual has the power to choose what is morally right for himself within whatever scope of awareness he possesses, and thus he can maintain his moral world intact as his awareness increases," as Trescott does, even as communities impel individuals to reject increased awareness (152).

In a similar vein, Gibson, Anthony Channell Hilfer, Eric Solomon, and Wolford all read the story as primarily an indictment of the limitations the community places upon its awareness, particularly by means of manners and other orthodox modes of behavior. Gibson makes the point that Crane presents Henry as clearly harmless after the fire; he only seems to be a monster to the townspeople because of his physical deformity and his being "unconstrained by the rigid system of manners" in which before the accident he had eagerly participated along with the rest of the town (138). Hilfer sees Crane as demonstrating that the popular myth of the small town—the belief that its "conventional thought patterns and moral judgments are *right*" (59)—is indeed only a myth, for with regard to Henry "conventional responses are the grounds of moral failure," as is the case when the conventional eulogies for the supposedly dead Henry turn to conventional horror when he is discovered to have survived in a disfigured condition, and when the ladies of the town's better social class show their disapproval of Dr. Trescott's protection of Henry by the highly conventional means of refusing to attend Mrs. Trescott's tea party (60–63). Solomon says that although Trescott is partly at fault due to his hubris and self-righteousness (a claim disputed by William K. Spofford [5–7]), the townspeople are chiefly to blame. They unjustifiably find Henry monstrous simply because of his "inability to comprehend the effect of his altered appearance"; what frightens them is that by this failure to acknowledge the importance of surfaces he "calls into question the social and religious hypocrisies that order men's lives" (195). In Wolford's comparable view, the point of the story is that society mediates "between the individual and chaos" by blocking out through its forms and rituals the reality of that chaos and thus giving the individual "a sense of security, order, and intelligibility" (*Anger* 88). Henry undermines that sense because, lacking "the familiar face, the veneer of civilization" (*Anger* 89), he is a reminder of chaos, of what all humans would be if "the artificially imposed rationality of their behavior were destroyed" (*Anger* 93). Trescott confronts this threat, but the rest of the community, lacking his sense of compassion and obligation, refuses to do so.

Kahn and Holton look at one particular segment of this community, the children, and assert that through this segment Crane anatomizes Whilomville as a whole. Kahn says that Jimmie and his friends, who eventually make a game of touching the addled, inoffensive Henry in order to prove their "courage" to one another, are "full of superstition, rumors, and misinformation"—in short, they simply imitate the behavior of their more culpable, supposedly more mature parents (43). Holton argues that this unsophisticated imitation is part of the corrosive myth of the American small town; such aping without fully understanding the ramifications of that behavior is innocent, and "in the American town childish innocence—no matter how destructive or cruel—is always permitted" (207).

Morace focuses on the fact that the boys' behavior is constructed as a game and asserts that three parallel, overlapping strands of metaphorical games carry the story's burden of significance. The first strand comprises the games the children and the "child-like" African-Americans play, such as Jimmie's pretending to be a train and Henry's self-consciously gallant courtship of Bella Farragut early in the story, as well as the later games at the children's birthday party and the boys' game of touch-the-monster, all of which, through their air of make-believe, are linked to the pointless and frequently cruel social games engaged in by the adults. The second strand is composed of games played by an individual alone that likewise mirror the games of the dominant white culture; the most obvious of these is Henry's mannerly courtship, which reflects the system of social illusions by which all the townspeople operate—their refusal to separate appearance and reality, their determination to "play games" in the sense of collaborating to agree that "reality" is whatever they wish it to be. The third strand, related to the second, consists of behaviors that are explicitly denoted as games and are played by conscious participants; these offer an ironic parallel to the conduct of the townspeople who, in their adherence to social forms, are equally participating in games with arbitrarily established rules but do not realize that fact, who fail to see their separation of appearance and reality and thus remain oblivious to the cruelty and suffering their unrealized rules inflict. The most crucial of these unconscious games, Morace says, are the melodrama of self-sacrifice, suffering, and noble death that the town constructs for Henry, in which he, "ungamesmanlike," refuses to participate by dying; and the ritual of ostracism constructed around Dr. Trescott when he refuses to abide by society's rules and send Henry away permanently (66–78).

Implicit in Morace's interpretation, as Wolford notes in an analysis separate from the one cited above, are the assumptions that the townspeople could abandon their vicious games if they chose to examine their behavior more closely and that therefore Crane's point in this story is the community's failure to live up to its true purpose of brotherhood and charity. Wolford argues that such a view stems from a misreading of Crane's theory about the nature of community. Wolford sees "Monster" as presenting a tripartite—and grim—purpose behind the formation of this or any such conventional society: "to shield people from reality, from the howling chaos of the universe; to curb the natural, chaotic barbarity of children; and to find acceptable channels for 'barbaric' expression that cannot be tethered entirely" (*Study* 44). Given these aims, Wolford argues, it is mistaken to assume that Crane regards the town as capable of making an ethical choice; rather, being only one step above a mob, such a community in fact exists, "in part, to *inhibit* ethical choice [emphasis added]." Only an individual can make such a choice, and when he or she does so the town opposes him or her as part of its very *raison d'être* (*Study* 47).

Two of the critics who see Crane as focusing on an individual—specifically, Dr. Trescott—rather than the town as protagonist base their arguments on Crane's choice of a peculiar name for one of the arbiters of Whilomville's opinions, John Twelve. Daniel Knapp and Gibson both regard this designation as Crane's way of pointing his reader to the twelfth chapter of the Gospel of St. John, an idea which gains considerable weight and, perhaps, considerable interpretive significance because of the subject matter of that chapter, Jesus' raising of Lazarus from the dead. This miracle, as Knapp points out, is the final confirmation of Jesus' divinity and is also the last one he performs, largely because it is the act that convinces the chief priests that he is a threat to their hegemony and therefore must be eliminated. Knapp sees Henry as enacting the role of Lazarus: like that resurrected man the rescued Johnson "is too compelling a testimony to be forgotten; his monstrous resurrection is unforgivable, and it brings doom not only on himself and Trescott, but on the entire community"—in terms, that is, of its moral ruin (262). As for Trescott, he "is more than Jesus, as Johnson is more than Lazarus; the doctor mimics both the Son of Man and the Father of Mankind, and Johnson mimics both Mankind and Mankind's Savior" (263), as is apparent in the story's final chapter. Knapp sees the empty tea-table as an ironic parallel of the Last Supper. All the disciples have failed to present themselves here, he argues: "Mrs. Twelve has come and gone," and "the only persons at the Love Feast are the father, the son—and Grace [Mrs. Trescott's Christian name]" (264). Viewed through these parallels, Knapp concludes, the story reveals that "Whilomville is not a Judah as yet unvisited by a savior; it is a Judah that cannot stand one when he comes" (266).

Gibson's explication of this connection is less elaborate, consisting chiefly of the point that Trescott is intended to be "Christlike" and, as such, undergoes no change in his character, being a model of sympathy and rectitude from beginning to end. However, Gibson also discerns the possibility of a certain ambivalence on Crane's part about such a figure. He notes that Lazarus's sister Martha served Jesus during his visit to their town, and that another Martha, by the suggestive last name of *Goodwin*, initially serves Trescott by scorning the townspeople who have worked themselves up over the imaginary dangers Henry Johnson poses, but then she lambastes the doctor as well. Perhaps, Gibson says, this inconsistency is merely reflective of Crane's frequent difficulties with maintaining a consistent tone, or perhaps he is purposefully proposing certain "reservations about the doctor's decision to follow the dictates of his conscience rather than to act pragmatically" (137–39).

Without arguing for intentionality on Crane's part, Wolford proposes another text that may shed interpretive light on Trescott, *Antigone*. The doctor, he argues, can be understood as a tragic hero facing the dilemma that Sophocles examines in this play, the conflicting imperatives of "private virtue and public order" (*Study* 44). In terms of the formula of Greek tragedy, Wolford explains, Trescott's *hamartia*—his error of judgment—is saving Henry, for his doing so is a noble action that the community cannot abide; his *peripeteia*—his reversal of circumstances—is the townspeople's demand that he send Henry away permanently after the "monster" escapes from his caretaker and wanders through town; and his *anagnorisis*—the discovery that leads him from ignorance to knowledge—is his seeing that his wife has been socially exiled as a result of his stance (*Study* 46).

James Hafley takes the view that Crane focuses primarily on neither the individual nor the community but instead evenly divides his attention between the two. Henry, "who becomes gradually symbolic of 'God,'" represents one pole of behavior, while the townspeople, who are characterized as comprising a "mechanical civilization [that] controls values" and who thus perceive Henry as both "monstrous and insane for his godlike virtues," represent the other. In this scheme, Trescott functions as a medial figure, occupying the center between these poles (159–60). Charles Child Walcutt and

Gullason do not dispute the concept of a split focus, but they read that split as producing not the kind of moral certainty that Hafley implies but rather a sense of insolubility. Walcutt reads the story as a "cosmic joke"—a situation in which there is no "human or decent solution." Regarding this condition as Crane's statement of his personal theory of naturalism, Walcutt says the point of the story is that "[a]ll the characters are bound by their virtues and limitations (it does not matter which) in the circumstances given, and apparently no will can extricate those involved from the social deterioration that ensues" (83–84). Gullason does not consider the characters as quite so trapped and bound, but he does note that none of them avoids "'the blunders of virtue'"— including Trescott, "the supposed hero of the story," who suffers from self-righteousness—with the result that the story is "paradoxical and allusive" rather than morally certain ("Permanence" 93–94).

Michael D. Warner explicitly rejects Hafley's clear-cut designations, as the aforementioned critics do implicitly, but he, unlike them, grounds this rejection in an intricate deconstructionist reading. He argues that, contrary to Hafley's formulation, Crane in fact evinces an "oddly contradictory attitude toward his characters" and that this attitude is a controlled effort "to register the difficulty of judication . . ., as it will be seen that he persists in signaling valuations even as he disables our mechanism of valuation" (77). Regarding Henry's apotheosis, Warner asserts that after Crane establishes Henry's god-like traits he systematically undermines them. When Jimmie and Bella ascribe divine qualities to him, for instance, the reader agrees, but in actuality these characters have very little reasonable basis for this judgment, since Henry is prone to bully Jimmie morally and Bella's opinion is based solely on Henry's superficial manners. More crucially, Warner says, in Henry's putatively most heroic moment, his rescue of Jimmie, "Crane circumscribes Henry's attentions in an astonishing way that causes us to suspect the moral value attached to his action": he presents Henry's rescue as essentially a "stock response" rather than an act of will, removing much of its ethical force, and he undermines it further by having Trescott complete the rescue by carrying Jimmie outdoors after Henry has fallen and dropped the boy in the burning laboratory (83). Trescott's saving Henry is equally undermined with regard to morality. Trescott's assumption is that saving a life is always good, and the reader agrees, Warner says, but Crane calls this assumption into question by proto-deconstructive means. When Trescott defends his saving of the maimed Henry by saying, "'He saved my boy's life. . . . What am I to do?'" Warner perceives Crane as intending both conjunction and disjunction between these two sentences. While Trescott "implies that his behavior is at once requisite and inscrutable, both eminently logical and quite inexplicable," by these statements, Crane's real point is that "'[c]onscience' and 'virtue' are insufficient to bridge the gap between the two sentences, and the whole ethical and legal tradition of locating judgments of morality in the quality of the intention becomes irrelevant." Thus, in Warner's view, "[o]ne can still point to moral agents and their acts, but Crane has put in question the kind of relation between those agents and their acts that we must assume in order to understand our machinery of valuation" (85–86).

The result of this questioning, what Warner terms "the problematic of agency," is that "Monster" is actually two stories. The first of these is the familiar one: "a black man risks his life for a boy, is saved by the moral courage of the boy's father, and then is made a martyr, together with the boy's father, by the social hypocrisy of the townsfolk." The second is "utterly antipathetic to the first." In it, "a man is trapped by instinct and fear, stripped of his identity but preserved as a living thing by another man who is himself trapped by debts of unaccountable gratitude," and while this double entrapment plays out, all the characters "suffer from the inability of their common code to comprehend the events of their lives, even as they, and we, perpetuate and endorse that code" (87). With the reader suspended between these two stories, reading "The Monster" becomes "a disconcerting and uncanny experience," and it is rendered even more disturbing by the implication of the second story that "the performance of a deed is not a simple matter of act following from will or intention." Instead, "Crane regards the relation of persons *to their own actions* as problematic. And if persons do not correspond exactly, in the relation of agency, to the events of which they are a part, how can determinations of value be made to adhere to them?" Warner asserts that this question is central not only to "The Monster" but to much of Crane's work, as is his awareness that it is finally unthinkable. "If there is a concept that we cannot do without," Warner says, "it is the concept of a moral. Crane knows that it will not work; the odd thing about it, however, is that it cannot *but* work." Crane's final point—a source of despair to him, in Warner's view—is that "no matter how clearly it might be demonstrated that the project of morality is inappropriate, moral judgments themselves will continue to seem no less serious, and no more appropriate means of evaluation will present itself" (87–88).

Andrew Delbanco takes a somewhat similar view. He too reads "The Monster" as a despairing comment on humans' need to formulate moral judgments, but he sees this despair as stemming not from the inappropriateness of this need *per se* but rather from humans' refusal to be objective, to whatever extent such a state is possible, in their process of formulation. He regards Crane's "descriptive austerity" in parts of the story as "a form of resistance to what he deemed the human predilection for turning phenomena into symbols." The central example of the dangers of this predilection, he says, is what the townspeople make of Henry's attempted rescue of Jimmie. This action is the clearest instance of Christian behavior in all of Crane's canon, yet they read Henry's wounds "not as stigmata, but as marks of Cain." Delbanco sees this response as exemplifying Crane's understanding of the mind, which differs crucially from that of his contemporary William James in being somewhat absurdist. According to James, Delbanco says, "the capacity of the mind to formulate new truths under the pressure of new experience (for example, black men can be heroic) was the measure of man's freedom and his improvisatory genius." Crane's perspective, on the other hand, is that even under the pressure of new experience "the productions of the mind are generally bad jokes at the expense of the observer and the observed" (35).

An element generally ignored or handled only as a side issue in the foregoing debates over Crane's focus in this story is the issue of race—the fact that the terrified community is dominated by whites and their "monster" is black. The explanation for this fact is that most of these writers are in accord with Gibson's view that the racial theme is significant but is finally subsumed into an examination of "human responsibility" in a larger sense (138). A number of other critics regard the race question as too much in the foreground to be handled so glancingly, but like the previous group they divide sharply over Crane's position on their subject as that can be inferred from the story, one faction praising Crane for his racial enlightenment and the other condemning him for insensitivity if not outright prejudice. Ralph Ellison, no stranger to the race issue, offers a measure of approval, calling "The Monster" a "more mature" work than *Maggie* and grouping it with *The Adventures of Huckleberry Finn* as "one of the parents of the modern American novel" (65). Stallman is more effusive; he asserts that "The Monster" is the first instance in American literature of a white American author depicting a black character as a hero in order to make "an appeal for brotherhood between white and black." This claim might come as a surprise to the creator of Huck Finn's friend Jim, a character who predates Henry by a decade; Stallman is on firmer ground when he argues that Crane's point is the juxtaposition of the fire in the laboratory that causes Henry's literal disfiguration with the allegorical fire of white society's cruelty that "consumes the moral face of the community." It was this "social irony," according to Stallman, that impelled R. W. Gilder to say that his *Century* could not publish the story for fear of ravaging the sensibilities of expectant mothers (334).

Whether or not Stallman is correct in his reading of Gilder's motives, at least two other critics regard him as correct in his racial reading of the juxtaposition of literal and symbolic facelessness in "The Monster," which they both place in a larger social/philosophical context without, like Gibson, arguing for its subsumption into that larger context. Holton says that Henry's promenade through town in his dress clothes on his way to court Bella Farragut, in the course of which a number of whites fail to recognize him because he is not in his more customary work attire, illustrates the way a black man "is denied identity by his fellow townspeople and even collaborates in that denial"; the townspeople's revulsion after the fire shows that Henry's now-literal facelessness "is at once the symbol of their denial and a tribute to the disorder which they have refused to acknowledge in their universe"—that is, the fact that all the social hierarchies by which they order their universe are ultimately meaningless, based as they are on such minor, racist considerations as the color and shape of one's face. "The center of the horror" of Henry's condition, Holton concludes, "is what it would disclose to the observer about himself." In other words, Henry "embodies the social reality" of ontological and moral facelessness that the town wishes to ignore and "to which the fire is the equivalent natural fact" due to its capacity for creating an all-too-suggestive physical facelessness (208–10).

Similarly, Charles W. Mayer says that the story's racial theme comes across clearly and powerfully because of Crane's having integrated it into a larger depiction of the failure of human compassion due to "the immense power of fear in sustaining a protective, imitative society dependent on theatricality and spectacle, sterile rituals and dead forms"—on putting on a good face, in other words—with those maneuvers producing "moral blindness and an atrophy of the heart." These rituals and forms, according to Mayer, are crucial to bolstering "man's false sense of his own importance in the scheme of things that prevents him from accepting or even wanting to understand the fact of his precarious foothold in the world of nature" (29). From the racial standpoint, Henry as a black man in a white-dominated town plays the many theatrical roles and enacts the many rituals demanded by the whites' illusions about themselves and him and by his own illusion that he is a gentleman. However, in the "supreme act of brotherhood and sacrifice" that is his rescue of Jimmie, Henry steps out of his socially imposed collection of roles and becomes simply a man, with the result that in his maimed state he can no longer resume the roles by which society sustains itself. Thus he becomes terrifying to others, since if he has no role he cannot be human by their limited, self-aggrandizing definition. His facelessness is, in effect, "the honest proof of nature's power" over human beings and therefore a negation of their illusions of importance, illusions predicated on essentially meaningless distinctions based on race and class. And it is this negation that causes Trescott to be ostracized as well, for he, not being like the rest "imprisoned in a false world of social forms that isolate men from the truth about themselves," is able to discern "something of his, and all men's, desperate condition in the world of nature [and] . . . to recognize Henry's humanity, to perceive and act upon the need for mutual help in the struggle to prevail in a hostile universe" (32–33).

Malcolm Foster makes some of the same points as Holton and Mayer, but he places them in a historical rather than philosophical context, reading the story as a conscious, sustained, condemnatory allegory of the specific circumstances of white America's treatment of blacks in the nineteenth century. At the outset, Foster says, Henry as companion to Jimmie and suitor to Bella plays the two most common roles forced on blacks by whites, those of the "benign and almost child-like Nigger Jim or Uncle Remus" and the "cake-walking minstrel-show comic dandy" (88). In its martial imagery, its destruction of a framed copy of the Declaration of Independence with a sound like a bomb, and its seemingly planned occurrence, the fire symbolizes the Civil War, while the rumor that circulates among the watching crowd that Henry started the fire correlates with the angry belief of many Northerners that the war was the fault of blacks. Henry's post-fire "facelessness and imprisonment" represent the "general dehumanization of black people" following the Compromise of 1876, and the townspeople's anger and fear at Henry's escape denote "the general role of the black as scapegoat" for all sorts of crimes in the period after this compromise, the period in which the story actually takes place (89–90).

If this reading seems somewhat forced, Foster is on equally uncertain ground when he asserts that within the allegory Trescott represents the worst kind of white Americans, the "weak-willed and compromising meliorists" (87). When Trescott takes him to Alek Williams's farm, Foster claims, Henry is essentially rational, "suffering only from a trauma-induced amnesia"; it is as a result of his inhumane treatment at the farm that he becomes genuinely unhinged (89). This claim is itself questionable; even more so, because of its basis in a failure to consider any of Trescott's behavior that might controvert it, is Foster's allegation that in these and other actions Trescott weakly abdicates his responsibilities to his black fellow man because of his wife's social anxieties.

Most of those critics who perceive a good deal less racial sensitivity and insight in the story do not accuse Crane of intentional bigotry, but rather view him as unfortunately a product of his times. Regarding Henry's genteel courtship of Bella Farragut and Alek Williams's shuffling, wheedling efforts to extract more money from Judge Hagenthorpe for Henry's care, Lillian Gilkes says that Crane exhibits "unconscious racism," partaking of the literary conventions of many authors of his period, who delighted in "representations of the Negro aping the white man, the Negro as buffoon." She finds it "painful" to be confronted with these stereotypes in "the otherwise magnificent realism of this richly textured story," and she considers it odd and lamentable that Crane, "the marvelous boy who stripped his mind of falsehoods, bombast, sentimentalisms and narrative stock-in-trade of every kind, should have employed such standardized expression in place of direct observation when writing about black people" (457). John R. Cooley takes a similar view. He argues that Crane's handling of Henry before the fire is acute and produces sharp social criticism, particularly in the scene in which Henry strolls through the center of town and metaphorically runs a gauntlet of whites who project their own ideas and fears of blackness onto him. Henry's literal facelessness after the fire might well serve tellingly as a metaphor for this white projection, Cooley continues, on a level with Ralph Ellison's metaphor of invisibility to describe the same syndrome in *Invisible Man*, but Crane fails to carry this metaphor through when he shifts his attention from Henry to Trescott, thereby obscuring Henry's humanity and rendering him faceless not only to the townspeople but to the reader. The story as a whole is thus a failure, and a particularly disappointing one; Crane's refusal or inability to permit himself and his reader to sustain an intimate identification with a black protagonist "reflects a sadly limited racial consciousness, despite all good intentions, in one of our most astute and compassionate social realists" (12–14).

Joseph Church carries such criticism somewhat further. Responding explicitly to Stallman's, Holton's, and Mayer's praise of Crane's alleged racial enlightenment, he notes that the author depicts the Farragut and Williams families in the most degradingly stereotypical terms and that, despite his presentation of Henry as courageous in the fire scene, he undermines that positive portrait, albeit mostly unintentionally, in a number of ways. Crucially, Church argues, Crane depicts Henry as not having the role of a true workman and thus lacking a "proper individual identity" in society, a condition that renders him "a kind of living signifier" that is "available to play parts in what amount to destructive white fantasies," in which, "in the black man's subjugated 'face' whites can imagine they see their own power" (378). More specifically, Church sets out three areas of relationship in which Henry is used and degraded in such fantasies. First, Jimmie, "in the absence of the intervening 'oedipal' father," uses Henry as a substitute "that finally serves fetishistic interests." Second, "the infantile white townsmen also use the black man in this manner." Third, "Crane's own stylistic (aesthetic) use of Johnson follows the same logic" (379).

Church relies heavily on a mixture of Freudian and postmodernist psychological-deconstructive literary theories to support these claims. For all three of the fetishizing agents, he says, Johnson's blackness marks him as different and therefore "other" and thus "useful for infantile fantasies" (381). With specific regard to Jimmie, he points out that Jimmie seeks comfort from Henry after his father scolds him for breaking the spine of a peony while he is pretending to be a train. Linking *peony* to *penis*, Church argues that this scolding carries heavily oedipal-phallic overtones, that Jimmie fetishizes Henry here in that he is in fact making Henry a substitute for his phallus, and that this process carries over to the fire scene, to Henry's detriment. At this moment, Trescott, the true father, is absent, and "the father's absence should damage the son (as it were his phallus); but Jimmie has already claimed a substitute and by a severe logic the damage is transferred to that site"—that is, Henry. In other words, Church says, "in this historical crisis the sins of the fathers are visited not on the sons but on the black man" (383).

Moving from Jimmie to the townsmen, Church sees the aged Judge Hagenthorpe, whose dominant characteristic is his dependence on his smooth-headed and hence phallic cane, similarly fetishizing Henry through his superior position to black men in general. "By an inverted reflection,"

Church says, "the inferior social position of blacks enables the judge and the other townsmen to imagine their own potency (a kind of imaginary phallus) in the black man's subjection" (382). The problem for this group arises when Henry's literal facelessness makes this process uncomfortably clear, and they are terrified as a result. The judge continues to see the black man as "merely a signifier . . . to be taken up or abandoned by the dominant culture as *it* thinks best," but this man's disfiguration "forces the townspeople to react to new circumstances and thus to disclose their latent values," something they wish to avoid at all costs (383–84). If Crane himself might thus far escape the charge of racism in this anatomizing of the deep psychological truth of Whilomville, Church argues, in making his attacks on "the torpid white fathers" of Whilomville, then the author, perhaps unconsciously, shows less interest in actually attacking racial injustice than he does in using a black man to attain his own artistic goals and thus equally fetishizing Henry in his own way. By the end of the story, Crane "seems to acknowledge that for him no arts can restore this permanent injury to the black race, but also that a (white) author can use this sad fact in symbolic ways," making the black man "a signifier he can re-mark; consequently, Johnson ultimately becomes a sign of Crane's power as an artist" (386–87).

Wolford and Halliburton are less elaborate and more temperate in their criticisms. Wolford argues that Crane does indict society on racist grounds in "The Monster" but is much more concerned with assailing the larger concept of community in general due to any such group's inevitably inhibitive effect upon ethically aware individuals. Therefore, he concludes, Crane should not be praised overmuch for his anti-racist attitude here, particularly given his unjustifiable trafficking in the grossest racial stereotypes in his handling of the African-American characters in another Whilomville tale, "The Knife" (*Study* 48). Halliburton sees Crane as honestly wrestling with the issue of race but unable to come to any workable conclusions. He argues that while Crane does offset his generic handling of most of the African-Americans in the story with his depiction of Henry as possessing "the highest form of freedom, the freedom to be brave," this fact is not a counter to racial stereotypes, not an assertion that African-Americans as a group possess this freedom. Rather, this capability belongs to Henry "as a man, irrespective of claims on him as a representative of his race," a fact that for Halliburton constitutes an evasion of racial questions through the "typically American solution . . . [of] the sovereign power of the individual" (191). And in any case, he continues, Crane ends up submerging the racial theme in Henry's accident, making the opposition in the story not white versus black but man versus monster. Seeing no symbolic connection between these two conflicts, despite the view of many other critics, Halliburton says that this submergence makes the ending of the story inconclusive. His own conclusion is that although Crane has not handled the racial theme decisively, although he "is not quite sure what he thinks," he nevertheless deserves a measure of credit for broaching this issue at all in the American 1890s (199).

Several other critics largely ignore the specifics of the racial question in favor of approaching the story from more or less doctrinaire psychological, theological, or philosophical perspectives. Maxwell Geismar follows Berryman's Freudian lead—detailed above in "Sources and Influences"—and reads "The Monster" as Crane's effort to work out his oedipal conflict and also his deep-seated guilt over his rejection of his family's Methodism. "Crane wrote so directly from his own need in these things, was driven so by inner necessity, and had really such a childish candor," Geismar says, "that it is impossible to ignore the symbols of his distress," such as the phallic serpent imagery suffusing the descriptions of the fire that destroys the Trescott family's home, which is for Geismar a clear indication of Crane's anxieties over his own sexuality in relation to his father and the rest of his family. Crane is at his best in working with such matters of "depth psychology," in Geismar's view; the story drops off in intensity and effectiveness when he shifts his concern to the town as a whole and to Trescott's dilemma over Henry, a "social and ethical conflict," which engages Crane's imagination less urgently than individuals' psychological traumas (116–19). Christopher Benfey also regards the story's intensity, which he argues does not dissipate when the focus shifts away from Henry, as a function of Crane's own psychological obsessions. However, in his view the fundamental "private theme" is not sexual or familial guilt but rather "how illness alienates its victims," an issue that Benfey regards as preoccupying the ailing author in the last years of his life (260).

George Monteiro sees the story as the culmination of one of Crane's religious obsessions: the nature and motivations of Christian charity and its practicability in the human realm. Like Warner, Monteiro points out that Henry does not complete his rescue of Jimmie, that Trescott is the one who finally brings the boy out of the house—a circumstance that for Monteiro raises the possibility that Trescott's saving Henry's life is not strictly a matter of repayment but rather "an act of disinterested benevolence," one that in fact turns out not to be benevolent, given Henry's altered mind and wretched physical state. Crane's goal, however, is not to pass a final judgment on this matter; he wishes simply to place it before the reader as a conundrum. Therefore, neither the doctor's nor the townspeople's position is rendered as entirely morally positive or negative. Trescott "exercises some form of Christian charity" in treating Henry but he may in fact be motivated by hubris, "while the townspeople fail to practice such charity" but "their response, given Henry's fate, can be interpreted, perversely, as more humane than the doctor's." Thus, "[w]ith subtlety and bite, Crane suspends both positions—the doctor's and the townspeople's—before the reader. Find a solution to this antinomy, challenges Crane, if you can" (103–04).

William B. Stein, on the other hand, sees Crane as taking a definite position with the story, a philosophical one. In his view, "The Monster" is, like much of Crane's work, proto-existential, depicting life and death as meaningless and thereby denying humans "the catharsis of tragedy," dooming them instead to clownishness that lacks the true clown's self-awareness. Trescott's situation is the prime example of this condition, Stein says. He has no doubts that the townspeople as a crowd are wrong when they reject his saving of Henry, but when Judge Hagenthorpe, whom Trescott regards as "the civil custodian of justice and reason," sides with them, Trescott experiences "the reduction of the rational to the irrational and of the irrational to the rational," which reveals to him and the reader "his own and the world's absurdity" (169). Wolford goes one step further and says that the story is not existentialist but nihilistic, an idea that Holton and several others imply but do not actually state; the true horror of Henry's facelessness, Wolford argues, is that it reminds all those who see it of "the vanity and chaotic nature of human life and endeavor," facts which they strongly prefer not to have called to their attention. Trescott "does all anyone can do" in the face of this situation, "and that is ultimately a losing battle" (*Study* 47).

John W. Shroeder sees an older school of philosophy informing "The Monster." He asserts that Crane's stories that are "centrally concerned with [the] antagonism of man and nature," as this one is, are infused with Naturalist ideology, positing man as essentially a mechanism and nature as utterly indifferent (122). Ordinarily, in Shroeder's view, Crane fatally mars such stories by applying this ideology too simplistically, too reductively, but in "The Monster" he avoids this drawback, offering a more complex and thus more persuasive Naturalistic vision, in which man is something more than a machine, through his depiction of acts of human brotherhood as deliberate functions of an individual's will that can oppose and to some extent mitigate nature's disinterest. The most significant of these acts are Henry's attempted rescue of Jimmie from the fire and Trescott's rescue of Henry from death; these are "two attempted salvations," with the second one expressly pro-claiming "Crane's recognition that salvation's validity inheres in its being a consciously willed readiness to accept the responsibility and consequences of the mythic battle" against unfeeling nature (128).

In addition to these various issues of interpretation, many critics pay atten-tion to Crane's technical accomplishments in this story. Cady says that "The Monster" is the best indication of the kind of technically proficient, con-trolled, and broadly insightful writer Crane might have developed into had he lived, and most others agree with this assessment, lauding especially Crane's style, his handling of structure, and his deployment of imagery and symbol-ism. In the area of style, Berryman asserts that the story "initiates a revolution in Crane's aesthetic," a revolution comprised of a largely toned-down, "delib-erately normal" style, in contrast to his previously somewhat ornate and fevered approach, coupled with a willingness to survey an entire community rather than just one or two individuals as in his earlier work (192). Bassan agrees, noting that in "The Monster" Crane manages to be "more sober and less sardonic than in the narratives of the early '90s" without sacrificing the effective bite of those narratives, for here—and in the best of the subsequent Whilomville stories as well—"Crane's eye for the savageness of the societal pressure to conform [is] as sharp as ever" (7). Frank Bergon is also in accord with this view, saying that this story is perhaps the best example of Crane's third and final style, more toned down and conventional than the first two, best represented by *The Red Badge* and "The Open Boat," respectively. This "normalized" style is particularly appropriate to Crane's subject matter here, "not war or the sea but society," Bergon says, a harmonizing of form and matter that still further suggests Crane's developing artistic control.

Several other critics point out, however, that Crane's toning down of his earlier style does not produce a uniform sobriety in the story but rather an ability to modulate purposefully and effectively between heat and coolness— an ability to be, in the words of Arno Karlen, "shrilly brilliant and reportorially calm by turns," or, in those of Halliburton, "chastened, more matter of fact, . . . closer to the Howells norm—though with colorful moments" (3). Holton focuses on Crane's extended description of the burning laboratory as a "garden of fire" as exemplifying this mature modulatory style, for in this passage he manifests the "visual vitality" of his earlier work in his handling of color, figures, and syntax, but in describing the deadly fire in delicate terms of flowers and jewels he creates an irony rare in descriptive sections of his previous stories, which makes the horror of the scene more subtle and thus more powerful in that it is associational rather than literal (155). Similarly, Gullason notes that to discuss the townspeople Crane uses a prosaic style that "perfectly fits the prosaic world" of Whilomville and to describe the fire he shifts smoothly to a consonantly wilder vein; in Gullason's view, this shifting style is appropriate not just to its subjects but to the theme that underlies those subjects: "the eternal battles between reason and passion, the material and the spiritual" ("True Road" 481). Solomon notes a difference in pace between the story's first and second halves accomplished through Crane's newly developed expertise in stylistic control. The first half moves rapidly due to its being "tightly filled with action and description," while the second half proceeds more slowly, focusing less on these elements and more on "analysis of motives." This formal shift is thematically appropriate, Solomon says, because it helps make the point that the "ethical drama" that comprises the second half—the "destruction of a man by prejudice"—is "more complicated and less dramatic than the destruction of a house by fire" (191).

As he does in considerations of style, Berryman also points the way in discussions of Crane's structural technique in "The Monster" with his comment that the "rescue-structure of the story is like a musical development:

Jimmie's attempt to rescue the flower, and punishment, Johnson's rescue of
him, and punishment, Dr. Trescott's rescue of Johnson, and punishment"
(323). Hafley likewise perceives a leitmotiv as the organizing principle. He
says that the story is constructed around the literal and metaphorical actions
of "losing face," with the paradox that those who lose face according to society's codes—Johnson and Trescott—concomitantly save it on the moral
level, while those who save it in the eyes of society—Jimmie in the game of
touch-the-monster, Alek Williams in his efforts to make money out of
Henry's condition, and Bella Farragut in her rejection of Henry after the accident—equally lose face in the moral realm (160). George W. Johnson proposes a somewhat different structural figure. He reads the story as a
meditation on the idea that society is "a group defining itself by the incongruities it is capable of accepting," and he argues that it is plotted as a set of
concentric circles, the inner ones enclosing small groups of individuals and
the outer enclosing larger clusters, that reflect "concentric rings of ceremony as society attempts to right itself" by adherence to pointless, incongruous
rules when Henry's disfiguration throws these circles out of their comforting
concentric orbits. Crane's point in this circle game, Johnson says, is that "[i]t
is all child's play, but it is all there is." Thus, the "doctor, the housewife, the
lawyer, the official, and the child must each finally abide by the rules" of his
or her particular circle, a requirement that reveals "both the necessity and
duplicity of decorum" (253–54).

    Gullason, LaFrance, and Charles B. Ives all look to Crane's chapter divi-
sions as keys to the story's design. Gullason sees chapters 1 through 9 as setting up Henry's injury and 10 through 24 as charting the town's "monstrous"
response to him, with several "minor climaxes" leading up to a major one in
each of these units, and with each chapter set up as a self-contained "dramatic scene" that contributes to these climaxes (663–64). Specifically, Gullason
says that chapter 1 establishes an "atmosphere of impending ostracism" in its
account of Jimmie's punishment by Dr. Trescott (a point also made by
Wolford, who regards this beginning as prefiguring the whole story [*Study* 45,
Anger 89]), chapter 2 connects Jimmie's fate with Henry's, and then 3 and 4
broaden the character of Henry's looming fate by detailing the townspeople's
mixture of friendliness and condescension in their response to Henry and creating an "atmosphere of potential disaster." Chapters 5 through 9 juxtapose
Henry's courageous response to the fire with the townspeople's comparatively inhumane desire to be entertained by this catastrophe, while 10 presents their initial positive response to Henry, which alters when he is
discovered to be alive, an alteration that Crane methodically charts in the rest
of the story. In 11, Hagenthorpe offers his negative response, which is followed in 12 and 13 by that of the Williams family. Chapters 14 through 23
then oscillate between groups and individuals reacting to Henry: the barber-
shop crowd is the focus in 14, Alek Williams is treated in 15, the terror of

Henry felt by the children at the birthday party and by the Farragut family are covered in 16 and 17, and this terror culminates in the "climax of fear" in the crowd's pursuit of Henry in 18. In 19, Crane returns to an individual, Martha Goodwin, and then in 20 he focuses on the children's community and their ritual of proving their courage by touching Henry. The individual is once again highlighted in 21 and 22, with the anger of Mr. Winter being the subject of the former and the hypocrisy of Martha Goodwin in dropping her defense of Trescott featured in the latter. The group makes its ultimate appearance in 23, in which the town's spokesman urges Trescott to get rid of Henry, and 24 reveals the final outcome of all these responses—the complete social ostracism of the Trescott family. The aggregate effect of this shifting structure, Gullason concludes, is the creation of a wavelike rhythm that produces a sense of "society's 'edge,' jagged like rocks" ("Unity" 665–68).

Like Gullason, LaFrance sees the story as divided into two parts, which he says comprise chapters 1 through 12 and 13 through 24, respectively. In this schema, the first half presents the appearance of a tranquil small town, and the second reveals the reality beneath that appearance. Within the first part, chapters 1 through 4 provide a "deceptively warm" introduction through their focus on Jimmie's childish concerns and Henry's cheerful courtship, 5 through 10 imply the sublimated cruelty of the townspeople in their descriptions of the pleasure these people take in the excitement of the fire, and 11 and 12 supply the climax by establishing Henry's condition and Trescott's dilemma. LaFrance breaks down the second half in a manner similar to Gullason's, asserting that in shifting back and forth between individuals and groups in chapters 13 through 24 Crane surveys the responses of the town to Henry, leading to the conclusion that no one except Trescott is able to get past his or her illusions about him and treat him with the compassion he deserves (207–09).

Ives also discerns a two-part structure in the story, with parallel features in each, and he asserts that it shares this form with Crane's two Bowery novels, *Maggie* and *George's Mother*, and *The Red Badge*. All these works are split in half by a turning point, Ives explains, each half is itself divided by a minor turning point, the chapters in each grouping thus created are linked by shared themes, and the entire work is tied together through repetition and anticipation (18). The first twelve chapters, Ives says, are devoted to the making of the monster, with 1 through 4 introducing seemingly tranquil Whilomville and the story's three main characters, 5 through 8 depicting the shattering of this apparent tranquility by the fire, and 9 through 12 presenting the townspeople's initial reactions to Henry. The second half of the story details the effect of the monster on the town, with 13 through 20 cataloguing various people's terrified and heartless behavior toward Henry, which climaxes with Jimmie's making a game of him, and 21 through 24 charting Trescott's ostracism, which progresses from an attack on him by one individual, through a discussion of him by two gossips and a visit paid to him by the town elders, to the climactic boycott of Mrs. Trescott's tea party by the thirteen women invited to it (18–26).

A considerable number of other critics argue that the most significant patterns in "The Monster" are to be found not in its plot structure but rather in its imagery. Holton notes Crane's frequent images and metaphors of sight, which he regards as typical of Crane's best work, and asserts that these combine to symbolize the characters' capacity for moral vision. In many instances, Holton points out, the townspeople literally cannot see clearly, as in the scene of the fire, and this lack of vision is ironically juxtaposed with frequent references to street lamps and other items involved in "the technology of seeing," with the point being that it is not only the eyes but also the hearts and minds of these people that fail them, as is most clear in their inability following the fire to "see" Henry as anything other than a monster (210–11).

Cooley sees Crane as getting his point across largely through "ironic contrasts between the Henry Johnson he portrays and the versions of Henry Johnson which grow in the white imagination . . . of Whilomville"; crucial to the reader's understanding of these contrasts are Crane's frequent images of "animality," "primitivism," and "savage natures being exposed," particularly in the fire scene, which Cooley reads as "Crane's microcosmic image of the town, and of human society, as predatory jungles both beautiful and hideous" (10). Ruth Betsy Tennenbaum likewise notes Crane's frequent use of images of animals, as well as of machines, to characterize the townspeople. In her view, he thereby powerfully underscores the bestiality, the "mindlessness and gratuitous ferocity," that constitutes the reality of their treatment of Johnson and Trescott, which they seek to conceal from themselves and others by their maintaining of socially acceptable forms and the conventional phrases and platitudes that comprise their speech (403).

Colvert looks at the story as a whole in terms of imagery, not at just one or two particular types, and praises Crane for using carefully established patterns of contrast throughout—for balancing strands of images of "domestic serenity" against strands of "mystical horror," strands of "generosity" against strands of "cruelty," and strands of "binding convention" against "strands of thought and feeling" (124). Conversely, Levenson and Bergon each focus on only one contrast as equal proof of Crane's artistic control. Levenson sees the heavy floral imagery in the fire scene as a "surrealist inversion of the peaceful domestic garden" that is the Trescott's lawn in the opening chapter, an inversion implying that in the story as a whole "violence weirdly triumphs over order" even though the townspeople see precisely the opposite as occurring (xx). Bergon concentrates on the tension between Henry's remaining visible eye and Judge Hagenthorpe's cane in Chapter 11; he asserts that these objects offer excellent examples of Crane's method of symbolism, which consists of providing "self-imposed definitions that rarely last for long." At the simplest symbolic level, Bergon explains, the eye represents "irrationality, nonconformity, or individuality," while the cane stands for the opposite concepts—"rationality, respectability, or social stability." However, despite the judge's belief that he thinks best when he is rubbing the head of his cane, doing so actually has a narcotic effect, since it enables him to lie with a clear conscience; the narrator, Bergon points out, says that Hagenthorpe only tells the truth when he has mislaid the cane. In this scene he has the cane, and so, Bergon asserts, he is holding back in his expressions of "the truth" about Trescott's and Henry's circumstances, while it is Henry's eye that acts as "a restraining force" on those expressions. Thus, Bergon concludes, these elements are not simply fixed symbols in a clear-cut dialogue of values, but rather "devices for suggesting a radically complex psychological portrait and interaction" (35–36).

Kahn notes that Crane does not limit himself to visual imagery in "The Monster"; he traces a meaningful pattern of aural imagery as well. The focus early in the story is on the conventionality of the townspeople, who judge all things by their appearance and thus give voice to many false rumors, such as the reports that circulate through the crowd of spectators at the fire that Henry and Jimmie are dead and that Henry caused the fire by knocking over a lamp while he sat up with a supposedly sick Jimmie. Crane, Kahn continues, links these voices to the many harsh sounds of the town—those of electric cars, fire engines, church- and school-bells, and the factory whistle that sounds the fire alarm like "'a giant voice in the night.'" Through this linking, Crane makes the point that it is this harsh, giant "voice made human that shouts down reason and compassion in Whilomville" (39–40).

Neal Osborn calls attention to still another technique, Crane's use of two names with thematic significance. The more obvious of these is Carrie Dungen, which is sharply appropriate for a neighborhood gossip. The aptness of the Tuscarora fire company, one of the units that responds to the blaze at the Trescott home, is less apparent; Osborn argues that this name suggests the words *tusk* and *roar* and thereby connects the fire crew to "the noisy, destructive, animal-like civilian mobs" that watch the fire and later persecute Henry and Trescott, making the point that beneath the facade of order and security everyone in Whilomville is bestial. Even the fire fighters, the town's supposedly heroic protectors of order, are in reality "subliminal subversives" (10).

Perhaps the most subtle commentary on Crane's technique comes from Max Westbrook, who focuses on "The Monster" and several other stories to refute the claim advanced by various critics, especially Warner Berthoff and Jay Martin, that Crane's art is incoherent due to a perceived lack of unity between the actions of his characters and his narrators' language—a sense that "the language invokes meanings the story cannot accommodate" (86). As an instance of this supposed problem in "The Monster," Westbrook points to the scene in which Jimmie and his friends turn touching the maimed Henry into a game by which they test their courage. When the narrator says that after Jimmie and another boy touch Henry these two boast as though "they had been decorated for courage on twelve battle-fields," this language may initially seem overblown, out of scale with the actions it describes, and thus inappropriate for both the boys and the narrator, but the critic must recognize that such imagery represents neither the boys' own thoughts nor Crane's straightforward judgment of the boys through his narrator, but rather constitutes the author's "ironic expression of the further implications of the characters' reactions"; in other words, it ironically describes not what the boys actually think or say but the nature of the "personal atmosphere" of exaggerated valor that their boasting projects (89–90). Once the critic grasps this concept and learns "to read [Crane's] coherent pattern of ironic interpretations" in this kind of "radical language," he or she will recognize that Crane's purpose in such language, particularly in his frequent use of it to characterize the actions of the adults in the story, is to reveal the human "image-making capacity . . . in its . . . distorted form" (96), which results from the adults' desires to create roles, personal atmospheres, for themselves through which they can avoid confronting the uncomfortable realities of their situations. These instances are more serious than those involving the boys because the adults are possessed of much greater awareness of what they are doing. "The boys, in play," Westbrook says, "cannot see that they are turning an instance of pathos into a game of heroics," but when Judge Hagenthorpe, in his confrontation with Trescott over the latter's saving of Henry, projects a personal atmosphere of exaggerated rationalism to suggest that the better course might have been to let Henry die, he, "with more guilt, blinds himself to ethical duty." As final proof that this critique of willfully distorted image-making is the intention behind Crane's radical language, Westbrook points out that this kind of language drops out when one character, Trescott, *does* face his ethical duty. When the doctor confronts his ostracism at the end by counting the unused teacups, Crane renders the moment in "straight and flat" terms, completely devoid of "the personal hyperbole of battlefields and rationalizations" (90–91).

Works Cited

Ahnebrink, Lars. *The Beginnings of Naturalism in American Fiction*. Cambridge: Harvard University Press, 1950.

Anderson, Margaret P. "A Note on 'John Twelve' in Stephen Crane's 'The Monster.'" *American Notes & Queries* 15 (1976):23–24.

Bassan, Maurice. Introduction. *Stephen Crane: A Collection of Critical Essays*. Ed. Maurice Bassan. Englewood Cliffs, N.J.: Prentice-Hall, 1967, 1–11.

Beer, Thomas. *Stephen Crane: A Study in American Letters*. New York: Knopf, 1923.

Benfey, Christopher. *The Double Life of Stephen Crane*. New York: Knopf, 1992.

Bergon, Frank. *Stephen Crane's Artistry*. New York: Columbia University Press, 1975.

Berryman, John. *Stephen Crane*. New York: Sloane, 1950.

Bowers, Fredson. Textual Introduction. *Tales of Whilomville*. Vol. 7 of The University of Virginia Edition of *The Works of Stephen Crane*. Ed. Fredson Bowers. Charlottesville: University Press of Virginia, 1968, 103–26.

Cady, Edwin H. Introduction. *Tales, Sketches, and Reports*. Vol. 8 of The University of Virginia Edition of *The Works of Stephen Crane*. Ed. Fredson Bowers. Charlottesville: University Press of Virginia, 1973, xxi–xli.

————. *Stephen Crane*. Rev. ed. New York: Twayne, 1982.

Church, Joseph. "The Black Man's Part in Crane's Monster." *American Imago* 5 (1988):375–88.

Colvert, James B. *Stephen Crane*. New York: Harcourt Brace Jovanovich, 1984.

Cooley, John R. "'The Monster'—Stephen Crane's 'Invisible Man.'" *Markham Review* 5 (1975):10–14.

Crane, Stephen. "The Knife." *Tales of Whilomville* 184–94.

————. "The Monster." *Tales of Whilomville* 7–65.

Deamer, Robert Glen. "Stephen Crane's 'Code' and Its Western Connections." *The Importance of Place in the American Literature of Hawthorne, Thoreau, Crane, Adams, and Faulkner*. New York: Edwin Mellen, 1990, 139–52.

Delbanco, Andrew. "The Disenchanted Eye." *New Republic* 199.2 (1988):33–36.

Ellison, Ralph. "Stephen Crane and the Mainstream of American Fiction." *Shadow and Act*. New York: Random House, 1964, 60–76.

Foster, Malcolm. "The Black Crepe Veil: The Significance of Stephen Crane's 'The Monster.'" *International Fiction Review* 3 (1976):87–91.

Fried, Michael. "Realism, Writing, and Disfiguration in Thomas Eakins's *Gross Clinic*, with a Postscript on Stephen Crane's Upturned Faces." *Representations* 9 (1985):33–104.

————. *Realism, Writing, Disfiguration: On Thomas Eakins and Stephen Crane*. Chicago: University of Chicago Press, 1987.

Geismar, Maxwell. *Rebels and Ancestors*. Boston: Houghton Mifflin, 1953.

Gibson, Donald B. *The Fiction of Stephen Crane*. Carbondale: Southern Illinois University Press, 1968.

Gilkes, Lillian. "Stephen Crane and the Biographical Fallacy: The Cora Influence." *Modern Fiction Studies* 16 (1970–71):441–61.

Gullason, Thomas A. "The Permanence of Stephen Crane." *Studies in the Novel* 10 (1978):86–95.

———. "Stephen Crane's Short Stories: The True Road." *Stephen Crane's Career: Perspectives and Evaluations*. Ed. Thomas A. Gullason. New York: New York University Press, 1972. 470–86.

———. "The Symbolic Unity of 'The Monster.'" *Modern Language Notes* 75 (1960):663–68.

Hafley, James. "'The Monster' and the Art of Stephen Crane." *Accent* 19 (1959):159–65.

Halliburton, David. *The Color of the Sky: A Study of Stephen Crane*. Cambridge: Cambridge University Press, 1989.

Hilfer, Anthony Channell. *The Revolt from the Village: 1915–30*. Chapel Hill: University of North Carolina Press, 1969.

Hoffman, Daniel G. *The Poetry of Stephen Crane*. New York: Columbia University Press, 1957.

Holton, Milne. *Cylinder of Vision: The Fiction and Journalistic Writings of Stephen Crane*. Baton Rouge: Louisiana State University Press, 1972.

Hughes, Rupert. "Rupert Hughes ('Chelifer') on Stephen Crane." *Stephen Crane's Career: Perspectives and Evaluations*. Ed. Thomas A. Gullason. New York: New York University Press, 1972, 57–72.

Ives, C. B. "Symmetrical Design in Four of Crane's Stories." *Ball State University Forum* 10 (Winter 1969):17–26.

Johnson, George W. "Stephen Crane's Metaphor of Decorum." *PMLA* 78 (1963): 250–56.

Kahn, Sy. "Stephen Crane and the Giant Voice in the Night: An Explication of *The Monster*." In *Essays in Modern American Literature*. Ed. Richard E. Langford. DeLand, Fla.: Stetson University Press, 1963, 35–45.

Karlen, Arno. "The Craft of Stephen Crane." *Georgia Review* 28 (1974):470–97.

Kazin, Alfred. "The Youth: Stephen Crane." *An American Procession*. New York: Knopf, 1984. 256–74.

Knapp, Daniel. "Son of Thunder: Stephen Crane and the Fourth Evangelist." *Nineteenth-Century Fiction* 24 (1969):253–91.

LaFrance, Marston. *A Reading of Stephen Crane*. Oxford: Clarendon, 1971.

Levenson, J. C. Introduction. *Tales of Whilomville* xi–lx.

Martin, John C. "Childhood in Crane's *Maggie*, 'The Monster,' and Whilomville Stories." *Midwestern University Quarterly* 2 (1967):40–46.

Mayer, Charles W. "Social Forms vs. Human Brotherhood in Crane's 'The Monster.'" *Ball State University Forum* 14 (Summer 1973):29–37.

Monteiro, George. "Stephen Crane and the Antinomies of Christian Charity." *Centennial Review* 16 (1972):91–104.

Morace, Robert A. "Games, Play, and Entertainments in Stephen Crane's 'The Monster.'" *Studies in American Fiction* 9 (1981):65–81.

Nagel, James. *Stephen Crane and Literary Impressionism*. University Park: Pennsylvania State University Press, 1980.

Osborn, Neal J. "'The Monster' and 'The Blue Hotel.'" *Explicator* 23 (1964):10.

Petry, Alice Hall. "Stephen Crane's Elephant Man." *Journal of Modern Literature* 10 (1983):346–52.

Pizer, Donald. "Stephen Crane's 'The Monster' and Tolstoy's 'What to Do?' A Neglected Allusion." *Studies in Short Fiction* 20 (1983):127–29.

Shroeder, J. W. "Stephen Crane Embattled." *University of Kansas City Review* 17 (1950):119–29.

Solomon, Eric. *Stephen Crane: From Parody to Realism*. Cambridge: Harvard University Press, 1966.

Spofford, William K. "Crane's *The Monster*." *Explicator* 36 (1977):5–7.

Stallman, R. W. *Stephen Crane: A Biography*. New York: George Braziller, 1968.

Stein, William B. "Stephen Crane's *Homo Absurdus*." *Bucknell Review* 8 (1959):168–88.

Tennenbaum, Ruth Betsy. "The Artful Monstrosity of Crane's Monster." *Studies in Short Fiction* 14 (1977):403–05.

Walcutt, Charles Child. *American Literary Naturalism: A Divided Stream*. Minneapolis: University of Minnesota Press, 1956.

Warner, Michael D. "Value, Agency, and Stephen Crane's 'The Monster.'" *Nineteenth-Century Literature* 40 (1985):76–93.

Weintraub, Stanley. *The London Yankees*. New York: Harcourt Brace Jovanovich, 1979.

Wertheim, Stanley. "Stephen Crane and the Wrath of Jehovah." *Literary Review* 7 (1963):499–508.

Wertheim, Stanley, and Paul Sorrentino. "Thomas Beer: The Clay Feet of Stephen Crane Biography." *American Literary Realism* 22 (Spring 1990):2–16.

————, eds. *The Correspondence of Stephen Crane*. 2 vols. New York: Columbia University Press, 1988.

Westbrook, Max. "Whilomville: The Coherence of Radical Language." *Stephen Crane in Transition: Centenary Essays*. Ed. Joseph Katz. DeKalb: Northern Illinois University Press, 1972, 86–105.

Wolford, Chester L. *The Anger of Stephen Crane: Fiction and the Epic Tradition*. Lincoln: University of Nebraska Press, 1983.

————. *Stephen Crane: A Study of the Short Fiction*. Boston: Twayne, 1989.

Moonlight on the Snow

Publication History

This story first appeared in America in the April 1900 issue of the magazine *Frank Leslie's Popular Monthly* (40:606–18). Unlike most of Crane's fiction, it did not run in any English magazine, nor was it published in any book during his lifetime; it was not collected until 1901, when Harper & Brothers released an English edition of their 1899 American book *"The Monster" and Other Stories* and added "Moonlight on the Snow" and three other pieces—"Twelve O'Clock," "Manacled," and "An Illusion in Red and White"—to this new version (Bowers clxxxvii). It was published again in 1927 in volume 12 of *The Work of Stephen Crane* (12 vols., New York: Knopf, 1925–27), edited by Wilson Follett, and Thomas A. Gullason included it in his 1963 *Complete Short Stories and Sketches of Stephen Crane* (Garden City, N.Y.: Doubleday).

Circumstances of Composition

J. C. Levenson has skillfully and persuasively tracked Crane's work on this story. He reports that Crane began it at his final English home, Brede Place, Sussex, in August 1899, at this point making his protagonist a barkeeper named Ignatius Burke, who is primarily responsible for the law against gunplay within the city limits and who is himself about to be punished for violating that law. However, Crane soon laid this manuscript aside to fulfill his immediate commitment to produce stories for his Whilomville series, which was then running in every issue of *Harper's New Monthly Magazine*, and to write some pieces based on his experiences in the Spanish-American War in the hope of persuading a publisher to give him an advance on a book of them. It was not until late September or early October that he returned to "Moonlight on the Snow," this time seeing it through but in the process changing his protagonist to the gambler Tom Larpent. A more reflective and ironic character than Burke, Larpent is "capable of being an interpreter" of his experience in the light of the laws of progress and the necessity of the passing of the Wild West, an attribute lacking in Burke in the earlier draft (cxxi–xxiv).

Crane finished and submitted the story before October 21, 1899. On that date Crane's common-law wife, Cora, wrote from Brede Place to Crane's British agent, James Pinker, to discuss the standing of Crane's account with him, and in the process of doing so she mentions "Moonlight" as one of several pieces that Pinker has received but not yet sold, a circumstance he confirms in his reply of January 9, 1900 (*Correspondence* II, 537, 580).

Sources and Influences

Crane's first biographer, Thomas Beer, asserts that Crane got the idea for this story from his observation of a professional gambler whom he encountered in May of 1898 in Key West, Florida, where he and a number of other press correspondents had taken up temporary residence while they waited for the American invasion force to cross over to Cuba at the outset of the Spanish-American War. "You should see the jay who runs the table here," Beer reports Crane writing to his friend Robert Barr. "He is straight out of a dime novel, moustache and all, with bunches of diamonds like cheap chandeliers on each hand" (qtd. in Beer 178). Crane's subsequent biographers John Berryman (219) and Robert W. Stallman accept this claim, with Stallman adding the further details that "the table here" to which Crane refers was the roulette table in an establishment called the Eagle Bird (604). However, this information must be taken with a degree of skepticism, since, as is often the case with Beer's assertions, no original of the letter Beer quotes has ever been found, nor has there been any other verification of what he says, raising the likelihood that he fabricated this missive in order to produce a dramatically satisfying confluence of Crane's life and art (*Correspondence* I, 6–10).

Stallman is on firmer ground when he turns to literary sources, for his statement that Larpent owes something to John Oakhurst, a gambler who figures prominently in Bret Harte's short story "The Outcasts of Poker Flat," has a good deal of credibility in light of the romanticized cynicism and self-awareness that these characters share. James L. Dean concurs with this view and adds that the other characters in "Moonlight" also appear to owe a debt to Harte, albeit a more general one, in that they, like many of Harte's characters, are "colorful, rough-hewn, simple souls (though drunks, thieves, and murderers) who take a childish pride in their sins" (261). Eric Solomon likewise links the characters in "Moonlight" broadly to Harte's works, noting that the scene in "Moonlight" in which the citizens who are about to lynch Larpent are abashed by the arrival of four newcomers from the East—a lovely young woman, two little girls, and a respectable-looking older gentleman—appears to be a parody of the behavior of many of Harte's "kindly ruffians" (279).

Milne Holton identifies another possible prototype in Mark Twain's *Adventures of Huckleberry Finn*: Colonel Sherburn, the well-dressed gentleman who shoots a man for insulting his honor and then cows the mob who come to hang him for this murder by holding a shotgun on them and, with cynicism much like Larpent's, pointing out that individually they are all cowards and back-shooters who have only plucked up the nerve to attempt a daylight lynching through a collective impulse toward sadism and a feeling that they are anonymous and thus safe within the crowd (242). Holton notes as well the probable influence of Henry James in Crane's selection of thematically resonant names for several characters, including "Larpent," which sounds to Holton's ear like "serpent," "Pigrim," suggestive of "pilgrim," and "Ike Boston" for the driver of the stagecoach that brings the Easterners to town (242). (Although he does not point to a specific source for this technique, Neal J. Osborn also notes the resemblance of "Larpent" to "serpent," an association that is strengthened, in his view, by Crane's imagistic linking of the gambler to devils and his description of him at one point as "forked-tongued." Osborn argues that this connection provides an interpretive cue not only to "Moonlight" but also to "Blue Hotel"; he contends that Larpent's "serpentine-satanic associations" carry over to the gambler in the latter story due to close resemblances in "theme, plot, and role" between these two tales, and that these associations should prompt the reader to "vigorously discount the chorus of sympathy for the gambler" in which the cowboy and the Easterner engage at the close of "Blue Hotel" [10].)

Two other critics agree that Crane draws on Sherburn for Larpent but identify additional sources. Levenson sees Larpent as an "ironical descendent" of Crane's nameless, equally respectable and equally deadly gambler in "The Blue Hotel"—a point also made by Solomon (276)—and he notes that his manner and speech seem to be those of Sherburn crossed with the "'certain mordant quality'" for which Crane himself was known (cxxiv–xxv). George Monteiro suggests that Crane draws not only on Mark Twain here but also on Twain's literary *bête noire*, Sir Walter Scott. While the townspeople debate his and their situations, Larpent occupies himself by reading Scott's *Fair Maid of Perth*, which, Monteiro says, cues Crane's reader to the theme of the story, since Scott's novel like "Moonlight" chronicles "the inevitable, yet not . . . entirely desirable, evolution [of a society] from a tribal state of communal existence into a more complex system which subsumes justice to law instead of loyalty" (125).

Relationship to Other Crane Works

"Moonlight," as Warren French points out, is one of only a handful of stories outside the Whilomville cycle in which Crane carries over characters from previous works. In this case, the central characters of "The Bride Comes to Yellow Sky," Jack Potter, now the sheriff of the county that takes in both Yellow Sky and the town in which "Moonlight" is set, War Post, and Scratchy Wilson, Potter's former antagonist who has now become his deputy, reappear with a warrant for Larpent's arrest for a prior crime of grand larceny, which saves him from being hanged for murder. French sees Crane's purpose in this narrative connection as identical to the one behind his decision to create a similar connection between his two stories featuring Henry Fleming, *The Red Badge of Courage* and "The Veteran": to present "unique glimpses of [his] ironic perception of the relationship between the individual and his culture" (156).

A number of critics address the precise nature of this relationship as it is constituted by the link between "Bride" and "Moonlight." If, as James B. Colvert says, "Moonlight" is like several of Crane's Westerns in its focus on the "theme of the conflict between the spirit of anarchy in the legendary West and the constraining influences of commercial and civic ambition" (148), then Potter's and Wilson's appearance in this story reveals such constraining influences as having extended their power since the events of "The Bride." Holton notes that in "Moonlight" Scratchy, no longer simply stunned into impotence by the marriage and thus domestication of his old adversary, as he is at the end of "The Bride," is now as Potter's deputy actively participating in the displacement of "the western way of seeing things" by the "opposed eastern order of apprehension and evaluation" (241–42). Similarly, Donald B. Gibson sees the men who are about to hang Larpent as being in the same position as Scratchy in his role of deputy, faced with the "impingement on the disordered West of the order of the more civilized East" and seeking in their own fashion to make obeisance "to the institutions of Western civilization" that can no longer be resisted (125).

Robert Glen Deamer places the impingement of East on West as it is detailed in these two stories within the larger context of Crane's Western tales. He sees Crane's major Westerns as forming two complementary triads, with the first—"The Five White Mice," "One Dash—Horses," and "A Man and Some Others"—celebrating Crane's discovery of the Western "code of self-reliant courage," and the second—"The Bride," "The Blue Hotel," and "Moonlight"—lamenting the passing of this code as Eastern civilization advances ("Myth" 121). Dean sees this theme of the passing code as indicating a larger dynamism in Crane's Westerns as a whole; in Crane's depiction, the West is constantly "mutable, . . . always in the process of becoming something else" (258). Frank Bergon likewise takes a broad view, seeing this story as related to almost all of Crane's Westerns through its focus on the theme of gambling as both occupation and ontological stance. Like Bill in "A Man and Some Others" and the gambler in "Blue Hotel"—and unlike Richardson in "One Dash" and the New York Kid in "Mice"—the professional gambler Larpent is a veteran, willingly engaging with the "vicissitudes of chance," despite his awareness that they are ultimately beyond his control, because of his ability to appraise the odds realistically and his confidence in his own skills. Thus, although he cannot finally control his fate, he can at least control himself (*Artistry* 120).

Two other critics, while acknowledging the place of the story in Crane's ongoing analysis of the myths and realities of the West, regard this place as being somewhat lower than that of the other stories in Deamer's and Bergon's schemata due to its artistic weaknesses. Marston LaFrance rates it and "Twelve O'Clock" as Crane's weakest Westerns due to their superficial characterizations, although he gives "Moonlight" higher marks within this pair for its somewhat deeper exploration of motivation. Levenson likewise sees Crane, in ill health and desperate for money at this point, as having intended to make "Moonlight" into the same kind of rapidly churned out "ironic anecdote" as "Twelve O'Clock" but somehow, despite the pressures on him, able to let this story ferment into a somewhat deeper treatment (cxxi).

Critical Studies

LaFrance and Levenson, quoted above, are not the only critics to regard "Moonlight" as one of Crane's less-successful works. French faults it for being an inferior repetition of the themes of "The Bride," largely because of Crane's heavy-handedness in his satire of the citizens' greed and his seeming idealization of the murderous Larpent. The gambler's escape from all punishment for his killing has the effect not of juxtaposing the worth of the Old West with the venality of the oncoming East, but rather of showing, unbeknownst to Crane himself, that "the West is really only exchanging one form of corruption for another. The easternization of the West will only mean the replacement of irresponsible individuals by dishonest institutions" (165). In two separate studies, Chester L. Wolford likewise sees "Moonlight" as suffering by the comparison to "The Bride" that Crane invites by writing Potter and Wilson into the latter story. Wolford regards the story as "quintessentially American" in its "violence, broad humor, sarcasm, stupidity, pretentious respect for women, and hyperbole" (*Anger* 117), and he considers Larpent, with his keen eye for the hypocrisy and violence beneath his fellow-citizens' veneer of civilization, Crane's "most sophisticated protagonist," except for Dr. Trescott in "The Monster" (*Study* 37). Nevertheless, he contends that "Moonlight" misses greatness because these positive qualities are undercut by a number of defects: the overly melodramatic quality of the anticlimax—the last-minute arrival of Potter and Wilson after the rope has already been placed around Larpent's neck (*Study* 37), the townspeople's lacking the individualized characterizations necessary "for the tragedy of the end of the heroic age in the West to have any force" (*Anger* 117), Larpent's being made to serve as "too much a jaded mouthpiece of the views of the narrator" (*Study* 37), and the absence of any of the elements drawn from "the epic tradition" that Crane uses in "The Bride" and "Blue Hotel" to give their events a universal significance (*Anger* 117).

Holton also finds the story finally somewhat unsatisfactory due to Crane's tendency in it to emphasize irony more than characterization, but unlike

French and Wolford he does not view it as an inferior companion-piece to "The Bride" but rather as one performed in a different key. "Moonlight" is the darker of the two stories; whereas "The Bride" provides an essentially comic vision of the coming of civilization to the West, "Moonlight" presents the grimmer side of this process in its focus on the greed-driven hypocrisy and cynicism behind the desire of War Post's citizens to adopt "civilized" values (241–42). Bergon makes much the same point, noting that "Moonlight" reverses the conflict between the encroaching East and the resistant West that is central to most Westerns, including "The Bride"; in this case, the Westerners actively seek Eastern encroachment because of the money it will bring (Introduction 6).

Similarly, and likewise implicitly controverting French's view that Crane unintentionally depicts the Old West as corrupt, Solomon sees Crane in "Moonlight" as employing a voice "drenched in a lyric irony, a comic contempt" to take up the defense of "the violent yet honest Old West against the law-abiding yet venal New West," which is the result of its inhabitants' allowing themselves to be "corrupted by Eastern motives, corrupted into accepting a set of moral standards that are a travesty of the mythic Western ideals of force and honor" (276–77). Dean largely echoes this view. Crane's handling of Larpent, he says, shows the author's attraction to his own idealized conception of Westerners—"rough and genuine men who, if not larger than life, seemed at least large in their lives because they were not trammeled in the artificialities of 'detestable culture'" (258).

In a somewhat different vein, more akin to French's except with regard to the question of authorial intent, Jamie Robertson argues that Crane purposefully conceives the story as "not a lamentation over the passing of the West"—nor, by extension, over the passing of Westerners such as Larpent—but rather as "a study of the replacement of lawless violence with lawful violence by a town full of hypocrites." The townspeople's hypocrisy is revealed in the motives behind their sudden desire for law. They are not eager that true justice be established but rather that a tranquil front be presented to Eastern real-estate interests; so eager are they for the latter that they are perfectly willing to ignore the former in their determination to lynch Larpent. Thus, Robertson concludes, as the new West comes to War Post "[t]he prognosis is not very promising: a new image has replaced the old 'wild West' one, but the reality remains as corrupt as ever" (255).

Several other critics in addition to Wolford have taken particular note of Crane's handling of character in this story. Like Wolford, Solomon notes that Larpent is Crane's "mouthpiece as cynical observer," but unlike Wolford he does not regard this fact as a drawback; he argues that Crane simultaneously achieves some distance from Larpent by giving him another, fuller dimension as well, that of "the protagonist as amoral hero" (277). Bergon sees this cynicism and non-aggressive amorality as crucial to Larpent's effectiveness and

272 Moonlight on the Snow

memorableness as a character. These qualities enable him to achieve a stance of detachment about the events unfolding around him and about himself as well, and "[b]y treating himself impersonally he achieves an eerie clarity of vision and also paradoxically asserts a unique personal authority that differentiates him from members of the crowd" (*Artistry* 106). Deamer takes a particular interest in Potter's character and its thematic dimension as those elements develop in "Moonlight" beyond their condition in "The Bride." In "The Bride," he says, Potter clearly embodies the classic paradox of the Western hero: in standing up for justice he makes his environment safe for civilization, and in so doing he quickly renders himself and his code of "courage and nonchalance in the face of death" obsolete. The ironic extension of this paradox in "Moonlight" can be discerned in the fact that here Potter is helping the civilizers rid themselves of Larpent, the one other figure who embodies Potter's own code (121).

Perhaps the most detailed reading of this story in the areas of both theme and technical skill comes from Monteiro. Writing in response to Solomon's theory that "Moonlight" is a parody of Bret Harte's tales, Monteiro agrees but cautions against letting this realization blind the reader to the story's thematic complexity and architectonic sophistication, which transcend the limits of mere parody. Monteiro points out in particular the townspeople's initial reluctance to execute Larpent, which reveals their "collective lack of the will to accept the consequences of their dedication to the new values of land speculation and economic prosperity" as a result of the pull their old values of the frontier and the clan still exert upon them (121). This dilemma leads to the irony that when Potter and Wilson take Larpent away the relieved townspeople—relieved that Larpent will be punished for a crime against property rather than murder, which is demonstrative of both their own and the new society's priorities—feel that they have managed to abide by the old values while effectively presenting the appearance of having adopted the new ones, whereas in reality Potter and Wilson's intervention reveals that "a greater law and outside authority encroach even as the clan thinks it has reasserted its traditional values" (122). The thematic significance of this irony is its revelation that, despite their belief in self-determination, the townspeople in fact have no power to accept or reject the society that encroaches with this law and authority; all they can actually do is "endorse the social process which has [already] engulfed [them]" (123).

The townspeople's behavior is also key, in Monteiro's view, to Crane's dramatic architecture. Subtly and sophisticatedly integrating the elements of plot, theme, and construction, Monteiro says, Crane structures the story around three tests of the values and sovereignty of the townspeople, all of which they fail. First, Larpent's crime tests their resolve in moving away from values of "friendship and personal privilege" and toward regularized civil law, a resolve that is found wanting in their hesitation to punish him. Second, the objections to the hanging voiced by the newly arrived Easterners further test this resolve, at which point the town's leaders, confused and embarrassed, irresolutely do nothing, failing to move in the direction of either set of values. And finally, Potter's intervention, although it seems to resolve the townspeople's problem by removing its proximate cause, Larpent, actually leaves it suspended, achieving only standoff, not concord, between the proponents of the older clan values and those of the newer principles of civilized respectability (123).

Works Cited

Beer, Thomas. *Stephen Crane: A Study in American Letters*. New York: Knopf, 1923.

Bergon, Frank. Introduction. *The Western Writings of Stephen Crane*. New American Library, 1979. 1–27.

———. *Stephen Crane's Artistry*. New York: Columbia University Press, 1975.

Berryman, John. *Stephen Crane*. New York: Sloane, 1950.

Bowers, Fredson. Textual Introduction. *Tales of Adventure*. Vol. 5 of The University of Virginia Edition of *The Works of Stephen Crane*. Ed. Fredson Bowers. Charlottesville: University Press of Virginia, 1970, cxxxiii–cxcv.

Colvert, James B. *Stephen Crane*. New York: Harcourt Brace Jovanovich, 1984.

Deamer, Robert Glen. "Stephen Crane and the Western Myth." *Western American Literature* 7 (Summer 1972):111–23.

Dean, James L. "The Wests of Howells and Crane." *American Literary Realism* 10 (1977):254–66.

French, Warren. "Stephen Crane: Moment of Myth." *Prairie Schooner* 55 (1981):155–67.

Gibson, Donald B. *The Fiction of Stephen Crane*. Carbondale: Southern Illinois University Press, 1968.

Holton, Milne. *Cylinder of Vision: The Fiction and Journalistic Writings of Stephen Crane*. Baton Rouge: Louisiana State University Press, 1972.

LaFrance, Marston. *A Reading of Stephen Crane*. Oxford: Clarendon, 1971.

Levenson, J. C. Introduction. *Tales of Adventure* xv–cxxxii.

Monteiro, George. "Stephen Crane's 'Yellow Sky' Sequel." *Arizona Quarterly* 30 (1974):119–26.

Osborn, Neal J. "'The Monster' and 'The Blue Hotel.'" *Explicator* 23 (1964): 10.

Robertson, Jamie. "Stephen Crane, Eastern Outsider in the West and Mexico." *Western American Literature* 13 (Nov. 1978):243–57.

Solomon, Eric. *Stephen Crane: From Parody to Realism*. Cambridge: Harvard University Press, 1966.

Stallman, R. W. *Stephen Crane: A Biography*. New York: George Braziller, 1968.

Wertheim, Stanley, and Paul Sorrentino, eds. *The Correspondence of Stephen Crane*. 2 vols. New York: Columbia University Press, 1988.

Wolford, Chester L. *The Anger of Stephen Crane: Fiction and the Epic Tradition*. Lincoln: University of Nebraska Press, 1983.

———. *Stephen Crane: A Study of the Short Fiction*. Boston: Twayne, 1989.

A Mystery of Heroism

Publication History

This story made its first American appearance in a two-part form that Bacheller syndicated to a number of newspapers—including the *Philadelphia Press*, the *Minneapolis Tribune*, the *Kansas City Star*, the *San Francisco Chronicle*, the *Omaha Daily Bee*, and the *Chicago Times-Herald*—most of which ran it on August 1 and 2, 1895. It was then collected in the book *"The Little Regiment" and Other Episodes of the American Civil War*, published in America by D. Appleton in October 1896 and in England by Heinemann in February 1897 (Bowers lxvii). In 1925, it appeared in volume 2 of *The Work of Stephen Crane* (12 vols., New York: Knopf, 1925–27), edited by Wilson Follett, and it was later included in *Stephen Crane: An Omnibus* (New York: Knopf, 1952), edited by Robert W. Stallman, and *The Complete Short Stories and Sketches of Stephen Crane* (Garden City, N.Y.: Doubleday, 1963), edited by Thomas A. Gullason.

Circumstances of Composition

There is no doubt that "A Mystery of Heroism" was the first Civil War story Crane wrote after finishing *The Red Badge of Courage*, and that Crane composed it before that novel had made its great success and brought him, as James B. Colvert puts it, "his disturbing fame" (Introduction xxv). There is, however, some disagreement over precisely when and where Crane worked on it. Stallman says that he wrote it at some point during his tour of the West as a correspondent for the Bacheller newspaper syndicate in the first half of 1895, most likely in mid-March, while he was staying at the Mahncke Hotel in San Antonio, Texas (137). While not explicitly controverting Stallman, Colvert says Crane probably wrote it shortly after his return from the West in May (Introduction xxv), perhaps while he was living at his brother Edmund's house in the upstate New York town of Hartwood. Milne Holton sees Colvert's hypothesis as "more plausible" than Stallman's (122), but a definitive determination is impossible—and perhaps unimportant in any case, given that the discrepancy is only a matter of a few months and seems ultimately to have no bearing on the final form the story took.

Sources and Influences

Like most of Crane's Civil War stories, "Mystery" does not appear to have any basis in events in Crane's own life or in the life of anyone whom he knew or spoke to directly. What it likely does stem from is his frustration with the reading on the Civil War that he did as research for *The Red Badge*. Crane's artist friend Corwin Knapp Linson recounts that in early 1893 Crane spent a great deal of time in Linson's studio reading a borrowed set of the four-volume collection of *Century* magazine articles *Battles and Leaders of the Civil War*. He found these pieces absorbing but also maddening due to the authors' limiting themselves to the external, impersonal aspects of their experiences in combat. Finally, Crane remarked exasperatedly, "'I wonder that *some* of these fellows don't tell how they *felt* in those scraps! They spout eternally of what they *did*, but they are as emotionless as rocks'" (37). "Mystery" can perhaps be regarded as one of his attempts, along with *The Red Badge*, "An Episode of War," and some of the other stories in "*The Little Regiment*," to work out for himself how those fellows *did* feel.

Despite Crane's supposed statement that he learned all he needed to know about fear and heroism in war on the football field, it seems more likely that literary sources gave him many of the ideas that he works with in this story. Lars Ahnebrink suggests Leo Tolstoy's *War and Peace* as one such source, noting that Tolstoy here takes the same approach toward heroism as Crane does in "Mystery," exploring the idea that it "sprang perhaps from man's vanity, from his desire to make an impression on other individuals at any cost," but offering no definitive pronouncements on the subject (357). James W. Gargano offers a Biblical analogue, noting that protagonist Fred Collins's dash through enemy lines for water may derive from Samuel 2.23.13–17. In this passage, with his army surrounded by the Philistines, David wishes aloud for a drink from the nearby well of Bethlehem, thereby prompting three of his men to race through the enemy's lines to get it for him. Upon their return, however, David refuses to drink, instead pouring out the water as an offering to God in tribute to their courage. Crane, Gargano says, alters this ending, having the water poured out in a pointless accident, to make Collins's supposed heroism "ludicrous," thus showing himself to be "an ironist who cannot accept the simple Old Testament idea that the performance of a hazardous action in itself constitutes heroism." Instead, in Collins's self-less act of giving the dying officer a drink, Crane links courage with fraternal charity and thus creates "an alternate and nobler concept of heroism" based on "the more responsible and humane code of conduct advanced by the New Testament" (22–23).

Also worthy of consideration are the various novels and memoirs, most of which do address the issue of how the writers felt in combat, that have been suggested as possible sources for *The Red Badge* and thus for Crane's Civil War writings as a whole: John W. DeForest's *Miss Ravenel's Conversion From Secession to Loyalty* (O'Donnell 578), Frank Wilkeson's *Recollections of a Private Soldier in the Army of the Potomac*, Warren Goss' *Recollections of a Private*, Wilbur F. Hinman's *The Adventures of Corporal Si Klegg and His Pard*, the frequent Civil War articles that ran in *Harper's Weekly* in the 1880s and -90s, and Ambrose Bierce's *Tales of Soldiers and Civilians* (Ahnebrink 97). Of this group, Hinman's and Bierce's works are the most likely as specific sources for "Mystery." H. T. Webster notes a number of parallels between *Si Klegg* and *Red Badge*—many similar incidents, a focus on the common soldier, a heavy use of vernacular dialect, and a central concern with the development of a raw recruit into a capable soldier—and it is possible to note some of these elements in "Mystery" as well. Most particularly, like Henry Fleming, Collins resembles Si Klegg in being a young man "much given to self-dramatization," as Webster characterizes Klegg and Fleming (285). Collins, however, does differ from these two as well by being, as Colvert says, more "reflective and critical, conscious of his vanity and its ethical and social significance" (*Stephen Crane* 94; *DLB* 117–18). As for Bierce, several of the stories in *Tales of Soldiers and Civilians*—"One Officer, One Man," "A Son of the Gods," and "Killed at Resaca"—are meditations on the nature of heroism that are conducted with an irony similar to Crane's in "Mystery," although Bierce tends to be more violent in his conclusions and more contemptuous of his protagonists' mistaken notions on this subject.

Allan Gardner Smith suggests a nonfiction source, the writings of William James. Although Crane cannot be definitively shown to have read any of James's works, his ideas were well known in the intellectual circles in which Crane moved, and Smith argues that certain elements in "Mystery" indicate a familiarity with and acceptance of them. He points specifically to two theories propounded in James's 1890 *Principles of Psychology*. First, James says that an idea produces action by "the urgency with which it is able to impel attention and dominate in consciousness" (qtd. in Smith 243), a principle, Smith points out, that can explain Collins's going for water when no one needs it: he does so "not because of any of the ordinary motivations given by writers for acts of heroism or [because of] extreme foolhardiness, but because," by their taunting, "his companions have managed to keep the idea of his doing so prominent in his consciousness." Second, James says that "the only thing that can neutralize an impulse . . . is an impulse the other way" (qtd. in Smith 243), a concept that accounts for Collins's returning to give a drink to the dying officer even though he initially said he could not do so.

Relationship to Other Crane Works

Despite its Civil War setting, several critics link this story most closely not to *The Red Badge* or any of the other pieces in *"The Little Regiment*," but rather, on the basis of its focus on a man who boasts until he has worked himself into the situation of either having to do something foolhardy or admit that he is afraid, to some of Crane's earliest work, the Sullivan County sketches, the plots of which generally center on the "little man" who places himself in this position. Holton and Marston LaFrance both identify the sketch "The Holler Tree," in which the braggart little man has to climb the tree of the title or else be branded a coward, as the most specific forebear, although Holton points out that Crane's treatment of this plot in "Mystery" is "considerably more mature and more profound" (Holton 31, LaFrance 30). Chester L. Wolford asserts that this superiority to the Sullivan County pieces stems from the fact that in "Mystery" the danger the protagonist faces is much greater, thus putting more at stake in the effort to save face and so producing a deeper meditation on the sources and meaning of courage (64–65).

Regarding Crane's other Civil War works, James Nagel sees this story as most closely related to "The Little Regiment." Both of these, in his view, derive the theme of foolish pride and the device of an ironically deflationary ending from the Sullivan County sketches, and they derive their shared theme of psychological development from fear to compassion within the mindless ferocity of battle from *The Red Badge* (8). He also sees "Mystery" as closely linked to "The Veteran" through their shared theme of courageous action carried out despite adversity and futility. In both of these stories, Nagel notes, Crane presents a situation in which the protagonist exercises compassion even though he himself is in jeopardy, and this behavior, regardless of its results, seems to be the true definition of heroism for Crane (10). Collins in "Mystery" cannot save the wounded lieutenant's life by giving him a drink, and Fleming in "The Veteran" stands very little chance of actually rescuing the colts in the burning barn, but in both instances these men risk their lives— and Fleming loses his—to make whatever effort they can, thus exhibiting the kind of grace under pressure that Crane most admired, the sort of unself-conscious human kindness that he once characterized as "[t]he final wall of the wise man's thought" (*Correspondence* I, 180).

Donald B. Gibson likewise discerns this thematic connection of grace under pressure between "Mystery" and several other *"Little Regiment"* stories.

278   A Mystery of Heroism

He notes that it resembles "An Indiana Campaign" in that both stories focus on a protagonist who must perform a foolhardy action in order to preserve his reputation, but he perceives as well a considerable difference between Collins and Major Tom Boldin, the protagonist of "Indiana," one that also links the latter story to "The Veteran." Both Boldin and the aged Henry Fleming are old soldiers, Gibson says, and thus they have already resolved the issue of their personal courage that Collins is just confronting. As a result, unlike Collins, "[n]either of the old soldiers has the least hesitation about doing what he does. Neither has the same tenacious hold on life [as Collins], though at the same time neither of the old men is simply foolhardy" (93). Beyond these differences, however, Gibson sees all three of these stories as carrying the same final meaning: "courageous action in the face of adversity is necessary and desirable despite the fact that it might or might not have some intimate relationship with the nature of things, that it might not accomplish what it was intended to accomplish" (94). Gibson also sees Crane continuing to engage with this theme in one of his Spanish-American War stories, "The Clan of No-Name." Like Collins, Boldin, and Fleming, the protagonist of this story, Manolo Prat, exemplifies the belief that "courage is its own justification for being" (100).

Wolford similarly links "Mystery" to "Indiana" on the basis of boasts that must be acted on for the sake of their protagonists' reputations. He also connects it to another of Crane's Spanish-American War pieces, "The Lone Charge of William B. Perkins," in that in both cases the protagonist makes a foolhardy gesture under enemy fire but manages to return safely to his own lines, with the narrator commenting more or less directly on the absurdity of a concept of heroism that drives men to such behavior. A major difference between the two, however, is that while Collins's comrades cheer his return and acclaim him a hero even if the narrator does not, no one cheers Perkins; the marines with whom he is associated would not have noticed if he had been killed in his wild charge, and they call him "'that crazy man'" when he makes his way back (*Tales of War* 118). The result of this change—possibly a function of Crane's having seen between the writing of these two stories how men under fire actually regard foolhardy gestures—is that, according to Wolford, the absurdity is presented more emphatically in "Lone Charge" than in "Mystery" (70).

LaFrance sees this theme as tying "Mystery" to still another area within Crane's corpus, his poetry. In this story as in many of his poems, LaFrance says, Crane makes the point that the only truly heroic action is one performed solely "for the sake of the action itself, when vanity is entirely absent" (195).

Colvert, however, disagrees with the initial premise underlying many of the preceding interpretations—the critical truism that this story and the others in "*Little Regiment*" are essentially direct outgrowths of the Sullivan County material and *The Red Badge*. "Mystery" and most of the others, he asserts, do not use "the mythic theme which Crane found most congenial to his imagination," which he discovered in the Sullivan County sketches and developed further in *The Red Badge*: that of the "poignantly alienated 'little man'" who spins out and confronts his own delusions within the mise-en-scène of indifferent nature. Instead, "Mystery" and the other *"Little Regiment"* stories feature protagonists who are closer in development to Henry Fleming at the end of *The Red Badge*, confronting "the world of men" as social beings (Introduction xxiv). "Mystery" is the best example of this change, Colvert says, because although it seems very similar to *The Red Badge* in terms of character and action it is actually quite different. Unlike that of *The Red Badge*, the setting here is not a series of hallucinatory images "projected upon the landscape from the demoralized fancy of the hero"; it is, rather, "merely a setting . . . adapted to a nonmythic dramatic situation" (xxv). And perhaps more important, Fred Collins is more reflective than Henry, being at least in some measure aware of his "self-serving pride" and seeing himself in "an ethical context, . . . [that] of the world of men and social conduct" (xxv–xxvi). (Colvert offers a similar analysis in a slightly later essay as well, "Stephen Crane: Style as Invention.")

Critical Studies

John W. Shroeder offers a wholly negative assessment of this story, judging it slight due to its focus on the single, reductive insight, derived from the spilling of the bucket, that the universe is indifferent. He regards this reductionism, "this error of writing to the service of empty revelations," as marring much of Crane's work; he ascribes it to what he sees as Crane's espousal of the Naturalist view of man as merely a thing in a disinterested cosmos (122).

Maxwell Geismar, on the other hand, takes a positive view. He finds most of the stories in the *"Little Regiment"* volume markedly inferior to *Red Badge* because in these stories Crane shifts from exploring the mindset of a raw recruit to celebrating, with no trace of irony, the professional killer's stoicism adopted by the veteran soldier. In Geismar's view, this shift indicates a "hardening and stratification of an attitude toward war (and toward the fresh and original amateur soldiers in Crane's own work) that one notices also in Kipling. . . . Here Crane descended to the rhetoric of heroism or the fervor almost of the dime novel" (90–91). However, he makes an exception for "Mystery" because Collins is not a veteran but rather, more like Fleming, "a blundering idiot, trapped by fate," whose predicament is "viewed with humor and a kind of desperate compassion" (91). Most critics agree with Geismar's assessment of the story as one of the best in its collection, but they disagree widely as to its meaning. Daniel Aaron asserts that its central point is simply the cruelty and purposelessness of war, which "turns men into animals or machines and blurs the distinction between fools and heroes" (218), but it is the issue of this distinction that is the source of most of the critical disputation.

Stallman, Eric Solomon, Bettina Knapp, and Frank Bergon essentially agree with Aaron, arguing that the blurring of heroism and foolishness is Crane's theme. Stallman says that what Collins and the reader learn is that "[h]eroism is not a predictable possession, but rather an impersonal gift thrust by chance upon a man at the wrong moment," a condition that renders him as much a fool as a hero, since the spilling of the bucket by the two joking lieutenants symbolically renders his action as empty as the bucket (335). Solomon sees "Mystery" as Crane's "most highly intellectualized war story" (102), an insightful study of the enigmatic nature of courage. He says that Collins's going for water is more gratuitous than brave, since no one is thirsty. His turning back to give a drink to the lieutenant who is in need *is* genuinely courageous, but the meaning of that action nevertheless remains mysterious, since the lieutenant dies regardless and the rest of the water is spilled. Thus, Solomon concludes, "[t]he 'heroism' of the title is parodic; the 'mystery' is realistic" (106). Knapp regards "mystery" as characterizing many things in the story: Collins's reasons for going to get water, his reasons for returning to the lieutenant, the reason the bucket is spilled, the question of whether this spilling indicates that his actions have no meaning. All these mysteries combine to imply that "certain acts during a time of crisis must remain unexplained" and that the "human personality is as unfathomable and baffling as the savagery—and, for Crane, the beauty—of war" (166). Bergon similarly argues that the sum of the story is that "the very conception of courage and heroism evaporate into mystery." We as readers "see all we can of the luck, will, chance, personality, thought, and everything else that make up an event, but we cannot reduce that event to any moral category," with the result that "[i]t is impossible to say whether . . . [Collins] is a fool or a hero" (20).

In contrast to Bergon's assertion, however, a number of critics have found it entirely possible to judge Collins as either wholly a fool or wholly a hero. On the side of fool, Wolford asserts that the bucket is already empty when Collins returns, rather than being emptied by the two lieutenants, and argues that the significance of this fact is that Collins's supposedly heroic action of fetching the water is in fact "as empty as the bucket; the 'mystery' of his 'heroism' is resolved by the recognition that egotism, pride, and saving face are at the heart of many . . . deeds commonly perceived as heroic" (66). In a similar but somewhat more complex reading, LaFrance also says that Collins's going to get the water stems only from vanity and thus lacks "worthy motivation" (193) but his foolishness lies deeper than that. Like Gargano, considered above in "Sources and Influences," and David Halliburton as well (150), LaFrance sees Crane as presenting a genuinely heroic action in Collins's stopping to give the dying officer a drink under fire, but Collins nonetheless remains a fool because he, along with the other men of his regiment, fails to see heroism in such a "willed and selfless act of charity" (194). Instead, he and his fellows continue to operate under a conventional, romanticized concept of heroism, as is borne out in the fact that, in LaFrance's view as in Wolford's, Collins himself spills the water before he returns to his own lines, thus symbolically revealing the emptiness of his action and his conception of heroism (194).

Leland Krauth's reading embraces much of what LaFrance says but takes it in a somewhat different direction, one that ultimately leads back to Geismar in that Krauth sees "Mystery" as not simply the artistic equal of *Red Badge* but rather a step forward from it. Krauth argues that the end of *Red Badge* is marred by an unresolved tension between the two conceptions of heroism that LaFrance notes in "Mystery": Crane himself regards heroic behavior as action motivated by "compassion and charitable self-sacrifice" (87), whereas the conventional military heroism that he has Henry Fleming display in the final charges stems from egotism, from his desire to prove himself to the general who referred to his regiment as "'mule drivers'" and "'mud diggers'"—an egotism that "is as reprehensible as it is useful" when one is under fire (89). In "Mystery," Crane resolves this tension by providing both kinds of behavior. Collins's initial effort is shown to be motivated purely by vanity, since it lacks any tactical objective, and then in Collins's selfless act of turning back to give the mortally wounded lieutenant a drink Crane overtly counterbalances the conventional definition of heroism with "his own moral redefinition" of it (91). Thus, Krauth says, this story is as much a "gloss" on the novel as "The Veteran" is, and in fact a more effective one, in that in "Mystery" Crane presents the selfless action without editorial comment, leaving it a "mystery," while in "The Veteran" he sentimentalizes and thereby weakens Fleming's comparable action with his concluding panegyric (92).

A number of other critics focus on the emptiness of the bucket, regardless of whose fault it is, as evidence of Crane's anticipation of twentieth-century philosophy. Gibson says that Crane's point is that the water itself is not important; what is meaningful is that in going to get it Collins proves to himself and others that he is heroic. Tacitly alluding to the death of Romanticism by the end of the nineteenth century, Gibson argues that what Crane is saying is that "even in a world where nature herself does not recognize the meaning and value of heroism, it is a significant value if only because it fulfills some yearning in men" (92). William Bysshe Stein notes more explicitly the proto-existentialist sense of absurdity implicit in such a reading of Crane's intent, asserting that the emptiness of the bucket is Crane's "measure of the significance of man's engagement to purpose in the scheme of this existence" (188).

With this sense of ultimate purposelessness in view, George W. Johnson sees "Mystery" as an early step in Crane's formulation of his mature philosophy that the human condition is "an untenable position between an unknowable world and incongruous ceremonies" such as "the decorum of the veteran" that Collins is learning about (251). What he learns is, first, that this decorum is "no more meaningful than the rituals of tea" (251), as evidenced when upon his return he "apparently abides by conventions and maintains decorum" and yet the water is spilled, revealing that "the conventions, like the bucket, are with terrible finality quite empty" (252). A corollary to this revelation, however, is that despite its meaninglessness this decorum "allows the veteran to accept incongruities which would otherwise overwhelm his imagination" (253), an insight that leads to the final, uncomforting realization that in the modern world "[f]ragmented men, fragmented action, are tied together only by meaningless rules" (256).

Florence Leaver still more overtly emphasizes the modern nature of Crane's work in this story. In her view, Collins's actions stem from conceit that is rooted in a sense of "the isolation of modern man, who has been sent to his unconscious to understand himself and even to find his God." Collins epitomizes this condition in that he, like twentieth-century humans, "has become the victim, aware or unaware, of the power of circumstance, the indifference of nature, the fading of tradition, and the weakening, if not loss, of faith. He feels terribly alone, with nowhere to go for absolutes" (522), and therefore he seeks to become part of an entity larger than himself, the regiment, by engaging in his meaningless acts of bravado (527).

"Mystery" has garnered considerable praise for its technical sophistication as well as for its thematic depth. Gullason calls it the best story in the *"Little Regiment"* volume, rating it as "Crane's first major story, and his first complex one," due to his "remarkable balance and counterpointing between the casual, trivial world of Collins and his thirst, and the deadly destruction of war," along with the "cinematic technique of isolating Collins, then losing him into the chaos of the larger world, and again focusing on him" to intensify "the relationship between man and war" (475–76). Holton is less enthusiastic. He too sees "Mystery" as the best story in *"The Little Regiment"*; however, he regards this group as a bad lot, lacking "the remarkably rendered dramatic impressionism, the grotesque apprehension of external reality, . . . [and] the intensity and focus" that distinguish *Red Badge* (141). He identifies "Mystery" as one of Crane's many stories about unwished-for confrontations but says that later ones in this vein, such as "The Bride Comes to Yellow Sky" and "The Blue Hotel," are more effective for concerning "higher stakes." Its individual merits lie, Holton concludes, in its presentation of Crane's ongoing interest in the effect fear has on a protagonist's ability to apprehend his circumstances clearly, although here, unlike in his later stories examining this theme, Crane focuses, less fruitfully, not so much on this apprehensional issue *per se* as on "the absurd meaninglessness of the event itself, . . . the gratuitous nature of reality" (141).

Nagel takes a position more akin to Gullason's than Holton's. He lauds Crane's skill in presenting a number of details in the opening of the story—the red flashes of the artillery, the artillerymen's white pants, the silhouettes of horses against the sky, the wounded lieutenant—that recur later, thus producing "referential unity" to develop his theme, a technique that in his view characterizes Crane's finest works (8). He notes as well Crane's "sustained pattern of nature images suggestive of destructive abnormality" to "establish a context of danger and destruction in which to measure Collins' act of heroism" (9), which leads to two possible measurements. On the one hand, this context reveals that the regiment does not need water and thus Collins acts out of pride. On the other hand, however, the context also suggests that Collins has "won a psychological victory over his own fear" and has shown charity to the dying lieutenant, suggesting the more positive insight that "true heroism, to the extent to which it is possible in the chaos of battle, consists not of massive destruction of the enemy but of the extension of compassion in a moment of danger" (10).

Works Cited

Aaron, Daniel. *The Unwritten War*. New York: Alfred A. Knopf, 1973.

Ahnebrink, Lars. *The Beginnings of Naturalism in American Fiction*. Cambridge: Harvard University Press, 1950.

Bergon, Frank. *Stephen Crane's Artistry*. New York: Columbia University Press, 1975.

Bowers, Fredson. Textual Introduction. *Tales of War*. Vol. 6 of The University of Virginia Edition of *The Works of Stephen Crane*. Ed. Fredson Bowers. Charlottesville: University Press of Virginia, 1970, xxxvii–cxci.

Colvert, James B. "Stephen Crane." *American Realists and Naturalists*. Vol. 12 of *Dictionary of Literary Biography*. Ed. Donald Pizer and Earl N. Harbert. Detroit: Gale Research, 1982, 100–24.

———. Introduction. *Tales of War* xi–xxxvi.

———. *Stephen Crane*. New York: Harcourt Brace Jovanovich, 1984.

———. "Stephen Crane: Style as Invention." *Stephen Crane in Transition: Centenary Essays*. Ed. Joseph Katz. DeKalb: Northern Illinois University Press, 1972, 127–52.

Crane, Stephen. "The Lone Charge of William B. Perkins." *Tales of War* 114–18.

Gargano, James W. "Crane's 'A Mystery of Heroism': A Possible Source." *Modern Language Notes* 74 (1959):22–23.

Geismar, Maxwell. *Rebels and Ancestors*. Boston: Houghton Mifflin, 1953.

Gibson, Donald B. *The Fiction of Stephen Crane*. Carbondale: Southern Illinois University Press, 1968.

Gullason, Thomas A. "Stephen Crane's Short Stories: The True Road." *Stephen Crane's Career: Perspectives and Evaluations*. Ed. Thomas A. Gullason. New York: New York University Press, 1972, 470–86.

Holton, Milne. *Cylinder of Vision: The Fiction and Journalistic Writings of Stephen Crane*. Baton Rouge: Louisiana State University Press, 1972.

Johnson, George W. "Stephen Crane's Metaphor of Decorum." *PMLA* 78 (1963): 250–56.

Knapp, Bettina L. *Stephen Crane*. New York: Ungar, 1987.

Krauth, Leland. "Heroes and Heroics: Stephen Crane's Moral Imperative." *South Dakota Review* 11 (Summer 1973):86–93.

LaFrance, Marston. *A Reading of Stephen Crane*. Oxford: Clarendon, 1971.

Leaver, Florence. "Isolation in the Works of Stephen Crane." *South Atlantic Quarterly* 61 (1962):521–32.

Linson, Corwin K. *My Stephen Crane*. Syracuse: Syracuse University Press, 1958.

Nagel, James. "Stephen Crane's Stories of War: A Study of Art and Theme." *North Dakota Quarterly* 43 (1975):5–19.

O'Donnell, Thomas F. "De Forest, Van Petten, and Stephen Crane." *American Literature* 27 (1956):578–80.

Shroeder, John W. "Stephen Crane Embattled." *University of Kansas City Review* 17 (1950):119–29.

Smith, Allan Gardner. "Stephen Crane, Impressionism, and William James." *Revue Française d'Études Américaines* 18 (1983):237–48.

Solomon, Eric. *Stephen Crane: From Parody to Realism*. Cambridge: Harvard University Press, 1966.

Stallman, R. W. *Stephen Crane: A Biography*. New York: George Braziller, 1968.

Stein, William B. "Stephen Crane's *Homo Absurdus*." *Bucknell Review* 8 (1959): 168–88.

Webster, H. T. "Wilbur F. Hinman's *Corporal Si Klegg* and Stephen Crane's *The Red Badge of Courage*." *American Literature* 11 (1939):258–93.

Wertheim, Stanley, and Paul Sorrentino, eds. *The Correspondence of Stephen Crane*. Vol. 1. New York: Columbia University Press, 1988.

Wolford, Chester L. *Stephen Crane: A Study of the Short Fiction*. Boston: Twayne, 1989.

One Dash—Horses

Publication History

This story made its first American appearance in a two-part form that Bacheller, Johnson & Bacheller syndicated to a number of newspapers— including the *Kansas City Star*, the *Buffalo Commercial*, the *Philadelphia Press*, and the *Nebraska State Journal*—most of which ran it on either January 3 and 4 or January 4 and 6, 1896. It was next published in the February 1896 number of the English magazine *New Review* (14:140–51), under the title "Horses," and then under its full title in the Bacheller-owned American *Pocket Magazine* for June 1896 (3:70–101). Its initial American book publication came in the 1898 Doubleday & McClure volume *"The Open Boat" and Other Tales of Adventure*; in England it appeared, again under the shortened title "Horses," in *"The Open Boat" and Other Stories*, also published in 1898 by Heinemann (Bowers cxliii). Editor Wilson Follett included it in volume 12, published in 1927, of *The Work of Stephen Crane* (12 vols., New York: Knopf, 1925–27), and it was also collected in *The Complete Short Stories and Sketches of Stephen Crane* (Garden City, N.Y.: Doubleday, 1963), edited by Thomas A. Gullason.

Circumstances of Composition

For a year and a half following his tour of the West and Mexico as a correspondent for the Bacheller newspaper syndicate, which lasted from January to May of 1895, Crane lived much of the time with his brother Edmund's family in Hartwood, a village in New York state. However, he also spent considerable periods with friends in New York City and Philadelphia (Levenson xl), and it was in the latter city that he composed "One Dash—Horses." In a letter of September 10, 1895, from there to a New York City friend, Willis Brooks Hawkins, Crane says, "I am engaged at last on my personal troubles in Mexico" (*Correspondence* I, 123), a reference to his finally having the time to transmute into literary form his own equestrian escape from Mexican outlaws the previous April or May.

Sources and Influences

Crane's first biographer, Thomas Beer, asserts that Crane closely modeled this story on his own encounter with a gang of Mexican bandits during his 1895 Western trip. Just as in the story, Crane and his guide, Miguel Itorbide, were threatened at an inn by the leader of this group, Ramón Colorado, saved when the arrival of a group of prostitutes diverted Colorado's attention, pursued next morning by the gang on horseback, and ultimately rescued by a patrol of *rurales*, Mexican cavalry, whose commander "sat cursing Colorado while the bandit tried to apologize for having annoyed a friend of the government" (116). Although Beer is not always the most reliable source for such information, given his predilection for inventing letters and episodes in order to create an aesthetically satisfying confluence of Crane's life and art (*Correspondence* I, 6–10), in this case most of what he says can be confirmed. Crane's letter to Hawkins, quoted above, that mentions his personal "troubles in Mexico" is one verification; Corwin K. Linson's memoir of Crane's telling him about these troubles is a second (87–88); and a letter of January 26, 1896, to Nellie Crouse, a young woman with whom Crane was in love, is a third, for here he mentions having sent her a copy of "Horses" earlier and explains that the story "celebrates in a measure my affection for a little horse I owned in Mexico" (*Correspondence* I, 185).

Subsequent biographers such as James B. Colvert (*Crane* 84), Robert W. Stallman, J. C. Levenson, and Charles W. Mayer add further details to Crane's adventure and its connection to the story. Stallman notes that at the time of his encounter with Colorado, Crane was even wearing clothes and accouterments very similar to those he gives Richardson, the protagonist of "Horses": sombrero, blanket, revolver, and spurs (149). Levenson says that this encounter can be dated with more precision than Beer realized, to either April or May of 1895 (xxxviii). And Mayer addresses the story's title in the context of Crane's Western trip, explaining that in the West in this period a *dash* meant not only a run for safety but also a roll of the dice, so that the title implies that Richardson hazards this latter kind of dash—relying on chance—in trusting the speed and endurance of his horse to make the former kind of dash (56).

To this wealth of biographical foundations, Frank Bergon adds the possibility of a literary source as well. He notes that Crane may have been familiar with the story "Kaweah's Run," which is a chapter of the popular 1872 book *Mountaineering in the Sierra Nevada*, by pioneering Western geologist and writer Clarence King. In this story King describes his own escape from Mexican bandits thanks to the speed and endurance of his horse, Kaweah. Bergon argues that this resemblance and the featuring of the horses prominently in both titles is unlikely to have been coincidental, but he also notes two significant differences between the stories: King presents his escape as entirely effected by the stamina of his horse and his own skill as a rider, and he maintains a serious, suspenseful tone throughout the piece; whereas Crane makes Richardson's escape a result of the combination of his horse's stamina and the pure luck of the *rurales'* appearing in the nick of time, and he routinely undercuts the dramatic tension of his tale with humorous asides and direct addresses to his reader. These differences indicate, in Bergon's view, that in blending his own experience with his literary background to produce this story Crane found that he could not wholly accept the heroic Western myth of the chase, as King does, but he could not entirely reject it, either (Introduction 12–14).

While not arguing for one specific source, Eric Solomon offers much the same assessment of Crane's ambivalence regarding the literary background on which he draws for "Horses." This story, Solomon says, is a "not wholly successful amalgam of parody and thriller." Crane effectively lampoons the stereotypically imperturbable Western hero by showing Richardson to be badly frightened, but in his depiction of the horse as the true hero, he "confuses the comic tone with some sentimental clichés out of *Black Beauty*" (240).

Relationship to Other Crane Works

Many critics discern thematic similarities between "Horses" and some of Crane's other Western tales. Robert Glen Deamer points out its close connections to "The Five White Mice" and "A Man and Some Others" in that all three affirm the Western "code of self-reliant courage" that Crane found highly admirable (118–20). Chester L. Wolford likewise sees "Horses" as linked very closely to these two stories through their common themes of "sheer chance, the apprehension of reality in danger and death, the cowardly bravado of groups, and the tenacity with which some people do what they do, all the while knowing the dire consequences" (41). He also notes that in some respects "The Wise Men" should be included in this group, since it shares with "Horses" and "Mice" an emphasis on the roles self-control and luck play along with chance in beating the odds and producing favorable outcomes. In "Horses," self-control comes in when Richardson refuses to let the outlaws see his fear when they threaten him in the cantina; luck plays its part in Richardson's happening to have a fast horse and to meet the *rurales* in time to be rescued (40).

Levenson takes a larger thematic view, one that embraces not only Westerns but a number of Crane's non-Western stories as well. He sees "Horses" as perhaps the clearest example of Crane's concern in all his early fiction more with the inner mental landscape of his protagonists, with "the chaotic, unpredictable flux of subjective experience," than with "the sense of fortuitously arranged, morally neutral objective nature," although both of these elements are present. In his later stories, such as "The Open Boat" and "The Blue Hotel," Levenson says, Crane reverses this emphasis (xvii). Levenson also points out that "Horses" lies at the midpoint of Crane's development of another theme through a number of his early stories, the threat of violence in a realm other than war. A revolver is "wildly brandished" in "The Pace of Youth," it is "seriously drawn and pointed" in "Mice" and "Horses," and at last fired in "Man," thereby finally yielding the moment to which Crane has built up in this group, the moment "when the horror of killing and the absoluteness of death are more important than the fear of dying, when the intensity of self-regard has given way to the perception of truths." Those truths, Levenson explains, are "the forms that live out from the incoherence, . . . the fragility of life, . . . [and] the dignity of death." And in creating this moment of insight under fire, Levenson concludes, Crane not only reaches the end of this sequence but also the limits of his ability to imagine the significances revealed by the imminent presence of death; "[i]n experience and in art he would here-after build on what he had done in his early Western tales" (xlix).

Critical Studies

A number of critics offer generally adverse assessments of this story. Neville Denny dismisses it as "slight" due to Crane's failure to develop fully his plot and theme and their significance, his apparent willingness to render only "a vague suggestion of the unpredictability and violence lurking at the heart of reality" (34). Donald B. Gibson concurs with this evaluation, saying that despite the basis of this story in Crane's own experience its plot is thin and the reader is given no insight into how this evidently harrowing event changes Richardson (123–24). Stallman sees Crane as more ambitious than Denny and Gibson, saying that he composed "Horses" "with the intent of out-stripping all other tales on the same subject," but he also sees Crane as failing to meet this goal, so that the story "has little significance other than its auto-biographical interest" (150). Bergon lays the story's putative failure to what would appear to be the opposite of ambition, a problem linked to Bergon's argument, noted above in "Sources and Influences," that Crane could neither accept nor reject the heroic dimensions of the myth of the Western chase. Writing out of this ambivalence, Bergon says, "Crane goes too far in his reluctance to take himself seriously" in transforming his own experience into Richardson's, and as a result "the story's self-effacement topples into extreme self-consciousness" (*Artistry* 102).

Raymund Paredes is likewise deeply critical of Crane's work in "Horses," but he faults it not for Crane's attitude toward himself but rather for his attitude toward others: he condemns the story, along with "The Five White Mice" and "A Man and Some Others," for what he regards as Crane's racist treatment of his Mexican characters. In all three stories, he says, Crane takes the view that "when Yankee confronted Mexican, mortal danger was the usual concomitant," and that this is the case because of the Mexican's "savage appetite . . . beyond all reason." However, Crane always presents this appetite as accompanied by a large streak of cowardice, a combination that causes the Yankee to react with a mixture of fear and contempt. At the moment of confrontation—as in the two instances in "Horses" when Colorado actively threatens Richardson—the Mexican crumbles, "totally bereft of dignity and nobility," while the Yankee responds to his own fear "with courage, reacting coolly and weighing his options, reacting quickly to stay alive." And Crane depicts the Yankee's subsequent contempt as warranted because the Mexican hides his cowardice "behind a colossal pretentiousness"; he seeks to bluff the Yankee but ultimately fails "because he has no bravery to fall back on," thus making "a mockery of an honest emotion." With these notions in view, Paredes offers perhaps the strongest denunciation to be found anywhere in the corpus of Crane criticism. In his Westerns, Crane constructs "a Darwinian world of constant and bitter struggle" in which the Mexican—sinister, treacherous, mysterious, and murderous—"is clearly the lowest form of humanity" and is thus destined to lose to the Yankee. And "the virulence of Crane's attitude toward the Mexican," Paredes concludes, "is even more meaningful and disturbing when viewed in the light of his own personal experience." In America, Crane "championed the destitute and disfranchised" and routinely "associated amicably with gamblers, dopeheads, and prostitutes." He was able to discern "virtue and dignity in some of the most unsavory characters of New York's Bowery," and yet, "with all his artistic sensibility," he failed ever to locate a single redeeming characteristic in any Mexican (31–38).

Cecil Robinson is in accord with this view, asserting that in "Horses" Crane presents two equally negative poles in his two major Mexican characters: Richardson's guide is wholly cowardly, and Colorado is both cowardly and bloodthirsty (192). A well-reasoned response to these charges, however, comes from Jamie Robertson. He begins by arguing that Crane arrived in the West at a date late enough to enable him to realize that the Western myth—"that individual courage gives meaning to life"—which was still being fostered in Western fiction by Eastern writers for Eastern readers, was in fact defunct. Thus Crane, aware of his Eastern outsider status in the West, creates protagonists much like himself in "Horses," "Mice," and "Man," protagonists who "participate in the convention of popular Western fiction" but nonetheless take an ironic view of that convention. Crane's goal in using this ironic stance toward the Western myth is to show that courage in confronting the unknown, which in these stories is the possibility of death in conflicts with Mexicans, does not in itself give meaning to life but rather leads to a larger insight into what for Crane is the desideratum of any person's individual development: "a humble awareness of one's own insignificance," like that which the correspondent in "The Open Boat" discovers in his contemplation of nature's indifference to his fate. And this fact absolves Crane from Paredes's charge of racism, Robertson says, because in all three of the stories in question, Yankees and Mexicans are not placed in hierarchy but rather united in their mutual recognition of their individual insignificance (244–46). In "Horses" in particular, according to Robertson's formulation, the key to understanding the non-racist nature of Crane's approach is to realize that Richardson is given the opportunity to recognize this unity when he and his guide together gallop for their lives but fails to achieve this recognition. Although the guide in fact behaves more capably and less fearfully than Richardson, the American continues to romanticize himself and look down on the Mexican, continues to subscribe to the Western romance cliché that all Mexicans are by definition inferior and pusillanimous. Thus, Robertson concludes, there is ironic distance between Richardson as protagonist and Crane as author; the bigoted illusions about Mexicans operative here "are Richardson's clichés, not Stephen Crane's" (248).

Colvert responds to one of the other charges levelled against "Horses," Gibson's criticism of its failure to indicate how its events change Richardson, by suggesting that viewing this character as the protagonist is in fact wrong-headed. Noting what Crane himself wrote to Nellie Crouse about the story's being a celebration of his "affection for a little horse I owned in Mexico," he asserts that Richardson's horse is the true hero due to his "admirable devotion" (*Crane* 84) and his "supreme courage and determination" (*DLB* 115). Viewed from this angle, the story is not lacking in insight but rather comes across as "a masterful evocation of a sense of crisis, furious motion, and rapport between horse and rider" (*DLB* 115). A considerable number of the many other critics who are favorably disposed toward "Horses" go even further than Colvert, arguing that significant insight *is* in fact present here, if somewhat difficult to discern due to Crane's characteristic understatement. Working from the story's autobiographical cast, John Berryman says that it dramatizes a key change in Crane's thinking, one that caused him to eliminate every trace of sentimentality from his writing. During his sojourn in the West, Berryman explains, Crane became more fully aware of the indifference of nature than he ever had been before, and this new awareness drove home to him the idea that one can rely only upon oneself. Therefore, "to find out what one was, how, that is, one would *act*," became of paramount importance to him, because that discovery provided the only measure of just how far one *could* rely upon oneself. And in Richardson, Berryman concludes, Crane dramatizes this process of self-discovery that he himself had just undergone in his real-life encounter with the bandits; like Richardson at the end of the story, he had "found that he was able to feel terror and act as if he did not feel terror and so survive," a realization that raised his view of human nature to the extent that "henceforth Crane could be an heroic writer" (104–07).

Deamer strongly agrees with Berryman; he considers "Horses" proof of his thesis that in the West Crane himself confronted true danger for the first time, discovered his own capacity for courage through those confrontations, and as a result renounced the ironic view of courage that he had maintained in *The Red Badge*. From an autobiographical perspective, Deamer says, Richardson's discovery of his ability to stare levelly back at Colorado and thereby keep him at bay when the bandit threatens the American at the inn re-enacts Crane's own realization that "manliness was not really such a mystery after all" (119). Levenson also regards the story as a reflection of Crane's own self-discovery in the West, but he sees this discovery as not simply a matter of self-reliance but rather as a lesson in the necessity of relying as well on certain entities besides oneself. Pointing to Crane's emphasis on the horse in both his title and his remarks to Nellie Crouse, along with the connection of *dash* to both a run for safety and a roll of the dice, Levenson says that the point of the story is that Richardson "must act in a world where the event cannot be foreknown, and when he sees that he cannot count on himself alone to make the event he wants, he takes the risk of counting on something outside himself"—his horse and luck. In this movement away from pure self-reliance, Levenson discerns "[t]he intensity of the youthful adventurer [giving] way to the understatement of the veteran" (xxxviii–xxxix). Edwin H. Cady likewise sees the story as indicative of expansion in Crane's sensibility as a result of his Western tour, but he regards this enlargement as occurring not only in Crane's understanding of himself but also in his response to his cultural context. Focusing particularly on its anticlimactic ending, Cady contends that "Horses" is a deflating response to the ideology of "neoromantic violence" that dominated the 1890s in the fiction of Owen Wister, the painting and drawing of Frederic Remington, and the posturing of Theodore Roosevelt (174). Despite his attraction to this ideology, Cady argues, Crane ultimately sides with the opposing ideas epitomized in the fiction of William Dean Howells, for by keeping the story constantly teetering on the edge of violence but concluding without the expected explosion of mayhem Crane purposefully refuses to present violence as the ultimate resolution; he seeks instead to establish a Howellsian "sensibility which is rational, compassionate, and reverential toward life" (180).

Taking a different tack, Bergon, implicitly rejecting the above readings, agrees with Gibson that Crane offers no particularly clear insight in "Horses" but argues that this trait is not an indication of the author's failure but rather a precise measure of his artistic and thematic success. Crane, Bergon says, is not a philosopher, ethicist, or aesthetician writing treatises but rather an explorer of consciousness. Therefore, he does not seek to inculcate specific, sharply articulated theories of life; instead, "[t]he kinds of responses Crane wants from the reader seem to be those very states of wonder, awe, or transcendence which he habitually attributes to his characters." A prime example of such a state, Bergon explains, is Crane's characterization of the blanket that covers the doorway between the rooms that Richardson and Colorado occupy at the inn, through which Richardson first hears Colorado's plan to rob and perhaps kill him, as "a horrible emblem." Staring at this blanket that veils a threat to himself the extent of which he cannot precisely know, Richardson "reaches a still point, his sense of self diminishes, and he becomes attuned to the outside world" in all its foreboding mystery (52–53). (Wolford tacitly accords with this reading of the "veiled" nature of reality in his description of the blanket as "a metaphor both for humanity's extremely limited understanding of reality and for fear of death" [40].)

Where Bergon *does* perceive an identifiably sharp change in Crane's thinking in "Horses" is in the realm of style. This is the first story, he says, in which Crane eschews the "extreme verbal excesses and syntactic dislocations" that are the hallmarks of his early works, especially *The Red Badge*, in favor of the "fluidity," "impassiveness," "firm narrative control," and "imaginative restraint" that distinguish his mature fiction (*Artistry* 119). Orm Overland also comments on Crane's style in this story, paying particular attention to the narrator's habit of imputing motion to inanimate objects, as when he says that houses "glided past" riders or "suddenly appeared squatting amid the bushes." Such formulations, in which the narrator "is recording a primary impression and rejecting logic," Overland says, are grounds for classifying Crane as an Impressionist, since one of the principal traits of literary Impressionism is precisely this "tendency to veil or neglect causal relations between objects, actions or phenomena described" in order to make the point that the "immediate impressions we receive of phenomena through our senses are often quite different from what we finally realize them to be"—that "[o]nly by applying logic and relying on experience can we make [our impressions] fit into the laws of cause and effect and other terms through which the surrounding world is meaningful to us" (264–65).

Milne Holton focuses not on Crane's handling of his narrator but on his use of Richardson as a third-person point-of-view character. This perspective, with its capacity to combine objective and subjective description, "makes it possible to report fear and experience simultaneously"—that is, to make the reader simultaneously aware of Richardson's fear when he encounters the bandits at the inn and on the plain and of the external actions he takes during those ordeals. Crane's goal in utilizing this approach, Holton says, is a frequent one in his stories: "recounting the experience of confronting alone a new, terrifying, and not entirely understandable reality." And as usual in his depictions of this condition, Crane uses literal sight as a metaphor for understanding or the lack thereof, as when Richardson's apprehension regarding the unknown is epitomized in his fear of what he cannot see beyond the blanket covering the doorway of his room at the inn. Here as in many of his later stories, Holton concludes, Crane draws the reader's attention to the fundamental human "terror of the unseen—to the power of blankness" (125–26).

Ben Merchant Vorpahl and Glen M. Johnson both examine another aspect of Crane's technique in "Horses," his handling of structure. Vorpahl discerns here the first use of a method of linking structure to theme that Crane employs in many of his later Western tales, most notably "Man" and "The Bride Comes to Yellow Sky": the deployment of contrasts within each setting to make a point about the passage of time. Each significant section of the story, Vorpahl explains, "contains two opposing elements: an artificial configuration—for which chronology appears to be irrelevant—and a chronological configuration—which suggests that such irrelevance is apparent only." For example, in the opening sequence the landscape is described in artificial terms, as when the narrator says that the "hills in the west were carved into peaks, and were painted the most profound blue" (*Tales* 13), giving it the timeless quality of a work of art, but then Richardson's first words express his immediate need for food and sleep, which reminds the reader that the sense that time stands still for nature or any of its creatures is merely an illusion, as Scratchy Wilson learns to his similar discomfort in "Bride" (201).

Johnson, in a very closely reasoned and meticulously detailed argument that shares certain features with Holton's analysis, sees "Horses" as a prime example of "Crane's characteristic method of structuring his fiction" in that although he appears to have "satiric" and "sensational" elements working at cross purposes here, he in fact harmonizes these two sets of elements in the service of one purpose: the creation of irony to accomplish "the realist's goal of providing usable insights into 'the way things happen.'" The satiric elements occur on the level of plot, in Crane's "refusal to provide the conventional violent climax"; and on the level of point of view in Crane's alternation between the subjective perspectives of Richardson and the outlaws and the objective, detached, ironic viewpoint of the narrator—an alternation that, in its emphasis on the limitations of subjectivity and creation of aesthetic distance, "tells the reader to relax, to think, and not to worry too much about the outcome," with the ultimate aim of achieving the realist's customary purpose of demolishing "the melodramatic view of existence." And beyond the level of satire, the sensational elements—sensational "in the sense of *enargia* or vividness"—create "an intensity or psychological violence not merely to be analyzed in certain characters, but to be experienced by the reader himself." In this intent, Johnson argues, Crane is expressionistic, in that like later dramatists and filmmakers he seeks here the "objectivization of the subjective," wherein "[t]he intense psychological condition of a character—or of the dramatist himself—is projected outward into the presented world of the drama to the extent that objective and subjective are inseparable if not identical." In the story's initial sequence, for example, Johnson says that the setting is expressionistic in that "qualities of instability and threat seem to inhere in the physical surroundings." This perception "may be a mental quality—may reflect Richardson's weariness and his consciousnes of isolation in an unfamiliar landscape—but it is impossible to isolate the quality in any perspective less inclusive than that of the total scene" (571–74).

These satiric and sensational levels then "work together in something like a dialectical process" during the story's climactic chase, Johnson says, and in doing so they create what he calls "realistic irony," which turns outward upon the reader rather than inward upon the artist, as romantic irony generally does, with the objective of showing the reader "the disastrous consequences of false interpretations of experience." The passages of "sensationalism" and those that more directly expose Richardson's subjectivity contrast with the narrator's detached perspective to reveal "distortions of fact" and "psychological violence," and in so doing these two sets create in the reader a concomitant conflict between his or her "'romantic' desire for vivid sensation and the 'realistic' desire to understand, and thus in some sense to control, experience." And in using these contrasts to point out "the potentially disastrous limitations of an interpretation of reality that sacrifices clear-headedness for sensation," Johnson concludes, Crane himself is clearly on the "realist" side of this conflict and wishes the reader to join him there (575–77).

Works Cited

Beer, Thomas. *Stephen Crane: A Study in American Letters*. New York: Knopf, 1923.

Bergon, Frank. *Stephen Crane's Artistry*. New York: Columbia University Press, 1975.

———. Introduction. *The Western Writings of Stephen Crane*. New American Library, 1979, 1–27.

Berryman, John. *Stephen Crane*. New York: Sloane, 1950.

Bowers, Fredson. Textual Introduction. *Tales of Adventure*. Vol. 5 of The University of Virginia Edition of *The Works of Stephen Crane*. Ed. Fredson Bowers. Charlottesville: University Press of Virginia, 1970, cxxxiii–cxcv.

Cady, Edwin H. *The Light of Common Day: Realism in American Fiction*. Bloomington: Indiana University Press, 1971.

Colvert, James B. "Stephen Crane." *American Realists and Naturalists*. Vol. 12 of *Dictionary of Literary Biography*. Ed. Donald Pizer and Earl N. Harbert. Detroit: Gale Research, 1982, 100–24.

———. *Stephen Crane*. New York: Harcourt Brace Jovanovich, 1984.

Crane, Stephen. "One Dash—Horses." *Tales of Adventure* 13–25.

Deamer, Robert Glen. "Stephen Crane and the Western Myth." *Western American Literature* 7 (Summer 1972):111–23.

Denny, Neville. "Imagination and Experience in Stephen Crane." *English Studies in Africa* 9 (1966):28–42.

Gibson, Donald B. *The Fiction of Stephen Crane*. Carbondale: Southern Illinois University Press, 1968.

Holton, Milne. *Cylinder of Vision: The Fiction and Journalistic Writings of Stephen Crane*. Baton Rouge: Louisiana State University Press, 1972.

Johnson, Glen M. "Stephen Crane's 'One Dash—Horses': A Model of Realistic Irony." *Modern Fiction Studies* 23 (1977):571–78.

Levenson, J. C. Introduction. *Tales of Adventure* xv–cxxxii.

Linson, Corwin K. *My Stephen Crane*. Syracuse: Syracuse University Press, 1958.

Mayer, Charles W. "Two Kids in the House of Chance: Crane's 'The Five White Mice.'" *Research Studies* 44 (1976):52–57.

Overland, Orm. "The Impressionism of Stephen Crane: A Study in Style and Technique." *America Norvegica* 61 (1966):239–85.

Paredes, Raymund A. "Stephen Crane and the Mexican." *Western American Literature* 6 (Spring 1971):31–38.

Robertson, Jamie. "Stephen Crane, Eastern Outsider in the West and Mexico." *Western American Literature* 13 (Nov. 1978):243–57.

Robinson, Cecil. *Mexico and the Hispanic Southwest in American Literature*. Tucson: University of Arizona Press, 1977.

Solomon, Eric. *Stephen Crane: From Parody to Realism*. Cambridge: Harvard University Press, 1966.

Stallman, R. W. *Stephen Crane: A Biography*. New York: George Braziller, 1968.

Vorpahl, Ben Merchant. "Murder by the Minute: Old and New in 'The Bride Comes to Yellow Sky.'" *Nineteenth-Century Fiction* 26 (1971):196–218.

Wertheim, Stanley, and Paul Sorrentino, eds. *The Correspondence of Stephen Crane*. Vol. 1. New York: Columbia University Press, 1988.

Wolford, Chester L. *Stephen Crane: A Study of the Short Fiction*. Boston: Twayne, 1989.

The Open Boat

Publication History

This story was first published in America in the June 1897 issue of *Scribner's Magazine* (21:728–40). Unlike most of Crane's fiction, it did not run in an English magazine as well; instead, it next appeared in the American volume *"The Open Boat" and Other Tales of Adventure*, published by Doubleday & McClure, and the English *"The Open Boat" and Other Stories*, published by Heinemann, both in April 1898 (Bowers clxvi). Wilson Follett collected it in volume 12, published in 1927, of *The Work of Stephen Crane* (12 vols., New York: Knopf, 1925–27), and it has appeared in numerous Crane anthologies since that time, including *Stephen Crane: An Omnibus* (New York: Knopf, 1952), edited by Robert W. Stallman, and *The Complete Short Stories and Sketches of Stephen Crane* (Garden City, N.Y.: Doubleday, 1963), edited by Thomas A. Gullason.

Circumstances of Composition

On December 31, 1896, Crane sailed out of Jacksonville, Florida, aboard the steamer *Commodore*. It was bound for Cuba, the site of a revolt against Spanish rule that Crane intended to cover as a correspondent for the Bacheller newspaper syndicate. However, the *Commodore* sank off the Florida coast in the early morning of January 2, 1897, and Crane and three members of the crew spent the next thirty hours in a dinghy before coming ashore, exhausted, near Daytona Beach. By January 6, back in Jacksonville, he had written a newspaper report of the sinking, which ran as "Stephen Crane's Own Story" in the *New York Press* for January 7, and over the next month he composed "The Open Boat," drawn from his experience in the dinghy. Another writer who was in Jacksonville at the time, Ralph D. Paine, recalled part of Crane's writing process for this story in his volume of reminiscences, *Roads of Adventure*, published in 1922. Once Crane had a draft completed, Paine says, he met at a hotel with Edward Murphy, captain of the *Commodore* and one of his mates in the dinghy, and read the story to him as a way of checking the accuracy of his account. Paine, who was having dinner at the hotel at the time, claims to have heard Crane say, "'Listen, Ed, I want to have this *right*, from your point of view. How does it sound so far?'" Murphy's response was "'You've got it, Steve. . . . That is just how it happened, and how we felt. Read me some more of it'" (qtd. in Stallman, *Biography* 257). As might be expected, there has been some question as to the truth of this suspiciously perfect recollection, but another journalist who was in Jacksonville at the time, Ernest McCready, confirmed it in 1934, identifying the locale of the meeting as the Hotel de Dreme, which was a well-known and high-class house of assignation run by Crane's then *inamorata* and later common-law wife, Cora Stewart. Paine had been unspecific about the meeting place, McCready explained, because he did not want his Jacksonville friends to know that he frequented such an establishment (qtd. in Randel, "Slate" 363).

Regardless of the doubts concerning the veracity of Paine's memoir, other evidence proves that Crane definitely did write "The Open Boat" in Jacksonville in January and February, for by February 24, shortly after he left Jacksonville for the swamps around the Indian River in a new attempt to get to Cuba (*Correspondence* I, 281), his agent in New York, Paul Revere Reynolds, had the story in hand and offered it to *Scribner's Magazine*, which accepted it on March 9 (Levenson, *Tales of Adventure* lxix).

Sources and Influences

Crane's principal source for this story was his own experience of being adrift in the *Commodore*'s dinghy with three other survivors. He remarks at the end of "Stephen Crane's Own Story," which describes the sinking of the ship, that "[t]he history of life in an open boat for thirty hours would no doubt be very instructive for the young, but none is to be told here now" (*Reports* 94); "The Open Boat" is a version of that history, with Crane himself as the prototype for the correspondent, Captain Murphy as the captain, and the two other crewmen in the dinghy, Steward Charles B. Montgomery and oiler William Higgins, as the cook and the oiler (Stallman, *Biography* 256). Many of the events of the story closely parallel the real-life castaways' situation: in both cases the four men in the dinghy were forced to abandon seven crewmen still on the wreck for fear of overloading their boat; Murphy injured his arm during the shipwreck just as the captain in the story is presented as having done; Higgins drowned in the surf just inches from safety, as Billie does in the story; and like the correspondent, Crane himself survived partly because Murphy helped direct his struggle through the surf and partly because a man on shore saw him and pulled him to safety—his name being John Kitchell (*Reports* 94).

Because of these and many other parallels, as well as Paine's report of Murphy's telling Crane that the story precisely described their shared ordeal, critics have frequently assumed that "The Open Boat" is an almost direct transcription of Crane's literal experience in the dinghy. However, others point out a considerable number of possible changes Crane made for the story, impute these changes to various motivations, and argue vociferously with one another on both these matters. John Berryman says that Crane reduced the number of men in the dinghy—that five rather than four made the actual trip through the sea and into the surf—and asserts further that Crane himself rescued this fifth man in the surf and left this event out of the story due to modesty (159–60), just as he made no mention in either "Story" or "The Open Boat" of Murphy's saying "'Crane is a man every inch of him, and he acted throughout with true grit'" (qtd. in Stallman, *Biography* 247). Berryman's sources for this view are the accounts Steward Montgomery gave in two newspaper interviews; however, two other literary detectives cast considerable doubt on Montgomery's reliability. Stallman points out that three dozen other newspaper stories gave the number of men in the dinghy as four, as did Murphy and the log of the revenue cutter *Boutwell*, which was nearby and recorded both the sinking of the *Commodore* and the rescue of her survivors (*Biography* 549–50). William Randel further questions Montgomery's claim by noting that at the legal inquiry into the sinking of the *Commodore* many of Montgomery's assertions in print were shown to be falsehoods that the steward had concocted to make his story more marketable ("Cook" 409–11).

Cyrus Day provides a more exhaustive account of Crane's alterations of the facts. He notes that the account in the story of cold weather and rough seas tallies with Montgomery's interviews but not with the records of the United States Weather Bureau, which report January 2 and 3 as having been relatively mild—between 58 and 75 degrees Fahrenheit, with the ocean running only swells or rollers—and that the claim of severe weather does not tally with the appearance of gulls at sea in the story itself, since if the weather were as bad as the story describes they would have stayed sheltered onshore (198–201). Day notes further that not only did the sea pose less of a threat to the dinghy than the story indicates but also this boat was more seaworthy than it is described as being. Ten-foot dinghies of this type were standard issue on British warships of this period and were designed for six men, a fact that leads Day to the conclusion that the *Commodore*'s boat "was probably seaworthy enough" to get four men ashore with relatively little difficulty in a calm sea (203–04). But if, in contradiction to Berryman's assessment, the castaways' physical ordeal was in reality less rigorous than the story indicates, Day continues, their psychological ordeal was likely greater, and this aspect of the experience motivated Crane's exaggeration of the physical dangers. In leaving behind seven crewmen, and doing so in an underloaded boat, Murphy might well have been accused of conduct unbecoming the captain of a ship, a failure compounded by his allowing the dinghy to sail for sixteen to eighteen hours rather than getting it ashore as quickly as possible and organizing efforts to rescue other still-surviving crew members. Thus, Day says, Crane in "The Open Boat" sidesteps the issue of the abandonment of some of the crew by referring only obliquely to "a scene in the grays of dawn of seven turned faces" (*Tales of Adventure* 69), and he dirties up the weather to make the process of getting ashore difficult enough to absolve Murphy of undue delay (204–205). In a line of thought more recently picked up by Christopher Benfey (190–93), Day notes that Crane may have been further impelled to these subterfuges by a sense that he shared Murphy's guilt, since in "Story" he depicts himself as having to cut loose from the dinghy the raft of an African-American stoker who, in a panic, endangered the dinghy by scrambling across the towline from his raft and attempting to board the boat. Day suggests that this incident may even have been an invention of Crane's to mask more calmly calculated decisions to abandon the men still on the sinking *Commodore* and not to risk taking the dinghy immediately to shore. Faced with these decisions, Day says, "Crane was *morally* tested at 4:00 on the afternoon of January 2, and in so far as he was a party to the decision not to land at once he was found wanting" (209) and was therefore eager to obscure the realities of his situation as he worked his way through "The Open Boat."

Such psycho-biographical speculations are reasonably well grounded and thought-provoking, but even before they were advanced Berryman provided a counter to the impulse to allow such ideas to condition completely one's reading of the story. At the end of his own discussion of Crane's biographical connections to it, he reminds the reader that to regard the story "as a *report* is to misunderstand the nature of [Crane's] work: it is an action of his art upon the remembered possibility of death" (291). Marston LaFrance makes this point still more emphatically, saying that "nothing more clearly illustrates the essential insignificance of external fact in a Crane story than a comparison of 'The Open Boat' with his own news report of the disaster," for in the report the reader gets only "the literal truth of the fact," whereas "Crane's structure imposed upon the fact in the work of art conveys the moral truth of the human experience" (195–96). This assertion leads to sources beyond the *Commodore* incident, for in making the sea the crucible in which this moral truth is rendered, Crane drew on much more of his own experience than just that of the most recent past. As Edwin Cady points out, Crane had spent enough of his boyhood and youth at Asbury Park on the New Jersey shore to be familiar with the threats the seacoast posed to human beings just beyond the elements of sun, sand, and surf that evoked a carefree, holiday mood in the throngs of summer visitors to that locale (*Tales, Sketches* xxxiii). As a young reporter for his brother Townley's Asbury Park branch of the *New York Tribune*'s news-gathering service he had written not only about the manners and mores of resort life but also about the terrors of shipwrecks. He had turned out articles such as "Ghosts on the Jersey Coast" and "The Ghostly Sphinx of Metedeconk," the imagery of which, in Eric Solomon's view, clearly prefigures that of "The Open Boat" (150–51), as well as "Six Years Afloat" and "The Wreck of the *New Era*" (*Tales, Sketches* 638–42, 645–48, 648–52, 580–84)—the last of which describes castaways drowning in sight of a crowd watching helplessly on shore, as James B. Colvert notes (*Stephen Crane* 27)—in doing so perhaps dipping into such popular works as R. Thomas's 1835 *Narratives of Remarkable Shipwrecks* to help him flesh out what he had observed firsthand (Benfey 193); he had also produced several more light-hearted but still threat-conscious pieces with a sea setting, such as "The Reluctant Voyagers" (*Tales, Sketches* 14–33). The consequence of such a background and such apprentice work, Cady points out, was that, though "obviously no blue-water sailor, Crane knew the coasts, . . . the shores and their often terrible surf," and he had acquired a fair degree of mastery at conveying these elements in his writing, with highly salubrious results for "The Open Boat" (*Tales, Sketches* xxxiii).

Earlier narratives of shipwrecks aside, the most obvious reference to a literary source in this story is the correspondent's recollection of Lady Caroline Norton's 1883 poem "Bingen on the Rhine." This work, with its focus on a French Foreign Legionnaire dying far from home, beneath an indifferent sun but with his hand grasping that of a comrade, seems to the correspondent to parallel his own perilous situation in the boat under a "high cold star on a winter's night" (*Tales of Adventure* 85) and thus leads him to feel "sorry for the soldier of the Legion who lay dying in Algiers" (86)—leads him, in essence, to a new understanding of the necessity for human sympathy in an uncaring universe. The fact that Crane misquotes this poem, dropping about twenty words from the passage he has the correspondent recall (Monteiro, "Text" 307), raises the question of whether Crane himself misremembered Norton's original or deliberately has the correspondent forget it in order to emphasize the point that he had never before regarded as important this piece he had had drummed into him as a grammar-school recitation (see also Jackson 77–81); however, this issue is ultimately less important than the question of the level of seriousness that Crane intends by this reference—whether he aims at straightforward pathos or irony in the correspondent's recollection of this rather mawkish verse.

Edward Stone argues for pathos. He notes that "Bingen" may in fact have served Crane earlier as a source for *The Red Badge of Courage*, since in both these works a poor youth joins the army in defiance of his mother, one soldier asks another to take his effects back to his family if he should not survive, and a soldier watches a valued friend die. If these parallels do indicate influence, Stone continues, then Crane obviously knew the poem well—probably, like the correspondent, from having had it dinned into him at school—and his point in using it again in "The Open Boat" is that it does not in truth enter the correspondent's head "mysteriously," as the correspondent himself believes, but rather quite logically because it is a moving expression of the correspondent's own new realization of "the overwhelming, abiding impersonality and inexorability of the transactions of the universe, and of the infinitely small importance of the individual in these transactions" (243).

Numerous other critics follow Stone's lead, likewise discerning no irony in this recollection. Max Westbrook sees the poem as crucial in conveying the central theme of the story, which he terms "the personal universal" (351)— the idea that abstract and thus universal concepts such as "courage, compassion, humility, pride, integrity" can only become meaningful to an individual through his or her personal experience. The abstract concept that Crane focuses on is compassion, to which the correspondent was introduced in childhood through the poem but which remained meaningless to him until now, when he links the poem's "cry for compassion" to his own condition in the boat. At this point, "after experience has provided personal terms for a universal value, he discovers that the poem is an objective reality" (355).

Herb Stappenbeck takes his cue from LaFrance's passing observation that the correspondent identifies with the dying Legionnaire; he details the precise terms of this identification and their effect on the story's meaning. Crane's description of the correspondent's recollection of the setting in which the Legionnaire dies, sand dunes in the foreground with distant buildings in the background, is very similar to what the correspondent himself is able to see of the shore, a connection that, in Stappenbeck's view, indicates that the correspondent "has projected himself into the soldier's situation in order to comprehend both himself and the soldier." What he comprehends is that as a child indifferent to the fate of the Legionnaire he took the same attitude that nature now takes toward him, a realization that leads him now to sympathy with the Legionnaire, and through this sympathy he moves beyond the personal. Heretofore, in his self-pity and his feelings of brotherhood for the other three castaways, he has been concerned only with the narrow scope of his own situation; in his compassion for someone outside that immediate situation he attains a higher level of feeling, "'a profound and perfectly impersonal comprehension' of his obligation to suffer with his fellow men" (41).

Edward Piacentino extends Stappenbeck's analysis, noting a number of further significant parallels between the correspondent and the Legionnaire. Both men are engrossed in meditations upon imminent death, both face that death with companions in attendance, both recall childhood as "a time of secure innocence when thoughts of death were presumably not of much immediate concern" (65). Through these resemblances, coupled with his courage and desire to be remembered after death, the Legionnaire becomes for the correspondent "a wished-for mirror image of himself, not just dying, but dying heroically, reconciled to his fate" (66). However, Piacentino continues, the most meaningful parallel of all, the one most indicative of Crane's artistic power, is the presence of moonlight in both cases, under which the Legionnaire dies and the correspondent survives. In Norton's hands, the moon is used merely as "a pathetic fallacy, a cheap strategy to cushion the pathos with which the poem concludes"; Crane, on the other hand, renders it, along with the "high cold star" that the correspondent feels is the answer to his prayer, a compelling "emblem of nature's indifference" (66).

If Westbrook, Stappenbeck, and Piacentino regard the correspondent's experience in the boat as deepening his understanding of the poem, Leedice Kissane and David Halliburton work from the opposite direction, arguing that the poem deepens his understanding of this experience. Kissane contends that Crane's depiction of the correspondent recalling this poem at a moment of extreme stress is one indication among many that Crane's true interest is not experience *per se* but rather consciousness, for, "[l]ike other figures of speech, literary allusion jets from deep in the subconscious. . . . [I]t is born not of an actual experience but of an intellectual impression" (413). Moreover, the poem helps produce a change in the correspondent's consciousness that, in Kissane's view, is a perhaps unconscious revelation of a change in Crane's own understanding of the "womanly" nature of solace. Up to this point in the story, Kissane notes, women have been denigrated in the castaways' personifications of Fate as "an old ninny-woman" and "an old hen," but in the poem a lack of women's comforting ministrations is one of the things that makes the Legionnaire's situation so pitiable, one of the things that evokes the correspondent's sympathy. In line with this change of attitude, at the end of the story the women who nurse the castaways are described as performing "sacred" relief activities. In the correspondent's new understanding of his experience in the light of the poem, then, Crane's "implication is clear: If man must venture into far lands and uncharted seas in his physical and psychic quests, he has need *in extremis* of the comfort of woman and the solace of her tears" (415).

Halliburton also sees Crane's use of the poem as charting a change in his attitude, but in his view the subject in question is not womanly solace but art. In *The Red Badge* Crane manifests a deep suspicion of art, Halliburton says, in that the books Henry Fleming read prior to his enlistment falsified the nature of war; only through his own experience does Henry come to a true understanding of combat. In "The Open Boat," in contrast, it is the poem, the work of art, that delivers to the correspondent the full meaning of his own ordeal, a shift that reveals Crane's revised understanding of art as "a mediating agency drawing its audience"—in this case, the correspondent—"to a higher order of experience" (248).

George Monteiro and J. C. Levenson, on the other hand, argue for irony. Monteiro points out that when the correspondent visualizes the scene of the Legionnaire's death after recollecting Norton's lines, he imagines a number of details that do not appear in the poem: blood from his wound flowing between the dying man's fingers, the skyline of a city in the distance, and a sunset as the overall setting. These details, Monteiro notes, are all to be found in the illustrations by William T. Smedley that accompanied the poem in a popular American edition, published in 1883 by Porter and Coates of

Philadelphia—the edition that Crane himself might well have been made to study in school and which he would thus logically have placed in the back of the correspondent's mind as well. This fact by itself would be of only minor interest, Monteiro says, but it gains ironic significance from a further connection between the story and vaguely recalled grammar-school lessons. In the running argument over the presence of life-saving stations nearby, when the narrator says that in fact there are none "within twenty miles in either direction" (*Tales of Adventure* 76), Monteiro theorizes that Crane is depicting the castaways as drawing on their memories of illustrated allegories in grammar-school readers, such as McGuffey's, in which life is symbolized as a sea voyage made safer by the lighthouses and life-saving stations of scripture and churches. That these "babes of the sea" (*Tales of Adventure* 83) cling in their current situation to childhood memories of such pictures, Monteiro concludes, is Crane's ironic comment on the power of infantile human wishfulness in the face of the brutal facts of the universe ("Text" 309–11).

Levenson sees Crane as less critical of human wishfulness *per se* than of the poem itself and the culture that produced it. Although he does regard the "longing for woman's nursing and woman's tears" as "childish," what Crane really seeks to reveal by the correspondent's recollection of this mawkish verse at this desperate moment, Levenson asserts, is "the near worthlessness of the prevailing culture as an instrument for finding the actual and reacting to it with the right emotions." Like Mark Twain before him and Ernest Hemingway after, Crane through this allusion "scorns the poetic throes of the safe, the comfortable, and the sentimentally bemused," who have so weakened their readers' emotional lives through the excesses, the sentimentality, and the generality of their outpourings that "it took a specific event, intensely and precisely felt, to provide meaning where the language by itself might not" (*Tales of Adventure* lxiii–lxiv).

Jules Chametzky and Halliburton provide useful examinations of less readily apparent literary influences. Chametzky links "The Open Boat" to Mark Twain's "Old Times on the Mississippi" due to the emphasis in both on the protagonists' lack of time for contemplation of the beauties of nature that Romantic reading may have conditioned them to see. Instead, both protagonists learn that "surviving shifting, changing, potentially destructive conditions require[s] a view that is clear-eyed, unsentimental, rooted in the situation you are *in*, not some other imagined or conventionally sanctioned perspective." Chametzky sees Crane as farther along than Mark Twain in an acceptance of this stance, given that Twain's narrator cogitates at length about the pilot's loss of the Romantic view of the river's beauty, whereas in saying only that the sea "was probably splendid, . . . probably glorious" Crane's narrator simply dismisses such a view (192). Chametzky also notes that given developments in science and philosophy as well as in literature during this period this attitude was becoming part of the *zeitgeist* (192), an idea Halliburton takes further by suggesting that "The Open Boat," along with other stories such as "The Veteran," "The Blue Hotel," and "The Monster," is Crane's meditation on the growing concern with the idea of aleatoriness in his era, expressed in the work of philosophers such as Heinrich von Kleist and Charles Sanders Peirce and in fictions by writers as different in other respects as Charles Dickens and Joseph Conrad (80–81).

Relationship to Other Crane Works

"The Open Boat" is most clearly connected to "Stephen Crane's Own Story," Crane's newspaper account of the sinking of the *Commodore*, and "Flanagan and His Short Filibustering Adventure," a short story based on this same ship-wreck but told from the point of view of its captain rather than that of a news-paper correspondent. As many critics note, since "Story" focuses almost entirely on the foundering of the ship and "The Open Boat" begins with the ship already sunk and limits itself to the ordeal of the survivors, Crane seems to have intended a complementary rather than redundant relationship between these two pieces. William Going argues this view on the basis of the fact that certain allusions in "The Open Boat," such as those to the captain's memories of "seven turned faces" and "a stump of a top-mast," cannot be understood unless the reader is familiar with "Story" (79). Richard Adams points out that at the end of "Story" Crane in fact provides a kind of "teaser" for "The Open Boat" in his remark that the "history of life in an open boat for thirty hours would no doubt be very instructive for the young, but none is to be told here now." Here, says Adams, Crane obviously recognizes perfect material for a popular short story and is cannily sharpening the reading pub-lic's appetite for it (138). Joseph Skerrett discerns a complementary differ-ence in character focus accompanying this difference in events. In "Story," he notes, Crane devotes most of his attention to the heroism of Edward Murphy and Billie Higgins, whereas in "The Open Boat" he concentrates on the char-acters based on himself and Higgins, relegating his Murphy character to third place in importance. Crane's purpose in this shift, Skerrett says, is to bring to the foreground the change in the correspondent's attitude from cynicism to an appreciation of "the human community of trust and goodwill"—his devel-opment, largely through his relationship with the Higgins character, of a vision of "other men as capable of nobility, even a kind of holiness" (23).

Halliburton argues that such divergences in these two works lead to a dif-ference in their epistemological stances as well. The focus in "Story," he says, is almost entirely on action, on doing, while in "The Open Boat" doing is pre-sented as "inseparable from the question of knowing and the question of being" (237). Working likewise along the line of the stories' communication of significance, Andrew Lytle notes a difference in their level of insight that favors "The Open Boat." This disparity, he says, can be inferred from this work's subtitle, "A Tale Intended To Be After the Fact." After the fact, Lytle explains,

> there is time for reflection, distance, and out of the act itself the growth of meaning. The immediate report of disaster is always too sensational and, as journalism, of necessity too hurried, too involved in the moment, too dependent upon clichés in the choice of the obvious in violence and sentiment. (60)

This difference between these two pieces is, in Lytle's view, paradigmatic of the general difference between journalism and fiction. A generalized journalistic report, he asserts, invariably fails to provide the reader with "the sense of having observed" the events in question; instead, it creates the impression "of receiving a rumor, the details of which are not quite to be believed." In such a case, "[t]he reader's position is always that of the stranger, the uninvolved." With fiction, by contrast,

> there is always a chorus, or what stands for a chorus, the enveloping action. This holds some essential archetypal explanation of experience, of which the action [focused on in the story] is one example. The sympathy between the reader, then, and the protagonist involves the reader, and lifts him from the accidents of life into some phase and understanding of the essence of things. (91)

James Nagel takes a similar view, asserting that "Story" is "a literal account of a thrilling physical adventure," whereas "The Open Boat" transmutes this adventure into "a unified drama of irony and poignancy with a psychological dimension which [gives] the story depth and thematic movement" ("Narrative Method" 409).

While not explicitly attacking Lytle or Nagel, two critics, Benfey and Phyllis Frus, take issue with this hierarchical treatment of fiction and journalism in the case of "Story" and "The Open Boat." Benfey questions the literal veracity of "Story," saying that in terms of invention and interpretation of events it "is no less 'literary' than the later story; in some ways it is more openly mythical and allusive," a result of what Benfey sees as Crane's use of it to confront his own culpability in "an episode more harrowing and morally ambiguous than any recorded in 'The Open Boat'"—his and his three companions' abandonment of the seven men for whom there was no room in the dinghy (189).

Frus like Lytle sees these two pieces as exemplifying a paradigm, but one that is essentially the opposite of his—that of "reified conventions" regarding the literary superiority of fiction to journalism. The conventional critical view, she says, is that journalism is simply composed "of events themselves" whereas fiction transforms those events into meaningful patterns, and this view affects "not only our categories of literature and nonliterary genres but our interpretations" (127). Both these pieces are in fact narratives, Frus asserts, and when they are tested "against the usual criteria for defining literature— fictional invention and aesthetic language—they do not fall into the literary and 'other' categories so easily" (128). In the area of invention, she argues, "The Open Boat" is not demonstrably different from "Story," in that both hew closely to the factual events and chronology of the *Commodore* disaster and that "Story" contains little more in the way of "journalistic particulars" than does "The Open Boat." Regarding aesthetic language, Frus notes that both pieces rely about equally on figures of speech and irony, although in "Story" the irony stems principally from the narrator's voice whereas in "The Open Boat" it is "distributed among several discourses, situations, and events" (131). Despite these "literary" similarities, she continues, expectations about the nature of journalism as opposed to that of fiction lead critics to see "Story" as objective and reportorial, and "The Open Boat" as subjective and impressionistic, when in fact the aforementioned similarities and Crane's use of first person in "Story" emphasize that this account is likewise subjective, is likewise an interpretation. Thus, she argues, critics err in regarding interpretation as solely the province of "fiction" (135).

However, Frus does not see the case as a simple matter of arguing that "journalism" ought to be reclassified as "fiction" or "literature." Rather, in her view a comparison of "Story" and "Boat" suggests that this whole system of classification is in fact meaningless. The "interpretation" of "Story," she says, is that life is characterized by "the absence of meaning, of a determinate commonsense explanation of experience," and this interpretation develops out of Crane's "conscious stylistic choice" to present the events of the sinking in a fragmented fashion, lacking explanations and transitions (136–37). This approach, Frus points out, is decidedly unconventional for what critics narrowly define as journalism, but it does not place "Story" within their equally narrow criteria for fiction, since this form of narration obviates fiction's usual structure of tension between what the reader senses will happen to the characters and what he or she wishes will happen to them (139). With this customary structure in view, as opposed to the fragmentation of "Story," Frus draws on Roland Barthes's and Emile Benveniste's theories to maintain that what cues the reader to regard "The Open Boat" as fiction is its expected use of "historical narration," a form that gives its events "the appearance of being related causally and of being ordered." Crane's use of third person in this piece—as opposed to first in "Story"—facilitates this appearance by creating "a source which becomes authoritative by hiding itself as discourse," and this authority backing the story's coherence implies that "all accidents of chance or fate have meaning simply because they are told, explained in a story" (143). Therefore, Frus argues, this form, coupled with realistic details and a sense of closure, impels critics to *find* the interpretations they expect within what already fits their definition of literature, something they do not expect of journalism. In fact, then, these interpretations "may simply be a function of the reader's desire for coherence and satisfaction rather than being provided by the text, and this desire may be fulfilled by the very expectations of unity that we bring to texts designated as fiction or literature" (144). And to further complicate the matter, Frus says, many texts designated as history or journalism utilize the same strategies as literary texts, so that once again clear distinctions between journalism and literature collapse.

The final significance of this lengthy and subtle comparison is Frus's proposal that in coming to "The Open Boat" the reader remain aware of the expectations its form creates and stay concomitantly "alert to the multiplicity of discourses and the possibility of reading them as contributing to the diversity and self-contradiction of the text." This approach "will make the short story more like the newspaper version (in its avoidance of disclosure and certainty)—not less fictional, but less a text of high realism and with all the difference in ideology that an open, skeptical reading implies" (145). And this approach will also impel the reader to give "Story," no longer devalued as mere journalism, more careful consideration, in so doing noting the "appeal to permanence and originality" it makes by "the way it questions the reality of its own illusion and by the way it subverts the reader's expectations [of journalism]" (149).

Like "Story," "Flanagan" is often regarded as a companion piece to "The Open Boat," most explicitly by Stallman (*Biography* 598). But in this case there is more general critical agreement that these two are comparable only in subject matter, not in level of achievement: Stallman's view is that "Flanagan" is an inferior companion piece to "The Open Boat," and no one has offered reasons to dispute this judgment. Levenson is persuasively specific about the causes of this disparity; sounding a note similar to Lytle's regarding "Story," he points out that whereas Crane allowed himself a good deal of time to work through "The Open Boat," "Flanagan" demonstrates "what could happen when he worked hurriedly under pressure" (*Tales of Adventure* lxxi). The result of these conditions is that "Flanagan" is simply a tale of adventure, not the fusion of adventure with interpretation by a thoughtful consciousness that Crane accomplishes in "The Open Boat." "Flanagan," Levenson concludes, effectively presents "acid ironies" in the fate of the sailors juxtaposed to the attitude of the hotel guests, who in their safe position refuse to consider that men may drown, and it is marked by "the colorful Crane style," but it ultimately lacks the symbolic resonance that produces the depth and universality of "The Open Boat"; instead, its events "define a world no bigger than the scene in which they take place" (*Tales of Adventure* lxxi–lxxii).

As noted above in "Sources and Influences," Crane's writing about shipwrecks and castaways was not limited to his experience with the *Commodore*, and a number of critics have traced links between "The Open Boat" and his earlier work on this subject. Many point to the early comical sketch "The Reluctant Voyagers," in which two young men bathing at the New Jersey seashore inattentively allow the raft on which they are floating to drift out to sea and then spend the night bickering over which of them is at fault, until a New York-bound ship rescues them. Chester L. Wolford notes that, despite the much lighter tone of this sketch, it is a precursor of "The Open Boat" in that both are about the interconnectedness in the human consciousness of "ego, pride, and survival" (17). Halliburton concurs, calling the sketch "apprentice work" for "The Open Boat" (71). In a more detailed examination, Frank Bergon says that "Voyagers," written before Crane had himself experienced ocean navigation in a tiny craft, is in fact much more closely related to "The Open Boat" than "Flanagan" is, despite the genesis of the latter two stories in the same experience. He points out that in both "Voyagers" and "The Open Boat" cigars are used as instruments of brotherhood, the castaways' crafts are described in terms of animal imagery, and the rescuers are regarded as miraculous, saintlike figures. These links lead Bergon to wonder whether Crane, "the great destroyer of preconceived notions," simply foresaw the truth of the experience of being adrift when he wrote "Voyagers," or if in fact he allowed what he imagined in this sketch to color his actual experience in the *Commodore*'s dinghy when he transmuted it into "The Open Boat" (38).

This line of speculation is the fundamental inquiry in Benfey's biography of Crane, and the relationship of "The Open Boat" to Crane's earlier seacoast writings is one of the linchpins of his argument that the overall pattern of Crane's life was first to write about a situation and then find a way to experience that situation—in the terms in which he had imagined it—for himself. Benfey notes that in his early journalism regarding shipwrecks Crane appears to draw as much on his father's frequent use of such disasters as metaphors in his sermons as he does on other sources, and that in this blending of influences he developed "techniques of style and emphasis that he would use to advantage" in framing his later experience in the dinghy (180). Colvert takes a broader view of the influence of Crane's prior thematic concerns in shaping his experience, pointing out that his ordeal in the boat and the story that came out of it in fact enact a theme that runs through a great deal of his earlier writing, including his sketches of Asbury Park and Sullivan County and his first volume of poetry, *The Black Riders*, "the plight of man in an alien and indifferent universe" (*Stephen Crane* 105). In a separate study, Colvert expands on this idea, arguing that Crane worked out not only his themes but also his "images, . . . motifs, and descriptive patterns" early in his career and that these dictated the nature of the rest of his work, and indeed the experience upon which that work was based. In essence, Crane "observed the world from a pre-established literary point of view, a view which largely determined what was seen and what the observed event signified" ("Invention" 130–31).

"The Open Boat" bears out this notion, Colvert says, in that the correspondent's astonishment at finding "the meaning of the problematical seascape so elusive" is very like the attitude of the protagonist of the Sullivan County sketches, known only as "the little man," in his encounters with nature ("Invention" 145).

William Spofford agrees with Colvert's assessment; he too sees this story as an illustration of Crane's habit of refracting his experience through "themes, motifs, and images" (321) developed at the outset of his writing life, and he offers a number of particulars to support this view. He points out that Crane was already preoccupied with the indifference of nature in "Coney Island's Failing Days," an article that ran in the *New York Press* for October 10, 1894, in which he contrasts the empty amusement park with "the unchangeable, ever imperturbable sea . . . with no thought for man or maid" (qtd. in Spofford 317), and in the early poems "To the Maiden," in which the sea appears as "dead grey walls" to a shipwrecked sailor (qtd. in Spofford 317), and "A Man Said to the Universe," in which the universe flatly states that the speaker's existence "'has not created in me / A sense of obligation'" (qtd. in Spofford 316). The futile anger that the correspondent displays in response to this indifference is already present in the Sullivan County sketch "The Black Dog," in which the little man curses fate and her offspring, and in *The Red Badge*, in which Henry begins to curse nature at the death of his friend Jim Conklin (318). The "high cold star on a winter's night" that the correspondent imagines as Nature's response to such imprecations first appears in this role in "In the Depths of a Coal Mine," a sketch Crane wrote for the August 1894 issue of *McClure's Magazine* (318). The sense of human brotherhood that the castaways in "Open Boat" discover among themselves is preceded by the realization of two men adrift on a raft in "The Reluctant Voyagers," an early, comic sketch, that "fear came to bind their souls together" (qtd. in Spofford 319). Even the broad vista of the sea and sky in the last section of "Open Boat," which Crane uses in contrast to the castaways' restricted vision of the sea alone in the first section to indicate their increased understanding of their position in the universe, serves a similar function in earlier works, the 1893–94 story "The Pace of Youth" and the 1895 poem "Small Glowing Pebbles" (320).

Wolford notes another, related, theme that links "The Open Boat" to Crane's early pieces, especially the Sullivan County sketches: the tendency of the protagonists to make the error of "attributing intelligence and purpose to nature" (5). Cady focuses more on technical than thematic connections between Crane's earlier seacoast work and "The Open Boat"; he argues that in newspaper pieces such as "The Wreck of the *New Era*" and "Ghosts on the Jersey Coast" Crane developed the stylistic aptitude that enabled him to provide in "The Open Boat" the "realizing sense of the real presence . . . of the comber and . . . the murderous surf" that gives the story much of its power—

an aptitude noticeably lacking, by comparison, in his depiction of war in *Red Badge*, which suffers due to "the absence from its combat scenes of any sense of the real presence of the bullet" (*Tales, Sketches* xxxiii).

Cady's opinion of the relationship between *Red Badge* and "The Open Boat" notwithstanding, at least three critics see these works as closely connected. Stallman calls them "identical" with regard to "theme, . . . patterns of imagery and leitmotif, and . . . form" (*Houses* 104), and in the matter of theme, LaFrance concurs. Both Henry Fleming and the correspondent, he says,

> learn of their own human weakness and fallibility, both learn that nature is amoral and apart from man's life of aspiration and suffering, both learn the value of brotherhood, and both end their dark journey with a quiet commitment to the group, mankind in general who, aware or unaware, are caught in the same human predicament. (159)

Colvert tacitly disagrees with this view. He argues that Fleming and the correspondent do indeed begin with the same assumptions but do not draw the same lessons from the ordeal that tests those assumptions. These two protagonists—and, for that matter, the protagonists of Crane's *Black Riders* poems about God—believe that "nature somehow holds the key to the mystery of existence," but the correspondent differs from these others in being "fully conscious and introspective, aware of his egotistical presumptions and of the multifarious ironies in his shifting perceptions of his plight." As a result, he takes a less certain view of the meaning of what he has endured than Henry does, for "[h]e knows, as Henry does not, that uncertainty of perception is central to the whole issue"—that the ambiguity of the seascape he confronts, which Colvert regards as an extension of the "metaphysical" landscape of *Red Badge*, is not fully resolvable ("Stephen Crane" 120).

Milne Holton is also of the opinion that "The Open Boat" and *Red Badge* are linked, but like Cady he sees the novel as suffering by this correspondence. "The Open Boat," Holton says, is a prime example of a pattern of storytelling that Crane developed in *Red Badge* and used in most of his works thereafter: a "movement from initiation to isolation, from isolation to confrontation with reality, and from confrontation to a return to community" (118). But in *Red Badge*, he continues, Crane fails to make the meaning of this movement—the need for human community in the face of nature's indifference—fully clear; he does so for the first time only in "The Open Boat" (159), a condition that might lead the puckishly inclined to term the story an artistic advance of the first water.

Numerous other critics link "The Open Boat" with another of Crane's major works, "The Blue Hotel." Donald Pizer notes that these two may readily be regarded as the complementary poles of Crane's career-long meditation on the idea of human community, since in both cases men threatened by the forces of indifferent nature can survive only by working together, which they do in "The Open Boat" and fail to do in "The Blue Hotel" (27). LaFrance makes a similar point, noting that despite their physical differences, both the hotel and the dinghy are simply pieces of "the world's external furniture, . . . and whatever each becomes depends upon human actions." Thus, through the actions of the characters the dinghy becomes a symbol of the accomplishment of human community, while the hotel becomes a concomitant symbol of the failure of community (224), a point Halliburton also makes in describing the stories' relationship as "dialogic" (71). Robert Gleckner takes a slightly different tack, focusing on the "conceit" of the Swede as he walks through the snowstorm, convinced that he can live without the community of the hotel, with which he has just engaged in acts of mutual rejection. Gleckner sees this passage as Crane's clearest statement of one of his most frequent themes, which is also apparent in "The Open Boat"—the human being's powerful if sometimes misguided will to continue to exist despite his or her utter insignificance in the realm of an indifferent and deadly universe (271).

Pizer links "The Open Boat" and "The Blue Hotel" to a third story, "The Bride Comes to Yellow Sky," asserting that Billie's death at the end of "The Open Boat" is closely related to the cash-register legend that appears over the dead Swede at the end of "The Blue Hotel" and to the deflation of Scratchy Wilson at the end of "Bride." In his view, all three of these moments epitomize Crane's reduction of "the violent and extraordinary to the commonplace, a reduction which indicates both his ironic vision of man's romantic pretensions and his belief in the reality of the fusion of the violent and the commonplace in experience" (25).

Two critics see "The Open Boat" as manifesting equally strong connections to another of Crane's Westerns, "A Man and Some Others," which Crane wrote shortly before his experience with the *Commodore*. Robert Glen Deamer notes that Joseph Conrad early on saw a connection between these two; he believes that Conrad was implicitly aware that they are thematically convergent, their point being that only experience yields true understanding, that "reality, [which encompasses] both nature's indifference and the brotherhood of the men, is felt rather than intellectualized or romanticized." Deamer considers these two stories Crane's most successful depictions—"The Five White Mice" and "One Dash—Horses" being lesser ones—of this necessity of experience to the attainment of felt and therefore genuine comprehension, and of the fact that only such comprehension truly affords "the possibility of human dignity, courage, heroism" ("Stance" 135–37). In a later study, Deamer expands on these points, explaining Crane's development of this stance as a function of his 1895 trip to the American West and Mexico as a correspondent for the Bacheller newspaper syndicate. Prior to this sojourn, Deamer says, Crane conceived of human life in deterministic terms, as evidenced by his depictions of his characters as essentially powerless to affect their fates in early works such as *Maggie: A Girl of the Streets* and *George's Mother*. What he saw of brave, tenacious human conduct in the West persuaded him that individuals could shape their own lives, at least to some extent, through the exercise of the "heroic"—and for Crane "Western"—virtues of "discipline, of responsibility, and of courage" ("'Code'" 143), and much of his later work is informed by this new code, both Westerns, such as "Man," and non-Westerns, such as "The Open Boat," in which the castaways, like the protagonist of "Man," display the "unselfishness, the discipline, and the courage which alone make dignity and meaning in man's life" ("'Code'" 145).

Nagel sees "Man" as anticipating "The Open Boat" not just thematically but in many technical respects as well: an opening paragraph that emphasizes the limitations of the individual's vision; the use of more than one protagonist and thus the employment of shifting narrative perspectives; a double plot of "physical adventure and psychological growth" that leads to the "related themes of nature's indifference to man and . . . the development of compassion in a moment of stress"; and the employment of a repeated refrain to chart the protagonists' growing awareness of nature's indifference ("Impressionism" 30). With these connections in view, Nagel regards "The Open Boat" as "essentially a sophistication of the devices and themes" Crane tried out in "Man," with the advance in sophistication residing partly in the fact that in "Man" only the narrator is fully aware of the indifference of nature at the story's end, whereas in "The Open Boat" the protagonist grasps it as well ("Impressionism" 33).

Robert Shulman likewise reads this story as "a deepening of the insights" of Crane's earlier work, but he compares it with two Bowery tales, "An Experiment in Misery" and "The Men in the Storm," rather than Westerns. All three of these pieces, he says, posit human community as the only viable response to adversity; where they differ is that in "The Open Boat" the adversity stems from "the impersonal violence of nature" rather than from "the human mortality and misery" operative in the Bowery pieces, and that in the Bowery stories the protagonists seem never to reach any conscious awareness of the power of community in the face of hardship, while the correspondent clearly does achieve such an understanding. It is this latter difference that prompts Shulman to praise "The Open Boat" as more deeply insightful than the other two (447).

Critics have not limited themselves to linking "The Open Boat" to other pieces of Crane's prose; as is clear from several passing references above, several have connected it to various of his poems. Alfred Kazin offers a general comparison in which he rates the story as superior because the poems "seem too easily satisfied with their contemptuous brevity" regarding the cosmos, whereas in the story "the universe is not that easily dismissed" (272). The poem most frequently mentioned in more specific comparisons is "A Man Adrift on a Slim Spar," which presents a situation markedly similar to that of the story: a castaway clings to a piece of driftwood in the sea and is depicted as being at the mercy of a deity utterly indifferent to his plight and to his death at the poem's end; its refrain, repeated four times, is "God is cold" (*Poems* 83). Stallman makes note of this correspondence (*Biography* 159), as does LaFrance, who draws a specific parallel between the poem's cold God and the "high cold star" that the story's narrator says is the answer to a man's prayers for rescue. The most detailed and illuminating comparison of these two pieces, however, is to be found in Daniel Hoffman's book on Crane's poetry. Hoffman notes that story and poem utilize many of the same devices—a "reiterated refrain, . . . parallel development of linked metaphors, and the tensions produced by a dialectic of opposite possibilities" (277), but he also asserts that they differ in several important respects. "The Open Boat," he says, focuses on the possibility of survival and of the formation of a community as ameliorations of the individual's aloneness in an indifferent universe, whereas "Slim Spar" concentrates on a man who is unquestionably doomed (271).

Hoffman also links "The Open Boat" to two other poems, "To the Maiden" and "When a People Reach the Top of a Hill." The first of these, he points out, uses multiple perspectives in much the same manner and to much the same purpose as the story: to dramatize the idea that what one makes of nature— whether one regards it as beautiful or hostile or indifferent—depends to a large degree on one's angle of vision (90–91). Just as the men in the dinghy regard the sea as "snarling" and "wrongfully and barbarously abrupt" while someone viewing the same sea from a balcony would find it "weirdly picturesque" (*Tales* 68–69), the maiden in the poem, safely on shore, pictures the sea as a "blue meadow / Alive with little froth people" while a shipwrecked sailor sees it as "dead grey walls" that, as they drown him, express "[t]he grim hatred of nature" (*Poems* 47). Once again, however, Hoffman also finds a point of divergence in the story's proffering of the potential for survival and community as opposed to the poem's straightforward denial of these possibilities (96). Regarding "Top of a Hill," Hoffman sees "the blue battalions" of this poem, led as they are by God, as possessed of "superhuman, unselfish, sacrificial" courage that connects them to Billie the oiler of "The Open Boat," who in Hoffman's view sacrifices himself so that his companions may survive. In both cases, Hoffman says, Crane's point is "that suffering is tolerable . . . when [and only when] it is sacrificial" (172).

LaFrance as well sees the story as closely related to Crane's poetry, although for reasons different from Hoffman's. Crane's usual story pattern, according to LaFrance, is to present a protagonist whose fear of the unknown causes his anticipation of an experience to grow wildly out of proportion to reality; when he *does* confront this new experience at the story's climax and discovers its true, lesser, proportions, he suffers abrupt deflation. "The Open Boat" is, in LaFrance's view, the one Crane story that violates this pattern, for in this case the protagonist—the correspondent—comes to an awareness of reality gradually rather than abruptly and receives the fruit of his confrontation—an understanding of nature's indifference—before the climax of the story in the castaways' run through the surf. The effect of this variation, LaFrance concludes, is that rather than winding neatly up, the story "open[s] outwards, as it were, to set forth the moral norm [of stoic humanism] implied by the poems" (198–99).

Working from a stylistic rather than formal perspective, Colvert links "The Open Boat" to "The Veteran," Crane's story of the aged Henry Fleming's courageous death. "The Veteran," he says, is Crane's first successful effort in moving away from the rhetorically showy style of *Maggie, Red Badge*, and his other early works and advancing toward the "spare, open, declarative" style that reaches its full development in "The Open Boat" (*Tales of War* xxx–xxxii). Levenson also points out a stylistic connection to *The Third Violet*, Crane's generally undistinguished novel of the lives and loves of a coterie of impoverished New York artists. He notes that in the name of the novel's protagonist, Billie, and in

> the curious fillips of thrice-repeated phrases [and] an occasional archness like swearing by "the nine mad blacksmiths of Donawhiroo," . . . Crane was preparing in this slight novel those elements of style which would stand in "The Open Boat" for what the human will can keep between itself and reduction to mere thing. (*Third Violet* xxx)

Critical Studies

As the above sections make clear, "Open Boat" is one of the most frequently discussed works in Crane's canon, and indeed in the entire canon of the American short story. It has also been one of the most highly praised, from the time of its initial appearance to the present. Joseph Conrad offered the first favorable judgment, writing Crane shortly after the story was published that he found it "immensely interesting. . . . You shock—and the next moment you give the perfect artistic satisfaction. The illusions of life come out of your hand without a flaw. It is not life—which nobody wants—it is art" (*Correspondence* I, 315). A few years later H. G. Wells pronounced "Open Boat" Crane's best story because of its combination of "the stark power" of its author's earlier work with a newly discovered sense of restraint. Crane's handling of color, Wells says, "is as full and strong as ever, fuller and stronger, indeed; but the chromatic splashes that at times deafen and confuse in 'The Red Badge,' those images that astonish rather than enlighten, are disciplined and controlled" (130).

Numerous more recent critics concur with Conrad's and Wells's assessments, often pointing to Crane's adept management of all the individual elements that comprise the totality of the story. Maurice Bassan places it among Crane's "most perfect tales" because of its well-thought-out and deft handling of point of view, "the clarity and precision of the prose as it clips and swells with the horizon and with the anxieties of the men," and the "muted, symbolic atmosphere." All these factors, Bassan says, produce "Crane's maturest vision of man's role in the cosmos" (7). Gullason notes the story's thematic richness—its encompassing of cynicism, human brotherhood, the "terrifying indifference" of nature, and the "agonizing process of rebirth"—coupled with its profusion of sophisticated techniques, such as the "incremental refrain," the organic color imagery that reveals "the passage of Time . . . and the beauty and terror of Nature," the use of dialogue to individualize the characters, the complexity of tone, the fusion of tragedy and comedy into tragicomedy, and the effective use of "symbolic overtones" ("True Road" 479). And Sergio Perosa says that through his "rigorous application of the point of view," his "balanced structure," and his "dramatic compression and impressionistic foreshortening," Crane "transfigures an actual occurrence into existential drama, and confers universal meaning and poetic value on the simple retelling of man's struggle for survival" (94).

Many critics rate the story highly for the last reason Perosa notes, its presentation of events in a manner both persuasively realistic and organically symbolic—its being, in Stallman's words, "a direct transcript of personal experience . . . transformed into an impersonal and symbolic representation of life: the plight of man tossed upon an indifferent sea" ("Revaluation" 247). Bert Bender asserts that no one but "an occasional unenlightened critic" would challenge the verisimilitude of Crane's portrayal of men adrift in a dinghy or claim that he exaggerates the physical sufferings involved in such an ordeal (74). The same point informs the valuation of Neville Denny; he says that the story "cannot be faulted for accuracy" and then expands upon this judgment by pointing out that through "selection, subtle shifts of emphasis, and above all in the metaphorical significance the tale is charged with, 'The Open Boat' is made to transcend the plane of photographic 'realism' and enter that of the indisputably artistic" (39).

Kissane similarly praises the story's realism, its closeness to Crane's actual experience, coupled with its artistry of selection. She notes that Crane purposefully tones down the more conventionally adventurous elements of his experience to focus on its metaphorical dimensions. Specifically, she says that Crane concentrates on the correspondent's consciousness in order to emphasize the universal overtones inherent in "his coming to realize the inequality of the struggle which is the condition of life, . . . his acceptance of it, and finally . . . his sensing of the solaces which make life under its inexorable condition bearable" (410). John T. Frederick likewise praises the story for being "something larger than its concrete terms" of a man's battle with nature, for being an examination "not only of man's ultimate relation to the planet which he inhabits and affects to govern and subdue, but of his relation to other men as well, and thus of the total fact of life itself" (14).

If critics are thus in general agreement that "Open Boat" is "an intense paradigm of the human situation as a whole" (Frederick 14), they disagree in many respects about the precise nature of this paradigm, about the attitude Crane expresses here toward the human situation as a whole. Probably the most frequently joined debate is between those who see Crane as taking a Naturalistic position and those who see him as espousing a belief in the efficacy of human will stronger than that which Naturalism will allow, with this debate complicated by disagreements among those in the Naturalist camp concerning the precise limits of that efficacy. That Naturalism and determinism are not necessarily synonymous terms is evident in Adams's reading of the story, which links Naturalism with Romanticism. "Open Boat" is Naturalistic, Adams says, in that it partakes of a "radical inconsistency" that characterizes most literature in this genre: on the one hand Crane creates a "feeling of extreme coldness and remoteness" with his metaphor of a "high cold star on a winter's night" as the response of the universe to a man's plea for mercy, while on the other hand he uses a great deal of personification and animistic imagery, which implies that "the natural things Crane says are indifferent are full of feeling." This inconsistency, Adams argues, is a function of the fact that most Naturalists, Crane included, operate upon "a submerged but still vital belief in the romantic world of warmth and relatedness" (140–41). As a result of this belief, Adams continues, Crane here, like most Naturalists in the bulk of their work, is unable to take the full-fledged Romantic view that human beings and nature exist in sympathetic harmony but nonetheless rejects the idea that the admitted indifference of nature toward humanity as a whole incontrovertibly dictates an equally indifferent relationship between individual human beings. Thus, Crane refuses to reduce his characters completely to "the terms of material cause and effect"; he is determined to have them work together and through their communal efforts to "find or save their souls," to "grow stronger, wiser, broader, or more mature" (143–44). Through these rejections and determinations, Adams concludes, Crane in "Open Boat" does what the best Naturalists—and indeed the best artists of any persuasion—do: he uses "the very tensions of an inconsistent or contradictory attitude," controlled by effective patterning of images of death and rebirth, to produce "an emergent synthesis of great power and beauty" (146).

W. T. Going discerns less inconsistency and thus less tension in the story and in Naturalism in general. He points out that the cause of the oiler's death—and indeed the death itself—is "strangely obscured" in both "Stephen Crane's Own Story" and "Open Boat" (79). In the former case, Going says, the explanation is likely journalistic integrity: Crane does not know how or why the oiler died, so he offers no explanation. In the latter case, Going sees Crane as transfiguring simple fact into universal significance, leaving the

oiler's death unexplained to make the mystery of his demise "the central symbol of the significance of the story," which is the indifference of nature to the
life and death of individuals (81–82).

Landon Burns essentially concurs with such a reading, but he offers a few
adjustments, mostly along the lines of Adams's position regarding the complex
character of Naturalism. The oiler's death, he argues, does not demonstrate
only nature's total indifference; it illustrates as well nature's principles of
"adaptability and survival of the fittest." The other three castaways, Burns
notes, seek the aid of life preservers and the overturned dinghy in getting
ashore, and they all rest in the course of their efforts. Billie, however, tries to
make the trip unaided and without rest, showing thereby that his instinct for
survival is less well-developed than that of his fellows. Thus, Burns argues, the
story is partly "a kind of Darwinian allegory about survival" (456). A corollary to
this allegory, according to Burns, is one "about the origin of life." The three
survivors only get help after they reach the shore by their own efforts, at which
point the first dispenser of this help is presented in imagistic terms that in
Burns's view suggest the figure of God in Michelangelo's creation panels in the
Sistine Chapel, symbolizing the active role that humans must play in their own
preservation. Whether one finally reads such details "on the level of Darwinian
allegory or on the level of spiritual rebirth," Burns concludes, they sort well
with the story's Naturalistic theme: "while Nature is indifferent to man's survival, mankind is not totally so. If one can, on his own, 'reach the shore,' then
he can enjoy the aid of and the welcome into the body of humanity" (457).

John Conder takes a similar view of the story and of the tenets of
Naturalism that it espouses. The correspondent's discovery, Conder says, is
twofold: he learns that nature is neither anthropomorphic nor symbolic but
utterly indifferent, and he learns that a man who acknowledges this reality
cannot create gods but can create community and society, which establish the
sense of mutual obligation that gives rise to ethics and morality. Conder
argues that Crane presents these realizations as wholly Naturalistic—not as
evidence that human beings are anything more than a part of nature, in other
words—by showing the development of a sense of mutual obligation to be
humans' *instinctive* response to the indifference of their environment (24).
However, in Conder's view the intellectual fearlessness of Crane's Naturalistic
vision extends well beyond this insight. If "nature is indifferent and societies
and their associated moral systems spring from man's instinct for survival,"
then the logical next step that Conder sees Crane taking is a realization that
"societies are fictions in the sense that works of art are fictions—that is, creations of man designed to interpret the world in human terms, to give human
meaning to a world without meaning," and, most important, to "impose
human order on a world whose natural order can be beneficent to man only
if its destructive aspects are controlled" (24).

Despite the potential grimness of such a discovery, the particular ramification of this insight that Conder reads as paramount in the story is ultimately positive. As a human creation, society like art requires aesthetic distance for the most accurate interpretation of its meaning, and it is precisely this distance, both literal and figurative, that the correspondent achieves in the boat. Specifically, this achievement occurs when he feels sorry for the soldier of the Legion, for here he attains "a consequent loss of self, rather than an identification that is strictly external because it projects one man's personal responses onto those of another." Such projection, Conder explains, occurs as society grows increasingly complex; its members lose sight of its original purpose, mutual preservation, and begin to act out of personal motives alone, thus relating to one another only externally, without the clear moral vision created by a strongly present sense of mutual obligation. In the starkly simple realm of the boat, the origins of society become clear for the first time to the correspondent, and this aesthetic distance enables him to develop his moral vision, his correct interpretation of the fiction that is society (25).

Clark Griffith sees a less positive result stemming from the castaways' new Naturalistic vision. The initial experience of being adrift is beneficial, he says, in that it forces them to abandon the assumption that they can earn survival in some way and to realize that survival is in reality wholly a matter of chance. Thus, they "give up a foolishly sentimental view of themselves, and . . . replace it with what, in Crane's eyes, would be the scientific view of experience, infinitely more difficult to maintain, but with the virtue of being truer and more credible." However, Griffith continues, the difficulty of maintaining such a view gives the story an ultimately negative cast. He points to the final sentence, in which the narrator says that the survivors "felt that they could then be interpreters" of nature (*Tales of Adventure* 92), as an indication that they are about to forget the scientific view in favor of one more flattering to their egos, the view that their becoming interpreters means that their survival has a purpose and that therefore, despite all the evidence to the contrary, they are, after all, important to the universe (84).

Maxwell Geismar does not dispute that Crane's vision in "Open Boat" is essentially Naturalistic, but he argues, contrary to most of the critics noted above, that his presentation of a "Darwinian cosmos of blind forces" is finally rather tame compared to the work of many other Naturalists. Despite his embrace of a scientific attitude toward experience, Geismar says, Crane casts the story in the highly conventional narrative pattern of sin followed by atonement to the father. The captain is the paternal character here; through his demeanor and the devotion of the other men to him he becomes "a dominant figure of divinity and mercy," a figure finally at odds with a Darwinian view of the cosmos. As an example of a more radical, "more ruthless application of the Darwinian code," Geismar points to the stories of Jack London, in which the father-figure is not cherished but rather "deposed, if not devoured, by the rebellious 'son-horde'" (100).

Whether the Naturalistic view at issue is radical or tame, an equal or greater number of critics read "Open Boat" as finally rejecting or at least mitigating it. Cady is the most extreme member of this group, arguing that Crane here presents his characters as other than nature rather than as part of it and that therefore he totally rejects the Naturalist position, since a view of humanity as no more than a part of nature is a *sine qua non* for that position (*Stephen Crane* 131). The majority of the other critics in this camp take a more medial stance, similar to that of Adams and Burns: like those two, they discern a purposeful tension between Naturalistic and non-Naturalistic elements, leading to an equal balance between them, or, in some cases, to a greater weight assigned to the non-Naturalistic ones.

Stanley Greenfield is one who sees equal balance. He discerns tension most markedly in the story's presentation of two planes of action, one governed by determinism and the other admitting the possibility of heroic action. The first plane comprises the parallel desires of the cook to eat pie and the shark to eat men, and the contrast between the water in the boat's jar as the source of life and the water surrounding the boat as an imminent source of death. These connections, Greenfield says, establish the deterministic character of "an indifferent universe [in which] one must eat or be eaten, one must drink or be drunk down." The second plane comprises the heroic efforts at survival that the men undertake both individually and collectively. That Billie behaves most heroically and most generously and then dies, Greenfield says, is Crane's way of suggesting that "while men's actions seem to have some value in deciding their fate, they are still limited by operating in an indifferent universe where chance can single out victims." On one plane, then, Greenfield continues, Crane asserts that "one must survive, and his struggle is dictated by circumstances; on another, one must do the right thing . . . demanded by the ethical considerations" of one's position. But neither of these assertions is the complete answer, in Greenfield's view; he sees Crane as "philosophically . . . refusing to guarantee that either a biologically or ethically motivated attempt at survival will produce the desired result." Thus, the two planes remain in tension, which is reinforced at the artistic level by the fact that in terms of plot Billie dies by chance whereas in terms of style Crane makes that death seem inevitable, fated. This tension, Greenfield concludes, Crane's admission of determinism balanced against his admiration for heroism, "gives the story its ultimate richness and meaning" (564–65).

Eric Solomon takes a similar but slightly more complex view, seeing not two planes of action but rather three sets of polarities developing the meaning of the story: man's egotistical belief in his own importance opposed to his actual helplessness, man's sense of nature's malevolence opposed to its true indifference, and the seemingly vast distance between the castaways and safety opposed to the literal nearness of the boat to shore. Through these antitheses, Solomon says, Crane depicts "the existential dilemma of the absurdity of man's immersion in the destructive element" (161), with the story's conclusion showing that consciousness of human community is the only means of coping with the polarities and ameliorating the dilemma. In the surf, the captain, the cook, and the correspondent all cling to a piece of the boat—"a relic of their fellowship," they remain aware of and help one another, and they survive (172). The oiler, on the other hand, swims strongly but alone, and he drowns, having failed to retain "the lesson of the sea that he learned while *in* the boat—the value of group action" (174).

Max Autrey offers a different reading of the conclusion, stemming from his view that three dissimilar attitudes rather than three sets of complementary oppositions develop the story's meaning, with each attitude embodied in one character's actions. The captain symbolizes "loss of control on both a personal and public level," Billie is the man of action who seeks to control his own destiny through that action, and the correspondent becomes "an embodiment of universal sympathy" (103–06). Due to these differing orientations, once in the surf the captain and the correspondent "place themselves at the mercy of fate" (106), accepting the greater power of nature and simply taking whatever assistance it offers, whereas Billie seeks to resist through his own strength alone, rejecting the assistance of nature or fate, and this course is the reason for his death. Self-reliance is thus shown to be futile; Billie can be understood "as revealing a weakness of man that is often disguised as a strength" (108). With this idea in view, the message out of the sea is for Autrey the "affirmation of a negation": all the struggles of individualism are futile, so that "life is to be either a frustrating experience, a groping, a search—or the resignation of . . . having reached a state of knowledge" (109). But within this condition Autrey detects a note of hope. If death is regarded as a liberation from this futility, then Billie's self-reliance has at least led him to this freedom, lending his struggle a modicum of nobility (110).

Both Westbrook and Donald B. Gibson, while not denying the power or indifference of nature and fate, discern a more equivalent tension between these forces and those of human will and thus a larger degree of hope in the story's action. The discovery of nature's indifference is not "a final conclusion" for the men in the dinghy, Westbrook argues, but rather "a preliminary—though important—discovery," important because it leads them to their realization of "the subtle brotherhood of men" that *is* the final conclusion, and which the characters act on in Billie's and the correspondent's spelling one another at the oars and in the captain's direction of the others in the surf. These actions produced by human will effect the survival of three of the four men, and thus, Westbrook concludes, "[t]he indifference of nature does not negate human value or will"; it is powerful and unavoidable, but "it is not the definitive factor of existence" (222–23). In a similar vein, Gibson points out that precisely because nature is indifferent it sometimes hurts the castaways but also sometimes helps them, as when they harness the wind by using the captain's coat for a sail, and that the implication of such moments is that a man "becomes free through the exercise of consciousness, will, against the nonconscious forces of nature" (131).

Leverett T. Smith sees this tension between nature and human will embodied in the narrator's differentiation between "nature in the wind, and nature in the vision of men" (*Tales of Adventure* 88). Smith argues that Crane regards the former as certainly indifferent but the latter as not, and that the story traces the correspondent's "conversion" to this tempered Naturalistic view (13). Smith does not use the word *conversion* here casually; he asserts that in limning the correspondent's change in understanding Crane is drawing on the ideas about religious conversion that he inherited from his parents and his other Methodist forebears, particularly the notion that the trials of life lead the non-elect to despair but give the elect a renewed will, a renewed sense of the worthiness of their combat for salvation. Transmuting the conversion experience in the story, preserving its basic form but stripping away its Methodist specifics, Smith says, Crane presents a three-part process that the men must and do undergo: first, they "must understand their own insignificance"; second, "they must be able to transcend hellish reality while remaining immersed in it"; and third, "they must experience a feeling of brotherhood" (24). This process of converting their human vision of nature, counteracting despair and strengthening the will, enables the cook and correspondent essentially to float to shore, to "transform the destructive element into the desired comfort"; accomplishing this transformation is thus, finally, "what one must do to be saved" (23).

LaFrance takes a similar view, seeing Crane as arguing for a fruitful understanding of the tension between nature as it is and nature as humans respond to it. He predicates his reading on Mordecai Marcus's outlining of a three-part progression in human awareness in the story, a progression from seeing nature as "malevolently hostile" to regarding it as "thoughtlessly hostile" to understanding it, finally, as "wholly indifferent" (Marcus 511). LaFrance concurs that Crane presents nature in this way, as "a moral blank" (199), but, like Conder and Westbrook in their separate ways, he argues that this vision is not for Crane the endpoint of human understanding and human morality; rather, the next step is for humans to recognize that, due to this blankness, any sense of union with nature is illusory and that, instead, only union with other people is real and serves as the ground of morality (199–200). These are the principles the correspondent discovers and acts on. He learns that the separation between nature and human is "absolute, and all that the aware and honest man can do . . . is accept it," and he learns as well that the "part of the relation which is not fixed, which is always capable of development or degeneration, is man's inner or moral reality of the mind as it copes with externality" (135). The result of this insight into the unfixed character of inner reality is the correspondent's increased awareness of and actions in accordance with the necessity of human community. With these ideas in view, LaFrance asserts that Crane intends no irony in the narrator's final statement that the men now feel that they can be "interpreters" of nature. This stance is in fact Crane's own, LaFrance says, since not only in this story but also in a number of other stories and poems Crane "obviously affirms both the view of external nature and the moral commitment that his spokesman here brings to the reader" (205). Further, this affirmation, part of "Crane's persistent emphasis upon the essential superiority of man's inner reality over all externals," places Crane squarely within "the humanistic tradition which reaches from Plato to Wallace Stevens" (135).

Denny, on the other hand, does perceive irony in this final statement, although not of the sort a reader might initially suspect. The men may be right that they are capable of being interpreters, he says, but they are wrong if they believe that their interpretations will affect the understanding of other men, for, as their own recent past should have shown them, only direct experience can truly alter human awareness. "[I]n the end, no matter how compellingly the 'interpreter,' the artist, say, may realize [the truth] for us or act as admittedly useful mediator," Denny argues, "it is rude and elemental experience itself, life willingly faced and committed to, that can establish the moral bearings that will have any real significance for us" (41).

Several other critics also regard the necessity of direct experience to reliable insight as one of the key themes of the story. Ralph Ellison asserts that the point here, as in much of Crane's work, is "the cost of moral perception, of achieving an informed sense of life, in a universe which is essentially hostile to man"; such perception requires "skill and courage and loyalty," which can be meaningfully tested only by a "plunge into the storm-sea-war of experience" (71). Holton sees the story as "a report of an experience of confrontation conducted within the metaphor of vision"—that is, an account of how experience gradually causes men to see differently both literally and figuratively—an approach he argues is typical in Crane's mature works. At the beginning, the characters do not know the color of the sky, a state that emblematizes their "visual innocence"; the rest of the story charts the progress of their metaphorical vision as that is linked to its literal counterpart (160). Gradually, with many oscillations between "blinding fear and illusory arrogance," the men come to "see" their fundamental estrangement from the universe. For the correspondent, this insight comes to him after the long, dark night, when he literally can see no "visible expression of nature" (*Tales of Adventure* 85) at which to jeer. Now he knows the color of the sky—he understands nature's indifference and humanity's concomitant need for community in the face of "universal absurdity" (165). Following this revelation, he seems to see a literal halo around the head of his rescuer, which at the metaphorical level suggests sainthood for this man, sainthood consisting of the ability not to defeat the indifference and absurdity of nature but rather to mitigate these characteristics to some degree by the exercise of human will (167). This experience of altered vision on two levels leads logically, Holton says, to the correspondent's and the others' final sense that they can now interpret nature. Unlike Denny, he does perceive irony of the expected variety here, a suggestion of a "subjective, even existential understanding of reality," in the narrator's saying that the men *feel* that they can be interpreters, not that they *are* interpreters; however, he argues that this irony is muted by the demonstrated power of experience to make the men's vision unquestionably more acute, as well as by the fact that "it is ultimately in interpretation that private perception achieves social significance"— in other words, that in returning to the community with an increased appreciation of it the correspondent will share his experience, his new understanding of nature and will, with others (168).

Nagel similarly focuses on the role of immediate experience in altering the protagonists' vision of their condition, in enabling them to perceive a difference between external and internal reality. He says that the refrain "'If I am going to be drowned'" that occurs in the middle of the fourth section and the beginning of the sixth (*Tales of Adventure* 77, 84) represents one stage of the men's thinking, but not the final stage. Their anger here, projecting their internal reality onto the external reality of nature, is "cosmologically presumptive" due to its basis in an assumption that whatever forces run the universe are hostile; it is a "tentative interpretation of the action later refuted by the events themselves" (*Impressionism* 82). These refuting events follow the refrain in section six and continue in section seven, Nagel says, when Crane shifts his point of view from the collective consciousness of the four men to the mind of the correspondent alone as he meditates upon his relationship to the universe and upon the wind-tower as representing "the serenity of nature amid the struggles of men—nature in the wind, and nature in the vision of men" (*Tales of Adventure* 88). At this point, Nagel contends, when the correspondent discerns a differentiation between nature as itself and nature as men see it, "the theme shifts from the concerns of action and danger to epistemology," and this change "parallels the alteration in the view of nature from hostile to indifferent" (*Impressionism* 83). One reason the men, prior to this moment, wished to view nature as malevolent, Nagel explains, is that such a view makes them important as the objects of that malevolence. When the correspondent abandons this interpretation for a grasp of nature's indifference, he concomitantly experiences despair at recognizing his own insignificance; however, the split between external and internal reality that impels these insights also offers hope, for when the correspondent feels sympathy for the legionnaire and ultimately feels that he can be an interpreter, he understands that "human beings are unimportant to the universe, [but] they can nevertheless be vitally important to themselves in their thoughts and feelings" (*Impressionism* 104).

Bergon dissents from this view of the story as linking experience and moral insight, arguing that Crane's relentless focus on the moment of perception itself produces "a psychological rather than a moral progression" (86). Levenson, however, offers even higher praise than Nagel for Crane's depiction of the interplay between external and internal realities, between experience and consciousness, leading finally to a change in moral vision. In Levenson's view, Crane's greatest achievement here is his "complex art" in fusing "the most external and the most inward of narrative forms, the tale of adventure and the fiction of consciousness" (*Tales of Adventure* lxvi). Normally, the tale of adventure simply recounts experience, but in subtitling this work "A Tale Intended To Be After the Fact" Crane announces that he will depict "the consciousness going over the facts of memory and trying to find some order, some meaning, by which to interpret the event" (lxvi). Crane accomplishes this fusion brilliantly, Levenson asserts, through his employment of a shifting point of view, by which he can dramatize not simply how the experience felt but "how it felt in all its multiplicity," and by which he can show that "beneath the brilliantly changing surface of experience, there are cumulative changes whereby men, though they cannot control what happens, can at least come to a rational perception of their fate" (*Tales of Adventure* lxvi–lxvii). Levenson uses the word *rational* advisedly here, for he does not regard Crane's shifting point of view as suggesting that "reality was constituted by the eye of the beholder or the language of the artist"; rather, he sees Crane asserting by this technique that humans learn the truth of their position through their progressive interpretation of the external world, which constitutes objective reality (*Tales of Adventure* lxvii–lxix).

Shulman concurs with Levenson regarding both the truth of the beholder's vision and Crane's artistry in this story; he sees these two as meaningfully interconnected, with the power of the artistry largely creating the reliability of vision. "Open Boat" is in his view "a culmination and turning point" (448) in Crane's evolution beyond *The Red Badge* because this story, unlike the novel, presents its protagonist's perception of and response to his experience as "basically convincing and reliable" (449); arguing against those who read the story as a study in the ultimate faultiness of all human perception, Shulman asserts that Crane conveys "exactly the experienced quality of the situation," makes that situation persuasively representative of human experience in general, and thereby renders the correspondent's insights "complex, precise, and convincing" (451). The result is that "all unpretentiously and believably, not larger than life, the ordinary men in the open boat affirm their—and our— shared humanity and vulnerable mortality in the face of arbitrary death and a threatening universe," with this affirmation leading finally to "a modern tragic vision" when coupled with the oiler's death, which reveals the limitations upon the saving power of shared humanity (454–55).

As noted above, Holton raises the possibility of an "existential understanding of reality" in the narrator's saying that the men *feel* that they can be interpreters. A large number of other critics discern more than possibility in this

area; they contend that "Open Boat" is unmistakably a precursor of this twentieth-century philosophical stance, leading to much grimmer implications
than Holton proposes. The earliest of this group is William Bysshe Stein, who
labels the story proto-Existentialist because of the characters' realization that
"the value categories of their culture fail to serve them in their predicament.
The idealistic virtues of bravery, fortitude, and integrity possess no meaning
in a world that denies the importance of man" (170). Stein asserts that Crane,
like Sartre and Camus after him, depicts God as withdrawn from humanity,
replaced by "the idiot forces of nihilism"; thus, there is no "moral function" in
distinctions between good and evil, and "there is no one to whom man is
responsible for his individual behavior" (171). From these premises, Stein
argues that the correspondent's discovery of human brotherhood and compassion is "merely self-deception—man torturing his imagination to find purpose in purposelessness, nobility in ignobility, dignity in degradation." This
reading is borne out, he says, by the oiler's death, in which the "brief comradeship" of the men in the boat "is unpityingly dissolved by contingent circumstance. . . . To die is simply to die. To live is to be absurd—in chilled
solitude to watch all trusted hopes and anticipations dissipate" (172).

Peter Buitenhuis arrives at the same conclusion by a slightly different path.
He discerns the story's proto-existentialist stance in its structure, which he
sees as composed of conflicts and paradoxes informing Crane's rhetoric and
symbolism. These elements initiate the correspondent into the indifference
of nature, and this initiation leads in turn to a new awareness of the absurdity
of life. The correspondent's refusal to fall into an equivalent indifference and
fatalism as a result, Buitenhuis says, is still further proof that Crane anticipates
existentialism, for by instead recognizing and acting upon the necessity of
human brotherhood, the correspondent "makes the affirmation of the absurd
man"—he demonstrates that he "is ready to realize existentially the responsibilities" of the human condition (249–50).

Donna Gerstenberger builds on this reading; she agrees with Buitenhuis
that the story develops a proto-existentialist position and then goes on to
argue that it focuses specifically on "the epistemological aspect of the existential crisis"—that from beginning to end it is "about man's limited capacities
for knowing reality" (557). With this argument in view, Gerstenberger differs
with Buitenhuis on one crucial point: she maintains that he is mistaken in
asserting that Crane erred in not presenting the story from one point of view.
Crane's intent, she says, is not simply to show the existential absurdity of the
universe but rather to reveal as well the subjectivity of every point of view—
to demonstrate that "the vision of any human being must of necessity be
false, *even if* that vision be a knowledge of the absurdity of the universe"
(558). Gerstenberger sees Crane communicating this idea through his frequent authorial intrusions offering views of the circumstances that differ from
the views of the men in the boat; through his authorial undercutting of any

hint of heroism in the correspondent's discovery of absurdity by emphasizing the ludicrous aspects of this discovery, such as a man's pathetic resolve that he would be "better and brighter during an introduction, or at a tea" (*Tales of Adventure* 88) if the universe were to give him another chance; and through his frequent use of the subjunctive mood in communicating the men's insights and observations. Through these means, Gerstenberger concludes, Crane suggests that "the final absurdity" of the story is

> the falsification of man's attempts to "interpret," an act in which he is betrayed by the very language he must use to conceptualize, by the narrowness of his vision, and by the further limitations of his need to frame, to formalize his apprehensions in a landscape, a poem, an irony, or a subjunctive statement of conditions that never were on land or sea. (561)

Thomas L. Kent, following Gerstenberger's lead in building on Buitenhuis, builds on Gerstenberger, concurring with her analysis and then examining how the epistemological uncertainty she identifies is generated in both the plot and the reader. The fourth section, the center of the story, is crucial in this process, he explains. Sight is the central metaphor throughout the story, and optimism changes to despair in this fourth section when the men in the boat cannot "see," either literally or metaphorically, the reason impelling the man on shore to wave his coat at them. They propose many theories about the meaning of this gesture, and the narrator offers no indication as to which of these theories is accurate, placing both characters and reader in an epistemologically uncertain condition. These parallel conditions persist throughout the story, Kent says. The reader may seem to have an interpretative advantage over the characters in being able to see those characters and their uncertainty as part of "the pattern of the narrative, . . . [of] an artistic text that has form, structure, and meaning," and thus being able to interpret the characters' "uncertainty and ignorance [as] the subject matter of the text," so that "the characters' uncertainty becomes the reader's certainty" (263); but this certainty is illusory. This interpretation of this section, Kent explains, partakes of the "traditional naturalistic" view, and when the reader moves on to interpret the whole text, he or she finds that it resists such an interpretation because that view is precisely the one the characters have now come to as well, and they have "consistently misinterpreted" their experience (263–64). Thus, the reader is once again plunged into uncertainty, the problem being not meaning *per se* "but rather how to *know* meaning, and the ultimate irony of 'The Open Boat' is aimed squarely at us." If we as readers "insist that the text must have some sort of overarching meaning—even a meaning that shows the universe to be existentially absurd—we place ourselves in the same boat as the deluded castaways," a circumstance that leads Kent to assert that the only point to be derived from the story with certainty is that "meaning in the universe is secondary to man's ability to perceive it" (264).

Bergon, Shulman, Halliburton, and Wolford likewise offer existential read-ings, but theirs are all a bit less radical than Gerstenberger's and Kent's. Bergon argues that Crane's employment of multiple narrative perspectives, coupled with his refusal either to say that the survivors are right to feel that they can now be interpreters or to specify what their interpretation is, does not constitute an unequivocal assertion of epistemological uncertainty but rather evinces a rejection of the idea that so powerful an experience can be reduced to a single meaning (87). Shulman comes closer to Gerstenberger and Kent, noting that the failure of the people on shore to respond to the castaways' distress signals illustrates "the generalized epistemological prob-lem" imposed by physical distance, but he takes this idea in a somewhat dif-ferent direction, arguing that this problem militates against interpreting the people's lack of response as "a moral failure of insufficient humanity." Instead, given this problem of long-distance interpretation, the story demon-strates that "at this level of generalization the barriers to human community are the mind and reality itself" (457).

Halliburton edges still closer to the hard existentialism of Gerstenberger and Kent but in the end similarly mitigates that stance. The lack of explana-tion of Billie's death, he contends, indicates Crane's belief that causality can-not be precisely determined, and the indeterminacies of the conclusion reinforce this idea, but only up to a point. Nietzsche "goes so far as to assert that there is no such thing as facts, only interpretations," whereas Crane, Halliburton says, although moving in the same direction, stops short of that conclusion. His final statement of the men's feeling that they can be inter-preters "neither denies the existence of facts nor affirms the existence of truthful interpretation. Crane remains with his characters on 'this' side of the problem, aware of the problem and therefore problematic in *his* interpreta-tion of *their* interpretation" (251–52). But despite these problems, Halliburton concludes, a note of certainty creeps in: Crane may intentionally place all other interpretations in doubt, but he equally intentionally leaves no doubt that the correspondent is correct in believing that his feeling of broth-erhood with the other men makes the ordeal in the boat the best experience of his life (254).

Wolford sees the unmistakable symbolic dimensions—the journey to shore as the archetypal voyage of discovery, the four men as "a microcosm of society or humanity"—as laying the story open to a vast number of interpre-tations, and he suggests that "the ambiguity that leads to so many interpreta-tions *is* perhaps the interpretation." As a result, the tale "seems to lead to the existential proposition that no one can know anything. . . . Ultimately, all that matters is the individual consciousness" (17). The path to existentialism here is made even clearer, Wolford continues, by the fact that the characters are presented as isolated from their environment rather than subsumed by it, as they would be if Crane were espousing Naturalism, and by the concomitant fact that Crane like the later explicit proponents of existentialism seems to argue that the world is meaningless and that, as an important corollary, "life is free" and so humans are free to make moral choices (25–26).

Bert Bender, on the other hand, disagrees with the contention (specifically, with Gerstenberger's contention) that Crane's central theme in this story is epistemological uncertainty. Focusing on the emphasis on direct experience, in a vein similar to that of Denny, Ellison, Holton, and Nagel, Bender argues that for Crane such experience can lead to certain knowledge, to the kind of hard-won insight "one feels and clings to in the face of death" (72). In "Open Boat" this insight is the need for compassion. The captain possesses this virtue from the outset due to his experience of suffering before the story begins, with both experience and compassion evinced in his sorrowful thoughts of the crewmen he was forced to leave on the sinking ship, but the correspondent only attains it when he stops raging at the imaginary "seven mad gods who rule the sea" (*Tales of Adventure* 84) and allows his feelings about his interaction with the other men in the boat to intermingle with the "mystery, emotion, and poetry" of his meditation upon the soldier of the legion. In effect, Bender says, this meditation scene, presenting a "mind's deep connection with actual experience" (74), constitutes an epiphany of the sort defined by William James two years later in *The Varieties of Religious Experience*—a moment of "'primal reality'" which "'the individual feels impelled to respond to solemnly and gravely, and neither by a curse nor a jest'" (qtd. in Bender 74–75). However, Bender continues, this is not a "conventional" religious experience but rather a revelation of what John Dewey in *A Common Faith* calls the "'religious values inherent in actual experience'" (qtd. in Bender 75).

Stallman, by contrast, takes a position completely opposed to that of the existentialists, arguing that Crane *does* intend for the reader to understand the correspondent's epiphany as a conventional Christian experience. In support of this view, he quotes certain of Crane's phrasings, saying that for the survivors "life now becomes 'sacred to their minds'" and that the oiler's death creates "'a terrible grace'" that purchases the rescue, the salvation, of the others ("Revaluation" 250). Stanley B. Greenfield, however, points out that this reading does not work because Stallman takes his probative phrases out of context: "sacred to their minds" refers not to the attitude of the survivors but to that of the women on the beach regarding the comforts that they offer to the survivors, and "a terrible grace" characterizes not the oiler's death at the story's end but rather the motion of the waves at its beginning (563).

LaFrance like Stallman takes note of conventional Christian imagery in this story, but what he makes of that imagery is closer to Bender's application of Dewey's principles. The first rescuer's being described as having a halo, he says, conjures up not traditional Christianity but rather the idea that this man "is the first person to act toward the castaways as an aware moral being should, and his sainthood is earned in terms of his enthusiastic practice of simple humanity toward a suffering brother" (203). Similarly, Billie's death is not a Christlike intentional sacrifice, for it is clearly a product of chance; as such, what it suggests, when it is coupled with his prior charitable cooperative efforts with the others, is "the immense value of brotherhood among living men, because, while contingency remains in externals"—most forcefully, in death—"the moral realities which make human life meaningful to the living are not in themselves contingent upon external effect" (204).

Randall Stewart, Robert Meyers, and Monteiro also discuss Crane's attitude toward Christianity as evinced in this story. Stewart sees it as largely significant by its absence; he regards "Open Boat" as "perhaps the first important American story to show man against the backdrop of the new universe of modern science"—a universe that thus lacks the comforting Christian belief in a benevolent God, as the correspondent discovers when the only response he receives to his supplications is "a high cold star on a winter's night" (*Tales of Adventure* 85) that men have discovered via the telescope. Here, Stewart points out, both correspondent and reader are confronted with the irony, probably unintended by Crane, of modern man dwarfed by the immensity of his own discovery of the universe (110).

Meyers and Monteiro, by contrast, see religion as not merely absent from the story but rather as specifically rejected. Meyers contends that Crane espouses Naturalism, "a new religion," in this story through a conscious inversion of the symbols and rites of an old, outworn Christianity. This process begins with the castaways' arguments over the possibility of help coming from the towns of New Smyrna and St. Augustine; since both these names can be read as references to the early history of the Christian church—Smyrna having been the site of one of the original seven churches of Asia—and since no help is actually forthcoming, Meyers sees Crane here as comparing "early, effective Christianity" to the etiolated church of his own day. The second inversion occurs when the castaways see a man on shore who waves his coat at them and they cannot comprehend the meaning of this gesture. Since this coat is black, the traditional color of clerical attire, Meyers says, this figure is "a parody of the black-frocked clergyman, looked to for directions but incapable of giving them." Faced with this ineffectuality, the castaways turn apostate with their refrain of "If I am going to be drowned"; given its repeated assertion that "the gods are all 'mad' and man's destiny is determined by nothing logical," Meyers regards this imprecation as a parody of a Christian devotional litany. The inversions continue when the men in the boat turn to Naturalism as a replacement for Christianity. What this new creed consists of is a reliance on courage and brotherhood, and in Meyers's view its presentation accompanied by Christian symbology—a halo around the head of the correspondent's rescuer, the characterization of the remedies the women bring as "sacred to their minds"—is Crane's way of asserting that this is indeed a new religious creed to these men, infused with all the intensity that Christianity once offered. Having rejected defunct Christianity in favor of "a religion which finds nothing important beyond man," the castaways at the conclusion, when they hear the voice of the sea, are now prepared to be the "apostles" of this new faith—its "hierophants," its "true interpreters" (60).

The reading that Monteiro offers is somewhat more limited; he discerns only a repudiation of Christianity, not a concomitant espousal of an alternative creed. He notes that, due to the story's close basis in Crane's own experience, critics rarely notice an "archetypal quality" in it. Nonetheless, he says, this quality is present: Crane wishes the reader to see the four men adrift in a fragile boat on a rough sea as symbolizing the human condition in general, and specifically to see through this symbolism a "rigorous and somewhat systematic repudiation of an unquestioning faith in Christ [as] the believer's certain protector" ("Logic" 330). The life-boat was a common symbol of the human condition in nineteenth-century Christian books and hymns, Monteiro points out, and that Crane was aware of this symbolism is clear from his ironic use of it in the poem "A Man Adrift on a Slim Spar" and from his specific mention of a hymn that employs it without irony, P. P. Bliss's "Pull for the Shore," also known as "The Life-Boat," in the short story "A Little Pilgrim" ("Logic" 331). By his use in "Open Boat" of such a craft drawn simultaneously from his own recent experience and his memories of early religious training, Monteiro concludes, Crane matches "his personal experience of shipwreck against the essentialist, allegorical teachings of nineteenth-century Protestantism as he knew them, and he [finds] their optimism decidedly wrong-headed" ("Logic" 334).

Lytle also reads the story in archetypal terms, but for him those terms embrace Christianity rather than undermine it. In his view, it is a version of the "dolorous quest" of Arthurian legend, in which ignorance must be transmuted into knowledge, "especially self-knowledge before a continuing precarious plight" (62). Initially, Lytle argues, although the men in the boat seem to be threatened only by water, they are in fact menaced by all four of the ancient basic elements—earth, fire, and air in addition to water—a fact that ultimately renders their quest a movement from a pagan to a Christian sensibility. The sea and the land together "contain the conflict, the threat of annihilation," while fire is represented by the high cold star that symbolizes nature's indifference to the correspondent, and air appears through the sky that "holds, as the winds blow it, the threat of death" (64). Through their dolorous quest, the men learn to see beyond these threats to the deeper ambiguity of the elements; they discover that the sky holds "the breath of life" as well as the threat of death and that land and sea together offer "the hope of salvation" along with the possibility of annihilation, as epitomized in the juxtaposition of the live body of the first rescuer with the dead body of the oiler. And at the end of the quest, at the story's conclusion, Lytle explains, the survivors reach beyond this ambiguity to an awareness of mystery, beyond a pagan sense that they are wholly at the mercy of the four elements to an understanding of a larger force that, while indefinable, carries Christian overtones through the halo that seems to enclose the head of the first rescuer and through the correspondent's new awareness of the need for charity and compassion. The air, in the voice of the wind, tells them that the elements themselves are indifferent "but the mysterious fateful circumstances depending upon the supernatural," beyond those elements, "can save or destroy. Those who escape and those who fall define [this] mystery" (74), and this fact enforces the need for the Christian virtues of sympathy and selfless love.

In addition to these myriad attempts to categorize Crane in terms of philosophy and theology on the basis of "Open Boat," a number of critics have tried to define him as a member of one or another aesthetic school. C. R. Metzger, proceeding from a definition of Realism as the presentation of experiences and insights that most readers can regard as possible in "real life," argues that this quality, along with a number of techniques customarily employed by Realists to achieve it, predominates in this story and that therefore in this instance Crane is a Realist. Among such techniques are an omniscient but not intrusive narrator who provides a considerable amount of factually grounded detail; the introduction of this material "in versions of the ways in which we apprehend facts in real life"—such as the apprehension of details of sight prior to definition, as when the correspondent is described as perceiving first a fin and a phosphorescent wake and then realizing that these phenomena add up to a shark; the use of "multiple perspectives, multiple interpretations, and the commission and correction of [perceptual] error"; the employment of preparatory repetition to make events credible, as in the frequently expressed fear that the boat will swamp before it actually does so; the use of repetition on the psychological level to depict the reality of recurring thoughts; and the deployment of irony as closely corresponding to the operation of the non-fictive world (49–54).

LaFrance, relying on a definition of Realism somewhat different from Metzger's, one more narrowly focused on the presentation of plausible physical experience, questions the adequacy of this label as a description of what goes on in this story. He notes that the concentration here, as always in Crane's work, is not so much on the experience itself as on the correspondent's thoughts about what happens. As a result, the story may be covered by a term such as "psychological realism," but, despite its genesis in Crane's own life, it certainly cannot be seen as a product of "the cult of experience" that constituted Realism for many of Crane's contemporaries (38).

Colvert is more doctrinaire, arguing that in this story Crane is not in any sense a Realist. Crane relies here, Colvert explains, on "image, metaphor, recurring motifs, contrasts in tone and mood, and other suggestive devices" ("Style" 39)—techniques far removed from the practices of textbook

Realism—to present a theme that in Colvert's view is equally removed from textbook Realism, "a theme so central to [his] consciousness that it can be taken almost as a definition of his world view, the vision of life governed by his profound sense of the consequences of our faulty perceptions of reality" ("Style" 39). In "Open Boat" as everywhere in Crane, Colvert says, the protagonists "struggle to bring into some kind of meaningful order the confusions and contradictions of experience"; but, possessing "a perceptual machinery which renders them incapable of reconciling all the apparently disparate elements in their experience," they "stand uncertain and defenseless in a flux of imperfectly comprehended events," reflecting Crane's own "perception of irreconcilable contradictions in reality" ("Style" 40). And, Colvert continues, Crane presents this condition principally through his ironic style and structure, particularly via his handling of point of view and imagery. Regarding point of view, for instance, Colvert says that by using words such as *seemed, probably, doubtless,* and *feels* to characterize the men's thoughts—as when the correspondent *feels* that the high cold star is nature's response to a man's supplications and the survivors "*felt* that they could then be interpreters" (*Tales of Adventure* 92)—Crane "always implicitly allows for errors of perception" ("Style" 42). Through various stylistic strategies that all make this allowance, Colvert concludes, Crane purposely keeps the meaning of the story open-ended. In the story's last lines, "charged with the cumulative meanings evoked in the poetic indirections of Crane's style, the final meaning of the men's experience escapes at last into mystery" ("Style" 45), and thus Crane escapes the purview of Realism.

Several other critics take similar note of Crane's emphasis on the subjective nature of perception and agree that it removes him from the Realist category, but they then implicitly extend Colvert's argument; they assert that this emphasis makes him an Impressionist—that is, an author who "presents materials as they appear to an individual temperament at a precise moment and from a particular vantage point rather than as they are presumed to be in actuality" (*Handbook* 244). These critics all take their initial cue from Conrad, who praised "Open Boat" by telling Crane that he was "a complete impressionist" (*Correspondence* I, 315), but they disagree regarding the precise sense in which this statement is meaningful. Orm Overland focuses on point of view. He notes that one technique frequently accepted as a hallmark of literary Impressionism is a narrator's pretense of not being omniscient in order to give readers "a greater illusion of being spectators to what is being described," and he then points out that Crane engages in just this pretense in "Open Boat." The characters are limited in view to "what at any moment they are able to grasp through their senses," and when the narrator reports something beyond that view he qualifies his information with phrases such as *must have been*, thereby preserving the illusion of immediate restriction to the characters' sense impressions (257).

Rodney O. Rogers also concentrates on point of view, but he contends that Crane does not use the Impressionists' techniques but rather appropriates their epistemological position—relativity of perception—and employs his own techniques to assert it. Crane's originality of technique, he says, resides in his use of a narrator who does not merely disclaim omniscience but explicitly emphasizes variations in perceptions created by differences in point of view. In some places this emphasis comes in a direct statement, as when the narrator points out that the condition of the men in the boat would look "weirdly picturesque" if it were "[v]iewed from a balcony" (qtd. in Rogers 296); in other places the narrator makes the point more indirectly, revealing the limitations of a viewpoint by "gradually or suddenly widening the angle of vision originating at a fixed point in space" (297), as when, upon the correspondent's awakening at dawn, the narrator provides a view of the beautiful sky and this "somewhat tranquil impression implicitly denies the malignancy which the correspondent previously had attributed to the sea" (298). Nagel likewise notes these changes between the point of view of the beleaguered men and that of the more detached narrator, but he does not see Crane as thereby rejecting the techniques of Impressionism while embracing its epistemology. He argues instead that through these shifts, which he terms "ironic narrative juxtapositions," Crane attempts, successfully, to "reconcile intrusive passages of omniscient comment," through which he makes the point that "moments of great intensity vary according to the perspective from which they are seen," with "the [more] restrictive assumptions of Impressionism" (*Impressionism* 72).

Two other critics rate the story's shifting point of view less successful as an artistic strategy. Buitenhuis contends that Crane's refusal to limit himself to the thoughts of one of the men in the boat causes problems by making all four men seem not only to share the same emotions about their experience but also to express those emotions in "similar formulations about the nature of existence"; such linguistic uniformity, Buitenhuis says, "presumes too much on the reader's willing suspension of disbelief" (246). Joseph X. Brennan discerns a more serious flaw: a habit on Crane's part of introducing his own ironic perspective into the thoughts and words of his characters, as a result of which "thematic intentions are blurred and character plausibility impaired" (184). Brennan sees this problem at work in much of Crane's canon, including *Maggie, George's Mother,* and *The Red Badge of Courage,* but he regards it as particularly widespread in "Open Boat." He notes, for instance, the undercutting of the emotions of the castaways due to Crane's use of "preposterous language and sentiments" in describing their thoughts on the possibility of drowning; rather than the genuine utterances of desperate men, these locutions "are the sentiments of the detached narrator-author, keenly aware in retrospect of the absurdity of all protestation and willing to sacrifice the verisimilitude of the actual experience to that dimension of present awareness" (193).

A similar problem occurs, Brennan continues, during two of the correspondent's meditations. By having the correspondent recognize the indifference of nature as symbolized in the wind-tower and then in response wish merely to "be better and brighter during an introduction, or at a tea" (*Tales of Adventure* 88), Crane purposefully causes his ironic narrator to subvert "the psychological plausibility and the supposed value of the experience"—to create the impression that "human understanding is so limited and relative as to render absurd any pretensions to moral or intellectual discrimination, or so incorrigible that a chance to do things over again would only result in the same vanities and inanities of the past" (196). Likewise, when the correspondent recalls the poem about the soldier of the Legion, irony abounds, for the poem is "patently sentimental and banal," and the correspondent's memory of it "is prompted by a self-indulgent sympathy that really amounts to veiled self-pity" (199). The cumulative effect of this irony, Brennan says, is to undercut the validity of the earlier straightforwardly intended passage on the "subtle brotherhood of men" that develops among the occupants of the dinghy and, more generally, to obscure whatever meaning Crane intends the story to convey (193).

These objections receive a tacit rejoinder in Cady's consideration of Crane's handling of point of view in this story. In Cady's reading, which has affinities with those of Greenfield, Autrey, Westbrook, Gibson, and others discussed near the beginning of this section, Crane intends to leave the story's meaning unresolved, to create a fruitful tension between the Naturalistic vision of the correspondent and the redemptive Christian vision that the oiler's possibly sacrificial death creates, in which a man may "rise superior to the pathos of his situation" (*Stephen Crane* 154); and this tension is most fully developed in Crane's controlled movements in and out of three separate points of view: that of the correspondent alone, that of the group—united in "a brotherhood of danger," and that of the neutral narrator (*Stephen Crane* 151). Largely through his adeptness with point of view, Cady concludes, Crane here achieves "the same sort of ambiguity . . . as that which we find in the greatest of Hawthorne's short stories" (*Stephen Crane* 154).

Charles A. Molle, Sura P. Rath, and Mary Neff Shaw likewise regard a measured ambiguity as Crane's ultimate goal in "Open Boat," and in so doing they likewise offer tacit rejoinders to charges of artistic ineptitude. Molle argues against what he calls the conventional reading of the story as "an account of futility" (105); he proposes that the reader instead follow Crane's own lead and adopt a stance of "negative capability," which enables one to "accept the intractability of negativism" that the story presents and then move beyond it (108). First defined by John Keats and expanded upon by Lionel Trilling, negative capability, as paraphrased by Molle, consists of the artist's "willingness to remain in uncertainties, mysteries, and doubts" rather than seeking to impose necessarily limited, partial meanings on complicated experiences—it is a manifestation of the artist's "seeing the full force and complexity of [his or her] subject matter" (109). In Molle's view, Crane fully acknowledges the bleak condition of his castaways but does not present this condition as the totality of their experience; as "a compassionate atheist," he maintains negative capability, and he implicitly challenges the reader to do the same, to overcome a detached pessimism and "move on to detect what hope may be offered to humanity" in his rendition of that experience (109).

Molle himself detects such hope in a three-stage alteration in the correspondent's point of view, a movement from simplistic cynicism to a more complex awareness that includes "the moral reality of brotherhood" (109). The first stage occurs early on, when the correspondent and his fellows discover that, in their grim situation, they are partaking of the "subtle brotherhood of men." The correspondent reaches the second stage when he links himself with and feels compassion for the dying Legionnaire in "Bingen on the Rhine," and at this point, Molle contends, Crane issues his subtle challenge to the reader. Molle points out that Crane here emphasizes that the Legionnaire is dying in Algiers and then near the end of the story, as the correspondent tries to swim through the surf, says that with part of his consciousness the correspondent observes his own struggles "as one who, in a gallery, looks at a scene from Brittany or Algiers" (qtd. in Molle 111). This repetition, Molle asserts, links the Legionnaire's death with the correspondent's potential death and in so doing turns the story's irony on the reader: just as the correspondent as a reader once regarded the Legionnaire with detachment, so the reader of the story may be regarding the correspondent—as nothing more than a figure on a page. The challenge is to go beyond this distanced point of view, as the correspondent himself has done with respect to the Legionnaire, and as he does with respect to humanity in general when he reaches the third stage, which takes place when he interprets the windtower as a symbol of nature's indifference to humankind and desires to amend his behavior, to "be better and brighter during an introduction, or at a tea" (qtd. in Molle 111). Rather than seeing the seemingly trivial terms in which this desire is stated as an indication of humanity's essentially pathetic condition, as Gerstenberger does (558–61), Molle reads them as part of Crane's effort to "maintain irony and ambiguity" and thus "avoid overt sentimentality and obvious preaching" (112)—in other words, to sustain Keats's negative capability.

Rath and Shaw, in a jointly written article, also argue against what they regard as a too-limiting conventional reading of "Open Boat," and they too draw on the ideas of a literary theorist to recover the controlled ambiguity, complexity, and deeper insight that this reading obscures. The traditional approach, they say, is to treat the story as ironic, with the chief ironies residing in the commentary of the narrator and in the death of the oiler even though he is "the one most favored to withstand the ordeal"; however, since much of the narrator's irony is directed at the ideas expressed by the men in the boat, this approach makes understanding the final meaning of the story difficult, for the survivors of the ordeal believe that they have learned something as a result of the oiler's death while the narrator undercuts this belief (96–97). This interpretative difficulty is not inherent in the text, Rath and Shaw contend, but rather arises from the critical habit of listening only to the narrator's voice and accepting its irony as normative. This "traditional analysis of irony" (95) ignores the fact that there are four other voices besides that of the narrator present in the story—those of the castaways—and that the narrator himself encompasses three versions of Crane's own consciousness, each of which possesses a different level of knowledge. There is, first of all, "Crane the 'correspondent'/character, who experiences the *Commodore* accident as a passenger on the wrecked ship" and who therefore "has no foreknowledge of how it will end." Second, there is "Crane the sailor/author, who relives the trauma by telling the story and who agonizes over his mate's death"—who, "privileged by his distance from the accident, can look upon the experience retrospectively and see the irony of its outcome." Finally, there is "Crane the author/narrator, who rewitnesses the accident for us as a fifth character observing himself and his companions," who "forges the correspondent and the author into one" and, in so doing, "must reconcile the dramatic unfolding of the events in time with his own foreknowledge of the narrative irony of the oiler's death" (95).

The complexity of these narrative circumstances, with four characters "passing through . . . three consciousnesses," Rath and Shaw say, can be confronted and resolved by the application of the theory that Mikhail Bakhtin, in his books *Problems of Dostoevsky's Poetics* and *The Dialogic Imagination*, calls "dialogism," by which he means, in Rath and Shaw's summary, an awareness of the "'independent and unmerged voices' that reach us *in spite* of the narrator's mediation" and thereby

> remind us that the characters exist not in one objective world "illuminated by a single authorial consciousness," but in a world not unlike our own, where a number of consciousnesses, "each with equal rights and each with its own world, combine but are not merged in the unity of the event" (94).

Such a reminder is, in Rath's and Shaw's view, exactly what Crane seeks through his handling of point of view in "Open Boat." In attempting to forge the correspondent and the author into one, Crane as narrator is "juggling . . . two polarized forces": on the one hand, his "conscious, objective self," which seeks to record accurately the events of the actual experience, and on the other hand, his "subconscious, subjective self, which questions the poetic justice of the oiler's death" (96). Rather than concealing this forging process, he builds his juggling into the narrative by at times allowing the voices of the sailors to escape the narrator's mediation and therefore his irony, for at such moments these voices are heard as "threatening—indeed compromising—Crane's fore-knowledge of the ending," and at other times keeping them under the narra-tor's control and thus making them "appear as ludicrous or pathetic victims of Crane's dramatic irony" (98). Through this negotiation of "alternate fore-grounding for the sailor and the author," this refusal to "effect a complete merg-ing of the witnessing 'I' in the acting 'he,'" Crane undermines the notion of "a single authoritative narrator" (99). Ultimately, Rath and Shaw explain, this undermining, created by the "polyphony of independent and 'unmerged voic-es,'" means that the story "envelops two plots, each developed and resolved independently of the other in the narrator's consciousness," these being the plot "defined by human values," embodied in the voices of the sailors—includ-ing that of the correspondent, "the acting 'he'"—and the plot of events, embod-ied in the ironic voice of the author—"the witnessing 'I'" (102). Through his or her awareness of the independence of these two plots, the dialogical reader recognizes that the narrator does not authoritatively undercut the conclusion the survivors reach, recognizes that the "audible voices of the 'others' through-out the story . . . render dubious the narrator's ironic stance," and recognizes therefore that "the men can indeed be interpreters of the sea" (104).

As the preceding discussions evince, Crane's work with point of view in "Open Boat" has elicited much critical commentary. It is not, however, the only aspect of technique to which critics have addressed themselves; imagery, style, and structure have been extensively examined as well, not only as com-ponents in a larger exegesis, which is how they have been handled in a num-ber of the analyses already covered, but also as elements worthy of individual consideration. James Napier praises Crane's skill in consistently employing imagery that depicts much of the sea voyage in terms of land, as in his descriptions of the ocean as "slate," the waves as "rocks," the boat as a "bath-tub" and a "broncho," and the men's efforts to change places as harder than stealing eggs from under a hen. Through this strategy, Napier says, Crane makes his imagery the chief element in generating the central irony of the story: the likelihood that the men will drown within sight of the safety of land, a circumstance that drives home the indifference of nature ("Land" 15). (Upon making these observations, Napier found himself in rough seas of his own, for Stallman responded to this work by charging that Napier had derived most of his observations from several already-published essays of Stallman's without acknowledging this debt ("Land-Sea" 15). In a note of reply append-ed to this attack, Napier said that he had been unaware of Stallman's work and apologized for his inadvertent failure of acknowledgment, but he also noted that Stallman had only remarked that Crane uses this type of imagery—that Stallman had not offered any insights about its thematic import—and that, therefore, Napier's reading of the imagery as emphasizing the "absurdi-ty" of drowning in sight of dry land was his own idea rather than an appropri-ation from Stallman ["Land-Sea" 15].)

338 The Open Boat

Kissane also notes Crane's use of land-based imagery, which she sees as drawn from his own boyhood domestic experience and which she regards him as employing for two purposes. First, the homespun nature of many of Crane's figures, such as his descriptions of the gulls as seeming to be made of "canton flannel" and of the waves as resembling "carpets on the line in a gale," shows the way the correspondent's consciousness works in attempting to come to grips with his current situation: he seeks reassuringly familiar equivalents for his dire circumstances (411). Second, the images metaphorically linking the men in the boat to what are conventionally regarded as lesser animals—ants in the passage about the correspondent's contemplation of the wind tower and, implicitly, mice in the frequent references to the men's nibbling "the sacred cheese of life"—emphasize the "puniness" and "paltriness" of these men as they confront the vast, indifferent universe (412).

Bergon implicitly agrees with the first part of Kissane's analysis, for he too says that Crane's frequent deployment of land metaphors is meant to show the castaways' efforts to define their terrifying new experience in comfortingly quotidian terms. Ultimately, however, Bergon continues, the nature of these metaphors in fact defeats such efforts, for their homely familiarity gradually serves only to "accentuate the gulf between commonplace experience and this grim exposure to sea and sky" (88). Gibson, on the other hand, sees the preponderance of land imagery not as emphasizing such a gulf but rather as implying that it does not exist, that what the men learn about the indifference of the sea applies to the land as well and thus to all of nature (130).

Levenson focuses attention on another strain of imagery, relating to children and childlike behavior—as when the waves, as viewed by the men in the boat, are characterized as "most wrongfully and barbarously abrupt," and when the captain is described as "soothing his children." These images, Levenson says, reveal "the inadequacy of popular culture for dealing with the world beyond the cheerful, grate-warmed living room" in which children play and in which parents seem capable of protecting them from any harm; further, they indicate the "absurdity" of not just their cultural but also their metaphysical circumstances. "Critically qualified by the ironic context," Levenson explains, "the childlike images provide bitter emblems of man's triviality and weakness when, having ventured from the safety of the living room, he makes his way through the chaos of the actuality beyond" (*Tales of Adventure* lxiv–lxv).

Holton accords with these views, lauding what he regards as a new sophistication in Crane's overall handling of figurative language in this story compared to his use of this technique in previous works. "Open Boat," he asserts, marks Crane's shift from using "bizarre" figures of speech as simple attention-getting devices to employing similes and metaphors that are "consciously organized to suggest a particular quality of perception in his speaker, to assert a theme, or to develop certain ironic attitudes toward material" (154–55). Holton does not limit himself to praise of this particular artistic development, however; he notes advances in style as well. In his view, "Open Boat" represents the first and perhaps the finest flowering of Crane's mature prose style, marked by a tempering of his earlier, "rather heavy-handed and mannered use of epithet"; a "less distorted, less grotesque syntax"; a greater number of active constructions along with "more energetic verbs"; a more subtle and exact use of color; and a skillful deployment of patterned repetition "to create a rhythmical sameness which charges a scene with an almost mesmeric quality of exhaustion" (150–53).

Bettina Knapp also praises Crane's handling of rhythms in "Open Boat," but she notes that he is capable not only of rhythmical sameness but also of rhythmic variations, created largely by the clustering of oddly punctuated sentences of varying lengths. This technique serves the story in terms of both physical intensity and thematic development, Knapp says, for in its aleatory jaggedness it "simulate[s] the heart beat of a man under extreme stress" and exemplifies "the utter senselessness of existence itself" (153–55).

Bergon and Gullason offer similarly favorable assessments of Crane's style in this story. Bergon identifies "Open Boat" as a prime example of the second of three stages, first formulated by Berryman, in Crane's stylistic development. The first stage, Bergon says, is best exemplified by *The Red Badge* and is notable for its abruptness and "relentless intensity," chiefly to be found in its imagery and "maintained by sheer willful invention" (4). In the second stage, Crane's prose is "more flexible," creating intensity through the more sophisticated method of "contrast and modulation." Concomitantly, Crane continues to use arresting figures but has now learned how to make them "thematically resonant" and "integral to a developing occasion" (4). The third stage is the style to be found in "The Monster"; quoting Berryman, Bergon describes it as "'much more closed, circumstantial, and 'normal' than the second'" (4).

Gullason catalogues the impressive number of formal devices Crane uses to great effect in "Open Boat," noting in particular his skillful handling of "ironic mood and tonal changes" and of the castaways' refrain "'If I am going to be drowned.'" This complaint, by virtue of its being "repeated and varied as in incremental poetry," creates a "pronounced and heightened rhythm that reflects on the monotony of [the castaways'] situation and their nearness to safety or disaster, on both the enclosing and liberating quality of the ocean." Thus, Gullason concludes, the refrain "links the world of man and nature" and powerfully unites the form and content of the story ("Renewal" 228).

Gregory Schirmer provides fuller remarks on Crane's handling of tone. Like Gullason, he notes the story's marked tonal shifts, and he argues that they are crucial in terms of thematic development. Critics have frequently pointed out, Schirmer says, that this development relies on a "constant tension and interplay" between two opposing views of man—as "a helpless and insignificant being adrift in a universe that is wholly indifferent to him," and as "part of a brotherhood that binds man to man in the face of that indifferent universe" (222). What critics have failed to notice, he continues, is that the tension between these views is largely produced by Crane's adept shifts through three distinct tones. The narrator's tone is primarily "distanced and ironic," and this attitude finds its counterpoint in that conveyed in the dialogue, which is expressive of "intimacy, loyalty, and a fundamental optimism in man's actions"; these two tones are then "modulated" by a second tone adopted by the narrator, one of neutrality rather than irony (222).

Gibson likewise notes these shifts and praises what he sees as Crane's unprecedented control over them. Much of Crane's work, he asserts, is marred by the author's lack of certainty regarding his own feelings about his characters and their situations, a lack that frequently causes him to shift tones without any guiding thematic principle. The most common manifestation of this condition, Gibson says, is that Crane turns his irony directly upon his characters, thereby "turning them into objects, into beings whose humanity he does not grant." His resistance of this impulse in "Open Boat," his surety of his own feelings about his creations, gives this story "a consistency of tone nearly unparalleled in Crane's major fiction" (127).

A number of critics regard the sophistication with which Crane connects structure to theme in this story as likewise nearly unparalleled. Colvert says that in this respect "Open Boat" is rivalled only by "Blue Hotel," *Maggie*, and *Red Badge*, these being, in his view, the only works in which Crane achieves a perfect harmony of structure and theme. The structure of each "is defined by the tension between two ironically divergent points of view: the narrow and deluding point of view of the actors and the enlarging and ruthlessly revealing point of view of the observer-narrator"; through this structural tension between self-deception and detached observation "Crane's essential theme" emerges—"the consequences of false pride, vanity, and blinding delusion" (200). In "Open Boat" in particular, this tension is created in the clash between the castaways' subjective view of their circumstances as momentously tragic and the narrator's more impersonal observation that their situation would look "picturesque" if seen from a balcony. Here, Colvert argues, the correspondent, like Henry Fleming in *Red Badge*, is able ultimately to attain the narrator's more objective stance and thereby survive, whereas in "Blue Hotel" and *Maggie* the protagonists resist abandoning their vainglorious illusions concerning their own importance and destroy themselves as a result.

Marcus sees the linkage of structure and theme in "Open Boat" as residing in a three-stage progression that the castaways undergo in their understanding of nature's attitude toward them (a schema briefly mentioned earlier, on p. 321, as a source for LaFrance's reading). In the first three sections of the story, Marcus says, Crane deploys "an abundance of animistic images" to convey that the men in the boat regard nature as "malevolently hostile" (512). Beginning in the fourth section, the repetitions of the "'If I am going to be drowned'" refrain mark their change to a view that nature's temper is not malevolent but rather "playfully and thoughtlessly cruel" (513). The first hint of their final, accurate conception of nature as indifferent comes as early as the second section, in Crane's depiction of the gulls who remain placid despite the sailors' desperation, but this awareness only fully develops in the correspondent's nighttime meditation in the sixth section and his interpretation of the wind tower in the seventh. This full development in turn brings to fruition the "profounder matter" of the men's deepening sense of the value of human community; this sense begins to evolve in the third section, when the men recognize their participation in "the subtle brotherhood of men," but it only fully crystallizes after the correspondent truly grasps nature's indifference and as a result feels compassion for the dying Legionnaire, and after the oiler's death, which reveals nature to be "accidentally destructive when circumstances permit" and the survivors thereby learn that they must "treasure brotherhood and life" (515).

Nagel also reads the story as "thematically structured" upon the correspondent's evolving understanding of nature, which is linked to the narrative structure of the boat's movement toward the shore. At the outset, Nagel says, the correspondent and his fellows have no understanding at all, as symbolized in the narrator's opening comment that they do not know "the color of the sky." They then progress through a malignant interpretation, expressed in their anger at the gulls; an incipient awareness of their "subtle brotherhood"; anger at fate, evinced in the "'If I am going to be drowned'" refrain; and finally reach an awareness of nature's aloofness and the concomitant need for human community, manifested in the correspondent's confrontation with the "high cold star on a winter's night" and his ensuing sympathy for the Legionnaire, which marks the completion of his "transformation from solipsism to solicitude" ("Narrative Method" 415). The precise nature of this transformation is crucial to a true understanding of the story, Nagel continues; the correspondent has achieved compassion—he has "overcome the limitations of a pride which allowed him to conceive of himself as the focal point of the hostility of the universe" ("Narrative Method" 417)—but a component of this achievement is a recognition of its limitations, an awareness that it is a valuable lesson but does not constitute omniscience. Due to Crane's linkage of structure and theme, of his connection between the gradual, halting nature of the castaways' physical progress toward shore and that of their perceptual development, "there is nothing in the story to suggest that proximity to death suddenly infuses a transcendent wisdom in the participants which lays bare to them the fundamental meaning of life itself. On the contrary, the emphasis throughout is on the *limits* of their point of view" ("Narrative Method" 417).

While Marcus and Nagel consider the "'If I am going to be drowned'" refrain a significant part of the story's linkage of structure and theme, Gibson, E. R. Hagemann, and Bender regard it as, one way or another, the essential, determining element. Gibson charts subtle variations in the refrain's repetitions that in his view reveal that the castaways move from blaming fate the first time it appears to acknowledging the indifference of nature the third time. For Crane, Gibson argues, the awareness of this metaphysical disinterest is in fact awareness of God, for Crane's belief is that God ultimately controls nature; in his poetry, he addresses his uncaring God directly, but in his fiction "Crane talks about God . . . in the only way his materials would allow him to—by talking about nature" (132).

Hagemann similarly analyzes changes in the refrain as an index to alterations in the castaways' thinking. In the story's first three sections, he says, the castaways rage against the injustice of nature, with their anger epitomized early in the fourth section in the first version of the refrain, in which they call fate an "old ninny-woman" and assert that their condition, the likelihood that they will drown after sighting land, "'is preposterous.'" Then, later in this fourth section, at the midpoint of the story, they encounter the man on shore who waves his coat at them, through which gesture, Hagemann says, they are being symbolically told, "you can't come in yet; you stay outside there and suffer; when your time comes you can come through; sorry, but that is the way it is" (74). This moment is in Hagemann's view the climax, after which the sailors' rage turns to acceptance, as expressed in the second and third refrains, at the end of the fourth and the beginning of the sixth section, in which the speakers no longer accuse fate or call their situation preposterous. This acceptance clears the way for the correspondent's further development in the sixth and seventh sections: it makes possible his discovery there of the bond of brotherhood that is forged by human compassion and courage.

Bender notes not changes within the refrain but rather its wholesale replacement by another recurrent utterance. This "refrain of rage," with its notes of self-centeredness and presumption, gradually gives way in the fifth and sixth sections to the correspondent's and the oiler's repeated requests to one another for relief at the boat's oars, "'[W]ill you spell me?'" This is the refrain of the "essential values" of compassion and brotherhood, Bender says, and both men unwaveringly honor it (79–80).

Clarence Walhout offers a more intricate if not ultimately more illuminating analysis of Crane's structural patterns and their thematic import. Focusing on what he terms the story's "internal structures," he identifies three major principles informing these structures: diachronicity, change occurring over an extended period of time; synchronicity, the complex of incidents occurring within a limited period of time; and referentiality, the relationship of events occurring in one time period to those occurring in another (363). Within the story's largest structural patterns, extended time—the overall movement of the narrative from day to night to a second day—and distance, the castaways are uncertain and ineffectual; when they "look into the distance or hear the sound of the distant surf, they are confused about their situation and their future, and they become angry and/or despairing." However, they can cope within the story's smaller structures, the more restricted temporal and spatial conditions of one moment at a time: "when they perceive sights and sounds close up, they do so clearly, and they grasp the reality of their situation" (365). Through these circumstances, Walhout says, Crane makes the point that human beings must begin with synchronicity and work only gradually toward a limited mastery of diachronicity. The story reveals, in other words, that "[t]he contours of reality beyond one's immediate situation are not clear or knowable; one can only struggle through the exigencies of the moment and accept whatever comes," through which struggle one can build "a more general understanding of what [one] should do," although that understanding will always be sharply bounded by the restricted nature of "human perception and effort" (365). This restrictedness chiefly resides in the fact that true knowledge depends upon direct experience, so that one's diachronic vision is always limited by the small amount of experience, compared to the range of extended time, that any individual can acquire. This point is borne out, Walhout says, in the story's third pattern, referentiality, which occurs when the correspondent relates his own circumstances to those of the Legionnaire in the poem and thereby for the first time truly comprehends the Legionnaire's plight. "This extratextual reference," Walhout concludes, "confirms the thematic patterns of the story as a whole by showing how interpretation of value depends on experience" (366).

John Ditsky also largely concerns himself with differing perceptions of time presented in "Open Boat," but he bases his examination on entirely different formal grounds. Using points of comparison set forth by author and composer Anthony Burgess in his book *This Man and Music*, Ditsky analyzes the story in relation to the structural principles of musical composition, arguing that Crane may not have had these principles consciously in mind but was at least not only a "literary craftsman" but "also by instinct a creator of music" (130). In general terms, Ditsky says, the story resembles a piece of music in that it uses a repetition of motifs to achieve many of its effects and that "it not only unfolds over a period of described time, clock time, but also delineates the ways in which a psychological predicament can alter one's time sense, and thus teach a person to tell time differently"—in this case, "to adopt the tempi set by a metronome of nature," the sea. More specifically, he argues that the story, with its five voices, those of the four characters and the narrator, can be understood as a "piano quintet" or a "concerto for quartet and orchestra, the sea serving as *tutti* [the direction for all instruments to perform together]," and that, with this idea in view, the story's seven sections can be read as the separate movements of this concerto, each with its own rhythm and mood but all thematically unified (121). The unifying principle here is the correspondent's gradual movement from discord to harmony with nature, his progressively clearer understanding of the cosmos and acceptance of the individual's small place in it; at the finale, Ditsky says, the correspondent's "experience of attending nature's concert . . . has left him humming nature's tune" (128).

Five critics offer even more tightly focused appreciations of Crane's technique in "Open Boat," calling attention not to style, imagery, or structure as a whole but rather to individual sentences and images as significant contributors to the story's themes. Bergon notes the meaningful construction of several sentences. The narrator's observation early in the story that "[m]any a man ought to have a bath-tub larger than the boat which here rode upon the sea" (*Tales of Adventure* 68), he says, exemplifies Crane's frequent strategy of interrupting "intense narratives with trite generalizations" for the purpose of shifting voice and perspective and thereby revealing that an experience that seems "intense, immediate, overwhelming, and wrong" can equally be regarded, from another perspective, as "small, silly, and insignificant." But Crane does not stop at that insight, Bergon contends; by observing that "many a man *ought* to have a bath-tub larger" rather than simply saying that "many a man *has* a bath-tub larger" he makes the further point that the men in the boat themselves find their condition ridiculous. Through his careful choice of verbs, Crane here "approaches the outraged cry of consciousness that often comes from his characters in moments of stress" (19–20).

In three later sentences, Bergon continues, Crane epitomizes another of his points regarding human consciousness, the inevitable relativity of its perceptual and interpretative processes. In describing the lighthouse that the castaways see in the story's third section, the narrator says that it "appeared like a little gray shadow on the sky" and that "[t]he man at the oars could not be prevented from turning his head rather often to try for a glimpse of this little gray shadow" (*Tales of Adventure* 74). By beginning and ending in this manner, Bergon says, with the way the lighthouse appeared to the men rather than the information that this shadow is in fact the lighthouse, Crane seeks to sustain "an immediate optical image" to emphasize to the reader that "this is the point at which perception begins, a point that people are rarely aware of and rarely remember." Conventional literary descriptions, such as one that would simply state that the men saw the lighthouse, "bypass both that tiny moment when objects strike human perception and that tiny moment when events become experience." Crane's more unorthodox approach concentrates attention on these moments, making the reader aware that "'experience' is a relational term, and an experience cannot be regarded apart from the experiencer" (15–16). This point is driven home, in Bergon's view, by the meticulous construction of the final sentence of the story: "When it came night, the white waves paced to and fro in the moonlight, and the wind brought the sound of the great sea's voice to the men on shore, and they felt that they could then be interpreters" (*Tales of Adventure* 92). The odd placement of *then* in this sentence, Bergon says "emphasizes time rather than inevitable causality" as the major factor in the men's interpretation and thus "introduces a gap—and perhaps a discrepancy—between the experience and the interpretation" (8).

Nagel takes note of the descriptive tags by which Crane identifies his castaways—"the captain," "the correspondent," "the cook," and "the oiler." This reliance on epithets is one of his frequent techniques, as in *The Red Badge*, which charts the actions of "the youth," "the loud soldier," "the tall soldier," and "the tattered soldier," but Nagel asserts that in "Open Boat" Crane uses them with unprecedented effectiveness to suggest "depth of character," particularly in the cases of the correspondent and the captain. *Correspondent*, Nagel says, conveys that character's "formulative powers and philosophical frame of reference," while *captain* explains that character's "'dejection and indifference'" due to the loss of the ship and much of the crew and also his "authority in commanding the boat" (*Impressionism* 120).

Eddy Dow and Daniel Muhlestein find considerable significance in the brief moment at the end of the third section when, in a burst of hope, the correspondent discovers that four of the eight cigars in his pocket are still dry and shares them with the others, one of whom has three dry matches. Dow reads the entire story in numerical miniature in this scene: the eight cigars represent the eight men that Dow says were aboard the sinking ship, the four soaked ones signifying the four who drowned and the four dry ones standing for the quartet in the dinghy; and the three dry matches represent the three members of that group who will reach the shore. The purpose of this symbolism, Dow says, is to make this moment when the castaways are at their most hopeful "complex and poignant" (48). Muhlestein makes much the same point. He does not read significance into the eight cigars—perhaps because Dow may be mistaken in asserting that the ship's complement was eight men (Dow bases his count on the narrator's saying that the captain recollects "seven turned faces" at the sinking of the ship, but most critics believe, based on the number of men involved in the actual *Commodore* disaster, that these seven are the men left behind on the wreck, not the entire crew)—but he too sees the four dry cigars and the three dry matches as respectively representing the four castaways currently alive and the three who will survive the surf, with the point of this numerical symbolism being an undercutting of the confidence of the four smokers, an ironic comment on "the illusions of men" (43).

The most elaborate—if not the most persuasive—reading predicated on a single image or sentence is proffered by Bill Brown. At the end of the story, when the men leap into the water and swim for shore, the correspondent is saved by being carried over the dinghy and close to land by a large wave; Brown's argument is that when the narrator observes, apropos of this event, that "[a]n overturned boat in the surf is not a plaything to a swimming man" (*Tales of Adventure* 91), Crane's intention is not simple irony, as one might assume, but rather an at least partly serious effort to make clear to the reader that this moment is a not a matter of sport but rather of life and death. Crane might fear that a reader would harbor this misconception, seeing the moment as playful—"ludic"—rather than serious—"agonistic," Brown contends, because of the social transformation taking place in America in the late nineteenth and early twentieth centuries. This is the era, Brown explains, of "the rise of organized recreation, enthusiasm for sport, and the commodification of leisure"—the era of "what the economist Simon Patten famously described (in 1907) as the transition from a 'pain' to a 'pleasure' economy" (25). One of the results of this transition is the common use of sports metaphors in all types of texts; Crane is thus aware of the manner in which, even in "serious" literature, "'the recreational' asserts itself, mediating the representation of human conflict" (24). For Crane, Brown says, such mediation is inappropriate to the life-and-death struggle he depicts in "Open Boat," and so he seeks to separate these two in his own discourse, as in his assertion that the boat is not a plaything. This very separation, however, threatens the opposite effect, in Brown's reading: Crane's "agonistic discourse expresses . . . the agony of the contest for survival, the agony of absolute unfreedom—but the story's ludic discourse, its images of recreation, contests the authority of that expression" (29).

This contesting in turn evinces anxiety about a deeper problem, Brown continues: the philosophical closeness of the ludic and agonistic—the possibility that what are life-and-death struggles form one perspective may be merely play from another. Brown sees Crane dramatizing this problem on the level of action when the spectators on shore assume the castaways are fishing—"playing"—rather than struggling for their lives, and when the castaways in turn cannot understand what one of those spectators means by waving his coat at them and conclude that "'He's just playing'" (*Tales of Adventure* 81). This valuation takes on still deeper, ontological import, Brown says, in that "the absence of signification, the lack of meaning" in this gesture constitutes the classical definition of *playing*, "non-purposive, ateleological activity," and that, by this definition, "'the unconcern of the universe'" regarding the castaways' plight "discloses a universe at play, . . . a universe that means nothing, wherein not-playing appears as the exception rather than the rule" (39).

Still another level of anxiety for Crane, in Brown's view, arises from the fact that, as a fiction, a story, "Open Boat" itself may be taken as the kind of play that he seeks to excise from its text; the story is a "a tale intended to be after the fact," as its subtitle asserts, but this intention, Brown says, cannot "prevent its consumption as no more than a tale" (40). The final effect of these levels of contested authority and anxiety, Brown concludes, is that "'man' names that being who dreams only of an end of play where there is no mistaking pain for play," an end where one can be certain that suffering has a purpose. *Dreams* is the operative word here because there is no such certainty even at the end of the story, for the survivors cannot be sure that the voice of the sea that they feel they can interpret is truly "a voice that does not play" (42).

Works Cited

Adams, Richard. "Naturalistic Fiction: 'The Open Boat.'" *Tulane Studies in English* 4 (1954):137–46.

Autrey, Max L. "The Word Out of the Sea: A View of Crane's 'The Open Boat.'" *Arizona Quarterly* 30 (1974):101–10.

Bassan, Maurice. Introduction. *Stephen Crane: A Collection of Critical Essays*. Ed. Maurice Bassan. Englewood Cliffs, N.J.: Prentice-Hall, 1967, 1–11.

Bender, Bert. "The Nature and Significance of 'Experience' in 'The Open Boat.'" *Journal of Narrative Technique* 9 (1979):70–80.

Benfey, Christopher. *The Double Life of Stephen Crane*. New York: Knopf, 1992.

Bergon, Frank. *Stephen Crane's Artistry*. New York: Columbia University Press, 1975.

Berryman, John. *Stephen Crane*. New York: Sloane, 1950.

Bowers, Fredson. Textual Introduction. *Tales of Adventure*. Vol. 5 of The University of Virginia Edition of *The Works of Stephen Crane*. Ed. Fredson Bowers. Charlottesville: University Press of Virginia, 1970, cxxxiii–cxcv.

Brennan, Joseph X. "Stephen Crane and the Limits of Irony." *Criticism* 11 (1969):183–200.

Brown, Bill. "Interlude: The Agony of Play in 'The Open Boat.'" *Arizona Quarterly* 45 (1988):23–46.

Buitenhuis, Peter. "The Essentials of Life: 'The Open Boat' as Existentialist Fiction." *Modern Fiction Studies* 5 (1959):243–50.

Burns, Landon, Jr. "'The Open Boat.'" *Studies in Short Fiction* 3 (1966):455–58.

Cady, Edwin H. Introduction. *Tales, Sketches, and Reports*. Vol. 8 of The University of Virginia Edition of *The Works of Stephen Crane*. Ed. Fredson Bowers. Charlottesville: University Press of Virginia, 1973, xxi–xli.

———. *Stephen Crane*. Rev. ed. New York: Twayne, 1982.

Chametzky, Jules. "Realism, Cultural Politics, and Language as Meditation in Mark Twain and Others." *Prospects* 8 (1983):183–95.

Colvert, James B. Introduction. *Tales of War*. Vol. 6 of The University of Virginia Edition of *The Works of Stephen Crane*. Ed. Fredson Bowers. Charlottesville: University Press of Virginia, 1970, xi–xxxvi.

———. "Stephen Crane." *American Realists and Naturalists*. Vol. 12 of *Dictionary of Literary Biography*. Ed. Donald Pizer and Earl N. Harbert. Detroit: Gale Research, 1982, 100–24.

———. *Stephen Crane*. New York: Harcourt Brace Jovanovich, 1984.

———. "Style and Meaning in Stephen Crane's 'The Open Boat.'" *Texas Studies in English* 37 (1958):34–45.

Conder, John J. *Naturalism in American Fiction: The Classic Phase*. Lexington: University Press of Kentucky, 1984.

Crane, Stephen. "A Man Adrift on a Slim Spar." *Poems and Literary Remains*. Vol. 10 of The University of Virginia Edition of *The Works of Stephen Crane*. Ed. Fredson Bowers. Charlottesville: University Press of Virginia, 1975, 83.

———. "Ghosts on the Jersey Coast." *Tales, Sketches, and Reports* 638–42.

———. "Six Years Afloat." *Tales, Sketches, and Reports* 648–52.

———. "Stephen Crane's Own Story." *Reports of War*. Volume 9 of The University of Virginia Edition of *The Works of Stephen Crane*. Ed. Fredson Bowers. Charlottesville: University Press of Virginia, 1971:85–94.

———. "The Ghostly Sphinx of Metedeconk." *Tales, Sketches, and Reports* 645–48.

———. "The Open Boat." *Tales of Adventure* 68–92.

———. "The Reluctant Voyagers." *Tales, Sketches, and Reports* 14–33.

———. "The Wreck of the *New Era*." *Tales, Sketches, and Reports* 580–84.

———. "To the Maiden." *Poems and Literary Remains*. Vol. 10 of The University of Virginia Edition of *The Works of Stephen Crane*. Ed. Fredson Bowers. Charlottesville: University Press of Virginia, 1975, 47.

Day, Cyrus. "Stephen Crane and the Ten-Foot Dingey." *Boston University Studies in English* 3 (Winter 1957):193–213.

Deamer, Robert Glen. "Remarks on the Western Stance of Stephen Crane." *Western American Literature* 15 (Summer 1980):122–41.

———. "Stephen Crane's 'Code' and Its Western Connections." *The Importance of Place in the American Literature of Hawthorne, Thoreau, Crane, Adams, and Faulkner*. New York: Edwin Mellen, 1990, 139–52.

Denny, Neville. "Imagination and Experience in Stephen Crane." *English Studies in Africa* 9 (1966):28–42.

Ditsky, John. "The Music in 'The Open Boat.'" *North Dakota Quarterly* 56 (1988):119–30.

Dow, Eddy. "Cigars, Matches, and Men in 'The Open Boat.'" *Re: Artes Liberales* 2 (1975):47–49.

Ellison, Ralph. "Stephen Crane and the Mainstream of American Fiction." *Shadow and Act*. New York: Random House, 1964, 60–76.

Frederick, John T. "The Fifth Man in 'The Open Boat.'" *CEA Critic* 30.8 (1968):1, 12–14.

Frus, Phyllis. "Two Tales Intended to Be 'After the Fact': 'Stephen Crane's Own Story' and 'The Open Boat.'" *Literary Nonfiction: Theory, Criticism, Pedagogy*. Ed. Chris Anderson. Carbondale: Southern Illinois University Press, 1989, 125–51.

Geismar, Maxwell. *Rebels and Ancestors*. Boston: Houghton Mifflin, 1953.

Gerstenberger, Donna. "'The Open Boat': Additional Perspective." *Modern Fiction Studies* 17 (Winter 1971–72):558.

Gibson, Donald B. *The Fiction of Stephen Crane*. Carbondale: Southern Illinois University Press, 1968.

Gleckner, Robert F. "Stephen Crane and the Wonder of Man's Conceit." *Modern Fiction Studies* 5 (1959):271–81.

Going, W. T. "William Higgins and Crane's 'The Open Boat': A Note about Fact and Fiction." *Papers on English Language and Literature* 1 (1965):79–82.

Greenfield, Stanley B. "The Unmistakable Stephen Crane." *PMLA* 73 (1958):562–72.

Griffith, Clark. "Stephen Crane and the Ironic Last Word." *Philological Quarterly* 47 (1968):83–91.

Gullason, Thomas A. "The New Criticism and Older Ones: Another Ride in 'The Open Boat.'" *CEA Critic* 31 (June 1969):8–9.

———. "The Short Story: Revision and Renewal." *Studies in Short Fiction* 19 (1982):221–30.

———. "Stephen Crane's Short Stories: The True Road." *Stephen Crane's Career: Perspectives and Evaluations*. Ed. Thomas A. Gullason. New York: New York University Press, 1972, 470–86.

Hagemann, E. R. "'Sadder Than the End': Another Look at 'The Open Boat.'" *Stephen Crane in Transition: Centenary Essays*. Ed. Joseph Katz. DeKalb: Northern Illinois University Press, 1972, 66–85.

Halliburton, David. *The Color of the Sky: A Study of Stephen Crane*. Cambridge: Cambridge University Press, 1989.

Hoffman, Daniel G. *The Poetry of Stephen Crane*. New York: Columbia University Press, 1957.

Holton, Milne. *Cylinder of Vision: The Fiction and Journalistic Writings of Stephen Crane*. Baton Rouge: Louisiana State University Press, 1972.

Jackson, David H. "Textual Questions Raised by Crane's 'Soldier of the Legion.'" *American Literature* 55 (1983):77–80.

Kazin, Alfred. "The Youth: Stephen Crane." *An American Procession*. New York: Knopf, 1984, 256–74.

Kent, Thomas L. "The Problem of Knowledge in 'The Open Boat' and 'The Blue Hotel.'" *American Literary Realism* 14 (1981):262–68.

Kissane, Leedice. "Interpretation Through Language: A Study of the Metaphors in Stephen Crane's 'The Open Boat.'" *Rendezvous* 1 (1966):18–22. Rpt. in *Stephen Crane's Career*, 410–16.

Knapp, Bettina L. *Stephen Crane*. New York: Ungar, 1987.

LaFrance, Marston. *A Reading of Stephen Crane*. Oxford: Clarendon, 1971.

Levenson, J. C. Introduction. *Tales of Adventure* xv–cxxxii.

———. Introduction. *The Third Violet* and *Active Service*. Vol. 3 of The University of Virginia Edition of *The Works of Stephen Crane*. Ed. Fredson Bowers. Charlottesville: University Press of Virginia, 1976, xi–lxii.

Lytle, Andrew H. "'The Open Boat': A Pagan Tale." *The Hero with the Private Parts*. Baton Rouge: Louisiana State University Press, 1966, 60–75.

Marcus, Mordecai. "The Threefold View of Nature in 'The Open Boat.'" *Philological Quarterly* 61 (1962):511–15.

Metzger, C. R. "Realistic Devices in Stephen Crane's 'The Open Boat.'" *Midwest Quarterly* 4 (Summer 1962):47–54.

Meyers, Robert. "Crane's 'The Open Boat.'" *Explicator* 21 (1963):60.

Molle, Charles A. "The Ironical Triumph of Stephen Crane's 'The Open Boat.'" *Wittenberg Review* 1 (1990):105–15.

Monteiro, George. "The Logic Beneath 'The Open Boat.'" *Georgia Review* 26 (1972):326–35.

———. "Text and Picture in 'The Open Boat.'" *Journal of Modern Literature* 11 (1984):307–11.

Muhlestein, Daniel K. "Crane's 'The Open Boat.'" *Explicator* 45 (1978):42–43.

Nagel, James. "Impressionism in 'The Open Boat' and 'A Man and Some Others.'" *Research Studies* 43 (1975):27–37.

———. "The Narrative Method of 'The Open Boat.'" *Revue des Langues Vivantes* 39 (1973):409–17.

———. *Stephen Crane and Literary Impressionism*. University Park: Pennsylvania State University Press, 1980.

Napier, James J. "Land Imagery in 'The Open Boat.'" *CEA Critic* 29, 7 (April 1967):15.

Overland, Orm. "The Impressionism of Stephen Crane: A Study in Style and Technique." *America Norvegica* 61 (1966):239–85.

Perosa, Sergio. "Naturalism and Impressionism in Stephen Crane's Fiction." *Stephen Crane: A Collection of Critical Essays*. Ed. Maurice Bassan. Englewood Cliffs, N.J.: Prentice-Hall, 1967, 80–94.

Piacentino, Edward J. "Kindred Spirits: The Correspondent and the Dying Soldier in Crane's 'The Open Boat.'" *Markham Review* 12 (1983):64–67.

Pizer, Donald. *Realism and Naturalism in Nineteenth-Century American Literature*. Rev. ed. Carbondale: Southern Illinois University Press, 1984.

Randel, William. "From Slate to Emerald Green: New Light on Crane's Jacksonville Visit." *Nineteenth-Century Fiction* 19 (1965):357–68.

———. "The Cook in 'The Open Boat.'" *American Literature* 34 (1962):405–11.

Rath, Sura P., and Mary Neff Shaw. "The Dialogic Narrative of 'The Open Boat.'" *College Literature* 18.2 (1991):94–106.

Rogers, Rodney O. "Stephen Crane and Impressionism." *Nineteenth-Century Fiction* 24 (1969):292–304.

Schirmer, Gregory A. "Becoming Interpreters: The Importance of Tone in Crane's 'The Open Boat.'" *American Literary Realism* 15 (1982):221–31.

Shulman, Robert. "Community, Perception, and the Development of Stephen Crane: From *The Red Badge* to 'The Open Boat.'" *American Literature* 50 (1978):441–60.

Skerrett, Joseph T., Jr. "Changing Seats in the Open Boat: Alternative Attitudes in Two Stories by Stephen Crane." *Studies in the Humanities* 4 (1982):22–27.

Smith, Leverett T. "Stephen Crane's Calvinism." *Canadian Review of American Studies* 2 (1971):13–25.

Solomon, Eric. *Stephen Crane: From Parody to Realism*. Cambridge: Harvard University Press, 1966.

Spofford, William K. "Stephen Crane's 'The Open Boat': Fact or Fiction?" *American Literary Realism* 12 (1979):316–21.

Stallman, R. W. "Crane's Short Stories." *The Houses That James Built*. East Lansing: Michigan State University Press, 1961, 103–10.

———. "The Land-Sea Irony in 'The Open Boat.'" *CEA Critic* 30 (May 1968):15.

———. *Stephen Crane: A Biography*. New York: George Braziller, 1968.

———. "Stephen Crane: A Revaluation." *Critiques and Essays on Modern Fiction: 1920–1951*. Ed. John W. Aldridge. New York: Ronald, 1952, 244–69.

Stappenbeck, Herb. "Crane's 'The Open Boat.'" *Explicator* 34 (1976):41.

Stein, William B. "Stephen Crane's *Homo Absurdus*." *Bucknell Review* 8 (1959): 168–88.

Stewart, Randall. *American Literature and Christian Doctrine*. Baton Rouge: Louisiana State University Press, 1958.

Stone, Edward. "Crane's 'Soldier of the Legion.'" *American Literature* 30 (1958):242–44.

Walhout, Clarence. "Ives, Crane, Marin, and 'The Mind Behind the Maker.'" *Christian Scholar's Review* 16 (1987):355–72.

Wells, H. G. "Stephen Crane: From an English Standpoint." *North American Review* 171 (August 1900):233–42. Rpt. in *Stephen Crane's Career: Perspectives and Evaluations*. Ed. Thomas A. Gullason. New York: New York University Press, 1972, 126–34.

Wertheim, Stanley, and Paul Sorrentino, eds. *The Correspondence of Stephen Crane*. Vol. 1. New York: Columbia University Press, 1988.

Westbrook, Max. "Stephen Crane and the Personal Universal." *Modern Fiction Studies* 8 (1962):351–60.

———. "Stephen Crane: The Pattern of Affirmation." *Nineteenth-Century Fiction* 14 (1959):219–29.

Wolford, Chester L. *Stephen Crane: A Study of the Short Fiction*. Boston: Twayne, 1989.

The Pace of Youth

Publication History

This story was first published with the title "The Pace of Youth" as a two-part feature syndicated to various American newspapers by Bacheller, Johnson, and Bacheller. It is known to have run on January 17 and 18, 1895, in the *Dayton, Ohio Daily Journal* and the *Kansas City Star*; on January 18 and 19 in the *New York Press*, the *Minneapolis Tribune*, and the *Nebraska State Journal*; and, without the two-part division, on June 30 in the *San Francisco Examiner* (Bowers, "Textual Introduction" cxxxix). The story had previously appeared, in a version only slightly different from that syndicated by Bacheller, under the title "The Merry-Go-Round" in the January 2, 1895, issue of a London weekly magazine, *The Sketch*. This initial publication was unknown to Crane scholars and bibliographers until Robert Morace rediscovered it in 1978. His explanation that Crane's alleged mention in a lost letter of a work called "The Merry-Go-Round" is actually a reference to this story rather than to a book by that title (147) put to rest the persistent rumor, begun in 1923 by Thomas Beer (183) and Vincent Starrett (9–10), that "The Pace of Youth" was actually a chapter of a lost novel to be called *The Merry-Go-Round*, which Crane supposedly worked on while reporting on the American blockading fleet off Cuba during the Spanish-American War in 1898 (Stallman 60–61), or while living in Cuba afterward (Starrett 10), or while dying at Brede Place in 1899 (Martin 147).

After the story ran as "The Pace of Youth" in the American press, it next appeared in the collection *"The Open Boat" and Other Stories*, published in London by William Heinemann on April 18, 1898 (Bowers, "Textual" cxxxv–xxxvi). In this volume it was listed as part of a group labeled "Midnight Sketches," the rest of which were pieces Crane had written about the Bowery. Its inclusion in this group thus seems odd, but there are two possible explanations. The first is that most of these Bowery sketches had originally been published in 1893 in the *New York Press*, the same paper in which "Pace" ran in 1895; perhaps Crane regarded the group that appeared in the Heinemann volume not as a Bowery collection but as a *Press* collection. A tangential bit of primary support for this possibility appears in a November 29, 1896, letter from Crane to his brother William, in which Crane mentions a never-fulfilled plan to publish a volume entitled *Midnight Sketches* that will consist of "fifteen or twenty short sketches of New York street life and so on" (*Correspondence* I, 265). The final phrase suggests that Crane might have intended this title to denote a work including but not limited to Bowery tales.

The second and probably more likely explanation is that Crane regarded the "Midnight Sketches" as mere filler in the Heinemann volume and thus was not concerned with their internal coherence. Crane had originally assembled a shorter version of this volume, lacking the "Midnight Sketches"; this version was published in America under the Doubleday and McClure imprint on the same day the Heinemann book was released in England. However, Heinemann had requested a longer collection, and so Crane supplied the publisher with these sketches, which seem to have been what he "had on hand at the moment, not necessarily what he wanted collected with his prime stories found in the Doubleday and McClure volume" (Bowers, Foreword vii).

Pioneering Crane editor Wilson Follett included "Pace" in volume 11, published in 1926, of *The Work of Stephen Crane* (12 vols., New York: Knopf, 1925–27), and Thomas A. Gullason also collected it in *The Complete Short Stories and Sketches of Stephen Crane* (Garden City, N.Y.: Doubleday, 1963).

Circumstances of Composition

The only information about when and where this story was written comes from Corwin Knapp Linson, a painter and illustrator who was one of Crane's close friends during the years Crane lived in New York City. Linson says that he arrived at Crane's rooms at 1064 Avenue A one morning during the spring of 1893 to find Crane completing "Pace" while wearing a wet towel turban-fashion on his head. The writer explained that he had worked on the story all night in a fever of inspiration; the towel "'cool[ed] the machinery'" (27–29). While no one has questioned the physical particulars of this charming anecdote, J. C. Levenson has suggested that Linson might have misremembered the date—that this encounter might actually have occurred in the spring of 1894 (xxiv).

Sources and Influences

Concerning his writing process, Willa Cather recalled Crane's explaining to her that "[t]he detail of a thing has to filter through my blood, and then it comes out like a native product, but it takes forever" (233). Levenson notes that "Pace" illustrates Crane's point here as graphically as any story in his corpus, for it emerged only gradually out of ten years of personal and journalistic experience (xx). Crane had lived on and off in the setting of this story, the New Jersey shore resort Asbury Park, since he was twelve, and he had been writing about it, for the news service that his older brother Townley ran there for the *New York Tribune*, since he was sixteen. He had first described the seaside merry-go-round that figures prominently in "Pace" in an 1892 *Tribune* piece entitled "Joys of Seaside Life," and he had initially addressed the story's main theme of youthful courtship in another feature from that same year, "On the Boardwalk." This latter article, Levenson further points out, also reveals the seashore genesis of two of the salient thematic features of "Pace," for it is here that Crane "began working out the ironies between summer-resort illusions and everyday facts . . . [and] combining his deflationary realism with his sense of the dazzle of appearances" (xx). Crane himself corroborated Levenson's point about long personal experience with specific regard to "Pace" in conversation with Linson, as recorded in Linson's memoir of Crane. Reading the manuscript of "Pace," Linson marveled at the accuracy with which Crane described his characters despite his not having been to Asbury Park in months. Crane responded, "'Can't you make sketches from memory? Of course. Well, haven't I known these types since I was a kid?'" (29)

But Crane, Linson, and Levenson all fail to mention that the story has its roots not merely in types but in a specific incident from Crane's Asbury Park years: his "courtship" of Lily Brandon Munroe (Stallman 60; Holton 22; Colvert 35–36). Crane first met and became infatuated with Munroe, an unhappily married woman several years older than he, at Asbury Park in the summer of 1892. He squired her around the resort, rode the merry-go-round with her, and tried to persuade her to leave her husband for him, a plea he renewed several times over the next few years but which she consistently rejected on the grounds of his youth and lack of promise as a steady provider. "Pace," given its ending with the lovers' happily defiant escape from the restrictions laid down by the heroine's father, appears to be Crane's "wish-fulfillment," to use Robert W. Stallman's words (60), of his relationship with Munroe, "Lily" in real life becoming "Lizzie" in the story. Stallman further notes the irony that on the weekend when "Pace" first appeared in the American press Crane was in Washington, D.C., making his final fruitless appeal to Munroe, urging her to accompany him on his impending trip to the West and Mexico; Stallman points out that this pattern of first writing a story with a desirable ending and then trying to live it out is characteristic of Crane (60).

If finding biographical sources for this story is relatively easy, discovering literary antecedents among the writers Crane admired is difficult. The only such influence anyone has noted is that of William Dean Howells; Levenson says that in making his lovers workers at the seashore rather than vacationers there and in creating obstacles between them rarely encountered in romances—the carousel animals, the children riding those animals, the wire front of the ticket booth, and the cashier's sign—Crane displays a "Howellsian instinct for the commonplace." The effect of this instinct, Levenson explains, is that like Howells, Crane is here "restoring the comedy of sentiment by getting rid of sentimentality": Crane gives the reader a situation that is "superficially the opposite of romantic but actually emphasize[s] the rightness of the heart's free choice" (xxvi). Levenson concludes, however, by asserting that when Stimson packs his gun for his pursuit of the lovers, Crane goes beyond the boundaries of Howells's middle-class realism and into his own particular territory, wherein is revealed "the possibility of violence that lies just behind the commonplace romance or the conventional role" (xxvii).

Christopher Wilson sees in this exceeding of Howells's precepts a problem with any attempt to point to conventional kinds of literary influences on Crane in this or any other story. Crane's work has consistently "eluded precise classification," Wilson says, because Crane mixes realism with "visual impressionism," producing a fluid, "playful" style marked by "exotic coloration, flamboyant imagery, and Alice-in-Wonderland inversions of scale and location" (31). Wilson proposes that this mixture points to a nonliterary source as Crane's primary influence: the "rhetoric of amusement" to be found in the seaside parks flourished during Crane's lifetime and with which, as "Pace" and some of his journalistic pieces make clear, he was quite familiar as both an attendee and a newspaper reporter. What Wilson means by "rhetoric of amusement" is not only the verbal but also the visual and emotional messages conveyed in such parks; these locales "familiarized Crane with the intricacies of an artistic 'pitch,' the self-conscious trickery, exoticism, and inflated rhetoric inherent in the drumming for customers on the boardwalk," and they also emphasized flamboyance, exuberance, and play through their attractions—rides, games, fabulous exhibits, and so on (34). This milieu was attractive to Crane on its own terms, Wilson argues, but it was made doubly so by the fact that both of his straitlaced Methodist parents condemned it in their writings on the proper conduct of Christian life, with the ultimate result that it "affected both his style and his moral outlook" (34). "Pace" in particular exemplifies Crane's application of "the rhetoric of amusement both philosophically and stylistically," Wilson says, by virtue of its being literally set in the realm of play—with this realm therefore presented as a place where serious matters can be addressed, by the exuberant stylistic figures Crane employs, and, perhaps most crucially, by Crane's use of the merry-go-round, one of the park's most prominent amusements, as the story's central symbol. The salient feature of this ride as Crane describes it is that, as Frank and Lizzie conduct their love affair around it covertly, under the watchful eye of Stimson, children ride on it, leaning out to grab at rings while their parents' cautioning cries are drowned out by the exuberant noises of play. Thus, Wilson says, Crane creates "a metaphor of courtship (reaching for rings) framed by failed communication between generations" (37), a metaphor that also informs the action of the second half of the story, for although Frank and Lizzie flee the literal merry-go-round and they in one carriage and Stimson in another are physically moving linearly, all three of these characters are still symbolically moving in the circle of the carousel, enacting the "universal comedy" of the unchanging cycles of love and of youth supplanting age (38).

Joseph Kwiat discerns influence of another nonliterary type; he asserts that this story is proof that Crane derived technical benefits from his close association with graphic artists during the period of its writing. Kwiat says that "in his skillful handling of the problems of perspective, composition, and color for the purpose of capturing a mood and an 'impression'" in the beach and amusement park scenes, Crane is applying verbal techniques that he adapted from the visual ones his friends employed in producing their drawings and paintings (334).

Relationship to Other Crane Works

This story is most closely connected with Crane's two other works that focus on young love and courtship—the short story "A Grey Sleeve" and the novel *The Third Violet*. That an author as prolific as Crane should have essayed this subject so rarely may seem surprising at first, but a reading of *Violet* and "Sleeve" alongside "Pace," and a perusal of the criticism on all three, provide a clear explanation: Crane had very little skill with this subject. Noting Crane's conventionally sentimental tone and the stilted dialogue of the lovers in *Violet*, John Berryman says Crane "stammers on this theme" (122), while Chester Wolford notes the equal lameness of tone and conversation in "Sleeve" (64). These critics, along with most others who have addressed these works, agree that "Pace" is Crane's only successful love story, due to four characteristics: its brevity (Berryman 123; Holton 132), its lightly parodic tone (Holton 132; Wolford 64), its use of Stimson to provide action (Berryman 123), and its paucity of talk between the lovers, which obviates Crane's ineptness with romantic dialogue (Colvert 91) and also adds a touch of realism and sympathy, since these characters' inarticulateness is natural and affecting at their ages and stations in life (Berryman 123).

A less obvious but perhaps more significant connection is to "The Bride Comes to Yellow Sky"; although the characters are older in this story than in "Pace," each tale presents a decision by a pair of lovers to be together in defiance of their society and details the consequences of that decision for the society (Levenson xvi). The result of these "two singular [for Crane] visions of happiness" in love (Berryman 265) is that one order is swept away by another—age by youth in "Pace," West by East in "Bride." Wolford finds a marked progression of artistry in this comparison. He notes that whereas "Pace" regards its lovers only in the context of their immediate situation, "Bride" presents its pair within the larger context of history; and that while "Pace" presents a simplistically optimistic triumph of young over old, "Bride" offers the more complex view that the triumphant Eastern order is in fact older and far less fresh and honest than its Western opponent (28).

Other critics have traced more general connections between "Pace" and the rest of Crane's output. Levenson charts an escalation in violence that begins in this story and runs through a number of others: in "Pace" a revolver is "wildly brandished," in "One Dash—Horses" and "The Five White Mice" it is "seriously drawn" and pointed, and in "A Man and Some Others" it is finally fired and kills (xlix). Frank Bergon says that one theme that stamps Crane as "modern" is his depiction of the dehumanization and depersonalization of the individual, often expressed as a growing similarity between men and machines. This idea is most particularly evident in *The Red Badge of Courage*, but it is clear in "Pace," for here Stimson "is a less animate character than is his giant machine, his merry-go-round" (146). David Halliburton discerns a third thematic pattern, this one encoded in the story's title. The idea of *pace* and differences in pace, conceived of as "a measure of competitive status, a way of telling who is winning or losing," is crucial to Crane's "agonistic" imagination (257), appearing in a central role not only in this story but also in "Five Mice," "The Wise Men," *Maggie: A Girl of the Streets, Red Badge,* and *Active Service* (258).

Stimson's behavior provides still another link to Crane's work as a whole. Halliburton points out that in his excitability, pugnacity, and pompous, swaggering language, Stimson closely resembles the "little man" of Crane's Sullivan County sketches, written early in his career (258). As is usually the case with that little man, these traits lead Stimson to humiliation at the end of the story, to the mortifying and therefore partly rejected awareness that he is not in fact master of his situation, as he had formerly believed. A connection here to Scratchy Wilson in "Bride" is readily apparent as well, but, as Marston LaFrance demonstrates, it is possible to see this "pattern of psychological action"—self-inflation followed by deflation and the possibility of increased self-awareness—as operative not just in these few works but in nearly all of Crane's writing (35). More specifically, according to LaFrance, Stimson is a typical Crane protagonist in that he begins with an illusion—that he can control Lizzie and Frank—and when he is forced to recognize it as merely an illusion he follows Crane's usual pattern, reacting first with rage and then with acceptance of this "deflating truth" (78).

Finally, James Nagel notes a connection of technique between "Pace" and several other Crane stories. As the lovers happily return from their first walk together, the narrator says that a line of "gay paper lanterns, flashing, fleeting and careering, sang to them, sang a chorus of red and violet and green and gold, a song of mystic lands of the future" (*Tales of Adventure* 10). This passage, Nagel says, is one of the earliest examples of Crane's use of a chorus as a "narrative evocation of mood," a device he subsequently employs to similar purposes in "A Man and Some Others" and "The Open Boat" (80), though the moods the choruses evoke in those stories are considerably darker than the one called forth in "Pace."

Critical Studies

Crane makes the theme of this story readily apparent in the narrator's description of Stimson's discomfiture and abandonment of pursuit at the end: youthful energy and desire inevitably and properly win out over the repressions of age (Stallman 60; Knapp 147; Wolford 14; Halliburton 257–58). Therefore, most critics have focused not on merely delineating this theme but rather on examining the techniques whereby Crane makes his statement of it engaging and moving rather than hackneyed and bathetic. Bergon, like Levenson (noted above in "Sources"), points to the effectiveness of Crane's strategy, unexpected in a romance, of making his lovers workers at the shore rather than vacationers there. The resulting discrepancy between these characters and the holiday atmosphere that surrounds them, Bergon explains, means that rather than having "to pump up a trite romance with an effulgence of emotional gush" about the lovers, Crane "can use this bright world to suggest with a minimum of statement the uncommon splendor of this romance." Against the carnivalesque backdrop, "the youngsters' common gestures and emotions acquire solidity and admirable strength" (154).

Broader-ranging discussions of Crane's techniques in "Pace" come from Milne Holton, Donald Vanouse, LaFrance, and G. C. Schellhorn. Holton lauds Crane's originality in having the lovers pursue their courtship with their eyes rather than with words, his succinctness of style, his "delicately controlled ironic distance," and his "fresh" and only unobtrusively symbolic imagery (23–24). Vanouse focuses on one example of such unobtrusive symbolism, pointing out that, in line with the story's theme of generational transition and succession, the carousel, by virtue of Stimson's ownership of it and the lovers' flight from it, subtly "seems to represent one generation's achievement and the meaninglessness of that achievement in the eyes of the second generation" (428). LaFrance also focuses on the carousel but provides a more detailed discussion of how Crane presents "commonplace facts" but uses his imagery to suffuse this essentially "simple tale" with "moral reverberations which thrust well beyond these facts" (76). In LaFrance's view, the carousel is both physically and symbolically linked to three elements that take in the whole story: the setting, the lovers' feelings for one another, and the analogies set up between the children on the carousel and Frank and Lizzie on the one hand and between these two and Stimson on the other. The upshot of these linkings is that "[t]he young lovers have seized the brass ring of the moral world—a feat which Stimson and his wife," given their unloving relationship, "seem to have missed," and that "the supervisory older generation is obliged to let Frank and Lizzie assume their rightful place on the larger merry-go-round" (77). This skillfully understated use of symbolic imagery, LaFrance concludes, makes this story "Crane's finest treatment of romantic love" (78).

Schellhorn likewise praises Crane's light touch with symbolism, citing this characteristic as crucial to the story's success; he asserts that the author's strongest accomplishment is his presentation of figures who are both realistically specific and symbolically universal. The young man is a believable individual due to the inarticulateness of his wooing, but he is also, by virtue of his namelessness early in the narrative, "all young men overwhelmed by the instinct to mate" (336). His paramour is specific in her occupation as ticket-seller for a carousel, but in her shyness and social clumsiness she is simultaneously emblematic of "all those dreamy, homely girls who are always getting left behind" (340). The final such convergence of realism and symbolism occurs when Stimson, forsaking his pursuit, overtly realizes that he is Age out-stripped by Youth, and for Schellhorn it is especially critical to the story's success, for the symbolic dimension here keeps the ending from collapsing into "cliched setpiece" (341). Schellhorn also rates the story highly for Crane's adept control of its form, always a hallmark of this author's best stories (334). He sees a two-part structure at work, with the first being a "predominantly descriptive prelude" that effectively sets up and contrasts with the frenzied dramatic action of the second (334).

Perhaps the subtlest among many insightful analyses comes from Levenson. Crane's narrative stance in this story, he says, departs from that of Howells in that it is marked by intentional internal divergences in the amount of commentary by the narrator, particularly in passages of visual description. In some of these "the author [is] adding something of his own to the thing seen, projecting his own interpretation," while in others "he deliberately adds nothing to the optical image." The result of this alternation, Levenson explains, is another hallmark of Crane's best and most original work: an awareness of epistemological uncertainty that "undermines the assumptions . . . [and] methods of common-sense realism" (xxv).

Works Cited

Beer, Thomas. *Stephen Crane: A Study in American Letters*. New York: Knopf, 1923.

Bergon, Frank. *Stephen Crane's Artistry*. New York: Columbia University Press, 1975.

Berryman, John. *Stephen Crane*. New York: Sloane, 1950.

Bowers, Fredson. Foreword. *Tales of Adventure*. Vol. 5 of The University of Virginia Edition of *The Works of Stephen Crane*. Ed. Fredson Bowers. Charlottesville: University Press of Virginia, 1970, vii–xi. 10 vols.

————. Textual Introduction. *Tales of Adventure* cxxxiii–cxcv.

Cather, Willa. "When I Knew Stephen Crane." *Library* (Pittsburgh) 1 (June 23, 1900):17–18. Rpt. *Prairie Schooner* 23 (Fall 1949):231–36.

Colvert, James B. *Stephen Crane*. New York: Harcourt Brace Jovanovich, 1984.

Halliburton, David. *The Color of the Sky: A Study of Stephen Crane*. Cambridge: Cambridge University Press, 1989.

Holton, Milne. *Cylinder of Vision: The Fiction and Journalistic Writings of Stephen Crane*. Baton Rouge: Louisiana State University Press, 1972.

Knapp, Bettina L. *Stephen Crane*. New York: Ungar, 1987.

LaFrance, Marston. *A Reading of Stephen Crane*. Oxford: Clarendon, 1971.

Levenson, J. C. Introduction. *Tales of Adventure* xv–cxxxii.

Linson, Corwin K. *My Stephen Crane*. Syracuse: Syracuse University Press: 1958.

Martin, Jay. *Harvests of Change*. Englewood Cliffs, N.J.: Prentice-Hall, 1967.

Morace, Robert A. "Stephen Crane's 'The Merry-Go-Round': An Earlier Version of 'The Pace of Youth.'" *Studies in the Novel* 10:146–53.

Nagel, James. *Stephen Crane and Literary Impressionism*. University Park: Pennsylvania State University Press, 1980.

Schellhorn, G. C. "Stephen Crane's 'The Pace of Youth.'" *Arizona Quarterly* 25 (Winter 1969):334–42.

Stallman, R. W. *Stephen Crane: A Biography*. New York: George Braziller, 1968.

Starrett, Vincent. *Stephen Crane: A Bibliography*. Philadelphia: Centaur Book Shop, 1923.

Vanouse, Donald. "Popular Culture in the Writings of Stephen Crane." *Journal of Popular Culture* 10 (1976):424–30.

Wertheim, Stanley, and Paul Sorrentino, eds. *The Correspondence of Stephen Crane*. Vol. 1. New York: Columbia University Press, 1988.

Wilson, Christopher P. "The Pace of Youth: Stephen Crane's Rhetoric of Amusement." *Journal of American Culture* 6 (1983):31–38.

Wolford, Chester L. *Stephen Crane: A Study of the Short Fiction*. Boston: Twayne, 1989.

The Price of the Harness

Publication History

This story was first published in America in the December 1898 issue of *Cosmopolitan* (26:164–72) under the title "The Woof of Thin Red Threads," a phrase drawn from the fifth section of the story by the magazine's editor, John Brisben Walker, who disliked Crane's original title (Bowers cvii). In a letter from Havana dated November 3, 1898, Crane expressed himself on this matter to Paul Revere Reynolds, saying, "Damn Walker. The name of the story is 'The Price of the Harness' because it *is* the price of the harness, the price men paid for wearing the military harness, Uncle Sam's military harness; and they paid blood, hunger, and fever" (*Correspondence* II, 373). Crane's feelings were honored in the first English publication of this story, for it ran under his title in the December 1898 number of *Blackwood's Edinburgh Magazine* (164:829–40). It also bore his title when it was collected in the volume *Wounds in the Rain*, which came out in September 1900, published in America by Frederick Stokes and in England by Methuen (Bowers cvii–cviii). Wilson Follett, editor of *The Work of Stephen Crane* (12 vols., New York: Knopf, 1925–27), included the story in volume 9, published in 1926; it also appeared in *The Complete Short Stories and Sketches of Stephen Crane* (Garden City, N.Y.: Doubleday, 1963), edited by Thomas A. Gullason.

Circumstances of Composition

"The Price of the Harness" is one of a number of stories and articles Crane wrote in Havana, Cuba, where he lived from mid-August until late December 1898. Crane had been in Cuba earlier that year, covering the Spanish-American War as a reporter first for Joseph Pulitzer's *New York World* and then William Randolph Hearst's *New York Journal*. He was in Puerto Rico at the war's end, but then instead of returning to his home and common-law wife, Cora, in England, where he faced considerable debts and what he seems to have regarded as excessively burdensome domestic and social obligations, he went to Havana to live quietly, first in a hotel and then in a lodging-house, and write steadily. He completed "The Price of the Harness" before September 27, for on that date he sent the story to his agent in New York City, Paul Revere Reynolds, with the note, "Now this is IT! If you dont [sic] touch big money for it I wonder!" (*Correspondence* II, 373).

Sources and Influences

Robert W. Stallman says that Crane derived most of the incidents of "The Price of the Harness" from what he had observed firsthand during the American army's successful assault on Kettle Hill during the Battle of San Juan, Cuba, on July 1, 1898 (385). Confirmation for this assertion can be found in Crane's newspaper account of this battle, which he filed on July 4 and which ran in the *World* under the headline "Stephen Crane's Vivid Story of the Battle of San Juan," for "Harness" is clearly a more detailed fleshing out of some of the events reported in this piece: the advancing American troops' passing of a line of wounded Cubans on their way to the rear ("San Juan" 156; "Harness" 100); the pointless deployment and swift demise of a bright yellow American observation balloon ("San Juan" 103; "Harness" 158); the Americans' discovery of a pagoda-like building in the center of the Spanish position ("San Juan" 157; "Harness" 104); the Spanish troops' ineffective volley firing of their rifles in response to the American artillery barrage out of frustration at their lack of any other, more significant countermeasure ("San Juan" 157; "Harness" 105); the rapid filling up of the American field-dressing station as the attack progresses ("San Juan" 160; "Harness" 107); the Spanish snipers' brutal concentration of their fire on the American wounded making their way to this dressing station ("San Juan" 159; "Harness" 108); and the speed and valor of the American mule-drivers and their animals in keeping the men on the battle line supplied with ammunition ("San Juan" 160; "Harness" 108).

What Crane chiefly adds in "Harness" to these incidents is a focus on the experiences of four individual American privates—Nolan, Watkins, Martin, and Grierson. His intention here is to show more particularly than in his newspaper account the dangers such men willingly face and the sacrifices they freely make, for at the end of the story Nolan is dead, Watkins is mortally wounded, and Martin suffers from both wounds and fever (113). Crane likewise drew these men and their fates from his personal observation, as is evidenced by a July 9 newspaper piece headlined "Regulars Get No Glory." As both Stallman (404) and David Halliburton (71) point out, in this article Crane uses the name Nolan, which Crane borrowed from a marine in Company C (Stallman 385), to designate a kind of Regular Private Everyman, "the common soldier in military harness" (Stallman 385), whose patient endurance, courage, and uncomplaining death are memorialized in the newspapers only by a figure in the casualty reports, while these papers devote most of their space to feature articles about higher-ranking and socially prominent volunteers such as "Reginald Marmaduke Montmorenci Sturtevant," explaining "how the poor old chappy endures that dreadful hard-tack and bacon" ("Regulars" 171). Stallman (404) and Milne Holton (259) also note that the Nolan character features prominently in two other of Crane's newspaper pieces from Cuba, "The Private's Story" and "Memoirs of a Private."

Given this wealth of evidence in his journalism regarding Crane's bio-graphical sources for "Harness," very few critics have looked for literary sources. Those who have, Lars Ahnebrink and Eric Solomon, both find evidence that in Crane's "glorification of battle" (Ahnebrink 344) and his idealization of the Regular private, in his "worship[ping] these men and envision[ing] them as symbols of military virtue" (Solomon 77), he is following in Rudyard Kipling's footsteps, despite his claim of having outgrown his "clever Rudyard-Kipling style" in 1894 (*Correspondence* I, 63).

Robert Glen Deamer proposes still another source, one postdating Crane's exposure to Kipling but predating his experiences in Cuba: his trip to the West and Mexico in 1895 as a correspondent for the Bacheller newspaper syndicate. Prior to this trip, Deamer says, Crane conceived of life in deterministic terms, as exemplified by his cynical depictions of the pathetic lives of the characters in his early works, especially the novels *Maggie: A Girl of the Streets* and *George's Mother*. However, what he witnessed of human behavior in the West convinced him that people could in fact shape their fates, at least to some extent, through attainment of the "heroic" virtues of discipline, responsibility, and courage—a shift in viewpoint borne out by the changed tone of many of his post-1895 Western stories, which tend to be studies of men who either exhibit these virtues and thus merit Crane's admiration or else reject them and therefore warrant his censure (143). The conduct of the men he observed under fire in Cuba, then, did not afford him a new insight, Deamer argues, but rather reinforced what he had discovered in the West, with the result that the stories in *Wounds in the Rain* generally take the same approach as these later Westerns, being either admiring portraits of men who live up to the code or disparaging renditions of those who fail to do so. "Harness" obviously falls into the former group, for Nolan and his fellows, privates and officers alike, willingly embrace the requirements of discipline and courage imposed on them as Regulars, recognizing that "what counts is man's conduct—man's code of life—as he fronts the onrush of death" and that by their adherence to this code they can "impose a self-created, albeit limited and finite, coherence upon a world of chaos and casualty" (148–49).

Relationship to Other Crane Works

John Berryman sees this story and the others in *Wounds in the Rain* as marking a shift in Crane's handling of war, a result of his having personally observed many of the events he treats in them. "They are much more matter of fact," Berryman observes, "less brilliant, more humanly funny . . . and affecting" than his earlier stories, *The Red Badge of Courage* and the pieces in *"The Little Regiment" and Other Episodes of the American Civil War.* (230). James B. Colvert tacitly agrees, saying that Crane's firsthand experiences in Cuba did not fundamentally alter the understanding of war that he had previously imagined in *Red Badge* and the *"Little Regiment"* tales, but they did give his Spanish-American War stories, of which "Harness" is a prime example, "a certain technical authority" lacking in the earlier works (xxxii). Crane's new fuller knowledge of armaments, tactics, terrain, combat journalism, and politics translated into the kinds of spare, realistic, rhetorically toned-down descriptions that pervade "Harness," in contrast to *Red Badge* and *Little Regiment*, in which "the things of war and the factual circumstances of military life are characteristically evoked, sometimes monotonously, in figurative rather than literal language" (xxxv). That Crane's essential understanding of war had not changed beneath this stylistic divergence, Colvert continues, is illustrated by the fact that despite the greater surface realism of "Harness" Crane still "obliquely defines war as the dark manifestation of a devil-corrupted world," just as he had done in *Red Badge*. Although this story is about a veteran rather than a raw recruit of Henry Fleming's ilk, its realism nevertheless "accommodates the myth that haunted Crane's imagination from first to last" (xxxv).

E. R. Hagemann sees "Harness" as perhaps the best example of two other themes that are pervasive from first to last in Crane's short fiction about war, and of a third that is new to *Wounds in the Rain*. The story's restriction of point of view to Nolan and his friends emphasizes Crane's frequent point that the individual line soldier has a severely limited view and conception of the events he is engaged in, in terms of both his immediate situation and the perspective of history (359). This limitation is closely tied to a second one that Crane frequently ruminates upon, the Regular's progressive loss of emotional responsiveness. In "Harness," Hagemann says, Crane makes this point chiefly through the Americans' lack of reaction to the cries of the Cuban wounded. This scene points up that combat veterans grow "emotionally hardened to the point of inhumaneness; so much have they seen and so much have they experienced, that little or nothing affects them in such a way as to penetrate the well-nigh impervious shell with which they cover themselves" (361). The new theme Hagemann discerns in *Wounds in the Rain*, particularly apparent in "'God Rest Ye, Merry Gentlemen'" and "The Lone Charge of William B. Perkins" as well as in "Harness," is an awareness of the attraction violence holds for many soldiers, possibly an outgrowth of their deadened emotions. Calling this attraction "the common and all-important . . . concomitant of war," which Crane evidently discovered in his firsthand experiences of combat, Hagemann asserts that these stories constitute

> a signal act of recognition on [Crane's] part that the simple brutal act of killing, the manipulation of the weapons of destruction, the sense of being in the presence of death—all of these and more—bring a terrifying feeling of joy, nay elation, to a man at war. (359)

James Nagel links "Harness" to one Civil War story that also features a lack of responsiveness on the part of the veteran, "An Episode of War," in which the protagonist is unable to feel any emotion regarding even his own wound ("War" 13). In both these cases, Nagel argues, Crane takes a condemnatory stance toward war; Harold Beaver, on the other hand, finds in a comparison of this story to another Civil War tale, "A Mystery of Heroism," evidence that Crane's exposure to combat caused him to shift to a more positive view of at least certain elements of war. In "Mystery," Beaver says, Crane appears to treat the idea of heroism ironically, undercutting the whole concept by having his protagonist, Fred Collins, naïvely believe that true heroes' behavior is "as deliberate and exact as [that of] so many watchmakers" (190). However, in "Harness" Crane's narrator and, presumably, Crane himself seem unambiguously admiring of precisely this kind of deliberateness under fire (193). Halliburton likewise sees a meaningful thematic opposition between these two stories. In his view, Collins in "Heroism" mistakenly believes that heroic behavior consists of distinguishing oneself from one's fellows, a view that leads to his daring but undisciplined and pointless dash for water, whereas Nolan in "Harness" understands that true heroism is simply remaining an essentially anonymous member of the unit and just calmly doing what one is told despite danger. Halliburton notes as well that this contrast in understanding extends beyond the privates to the officers: in "Heroism" they are excitable and immature, while in "Harness" they are calm and focused (153). Hagemann too notes Crane's espousal of unspoken devotion to duty for its own sake as the ideal soldier's highest value in this story, which in his view links it thematically to two other post-eyewitness pieces in *Wounds in the Rain*, "The Clan of No-Name" and "Virtue in War" (363). To this list Marston LaFrance adds "The Second Generation" and the earlier Civil War story "The Little Regiment" (185).

Gullason and Chester L. Wolford are both more expansive than LaFrance and Hagemann concerning the connections between "Harness" and "Virtue" that seemingly result from Crane's own participation in the Spanish-American War. Gullason argues that all the stories in *Wounds in the Rain* are thematically linked in that Crane intends them all to be regarded as "wounds" of one sort or another—"an aggravation, a complaint, a satire, a shock"—and that within this schema "Harness" and "Virtue" are alike in being "'tragic complaints'": the most pointed presentations of "the futility of war and the terrible price of patriotism to one's country," that price being a death that goes unappreciated by everyone except the soldier's close compatriots ("Wounds" 238). In a similar vein, Wolford says that both these stories seek to communicate two new insights at which Crane had arrived: heroism is simply the performance of one's job despite the imminent presence of death, and such heroism is its own reward. This second insight comes across through Crane's ironic undercutting of any further accolade for heroism at the end of each story. That heroic behavior might stem from or result in patriotic fervor is denied at the conclusion of "Harness," when one of the wounded in a hospi-tal tent sings "The Star-Spangled Banner" as a sarcastic comment on his own sufferings and those of the men around him; and the idea that courage may result in general public acclaim is demolished at the end of "Virtue" when the correspondents display much more interest in the merits of varieties of mint juleps than in Major Gates's heroic death (Wolford 73–74). Somewhat earlier, Berryman made much the same point regarding the emphasis on the true nature of heroism in "Harness" and "Virtue," but he regards these stories less highly than Wolford, owing to his belief that both "insist a little too much, as the titles insist: the price is death, the virtue, doing one's duty in silence, the duty being courage" (253).

In the area of technique, Halliburton discerns a connection to several other stories in Crane's use of the image of wearing the harness to characterize the men as well as the horses and mules. Here and in "Heroism," "One Dash—Horses," and "The Veteran," he says, soldiers and their animals are closely and positively linked through this image, Crane's point being that they are all mutually devoted members of the "fraternity of martial experience" (148). Stallman notes two further connections of imagery between this story and another Crane work. The "triangle of raw gold light" that shines on the side of a tent during Nolan's death scene, he says, is "a supernatural sign" on the order of the "fierce red wafer" of the sun that shines down on Jim Conklin's death in *Red Badge*, and the image of the soldiers as a "woof of thin red threads" makes the army a loom, giving it the same machine-like character that Crane ascribes to it in *Red Badge* (396). Stallman also points out a con-nection in terms of action: like the protagonist in "Episode," when Private Martin in "Harness" is wounded, he first feels disoriented and sad, and he then walks down a road to the rear, where he is accosted by a surgeon who, overwhelmed by his workload, seems angry at the sufferer for having got him-self wounded (396).

Critical Studies

Critics differ sharply as to the merits of "Harness," with the dividing line gen-erally being an issue that, as is clear in many of the comments noted in the "Relationship to Other Crane Works" section, is almost unavoidable in any discussion of this story: whether Crane's attitude toward his protagonists is straightforward or ironic. Those who regard it as straightforward see that fact as irreparably damaging the story. Edwin Cady argues that throughout his life Crane was torn between an ironic, "complex, mature vision of a responsible and humane life and art," as embodied by William Dean Howells (378), and the unreflective, juvenile ideals of the "strenuous life"—the "muscular, buoy-ant" approach in which all life, including war, is the Great Game in which one constantly tests his masculinity, an approach disseminated most prominently by Kipling, Theodore Roosevelt, Frederic Remington, and Owen Wister (379). In "Harness," as in most of the Greco-Turkish and Spanish-American War stories, Cady says, the strenuous strain wins out and Crane succumbs to its simplistic code, embodied in the Regulars' unquestioning performance of their duty.

Solomon begins his assessment more favorably, praising "Harness" as the most successful of the generally weak *Wounds in the Rain* group due to its realism regarding the quotidian details of warfare; he sees it as the best account of such matters to be found in nineteenth-century fiction. However, he then says that the story is deeply flawed due to Crane's failure to give his protagonists distinctive personalities and his concomitant presentation of them as behaving automatically and unreflectively, a complete—and negative—turnabout from his handling of Henry Fleming. These weaknesses, Solomon continues, are a result of Crane's desire at this point in his life to idealize "the capable, professional workman who does his dangerous job without the slightest hint of heroics, accepts his wounds quietly, his death silently." In giving in to this desire, Solomon laments, the "newspaperman Crane, like the civil servant Kipling, has succumbed to the glamour of the soldier" (76–77). According to Solomon, at the end of the story "[t]he author insists that the price of the harness"—an essentially meaningless death—"must be paid, and gladly, by all soldiers, since life is cheap in war," an attitude that moves Solomon to conclude that "[t]here is something distasteful about the easy moral. Crane's simplistic view of life and death in war does not ring true" (77–78). (Solomon also offers this assessment on pp. 120–24 of his book-length study *Stephen Crane: From Parody to Realism*.) Colvert is more restrained but nonetheless critical as well. He finds nothing inherently distasteful about Crane's focus in "Harness" on his frequent theme of "courage in unfaltering performance of duty," but he asserts that Crane could have found better exemplars of such courage than those he presents here, for he argues that this theme "is diluted by [Crane's] topical interest in the stoical professionalism of the regular army soldier at Santiago" (140).

Joseph Conrad is chronologically the first of the critics who rate this story highly. In a letter to Cora shortly after its publication, he pronounces it as good as or better than *The Red Badge*. It indicates, he says, that Crane "is maturing" and "expanding. There is more breadth and somehow more substance in this war picture. . . . It is Stephen all himself—and a little more. It is the very truth of art" (*Correspondence* II, 396). To Crane himself in a subsequent letter, Conrad says, "[t]here is a mellowness in the vigour of that story that simply delighted me" (*Correspondence* II, 417). Gullason agrees with these early assessments, singling "Harness" out as the best exemplar of the more disciplined prose style Crane developed in his war fiction following his firsthand observations of battle, a fact that makes it, in Gullason's view,

Crane's finest war story ("Wounds" 236). This accomplishment, Gullason continues, controverts the common view of Crane's later battle writings as a descent from the heights of *The Red Badge;* it proves that his powers in fact grew in his last years. "His writing gained in depth," Gullason says. "[H]is style was no longer obtrusive; his cynicism gave way to a mellow worldliness; his vision and range of perspective showed gains by his broader, more skillful blending of political, social, and individual insights" ("Wounds" 242). Gullason also praises the convincing qualities of the characters, settings, and actions, and Crane's presentation of the "monotonous" as well as the "tragic" elements of war; the only flaw he finds, in contradiction of Cady, Solomon, and Colvert, is that the ending is ironic, in an "unnecessary and obtrusive manner" ("True Road" 485).

Nagel and Wolford share Gullason's favorable estimation of the story, but for them irony is not a flaw but rather a necessary component of its accomplishment. Somewhat less enthusiastic than Gullason, Nagel says that "Harness" is "not as carefully drawn" as Crane's best work, nor as effectively unified, and thus not as "artistically important"; but he asserts that it is nevertheless significant for its pervading antiwar stance, which stems from its emphasis on the deadening psychological effect that war produces, its "bleak juxtapositions of humor and tragedy," and its "dramatically ironic conclusion" ("War" 13). Wolford notes that at first glance the story suggests that Crane has indeed changed his outlook on war from what it was in *The Red Badge*, and has come to value the group over the individual, particularly if Nolan's love for the regiment and the army is seen as presented without irony. But in Wolford's view this love *is* meant to be taken with irony, due to Crane's juxtaposition of the gruesome details of Nolan's death with the wounded man's "ironically" rendered version of "The Star-Spangled Banner," and due to the link between the mules who blindly follow the bell-mare and the men who perform with equal blindness in their harness. With these facts in mind, Wolford tacitly agrees with Cady and Solomon that Crane has now come to see heroism as the "individual act of simply performing one's 'duty,'" but he feels that the ironic framing of such heroism indicates that Crane has not actually succumbed to the Roosevelt-Kipling cult of patriotic duty (72–73).

Four other critics, Holton, LaFrance, Bettina Knapp, and Halliburton, read "Harness" as lacking irony but nonetheless regard it as artistically successful. Like Solomon, Holton sees this story as indicative of a change in Crane's thinking about warfare and heroism, for unlike Fleming or Peza in "Death and the Child" Nolan is not very perceptive and lacks a desire to apprehend the full reality of war, but perceptiveness and ontological curiosity are no longer Crane's criteria of value, his locus having shifted to the soldier's "capacity to perform his duty selflessly," by which measure Nolan rates highly. Unlike Solomon, however, Holton does not see this change as a drawback. Whereas the communities of soldiers to which Fleming and Peza belong are broken by their own bad behavior and flight, Nolan's courage and constancy—as well as that of his friends—mean that his community is broken only by death, through which change Crane emphasizes his new understanding of "the superior importance of human love to circumstantial fact" (259–60).

LaFrance lauds the story in a similar manner, pointing out that it is Crane's fullest presentation of his newly formulated code of the Regular soldier, which is never overtly discussed and which its adherents freely choose. The true harness of the title, this code comprises "a competent professionalism," which is "the practical ability to do efficiently whatever the situation requires"; the capacity for "stoic endurance of whatever suffering the situation may bring"; a readiness to follow orders; and, most crucially, "selfless identification with one's brothers so that the regiment can function in combat as a unit" (182–83). Knapp also sees selfless brotherhood as Crane's key theme here. The story's point, she says, is the Regulars' subordination of their individuality to the demands of the regiment, as exemplified by the fact that the four protagonists, Nolan, Watkins, Grierson, and Martin, "actually compose one being, each [man] having divested himself of his subjectivity, personal needs, and desires so as to fulfill the needs of the collective" (171).

Halliburton, like LaFrance, focuses on the positive symbolic overtones of the harness. On a stylistic level, he sees the rhythms of the soldiers' work as underlying the story, with Crane thereby making the point that the regiment's unity comes through the discipline of various kinds of labor. This discipline enables the soldiers to treat battle as simply another form of work, an approach that gives them "the relief of automatism" (152). Thus, the import of the story is that in the face of death "courage has become routine. Only a brave man wears the harness [of discipline] and the harness keeps him brave" (157).

Other stylistically based analyses come from Rodney O. Rogers and Nagel. Rogers notes in particular Crane's use of what Rogers calls a "domestic trope" in his image of celestial heat "'frying this part of the world,'" which in Rogers's reading "reduces the immediate world to the size and perhaps to the shape of a kitchen, qualifying drastically the impression that a battle of grand proportions is being waged." In Rogers's view, this technique, emphasizing relativity of perception, reveals Crane's adherence to an Impressionist-derived theory of epistemology (300). Nagel likewise regards Crane as an Impressionist, but he judges "Harness" lacking in terms of the criteria of this movement. He argues that Crane's central metaphor, the battle as a "great grand steel loom" that weaves "a woof of thin red threads, the cloth of death" ("Harness" 109), constitutes a crucial failure of Impressionist artistic control in that it comes directly out of the narrator's own mind rather than being part of the dramatic presentation. Thus, it is in fact overt editorializing as are the narrator's comments on duty and pride—a cardinal sin by the tenets of Impressionism (*Impressionism* 42).

Works Cited

Ahnebrink, Lars. *The Beginnings of Naturalism in American Fiction*. Cambridge: Harvard University Press, 1950.

Beaver, Harold. "Stephen Crane: The Hero as Victim." *Yearbook of English Studies* 12 (1982):186–93.

Berryman, John. *Stephen Crane*. New York: Sloane, 1950.

Bowers, Fredson. Textual Introduction. *Tales of War*. Vol. 6 of The University of Virginia Edition of *The Works of Stephen Crane*. Ed. Fredson Bowers. Charlottes-ville: University Press of Virginia, 1970, xxxvii–cxci.

Cady, Edwin H. "Stephen Crane and the Strenuous Life." *ELH* 28 (1961):376–82.

Colvert, James B. Introduction. *Tales of War* xi–xxxvi.

———. *Stephen Crane*. New York: Harcourt Brace Jovanovich, 1984.

Crane, Stephen. "The Price of the Harness." *Tales of War* 97–113.

———. "Regulars Get No Glory." *Reports of War*. Vol. 9 of The University of Virginia Edition of *The Works of Stephen Crane*. Ed. Fredson Bowers. Charlottesville: University Press of Virginia, 1971. 170–73.

———. "Stephen Crane's Vivid Story of the Battle of San Juan." *Reports of War* 154–56.

Deamer, Robert Glen. "Stephen Crane's 'Code' and Its Western Connections." *The Importance of Place in the American Literature of Hawthorne, Thoreau, Crane, Adams, and Faulkner*. New York: Edwin Mellen, 1990, 139–52.

Gullason, Thomas A. "Stephen Crane's Short Stories: The True Road." *Stephen Crane's Career: Perspectives and Evaluations*. Ed. Thomas A. Gullason. New York: New York University Press, 1972, 470–86.

———. "The Significance of *Wounds in the Rain*." *Modern Fiction Studies* 5 (1959):235–42.

Hagemann, E. R. "Crane's 'Real' War in His Short Stories." *American Quarterly* 8 (1956):356–67.

Halliburton, David. *The Color of the Sky: A Study of Stephen Crane*. Cambridge: Cambridge University Press, 1989.

Holton, Milne. *Cylinder of Vision: The Fiction and Journalistic Writings of Stephen Crane*. Baton Rouge: Louisiana State University Press, 1972.

Knapp, Bettina L. *Stephen Crane*. New York: Ungar, 1987.

LaFrance, Marston. *A Reading of Stephen Crane*. Oxford: Clarendon, 1971.

Nagel, James. "Stephen Crane's Stories of War: A Study of Art and Theme." *North Dakota Quarterly* 43 (1975):5–19.

———. *Stephen Crane and Literary Impressionism*. University Park: Pennsylvania State University Press, 1980.

Rogers, Rodney O. "Stephen Crane and Impressionism." *Nineteenth-Century Fiction* 24 (1969):292–304.

Solomon, Eric. *Stephen Crane: From Parody to Realism*. Cambridge: Harvard University Press, 1966.

———. "Stephen Crane's War Stories." *Texas Studies in Literature and Language* 3 (1961):67–80.

Stallman, R. W. *Stephen Crane: A Biography*. New York: George Braziller, 1968.

Wertheim, Stanley, and Paul Sorrentino, eds. *The Correspondence of Stephen Crane*. 2 vols. New York: Columbia University Press, 1988.

Wolford, Chester L. *Stephen Crane: A Study of the Short Fiction*. Boston: Twayne, 1989.

The Revenge of the *Adolphus*

Publication History

This story was first published in America in the October 28, 1899, issue of *Collier's Weekly* (24:13–14, 19, 24–25). It next ran in England in the December 1899 issue of *Strand Magazine* (18:724–33), and it was then included in the collection *Wounds in the Rain*, which was published in America by Frederick Stokes in September 1900 and in England by Methuen in the same month (Bowers cxxx–cxxxi). It appeared in volume 9, published in 1926, of *The Work of Stephen Crane* (12 vols., New York: Knopf, 1925–27), edited by Wilson Follett; and Thomas A. Gullason collected it again in his 1963 *Complete Short Stories and Sketches of Stephen Crane* (Garden City, N.Y.: Doubleday).

Circumstances of Composition

Crane evidently wrote "The Revenge of the *Adolphus*" at Brede Place, Sussex, his final English residence, in the late winter or spring of 1899; Fredson Bowers pinpoints April and May as the most likely period (lxxxviii). In any case, he had finished a draft of it before May 27, for on that date he received a letter from Commander J. C. Colwell, USN, a friend from his days as a newspaper correspondent during the Spanish-American War (Stallman 452) who was now a naval attaché at the American embassy in London and who had visited at Brede, in which was enclosed a copy of the story, which Colwell says he read "with much amusement and pleasure" (*Correspondence* II, 484). Crane had apparently given Colwell the story for an appraisal of its verisimilitude, since Colwell ends his letter by saying that if Crane has "any more stories of the same ilk I would be glad to read them and give a professional judgment—though literary criticism is not exactly in my line" (485).

Regarding his professional judgment of Crane's depiction of naval operations in *this* story, Colwell says that "[y]ou have hit off the local color of that sort of thing admirably and the unconscious humour of the actors on the little stage is quite true to life," but he then offers a number of suggestions for improvement. Most notably, he points out that Crane errs in having the crew of the cruiser *Chancellorville* brought to quarters by a boatswain's whistle and the orders of the boatswain's mate; a ship this large would have buglers and drummers on board to signal such commands. Colwell concludes this part of his critique by actually rewriting the offending section (484–85). Crane did not go so far as to use Colwell's passage verbatim, but he did incorporate his drummers and buglers and, as Bowers notes, corrected a number of other inaccuracies the officer detailed (cxxxii).

Sources and Influences

Robert W. Stallman says that this story is based on Crane's own experiences as a correspondent for Joseph Pulitzer's *New York World* during the early stages of the Spanish-American War. At this point Crane and a number of other correspondents were aboard two tugs, the *Three Friends* and the *Triton*, which were being used as press boats accompanying the American naval fleet during its blockade of the Spanish fleet in the waters around Cuba. Stallman asserts that Crane only lightly alters actual events, primarily just changing the names of people, ships, and places in such a way as to create "a humorous and spoofing tone which of course was not suitable for [his] war dispatches" (452). Thus Ernest W. McCready, correspondent for the *New York Herald*, becomes Shackles, who is the central consciousness in this story; the *Three Friends* becomes the *Adolphus*; and the two small American gunboats are given the unlikely names *Chicken* and *Holy Moses*. However, none of Crane's published dispatches reports the central incident of this story, the sinking of two Spanish gunboats by two American ones in a harbor while an American cruiser engages the guns of the harbor's batteries. The most closely parallel incident is to be found in "Chased by a Big Spanish Man-o'-War" (*Reports of War* 124–28), in which a press tug is pursued not by small gunboats but rather by the large battleship of the title and is saved by the timely appearance of an equally large American auxiliary cruiser, the *St. Paul*.

Relationship To Other Crane Works

"Adolphus" is linked to another Spanish-American War tale from *Wounds in the Rain*, "'God Rest Ye, Merry Gentlemen,'" in terms of some narrative details: the same group of correspondents appears in both—although only one, Shackles, is mentioned by name in *"Adolphus"*; both are set on the ships of the squadron blockading Cuba, with the *Adolphus* figuring by name; and the action of both takes place during the early stages of the war. However, the only connection any critic notes between *"Adolphus"* and any of the rest of Crane's stories is a perceived lack of merit that it shares with several other pieces in *Wounds in the Rain*, particularly "'God Rest Ye'" and "Marines Signaling Under Fire at Guantánamo." Milne Holton lumps these pieces together as "inferior work written in a time of illness and need, . . . framed out of Crane's reportage by means of a weak plot, with hardly any discernible form or theme and with only occasional sparks of good writing" (257).

Critical Studies

However much Commander Colwell may have admired the realism of Crane's details in this story, few other critics have found anything in it worthy of praise. Indeed, few have found it even worthy of comment; aside from Holton's negative appraisal, noted above, comments by Stallman and Chester L. Wolford are the only specific criticisms to be found. Stallman judges it "one of the least interesting pieces in *Wounds in the Rain*" (452) and says that it is in fact not even a story but rather only a sketch—"a series of vignettes, a descriptive account of what happened"; to be a story it would require what in Stallman's view it most conspicuously lacks: "the ingredient of thematic import by which . . . a short story [such] as 'The Price of the Harness' [another Spanish-American War piece] transcends mere reporting" (615). Wolford, on the other hand, while not arguing that *"Adolphus"* is a masterpiece, tacitly disagrees with Stallman by asserting that it does have a discernible theme, one that is of a piece with Crane's praise for the common soldier in the rest of *Wounds*. This theme is linked to the title, in that the humble, ordinary sailors comprising the crew of the *Adolphus* get a twofold revenge, on the Spanish and on their compatriots manning larger vessels, that reveals their worth. First, they play a role in the sinking of the Spanish gunboats despite the minor, seemingly negligible character of their craft; and second, the correspondents aboard the *Adolphus* leave the cruiser *Chancellorville* out of their reports of the sinking, relating only the actions of the two other, much smaller ships involved in this engagement, the *Chicken* and the *Holy Moses*—a slap at the "phony heroism . . . created by the good press coverage big things, such as regiments and battle cruisers, receive." Crane's point here, Wolford concludes, is that "[t]rue heroism . . . is the sole property of small things, such as individuals and small boats" (71).

Works Cited

Bowers, Fredson. Textual Introduction. *Tales of War*. Vol. 6 of The University of Virginia Edition of *The Works of Stephen Crane*. Ed. Fredson Bowers. Charlottesville: University Press of Virginia, 1970, xxxvii–cxci.

Holton, Milne. *Cylinder of Vision: The Fiction and Journalistic Writings of Stephen Crane*. Baton Rouge: Louisiana State University Press, 1972.

Stallman, R. W. *Stephen Crane: A Biography*. New York: George Braziller, 1968.

Wertheim, Stanley, and Paul Sorrentino, eds. *The Correspondence of Stephen Crane*. Vol. 2. New York: Columbia University Press, 1988.

Wolford, Chester L. *Stephen Crane: A Study of the Short Fiction*. Boston: Twayne, 1989.

The Second Generation

Publication History

This story first saw print in America in the *Saturday Evening Post* for December 2, 1899 (172:449–52); its initial English publication came in the December 1899 issue of *Cornhill Magazine* (n.s. 7:734–53). It was then collected in the book *Wounds in the Rain*, which came out in September 1900, published in America by Frederick Stokes and in England by Methuen (Bowers clxiii). It was placed in volume 2, published in 1925, of *The Work of Stephen Crane* (12 vols., New York: Knopf, 1925–27), edited by Wilson Follett, and Thomas A. Gullason included it in his 1963 *Complete Short Stories and Sketches of Stephen Crane* (Garden City, N.Y.: Doubleday).

Circumstances of Composition

Fredson Bowers points out that "The Second Generation" and "Virtue in War" appear to have been linked for some reason in the mind of James Pinker, Crane's English agent, and perhaps in Crane's mind as well, a circumstance suggesting that these works were composed around the same time (clxii).

This would seem to have been the summer of 1899, while Crane was ensconced in his last British home, Brede Place, Sussex, since Crane submitted an early, short version of "Virtue," then entitled "The Making of the 307th," to Pinker on July 21 of that year (*Correspondence* II, 490), followed by both its full version—the title now evidently changed to "West Pointer and Volunteer; Or, Virtue in War"—and "The Second Generation" in August or early September (Bowers cxlvi–xlvii), actions that probably occasioned the aforementioned linking and definitely provoked a good deal of confusion. On September 14, 1899, Pinker wrote Crane to tell him that he had sold the American serial rights for "Generation" to the *Saturday Evening Post* (*Correspondence* II, 517); shortly thereafter, in a letter that has been lost, he added that he had sold the American serial rights for "Virtue in War" to Tillotson's newspaper syndicate. Crane's response has been lost as well, but he evidently wired Pinker that he could not remember which recent war story had had its name changed and therefore feared that "Virtue" and "Generation" were the same story, which meant that Pinker had sold its American serial rights twice. Pinker replied on September 21 that "'Virtue in War' is the story the American serial rights of which I sold to Tillotsons. It is not the same story as 'The Second Generation'" (*Correspondence* II, 517).

Crane was not completely reassured, however, for on September 30 he wrote Pinker, "I cannot express how worried I am over 'Virtue in War' and 'The Second Generation.' I can only remember writing *one* story and I would almost bet the two titles cover one story. We may be making a hideous blunder. Please find out." And two days later, probably before Pinker had had a chance to offer further reassurance, Crane wrote him again to say, "I am still nervous about Virtue in War and The Second Generation [sic]" (*Correspondence* II, 526, 528). This is Crane's last surviving word on this subject; whether Pinker finally managed to set his mind at rest or he simply forgot the problem in the press of his other concerns is open to speculation. He mentions "Generation" only once more, in a letter to Pinker of November 4, 1899, in which he expresses his pleasure at the agent's sale of the English serial rights for the story to *Cornhill Magazine* (*Correspondence* II, 544).

Sources and Influences

James B. Colvert says that Crane could not have written "Generation" before observing war firsthand in Cuba, because it was that experience that gave him an understanding of "the politics of war" (xxxii), which is his primary concern in this story. However, if Crane's first biographer, Thomas Beer, is to be believed, Crane did not in fact get the political initiation that led to this story until after the Spanish-American War. Beer says that, passing through Washington, D.C., on his way from Havana to England in late 1898, following his coverage of the war for the *New York World* and the *New York Journal*, Crane encountered a blowhard senator who expatiated upon the supposed privations his well-born nephew had endured as a member of the Rough Riders (199–200). Despite Beer's frequent unreliability in such matters (*Correspondence* I, 6–10), Crane's later biographers John Berryman and Robert W. Stallman accept this anecdote as factual and assert that this conversation prompted Crane to writing a story unfavorably comparing the demeanor of a pampered Volunteer to that of the Regulars, whose stoic professionalism had aroused his highest admiration. Berryman points out, however, that in the story Crane makes the senator-father a more admirable figure than he was in life and heaps the greater measure of irony on the son (232), a circumstance Stallman explains by linking the story to Crane's own filial feelings. In his view, the story in general, and the senator's saying to his son in it, "'I guess you are no damn good'" (*Tales of War* 284) in particular, may have more to do with Crane's sense of his own failure to live up to his deceased father's "nobility of spiritual outlook" than with his experiences in Cuba and Washington (14). Stallman hastens to add that the elder Crane had not in fact regarded his son a failure, but the "sense of guilt and isolation resulting from Stephen Crane's rebellion against his father's dogmas . . . found expression in all his writing" (17).

Regardless of whether Beer, Berryman, and Stallman are correct in their surmises, while Crane was with the American invasion force in Cuba he certainly witnessed upper-class Volunteers behaving badly in the manner of young Caspar Cadogan, and he raged over the great interest most of the press corps and their readers took in such society soldiers at the expense of the Regulars, as he expresses most vehemently in the July 9, 1898, article "Regulars Get No Glory." "The public," Crane fumes,

> wants to learn of the gallantry of Reginald Marmaduke Maurice Montmorenci Sturtevant, and for goodness sake how the poor old chappy endures the dreadful hard-tack and bacon. Whereas, the name of the regular soldier is probably Michael Nolan and his life-sized portrait was not in the papers in celebration of his enlistment. (*Reports of War* 171)

In addition to drawing on this general experience for "Generation," in at least one instance Crane was more specific in his selection, for the character of General Reilly here is recognizably modeled on Captain Bucky O'Neill, who also appears as a nameless veteran captain in the story "'God Rest Ye, Merry Gentlemen'" and who was killed on July 1, 1898, at the battle of Kettle Hill (Stallman 380–81).

These direct sources notwithstanding, Robert Glen Deamer argues that "Generation" had its true genesis, at least in terms of theme, in one of Crane's earlier experiences, his 1895 trip to the West and Mexico as a correspondent for the Bacheller newspaper syndicate. Prior to this trip, Deamer says, Crane conceived of human existence in deterministic terms, as illustrated by his sardonic treatment of the pathetic lives of the characters in his early works, particularly the novels *Maggie: A Girl of the Streets* and *George's Mother*. However, his witnessing of the undaunted behavior of many Westerners in the face of natural disasters convinced him that people could in fact shape their fates, at least to some extent, through attainment of the "heroic" virtues of discipline, responsibility, and courage—a shift in viewpoint borne out by the changed tone of many of his post-1895 Western stories, which tend to be studies of men who either exhibit these virtues and thus merit Crane's admiration or else reject them and therefore warrant his censure. The conduct of the men he observed under fire in Cuba, then, did not give Crane new insight, Deamer asserts, but rather reinforced what he had already discovered in the West, with the result that the stories in *Wounds in the Rain* generally take the same approach as these later Westerns, being either admiring portraits of men who live up to the code or disparaging renditions of those who fail to do so. "Generation" belongs to the latter group, for Caspar "violates the very essence of Crane's code for human performance" when he complains that he cannot stand the privations of war and refuses to act generously toward his compatriots (143).

There have been fewer probings into possible literary influences on this story. In fact, the only critic who identifies any is Lars Ahnebrink, who notes, first, that Rudyard Kipling's poem "The White Man's Burden" is mentioned in the story and thus infers that Kipling's emphasis on the admirable qualities of common professional soldiers may have helped to inform Crane's attitude here (104), and, second, that Crane might have derived his generational theme from Leo Tolstoy's story "The Two Hussars," since like Crane Tolstoy in this work focuses on a father who is competent and brave and a son who is arrogant and cowardly (357).

Relationship To Other Crane Works

Marston LaFrance and E. R. Hagemann are the only critics to address the possible connections between this story and other Crane pieces, and what they say implies that Pinker and Crane may have confused "Virtue" with "Generation" not only because of their closeness in time of composition but also due to marked thematic and technical similarities. LaFrance notes that both draw comparisons between those who do and those who do not live up to Crane's code of the Regulars—the steady, focused, unostentatious performance of whatever task must be done regardless of the dangers involved. The acceptance of this "moral harness," LaFrance says, "develops logically as the moral answer" to the incompetence of volunteers and the venality of those in positions of power; it constitutes virtue in war, and those who do accept it recognize one another immediately and can equally readily spot the men who will never do so. In LaFrance's view, however, "Generation" and "Virtue" are less effective meditations on this theme than several other stories, such as "The Price of the Harness," because in the former cases Crane overdoes his contempt for the poltroons, making them caricatures rather than convincing characters (182–87).

LaFrance also points out that this concept of a moral harness ties into the moral principles that pervade Crane's poetry. Following the lead of Daniel Hoffman (153–54), LaFrance says that in his poems and stories Crane develops the same code through his use of the same classes of characters. There are, first of all, in the poems "the personally dishonest men who have met their death in the enchanted forest"; these become the poltroons in the stories, such as Caspar Cadogan in "Generation." Then there are "the drones of the huddled procession who never enter the forest" in the poems, who are transmuted into "the innocent volunteers" in the stories. And finally, there are "the good men who successfully negotiate the forest" in the poems and become the Regulars, like General Reilly and the men of the Sixth Infantry in "Generation" (185).

Hagemann, while acknowledging the thematic similarity between "Generation" and "Virtue," focuses on a technical connection. He notes that in both of these stories Crane consciously personifies death, as in the sentence "Death smote them," from "Virtue," a technique he did not use in his earlier Civil War fiction. This change, Hagemann argues, is a function of Crane's having experienced battle at first hand in the interval between these two groups of stories. Through this personal observation Crane "came to realize the presence and personification of death" on the battlefield and sought to convey this new realization in his later war fiction (364).

One other possible connection is with one of Crane's Civil War tales, "A Mystery of Heroism." Here, a Union private by the name of Fred Collins asserts that he is willing to fetch water from a nearby well for his company, even though no one needs the water and the company's position is under heavy enemy fire. Collins's comrades goad him into the actual performance of this act by calling him a coward for only saying he will do so, but such behavior is not heroism, because it is motivated purely by vanity, lacking any tactical objective. However, after Collins gets the water, as he is racing back to his own lines through a hail of bullets, he encounters a mortally wounded Union officer who begs him for a drink, which Collins stops to provide despite the danger to himself. By this selfless act of compassion, Leland Krauth says, Crane provides his own index of heroism (91). And it is according to exactly this index that Caspar Cadogan is found wanting, for his fellow officers reject further association with him when, not even under fire, he refuses to give a drink from his full canteen to a soldier suffering from fever (*Tales of War* 277–78).

Critical Studies

For various and in some cases seemingly contradictory reasons, a number of critics have judged "Generation" one of the weaker pieces in Crane's canon. In a reading similar to Stallman's, noted above in "Sources and Influences," Maxwell Geismar sees Crane's contrasting the father's virtues with the son's vices here, coupled with his unironic admiration for the virtues of military professionalism—especially unquestioning obedience of orders—as constituting Crane's return to the father and "tribal mores" after his revolt from those values, the consequences of which he explored in "The Blue Hotel" and "The Monster" (128). This motif of filial return, in Geismar's view, illustrates Crane's artistic limitations, for it reveals him as incapable of seeing war in impersonal terms, as a product of history or of humans' essential nature. Instead, for Crane war is only "the projection of a cataclysmic interior conflict. The single issue was how men would behave in the heat of the inferno he had projected outward," and once he resolves this issue, he has nothing further to explore in war (133).

Gullason and James Nagel share Geismar's low opinion of "Generation," but their judgments are based on an alleged lack of the psychological-symbolic dimension that Geismar finds oppressively present. Nagel considers the story "shallow" compared to Crane's best work because of his eschewal of psychological penetration here in favor of a broadly drawn protest against wartime nepotism (16). Similarly, in line with LaFrance's criticism of caricatures in this story, Gullason says that it begins as a sharp treatment of military-political patronage, a theme of much currency during the Spanish-American War, but "dwindles into a fragile allegory" on this subject due to Crane's overly simplistic delineations of the characters ("True Road" 485).

Despite this negative judgment, in a separate essay Gullason aligns himself with those who take a more positive view of "Generation." He cites its expert blend of comedy and seriousness and, in contrast to Berryman's and Stallman's views, the pointedness of its ridicule and criticism of not only Caspar Cadogan but also his senator father, whom Gullason sees as guilty of mismanaging the war in his egotistical use of his power to get Caspar a place in the army when he knows his son is unfit for such duty ("Wounds" 240). Chester L. Wolford tacitly agrees with this reading of Crane's attitude toward the father and thus likewise sees the story as more complex than most critics have noted. The senator is right, Wolford says, that Caspar is "'no damn good,'" but he fails to see that his son's lack of worth does not stem from his refusal to stay in the army but rather from his being nothing more or less than "the selfish prig he was raised to be" by the senator himself (72).

Milne Holton focuses solely on Caspar in praising "Generation" as "perhaps Crane's most sardonic war story." Its bitter quality derives, he says, from a greater depth than critics have generally acknowledged, residing in Caspar's failure not only in his soldierly responsibilities but also, more importantly, in the area of human brotherhood, particularly when out of pure selfishness he refuses to give the fever-wracked soldier a drink from his canteen. Caspar's subsequent ostracism by "the military brotherhood," Holton concludes, renders him "perhaps the ultimately degraded apprehending hero" in Crane's canon—apprehension of the reality of one's circumstances and one's response to that apprehension being in Holton's view Crane's primary concern in all his work (258).

Works Cited

Ahnebrink, Lars. *The Beginnings of Naturalism in American Fiction*. Cambridge: Harvard University Press, 1950.

Beer, Thomas. *Stephen Crane: A Study in American Letters*. New York: Knopf, 1923.

Berryman, John. *Stephen Crane*. New York: Sloane, 1950.

Bowers, Fredson. Textual Introduction. *Tales of War*. Vol. 6 of The University of Virginia Edition of *The Works of Stephen Crane*. Ed. Fredson Bowers. Charlottesville: University Press of Virginia, 1970, xxxvii–cxci.

Colvert, James B. Introduction. *Tales of War* xi–xxxvi.

Crane, Stephen. "Regulars Get No Glory." *Reports of War*. Vol. 9 of The University of Virginia Edition of *The Works of Stephen Crane*. Ed. Fredson Bowers. Charlottesville: University Press of Virginia, 1971, 170–73.

———. "The Second Generation." *Tales of War* 264–84.

Deamer, Robert Glen. "Stephen Crane's 'Code' and Its Western Connections." *The Importance of Place in the American Literature of Hawthorne, Thoreau, Crane, Adams, and Faulkner*. New York: Edwin Mellen, 1990, 139–52.

Geismar, Maxwell. *Rebels and Ancestors*. Boston: Houghton Mifflin, 1953.

Gullason, Thomas A. "Stephen Crane's Short Stories: The True Road." *Stephen Crane's Career: Perspectives and Evaluations*. Ed. Thomas A. Gullason. New York: New York University Press, 1972, 470–86.

———. "The Significance of *Wounds in the Rain*." *Modern Fiction Studies* 5 (1959):235–42.

Hagemann, E. R. "Crane's 'Real' War in His Short Stories." *American Quarterly* 8 (1956):356–67.

Hoffman, Daniel G. *The Poetry of Stephen Crane*. New York: Columbia University Press, 1957.

Holton, Milne. *Cylinder of Vision: The Fiction and Journalistic Writings of Stephen Crane*. Baton Rouge: Louisiana State University Press, 1972.

Krauth, Leland. "Heroes and Heroics: Stephen Crane's Moral Imperative." *South Dakota Review* 11 (Summer 1973):86–93.

LaFrance, Marston. *A Reading of Stephen Crane*. Oxford: Clarendon, 1971.

Nagel, James. "Stephen Crane's Stories of War: A Study of Art and Theme." *North Dakota Quarterly* 43 (1975):5–19.

Stallman, R. W. *Stephen Crane: A Biography*. New York: George Braziller, 1968.

Wertheim, Stanley, and Paul Sorrentino, eds. *The Correspondence of Stephen Crane*. Vol. 2. New York: Columbia University Press, 1988.

Wolford, Chester L. *Stephen Crane: A Study of the Short Fiction*. Boston: Twayne, 1989.

The Serjeant's Private Mad-house

Publication History

This story was first published in America in the September 30, 1899 issue of the *Saturday Evening Post* (172:214–15). It then appeared in England in the *English Illustrated Magazine* for December 1899 (22:243–49). Its first book publication came in *Wounds in the Rain*, published in America by Frederick Stokes in September 1900 and in England by Methuen the same month (Bowers cxl–cxli). It was published again in 1926 in volume 9 of *The Work of Stephen Crane* (12 vols., New York: Knopf, 1925–27), edited by Wilson Follett, and also in *The Complete Short Stories and Sketches of Stephen Crane* (Garden City, N.Y.: Doubleday, 1963), edited by Thomas A. Gullason.

Circumstances of Composition

When and where Crane wrote this Spanish-American War story is open to speculation. He may have composed it in Havana, where he lived from August through December of 1898, following his coverage of the war for the *New York World* and the *New York Journal*, or he may not have taken it up until he returned to his home in England in January of 1899. Fredson Bowers hypothesizes that it was composed in April or May of 1899, or perhaps even later (lxxxix), but all that can be definitively determined is that Crane finished it by sometime in August or early September of 1899, since the sole surviving reference to it occurs in a letter of around October 23 of that year, in which Crane tells his agent in England, James Pinker, "By the Phila. Sat Evening Post printing 'The Serjeant's Private Mad-House' on Sept 30, the English copyright of it is lost of course [sic]" (*Correspondence* II, 539). However, Crane was mistaken in this notion regarding the copyright; as noted above in "Publication History," Pinker placed it in a British periodical shortly thereafter.

Sources and Influences

Most of Crane's stories about the Spanish-American War can be readily traced to his own experiences during that conflict, for they clearly draw their events and characters from the dispatches he wrote for the *New York World* and the *New York Journal*. However, this is not the case with "Serjeant's." Crane was present on several occasions when Spanish forces launched the kind of surprise night attack on an American outpost that the Spanish attempt in this story, two of which he reported on June 12 and July 4, 1898 (*Reports* 128–30, 153–54), but in these cases the attacks succeeded and a number of Americans were killed in each; there was no "'useful-crazy-man'" like "Serjeant's" Dryden to unnerve the enemy and thwart their purpose with his wild singing. The kind of absurdity recounted in "Serjeant's" is of course not uncommon in any theater of war, but for this particular story Crane may have drawn on a literary rather than a personal source, for the ironic, tension-producing mix of absurdity and threat he develops here is similar to Rudyard Kipling's approach in a number of his stories of warfare in India. Two examples are "The Drums of the Fore and Aft," in which two British drummer boys made foolhardy by drink put to shame the performance of the rest of their regiment, and "The Taking of Lungtungpen," in which British troops shed their clothes in order to cross a river quickly before making a night attack and then capture the town of the title while they are stark naked. Eric Solomon notes with regard to *Wounds in the Rain* that Crane declared in 1894 that he had outgrown his "'clever, Rudyard-Kipling style'" but a good deal of the English writer's influence is nevertheless evident in many of the stories in this volume (78). Solomon does not mention "Serjeant's" specifically as one of this group, but it may well offer further support for his argument.

Relationship To Other Crane Works

Milne Holton sees this story as of a piece thematically with all the stories in *Wounds in the Rain* in its focus on the absurdity of most of the events of war. He also asserts that it is linked to the Greco-Turkish War story "Death and the Child" in that both are meditations on the dangers that an imaginative man poses to himself and others when he faces the stresses of combat. Holton regards "Serjeant's" as less successful than "Death," however, due to its comparative lack of "thematic focus" (257–58). James Nagel likewise rates this story as undistinguished in the context of Crane's work as a whole, but he notes that it is nonetheless typical of Crane in "structure, method, and theme." Like many of Crane's works, it "begins with an impressionistic description of scene and ends with a twist"; the mode in which it is written is "persistently ironic"; and "its psychological themes emerge from fear" (15).

Critical Studies

Aside from Holton's and Nagel's analyses noted above, only Donald B. Gibson offers any specific commentary on this story. His opinion of it is similar to theirs—that it is competent but pedestrian. He points to a lack of depth, resulting from Crane's focus on a "situation rather than a character," as a serious weakness, but he goes on to say that within this limitation the story is well done: "Slight though the ideational content may be, Crane here has his materials well in hand, seeming aware at each moment of what he intends to do" (98).

Works Cited

Bowers, Fredson. Textual Introduction. *Tales of War*. Vol. 6 of The University of Virginia Edition of *The Works of Stephen Crane*. Ed. Fredson Bowers. Charlottesville: University Press of Virginia, 1970, xxxvii–cxci.

Crane, Stephen. "In the First Land Fight Four of Our Men Are Killed." *Reports of War*. Vol. 9 of The University of Virginia Edition of *The Works of Stephen Crane*. Ed. Fredson Bowers. Charlottesville: University Press of Virginia, 1971, 128–30.

———. "Night Attacks on the Marines and a Brave Rescue." *Reports of War* 153–54.

Gibson, Donald B. *The Fiction of Stephen Crane*. Carbondale: Southern Illinois University Press, 1968.

Holton, Milne. *Cylinder of Vision: The Fiction and Journalistic Writings of Stephen Crane*. Baton Rouge: Louisiana State University Press, 1972.

Nagel, James. "Stephen Crane's Stories of War: A Study of Art and Theme." *North Dakota Quarterly* 43 (1975):5–19.

Solomon, Eric. "Stephen Crane's War Stories." *Texas Studies in Literature and Language* 3 (1961):67–80.

Wertheim, Stanley, and Paul Sorrentino, eds. *The Correspondence of Stephen Crane*. Vol. 2. New York: Columbia University Press, 1988.

Shame

Publication History

This story first appeared in the January 1900 issue of *Harper's New Monthly Magazine* (100:321–25), the sixth in that magazine's thirteen-part series, running in every issue from August 1899 through August 1900, of Crane's Whilomville tales. Like the rest of this series, it was then included in the collection *Whilomville Stories*, published by Harper & Brothers in America in August 1900 and in England in November of the same year (Bowers 103). Wilson Follett, editor of *The Work of Stephen Crane* (12 vols., New York: Knopf, 1925–27), placed the story in volume 5, which appeared in 1926, and Thomas A. Gullason also included it in his *Complete Short Stories and Sketches of Stephen Crane* (Garden City, N.Y.: Doubleday, 1963).

Circumstances of Composition

There is very little evidence to pinpoint the location and date of the composition of "Shame." The most probable hypothesis is that Crane wrote it at his final English residence, Brede Place, in Sussex, at some point in the early summer of 1899. The support for this theory is that, as J. C. Levenson notes, the story is not listed in two inventories of material that Crane compiled in March of that year but does appear in a list he drew up sometime that summer (liii–liv). If this hypothesis is correct, then "Shame" occupies the same place in the order of composition as in the order of publication of the Whilomville stories—sixth. (Levenson points out that the extant evidence suggests that Crane wrote all of the third through thirteenth Whilomville stories in the order in which they were published [liii].)

Sources and Influences

Although various biographers have identified incidents in Crane's own life as sources for many of the Whilomville tales, no one has offered any such connections in the case of "Shame." Possible literary antecedents are the short stories that Crane's mother, Mary Helen Peck Crane, wrote in the late 1880s for publication in several New Jersey newspapers. As Gullason points out, these stories, with titles such as "How Jonathan Saved the Ash Barrel" and "Thanksgiving or Christmas. Which?" display the same understanding of children's fragile sensitivities and the ease with which those sensitivities may be injured by other children's teasing that marks Crane's Whilomville stories ("Cache" 72)—an understanding that is particularly acute in "Shame."

Relationship to Other Crane Works

All the Whilomville stories are loosely connected in that all focus on Jimmie Trescott and his family and friends, a circumstance that leads Gullason to propose that they be read as a sort of episodic novel that presents "a vibrant and full world" and "demonstrates further . . . Crane's range and versatility" ("True Road" 483). However, "Shame" is more closely related to "The Lover and the Tell-Tale," "'Showin' Off,'" "The Trial, Execution, and Burial of Homer Phelps," "The Fight," and "The City Urchin and the Chaste Villagers" than to the others because these stories all focus explicitly on the somewhat arbitrary norms by which children, implicitly just like adults, establish their communities and ostracize certain people from them—in the case of "Shame," the measure of social acceptability is the kind of container in which one carries one's lunch—as well as the desolation the exiles feel as a result and the desperate measures to which they will go to be reaccepted into the group. Milne Holton notes that this theme is one of Crane's abiding interests in writing about Whilomville, since he began working with it even before the *Harper's* series, in "His New Mittens," the second story, after "The Monster," set in this town. Given this orientation, Crane's goal in "Shame" and the others, Holton says, is to illustrate the great extent to which environment forms the individual's imagination, and thus to reveal "the growth, nurture, and shaping of an American delusion" by the force of communal standards. In all three of the communities within Whilomville with which Crane is concerned—white adult, white child, and African-American adult—"everything seems to turn upon individual acceptability to the group and individual status within it," which has the effect of limiting not only the individual's behavior but also his or her imagination, for "no one in Whilomville asserts original fantasies or experiments with direct confrontations with reality or with new ways of seeing" (215–16).

Eric Solomon like Gullason argues that the Whilomville tales comprise a novel; in his view the central theme that ties them together is Jimmie Trescott's development from innocence to experience—his gradual education, from one story to the next, in the hypocrisies of the adult world. With this theme in view, Solomon sees "Shame" as most closely linked to the third story in the series, "Tell-Tale," in that both focus directly on an ostracism of Jimmie by his peers, with the differences between these two versions of this experience marking the progress of Jimmie's education. In "Tell-Tale," Solomon points out, Jimmie's exile takes place on the playground, with only children present, and he is able to resort to fisticuffs to win back his place in the group. In "Shame," on the other hand, grownups are present at the picnic when Jimmie suffers expulsion, and as a result fighting is precluded as a method of restoring his social standing, as will be the case for him from now on, as he moves into adult society. His rescue provides another lesson in hypocrisy, for in Solomon's view Crane treats it ironically, making clear to the reader, if not to Jimmie himself at this point, that Jimmie's "pretty guardian angel is manipulating his responses and con-descending to him"—in other words, that where the boy perceives roman-tic interest there are only maternal instincts at work, and that those are of questionable motivation (218).

Critical Studies

Levenson says that as a group the Whilomville tales offer the happiest outlook to be found in Crane's canon, largely because of their focus on children in an economically and socially secure middle-class environment, but he notes as well that several of the stories—"The Fight" "The City Urchin," "A Little Pilgrim," and especially "Shame"—also convey darker intimations regarding the sources of the security to be found in this world. In "Shame," he says, Crane provides the clearest view in the series of the fact that the prime force for the order and seeming tranquility of Whilomville is a ruthlessly maintained social hierarchy. Specifically, when Jimmie Trescott appears at the picnic with his lunch in a pail, the "badge of the working class," and is mercilessly teased, he is initiated into "the terrible power of exclusion which Crane knew to be an instrument of middle-class stability." With this point in view, Levenson says, Crane shows that a great deal of pain inflicted on certain individuals is the price of the "general freedom from pain on which the social order of Whilomville rests" (lvi). In line with this argument about the pain of individu-als, Marston LaFrance asserts that "Shame" exemplifies a distinguishing trait of all the Whilomville stories: "Crane's refusal to make light of the child's values and desires when they are considered from the child's own point of view." When the other children turn on Jimmie, LaFrance says, "no character in all Crane's fiction is [presented as] more desolate than he is" (185).

Various critics have found one or another of the Whilomville stories, or even the entire group, to be subpar for Crane. H. E. Bates says the series is "commonplace as calico," could have been turned out by "any tenth-rate provincial reporter without the wit to determine whether what he is doing is good or bad," and is thus primarily an index to the deterioration of Crane's abilities at the end of his life (148). Somewhat less severely, James B. Stronks finds the Whilomville pieces "thin and slight," largely because of their focus on mundane situations that do not evoke the "nerveless intensity" of Crane at his best, but he asserts that they are nevertheless preferable to most late-Victorian literature about children (343). These criticisms acknowledged, however, Holton and Chester L. Wolford rate "Shame" among the best of this somewhat weak collection. Holton praises it as "one of the more complex and profound" of the Whilomville tales in that it unsentimentally depicts Jimmie, like Horace in "His New Mittens," as trapped between conflicting sets of expectations, a condition that leaves him no positive alternative. He knows that if he does not show up at the picnic the adults will be angry with him, he knows that if he does show up the children will ridicule him for carrying his lunch in a pail, and even his seeming rescue from the latter ignominy by the beautiful lady is only temporary, since at the conclusion he is still trapped by sets of expectations, waiting to be confronted and punished by his father for not eating his sandwich (219–21). Wolford takes a very similar view of the story's complexity and profundity. He too sees Jimmie as trapped, "caught between two groups of women" (54): the adults who demand that he go to the picnic and the little girls he knows will make fun of him if he does. And he too sees Jimmie's rescue as ultimately illusory, for a permanent escape into romance with the girl of his dreams is not really viable in light of the frightening way in which the older women are depicted in this story (54–55).

Works Cited

Bates, H. E. "H. E. Bates on Stephen Crane." *Stephen Crane's Career: Perspectives and Evaluations*. Ed. Thomas A. Gullason. New York: New York University Press, 1972, 146–50.

Bowers, Fredson. Textual Introduction. *Tales of Whilomville*. Vol. 7 of The University of Virginia Edition of *The Works of Stephen Crane*. Ed. Fredson Bowers. Charlottesville: University Press of Virginia, 1968, 103–26.

Gullason, Thomas A. "A Cache of Short Stories by Stephen Crane's Family." *Studies in Short Fiction* 23:71–106.

———. "Stephen Crane's Short Stories: The True Road." *Stephen Crane's Career: Perspectives and Evaluations*. Ed. Thomas A. Gullason. New York: New York University Press, 1972, 470–86.

Holton, Milne. *Cylinder of Vision: The Fiction and Journalistic Writings of Stephen Crane*. Baton Rouge: Louisiana State University Press, 1972.

LaFrance, Marston. *A Reading of Stephen Crane*. Oxford: Clarendon, 1971.

Levenson, J. C. Introduction. *Tales of Whilomville* xi–lx.

Solomon, Eric. *Stephen Crane: From Parody to Realism*. Cambridge: Harvard University Press, 1966.

Stronks, James B. "Stephen Crane's English Years: The Legend Corrected." *Papers of the Bibliographical Society of America* 57 (1963):340–49.

Wolford, Chester L. *Stephen Crane: A Study of the Short Fiction*. Boston: Twayne, 1989.

"Showin' Off"

Publication History

This story made its first appearance in the issue of *Harper's New Monthly Magazine* for November 1899 (99:855–60). It was the fourth piece in the thirteen-part series of Crane's tales of Whilomville that was published in *Harper's* between August 1899 and August 1900. Like the rest of this series, the story was subsequently included in the book *Whilomville Stories*, which Harper & Brothers published in America in August 1900 and in England in November of the same year (Bowers 103). It subsequently appeared in volume 5, published in 1926, of *The Work of Stephen Crane* (12 vols., New York: Knopf, 1925–27), edited by Wilson Follett, and in Thomas A. Gullason's *Complete Short Stories and Sketches of Stephen Crane* (Garden City, N.Y.: Doubleday, 1963).

Circumstances of Composition

No references to "'Showin' Off'" occur in Crane's extant correspondence, which makes determining the location and date of its composition difficult. The best conjecture is Brede Place, Sussex, Crane's final British residence, during March 1899; J. C. Levenson notes that this title appears for the first time on two lists of stories that Crane compiled at Brede that month. This circumstance makes "'Showin' Off'" the fourth composed as well as the fourth published of Crane's stories set in the fictional village of Whilomville. (As Levenson points out, the possibility is strong that Crane wrote all of the third through thirteenth Whilomville stories in the order in which they were published [liii].)

Sources and Influences

Various biographers have tied the events of most of the Whilomville stories to incidents in Crane's own life. No one, however, has done so with "'Showin' Off.'" Nevertheless, it is not hard to imagine Crane, a "preacher's kid" anxious to head off accusations of effeteness or even refinement, engaging in the kind of boyhood brinksmanship that Jimmie Trescott and Horace Glenn goad each other into in this story. Robert W. Stallman may afford a clue in his noting that Crane spent much of the summer of 1894 playing uninhibitedly with eight small nieces, the daughters of his brothers Edmund and William, and that these frolics "bore fruit later in his *Whilomville Stories*" (113). We can only guess, but given that William, an attorney and later a judge, was in his own way even more straitlaced than his minister father, Crane might well have had memories of proving his toughness brought sharply back to him while playing with this staid brother's offspring—memories that thus revived would have readily worked their way into a story when, a few years later, he turned to childhood as a subject.

Relationship to Other Crane Works

All the Whilomville stories are loosely connected in that all focus on Jimmie Trescott and his family and friends, a circumstance that impels Gullason to propose that the series be regarded as a kind of episodic novel that presents "a vibrant and full world" and in so doing effectively "illuminate[s] a number of universal truths about children, family life, and one's former home town" (483). Viewed in this light, "'Showin' Off'" may be seen to focus, like a number of the other stories, on the nature of childhood perception and behavior. Jimmie's agony over his supposedly unrequited admiration for the little girl Abbie, Abbie's awareness of his feelings and her pleasure in manipulating him by her air of indifference, Jimmie's assumption of the top place in the pecking order of his set by virtue of his having the velocipede with the largest wheel, his verbal bullying of other boys and willingness to resort to physical demonstrations to maintain that place and impress Abbie—all these figure one way or another in most of the Whilomville tales. The result, as Marston LaFrance points out, is that Crane in this story and the series in general takes an "absolutely unsentimentalized" look at children, presenting them as "amoral, selfish, mean, vain, loud-mouthed, cowardly, fickle, infinitely romantic, and given to brutal mob action" (187). These traits, LaFrance notes, are precisely the ones that cause Crane to condemn adults in most of his work, but he does not condemn these children; he presents them instead as not yet having developed the moral awareness to make a conscious choice to behave in such a fashion. Without the element of moral condemnation, LaFrance explains, these stories generate "warm humour," revealing that "the child's world is one of illusion, and its only boundaries are physical limitations such as fatigue, hunger, chance, . . . parental authority, and superior force" (187–88). Given this composition of the child's world, LaFrance concludes, the stories are structured around the protagonist's crashing against one of these limits in the pursuit of some desire or other (187); and in this respect "'Showin' Off'" is again paradigmatic of the series, for its conclusion is Horace Glenn's bone-jarring confrontation with the laws of physics when, in pursuit of status, he attempts to ride his velocipede down a six-foot bank.

Eric Solomon similarly regards Crane as depicting the children in this story and the Whilomville series as a whole as prone to highly unpleasant behavior but still essentially innocent, unlike their parents. Crane's purpose, Solomon contends, is to indict adult society by showing the children's world as simply an imitation of it—or, particularly in the case of "'Showin' Off,'" by implicitly presenting the adult world as an older but no more mature version of the children's society. The point of the story, even though no adults actually appear in it, Solomon says, is that the behaviors in which Jimmie and Horace and their peers engage, "[v]anity and pride in possessions, pompous and boastful words, gratuitous flaunting of personal strength," are frequently deemed childish, but adults are actually even more prone to these "foibles" than their offspring (216).

Chester L. Wolford links "'Showin' Off'" more specifically to one of the other Whilomville stories, "The Lover and the Tell-Tale," in which Jimmie Trescott resorts to physical violence to maintain his status in the world of Whilomville's children after a girl, Rose Goldege, exposes him to merciless teasing from his whole society by revealing that he has written a love letter to another girl. In both these cases, Wolford says, Crane shows "the power of communal standards over individual behavior." The main difference between the two is that in "Tell-Tale" the punishment comes actively and directly from the girl herself, Rose, whereas in "'Showin' Off'" the loser, Horace, brings his punishment on himself through his efforts to impress the disdainful Abbie (56).

Several connections between "'Showin' Off'" and stories outside the *Harper's* 1899–1900 Whilomville series are also worthy of note. One such link is to one of the two earlier stories Crane set in Whilomville, the 1898 piece "His New Mittens." The protagonist here, like the antagonist in "'Showin','" is named Horace, and although Crane gives him no last name in "Mittens" he may well have regarded Horace Glenn in the later story as the same person, particularly since in both cases the story's conflict arises from the Horace character's determination to defy the immutable laws of his world—in "Mittens" maternal rather than physical ones—to prove to his taunting peers that he is not afraid and thus maintain his place in their community. Milne Holton links this same theme to one of Crane's war stories, "A Mystery of Heroism," and one of his Westerns, "The Five White Mice." These two stories, Holton says, are Crane's meditations on adults' willingness to accept dares, to do foolhardy things, to maintain their standing in their communities; "'Showin' Off'" constitutes an assertion that such behavior is formed by one's childhood relationships (219).

John C. Martin links this story, and the Whilomville tales in general, not only to "Mittens" and "Monster" but also to Crane's first novel, *Maggie: A Girl of the Streets*. Taken together, he says, these works offer a consistent view of childhood spanning Crane's whole career, from the very early *Maggie* through the middle-period "Mittens" and "Monster" and on to the late Whilomville stories. Among the principal recurrent elements in this view are the cruelty that groups of children display toward outsiders, as when the crowd in "'Showin' Off'" taunts Horace for boasting about his prowess on the velocipede, and the concomitant desperation of those outsiders to achieve or regain acceptance by the group, which Horace manifests when in response to these taunts he tries to live up to his boasts despite his abject terror at doing so (45–46).

Critical Studies

Like LaFrance, Levenson sees the Whilomville cycle as offering the sunniest vision and the mellowest humor to be found anywhere in Crane's canon (lvi). Sunniness and mellowness notwithstanding, however, critics have frequently found these stories artistically lacking. H. E. Bates calls the series "as commonplace as calico" and says it could have been produced by "any tenth-rate provincial reporter without the wit to determine whether what he is doing is good or bad." This being the case, Bates argues that these stories are nothing more than an indication of the diminished state of Crane's powers at this late stage of his life (148). More moderately, James B. Stronks regards the Whilomville pieces as "thin and slight" because of their focus on mundane situations that do not evoke the "nerveless intensity" of Crane at his best, but he points out that they are nevertheless preferable to most late-Victorian literature about children (343). No one has singled out "'Showin' Off'" as exceptionally faulty within this context, but neither has anyone praised it for exceptional thematic or aesthetic achievement; the most that has been said is that, as is noted above in "Relationship to Other Crane Works," its concerns are consistent with those Crane evinces in other stories, both about Whilomville and about the larger world beyond this seemingly idyllic enclave.

Works Cited

Bates, H. E. "H. E. Bates on Stephen Crane." *Stephen Crane's Career: Perspectives and Evaluations*. Ed. Thomas A. Gullason. New York: New York University Press, 1972, 146–50.

Bowers, Fredson. Textual Introduction. *Tales of Whilomville*. Vol. 7 of The University of Virginia Edition of *The Works of Stephen Crane*. Ed. Fredson Bowers. Charlottesville: University Press of Virginia, 1968, 103–26.

Gullason, Thomas A. "Stephen Crane's Short Stories: The True Road." *Stephen Crane's Career: Perspectives and Evaluations*. Ed. Thomas A. Gullason. New York: New York University Press, 1972, 470–86.

Holton, Milne. *Cylinder of Vision: The Fiction and Journalistic Writings of Stephen Crane*. Baton Rouge: Louisiana State University Press, 1972.

LaFrance, Marston. *A Reading of Stephen Crane*. Oxford: Clarendon, 1971.

Levenson, J. C. Introduction. *Tales of Whilomville* xi–lx.

Martin, John C. "Childhood in Crane's *Maggie*, 'The Monster,' and Whilomville Stories." *Midwestern University Quarterly* 2 (1967):40–46.

Solomon, Eric. *Stephen Crane: From Parody to Realism*. Cambridge: Harvard University Press, 1966.

Stallman, R. W. *Stephen Crane: A Biography*. New York: George Braziller, 1968.

Stronks, James B. "Stephen Crane's English Years: The Legend Corrected." *Papers of the Bibliographical Society of America* 57 (1963):340–49.

Wolford, Chester L. *Stephen Crane: A Study of the Short Fiction*. Boston: Twayne, 1989.

The Shrapnel of Their Friends

Publication History

This story was not published in America during Crane's lifetime; it first appeared in England in the May 1900 issue of *Ainslie's Magazine* (5:303–305) and was collected for English book publication in the posthumous *Last Words*, which Crane's common-law wife, Cora, assembled and which was published by Digby, Long in 1902 (Bowers clxxxii–lxxxiii). It appeared again in 1926 in volume 9 of *The Work of Stephen Crane* (12 vols., New York: Knopf, 1925–27), edited by Wilson Follett. Thomas A. Gullason also included it in his 1963 *Complete Short Stories and Sketches of Stephen Crane* (Garden City, N.Y.: Doubleday).

Circumstances of Composition

Fredson Bowers has argued convincingly that all four of Crane's tales about the Twelfth Regiment of the army of the fictional country of Spitzbergen, the series to which this story belongs, were written in England, at Crane's successive homes Ravensbrook, in Surrey, and Brede Place, in Sussex, at some point between January 13, 1899, and early November of that year. Bowers's evidence for this dating is that on January 13 Joseph Conrad in a letter to Crane refers to one of the stories, "The Upturned Face," as an idea that Crane has not yet had time to work on, and that in early November Crane began sending these pieces to his British agent, James Pinker (clxxii). "The Shrapnel of Their Friends" was probably composed second in this series, given that in a letter of January 9, 1900, Pinker refers to it as "the second Spitzbergen story" (qtd. in Bowers clxxx).

Sources and Influences

Eric Solomon says that Crane's experiences in the Greco-Turkish and Spanish-American Wars underlie "Shrapnel," as well as the other Spitzbergen tales, in a general way, in that from his firsthand observations of these conflicts Crane drew the realistic details that make his depiction of combat in this story authoritative (79), but no one has identified any of the specific events in which he participated in Greece and Cuba as direct sources for the situation he presents here. In fact, as Solomon argues, this lack of specific sources may well have been a conscious artistic choice on Crane's part; it may indicate his desire in this and the other Spitzbergen stories to create "his own picture of war, this time without . . . the restraint of historical fact"—in other words, to write "war fiction as [he] believed it should be organized," with the goal of emphasizing the universal characteristics of all wars, of revealing that "[t]he baptism of fire, fear, death, courage, [and] horror are qualities of all war and all war fiction" (79). Two details that *can* be traced to specific sources are the names Crane gives his mythical country and its enemy in this series. Spitzbergen and Rostina, as Robert W. Stallman points out, are Norwegian islands in the Arctic Ocean (605).

Relationship to Other Crane Works

"Shrapnel" is most closely linked to the other three Spitzbergen tales, "The Kicking Twelfth," "'And If He Wills, We Must Die,'" and "Face." A number of critics have argued that this connection is based on more than just the same regiment's appearing in all four of these stories and Lieutenant Timothy Lean's being the protagonist in three; they read the stories as stages in a single narrative line that is so clear that Chester L. Wolford proposes that they collectively be regarded as forming a "composite novel" that moves from a focus on the whole, fully manned regiment in "Kicking Twelfth," to the regiment decimated by combat in "Shrapnel," to sixteen men in "'If He Wills,'" to just two men, Lean and the adjutant, in "Face," with each stage in this tightening of focus moving the reader closer to "'the real thing'" of combat (77). Milne Holton sees the stories as combining to depict the gradual education of the whole regiment in "the awful reality of war." In "Kicking Twelfth," he explains, the men engage in two attacks that end in victory with relatively little loss of life, so that at this point they regard combat as rather easy and highly exhilarating. In "Shrapnel" they encounter the "absurdity" of being mistakenly fired on by their own artillery, which introduces them to a "less orderly, less safe, less reasonable" dimension of war, and although their situation ultimately works out satisfactorily, they have been through a far more unnerving stage of their initiation than the one they underwent in "Kicking Twelfth," a stage that effectively sets up their still more intense confrontations with death under fire in "'If He Wills'" and "Face."

Solomon sees the stories similarly, but he regards them as focused not on the regiment as a whole but more specifically on Timothy Lean and his personal education into the nature of battle. In "Kicking Twelfth," he says, Lean learns about the satisfying side of combat through his participation in the regiment's first two engagements, while in "Shrapnel" he discovers the illogical side of war when the regiment breaks and runs under the stress of friendly fire. In "'If He Wills'" Crane moves from the illogic of combat to its patent injustice in depicting the deaths of fifteen brave men and a sergeant who is "a perfect soldier who obeys his impossible orders in the best tradition of the service." Although Lean does not appear in this story, Solomon asserts that "it seems clear that the episode is meant to be part of the lieutenant's military education" in its revelation of "the ugly side of war," of "the reality of violent painful death." Then in "Face" Lean reappears to confront this reality directly in having to bury a friend under fire (79–80).

Solomon is also the only critic to address the possibility of connections between "Shrapnel" and Crane's non-Spitzbergen works about war. He notes that in this story and the other three in the series Crane turns away from the techniques and concerns that occupied him in the stories of *The Little Regiment* and *Wounds in the Rain* and returns to "the approach that produced *The Red Badge of Courage*"—that is, he focuses only on the moment of combat, showing "the Spitzbergen army set apart from history or society. The sole field of endeavor is the battlefield; everything else is extraneous" (78). The point of this full-circle movement in his final war stories, away from "the insensitivity of *Wounds in the Rain*" and back to the "great care for human values" that marks *The Red Badge*, Solomon concludes, is that Crane has discovered "a middle way that conceives of war, like life, as both a glory and an obscenity." Crane himself has learned, as he has Lean discover, that "war is all things to all men—beauty, a test, a muscular way of life, and, finally, a horror" (80). (Solomon also offers this analysis of the Spitzbergen tales' links to one another and their collective relationship to the rest of Crane's war canon on pp. 125–28 of his book *Stephen Crane: From Parody to Realism*.)

Critical Studies

Almost all of what critics have to say about this story in terms of plot and theme links it with the other three Spitzbergen tales and therefore is covered immediately above in "Relationship to Other Crane Works." In the area of technique, "Shrapnel" is equally of a piece with the others: Holton points out that in it Crane uses the "purified style"—distinguished by darkened imagery, "bare and functional" language, and a "relentlessly closing" focus—that he employs throughout the Spitzbergen series (266–67).

Works Cited

Bowers, Fredson. Textual Introduction. *Tales of War*. Vol. 6 of The University of Virginia Edition of *The Works of Stephen Crane*. Ed. Fredson Bowers. Charlottesville: University Press of Virginia, 1970, xxxvii–cxci.

Holton, Milne. *Cylinder of Vision: The Fiction and Journalistic Writings of Stephen Crane*. Baton Rouge: Louisiana State University Press, 1972.

Solomon, Eric. *Stephen Crane: From Parody to Realism*. Cambridge: Harvard University Press, 1966.

———. "Stephen Crane's War Stories." *Texas Studies in Literature and Language* 3 (1961):67–80.

Stallman, R. W. *Stephen Crane: A Biography*. New York: George Braziller, 1968.

Wolford, Chester L. *Stephen Crane: A Study of the Short Fiction*. Boston: Twayne, 1989.

The Stove

Publication History

This story first appeared in the April 1900 number of *Harper's New Monthly Magazine* (100:798–804). It was the ninth installment in the series of thirteen Crane stories set in the fictional town of Whilomville that *Harper's* published from August 1899 through August 1900. Like the other tales in this series, it was then included in the collection *Whilomville Stories*, which Harper & Brothers published in America in August 1900 and in England in November of the same year (Bowers 103). Wilson Follett, editor of *The Work of Stephen Crane* (12 vols., New York: Knopf, 1925–27), placed this story and the rest of the Whilomville tales in volume 5, published in 1926; and Thomas A. Gullason collected it again in 1963 in his *Complete Short Stories and Sketches of Stephen Crane* (Garden City, N.Y.: Doubleday).

Circumstances of Composition

There is very little evidence by which to date "The Stove." The most likely surmise is offered by J. C. Levenson: that Crane wrote it at his last home, Brede Place, in Sussex, England, in September of 1899. Levenson notes that in a letter dated September 22 of that year to his English agent, James Pinker, Crane says he is finishing an unnamed story for Harper, the publisher of the Whilomville series, which he posted, accompanied by another letter, the next day. Because it does not appear in a list of completed works, including all the Whilomville stories to date, that Crane compiled at some point in the summer of 1899, and because most of the later stories can be identified by some other means, Levenson says that "The Stove" is probably the story to which Crane refers in these missives (liv), an identification with which the editors of Crane's letters concur (*Correspondence* II, 518–20).

Sources and Influences

Like the second and third Whilomville stories, "The Angel-Child" and "The Lover and the Tell-Tale," this one features Jimmie Trescott's distant cousin, the beautiful, spoiled Cora, and her parents, an unassertive artist and a highly assertive society matron. Levenson has noted that an "aura of shared reminiscence" hangs over this cluster of tales because these three characters are based not on figures from Crane's own childhood but rather on his common-law wife Cora and her own parents, John and Elizabeth Howorth, as she described herself as a child and them to him (xliv–xlv). It is possible that the central incident of the story, the ruination of a party due to the children's imitations of adults' behavior, also derives from Cora's past, given that Edith Richie (subsequently Edith Richie Jones), a houseguest of the Cranes during the period in which Stephen was writing the Whilomville series, later recalled his telling her that most of these tales "were founded on stories Cora had told him of her childhood" (60).

Relationship to Other Crane Works

All the Whilomville stories are loosely connected in that all focus on Jimmie Trescott and his family and friends, a fact that leads Gullason to argue that they should be read as a kind of loose novel that presents "a vibrant and full world" and in so doing effectively "illuminate[s] a number of universal truths about children, family life, and one's former home town" (483). More specifically,

"The Stove" is most closely linked to "The Angel-Child" and "The Lover and the Tell-Tale" because these three work variations on the same subjects: Jimmie's love-hate relationship with Cora and the havoc she wreaks in both the child and adult worlds of Whilomville—in "The Stove" by persuading Jimmie to mimic the tea party his socially ambitious mother is holding, an activity that includes cooking turnips on the furnace, the smell of which breaks up the party and thus derails his mother's quest to rise among the town's elite. Crane's focus on the tea party here as the primary means by which women achieve or fail to achieve social prominence also links this story to one of the two tales set in Whilomville that are not part of the *Harper's* series of 1899–1900, "The Monster," for the final section of that story concludes with Mrs. Trescott's loss of status as a result of her friends' failure to attend a similar tea party, by which they show their disapproval of Dr. Trescott's refusal to ship the mentally and physically impaired Henry Johnson out of town.

While this social function is treated much more lightly in "The Stove" than in "The Monster," in both cases, as Robert W. Stallman notes, Crane presents the tea party as "a pagan ritual where latent enemies greet each other in a fanfare of empty affections" while subtly seeking ways to cut one another in matters of fashion and refinement (482). This use of the tea party alongside Cora's imitation of it leads also, in Stallman's view, to thematic connections between "The Stove" and many of the other *Harper's* Whilomville tales—including "The Fight," "'Showin' Off,'" "Shame," and "The Trial, Execution, and Burial of Homer Phelps"—for in all of these Crane parallels the behavior of adults and children to show that both groups are governed by the same motive: self-aggrandizement at the expense of toleration, forbearance, and charity. Stallman sees "The Stove" as employing the "most subtly designed" of these parallels, leading the reader to understand that "[t]he stench from the burnt turnips" cooked at the "party" concocted by the capricious, tyrannical Cora "is Crane's commentary on the social stench of the party upstairs" (482).

The comic tone of this story leads Levenson to a less severe conclusion, for in his view this story is related to all the 1899–1900 *Harper's* Whilomville tales in depicting

> an ideal American society, not faultless by any means, . . . but basically humane, equalitarian, and peaceful. It is a middle-class utopia, in which the state has virtually disappeared along with all evidence of public life. Here the concerns of men center in private interest and domestic life. Here, also, the rule of equality provides that even children and their desires and feelings are to be taken seriously. (xiv)

Critical Studies

Russell B. Nye's, Eric Solomon's, and James Nagel's views of "The Stove" and of the Whilomville tales as a group are akin to that of Stallman as noted above; they too see these stories as deriving much of their meaning from Crane's presentation of parallel patterns of behavior in the adults' and children's worlds. For Crane, Nye says, "the child's society was . . . a microcosmic representation of the greater society he probed in his other stories," and, perceiving the presence of all the ills of the greater society within this microcosm, he wrote the Whilomville series partly to account for those ills, to discover their sources. His conclusion in such stories as "The Stove," Nye argues, looking at the adult party and Cora's and Jimmie's version of it, is that these ills are not inborn in people but rather "develop as the child begins to merge his individuality with the greater pattern of society" (52). Solomon offers a logical extension of this theory: if children's behavior stems from their observations of adult society, then it stands to reason that adults' supposedly mature behavior is actually as childish as that of the children. Solomon sees this idea as the fundamental theme of the entire Whilomville cycle, but he regards "The Stove" as Crane's most overt presentation of it. The children's cooking of turnips and pretending they are puddings is absurd, he says, but so is the ladies' tea party, because the participants do not actually like tea, drinking it only for the refinement they believe they display in doing so, and because they use this ostensibly friendly gathering primarily to jockey subtly but viciously for social advantage at one another's expense. Through these parallel plots, Solomon asserts, Crane makes the point that the "innocent destructiveness" of the children is ultimately less disturbing than the more quietly perpetrated "experienced hypocrisy" of their parents (220). Similarly, Nagel asserts that in performing their own interpretation of the adult social event, the children are creating a fantasy, which sheds ironic light on what the adults are doing, for their "social pretensions" are equally the stuff of fantasy and are just one example of the many "common illusions of adult life" (94).

Chester L. Wolford likewise sees the significance of the story as deriving from its parallel plotting, but his interpretation of that significance and of the source of society's ills is a bit narrower. The most striking feature of this parallel structure, he says, is that in both plots the males are dominated by the females. What Crane is after, he concludes—in a view consistent with some readings of another Whilomville piece, "His New Mittens"—is a realization of the way boys and men in the middle-class world are cowed and dominated by "the power of feminine rituals" (54).

Works Cited

Bowers, Fredson. Textual Introduction. *Tales of Whilomville*. Vol. 7 of The University of Virginia Edition of *The Works of Stephen Crane*. Ed. Fredson Bowers. Charlottesville: University Press of Virginia, 1968. 103–26.

Gullason, Thomas A. "Stephen Crane's Short Stories: The True Road." *Stephen Crane's Career: Perspectives and Evaluations*. Ed. Thomas A. Gullason. New York: New York University Press, 1972, 470–86.

Jones, Edith R. "Stephen Crane at Brede." *Atlantic Monthly* 194 (1954):54–61.

Levenson, J. C. Introduction. *Tales of Whilomville* xi–lx.

Nagel, James. *Stephen Crane and Literary Impressionism*. University Park: Pennsylvania State University Press, 1980.

Nye, Russell B. "Stephen Crane as Social Critic." *Modern Quarterly* 11, 6 (Summer 1940):48–54.

Solomon, Eric. *Stephen Crane: From Parody to Realism*. Cambridge: Harvard University Press, 1966.

Stallman, R. W. *Stephen Crane: A Biography*. New York: George Braziller, 1968.

Wolford, Chester L. *Stephen Crane: A Study of the Short Fiction*. Boston: Twayne, 1989.

This Majestic Lie

Publication History

This story first appeared in America on June 10, 1900, syndicated by an unknown organization to the *Cincinnati Enquirer*. It also ran on June 24 in the *St. Louis Daily Globe-Democrat*, and, in a two-part form, on June 24 and July 1 in the *New York Herald* and the *Chicago Tribune*. It next appeared in the book *Wounds in the Rain*, published in America by Frederick Stokes in September 1900 and in England by Methuen in the same month (Bowers clii–cliii). Pioneering Crane editor Wilson Follett placed it, under the title "His Majestic Lie," in volume 2, published in 1925, of *The Work of Stephen Crane* (12 vols., New York: Knopf, 1925–27). It also appeared, under its original title, in Thomas A. Gullason's *Complete Short Stories and Sketches of Stephen Crane* (Garden City, N.Y.: Doubleday, 1963).

Circumstances of Composition

Conflicting opinions have been advanced regarding the time and place of Crane's work on "This Majestic Lie." Robert W. Stallman asserts that Crane wrote it in Havana, Cuba, where he elected to stay from August through December 1898, after covering the Spanish-American War for the *New York World* and the *New York Journal*, rather than return to his home, his common-law wife, Cora, and mounting debts in England. Stallman dates the story to October, since on the 20th of that month Crane sent to his American agent, Paul Revere Reynolds, what he describes as "a 'personal anecdote' thing" (*Correspondence* II, 380), which Stallman identifies as "Lie" on the basis of Crane's description in this story of a lodging-house very similar to the one in which he himself was staying at that point (425). Fredson Bowers, on the other hand, dates the story, at least in its final form, to sometime after August 31, 1899, since a word count that Cora sent to Crane's British agent, James Pinker, on that date seems not to include a figure for this story (lxxxix). (And further, it is more probable that when Crane mentions the "'personal anecdote' thing" he is referring to another story, "Marines Signaling Under Fire at Guantánamo," rather than "Lie," since Crane tells Reynolds that this "'thing'" should go to *McClure's Magazine* [*Correspondence* II, 380], which is where "Marines" first appeared, whereas "Lie" was syndicated to newspapers.)

Bowers's view is strengthened by the able detective work of Paul Sorrentino, who notes that a list of stories appears on the verso of leaf 6 of the manuscript of "Lie," a manuscript that had not yet been found when Stallman and Bowers formulated their hypotheses. Among others on this list are "'God Rest Ye, Merry Gentlemen,'" "The Revenge of the *Adolphus*," and "Twelve O'Clock," all of which can be reliably dated between January and August 1899. This circumstance, Sorrentino concludes, points to composition—or at least completion—of "Lie" in England in September of that year (222–23).

Regardless of when and where "Lie" was begun, it was finished before September 23, 1899. On that date Frederick Stokes, the American publisher of the book in which the story was slated to appear, wrote Crane that he had received a copy of it from Pinker (*Correspondence* II, 523).

Sources and Influences

Stallman says that the protagonist of this story, Johnnie, an American spy in Havana during the Spanish-American War, was based on an actual American agent, Charles H. Thrall, who was also, like Crane, a correspondent for the *New York World* (353). Crane interviewed him on May 4, 1898, reported some of this encounter on May 8 as "Stephen Crane's Pen Picture of C. H. Thrall" (*Reports* 108–09), which appeared in the *World* on the same page as Thrall's own story, "Thrilling Account of World Scout in Cuba," and then used some aspects of Thrall's circumstances in creating Johnnie: like Thrall,

Johnnie is involved in the sugar trade in civilian life and lives in a boarding-house run by an Irishwoman, changed for the story from the actual Mary Horan to Martha Clancy.

Beyond such circumstantial details, Crane also drew heavily on Thrall's personal characteristics, as reported in his article, for Johnnie. In particular, Johnnie possesses Thrall's quiet courage and air of anonymity, as well as his taciturnity and melancholy mien. Stallman asserts that Crane was moved to this modeling because these were traits he sought in himself (353), and such an assessment seems highly probable in light of Crane's epistolary characterization of himself as one who wished to "go through life unexplained" (*Correspondence* I, 171) and his only partly apologetic observation that "[a]fter all, I cannot help vanishing and disappearing and dissolving. It is my foremost trait" (*Correspondence* I, 213). In fact, Crane seems to have identified so closely with Thrall, perceiving in him "the same conflict of ironic selfhood" that he saw in his own character (Stallman 353), that he actually tried to assume the spy's identity, "retracing his footsteps," as Christopher Benfey says, by slipping into Havana before the war was officially over, living anonymously in Mary Horan's boardinghouse, perhaps in what had been Thrall's very room, and possibly eating dinner with Thrall sometime in October (Benfey 254), although the only evidence for such a meeting is in the story.

However, devoting a great deal of energy to trying to pinpoint which specific elements of Johnnie's character and actions derive from Thrall and which derive from Crane himself is perhaps not as illuminating as simply understanding the story to be a manifestation of Crane's impulse toward wish-fulfillment concerning himself and Thrall and then moving on to a consideration of other influences and themes. Gullason suggests one of these, identifying a possible further source for the story in Crane's disgust at having encountered many so-called "war correspondents" who never set foot in Cuba. These men preferred to remain far away, in safer and more comfortable conditions, and invent inaccurate but thrilling stories about the battles, stories that brought them fame with readers on the homefront, while the men such as Johnnie who really knew Cuba and played significant parts in the conflict there languished in obscurity (206).

Relationship to Other Crane Works

Perhaps because "Lie" focuses on a spy rather than soldiers, critics generally regard it as anomalous among Crane's war writings and thus do not offer examinations of its connections to those writings. However, while it is true that Johnnie's circumstances are quite different from those of the more immediately engaged combatants in "The Price of the Harness," "War

Memories," "Virtue in War," "The Second Generation," "The Clan of No-Name," and "Marines Signaling Under Fire at Guantánamo," it is equally possible to regard it as related to these stories in at least two respects. Like the protagonists in all these pieces, Johnnie carries out his assignments not out of a desire for glory or even out of patriotism but because of his devotion to duty for its own sake, and like them he performs his heroic actions without expecting or receiving credit from the press. As Chester L. Wolford points out with regard to "Harness" and "Virtue" in particular, Crane's firsthand observations of the conduct of American Regulars in Cuba led him to realize that men were truly capable of this kind of selfless behavior, which he regarded as the highest manifestation of virtue and thus celebrated in these stories (73–74); it seems reasonable to include his laudatory tale of a spy, a "Regular" beyond the battle line rather than on it, in this group.

Critical Studies

Although Milne Holton dismisses this story as "trivial" (256), several other critics hold it in considerably higher esteem, largely because of its seeming to be, through Crane's characterization of Johnnie, one of his most revealing statements of his own ironic philosophy. Stallman argues that the heart of this philosophy is the blend of admiration and compassion Crane expresses for Johnnie in the title of the story. Johnnie's lie is majestic, Stallman says, "not only because as a spy he conceals his identity, but also because he risks his life for an ideal that fails him," patriotism (353). Implicit in this reading is the thesis frequently advanced in interpretations of Crane's Spanish-American War material as a whole: there is no cause that truly warrants the kind of courage that Johnnie possesses; it is that courage itself—courage for its own sake—that is, finally, the only worthy ideal. Benfey is one who explicitly takes this stance regarding "Lie," saying that one of the sources of Crane's admiration for Johnnie is the "futility" of his efforts, his "willingness to risk all for nothing," and that Crane sees himself in the same terms, likewise leading a daringly futile life (255–56).

In Stallman's and Benfey's view, then, Crane is ironic about Johnnie's causes but not about Johnnie, nor, by extension, about himself. Edwin Cady, on the other hand, sees Crane's irony and concomitant self-knowledge as cutting more deeply. In his view, Crane presents Johnnie as capable of being ironic not only about other people, his nation, and God, but also about himself. And yet, Cady continues, Crane is thereby only "*almost* . . . defining himself in the character of the hero [emphasis added]"—*almost* because Cady regards Crane as at least partly satirizing even his own ironic stance toward life in his creation of the ironic Johnnie, thus demonstrating his ability "to revolt against his own revolt—because that, too, was based on vanity" (96).

Works Cited

Benfey, Christopher. *The Double Life of Stephen Crane*. New York: Knopf, 1992.

Bowers, Fredson. Textual Introduction. *Tales of War*. Vol. 6 of The University of Virginia Edition of *The Works of Stephen Crane*. Ed. Fredson Bowers. Charlottesville: University Press of Virginia, 1970, xxxvii–cxci.

Cady, Edwin H. *Stephen Crane*. Rev. ed. New York: Twayne, 1982.

Crane, Stephen. "Stephen Crane's Pen Picture of C. H. Thrall." *Reports of War*. Vol. 9 of The University of Virginia Edition of *The Works of Stephen Crane*. Ed. Fredson Bowers. Charlottesville: University Press of Virginia, 1971, 108–09.

Gullason, Thomas A. "Stephen Crane's Private War on Yellow Journalism." *Huntington Library Quarterly* 22 (1958):201–08.

Holton, Milne. *Cylinder of Vision: The Fiction and Journalistic Writings of Stephen Crane*. Baton Rouge: Louisiana State University Press, 1972.

Sorrentino, Paul. "Stephen Crane's Manuscript of 'This Majestic Lie.'" *Studies in Bibliography: Papers of the Bibliographical Society of the University of Virginia* 36 (1983):221–29.

Stallman, R. W. *Stephen Crane: A Biography*. New York: George Braziller, 1968.

Wertheim, Stanley, and Paul Sorrentino, eds. *The Correspondence of Stephen Crane*. 2 vols. New York: Columbia University Press, 1988.

Wolford, Chester L. *Stephen Crane: A Study of the Short Fiction*. Boston: Twayne, 1989.

Three Miraculous Soldiers

Publication History

This story made its first appearance in a shortened version syndicated by the McClure organization to various newspapers, which ran it on either March 14 or 15, 1896. These papers included the *Philadelphia Enquirer*, the *Pittsburgh Leader*, the *Chicago Inter-Ocean*, the *St. Paul Pioneer Press*, the *Kansas City Star*, the *Denver Republican*, and the *San Francisco Examiner*. The same cut version ran in Britain in the May 1896 number of the *English Illustrated Magazine* (15:104–15). The story first came out in its full form in the book *"The Little Regiment" and Other Episodes of the American Civil War*, published in America by D. Appleton in October 1896 and in England by Heinemann in February 1897 (Bowers lviii–lix). The full version also appeared in volume 2, published in 1925, of *The Work of Stephen Crane* (12 vols., New York: Knopf, 1925–27), edited by Wilson Follett, and in *The Complete Short Stories and Sketches of Stephen Crane* (Garden City, N.Y.: Doubleday, 1963), edited by Thomas A. Gullason.

Circumstances of Composition

"Three Miraculous Soldiers" was one of five stories with Civil War settings that Crane wrote between October 1895 and February 1896, while living at his brother Edmund's home in the rural town of Hartwood, New York, in response to a request from the McClure newspaper syndicate for more Civil War material to capitalize on the current success of *The Red Badge of Courage* (Colvert xiii–xiv). He finished and submitted this piece before January 27, 1896, for in a letter of that date from Hartwood to S. S. McClure, the head of the syndicate, he says, "I dont [sic] know how much you were going to pay me for the little 'Three Miraculous Soldiers' but if you can send me twenty-five more dollars to last until my February ship comes in, it would assist the Cranes of Sullivan County very greatly" (*Correspondence* I, 192).

Sources and Influences

Very little has been written regarding Crane's inspiration for this story. No one has identified any incidents in Crane's own life that might have given him the idea for it, and the only probing of its possible literary antecedents is a brief remark by Lars Ahnebrink, following several pages devoted to drawing extensive parallels between *The Red Badge of Courage* and Tolstoy's *Sebastopol*, including a tendency to regard enemy soldiers not as bloodthirsty monsters but rather as fellow human beings, possibly equally frightened but in any case capable of warmth and sympathy and thus deserving sympathy in return (352–58). Ahnebrink concludes by noting that Crane exhibits the same attitude in "Soldiers," particularly at the end, in his depiction of Mary's sorrow and compassion over the injured Union soldier and in the kindly Union lieutenant's explanation that he understands why she feels this way about her supposed enemy: "'War changes many things, but it doesn't change everything, thank God'" (Crane 47; Ahnebrink 354).

Relationship to Other Crane Works

Gullason links "Soldiers" with another story in *"The Little Regiment,"* "A Grey Sleeve," as examples of Crane's sentimental side. Both focus on young Southern women confronted by only slightly older Yankee officers, although the romantic attraction between the two is much more marked in "Sleeve," and in both cases this situation impels Crane to produce clichéd melodrama that he intends seriously. "[A] maturer Crane would have parodied all this," Gullason asserts; that he does not do so in these stories results in artistic failure (475).

Marston LaFrance is less harsh. He too connects "Soldiers" with "Sleeve" as the first in a considerable line of "conventional adventure-suspense" tales, well crafted and enjoyable but superficial, that Crane turned out for sure and quick sales. This superficiality derives from Crane's use in these stories of what LaFrance sees as his characteristic narrative pattern—fear of something unknown that produces exaggerated illusions about that thing, followed by a deflating discovery that the thing is not so fearful—simply to generate suspense, whereas in his better, more insightful stories he uses it to reveal the character of his protagonists (181).

James B. Colvert is even less critical than LaFrance, perhaps reflecting his view that "Soldiers" represents an amelioration of criticism on Crane's own part. In his early Sullivan County sketches, Colvert says, Crane directs "relentless" irony at the heroic self-image of his protagonist, known only as "the little man," and this practice carries over to his treatment of Henry Fleming in *The Red Badge*. Like these characters, Mary, the protagonist of "Soldiers," has "certain heroic ambitions," but in her case Crane leavens them with "homely common sense [that] keeps her firmly attached to the real world of cause, effect, and probability." As a result, Crane does not flay her as he does the little man and Henry when she realizes that her actual conduct has fallen far short of her heroic illusions; instead, he treats her with "a tender, ironic circumspection" (xxvii).

Critical Studies

Almost all critics who address this story comment on its being related, as noted above, to many of Crane's other works by its focus on the theme of illusion versus reality, but, as is also the case above, these critics differ widely in their assessments of its merits. Chester L. Wolford praises Crane's effort to create in Mary a woman who embarks with bravery and intelligence on the quest to determine the difference between illusion and reality that engages Crane's major male protagonists, such as the correspondent in "The Open Boat" and Dr. Trescott in "The Monster," but he asserts that this effort ultimately fails because of Crane's inability to write natural and affecting dialogue between men and women, which prevents him from lifting Mary out of the stereotype of the romantic heroine (64). Milne Holton sidesteps this problem of characterization, choosing to focus instead on the effectiveness of Crane's irony. He says that "Soldiers," like all of Crane's major works, is chiefly concerned with the ironic aspects of the difference between the vision of the protagonist and that of the narrator and reader. In this case, the irony stems from the "disparity between the fantasizings of the girl, . . . who casts herself . . . as 'heroine,' and the [unheroic] reality of the situation which confronts her"; in Holton's view Crane gets his point across quite sharply and meaningfully, particularly when the girl weeps over the injuries of the Yankee who has been knocked unconscious, failing to realize that this act of sympathy is not consonant with her chosen role as a Southern heroine (142).

Two other critics, Charles W. Mayer and James Nagel, take an even more positive view, arguing that in terms of technique "Soldiers" ranks among Crane's greatest achievements. Both regard Crane's technique as essentially Impressionistic—that is, aimed at demonstrating the ways in which a character's apprehension of reality is restricted by the data of his or her own senses as conditioned by his or her mental state. Thus they, like Wolford and Holton, see Crane as primarily concerned with exploring the relationship between illusion and reality, and they see him doing so most powerfully in "Soldiers." Mayer points to Crane's creation of "descriptive imagery that, against the backdrop of sharp extremes of light and dark, becomes an equivalent for the romantic dream state" of the protagonist, a state that "transmutes an ordinary scene of war into an unreal world of marvels and mystic experiences that reaches hallucinatory extremes before finally giving way to common truth and reality" (130–31). Unlike Holton, Mayer argues that Mary does come to see the disjunction between her conception of herself as a heroine and her feelings for the injured Yankee; what she discovers this reality to be, Mayer says, constitutes one of Crane's central truths, which his protagonists usually distort through their impressionistic vision: "men do not cease to be human because they fight on the wrong side." She now understands that the actual, fundamental facts of war "are violence and death, not heroic acts of self-sacrifice," and that "[i]n the face of these facts all men are vulnerable, even helpless, and all suffer, regardless of their colors." With these discoveries made, Crane's final point is that, contrary to Mary's original impression, "heroism is at last only sympathy, compassion, and commonplace help for those in trouble" (133).

Nagel is even more laudatory. He notes that, in line with Impressionism's focus on the limitations of awareness imposed on an individual by his or her sensory apprehensions, Crane here limits himself almost totally to the data of Mary's senses and in so doing emphasizes the priority of apprehension over cognition, as when, early in the story, Mary is depicted as first seeing black dots on the road leading to the farm, then realizing these dots are horsemen, and then grasping that these horsemen are soldiers (Nagel 44–45). This technique, Nagel says, makes the story "artistically and ideologically a study in the limitation of sensory data," the most radical such study within Crane's canon and, perhaps, outside that canon as well, for the long section in which Crane describes only what Mary can apprehend as she spies on the Yankees through a knothole "constitute[s] one of the most remarkably limited narrative perspectives in American literature" (48).

Works Cited

Ahnebrink, Lars. *The Beginnings of Naturalism in American Fiction*. Cambridge: Harvard University Press, 1950.

Bowers, Fredson. Textual Introduction. *Tales of War*. Vol. 6 of The University of Virginia Edition of *The Works of Stephen Crane*. Ed. Fredson Bowers. Charlottesville: University Press of Virginia, 1970, xxxvii–cxci.

Colvert, James B. Introduction. *Tales of War* xi–xxxvi.

Crane, Stephen. "Three Miraculous Soldiers." *Tales of War* 22–47.

Gullason, Thomas A. "Stephen Crane's Short Stories: The True Road." *Stephen Crane's Career: Perspectives and Evaluations*. Ed. Thomas A. Gullason. New York: New York University Press, 1972, 470–86.

Holton, Milne. *Cylinder of Vision: The Fiction and Journalistic Writings of Stephen Crane*. Baton Rouge: Louisiana State University Press, 1972.

LaFrance, Marston. *A Reading of Stephen Crane*. Oxford: Clarendon, 1971.

Mayer, Charles W. "Stephen Crane and the Realistic Tradition": 'Three Miraculous Soldiers.'" *Arizona Quarterly* 30 (1974):127–34.

Nagel, James. *Stephen Crane and Literary Impressionism*. University Park: Pennsylvania State University Press, 1980.

Wertheim, Stanley, and Paul Sorrentino, eds. *The Correspondence of Stephen Crane*. Vol. 1. New York: Columbia University Press, 1988.

Wolford, Chester L. *Stephen Crane: A Study of the Short Fiction*. Boston: Twayne, 1989.

The Trial, Execution, and Burial of Homer Phelps

Publication History

This story was first published in *Harper's New Monthly Magazine* for May 1900 (100:963–68), the tenth in Crane's cycle of thirteen tales of Whilomville that ran in *Harper's* between August 1899 and August 1900. Like the rest of this series, it then appeared in the volume *Whilomville Stories*, which Harper & Brothers published in August 1900 in America and in November of the same year in England (Bowers 103). Editor Wilson Follett placed it, along with the other Whilomville stories, in volume 5, published in 1926, of *The Work of*

Stephen Crane (12 vols., New York: Knopf, 1925–27). It was collected again by Thomas A. Gullason in his 1963 *Complete Short Stories and Sketches of Stephen Crane* (Garden City, N.Y.: Doubleday).

Circumstances of Composition

The evidence for dating this story is scanty, as it is with many others in the series of tales of Whilomville that Crane turned out rapidly in 1899. J. C. Levenson notes a letter Crane wrote from his last home in England, Brede Place, Sussex, to his British agent, James Pinker, in which he says that an unnamed Whilomville story of a length consistent with that of "The Trial, Execution, and Burial of Homer Phelps"—3,230 words—is enclosed, but the letter is not dated (liv). The editors of Crane's correspondence, Stanley Wertheim and Paul Sorrentino, agree that "The Trial" is the story Crane mentions in this letter, and they conjecturally date it to September 28, 1899 (*Correspondence* II, 525). If these surmises are correct, the story was written sometime between September 22, when Crane probably finished the previous Whilomville piece, "The Stove" (Levenson liv), and September 28, making it the tenth tale in the series in terms of composition as well as publication.

Sources and Influences

Almost all of Crane's biographers, including Thomas Beer, John Berryman, Robert W. Stallman, and James B. Colvert, assert or imply that this story derives from a hilarious but unconfirmed episode in Crane's own childhood. In Berryman's version, the eleven-year-old Crane and some other boys, likely acting out a story they had heard from a Civil War veteran, "interred" a friend in the sand on the beach at Asbury Park, New Jersey, and then "exhumed" him, with Crane explaining to the friend's horrified aunt that he and his "fellow-soldiers" wished to retrieve a full canteen of whiskey that the "corpse" still had on him (13). Stallman and Colvert both add that the aunt, Olive Brett, spanked Crane but then some years later played a more encouraging role in his career in Civil War mimetics by loaning him the four volumes of *Battles and Leaders of the Civil War* when he was researching *The Red Badge of Courage* (Stallman 8; Colvert 53).

Relationship to Other Crane Works

All the Whilomville stories are loosely connected in that all focus on Jimmie Trescott and his family and friends, a fact that impels Gullason to argue that they should be understood as comprising an episodic novel that presents "a vibrant and full world" and "demonstrates further . . . Crane's range and versatility" (483). However, "The Trial" has its closest specific narrative links to "The Angel-Child," through the Margate twins' and Homer Phelps's appearance in both stories, and to "The Carriage-Lamps," "The City Urchin and the Chaste Villagers," and "Lynx-Hunting" through the fact that in all four of these the character who causes much of the trouble is Jimmie's friend Willie Dalzel. This trouble in all cases stems from Willie's determination, very similar to Tom Sawyer's, to maintain his position as "chieftain" of his little world by devising games for which he dictates the rules, based on his reading of dime-novels and other forms of romantic fiction. In "The Carriage-Lamps," for instance, he insists that the boys' efforts to "rescue" Jimmie from paternally imposed confinement be conducted according to his recent reading of *The Red Captain: A Tale of the Pirates of the Spanish Main* (*Tales of Whilomville* 179), while in "The Trial" his demand that Homer "'play it right'"—that is, "according to the books" (208)—leads to Homer's willingness to be executed and buried to prove that he is a worthy member of the Red Raiders and deserving of a eulogy from their leader, "Dead-shot Demon" Dalzel (213), who obliges with this oration over the "grave": "'[P]ards, we've got one more debt to pay them murderin' red-skins. Bowie-knife Joe was a brave man an' a good pard but—he's gone now—gone'" (215).

The ripe comedy of such behavior and language notwithstanding, Milne Holton sees this as the "most ominous" of Crane's Whilomville stories, partly because within six weeks Crane would write the "adult" version of it, the grimly ironic "The Upturned Face" (221), which deals with the efforts of two soldiers to conduct an actual burial of a comrade "according to the books," and partly because "The Trial" seems itself to be a rather grimly ironic commentary on life in Whilomville as presented in the other tales. In all the strata of this town depicted in the various stories, Holton says, "everything seems to turn upon individual acceptability to the group and individual status within it" (215). In this context, he sees the mock death to which Homer submits in order to regain his place in the group as a "cruel ritual, . . . chilling in its implications, for the burial suggests just how high the price of acceptance in Whilomville can sometimes be" (221).

John C. Martin implicitly concurs with Holton, but argues that this grim vision of childhood is not limited to "The Trial" and the rest of the Whilomville series. In his view, the cruelty of the group to a scapegoat and the scapegoat's desperation to return to the group's good graces that feature so prominently here inform Crane's depiction of children's behavior from the outset of his career, in the novel *Maggie: A Girl of the Streets*, through its middle phases, in the stories "His New Mittens" and "The Monster," and on into the late Whilomville tales (40–46).

Critical Studies

A number of critics have dismissed the Whilomville stories as a group as Crane's least accomplished writing. H. E. Bates says they are "as common-place as calico" and could have been written by "any tenth-rate provincial reporter without the wit to determine whether what he is doing is good or bad"; in his view they are nothing more than an indication of the failure of Crane's diminished artistic faculties at the end of his life (148). More moder-ately, James B. Stronks acknowledges that these pieces are "thin and slight" because of their focus on mundane situations that do not evoke the "nerve-less intensity" of Crane at his best, but he also points out that they are still preferable to most late-Victorian literature about children (343). However, "The Trial" has generally been exempted from such negative responses, large-ly because of the implicit seriousness of its theme, which links it with some of Crane's higher-caliber work, and which, as in Holton's view noted above, is discerned in the ritualistic and metaphorical aspects of Homer's mock-burial. Max Westbrook, for instance, says that the point of the story is Homer's humorously presented but fundamentally bleak realization that life in society is a game, but a game played for deadly serious stakes and offering no happy alternatives. Homer's experience demonstrates to him and to the reader that "[r]efusal to play the game leads to isolation; acceptance of society's terms leads to a figurative death." This discovery, Westbrook argues, makes Homer a more humorous version of the eponymous protagonist of *Maggie: A Girl of the Streets*, another innocent given no opportunity happily to escape society's rules, and also ties the story to the adult world of the grimmest and most highly esteemed Whilomville tale, "The Monster," in which Dr. Trescott and Judge Hagenthorpe acknowledge, in Westbrook's words, that "society's unre-alistic rules are only too real in their existence as a powerful force in man's life" (226). (Westbrook offers a similar analysis on p. 103 of another essay, "Whilomville: The Coherence of Radical Language.")

Ellen A. Brown and Chester L. Wolford likewise see "The Trial" as making a disquieting link between the games of childhood and the rules of adulthood. Brown notes that here, as in all the Whilomville stories, the characters are pre-sented, seemingly soothingly, as average, ordinary children, but their "very commonality . . . strikes a chilling keynote of irony," for if "these children are typical, Crane must be saying that regardless of environment, all the world is populated with tiny barbarians, savages." And, Brown concludes, "[e]ven more frightening is Crane's implicit comment that these little savages are merely miniatures of adults in this 'normal' world" (106). Wolford takes a similar view of the children as miniatures of "normal" adults. He says that "[t]he story is about initiation into the same group that . . . will form when its members grow up, the community of Whilomville. The price is high: utter conformity and rit-ual death," with the latter symbolizing "the death of individuality" (58).

Works Cited

Bates, H. E. "H. E. Bates on Stephen Crane." *Stephen Crane's Career: Perspectives and Evaluations*. Ed. Thomas A. Gullason. New York: New York University Press, 1972, 146–50.

Beer, Thomas. *Stephen Crane: A Study in American Letters*. New York: Knopf, 1923.

Berryman, John. *Stephen Crane*. New York: Sloane, 1950.

Bowers, Fredson. Textual Introduction. *Tales of Whilomville*. Vol. 7 of The University of Virginia Edition of *The Works of Stephen Crane*. Ed. Fredson Bowers. Charlottesville: University Press of Virginia, 1968, 103–26.

Brown, Ellen A. "Stephen Crane's *Whilomville Stories*: A Backward Glance." *Markham Review* 3 (1972):105–09.

Colvert, James B. *Stephen Crane*. New York: Harcourt Brace Jovanovich, 1984.

Crane, Stephen. "The Carriage-Lamps." *Tales of Whilomville* 173–83.

———. "The Trial, Execution, and Burial of Homer Phelps." *Tales of Whilomville* 207–15.

Gullason, Thomas A. "Stephen Crane's Short Stories: The True Road." *Stephen Crane's Career: Perspectives and Evaluations*. Ed. Thomas A. Gullason. New York: New York University Press, 1972, 470–86.

Holton, Milne. *Cylinder of Vision: The Fiction and Journalistic Writings of Stephen Crane*. Baton Rouge: Louisiana State University Press, 1972.

Levenson, J. C. Introduction. *Tales of Whilomville* xi–lx.

Martin, John C. "Childhood in Crane's *Maggie*, 'The Monster,' and Whilomville Stories." *Midwestern University Quarterly* 2 (1967):40–46.

Stallman, R. W. *Stephen Crane: A Biography*. New York: George Braziller, 1968.

Stronks, James B. "Stephen Crane's English Years: The Legend Corrected." *Papers of the Bibliographical Society of America* 57 (1963):340–49.

Wertheim, Stanley, and Paul Sorrentino, eds. *The Correspondence of Stephen Crane*. Vol. 2. New York: Columbia University Press, 1988.

Westbrook, Max. "Stephen Crane: The Pattern of Affirmation." *Nineteenth-Century Fiction* 14 (1959):219–29.

———. "Whilomville: The Coherence of Radical Language." *Stephen Crane in Transition: Centenary Essays*. Ed. Joseph Katz. DeKalb: Northern Illinois University Press, 1972, 86–105.

Wolford, Chester L. *Stephen Crane: A Study of the Short Fiction*. Boston: Twayne, 1989.

Twelve O'Clock

Publication History

This story was first published in England in the December 1899 number of *Pall Mall Magazine* (19:462–68). It did not appear in any American magazine or book; it came out in book form only in 1901, when, after Crane's death, Harper & Brothers published an English edition of their 1899 American collection *"The Monster" and Other Stories* and added "Twelve O'Clock" and three other pieces—"Moonlight on the Snow," "Manacled," and "An Illusion in Red and White"—to this new version (Bowers clxxxvi). It appeared again in 1927 in volume 12 of *The Work of Stephen Crane* (12 vols., New York: Knopf, 1925–27), edited by Wilson Follett, and in 1963 in *The Complete Short Stories and Sketches of Stephen Crane* (Garden City, N.Y.: Doubleday), edited by Thomas A. Gullason.

Circumstances of Composition

Very little can be determined with certainty about when and where Crane wrote "Twelve O'Clock," since there are few references to it in his surviving correspondence. J. C. Levenson places it in the first eight months of 1899, after Crane had taken up residence in England, first at Ravensbrook, in Surrey, and then at Brede Place, in Sussex (cxx). What is certain is that Crane had finished the story and submitted it to his British agent, James Pinker, before August of that year, for in a letter conjecturally dated August 1 he tells Pinker that he is currently working on three series of short stories: tales of the fictional American town of Whilomville, tales of war, and "[t]ales of western American life similar to 'Twelve O'Clock'" (*Correspondence* II, 492).

Sources and Influences

Robert W. Stallman says that many of the physical details of the Placer Hotel, the principal setting for this story, probably derive from the Mahncke Hotel in San Antonio, Texas, where Crane stayed in March 1895, during his Western sojourn as a correspondent for the Bacheller syndicate (137). However, neither Stallman nor anyone else identifies any specific actual incident of violence like the one culminating this story that Crane might have witnessed or heard about and used as a basis for his plot. Stallman argues that in fact the story stems from Crane's life in England during the period of its composition. Citing Crane's customary closely brushed hairstyle and his well-documented fondness for Western appurtenances during his tenancy at Brede Place, particularly his habit of wearing and brandishing a large revolver, Stallman argues that the young cowboy who comes into the store in search of tobacco, wearing huge spurs and a hefty six-shooter and with his hair soaked with water and plastered down, is a parodic self-portrait (139). Stallman explains Crane's motivation for placing such a version of himself in this story by asserting that the triple murder with which it concludes is a function of Crane's obsession with death at the late stage of his life during which he wrote it (493).

The few other critics who have traced influences have looked at literary rather than autobiographical possibilities. Marston LaFrance sees the story as a parody of Bret Harte's tales of the West, albeit a clumsy and obvious one and as a result the weakest of Crane's Westerns (189). Lars Ahnebrink ranges farther afield, suggesting that Crane's emphasis in this story on "a series of irrational circumstances" rather than heredity or environment as the cause of the trouble may stem from the similar philosophy Leo Tolstoy espouses in *War and Peace* (359).

Relationship To Other Crane Works

"Twelve O'Clock" is clearly related to most of Crane's other Western tales in its focus on the unexpected emergence of violence from a seemingly innocuous situation—as in "One Dash—Horses," "The Blue Hotel," "The Bride Comes to Yellow Sky," and "The Five White Mice"—and on the conflict between Eastern and Western modes of perception and codes of conduct—as in "Hotel," "Bride," "A Man and Some Others," and "Moonlight on the Snow." However, it is also the least of these stories, due to its sketchy characterizations and thin plot, which make the violence seem more an arbitrary imposition than an organic result of the story's conflicts. Levenson sees these flaws as most evident in a comparison of "Twelve O'Clock" with "Blue Hotel." He points out that both stories present Easterners as deeply complicit in the violence, that "Twelve" has the incongruous pink counter where "Hotel" has the oddly painted building of the title, and that "Twelve" has the cuckoo sounding over the corpse where "Hotel" has the cash-register legend commenting on the dead Swede. And in both stories these elements emphasize the mystery, fragility, and meaninglessness of life, but "Twelve" lacks the multiplicity of significances that develop out of this theme in "Hotel." In "Twelve,"

> it seems as if not character but incompetence is fate; there is no shadowing doubt about the Philadelphia cowboy's involvement; the absurdity of

the pink counter lacks the vital assertiveness of Scully's feat with blue paint; . . . [and] the well-made plot ends with the finality of Q. E. D. The unanswered questions that art and life tend to raise are missing. There is no need for interpreters. (cxxi)

Critical Studies

In line with Levenson's remark that this story does not need interpreters, critics generally agree on the insights Crane intends to communicate here; the only point of disagreement concerns the aesthetic merit of that communication. Although no one places "Twelve" in the first rank of Crane's works, Jamie Robertson and Chester L. Wolford regard it rather favorably. Robertson sees it as a reasonably successful companion-piece to "Bride" in that both stories study "the foolish violence that results from too slavish an imitation of the Western myth," with "Bride" taking a comic approach and "Twelve" a tragic one. In contrast to Scratchy Wilson's childishly petulant but nonviolent abandonment of his long-running gunplay game with Jack Potter in "Bride," "Twelve" demonstrates that carnage may equally be the result of the gap between the wild image of the cowboy myth and "the child-like foolishness that really characterizes these young, dangerous cowboys" (252–53). Wolford offers some criticisms of the story in one study, saying that Crane here substitutes some flat "editorializing" from his characters for the "classical forms and . . . universalizing epical descriptions" that he uses to develop his themes in the best of his Westerns (*Anger* 114), but in another study he provides a positive analysis. Like Levenson, he points to the thematic similarity of the cuckoo in "Twelve" to the cash-register legend in "Hotel," but unlike Levenson he considers these devices roughly equally effective in making the point that the action preceding their appearance has been essentially meaningless, that "in a world of chance . . . people pay with their lives for nothing" (*Short Fiction* 37).

Arno Karlen, on the other hand, considers this echo of "Hotel" an "unintentional self-parody" of the earlier story and thus an index to Crane's artistic decline in the waning days of his career (481), a view that accords with John Berryman's earlier, more general estimation that in comparing "Twelve" with "Hotel" the reader discerns Crane's imagination in the act of "parodying itself, without meaning now" (248). Without pointing explicitly to self-parody, whether intentional or not, LaFrance and Milne Holton offer equally adverse estimations that focus on the cuckoo. LaFrance dismisses this symbol and the story as a whole as making only the "familiar" point that "violence, suffering, and death are stupidly gratuitous when they result merely from human weakness" (189). Holton suggests that at first glance the cuckoo offers a historical resonance lacking in the cash-register legend, since the legend refers only to the end of the Swede whereas the cuckoo, as part of an instrument that measures the passage of time, sounds "the end of an order"—that of Western rituals and ways of seeing the world. However, Holton continues, this potential thematic richness is undercut by the story's lack of Crane's usual "distancing irony," which creates a tone that is "much too desperate" and perhaps indicates "an almost complete surrender to a vision of the absurd which, in the final year, was becoming increasingly significant in Crane's imagination" (243).

Eric Solomon also sees the story as constituting a surrender to the absurd, although he is less critical of that gesture than Holton. He reads Crane's absurdist stance as developing through three actions that succeed each other as determiners of the story's meaning. When Watson shoots Placer, the clear implication is that "the Old West represented by a six-shooter" has won, "has destroyed the New West represented by a ledger and an inkstand." However, the other cowboys' turning Watson over to the law seems to reverse this meaning, showing the Old West to be anachronistic after all, with such "kicks at progress" as Placer's murder being pointless. But the cry of the cuckoo introduces another, inclusive reversal; it negates both the Old and New Wests, making "[v]iolence and order seem equally meaningless" (276).

Donald B. Gibson offers a somewhat more thoroughly considered assessment, one that embraces elements of the views offered by Levenson, LaFrance, and Holton, whose remarks in fact all postdate Gibson's. Like Levenson, Gibson notes that the characters in "Twelve" are unignorably one-dimensional, but unlike Levenson he argues that this trait is intentional, that it is of a piece with Crane's goals in the story. Crane intends, Gibson says, to focus on "the irony of fate" and "the coming of law and order to the West," so that he purposely gives plot prominence over character. With this aim in mind, Crane seeks to produce "a parody of Western melodrama," but like LaFrance, Gibson asserts that he fails to bring this parody off successfully. And once again Levenson's remarks are relevant here: whereas Levenson says that the story fails for lack of multiplex meanings, Gibson argues that a simplistic conclusion is precisely what Crane seeks in a parody of a genre as simple-minded as melodrama but that he misses this one-dimensional finish precisely because, as Holton later notes, the cuckoo's cry is in fact multiplex in its meanings. It is intentionally "overly dramatic," as is appropriate to melodrama, but in its commentary on both the stupidity of the behavior of the individuals directly involved in the story and the end of the era of wild-West lawlessness that this behavior epitomizes, the sound of the cuckoo offers more complexity than melodrama allows (122–23).

Robert Glen Deamer agrees with Gibson that the story is largely melodramatic, but he argues that this fact arises not from parodic intentions but from Crane's attraction to the Western myth, his unironic attachment to the idealized "Western code of manliness and courage." Deamer says that in his first-rate Western stories—such as "A Man and Some Others," "Hotel," and "Bride"—Crane works effectively with this myth by focusing on conflicts and dangers that evoke genuine courage and heroism, or else on the inroads of civilization that obviate opportunities for the exercise of these virtues. In "Twelve," however, Crane focuses only on "raw violence" rather than these more resonant conflicts, thereby producing nothing more than "slight melodrama" (117).

Works Cited

Ahnebrink, Lars. *The Beginnings of Naturalism in American Fiction*. Cambridge: Harvard University Press, 1950.

Berryman, John. *Stephen Crane*. New York: Sloane, 1950.

Bowers, Fredson. Textual Introduction. *Tales of Adventure*. Vol. 5 of The University of Virginia Edition of *The Works of Stephen Crane*. Ed. Fredson Bowers. Charlottesville: University Press of Virginia, 1970, cxxxiii–cxcv.

Deamer, Robert Glen. "Stephen Crane and the Western Myth." *Western American Literature* 7 (Summer 1972):111–23.

Gibson, Donald B. *The Fiction of Stephen Crane*. Carbondale: Southern Illinois University Press, 1968.

Holton, Milne. *Cylinder of Vision: The Fiction and Journalistic Writings of Stephen Crane*. Baton Rouge: Louisiana State University Press, 1972.

Karlen, Arno. "The Craft of Stephen Crane." *Georgia Review* 28 (1974):470–97.

LaFrance, Marston. *A Reading of Stephen Crane*. Oxford: Clarendon, 1971.

Levenson, J. C. Introduction. *Tales of Adventure* xv–cxxxii.

Robertson, Jamie. "Stephen Crane, Eastern Outsider in the West and Mexico." *Western American Literature* 13 (Nov. 1978):243–57.

Solomon, Eric. *Stephen Crane: From Parody to Realism*. Cambridge: Harvard University Press, 1966.

Stallman, R. W. *Stephen Crane: A Biography*. New York: George Braziller, 1968.

Wertheim, Stanley, and Paul Sorrentino, eds. *The Correspondence of Stephen Crane*. Vol. 2. New York: Columbia University Press, 1988.

Wolford, Chester L. *The Anger of Stephen Crane: Fiction and the Epic Tradition*. Lincoln: University of Nebraska Press, 1983.

———. *Stephen Crane: A Study of the Short Fiction*. Boston: Twayne, 1989.

The Upturned Face

Publication History

This story made its initial appearance in England in *Ainslee's Magazine* for March 1900 (6:108–10). It did not run in any American periodical or book; it was next published in England in 1902, when Digby, Long brought out the collection *Last Words*, which Crane's common-law wife, Cora, had compiled after his death (Bowers clxxx). It appeared again in 1926, in volume 9 of *The Work of Stephen Crane* (12 vols., New York: Knopf, 1925–27), edited by Wilson Follett; in 1952, in Robert W. Stallman's *Stephen Crane: An Omnibus* (New York: Knopf); and in 1963, in Thomas A. Gullason's *Complete Short Stories and Sketches of Stephen Crane* (Garden City, N.Y.: Doubleday).

Circumstances of Composition

Fredson Bowers has argued convincingly that all four of Crane's tales about the Twelfth Regiment of the army of the fictional country of Spitzbergen, the series to which "The Upturned Face" belongs, were written in England, at Crane's successive homes Ravensbrook, in Surrey, and Brede Place, in Sussex, at some point between January 13, 1899, and early November of that year (clxxii). The first surviving reference to any of them is to "Face," which Joseph Conrad mentions in a letter to Crane on January 13. Welcoming Crane back to England after his extended sojourn in Cuba reporting the Spanish-American War, Conrad opines that this adventure must have given him many new ideas for stories, saying, "[y]ou must be full of stuff. I suppose the 'Dead Man' story will have to wait until you unload your new experience" (*Correspondence* II, 417).

This statement, as Bowers notes, suggests that at this point "Face" was simply an idea that Crane had not yet begun to work up (clxxii). Bowers asserts that it was the last to be written of the Spitzbergen tales (clxxx), but whether or not this is the case, Crane finished it by November 4, 1899. On that date he sent the story to his British agent, James Pinker, describing it as "a double extra special good thing" and saying he was also sending a copy to Sir Johnston Forbes-Robertson, a leading English actor of the period, "in an attempt to make him see that in a thirty minute sketch on the stage he could so curdle the blood of the British public that it would be the sensation of the year, of the time" (*Correspondence* II, 543). Forbes-Robertson evidently found curdling his audience's blood a less exciting prospect than Crane did, for nothing came of this effort.

Sources and Influences

Unlike the other three Spitzbergen tales—"The Kicking Twelfth," "The Shrapnel of Their Friends," and "'And If He Wills, We Must Die'"—which are based only generally on Crane's experiences as a correspondent during the Spanish-American War (Solomon 79), "Face" was inspired by a specific incident in that conflict, the death of Marine Surgeon John Blair Gibbs. As Crane explains in his treatment of this event in a newspaper account (*Reports of War* 128–29) and in the story "War Memories"—in which he devotes most of his attention to Gibbs's gradual, horrifying expiration, whereas in "Face" the man to be buried is already dead when the story begins—he and Gibbs became friendly while both were at Camp McCalla, the position the Marines had established above Guantánamo Bay upon first coming ashore in Cuba in June of 1898. During a Spanish counterattack on this outpost on the night of June 9, Gibbs was shot and died near the spot where Crane had taken cover, near enough that Crane could hear his dying wheezes ("War Memories" 226–27). The next day Crane and several others buried Gibbs and the rest of the night's dead in a service conducted, like the one in "Face," under sporadic enemy fire (227). Among those in the burial group with Crane was a young adjutant, First Lieutenant Herbert Draper, who according to Stallman was the model for the adjutant in "Face" (*Stephen Crane* 363). However, in another context Stallman and E. R. Hagemann assert that Draper was the prototype for the protagonist of this story, Timothy Lean (*War Dispatches* 150). What seems most probable is that Crane drew on both Draper and himself for Lean, since Lean, like Crane at Gibbs's death, is just coming to understand the individual and group psychological effects of seeing a friend die for no good reason and having to perform some kind of ritual to memorialize that friend at the risk of one's own life.

Relationship to Other Crane Works

"Face" is most closely linked to the other three Spitzbergen stories. A number of critics have noted that this connection is based on more than just the same regiment's appearing in all four and Lieutenant Timothy Lean's being the protagonist in three of them; they read the stories as stages in a single narrative line that is so clear that, as Chester L. Wolford proposes, they should be regarded as collectively forming a "composite novel" that moves from a focus on the whole, fully manned regiment in "Kicking Twelfth," to the regiment decimated by combat in "Shrapnel," to sixteen men in "'If He Wills,'" to just two men, Lean and the adjutant, in "Face," with each stage in this tightening of focus moving the reader closer to "'the real thing'" of combat (77). Milne Holton and Eric Solomon also take this composite view. Holton sees the stories as combining to depict the gradual education of the whole regiment in "the awful reality of war" (268), while Solomon sees them as focused more specifically on Lean's education. In "Kicking Twelfth," he says, Lean learns about the exhilarating side of combat through his participation in the regiment's first two, successfully concluded, engagements. In "Shrapnel" he begins to discover the illogical side of war when the regiment breaks and runs after being mistakenly shelled by their own army's artillery. In "'If He Wills'" Crane moves from the illogic of combat to its patent injustice, "in sharp contrast to the earlier tales of the series," in depicting the deaths of fifteen brave men and a sergeant who is "a perfect soldier who obeys his impossible orders in the best tradition of the service." Although Lean does not appear in this story, Solomon asserts that "it seems clear that the episode is meant to be part of the lieutenant's military education," revealing "the ugly side" of battle, "the reality of violent painful death." Then in "Face" Lean reappears to confront this reality directly in having to bury a friend under fire (79–80). (Solomon also offers this assessment in his later book-length study, *Stephen Crane: From Parody to Realism*, pp. 125–28.) How this "composite novel" might have been altered in meaning had Crane lived to finish "The Fire-Tribe and the White-Face," another Spitzbergen tale that he began during the last few months of his life, one that focuses on Lean's adventures as a captain in the now-victorious Spitzbergen Army during its postwar occupation of Rostina, is open to speculation.

Many critics also address the possibility of connections between "Face" and Crane's non-Spitzbergen works. Solomon notes that in this story and the other three in the series Crane turns away from the techniques and the social and political issues that occupied him in the Civil War stories of *"The Little Regiment"* and the Spanish-American War narratives of *Wounds in the Rain* and returns to "the approach that produced *The Red Badge of Courage*"— that is, he focuses only on the moment of combat, showing "the Spitzbergen army set apart from history or society. The sole field of endeavor is the battlefield; everything else is extraneous" (78). The point of this full-circle movement in his final war stories, away from "the insensitivity of *Wounds in the Rain*" and back to the "great care for human values" that marks *The Red Badge*, Solomon says, is that Crane has discovered "a middle way that conceives of war, like life, as both a glory and an obscenity." Crane himself has learned, as he has Lean discover, that "war is all things to all men—beauty, a test, a muscular way of life, and, finally, a horror" (80).

Wolford links "Face" with the Greco-Turkish War story "Death and the Child" in that both indicate Crane's gradual movement toward an embrace of ritual as a literal expression of grace under fire, an expression that constitutes for him the only acceptable answer to the apparent meaninglessness of life and the universe. Wolford regards "Face" as a step much farther in this direction than "Death"; he sees "Face" as Crane's first real confrontation with "the great horror of death" in his work. Citing the behavior of Richardson in "One Dash—Horses," Peza in "Death," and the townspeople in "The Monster," Wolford says that up to this point Crane's protagonists have desperately avoided the contact with the maimed and dead that Lean resolutely faces. And in the burial service Lean discovers that ritual is "without pretension," "performs as a kindness," and is "a way of creating order out of chaos, a way of giving comfort and meaning, even as it creates horror and, in this case, danger. . . . Death remains horrible—ritual does not lessen its horror—but ritual enables one to face it" (79–81).

Holton seems implicitly to disagree with Wolford that "Face" represents Crane's first true confrontation with death, for he identifies the minor tale "The Snake," probably written in 1894, in which a man is terrified by a rattlesnake and responds to this terror by nerving himself to kill it, as a precursor of "Face" in that both present "a confrontation with an ultimate reality—a rational, absurd, yet terribly dangerous reality." And in both cases, this confrontation is "conditioned by emotions which go deep, deeper than individual psychology" (33). Holton also implicitly disagrees with Solomon's assertion that in "Face" Crane turns away from the themes that preoccupied him in his Civil War short stories, for he links this story with "An Episode of War." In both these pieces, he says, Crane focuses on "the paradox of apprehension and love"—that is, the tension between forming a meaningful relationship with another person and the terrifying awareness of death which that person's being killed or wounded produces (266). William B. Dillingham sees perhaps less obvious connections between "Face" and "The Bride Comes to Yellow Sky." In both of these stories, he points out, the protagonists are highly capable in one realm—law enforcement in "Bride," battle in "Face"—but they are childishly, laughably inept when that realm changes, to civilization in "Bride," to death in "Face." Just as Jack Potter is discomfited by the train and Scratchy Wilson by marriage, so are Lean and the adjutant by the necessity of having to bury their friend themselves, and they "handle this situation about as well as Scratchy Wilson copes with Jack Potter's marriage, and they are only slightly less comic" (328–29).

Michael Fried notes that this story and "The Monster" are connected in that both focus on an upturned face—the corpse's in "Face," Henry Johnson's in "The Monster"—which is disfigured, the corpse's by the dirt of burial and Johnson's by burning chemicals. In Fried's view, these faces "are at once synecdoches for the bodies of those characters and singularly concentrated metaphors for the sheets of writing paper that the author had before him," with Crane's goal in creating these metaphors being an allegory of the act of writing and the inevitable disfiguring of reality involved in that act. With this possibility in mind, Fried continues, "one way of accounting for the peculiar horror of the violence that befalls the faces . . . is as the writer's response *as reader* to the deathliness of the blank upward-staring page," which the writer is intuiting as "a sign that the natural world has died and cannot be resuscitated . . ., though by the force of art—of literary writing—it can at least be consumed or buried (his solution to Romanticism)" ("Gross Clinic" 94–95). In a later study Fried expands on this idea, arguing that the horizontal position of the face, like that of a sheet of paper on a writing-desk, and the similarity between the names "Lean" and "Crane" render the story "a sustained if displaced representation of the act of writing." The depositing of dirt on the face/page, Fried says, "defines the enterprise of writing—of inscribing and thereby in effect covering the blank page with text—as an 'unnatural' process that undoes but also complements an equally 'unnatural' state of affairs," the necessity of burying a friend (*Realism* 100). Crane presents writing as unnatural here, as well as in *Red Badge*, "Death," and "The Monster," Fried explains, because of his uncertainty about the efficacy of writing as a way of recreating the natural world for the reader, his doubts concerning "his own extreme version of the 'impressionist' enterprise" of making the reader see, both literally and figuratively, what he himself saw (*Realism* 115). (Fried's theories have been subjected to a good deal of criticism due to what some other readers of Crane consider the questionable nature of his methodology; see Raymond Carney's "Crane and Eakins" and James B. Colvert's "Stephen Crane and Postmodern Criticism" for examples.)

In addition to these narrative and thematic links, Holton also discerns a significant one in the area of technique. He notes that Crane's making the corpse's face blue in this story is consonant with his use of that color for objects in many other works—the eponymous building in "The Blue Hotel," the sky in "The Open Boat," the battle line in *The Red Badge*, the battalions in one of his better poems. In all these instances blue is simultaneously "the color which constantly reminds Crane's characters of their insignificance," the color that masks "some terrible and supreme reality . . . necessarily incomprehensible to man," and "the color of the absurd" (271).

Critical Studies

Critics generally agree that "Face" is one of Crane's best stories. John Berryman says that it is unique in Crane's canon in that "though perfectly naturalistic in technique, it affects one as pure symbol, senseless and ghastly, like one of Goya's last etchings, and has the posthuman quality of certain late art by other masters" (257). Stallman calls it a "slight thing but a perfection"; he argues that this quality stems from the story's being constructed on the paradox that "the ritual of burying a dead man is exposed as a ghastly outrage, more real than riflefire itself" ("Revaluation" 258). In a separate study he expands on this idea of outrage, describing the burial as a "maimed ritual" in the sense that even as Lean and the adjutant seek to honor their dead friend with a "proper" military burial, they dishonor him by using an inappropriate service, the one prescribed for burial at sea rather than on land, and, more crucially, by the necessity of having to throw dirt onto his face (*Stephen Crane* 364). These facts, Stallman says in yet another study, are what render the sound of shoveled earth louder than that of rifles, for in this sound Crane shows that Lean and the adjutant's putative ceremony of consecration of their friend is in fact "a desecration: the ritual consecrates him, but the act of the ritual [the physical burial] desecrates him ("Short Stories" 109). Thus, in Stallman's view, the story is one of Crane's last explorations of one of his most frequent themes, "illusion shattered by realities." Just as is the case for Lean and the adjutant regarding their friend, so "all relationships . . . involve that shock of reality by which intentions are contradicted by the act" ("Short Stories" 109).

Donald B. Gibson calls "Face" one of Crane's best stories about war. Like Berryman, he considers it unique in Crane's canon; for him this quality stems from the absence in it of "simple animal aversion to physical destruction," which he regards as the focus of all Crane's other stories about death, in favor of a concentration on the "more subtle" problem of accepting death in a philosophical sense (105). Unlike Henry Fleming, or Peza in "Death and the Child," Gibson says, Lean and the adjutant are not afraid of physical harm. Rather, "[w]hat they cannot accept . . . is the clear and present existential necessity of realizing the finality of death, a problem to these men, who have seen many dead bodies, because the corpse is of an intimate friend whom they must bury with their own hands." Given these conditions, Gibson says, in a vein similar to Stallman's, the need for burial, not the actual shooting and killing, is what makes their friend's death real to Lean and the adjutant (104). Neville Denny takes this view as well, asserting that the point of the story is the protagonists' discomfiture at having to do the burying themselves—at being "faced with the rude actuality" of "a friend in a hole"—rather than being, as is more customary, screened off from the death by "the ritualistic funeral trappings—handsome coffin, litany, formal movements" (38).

Bettina Knapp goes one step further, arguing that the most disturbing aspect of this hands-on interment for Lean and the adjutant is not simply the lack of screening from death as an idea but the lack of screening from that idea as it applies specifically to them. In the body and especially the face of their friend, "they see themselves, unconsciously, in projection," and it is this identification, coupled with their awareness of the body's vulnerability to decomposition, that underlies their reluctance to complete the burial. It is also this identification, extended to the reader, Knapp says, that produces the emotional power of the story's climax, which "transcends the individual act and takes on mythical status" (173–74).

A number of other critics are equally laudatory but focus not only on the story's themes but also on the technical expertise with which Crane deals with those themes. James B. Colvert ranks "Face" with Crane's best work because of "its precision and perfect economy, its flawless representation of the gesture, posture, and inarticulate speech of extreme mental distress" (*Stephen Crane* 157). Colvert also regards the story as perhaps the best example of Crane's late prose style, which he characterizes as "lean, open, and sardonically understated" and by means of which he sees Crane attenuating "his essentially mythic sense of war so severely that it seems all but absent except in the broad context of his characteristic feeling for the ambiguous crossing of horror and humor in a dreamlike suspension of the movement of time" ("Style" 131). James Nagel similarly praises the story for its brevity, unity, well-thought-out structure and psychological penetration, but he singles out two further attributes for particular notice. The first of these is the story's "rich duality"—the fact that "the narration is objective, external, detached" and yet "the significance is subjective, internal, psychological"; the second is the power of the conclusion, at which point the "plop" of the earth striking the corpse's face becomes "essentially an objective correlative for a powerfully realized emotion, one symbolically indicating the undesirable presence and fact of death" (17–18).

Frank Bergon also takes note of this onomatopoeia and goes on to point out that it is one manifestation of a conscious and effective artistic decision. Whereas Crane customarily relies most heavily on visual imagery, there is very little of it in "Face"; he works here mostly with aural and tactile images, with the goal of "disproportion[ing] the senses by restricting some and stressing others, just as dreams often do," thereby creating a world that physically as well as mentally bears the characteristics of a nightmare (37). What Crane *does* do with visual effects in this story has been explored by Christopher Benfey, who calls it "one of Crane's masterpieces of concentration" (264); it gets much of its force, in his view, from Crane's handling of sharp visual contrasts of vertical with horizontal, such as those between the two "'upright'" officers and the two lowly privates who are first supposed to bury the dead man and between the standing survivors and the recumbent corpse (266).

Marston LaFrance and Charles Swann concentrate on other stylistic features of "Face." LaFrance notes Crane's tense prose style here, which conveys that Lean and the adjutant are on the verge of hysteria over having to bury their friend themselves when they have not yet accepted the fact of death. This condition is for LaFrance consonant with his discernment in nearly all of Crane's significant works of a pattern of great fear of the unknown followed by deflation and then absurdity. In this case, performing the burial is the unknown experience the protagonists fear so greatly, and their hysteria is deflated and rendered absurd when they finally throw earth on the corpse's face, for that action reveals to them that "[t]his corpse was after all but a corpse, . . . and whatever happened to it could happen to any other piece of inanimate clay with exactly the same significance"—none (240). Swann sees the tenseness of the prose as conveying the idea that "[o]ne of the challenges of death is that it is beyond or beneath language." The two officers struggle to remember the words of the burial service, which is "a metaphysical, ordered linguistic statement about the immortality of the soul, but which is dreadfully contradicted by the presence of the corpse." What preoccupies Lean and the adjutant "is not that half-remembered fiction" of the burial service, but rather "the actuality of the face of the dead man—a reality with which language cannot cope." This inability, Swann says, is the reason that the story concludes not with a word but with an onomatopoeia, "something prior to language" (101).

Two other critics take as their main consideration the story's terminal position in Crane's *oeuvre*. George W. Johnson sees it as a summation of Crane's philosophy: in their efforts to adhere to "some notion of ultimate propriety," in their effort in the burial ritual to "phrase a metaphor of man's relationship to the cosmos" (252), Lean and the adjutant provide a final illustration of Crane's belief that the human condition is entrapment between "an unknowable world and incongruous ceremonies" (251), a condition in which those ceremonies, despite their ultimate meaninglessness, enable their practitioners to "accept incongruities which would otherwise overwhelm [their] imagination" (253). Similarly, Holton emphasizes the necessity of reading this story not in isolation but as the last of the four Spitzbergen tales, since it only makes full sense as the final step in the Twelfth Regiment's initiation into the absurdity of war, a process that all four tales progressively illuminate, and since this cycle of tales only makes its fullest impact when it is understood as the logical culmination of much of Crane's life and work devoted to confronting the reality of war and death. In terms of this confrontation, Holton argues that "Face" presents the final, most horrible initiation into these subjects, in that the burial here requires Lean to touch the corpse and look into its face even as bullets whine around him, thus forcing him to recognize "the mutability which one shares with the dead" (269). And along with this recognition comes a concomitant understanding of burial as a ritual that serves as "a means of dealing with chaos, a means of asserting order," and as a ritual that "requires confrontation even as it makes such confrontation bearable" (269). When Lean takes over the actual task of burial and thus confronts the face, Holton says, he, in parallel with Crane himself at this late stage of his life, "has earned the right, finally, to cover over the reality of death and to turn away" (271).

In partial controversion of unrelievedly grim views such as Holton's, Dillingham argues that one must be aware of the comic elements of "Face," derived from its pairings of the grisly and the laughable, to understand its full impact. Among such elements, Dillingham says, are the adjutant's ineffectuality at managing the burial when an adjutant's express function is to manage (325); the characters' frequent indecisive stares at one another in juxtaposition with the corpse's sightless stare, which creates "a farcical pantomime" (327); and Lean's and the adjutant's helplessness when confronting the details of death because they are accustomed to having a mortician and minister present to take care of those (329). Crane's intent with this comedy, Dillingham says, is "to point up man's utterly irrational attitudes toward death, to show what happens when man, a somewhat ridiculous creature anyway, is transplanted from an environment where death can be clothed in euphemisms to one where he is forced to face death directly" (324).

In response to Dillingham's argument, Bill Christophersen acknowledges Crane's incongruous juxtapositions but asserts that these make the story not comic—nor indeed Naturalistic or Impressionistic, the labels most frequently applied to Crane's fiction—but rather Expressionistic. Using Berryman's comment that this story is unique in Crane's canon by virtue of its affinities with Goya's late etchings, which are precursors of Expressionism, Christophersen systematically draws a number of specific parallels between "Face" and this twentieth-century visual-arts movement. Expressionism, he explains, is an effort to create "an assertion of the individual ego in a machine age which has all but annihilated the ego and individual response" (152–53) by depicting the emotional content contained in a scene, usually through exaggeration and symbolism, rather than simply reproducing its surface reality, and he sees Crane taking precisely this approach in "Face." Crane symbolically "concretize[s] and concentrates" fear of death and the unknown in the chalk-blue color of the corpse's mask-like face (153), and Lean's outburst at the adjutant's indecision is "the Expressionist shriek par excellence—a cry of mutiny, conveying the affronted sensibility of man at that moment [when] the modern world dawns on him in all its senselessness and horror" (154). Christophersen further notes Crane's seeming anticipation of a number of the techniques of Expressionist theater, such as "lurid visual effects, . . . an ambience of darkness, grotesqueness, and unreality, . . . disturbing aural effects, . . . [and] the ambiguous rendering of setting and character" (155). Crane's use of such techniques, Christophersen says, stems from his grounding in the ideas of Impressionism—its focus on the "inscrutability and mutability of reality as perceived by the senses"; Crane's version of Expressionism in "Face," his determination to dig beneath the inscrutable, mutable surface of reality, constitutes his rejection of the "bitter implications," epistemologically speaking, of Impressionism (160).

Still one more proposed artistic label for this story comes from Wolford. He points out Crane's uncharacteristic lack of "odd details" in describing death here, his use of only the corpse's buttons and its face, and notes that this extreme spareness is more evocative than a profusion of gory effects would be. Such "excruciating economy," Wolford says, makes the story a forerunner of Modernism or perhaps even Postmodernism (79).

Works Cited

Benfey, Christopher. *The Double Life of Stephen Crane*. New York: Knopf, 1992.

Bergon, Frank. *Stephen Crane's Artistry*. New York: Columbia University Press, 1975.

Berryman, John. *Stephen Crane*. New York: Sloane, 1950.

Bowers, Fredson. Textual Introduction. *Tales of War*. Vol. 6 of The University of Virginia Edition of *The Works of Stephen Crane*. Ed. Fredson Bowers. Charlottesville: University Press of Virginia, 1970, xxxvii–cxci.

Carney, Raymond. "Crane and Eakins." *Partisan Review* 55 (1988):464–73.

Christophersen, Bill. "Stephen Crane's 'The Upturned Face' as Expressionist Fiction." *Arizona Quarterly* 38 (1982):147–61.

Colvert, James B. *Stephen Crane*. New York: Harcourt Brace Jovanovich, 1984.

———. "Stephen Crane and Postmodern Criticism." *Stephen Crane Studies* 1 (1992):2–8.

———. "Stephen Crane: Style as Invention." *Stephen Crane in Transition: Centenary Essays*. Ed. Joseph Katz. DeKalb: Northern Illinois University Press, 1972, 127–52.

Crane, Stephen. "In the First Land Attack Four of Our Men Are Killed." *Reports of War*. Vol. 9 of The University of Virginia Edition of *The Works of Stephen Crane*. Ed. Fredson Bowers. Charlottesville: University Press of Virginia, 1971, 128–30.

———. "War Memories." *Tales of War* 222–263.

Denny, Neville. "Imagination and Experience in Stephen Crane." *English Studies in Africa* 9 (1966):28–42.

Dillingham, William B. "Crane's One-Act Farce: 'The Upturned Face.'" *Research Studies* 35 (1967):324–30.

Fried, Michael. "Realism, Writing, and Disfiguration in Thomas Eakins's *Gross Clinic*, with a Postscript on Stephen Crane's Upturned Faces." *Representations* 9 (1985):33–104.

———. *Realism, Writing, Disfiguration: On Thomas Eakins and Stephen Crane*. Chicago: University of Chicago Press, 1987.

Gibson, Donald B. *The Fiction of Stephen Crane*. Carbondale: Southern Illinois University Press, 1968.

Holton, Milne. *Cylinder of Vision: The Fiction and Journalistic Writings of Stephen Crane*. Baton Rouge: Louisiana State University Press, 1972.

Johnson, George W. "Stephen Crane's Metaphor of Decorum." *PMLA* 78 (1963): 250–56.

Knapp, Bettina L. *Stephen Crane*. New York: Ungar, 1987.

LaFrance, Marston. *A Reading of Stephen Crane*. Oxford: Clarendon, 1971.

Nagel, James. *Stephen Crane and Literary Impressionism*. University Park: Pennsylvania State University Press, 1980.

Solomon, Eric. *Stephen Crane: From Parody to Realism*. Cambridge: Harvard University Press, 1966.

———. "Stephen Crane's War Stories." *Texas Studies in Literature and Language* 3 (1961):67–80.

Stallman, R. W. "Crane's Short Stories." *The Houses That James Built*. East Lansing: Michigan State University Press, 1961, 103–10.

———. "Stephen Crane: A Revaluation." In *Critiques and Essays on Modern Fiction: 1920–1951*. Ed. John W. Aldridge. New York: Ronald, 1952, 244–69.

———. *Stephen Crane: A Biography*. New York: George Braziller, 1968.

Stallman, R. W., and E. R. Hagemann, eds. *The War Dispatches of Stephen Crane*. New York: New York University Press, 1964.

Swann, Charles. "Stephen Crane and a Problem of Interpretation." *Literature and History* 7 (1981):91–123.

Wertheim, Stanley, and Paul Sorrentino, eds. *The Correspondence of Stephen Crane*. Vol. 2. New York: Columbia University Press, 1988.

Wolford, Chester L. *Stephen Crane: A Study of the Short Fiction*. Boston: Twayne, 1989.

The Veteran

Publication History

This story was first published in America in the August 1896 issue of *McClure's Magazine* (7:222–24); it was then included in the D. Appleton book *"The Little Regiment" and Other Episodes of the American Civil War*, which came out in October of 1896. In England, it first ran in the Christmas 1896 number of *St. James's Budget* (81–82) and then appeared in the English version of *"The Little Regiment" and Other Episodes of the American Civil War*, which Heinemann published in February 1897 (Bowers lxxvii–lxxviii). Pioneering Crane editor Wilson Follett placed it in the first volume, published in 1925, of *The Work of Stephen Crane* (12 vols., New York: Knopf, 1925–27), and in 1963 Thomas A. Gullason included it in his *Complete Short Stories and Sketches of Stephen Crane* (Garden City, N.Y.: Doubleday).

Circumstances of Composition

"The Veteran" was one of five stories related to the Civil War that Crane wrote, in response to the McClure newspaper syndicate's request for such material to capitalize on the current success of *The Red Badge of Courage*, while he was living at his brother Edmund's home in Hartwood, a village in New York State, between October 1895 and February 1896 (Colvert xiv). The editors of Crane's correspondence hypothesize that Crane may be referring to "The Veteran" in a letter of January 28, 1896, from Hartwood to syndicate head S. S. McClure in New York City, when he says, "I feel for you when I think of some of the things of mine which you will have to read or have read. If you dont [sic] like the enclosed [story] please return it to me here" (*Correspondence* I, 194).

Sources and Influences

No one has identified any sources for this story in Crane's conversations with actual veterans or in his reading; James B. Colvert asserts that it "is composed of elements obliquely drawn from his mythic imagination" (xxx). However, two critics, John Berryman and Nicholas Delbanco, speculate interestingly on what specific personal thoughts and feelings might have turned his imagination to this particular subject and impelled him to make this particular myth from it. Berryman reads the story in Freudian terms, as one of Crane's efforts to deal with his Oedipal guilt. He says that here Crane splits his identity between two masks he has used for himself in other stories—Henry Fleming from *Red Badge* and a Swedish farmhand, who stands in for the panic-stricken, death-obsessed Swede of "The Blue Hotel"—and has these two masks meet in order to force a confrontation between himself and his father, the aged Henry now serving not just as Crane himself but as his father as well. Through this imaginative confrontation, Berryman argues, Crane enables himself to come to grips with his feelings of "aggression against the father, the wish to be the father, and the solution for panic." As further confirmation of this theory, he points out that Henry dies trying to save horses, animals that Berryman interprets, following Freud's lead, as being linked in a number of stories to Crane's Oedipal guilt (324).

Delbanco sees the story as rooted in another source of guilt. Henry's decision to go back for the colts, he suggests, is a product of Crane's own "guilt of the survivor" due to his having been born too late for the Civil War, a feeling that "is characteristic of those American authors who missed the Civil War." Owing to this condition, Crane's "imaginative reconstruction" of Henry Fleming's behavior during and after the war "is powered by a sense of loss. Henry Fleming in *The Red Badge of Courage* is at the edge of action only, a pampered child. The pale cast of thought has sicklied him." However, "conscience can make heroes of us all," Delbanco continues, which is what Crane finally has happen to Henry in "The Veteran" when he goes back for the colts, constituting the fulfillment of the author's wish to make amends for his own inability to have been even at the edge of the action during the war (50).

Relationship to Other Crane Works

Since Henry Fleming's old age and death are the subjects of this story, many critics regard it as Delbanco does, as deriving its meaning almost wholly from being Crane's epilogue to *Red Badge* and in that capacity providing the kind of clear-cut explanation of the significance of Henry's experience that the novel withholds at its end. Thus, they tend to look for explicit links between novel and story that may be seen to bear on this explanation. Colvert, for example, sees the "satanic" imagery that Crane uses in "The Veteran" to describe the fire in the barn as a conscious repetition of the "demonic" imagery through which he characterizes battle in *Red Badge*, Crane's point in setting up this connection being that in the story "Henry at last charges the enemy he was permitted to evade at the end of *The Red Badge*," thereby creating a more clearly redemptive resolution than the novel affords (xxix). Colvert also sees the story as a clarification of the novel in terms of style, for in his view "The Veteran" exemplifies Crane's development of a "lean, open, disciplined" prose that dispenses with the "rhetorical flourishes [and] studied elaboration of chiaroscuro imagery" that mark *Red Badge* and much of his other early work (xxviii–xxix). (Colvert also offers this assessment on p. 148 of a later essay, "Stephen Crane: Style as Invention.")

John W. Shroeder and Michael Fried likewise read the story as a clarification of the novel. Shroeder contends that Crane doubted the efficacy of the transformation and salvation that he had put Henry through—that he came to feel that, though he intended Henry's redemption in *Red Badge* to be genuine, he might have missed that mark. Viewed in this light, Henry's death while trying to rescue the colts strikes Shroeder as "both afterthought and act of expiation," as Crane's way of giving Henry a second, unambiguous chance at redemption (126). Fried too sees "The Veteran" as Crane's effort to resolve what he left ambiguous in *Red Badge*. Where Henry's level of insight into himself in *Red Badge* remains uncertain, in the "The Veteran" he definitely possesses "an ironic self-knowledge that far surpasses his most enlightened moments in the novel," and his willingness to confront death in his attempt to rescue the colts renders him unquestionably heroic. What Fried finds most significant here is the idea that in writing this unambiguous story Crane himself enacts the process that most of his later readers have gone through regarding *Red Badge*: he takes an indeterminate, multiplex novel and imposes a single interpretation on it. In postmodern parlance such in act is called "totalizing," and in Fried's view "The Veteran" reveals Crane emerging as

> the first (or among the first) of his totalizing readers, who traditionally have felt compelled to subsume under a univocal moral and/or psychological interpretation not only as many of the events of a given narrative as could be made to fit but also the overall shape of that narrative considered as a simultaneous unity. (160)

Eric Solomon and Warren French also read "The Veteran" as a commentary of sorts on *Red Badge*, but in their view this commentary is not a resolution of a lack of clarity in the novel but rather an extension or refinement of ideas that are already made plain there. Solomon sees the youthful Henry as learning in *Red Badge* to let go of his incorrect preconceptions about the nature of heroism and to focus simply on the performance of his duty as a soldier's highest achievement, and he contends that "The Veteran" shows the aged Henry still acting upon that lesson. He dies, Solomon says, "as a calm, unheroic individual doing his best for society," and he thereby evinces "the quiet devotion to duty [that] leads to the real glory and [the] selflessness [that] raises one above the mass of men" (113). (Solomon repeats this assessment in his later book-length study *Stephen Crane: From Parody to Realism*, p. 98.)

French interprets the aggregate significance of the novel and story somewhat differently. In his view, Henry in *Red Badge* does not learn to see the world as it is but rather discovers that he can mold it to his own benefit. When his comrades accept his fiction about having been wounded he becomes what he wishes to be, a hero, rather than what he has in fact been. He thus learns "to reshape reality for his own purposes," and with this fact in view "The Veteran" "offers several important insights into Crane's conception of the hero in a self-conscious age," thereby providing a capstone to the novel's open ending (161). In French's reading, the opening of the story shows that Henry after the war continues to shape reality for his own benefit, since his willingness now to admit his early fear makes a more favorable impression on his neighbors than would bragging about his supposed exploits, but it also shows that he has not used this ability to aggrandize himself excessively as a politician or entrepreneur. And in line with this wise use of the power he discovered in battle, the end of the story shows Henry achieving mythological stature. If he were simply to die and be buried, "returned to the nature in which in his moment of defeat he had sought refuge" in *Red Badge*, Henry would be seen as being defeated by "the very forces of preordination that [he] had vanquished" in the novel (163). Instead, with Henry's death in the fire, with the metaphor of the genie emphasizing his transcendence of the material world, Crane moves his hero "out of any particular place and time, suggesting that his spirit is untouchable by any physical powers." The reader may not be completely convinced by Crane's "incantation" here, French acknowledges, but the author is unmistakably "bent on myth-making" (163).

Donald B. Gibson, on the other hand, argues that the reader should resist making such clear-cut connections between "The Veteran" and *Red Badge*. In his view, the novel is tonally confused, so that grasping Crane's intentions in it, or inferring them from "The Veteran," is impossible; moreover, "Crane had no obligations in writing ['The Veteran'] to interpret the meaning of the earlier work. The tale is external evidence, and thus subject to the limitations of all other external evidence" (90). Henry ends up courageous in *Red Badge*, Gibson says, but the meaning of this courage is unclear, whereas in "The Veteran" the end of the story asserts that courage is "desirable and worthwhile" (91), as is likewise the case in "A Mystery of Heroism" and "The Clan of No-Name" (100). Gibson also links "The Veteran" with another of the stories in "*The Little Regiment*," "An Indiana Campaign," in that in both these cases the protagonist is an old soldier who long ago resolved the issue of his own courage that the Henry of *Red Badge* and Fred Collins, the protagonist of "Mystery," are just confronting. As a result, unlike young Henry and Collins, "[n]either of the old soldiers has the least hesitation about doing what he does. Neither has the same tenacious hold on life [as the younger men], though at the same time neither of the old men is simply foolhardy" (93). Beyond these differences, however, Gibson sees "The Veteran," "Indiana," and "Mystery" as all carrying the same final meaning: "courageous action in the face of adversity is necessary and desirable despite the fact that it might or might not have some intimate relationship with the nature of things, that it might not accomplish what it was intended to accomplish" (94).

James Nagel agrees that "The Veteran" is not simply a gloss on *Red Badge* and that it is in fact more closely linked to "Mystery" on the basis of courageous action carried out despite adversity and futility. In both of these stories, he notes, Crane presents a situation in which the protagonist exercises compassion even though he himself is in jeopardy, and this behavior, regardless of its results, seems to be the true definition of heroism for Crane ("War" 10). Collins in "Mystery" cannot save the wounded lieutenant's life by giving him a drink, and Fleming stands very little chance of actually rescuing the colts in the burning barn, but in both instances these men risk their lives—and Fleming loses his—to make whatever effort they can, thus exhibiting the kind of grace under pressure that Crane most admired, the sort of unself-conscious human kindness that he once characterized as "[t]he final wall of the wise man's thought" (*Correspondence* I, 180).

Critical Studies

Several critics believe that Crane accurately assesses the merits of "The Veteran" when he expresses sympathy for McClure regarding "some of the things of mine which you will have to read or have read." Marston LaFrance dismisses it out of hand as "an unnecessary epilogue" to *Red Badge* (179), while Gullason identifies its flaws more specifically: a focus on "incident and plot" rather than "character and life," and a lack of a truly tragic dimension in the ending because Henry sacrifices himself for animals rather than people (475). Frank Bergon's opinion is equally low; in his view, the story "resorts to conventional expressions of conventional attitudes in a way that Crane's more alert fiction does not" (95).

A number of other critics do not find "The Veteran" wanting alongside most of Crane's other fiction, as is evident in the "Relationship to Other Crane Works" section, and still others rate the story favorably on its own merits alone. However, given the fact of Henry Fleming's being the protagonist of two works, even those critics who wish to concentrate solely on the merits and import of "The Veteran" cannot avoid reading it with some reference to Henry's behavior in *Red Badge*. Tracing from the novel to the story, Joseph Katz says that, in contrast to his youthful self, Henry in "The Veteran" is "the man who has solved himself." Starting in *Red Badge* and concluding in "The Veteran," his process of maturation "involved successive stages in which his preconceptions were established, then shaken, then tested against his experience, and finally modified to conform more closely with his insight into reality" (xxv). J. C. Levenson likewise sees a process begun in *Red Badge* and concluded in "The Veteran," but he is less positive about the satisfactoriness of that conclusion. Henry's grandson's being named Jimmie is an indication that Henry is aware that he still owes a debt to Jim Conklin, which he discharges in his final act of self-sacrifice in attempting to rescue the colts, Levenson says, but he also opines that this resolution of Henry's problem "is so neat as to require more mythic belief than a reader may be willing to lend" (xxiii).

Milne Holton takes the view that Crane may have wanted the reader to view this resolution as too neat and to understand thereby that Henry has still not reached full knowledge in the moment of his death. The story is "a kind of gloss on *The Red Badge*" in that here Henry is willing to admit his own fear in battle and to recall his friend Conklin but still represses his memories of his encounter with the corpse in the forest and the grisly manner of Conklin's death, circumstances that suggest to Holton that, veteran though Henry may be, his initiation into a full understanding of courage in the face of death is still incomplete. Therefore, Holton argues, Henry's behavior during the barn fire shows that "he can behave bravely—he can act efficiently and courageously to save horses and the Swede—but he cannot save himself." Saving himself, "accepting the absurd and horrible fact of the destruction of the colts which remain in the burning barn," would in Holton's view constitute full initiation. Instead, however, Henry "recklessly" returns to the barn to bring the colts out, in which action "[w]e see Henry's courage, the courage which he earned at Chancellorsville, but we also see the ultimate uselessness of that courage." And here as in *Red Badge*, "Crane's closing rhetoric has an ironically hollow ring" (116–17).

Three other critics as well take up the question of intentional irony in Crane's rhetorically charged ending:

> When the roof fell in, a great funnel of smoke swarmed towards the sky,
> as if the old man's mighty spirit, released from its body—a little bottle—
> had swelled like the genie of fable. The smoke was tinted rose-hue from
> the flames, and perhaps the unutterable midnights of the universe will
> have no power to daunt the color of this soul. (86)

Chester L. Wolford is in accord with Holton's view that Crane does intend irony here, emphasizing the meaninglessness of Henry's death; he predicates this stance on the fact that all the rest of what he calls Crane's "lyrical" endings—of *Red Badge*, "The Bride Comes to Yellow Sky," "The Blue Hotel," and "The Open Boat"—are frequently regarded as ironic (67). Bettina Knapp, on the other hand, reads this passage straightforwardly, arguing that the final sentence in particular sums up the merit of Henry's last effort at heroism and also concentrates attention upon "the poignancy of *feeling* in this old man who, at the outset of the story," in his explanation of his fear and recovery on his first battlefield, "so movingly touched upon universal values and ideas" (168). David Halliburton offers a third possibility; he takes the view that Crane intends for the reader not to decide whether his "panegyric" to Henry is sincere or ironic, his goal thereby being to leave intact the ultimately insoluble mystery of the sources and nature of heroism (146–47).

Rather than concentrating on the ending, Nagel considers the style of the story as a whole and, in so doing, concludes that Crane's final vision of Henry is not ironic. He notes first Crane's skill in creating imagistic unity and contrast by setting up details that contribute to the tranquility of the first scene but metamorphose into indications of threats later on, threats which Henry faces with tranquility. The church belfry that is visible in the opening, for instance, becomes audible as a fire alarm when the action rises, while the yellow sunshine of the initial scene is transformed into the yellow flame of the barn fire (*Impressionism* 136). Nagel then points out the battle imagery that Crane uses to describe Henry's conduct during the fire, which creates a larger unity, with the combat scenes of *Red Badge*, a unity that enables the reader to see Henry's progression from cowardice in the early stages of that novel to unwavering courage at the close of this story (*Impressionism* 138–39).

Works Cited

Bergon, Frank. *Stephen Crane's Artistry*. New York: Columbia University Press, 1975.

Berryman, John. *Stephen Crane*. New York: Sloane, 1950.

Bowers, Fredson. Textual Introduction. *Tales of War*. Vol. 6 of The University of Virginia Edition of *The Works of Stephen Crane*. Ed. Fredson Bowers. Charlottesville: University Press of Virginia, 1970, xxxvii–cxci.

Colvert, James B. Introduction. *Tales of War*, xi–xxxvi.

————. "Stephen Crane: Style as Invention." *Stephen Crane in Transition: Centenary Essays*. Ed. Joseph Katz. DeKalb: Northern Illinois University Press, 1972, 127–52.

Crane, Stephen. "The Veteran." *Tales of War*, 82–86.

Delbanco, Nicholas. *Group Portrait: A Biographical Study of Writers in Community*. New York: William Morrow, 1982.

French, Warren. "Stephen Crane: Moment of Myth." *Prairie Schooner* 55 (1981):155–67.

Fried, Michael. *Realism, Writing, Disfiguration: On Thomas Eakins and Stephen Crane*. Chicago: University of Chicago Press, 1987.

Gibson, Donald B. *The Fiction of Stephen Crane*. Carbondale: Southern Illinois University Press, 1968.

Gullason, Thomas A. "Stephen Crane's Short Stories: The True Road." *Stephen Crane's Career: Perspectives and Evaluations*. Ed. Thomas A. Gullason. New York: New York University Press, 1972, 470–86.

Halliburton, David. *The Color of the Sky: A Study of Stephen Crane*. Cambridge: Cambridge University Press, 1989.

Holton, Milne. *Cylinder of Vision: The Fiction and Journalistic Writings of Stephen Crane*. Baton Rouge: Louisiana State University Press, 1972.

Katz, Joseph. Introduction. *Stephen Crane in the West and Mexico*. Kent, Ohio: Kent State University Press, 1970, ix–xxv.

Knapp, Bettina L. *Stephen Crane*. New York: Ungar, 1987.

LaFrance, Marston. *A Reading of Stephen Crane*. Oxford: Clarendon, 1971.

Levenson, J. C. Introduction. *Tales of Whilomville*. Vol. 7 of The University of Virginia Edition of *The Works of Stephen Crane*. Ed. Fredson Bowers. Charlottesville: University Press of Virginia, 1968, xi–lx.

Nagel, James. *Stephen Crane and Literary Impressionism*. University Park: Pennsylvania State University Press, 1980.

————. "Stephen Crane's Stories of War: A Study of Art and Theme." *North Dakota Quarterly* 43 (1975):5–19.

Shroeder, John W. "Stephen Crane Embattled." *University of Kansas City Review* 17 (1950):119–29.

Solomon, Eric. *Stephen Crane: From Parody to Realism*. Cambridge: Harvard University Press, 1966.

————. "A Gloss on *The Red Badge of Courage*." *Modern Language Notes* 75 (1960):111–13.

Wertheim, Stanley, and Paul Sorrentino, eds. *The Correspondence of Stephen Crane*. Vol. 1. New York: Columbia University Press, 1988.

Wolford, Chester L. *Stephen Crane: A Study of the Short Fiction*. Boston: Twayne, 1989.

Virtue in War

Publication History

This story was first published in America in *Frank Leslie's Popular Monthly* for November 1899 (49:88–101), under the title "West Pointer and Volunteer; Or, Virtue in War." It appeared with this same title in England in the June 16, 1900, issue of the *Illustrated London News* (116:809–11). The title was probably shortened to its current form by an editor with the Frederick Stokes company when the story was included in the Stokes book *Wounds in the Rain*, published in America in September 1900; the story also ran under its current title in the English edition of this collection, which Heinemann published concurrently with the Stokes American edition (Bowers cxlviii–cxlix). It appeared again, with the title "Virtue in War" firmly established, in volume 2, published in 1925, of *The Work of Stephen Crane* (12 vols., New York: Knopf, 1925–27), edited by Wilson Follett. It was also collected in 1963 in *The Complete Short Stories and Sketches of Stephen Crane* (Garden City, N.Y.: Doubleday), edited by Thomas A. Gullason.

Circumstances of Composition

Fredson Bowers notes that "Virtue in War" and another Spanish-American War story, "The Second Generation," were for some reason linked in the mind of James Pinker, Crane's English agent, and in Crane's own mind as well, a condition suggesting that they were composed around the same time (clxii). This appears to have been the summer of 1899, while Crane was living in his final English home, Brede Place, Sussex, since Crane submitted an early, short version of "Virtue in War," then entitled "The Making of the 307th," to Pinker on July 21 of that year, calling it "a rattling good war story" (*Correspondence* II, 490). In late August or the beginning of September he sent Pinker both the full version of the story as it was eventually published—the title now evidently changed to "West Pointer and Volunteer; Or, Virtue in War"—and a copy of "The Second Generation" (Bowers cxlvi–xlvii). It was probably this essentially concurrent submission that occasioned the aforementioned linking; in any event, it definitely provoked a good deal of confusion. On September 14, 1899, Pinker informed Crane that he had sold the American serial rights for "Generation" to the *Saturday Evening Post* (*Correspondence* II, 517), and shortly thereafter, in a letter that has been lost, he added that he had sold the American serial rights for "Virtue in War" to Tillotson's newspaper syndicate. Crane's response has been lost as well, but he apparently wired Pinker that he could not remember which recent war story had had its name changed and therefore feared that "Virtue" and "Generation" were the same story, meaning that Pinker had sold its American serial rights twice. Pinker replied on September 21 that "'Virtue in War' is the story the American serial rights of which I sold to Tillotsons. It is not the same story as 'The Second Generation'" (*Correspondence* II, 517).

This letter did not ease Crane's mind completely, however, for on Sept. 30 he wrote Pinker, "I cannot express how worried I am over 'Virtue in War' and 'The Second Generation.' I can only remember writing *one* story and I would almost bet the two titles cover one story. We may be making a hideous blunder. Please find out." Two days later, probably before Pinker had had a chance to offer further reassurance, Crane wrote him again to say, "I am still nervous about Virtue in War and The Second Generation [sic]" (*Correspondence* II, 526, 528). This is Crane's last surviving word on this subject; whether Pinker finally managed to set his mind at rest or he simply forgot the problem in the press of his other concerns is open to speculation.

Ironically enough, Crane's fears were justified: his faulty memory about the name change of this story did in fact cause a problem, although not the one he suspected, but he did not live long enough to realize it. On June 15, 1900, ten days after Crane died of tuberculosis in a sanitarium in Badenweiler, Germany, Pinker received a letter from the American publisher Frederick Stokes, who was preparing to release *Wounds in the Rain*, the volume of Crane's Spanish-American War stories in which "Virtue" was to be included. Stokes reminds Pinker that Crane had contracted for a book of 80,000 words, a goal that Crane thought he had met. However, Stokes says, the actual total is only 75,735, since "two stories in Mr. Crane's own list, given by him as 'The Making of the 307th,' and 'Virtue in War,' respectively, are one and the same story" (*Correspondence* II, 532).

Sources and Influences

Crane got the germ for the central conflict in this story—the clash between the thoroughly professional veteran Major Gates and the informally inclined recruit Lige Wigram that develops when Wigram is assigned to Gates's unit at the outset of the Spanish-American War—from an anecdote that Edward Marshall, a war correspondent for the *New York Journal*, passed along to him. (Crane himself began the war as a corespondent for the *New York World*, but he moved to the *Journal* after a dispute with the *World*'s editors.) At one point early in the war, Marshall reported, an Army surgeon casually asked Lieutenant Colonel Theodore Roosevelt who he was; Roosevelt angrily replied, "'I'm your superior officer, sir. Stand at attention, salute, and take your hat off'" (Stallman 386). Gates's anger at Carmony, the battalion commander whose disorganized troops block Gates's own battalion during an uphill assault, was also derived from a situation in which Roosevelt was the principal actor. As his Rough Riders advanced into battle on July 1, 1898, Roosevelt found their way blocked by another regiment, the Tenth Cavalry. He ordered the nearest officer of that regiment, a Captain Hamilton, to move his men, but Hamilton refused, saying he would take orders only from his own colonel. Roosevelt allegedly replied either, "Then let my men through, sir," or "If you're not going up, get out of my way, for I am" (Stallman 391), and led his troops through the ranks of the Tenth and on to the successful charge up Kettle Hill that won fame for him and the Rough Riders, although they are frequently erroneously credited with having charged up nearby San Juan Hill instead. Crane alters Roosevelt's words to Gates's implicitly more pungent "'—— it, man, if you can't get your people to deploy, for —— sake give me a chance'" (*Tales* 189), and he alters Roosevelt's destiny as well by having Gates die in the attack, appreciated for his courage and professionalism not by the whole nation but, finally, by Wigram alone (191–92).

The aftermath of Gates's heroic death—the reason the nation will not celebrate him—also likely derives from actual events of the war. According to Gullason, the closing scene of the story, in which three correspondents remark momentarily on Gates's death, with one of them saying condescendingly, "'Poor old Gatesie!'" (*Tales* 192), and then consign him to oblivion as they resume an interrupted argument about where the best mint juleps in the world are made, reflects Crane's anger at the behavior of many of his fellow-correspondents in Cuba. He felt that they exhibited precisely this kind of misplacement of priorities, valuing their personal comfort over the true courage of the soldiers whose actions they were supposed to be reporting to their readers (Gullason 206).

Relationship to Other Crane Works

Marston LaFrance and E. R. Hagemann implicitly suggest that Pinker and Crane may have confused "Virtue in War" with "The Second Generation" due to marked thematic and technical similarities between these stories. LaFrance says that both draw comparisons between those who do and those who do not live up to Crane's code of the Regulars—that code being the steady, focused, unostentatious performance of whatever task must be done regardless of the dangers involved. The acceptance of this "moral harness," LaFrance continues, "develops logically as the moral answer" to the incompetence of volunteers and the venality of those in positions of power; it constitutes virtue in war, and those who do accept it recognize one another immediately and can equally readily spot the men who never will, the "poltroons" such as Caspar Cadogan, a spoiled officer of Volunteers in "Generation." However,

LaFrance concludes, "Virtue" and "Generation" are less effective meditations on this theme than several of Crane's other Spanish-American War stories, such as "The Price of the Harness," because in these two Crane overdoes his contempt for the poltroons, making them caricatures rather than convincing characters (182–87)—an assessment shared by Eric Solomon (118).

Hagemann, while acknowledging this thematic similarity, focuses on a technical connection. He notes that in "Virtue" and "Generation" Crane consciously personifies death, as in the sentence "Death smote them," from "Virtue," a technique he did not use in his earlier battle fiction, set during the Civil War. This change, Hagemann argues, is a function of Crane's having experienced combat at firsthand in the interval between these two groups of stories. Through this personal observation Crane "came to realize the presence and personification of death" on the battlefield and sought to convey this new realization in his later war fiction (364).

Chester L. Wolford is more expansive than LaFrance concerning connections between "Virtue" and "The Price of the Harness." Both these stories, he says, seek to communicate two new insights at which the author had arrived: first, heroism is simply the performance of one's job despite the imminent presence of death, and second, such heroism is its own reward. The second insight comes across through Crane's ironic undercutting of any external reward for heroism at the end of each story. That heroic behavior might stem from or result in patriotic fervor is denied at the conclusion of "Harness," when one of the wounded in a hospital tent sings "The Star-Spangled Banner" as a sarcastic comment on his own sufferings and those of the men around him; and the idea that courage may result in general public acclaim is demolished at the end of "Virtue" when the correspondents display more interest in the merits of various mint juleps than in Gates's heroic death (Wolford 73–74). Somewhat earlier, John Berryman made much the same point regarding the emphasis on the true nature of heroism in "Harness" and "Virtue," but he regards these stories less highly than Wolford, owing to his belief that both "insist a little too much, as the titles insist: the price is death, the virtue, doing one's duty in silence, the duty being courage" (253).

James Nagel connects "Virtue" as a meditation on heroism to one more of Crane's Spanish-American War stories, "The Clan of No-Name," and in so doing he comes to a conclusion regarding Crane's attitude toward this subject that differs from those above. In his view, both these stories take not only an "antigovernment" but also an "antiwar" stance, leading to the insight that Gates and Manolo Prat, the protagonist of "Clan," are not so much truly heroic as "inordinately idealistic and out of tune with reality." Both men die "with steadfast adherence to the code" of stoically silent professionalism, but in both cases "the code seems out of touch with reality and the story ends ironically," with the lack of appreciation or understanding of this code by others not making the point that such courage is its own reward but rather indicating that it is in fact meaningless (14–15).

Critical Studies

Although commentators generally consider the stories in *Wounds in the Rain* to be second-rate Crane, indications of his artistic decline toward the end of his life, several critics regard "Virtue" quite highly. Berryman says that despite its overly insistent character it is Crane's only story from 1899 that "shows undiminished power of conception and execution"; he sees it as a stylistic advance over even the more frequently praised "Monster" in terms of the "laconic perfection of mannerless phrasing which is one ideal of prose since Crane" (252–53). Milne Holton, controverting Berryman's judgment of the story as too insistent, praises Crane's lack of didacticism in this story, his willingness to let the reader make up his or her own mind, in contrast to his tone in a number of the other pieces in *Wounds*, in which he tends to preach about the nature and meaning of heroism. Here, Holton says, Crane employs two protagonists, Gates and Wigram, with opposing values but does not argue for the superiority of one over the other. While Crane clearly intends for the reader to admire the capability and professionalism Gates displays, Wigram is not presented as a counterbalancing negative figure. Rather, in Wigram's sense of comradeship that "transcends rank" and "ignores the imperatives of command," the reader may be given alternative positives, since it is this sense that impels Wigram to attempt to save Gates and then to identify his body when that attempt fails, acts proceeding from the sort of selfless compassion that Crane focuses on in many other stories. Thus, Holton concludes, Crane's intent may be not to make definitive statements but rather to ask the reader to consider what exactly does constitute "virtue in war" (262).

Robert W. Stallman, on the other hand, lauds the story for what he sees as the definitiveness of its statement. Crane's ideal of "virtue in war" here, according to Stallman, is clearly the fealty that Wigram displays to the dead Gates. He argues that Crane purposely chooses Wigram's odd first name, Lige, because it is derived from the Old French word *liège*, a vassal who owes service to a lord, and that Wigram dutifully discharges this service by burying Gates with a paper inscribed with his name and regiment to ensure that, when the body is disinterred for a more proper burial at a later date, the major will get the recognition he deserves for his professionalism and loyalty to the regiment (385–86).

Works Cited

Berryman, John. *Stephen Crane*. New York: Sloane, 1950.

Bowers, Fredson. Textual Introduction. *Tales of War*. Vol. 6 of The University of Virginia Edition of *The Works of Stephen Crane*. Ed. Fredson Bowers. Charlottesville: University Press of Virginia, 1970, xxxvii–cxci.

Crane, Stephen. "Virtue in War." *Tales of War* 180–93.

Gullason, Thomas A. "Stephen Crane's Private War on Yellow Journalism." *Huntington Library Quarterly* 22 (1958):201–08.

Hagemann, E. R. "Crane's 'Real' War in His Short Stories." *American Quarterly* 8 (1956):356–67.

Holton, Milne. *Cylinder of Vision: The Fiction and Journalistic Writings of Stephen Crane*. Baton Rouge: Louisiana State University Press, 1972.

LaFrance, Marston. *A Reading of Stephen Crane*. Oxford: Clarendon, 1971.

Nagel, James. "Stephen Crane's Stories of War: A Study of Art and Theme." *North Dakota Quarterly* 43 (1975):5–19.

Solomon, Eric. *Stephen Crane: From Parody to Realism*. Cambridge: Harvard University Press, 1966.

Stallman, R. W. *Stephen Crane: A Biography*. New York: George Braziller, 1968.

Wertheim, Stanley, and Paul Sorrentino, eds. *The Correspondence of Stephen Crane*. Vol. 2. New York: Columbia University Press, 1988.

Wolford, Chester L. *Stephen Crane: A Study of the Short Fiction*. Boston: Twayne, 1989.

War Memories

Publication History

This story received its first English publication in the December 1899 issue of the *Anglo-Saxon Review* (10:10–38). It did not run in any American periodical; instead, it next appeared in the collection *Wounds in the Rain*, which was published in September 1900 by Frederick Stokes in America and Methuen in Britain (Bowers cliv). Pioneering Crane editor Wilson Follett placed it in volume 9, published in 1926, of *The Work of Stephen Crane* (12 vols., New York: Knopf, 1925–27).

Circumstances of Composition

On July 24, 1899, Lady Randolph Churchill wrote Crane at his final English home, Brede Place, in Sussex, to ask him to write for the second number of her *Anglo-Saxon Review*, suggesting a piece of 6,000–10,000 words "on perhaps your experiences in Crete or Cuba" (*Correspondence* II, 491)—that is, his experiences as a newspaper correspondent in the Greco-Turkish or Spanish-American Wars. Crane agreed and decided to develop her suggestion into "War Memories," writing on August 4 to his British agent, James Pinker, to explain that this work "is not a commercial transaction"—in other words, there will be no agent's fee coming to Pinker for this piece because Crane is going to write it for free (*Correspondence* II, 493). Lady Churchill was apparently in dire need of copy at this point, for she wrote Crane again on August 8 to urge him to begin work immediately (*Correspondence* II, 495) and then once more on August 9 to tell him she wants the story for her September number but can "give you a little extra time if you want it" (495). Crane did get to work in short order, for C. Lewis Hind, an editor for the English periodical *Academy* and a visitor to Crane's home during this period, later recalled Crane's struggle with this piece in the summer of 1899. Laboring on what ultimately became the second paragraph of the story, Crane "seemed over-anxious about the right description of that huddle of bananas; and it seemed strange to find this fair, slight, sensitive youth sitting in the quiet of Brede Place writing about wild deeds in outlandish places" (qtd. in Berryman 243).

In a revealing glimpse of the difficult conditions of his life in this period, Crane notes in a letter of September 26 to Moreton Frewen, his landlord at Brede, that his work on "Memories" was interrupted when he had to escort his niece Helen to school in Switzerland in early September, and the interruption was compounded by one of his recurrent bouts with malaria while he was returning (*Correspondence* II, 524), and then by his need to stop over in Paris, still ill, and write another story to raise the money for his passage back to England (Stallman 474–75). But despite these setbacks, Crane evidently managed to meet Lady Churchill's deadline—to no purpose, as it turned out, for in a letter of October 10 she apologizes to him for her failure to run the story in either the September or the October number "owing to too much material being here set up & printed." She promises that it will appear in the December number, "which I am trying to make exceptionally good," a statement presumably intended as mollification (*Correspondence* II, 533).

If Crane required such placating, it probably came less from these words than from the fact that, his offer to work gratis notwithstanding, Lady Churchill paid him £52.10 on October 25 (*Correspondence* II, 540). Her reason for doing so is open to speculation. It may have been simply that she was compassionately aware of Crane's dire financial straits. Or it may have been an October 21 letter to Pinker from Crane's common-law wife, Cora, in which, displaying the Cranes' usual disregard for earlier promises in the face of their chronic insolvency, she claims that John Lane, Lady Churchill's publisher, owes Crane "*at least*, £50" for the story (*Correspondence* II, 537).

Sources and Influences

As Robert W. Stallman has shown, this story is composed of Crane's own war memories, his recollections of events in which he participated during the Cuban campaign of the Spanish-American War, as can be verified in most cases by cross-checking the story with various of Crane's Cuban newspaper dispatches. The near-collision of the narrator's unnamed ship with the U.S. gunboat *Machias*, for instance, is a version of what occurred on the night of May 14, 1898, between the *Machias* and the tug *Three Friends*, which had been pressed into service as a correspondents' transport, as Crane reported that episode in "Narrow Escape of the Three Friends" (*Reports* 118–20), filed in Key West on May 20 (Stallman 356). The account in "Memories" of the Spanish attacks on Camp McCalla, the U.S. Marine beachhead above Guantánamo Bay, follows closely Crane's description of the Spanish assaults on this position on the night of June 7–8 in the article "In the First Land Fight Four of Our Men Are Killed" (*Reports* 128–30), filed on June 20 (Stallman 362–63); the principal difference is that in the newspaper account Crane devotes more space to the tactics of the fight while in the story he provides more particulars of the death of Marine Surgeon John Blair Gibbs, with whom he had become friends.

Crane follows this episode in "Memories" with a description of the Marines' efforts on June 14–18 to dislodge the Spanish from their positions surrounding Camp McCalla, an engagement that came to be known as the Battle of Cuzco. This section tallies with Crane's June 22 dispatch on those events, "The Red Badge of Courage Was His Wig-Wag Flag" (*Reports* 134–42). The main difference between these two versions—a third is found in the story "Marines Signaling Under Fire at Guantánamo"—is that in "Memories" he gives a fuller account of the battle and of the heroics of two Marine signalmen, in reality Private John Fitzgerald and Sergeant John Quick (Stallman 371), who repeatedly risked their lives by standing up amid heavy enemy fire to transmit semaphore messages to the Navy ship *Dolphin*, which was acting as offshore support. What Crane leaves out of all these accounts is his own heroism, for during the early stages of this engagement he acted as an aide to Captain George F. Elliott, who praised him highly in his official report (Stallman 369).

The next episode in "Memories," a trip on horseback taken by the narrator and another correspondent from Guantánamo to Santiago Bay in search of the hitherto elusive Spanish fleet, is based on a similar and similarly successful expedition Crane undertook on June 17–18 with Sylvester Scovel, who was the head correspondent for the *New York World*, for which Crane was also reporting at this point (Stallman 373–74). Crane's own account of the Battle of San Juan on July 1 and the Americans' subsequent capture of the town of El Caney and advance on Santiago, "Stephen Crane's Vivid Story of the Battle of San Juan" (*Reports* 154–66), dated July 4, is his source for his treatment of those events in "Memories," the main difference being greater detail in

"Memories," particularly in the description of the church of San Luis de Caney, which the Americans had taken over for use as a hospital for the wounded the retreating Spanish had abandoned. The narrator's description of the unaccountable craving he developed for orange soda and of his return to Norfolk, Virginia, on a transport filled with the sick and wounded is, as David Halliburton points out (179), a fleshing out of a newspaper dispatch entitled "The Private's Story" (*Reports* 196–98). And finally, the narrator's recollection of the man who developed a similarly unaccountable but all-consuming craving for canned peaches derives from the real-life behavior of a fellow member of the press corps, Burr McIntosh, a photographer for *Leslie's Weekly* (Stallman 405).

Given this wealth of biographical sources, relatively few critics have explored possible literary antecedents on which Crane might have drawn for this story. One who has, Lars Ahnebrink, calls attention to the description of a red-headed Spanish corpse that the narrator observes in the aftermath of the Battle of San Juan. "He was irrevocably dead," the narrator says,

> [a]nd to what purpose? The honor of Spain? Surely the honor of Spain could have existed without the violent death of this poor red-headed peasant? Ah well, he was buried when the heavy firing ceased and men had time for such small things as funerals. The trench was turned over on top of him. . . . Sleep well, red-headed peasant. You came to another hemisphere to fight because—because you were told to, I suppose. Well, there you are, buried in your trench on San Juan Hill. That is the end of it. Your life has been taken—that is a flat, frank fact. And foreigners buried you expeditiously while speaking a strange tongue. Sleep well, red-headed mystery. (*Tales* 249–50)

Such an attitude, Ahnebrink says, with the narrator regarding war as meaningless and horrible and seeing men nevertheless going into it and dying for no reason that he can discern, is very similar to the stance Leo Tolstoy adopts in much of his war fiction, including *Sebastopol*, which Crane is known to have read, and *War and Peace*, which he may have read (345).

Another possible source is Rudyard Kipling. Although Crane claimed to have outgrown his "clever Rudyard-Kipling style" by 1894 (*Correspondence* I, 63), Eric Solomon notes that many of his Spanish-American War articles and stories partake of a distinctly Kipling-like idealization of the matter-of-fact courage of the common professional soldier, although this may be a result of Crane's and Kipling's sharing the same temperament rather than a case of direct literary influence. At one point in "Memories," for instance, the narrator describes a body of American troops advancing under fire as follows:

> There wasn't a high heroic face among them. They were all men intent on business. That was all. It may seem to you that I am trying to make everything a squalor. That would be wrong. I feel that things were often sublime. But they were *differently* sublime. They were not of our shallow and pre-

> posterous fictions. They stood out in a simple, majestic commonplace. . . .
> One cannot speak of it—the spectacle of the common man serenely doing
> his work, his appointed work. It is the one thing in the universe which
> makes one fling expression to the winds and be satisfied to simply feel.
> Thus they moved at San Juan—the soldiers of the United States Regular
> Army. One pays them the tribute of the toast of silence. (*Tales* 249)

In expatiations such as this, Solomon says, in which Crane falls into the unintended irony of concluding that he will pay tribute with silence to a subject to
which he has just devoted a lengthy and somewhat gushing paragraph, "[t]he
newspaperman Crane, like the civil servant Kipling, has succumbed to the
glamour of the soldier" (77).

Perhaps the most logical suggestion in the realm of literary influence is
Charles Swann's linking of Crane's work here to that of Joseph Conrad.
Swann points out that Crane's well-documented friendship with Conrad was
based, as their correspondence makes clear, on esteem for one another's
work and a belief that their approaches to art, epistemology, and the relationship between these two were closely aligned. With these facts in view, Swann
says that the attitude expressed at both the beginning and the end of
"Memories" regarding the gap between literature and life may stem from
Conrad. A war correspondent named Vernall, who may or may not be the
first-person narrator of the rest of the story, opens the story with an exclama-
tion that "'to get the real thing'" about war "'seems impossible! It is because
war is . . . simply life, and an expression of life can always evade us. We can
never tell life, one to another, although sometimes we think we can'" (*Tales*
221). And the narrator concludes this lengthy story by informing the reader
that "you can depend upon it that I have told you nothing at all, nothing at all,
nothing at all" (*Tales* 263). By way of comparison, Swann quotes an assertion
made by a character in Conrad's early masterpiece *Heart of Darkness*: "'it is
impossible to convey the life sensation of any given epoch of one's existence.'" Swann says that even though this particular story was not published
until 1902, two years after Crane's death, this sentiment accords with
Conrad's attitude during his period of close association with Crane and very
likely made a strong impression upon the younger Crane (99–100).

Another passage in "Memories" is frequently cited in the argument over
the theory, advanced by Thomas Beer and Stallman, and examined most thoroughly by Orm Overland, James Nagel, and Joseph J. Kwiat (331–38), that
Crane was heavily influenced by visual-arts techniques, especially those of
Impressionist painting. This passage describes the narrator's observation of
the field hospital the Americans had hastily set up in the church of San Luis
de Caney. "The interior of the church," he explains,

> was too cavelike in its gloom for the eyes of the operating surgeons, so
> they had had the altar-table carried to the doorway, where there was a

bright light. Framed then in the black archway was the altar-table with the figure of a man upon it. He was naked save for a breech-clout, and so close, so clear was the ecclesiastic suggestion, that one's mind leaped to a fantasy that this thin pale figure had just been torn down from a cross. The flash of the impression was like light, and for this instant it illumined all the dark recesses of one's remotest idea of sacrilege, ghastly and wanton. I bring this to you merely as an effect—an effect of mental light and shade, if you like; something done in thought similar to that which the French Impressionists do in color; something meaningless and at the same time overwhelming, crushing, monstrous. (*Tales* 254)

Although John Berryman asserts that Crane derived his theory of color deployment from reading Goethe and "owes nothing whatever, apparently, to painting" (289), this passage certainly suggests awareness if not influence, and Overland argues for both. He says that this description and explanation prove that Crane was conversant with and influenced by visual Impressionism, and that he may be counted as a literary Impressionist if one accepts the definition of *Impressionism* as the effort to show "the meeting of the outer world and the inner ego" (240); for in this passage Crane's narrator is presenting both "his own state of mind and the different components of outer reality coming into his vision . . ., explaining first how [this scene] came into his mind and then telling us what he has done or tried to do with it in his writing" (247). Similarly, Nagel notes that this passage demonstrates Crane's effective modification of the principles of French Impressionist painting to the needs of a literary exploration of individual consciousness. Perception is here presented as "originating from within the fiction itself and as having been perceived by the narrator," so that Crane as author "records what the center of intelligence experiences and thinks and nothing else." Crane thereby creates "a good example of how an established center of intelligence can relate not only sensory data but cognitive and associative mental activity as well" (43–44).

Three other critics dispute this influence. Responding expressly to Kwiat's assertion that Crane's mention of French Impressionism leads logically to the conclusion that Crane possessed technical familiarity with works in that genre, Stanley Wertheim contends that he actually derived his understanding of Impressionism in both painting and literature as a "subjective conception of truth," an "attempt to reproduce objects in the external world in the precise manner in which they impressed the beholder," from the American writer and critic Hamlin Garland, with whom he was friendly in the early 1890s (25). Allan Gardner Smith concurs with Wertheim's judgment that Crane evidently had little firsthand knowledge of the theory and techniques of the visual arts, but he identifies a source other than Garland for the idea that Crane expresses in the passage in question, that the apprehension of "reality" consists of "the subjective experience of the individual in responding to sensory data and combining them into an impression" (240). This concept may parallel the epistemological stance of French Impressionism, Smith says, but a more likely source is the philosophical and psychological *zeitgeist* of Crane's era, best represented by William James's 1890 *Principles of Psychology*, in which consciousness is described as follows:

> Out of what is in itself an indistinguishable, swarming *continuum*, devoid of distinction or emphasis, our senses make for us, by attending to this notion and ignoring that, a world full of contrasts, of sharp accents, of abrupt changes of picturesque light and shade. (qtd. in Smith 242)

Despite the similarity of this phrasing to Crane's in places, Smith does not argue that Crane necessarily read this work; he points out that James's ideas were in the air in the intellectual circle in which Crane moved, which included James's brother Henry, so that Crane could scarcely have missed them.

Bert Bender takes a somewhat different tack, arguing that if the San Luis de Caney chapel passage reveals that Crane was aware of the works of some Impressionist painters, it reveals equally that he never contemplated those works with any high degree of insight, for the Impressionist aesthetic is in Bender's view much different from the one Crane espouses here and calls Impressionism. The Impressionists, Bender explains, "are concerned with the reality of their sensations, a reality which is objectively verifiable on the lighted surfaces of things and which is inextricably involved with their techniques of rendering it" (50), whereas Crane in this passage as elsewhere is concerned with "metaphysics, not the physics of light; his 'mental' or spiritual 'light and shade' affect his soul, not his retina, as do the received sensations of lighted surfaces recorded by the impressionists" (52).

Relationship to Other Crane Works

Milne Holton notes that the two scenes in this story in which the narrator contemplates a corpse seem to have antecedents in Crane's earlier war writings. The image of a number of men exhausted after the attack on Camp McCalla, lying around Surgeon Gibbs's corpse recalls a similar scene in a Greco-Turkish War dispatch, "Stephen Crane Tells of War's Horrors" (*Reports* 53–56), in which dead and wounded soldiers lie intermingled on a troop transport. In "Memories," though, Holton says, Crane makes his point more clearly, that here is "the center of war's reality—death hidden among the unseeing, sleeping soldiers" (252). The image of the red-headed Spaniard killed at San Juan links to the corpse in the forest chapel scene in *The Red Badge of Courage* and to one of a Greek youth in another Greco-Turkish dispatch, "A Fragment of Velestino" (*Reports* 27–44). Again, however, Holton discerns differences as well as similarities among these three scenes. Whereas in *Red Badge* Crane uses the corpse to evoke "the grotesque terror of the event of apprehension" and in "Velestino" to reveal the "delusion which leads the soldier to his death," in "Memories" his point is precisely that there is no meaning, not even the revelation of a delusion, in the Spaniard's death (254).

Halliburton sees a similarly purposeful progression to a lack of meaning in the relationship between the forest chapel scene in *Red Badge* and the scene in the chapel of San Luis de Caney in "Memories." The ecclesiastical aspect of the former situation, Halliburton notes, is figurative, produced in Henry's mind, while in the latter the fact that the chapel is literal indicates Crane's view that this scene that *ought* to have figurative meaning does not—that instead the suffering of the wounded lacks any higher meaning, or any meaning at all; the narrator himself, as Halliburton points out, says that the image he has just described is meaningless and simultaneously "overwhelming, crushing, monstrous," perhaps precisely because it is meaningless (177–78).

Several critics have traced connections as well between this story and Crane's non-war fiction. James B. Colvert says of the chapel scene that it demonstrates that Crane's imagination conditioned what he chose to see and report on when he experienced war for himself, for the main imagistic elements of this scene—"the altar, the gloomy cave, the priestlike spectral man, the garish lights, and the vague aura of sacrilege"—are all present in one of Crane's earliest pieces, the Sullivan County sketch "Four Men in a Cave," written in 1892. Thus, Colvert concludes, these elements are not simply products of Crane's firsthand observation at El Caney; rather, they are primarily "radical elements of Crane's imagination" (xxxii–xxxiii). (Colvert also makes this point on p. 148 of another essay, "Stephen Crane: Style as Invention.") Marston LaFrance links the story to another fairly early piece, the 1894 "Experiment in Misery," in that both are framed by comments from the protagonist about the difficulties involved in communicating "'the real thing,'" experience, to anyone else, with the difference that in the more mature "Memories" these remarks are more subtle and more self-reflexively ironic (232–33).

Holton addresses perhaps the broadest parallels. He views "Memories" as one of a set of stories, also including "The Five White Mice," "Flanagan and His Short Filibustering Adventure," and "An Episode of War," which have ironic endings that "deny the very [stories] they conclude" (83–84); further, he discerns a link between this story, as well as all the others in *Wounds in the Rain*, and the Whilomville tales. These two groups, he says, are alike in being relatively lengthy story cycles to which Crane turned late in his life for specific reasons: the stories of Whilomville are his "coming to terms with the communally shaped delusions of his past," while "Memories" and *Wounds* as a whole constitute an effort to come to terms with the present, "a summary attempt to order the experiences and significances of his confrontation with an absurd reality" in the maelstrom of war (256).

Critical Studies

Beginning with Crane's early biographer Beer, a number of critics have judged this story a failure. Beer traces its problem to what he feels is Crane's weakness of tone, his assumption of the attitude of "a nervous and embarrassed spectator at an imbecile and ill-rehearsed show," possibly a result of his having seen for himself in the events on which "Memories" is based the true mental and physical horrors of war (198). E. R. Hagemann likewise locates the flaw in Crane's attitude, asserting that Vernall's complaint about his inability "'to get the real thing'" stems from Crane's own feelings of inadequacy regarding his ability to understand and report war. Such feelings are unwarranted, Hagemann argues, given the high degree of realism in Crane's Spanish-American War material (357), but they may be seen as having a constricting effect on Crane's artistic powers nonetheless, impelling him to confine himself to realism defined strictly as an accurate rendering of external physical details, eschewing imaginative sympathy with and psychological insight into his characters.

Two critics focus on this particular problem in the *Wounds in the Rain* stories. Donald B. Gibson says that, despite their basis in Crane's personal experience, none of this group possesses "outstanding merit" due to their all being "only surface accounts of human experience" (97). Solomon examines this issue in more detail with specific reference to "Memories." Taking note of numerous passages describing the American regular troops in action, such as "One cannot speak of it—the spectacle of the common man serenely doing his work, his appointed work. It is the one thing in the universe which makes one fling expression to the winds and be satisfied to simply feel," quoted more fully above in the "Sources and Influences" section, Solomon argues that they constitute a refusal on Crane's part to "apply any further analysis to motives or to the meaning of courage and fear in war." As a result, Solomon concludes, Crane forfeits "the power of sympathetic projection that accounts for the brilliant portraits of Fleming, Collins, and Peza" in *The Red Badge of Courage*, "A Mystery of Heroism," and "Death and the Child," respectively, a loss that renders "Memories" and the rest of the *Wounds in the Rain* pieces nothing more than "grim, inflexible sketches, totally lacking the tension and emotional complexity of his previous war fiction" (74).

In another camp, however, many readers find this story quite successful due to Crane's choices of tone and point of view. Stallman rates it the best piece in *Wounds in the Rain* due to its tight-lipped realism and concomitant lack of sentimentalism, leavened by his mellow attitude—his willingness to recall "the finer side of warfare" and to praise generously most of his former colleagues—which Stallman considers a result of his temporal distance from the events in question by the time he got around to recounting them here, over a year after the fact (397). Regarding point of view, Edwin Cady argues that Vernall's "Shelleyan cries and the self-consciousness about expression and the real thing" that open the story are not indications of a sense of inadequacy on Crane's part but rather "a strategic insincerity" to alert the reader to Crane's definition of "'the real thing'" in literature. Specifically, they serve notice that the author "is embarking on a long series of pictures which will not 'tell life' but present it unmistakably to a reader" (135), an approach that, in not only Cady's view but also LaFrance's, does not obviate sympathetic projection into the characters on either Crane's or the reader's part but rather increases the emotional response. Noting the narrator's comment that the sight of American Regulars attacking San Juan Hill in a calm, matter-of-fact manner "is the one thing in the universe which makes one fling expression to the winds and be satisfied to simply feel" (*Tales* 249), LaFrance says that Crane's point is that "[t]he real thing is never seen or heard: it is the moral reality which the aware mind perceives within or beyond the literal event, the life which is masked by the mere fact" (233). Thus, LaFrance continues, when the narrator concludes with the disclaimer that he has told the reader nothing, he is correct in the sense that "the nameless Regular's expert professionalism, his stoic acceptance of suffering, his brotherhood, his quiet courage in the face of death, and Crane's overwhelming response to such realities are not *things* which can be communicated in factual reports," but Crane's achievement in this story is that he presents the mere facts in such a way that a reader possessed of an aware mind "never has to probe beyond this surface to respond to the force of the writing" (234). Crane evokes this response, LaFrance explains, by means of structure and imagistic technique. Each of the incidents in the story "begins with the external event . . . and it progresses to the moral reality beyond the literal event." This reality, which is the narrator's mental grasp of and emotional response to the literal event, "is communicated by bringing each episode to a taut emotional climax expressed either in images of intense silence"—as in the description of the Regulars' attack on San Juan Hill—"or in images which exist only within Vernall's haunted mind as it leaps beyond the observed event"—as in the comparison to French Impressionism that concludes the description of the church of San Luis de Caney (234).

Holton, Halliburton, and Chester L. Wolford share Cady's and LaFrance's high estimation of Crane's technical skill in this story, but they argue that this skill is purposefully aimed at producing ambiguity, not clear emotional insight. Holton says that the "flat and negative" nature of the ending is not the culmination of a strategic insincerity leading to intimations of moral reality but rather an assertion that for the narrator, and presumably for Crane himself, "the absurd reality of war is even less understandable as one increases his temporal and spatial distance from it" (255). Halliburton, like LaFrance, takes note of the episodic character of "Memories," but he sees it as "organized around scenes in which key figure-types are represented as sublime or ironic, or both" (173), a design of paradox whereby the narrator is depicted "as a man in a dream experiencing brief interludes of reality that, far from providing an overview of his situation, merely tell him about his immediate physical state" (176).

Wolford notes the connection of the name "Vernall" to *vernal*, green, which describes the correspondent's state relative to war at the outset; the story details his progression from that condition of innocence to experience. Such a journey is customary for Crane's protagonists, Wolford notes, but he points out further that in this case experience does not lead to an insight into truth. Vernall's remarks on the impossibility of getting "'the real thing,'" Wolford says, show that now "misperception is taken for granted," that "Crane no longer rails against those trying to create false order out of chaos, no longer believes that he can discover meaning . . . in the temporary apprehension of reality in a fragment of time" (74). With this failure of belief in epiphany in view, Crane employs an episodic structure here not to "build toward such an apprehension. Instead, . . . Crane now provides a series of events designed for a cumulative effect. No one of these will get the real thing, but perhaps in the accumulation there will be something" (74–75).

The first aspect of this "something" emerges, according to Wolford, in the early episode in which the narrator and several fellow-correspondents on a press boat are knocked in various directions by a bunch of bananas that hangs in their stateroom and swings around wildly in response to the pitching of the ship, an encounter that the narrator compares to the causes and effects of war: "You see? War! A bunch of bananas rampant because the ship rolled" (*Tales* 222). With war thus established as merely a dangerous product of chance, the second aspect of "something" takes shape in the episodes describing Regulars under fire, which reveal Crane's new understanding, totally without irony, of simply doing one's duty in absurd conditions of chance as the highest form of heroism; his admiration for the Regulars' discharging of their responsibilities, Wolford notes, stems from his recognition that "the group behaves well for no apparent reason" (76). Allied to this proto-existentialist stance, the third aspect comes across in the ending of the story—"several pages describing confusion and chaos" and the narrator's protests that he has revealed nothing, which collectively reveal that "the only certainty is a lack of certainty" (76).

In addition to his remarks noted above, Holton offers some further illuminating insights into Crane's technique in "Memories." Specifically, he sees this story as exemplifying a new development in Crane's handling of images. Whereas in his previous work Crane relied heavily on "the purely descriptive image—the image as element in purely impressionistic rendering," in "Memories" such images occur with less frequency, giving way to images that are not parts of a larger descriptive whole but rather are "set apart from their background," seeming isolated and gratuitous (250). Crane's goal here, Holton says, is twofold. First, the isolation of these images is designed to present them "almost as if they are the real concretization of recollection," a characteristic by which he seeks to "dramatize the process of memory," showing it fixing upon seemingly meaningless objects that nonetheless carry meaning within the memory of the individual (250). Second, and allied to their burden of meaning, these images function, almost expressionistically, as "parts of a system which bear crucial thematic import" (250), as is the case when Crane fixes upon the simultaneous gratuitousness and dangerousness of the bunch of swinging bananas to emblematize war, and when he uses the near-ramming of the press boat by the gunboat *Machias* to symbolize "the massive blindness of the force of war" (251).

Swann also scrutinizes the imagery of "Memories" for its simultaneous conveyance of gratuitousness and danger. Unlike Holton, however, he sees it doing so as part of an impressionist rendering that he regards as not purely descriptive. Regarding the description of the church of San Luis de Caney, he says that "[t]he impressionist technique, for Crane, is not an end in itself. The method is to one end—to achieve an effect which will render a perception that the world is at once without meaning *and* threatening" (99). This perception, Swann argues, conveys Crane's major insight in the area of epistemology, for its ultimate implication is that "[t]he world that Crane sees is one without sense, in which any impression of order or control comes from the imposition of a fictional pattern—but in which that fiction is itself illusory and should be perceived as such" (100).

Works Cited

Ahnebrink, Lars. *The Beginnings of Naturalism in American Fiction*. Cambridge: Harvard University Press, 1950.

Beer, Thomas. *Stephen Crane: A Study in American Letters*. New York: Knopf, 1923.

Bender, Bert. "Hanging Stephen Crane in the Impressionist Museum." *Journal of Aesthetics and Art Criticism* 35 (1976):47–55.

Berryman, John. *Stephen Crane*. New York: Sloane, 1950.

Bowers, Fredson. Textual Introduction. *Tales of War*. Vol. 6 of The University of Virginia Edition of *The Works of Stephen Crane*. Ed. Fredson Bowers. Charlottesville: University Press of Virginia, 1970, xxxvii–cxci.

Cady, Edwin H. *Stephen Crane*. Rev. ed. New York: Twayne, 1982.

Colvert, James B. Introduction. *Tales of War* xi–xxxvi.

———. "Stephen Crane: Style as Invention." *Stephen Crane in Transition: Centenary Essays*. Ed. Joseph Katz. DeKalb: Northern Illinois University Press, 1972, 127–52.

Crane, Stephen. "In the First Land Fight Four of Our Men Are Killed." *Reports of War*. Vol. 9 of The University of Virginia Edition of *The Works of Stephen Crane*. Ed. Fredson Bowers. Charlottesville: University Press of Virginia, 1971, 128–30.

————. "Narrow Escape of the Three Friends." *Reports of War* 118–20.

————. "The Private's Story." *Reports of War* 196–98.

————. "The Red Badge of Courage Was His Wig-Wag Flag." *Reports of War* 134–42.

————. "Stephen Crane Tells of War's Horrors." *Reports of War* 53–56.

————. "Stephen Crane's Vivid Story of the Battle of San Juan." *Reports of War* 154–66.

————. "War Memories." *Tales of War* 222–263.

Gibson, Donald B. *The Fiction of Stephen Crane*. Carbondale: Southern Illinois University Press, 1968.

Hagemann, E. R. "Crane's 'Real' War in His Short Stories." *American Quarterly* 8 (1956):356–67.

Halliburton, David. *The Color of the Sky: A Study of Stephen Crane*. Cambridge: Cambridge University Press, 1989.

Holton, Milne. *Cylinder of Vision: The Fiction and Journalistic Writings of Stephen Crane*. Baton Rouge: Louisiana State University Press, 1972.

Kwiat, Joseph J. "Stephen Crane and Painting." *American Quarterly* 4 (1952):331–38.

LaFrance, Marston. *A Reading of Stephen Crane*. Oxford: Clarendon, 1971.

Nagel, James. *Stephen Crane and Literary Impressionism*. University Park: Pennsylvania State University Press, 1980.

Overland, Orm. "The Impressionism of Stephen Crane: A Study in Style and Technique." *America Norvegica* 61 (1966):239–85.

Smith, Allan Gardner. "Stephen Crane, Impressionism, and William James." *Revue Française d'Études Americaines* 18 (1983):237–48.

Solomon, Eric. "Stephen Crane's War Stories." *Texas Studies in Literature and Language* 3 (1961):67–80.

Stallman, R. W. *Stephen Crane: A Biography*. New York: George Braziller, 1968.

Swann, Charles. "Stephen Crane and a Problem of Interpretation." *Literature and History* 7 (1981):91–123.

Wertheim, Stanley. "Crane and Garland: The Education of an Impressionist." *North Dakota Quarterly* 35 (1967):23–28.

Wertheim, Stanley, and Paul Sorrentino, eds. *The Correspondence of Stephen Crane*. 2 vols. New York: Columbia University Press, 1988.

Wolford, Chester L. *Stephen Crane: A Study of the Short Fiction*. Boston: Twayne, 1989.

The Wise Men

Publication History

This story made its first appearance in America on pages 1–19 of *The Lanthorn Book*, a collection of pieces that various writers had read at the Lanthorn Club, a New York City literary society to which Crane belonged. This volume, privately published in 1898, was limited to 125 copies, all of which were signed by the authors represented. In England, the story first ran in the April 1898 issue of the *Ludgate Monthly* (594–603). It was then collected in the American book *"The Open Boat" and Other Tales of Adventure*, published by Doubleday & McClure in April 1898, and in the English volume *"The Open Boat" and Other Stories*, published the same month by Heinemann (Bowers cxlix). Wilson Follett, editor of *The Work of Stephen Crane* (12 vols., New York: Knopf, 1925–27), placed it in volume 12, published in 1927; and Thomas A. Gullason included it in his 1963 *Complete Short Stories and Sketches of Stephen Crane* (Garden City, N.Y.: Doubleday).

Circumstances of Composition

In a June 1897 letter from England, Crane asks his brother Edmund to search for the manuscripts of two stories, "The Five White Mice" and "The Wise Men," among the possessions he left at Edmund's house in the village of Hartwood, New York, and to send them to him immediately, presumably so that he could prepare them for sale (*Correspondence* I, 292). On the basis of this letter and several other circumstances, J. C. Levenson persuasively deduces that Crane wrote "Wise Men" while he was staying with Edmund and his family in Hartwood during the spring and summer of 1896. Levenson points out that Crane could not have written the story earlier than this period, because after his trip to the West and Mexico in the early months of 1895 as a correspondent for the Bacheller syndicate, which gave him the basis for it, he was occupied first with completing his novel *George's Mother* and then with writing and publishing journalistic accounts of the trip, as well as with other matters that kept him busy until he left New York City for Hartwood in the spring of 1896. After his return to the city following this period of rustication, Levenson continues, Crane was equally preoccupied, first defending himself against the harassments of the metropolitan police resulting from his accusations that the arrest of an acquaintance of his, Dora Clark, for prostitution was groundless, and then attempting to deal with the allegations of an actress and theater critic, Amy Leslie, that he had jilted and defrauded her (xli–xlii). These problems and other matters impelled Crane to leave the city and state of New York permanently, aside from a few brief visits, in November of 1896. Therefore, Levenson concludes, he would have had no chance to leave manuscripts at Edmund's house after his 1896 sojourn there—a fact that, in combination with the other conditions detailed above, makes this sojourn the only logical period in which Crane could have composed those manuscripts (xli).

Sources and Influences

Various of Crane's biographers have noted the close connections between this story and his own experiences during his trip to the West and Mexico. Levenson, Robert W. Stallman, and Milne Holton all assert that the protagonists, the New York Kid and the San Francisco Kid, are based respectively on Crane himself and Charles Gardner, a young engineer from Chicago with whom Crane traveled from San Antonio to Mexico City and who also appears as the "Chicago capitalist" in several of the newspaper sketches Crane wrote about the trip (Levenson xxxvi–xxxvii; Stallman 147; Holton 122). While not explicitly disagreeing with these identifications, John Berryman suggests that the two Kids are Crane's division of the two parts of his own nature, the Eastern and the Western. Berryman also adds another identification, although from a different part of Crane's past: he says that the Kids' antagonist, Wilburson, who, the narrator says, "worked; not too much, though" (*Tales* 32), is based on Crane's own "indolent" brother Wilbur (112).

Despite these particulars of character, no one has discovered any mention by Crane of a specific event of gambling on foot races during his trip from which he might have derived the plot of this story. It is not hard to imagine him taking part in such an escapade, but the link between story and trip is clear enough without this kind of one-to-one correspondence. As Levenson notes, the lighthearted "Wise Men" plainly stems in a general way from the sense of liberation that Crane, a preacher's kid from small-town America, felt upon discovering that in Mexico City—in the larger world, that is—many people regarded drinking and gambling as "play rather than corruption" (xlii).

Relationship to Other Crane Works

Surprisingly, given that "Wise Men" shares a number of elements with "The Five White Mice"—including the New York and San Francisco Kids, Freddie the bartender, a Mexico City setting, and a focus on games of chance—very little has been written about the relationship between these two, or between

"Wise Men" and any other Crane story. This circumstance may be a result of a general consensus that this story is rather slight. Chester L. Wolford asserts, for example, that by itself it seems to have little meaning "other than that of dumb luck making an ironical comment on the 'wisdom' of the title" (38). But this assessment should actually make clear the need for more study of the story in the context of Crane's other work; as Wolford goes on to note, when it is read in "counterpoint" to "White Mice," with the latter story's focus on violent death averted by the New York Kid's trusting to chance, as opposed to the concentration in "Wise Men" on the role of chance in the outcome of a mere foot race, what emerges is the point that chance rules in all the games of life, whether those games are insignificant or vital. With this fact in view, these stories combine to assert that the key to obtaining the most favorable odds in any such game is maintaining self-control through recourse to ritual: the two Kids' conscious preservation of a façade of nonchalance in "Wise Men" and the New York Kid's repetition of the "five white mice of chance" refrain in "White Mice" (Wolford 38).

Critical Studies

In a eulogy for Crane, H. G. Wells expressed great admiration for this story, calling it "a perfect thing" and saying that "I cannot imagine how it could possibly have been better told" (qtd. in Gullason 131). Many subsequent critics, however, while not disputing that the story is an excellent example of its kind, are in accord with Wolford's opinion, noted above, that this kind, with its limitation to an ironic focus on the connection between luck and perceived wisdom—to the insight that "[a]ccident dominates an inchoate society," in Thomas Beer's formulation (216)—is itself distinctly minor. In direct response to Wells, Stallman says of "Wise Men" that "[a]part from its autobiographical interest, it is scarcely worth mentioning" (147). Holton concurs with this view, judging the story to be "little more than a sardonic report of a remembered event" that lacks both a consistent point of view and a meaningful insight of any sort (131–32).

Marston LaFrance offers an assessment that agrees more closely with Wells's; he rates the story as "slight" but goes on to note that "it is one of Crane's happiest," sustaining "the warmest tone to be found in his work" and exemplifying the best traits of his humor (72). Only Levenson regards "Wise Men" as providing more than a minor statement about dumb luck. He argues that Crane intends for the reader to perceive the Kids' wisdom as located "not so much in their discernment or their luck as in their style." In a vein similar to Wolford's assertion, noted above in "Relationship to Other Crane Works," that "Wise Men" and "White Mice" together make the point that the secret of success in a world of chance is maintaining control of oneself, Levenson says that the effective style the Kids discover here is understatement, the conscious preservation of an appearance of nonchalance, which constitutes "the test of self-discipline . . . in the midst of purported vice" (xliii).

Works Cited

Beer, Thomas. *Stephen Crane: A Study in American Letters*. New York: Knopf, 1923.

Berryman, John. *Stephen Crane*. New York: Sloane, 1950.

Bowers, Fredson. Textual Introduction. *Tales of Adventure*. Vol. 5 of The University of Virginia Edition of *The Works of Stephen Crane*. Ed. Fredson Bowers. Charlottesville: University Press of Virginia, 1970, cxxxiii–cxcv.

Crane, Stephen. "The Wise Men: A Detail of American Life in Mexico." *Tales of Adventure* 26–38.

Holton, Milne. *Cylinder of Vision: The Fiction and Journalistic Writings of Stephen Crane*. Baton Rouge: Louisiana State University Press, 1972.

LaFrance, Marston. *A Reading of Stephen Crane*. Oxford: Clarendon, 1971.

Levenson, J. C. Introduction. *Tales of Adventure* xv–cxxxii.

Stallman, R. W. *Stephen Crane: A Biography*. New York: George Braziller, 1968.

Wells, H. G. "Stephen Crane from an English Standpoint." *North American Review* 171 (August 1900):233–42. Rpt. in *Stephen Crane's Career: Perspectives and Evaluations*. Ed. Thomas A. Gullason. New York: New York University Press, 1972, 126–34.

Wertheim, Stanley, and Paul Sorrentino, eds. *The Correspondence of Stephen Crane*. Vol. 1. New York: Columbia University Press, 1988.

Wolford, Chester L. *Stephen Crane: A Study of the Short Fiction*. Boston: Twayne, 1989.

General Index

Aaron, Daniel, 201, 202, 279, 280, 283
Absurdism, 149, 150, 250
Academy, 441
Adams, Richard, 304, 316, 317, 319, 347
Ahnebrink, Lars, 14, 25, 26, 54, 101, 111, 116, 125, 130, 136, 144, 156, 197, 202, 238, 262, 275, 283, 363, 370, 377, 380, 404, 407, 413, 416, 443, 451
Ainslee's Magazine, 181, 392, 417
Alger, Horatio, 228
Anderson, Margaret, 239, 262
Anderson, Warren D., 95, 98
Anglo-Saxon Review, 440, 441
Askew, Melvin, 40, 54
Atlantic Monthly, The, 11, 178
Audubon, John James, 53–54
Autrey, Max, 320, 334, 347

Bacheller, Irving, 167
Bacheller newspaper syndicate, 12, 63, 95, 115, 143, 159, 177, 178, 221, 238, 274, 285, 296, 311, 352, 363, 376, 412, 453
Baker, Louise, 114
Bakhtin, Mikhail, 336
Balaclava, Battle of, 218
Barnes, Robert, 66, 78
Barr, Mark, 182
Barr, Robert, 267
Barthes, Roland, 306
Bassan, Maurice, 15, 45, 55, 63, 78, 108, 111, 124–25, 126–27, 131, 132, 133, 136, 257, 262, 315, 347
Bates, H. E., 7, 9, 83, 84, 87, 88, 140, 142, 187, 188, 215, 218, 219, 386, 387, 391, 410, 411
Beaver, Harold, 365, 370
Beer, Thomas, 5–6, 9, 12, 13, 14, 55, 69,

78, 82, 84, 97, 99, 101, 111, 116, 128–29, 131, 136, 144, 149, 150, 156, 172, 176, 212, 221, 229, 234, 235, 237, 262, 267, 273, 286, 294, 352, 359, 375–76, 380, 408, 411, 444, 448, 451, 455, 456
Bellman, Samuel I., 62, 78
Bender, Bert, 47, 55, 315, 328, 341, 342, 347, 446, 451
Benfey, Christopher, 18, 45–46, 55, 61, 78, 103, 111, 172, 176, 233, 255, 263, 299, 300, 305, 308, 347, 401, 402, 403, 423, 426
Bennett, Sanford, 235
Benveniste, Emile, 306
Bergon, Frank, 15, 17, 20, 22, 24, 34, 35, 43, 53, 54, 55, 67, 69, 72, 76, 78, 109, 110, 111, 133, 136, 151, 155, 156, 226–27, 229, 257, 260–61, 263, 269, 270, 271, 273, 280, 283, 286–87, 288, 291–92, 294, 308, 323, 327, 338, 339, 344, 347, 357, 358, 359, 423, 426, 432, 433
Bernard, Kenneth, 66, 78
Berryman, John, 8, 9, 14, 18, 39, 44, 55, 61, 78, 97, 98, 99–100, 111, 116, 121, 145, 150, 156, 158–59, 162, 163, 169, 170, 172, 176, 217, 219, 236, 256, 257, 263, 267, 273, 290, 291, 294, 298, 299, 339, 347, 356, 357, 360, 363, 366, 370, 376, 379, 380, 408, 411, 414, 416, 421, 422, 426, 428, 433, 438, 439, 441, 445, 451, 454, 456
Berthoff, Warner, 176, 261
Bierce, Ambrose, 2, 104, 197–98, 276
Black and White, 89, 99
Blackwood's Edinburgh Magazine, 7, 204, 361

Bliss, P. P., 330
Bonner, Thomas, Jr., 135, 136
Borodino, Battle of, 101, 116
Boutwell, 298
Bowers, Fredson, 1, 4, 5, 9, 11, 55, 60,
    78, 81, 84, 88, 89, 98, 99, 111, 113,
    114, 121, 123, 136, 138, 142, 143,
    156, 158, 163, 164, 166, 167, 170,
    171, 176, 178, 180, 181, 182, 184,
    185, 188, 189, 194, 195, 202, 203,
    204, 206, 207, 211, 215, 216, 219,
    220, 229, 233, 234, 263, 266, 273,
    274, 283, 285, 294, 296, 347, 352,
    353, 360, 361, 370, 371, 372,
    374–75, 380, 381, 383, 384, 387,
    388, 391, 392–93, 395, 398, 399,
    400, 403, 407, 411, 412, 416, 417,
    426, 427, 434, 435, 439–40, 451,
    453, 456
Brennan, Joseph X., 333–34, 347
Brett, Olive, 408
Bridgman, L. J., 114
Brown, Bill, 345–46, 347
Brown, Ellen A., 8, 10, 141, 142, 175,
    176, 190, 195, 410, 411
Buffalo Commercial, 177, 285
Buitenhuis, Peter, 325, 326, 333, 347
Bunner, H. C., 125
Burgess, Anthony, 343
Burnett, Frances Hodgson, 8
Burns, Landon, 317, 319, 347
Burns, Shannon, 66, 72–73, 74, 78

Cady, Edwin H., 6, 10, 12, 13, 20, 27, 35,
    43, 54, 55, 66, 78, 90, 94, 98, 129,
    136, 149, 157, 233, 234, 243, 256,
    263, 291, 294, 299, 300, 309, 310,
    319, 334, 347, 366–67, 368, 370,
    402, 403, 448–49, 451
Camus, Albert, 325
Carney, Raymond, 421, 426
Cate, Hollis, 51–52, 55
Cather, Willa, 166, 353, 360
*The Century Illustrated Monthly
    Magazine,* 11, 116, 125, 178, 197,
    220, 221, 234, 250, 275
Cervera, Pascual, 165
Chametzky, Jules, 14, 55, 303, 347
Chancellorsville, Battle of, 197, 432
Chapman, George, 23
Chapman's Magazine, 60, 195
Chicago Inter-Ocean, 403

Chicago Times-Herald, 89, 167, 274
Chicago Tribune, 399
Christophersen, Bill, 425, 426
Church, Joseph, 253–54, 263
Churchill, Lady Randolph, 440, 441
Cincinnati Enquirer, 399
Civil War, 91, 115, 116, 167, 168, 178,
    196, 197, 198, 199, 201, 205, 252,
    274, 275, 276, 277, 365, 378, 404,
    408, 419, 420, 428, 438
Clark, Dora, 143, 236, 237, 238, 453
Clarke, Willis B., 212
Collier's Weekly, 10, 165, 371
Collins, Michael, 41, 42, 55, 72, 73–74,
    79, 149–50, 157
Colorado, Ramon, 286
Colvert, James B., 12, 13, 16–17, 55, 62,
    67, 79, 102–03, 111, 115, 122, 125,
    126, 131, 133, 136, 159, 163, 168,
    169, 170, 178, 180, 196, 199, 200,
    202, 204, 205, 206, 232, 234, 236,
    239, 260, 263, 269, 273, 274–75,
    276, 278–79, 283, 286, 290, 294,
    300, 308–09, 310, 314, 331–32, 340,
    347, 354, 356, 360, 363–64, 367,
    368, 370, 375, 380, 404, 405, 407,
    408, 411, 421, 423, 426, 428, 429,
    434, 447, 451
Colwell, J. C., 371–72, 373
Commodore, 61, 159, 160, 162, 296,
    297, 298, 299, 304, 306, 307, 308,
    311, 336, 345
Conder, John J., 26–27, 55, 317–18, 321,
    348
Conrad, Joseph, 1, 40, 47, 101, 181, 223,
    235, 243, 304, 311, 314, 367, 393,
    417, 444
Cook, Robert G., 75, 79
Cooley, John R., 252, 260, 263
Cornhill Magazine, 164, 171, 374, 375
Cosmopolitan, 361
Cox, James T., 26, 31, 55
Crane, Cora—see *Stewart, Cora
    Howorth*
Crane, Edmund (brother), 5–6, 8, 60,
    115, 143, 144, 178, 196, 220, 235,
    275, 285, 389, 404, 428, 453, 454
Crane, Helen (niece), 182, 441
Crane, Jonathan Townley (brother),
    299, 354
Crane, Mary Helen Peck (mother), 384
Crane, Wilbur (brother), 454

Crane, William (brother), 60, 159, 207, 235, 353, 389
The Criterion, 243
The Critic, 196
Crouse, Nellie, 168, 286, 290, 291
Cuzco, Battle of, 231, 232, 233, 442

Daily Journal (Dayton, Ohio), 352
Darwinism, 148, 224, 289, 317, 318
Davidson, Richard A., 30–31, 56
Davis, Richard Harding, 90, 166
Day, Cyrus, 298–99, 348
De Forest, John William, 116, 197, 276
Deamer, Robert Glen, 15, 21–22, 37, 43, 56, 63, 66–67, 79, 95–96, 98, 144, 148, 150–51, 157, 221, 222, 223, 229, 238, 263, 269, 270, 272, 273, 287, 291, 294, 311, 348, 363, 370, 376–77, 380, 415, 416
Dean, James L., 21, 56, 64, 79, 145, 157, 267, 269, 271, 273
Deconstruction, 248, 253
Degas, Edgar, 102
Delbanco, Andrew, 249–50, 263
Delbanco, Nicholas, 116, 122, 428–29, 434
Denny, Neville, 70–71, 79, 87, 88, 140, 141, 142, 175, 176, 212, 215, 221, 229, 288, 295, 315, 322, 323, 328, 348, 422, 426
Denver Republican, 403
Dewey, John, 328
Dickens, Charles, 304
Dillingham, William B., 32–33, 56, 420, 424–25, 426
Ditsky, John, 343–44, 348
Dolmetsch, Carl, 178
Dolphin, 232, 442
Dow, Eddy, 345, 348
Draper, Herbert, 418
Dreiser, Theodore, 129

Earp, Wyatt, 74, 78
Eliot, T. S., 23
Elliott, George. F., 232–33, 442
Ellis, James, 36, 56
Ellison, Ralph, 15, 56, 74, 79, 240, 250, 252, 263, 322, 328, 348
English Illustrated Magazine, 63, 167, 177, 381, 403
Existentialism, 36, 46, 74, 108, 154, 226, 228, 256, 281, 315, 319, 323, 324–28, 450

Expressionism, 53, 293, 425, 451

Faulkner, William, 45
Ferguson, S. C., 66, 79
Fiedler, Leslie, 8, 10
Fitzgerald, John, 232, 442
Flynt, Thomas, 125
Follett, Wilson, 1, 5, 11, 60, 81, 85, 89, 99, 115, 123, 138, 143, 158, 164, 167, 171, 178, 181, 185, 189, 195, 203, 207, 211, 216, 220, 230, 234, 266, 274, 285, 296, 353, 361, 371, 374, 381, 384, 388, 392, 395, 399, 404, 407, 412, 417, 427, 435, 440, 453
Forbes-Robertson, Johnston, 417
Ford, Ford Madox, 47, 56, 61, 155, 157
Foster, Malcolm, 251–52, 263
Frank Leslie's Popular Monthly, 1, 266, 435
Frederic, Barry, 212
Frederic, Harold, 61, 101, 103, 112, 182, 208, 212, 234–35, 243
Frederic, Helen, 207
Frederic, Héloise, 212
Frederick, John T., 315, 316, 348
Fredericksburg, Battle of, 196, 197
French, Warren, 268, 270, 271, 273, 430, 434
Freud, Sigmund, 41, 42, 73, 111, 428
Freudianism, 39–40, 73, 97, 105, 155, 236, 253, 255, 428
Frewen, Moreton, 441
Fried, Michael, 110–11, 112, 242, 263, 420–21, 426, 429–30, 434
Frus, Phyllis, 305–07, 348
Frye, Northrop, 42, 73, 149

Gardner, Charles, 145, 454
Gargano, James W., 275, 280, 283
Garland, Hamlin, 172, 199, 445
Garnett, Edward, 105, 112, 132, 136, 174, 177
Geismar, Maxwell, 18, 56, 65, 79, 105, 107, 108, 112, 115, 122, 174, 177, 200, 201, 202, 255, 263, 279, 281, 283, 318, 349, 379, 380
The Gentlewoman, 113, 114
Gerlach, John, 76, 77, 79
Germanic, 171
Gerstenberger, Donna, 325–26, 327, 328, 335, 349

Gibbs, John Blair, 2, 418, 442, 446
Gibson, Donald B., 20, 38–39, 56, 68,
    69, 79, 91, 97, 98, 104, 107, 112,
    118, 120, 122, 131, 136, 147–48,
    157, 179, 180, 198, 200, 201, 202,
    227, 228, 229, 243, 244, 246, 247,
    250, 263, 269, 273, 277–78, 281,
    283, 288, 290, 291, 295, 320, 334,
    338, 340, 341, 342, 349, 383, 415,
    416, 422, 426, 431, 434, 448, 452
Gilder, Richard Watson, 220, 234, 243,
    250
Gilkes, Lillian, 95, 98, 252, 263
Girard, René, 43–44
Gleckner, Robert F., 16, 35–36, 49, 56,
    311, 349
Goethe, Johann Wolfgang von, 44, 445
Going, William, 304, 316, 349
Gordon, Frederic, 124
Goss, Warren, 197, 276
Goya, Francisco José de, 421
Greco-Turkish War, 1, 16, 100, 182, 367,
    382, 393, 419, 441, 446
Greene, Nelson, 167, 168
Greenfield, Stanley B., 28–29, 30, 56,
    319, 328, 334, 349
Grenberg, Bruce L., 30–31, 56
Griffith, Clark, 37, 56, 318, 349
Gross, David S., 42–43, 56, 228–29
Gullason, Thomas A., 1, 5, 8, 10, 11, 20,
    35, 56, 60, 72, 79, 81, 83, 84, 85, 88,
    89, 99, 104, 112, 115, 123, 132, 137,
    138, 141, 142, 143, 158, 164, 166,
    167, 169, 171, 173, 174, 177, 178,
    180, 181, 185, 187, 188, 189, 193,
    195, 198, 200, 202, 203, 204, 206,
    207, 210, 211, 214, 215, 216, 217,
    219, 220, 223, 229, 234, 248, 257,
    258–59, 263–64, 266, 274, 282, 283,
    285, 296, 315, 339, 349, 353, 361,
    365, 367–68, 370, 371, 374, 379,
    380, 381, 384, 385, 387, 388, 389,
    392, 395–96, 399, 401, 403, 404–05,
    407, 408, 411, 412, 417, 427, 432,
    434, 435, 437, 440, 453, 455,
Gunn, Drewery Wayne, 146, 157

Hafley, James, 247, 248, 258, 264
Hagemann, E. R., 91, 98, 165, 166, 199,
    202, 205, 206, 341, 342, 349, 364,
    365, 370, 377, 378, 380, 418, 437,
    438, 440, 448, 452

Halliburton, David, 9, 10, 19, 36, 56, 64,
    65, 68, 79, 86, 88, 103, 106, 112,
    140, 141, 142, 152–53, 156, 157,
    186, 188, 189, 239, 254, 257, 264,
    280, 302, 303, 304, 308, 311, 327,
    349, 357, 358, 360, 362, 365, 366,
    368, 369, 370, 433, 434, 443, 447,
    449, 452
Hare, James, 165
Harper's New Monthly Magazine, 5, 11,
    81, 84, 138, 171, 173, 185, 187, 189,
    207, 211, 213, 216, 234, 266, 384,
    385, 388, 390, 395, 397, 407
Harper's Weekly, 99, 197, 276
Harris, Catherine, 128
Harte, Bret, 267, 272, 413
Hawkins, Willis Brooks, 196, 285, 286
Hawthorne, Nathaniel, 334
Hearst, William Randolph, 89, 100, 203,
    204, 231, 361
Heidegger, Martin, 156
Hemingway, Ernest, 303
Hernlund, Patricia, 190, 195
Herzberg, Max, 167
Hickock, Wild Bill (James Butler), 66,
    74, 78
Higgins, William, 297, 304
Hilfer, Anthony Channell, 244, 264
Hind, C. Lewis, 441
Hinman, Wilbur F., 197, 276
Hoffman, Daniel G., 91, 92, 94, 98, 129,
    137, 146, 157, 240, 264, 313, 349,
    378, 380
Hogarth, William, 126
Holton, Milne, 3, 4, 6, 10, 15, 19, 29–30,
    35, 51, 57, 63, 67, 70, 74, 75, 79, 82,
    84, 87, 88, 96, 97, 98, 106–07, 108,
    112, 118, 119, 122, 128, 137, 141,
    142, 145, 152, 153, 157, 161–62,
    163, 165, 166, 169, 170, 172–73,
    175, 177, 179, 180, 183, 184, 186,
    188, 189, 190, 193, 194, 195, 201,
    202, 205, 206, 210, 211, 215, 218,
    219, 227, 229, 232, 233, 234, 238,
    239, 241, 245, 250–51, 253, 257,
    260, 264, 267–68, 269, 270, 273,
    275, 277, 282, 284, 292, 293, 295,
    310, 322–23, 324–25, 328, 338, 349,
    354, 356, 358, 360, 362, 368, 370,
    373, 374, 379–80, 382–83, 385, 387,
    390, 392, 394, 395, 402, 403,
    405–06, 407, 409, 410, 411, 414–15,

416, 419, 420, 421, 424, 426, 432, 433, 434, 439, 440, 446, 447, 449, 450, 451, 452, 454, 455, 456
Homer, 41, 95, 96
Horan, Mary, 401
Hough, Robert L., 53–54, 57
Howorth, Elizabeth, 396
Howorth, John, 396
Howells, William Dean, 35, 125, 199, 243, 257, 291, 355, 359, 366
Hughes, Rupert ("Chelifer"), 243, 264
Hume, Levi, 235, 237

Ibsen, Henrik, 238–39
Illustrated London News, 1, 158, 435
Impressionism, 44, 47, 48–49, 51, 65, 75, 110, 111, 121, 126, 134, 155, 162, 198, 199, 206, 292, 306, 315, 332–33, 355, 369, 406, 421, 425, 444–46, 450, 451
Itabashi, Yoshie, 129–30, 137
Itorbide, Miguel, 286
Ives, Charles B., 197, 198, 202, 258, 259, 264

Jackson, David H., 300, 349
James, Henry, 13, 77, 268, 446
James, Overton P., 68–69, 74, 79
James, William, 156, 250, 276–77, 328, 446
Johnsen, William A., 43–44, 57
Johnson, Clarence O., 135–36, 137
Johnson, George W., 24, 57, 69, 79, 120, 122, 258, 264, 281, 284, 424, 426
Johnson, Glen M., 293–94, 295
Jones, Edith Richie, 6, 10, 182, 396, 399
Joyce, James, 23
Jung, Carl, 41, 42, 174
Jungianism, 73

Kahn, Sy, 236, 237, 241, 245, 261, 264
Kansas City Star, 167, 177, 274, 285, 352, 403
Karlen, Arno, 121, 122, 257, 264, 414, 416
Katz, Joseph, 12, 57, 197, 202, 432, 434
Kazin, Alfred, 243, 264, 312, 349
Keats, John, 334, 335
Keenan, Richard, 26, 57
Kent, Thomas L., 51, 52, 57, 326, 327, 349
Kettle Hill, battle of, 376, 437

Kimball, Sue L., 52, 57
King, Clarence, 286–87
Kinnamon, Jon M., 13, 57
Kipling, Rudyard, 90–91, 94, 96, 200, 235, 279, 363, 367, 368, 377, 382, 443–44
Kissane, Leedice, 302, 315, 338, 349
Kitchell, John, 297
Kleist, Heinrich von, 304
Klotz, Marvin, 47, 57
Knapp, Bettina L., 54, 57, 71, 79, 107, 112, 119, 120, 121, 122, 134, 137, 175, 177, 180, 201, 202, 226, 229, 280, 284, 339, 350, 358, 360, 368, 369, 370, 422, 426, 433, 434
Knapp, Daniel, 44–45, 57, 246–47, 264
Krauth, Leland, 281, 284, 378, 381
Kronegger, M. E., 47, 57
Kwiat, Joseph J., 47, 57, 126, 137, 220, 229, 356, 444, 445, 452

Lacan, Jacques, 42
LaFrance, Marston, 16, 27–28, 29, 36–37, 57, 70, 79, 91, 95, 98, 107–08, 112, 117, 118, 119, 120, 122, 126, 127, 129, 137, 146, 147, 157, 169–70, 179, 181, 199, 202, 226, 228, 229, 241, 244, 258, 259, 264, 270, 273, 277, 278, 280–81, 284, 299, 301, 310, 311, 313–14, 321–22, 328, 331, 340, 350, 357, 358–59, 360, 365, 368, 369, 370, 377–78, 379, 381, 386, 387, 389, 391, 392, 405, 407, 413, 414, 415, 416, 423, 426, 431, 434, 437–38, 440, 447, 449, 452, 455, 456
Lane, John, 441
The Lanthorn Book, 453
Leaver, Florence, 46–47, 57, 282, 284
Leslie, Amy, 143, 454
Leslie's Weekly, 165, 443
Levenson, J. C., 5, 6, 7, 8, 10, 11, 12, 15–16, 33–34, 57, 61, 64, 65, 70, 79, 81, 84, 85, 87, 88, 100, 101, 103, 109, 112–13, 116, 122, 141, 142, 143–44, 145, 146, 151–52, 153, 155, 157, 159, 161, 163, 172, 173, 174, 175, 177, 185, 186, 187, 188, 189, 190, 192, 195, 207, 208, 210, 211, 212, 213, 214, 216, 219, 220, 222–23, 229, 235, 236, 241, 243, 260, 264, 266, 268, 270, 273, 285,

Levenson, J. C., *(continued)*, 286, 287–88, 291, 295, 297, 302, 303, 307, 324, 338, 350, 353, 354, 355, 356, 357, 358, 359, 360, 384, 386, 387, 388, 391, 392, 396, 397, 399, 408, 411, 412, 413–14, 415, 416, 432, 434, 453–54, 455, 456
Levernier, James A., 66, 72–73, 74, 78
Linder, Lyle, 186, 188, 189
Linson, Corwin Knapp, 116, 122, 124, 137, 275, 284, 286, 295, 353, 354, 360
London, Jack, 318
Lothrop, Harriet, 8
Ludgate Monthly, 453
Lyon, Kate, 182, 235
Lytle, Andrew, 304–05, 307, 330, 350

Machias, 442, 451
MacLean, Hugh, 31, 32, 57
Manet, Edouard, 102
Marcus, Mordecai, 321, 340, 341, 350
Marovitz, Sanford, 77, 78, 80
Marshall, Edward, 165, 436
Martin, Jay, 176, 261, 352, 360
Martin, John C., 140, 142, 173, 174, 177, 241–42, 264, 390, 392, 409, 411
Masterson, Bat (William Barclay), 74
Matthews, Brander, 125
Mayer, Charles W., 153–54, 157, 251, 253, 264, 286, 295, 406, 407
McCalla, Camp, 2, 231, 232, 418, 442, 446
McClure newspaper syndicate, 115, 159, 168, 178, 196, 203, 403, 404, 428
McClure, S. S., 196, 212, 231, 404, 428, 431
McClure's Magazine, 60, 158, 171, 195, 204, 230, 309, 400, 427
McCready, Ernest W., 165, 297, 372
McFarland, Ronald, 41, 57
McIntosh, Burr, 165, 443
Mencken, H. L., 20, 57
Merrick, John, 237
Metzger, C. R., 331, 350
Meyers, Robert, 329, 350
Michelangelo, 317
Minneapolis Tribune, 167, 177, 274, 352
Modernism, 43, 228, 425
Molle, Charles A., 334–35, 350
Monteiro, George, 17, 48, 57, 193, 195,

217, 218, 219, 255, 264, 268, 272, 273, 300, 302–03, 329, 330, 350
Montgomery, Charles B., 297, 298
Morace, Robert, 239, 240, 245–46, 264, 352, 360
Muhlestein, Daniel, 345, 350
Munroe, Lily Brandon, 354
Murphy, Brenda, 14, 58
Murphy, Edward, 159, 160, 161, 296, 297, 298–99, 304

Nagel, James, 9, 10, 19, 45, 48, 58, 65, 75–76, 80, 92, 97–98, 102, 103, 110, 113, 120–21, 122, 126, 127, 132–33, 137, 156, 157, 169, 170, 198, 201, 202, 206, 215, 216, 219, 223, 230, 242, 243, 265, 277, 282, 284, 305, 312, 323, 324, 328, 333, 341, 345, 350, 357–58, 360, 365, 368, 369, 370, 379, 381, 383, 397, 398, 399, 406, 407, 423, 427, 431, 433, 434, 438, 440, 444, 445, 452
Napier, James J., 337, 350
Narveson, Robert, 37–38, 58
Naturalism, 25–26, 28, 47, 75, 92, 109, 121, 134, 135–36, 153, 200, 201, 248, 256, 279, 316–19, 321, 326, 327, 329, 334, 421, 425
Nebraska State Journal, 177, 285, 352
Neglia, Erminio G., 13, 58
New Review, 285
New York Herald, 89, 165, 372, 399
New York Journal, 89, 100, 101, 165, 203, 231, 361, 376, 381, 382, 400, 436
New York Press, 123, 126, 241, 296, 309, 352, 353
New York Tribune, 145, 299, 354
New York World, 89, 143, 164, 165, 171, 203, 231, 361, 362, 372, 376, 381, 382, 400, 436, 442
Nietzsche, Friedrich, 327
Nihilism, 256
Norris, Frank, 125
Norton, Lady Caroline, 300, 301, 302
Noxon, Frank, 44
Nye, Russell B., 17, 58, 130, 137, 397, 398, 399

O'Donnell, Thomas F., 116, 122, 197, 202, 276, 284
Omaha Daily Bee, 274

O'Neill, Bucky, 165, 376
Osborn, Neal J., 19, 58, 92–93, 98, 261, 265, 268, 273
Overland, Orm, 292, 295, 332, 350, 444, 445, 452

Page, Walter Hines, 178, 180
Paine, Ralph D., 204, 206, 296, 297
Pall Mall Magazine, 181, 412
Paredes, Raymund A., 148–49, 157, 224–25, 230, 288–89, 290, 295
Parkman, Francis, 62
Patten, Simon, 346
Pease, Margery, 208
Pease, Michael, 207–08
Peck, George (grandfather), 190
Peck, Jonathan Kenyon (cousin), 190
Peirce, Charles Sanders, 304
Peirce, J. F., 53, 58
Perosa, Sergio, 133, 137, 315, 350
Peterson, C. T., 53–54, 58
Petry, Alice Hall, 77–78, 80, 126, 137, 237, 265
Philadelphia Enquirer, 403
Philadelphia Press, 274, 285
Phillips, John, 196
Piacentino, Edward, 301, 302, 350
Pilgrim, Tim A., 50, 58
Pinker, James B., 1, 7, 81, 85, 138, 164, 181–82, 185, 190, 266–67, 374–75, 377, 382, 393, 396, 400, 408, 412, 417, 435–36, 438, 441
Pittsburgh Leader, 403
Pizer, Donald, 16, 58, 239, 265, 310, 311, 350
Plato, 322
Pluralism, 130, 151–54
Pocket Magazine, 167, 177, 285
Poe, Edgar Allan, 116, 239
Postmodernism, 43, 228, 253, 425, 430
Pound, Ezra, 215
Pratt, Lyndon Upson, 144, 158
Proudfit, Charles, 40–41, 58
Pulitzer, Joseph, 89, 164, 171, 203, 204, 230, 361, 372

Quick, John, 232, 442

Ralph, Julian, 125
Randel, William, 297, 298, 350–51
Rath, Sura P., 334, 335–37, 351
Realism, 51, 52, 75, 199, 206, 331–32

Remington, Frederic, 291, 367
Reynolds, Paul Revere, 5, 11, 60, 89, 99, 164, 171, 204, 207, 212, 220, 231, 240, 297, 361, 400
Riis, Jacob, 125
Robertson, Jamie, 21–22, 43, 58, 63, 70, 80, 148–49, 152, 153, 158, 224–25, 226, 228, 230, 271, 273, 289–90, 295, 414, 416
Robinson, Cecil, 289, 295
Rogers, Rodney O., 47–48, 58, 109–10, 111, 113, 162–63, 333, 351, 369, 371
Romanticism, 242, 281, 303, 316, 421
Rooke, Constance, 32–33, 58
Roosevelt, Theodore, 220, 224, 233, 291, 367, 368, 436–37

St. James's Budget, 427
St. Louis Daily Globe-Democrat, 399
St. Paul, 372
St. Paul Pioneer Press, 403
San Francisco Chronicle, 167, 274
San Francisco Examiner, 89, 352, 403
San Juan, battle of, 362, 442, 443, 444, 446, 449
Sartre, Jean-Paul, 325
Satterwhite, Joseph N., 32, 58
Saturday Evening Post, 164, 374, 375, 381, 382, 435
Schellhorn, G. C., 358, 359, 360
Schirmer, Gregory, 339, 351
Schoberlin, Melvin, 208
Scott, Sir Walter, 268
Scovel, Sylvester, 165, 442
Scribner's Magazine, 11, 296
Shakespeare, Wiliam, 71
Shaw, Mary Neff, 334, 335–37, 351
Shroeder, John W., 25, 58, 109, 113, 256, 265, 279, 284, 429, 434
Shulman, Robert, 128, 131–32, 137, 312, 324, 327, 351
Sidbury, Edna Crane (niece), 235
Skerrett, Joseph T., 160–61, 162, 163, 304, 351
The Sketch, 352
Slote, Bernice, 12, 13, 58
Slotkin, Alan R., 135, 137
Smedley, William T., 302
Smith, Allan Gardner, 276–77, 284, 445–46, 452
Smith, Leverett T., 321, 351

Sojka, Gregory, 193
Solomon, Eric, 2, 3, 4, 9, 10, 25, 58, 72,
    80, 83, 84, 90, 91, 94, 98, 99,
    105–06, 107, 113, 121, 122, 141,
    142, 150, 158, 162, 163, 182,
    183–84, 187, 188, 189, 193, 194,
    195, 208, 210, 211, 214, 216, 227,
    228, 230, 244, 245, 257, 265, 267,
    268, 271, 272, 273, 280, 284, 287,
    295, 299, 319, 351, 363, 367, 368,
    371, 382, 383, 385–86, 387, 390,
    392, 393, 394, 395, 397, 398, 399,
    415, 416, 419, 420, 427, 430, 434,
    438, 440, 443–44, 448, 452
Somers N. Smith, 165
Sophocles, 247
Sorrentino, Paul, 10, 12, 59, 69, 80, 84,
    88, 99, 113, 114, 122, 123, 128, 137,
    138, 142, 158, 163, 166, 168, 170,
    171, 177, 181, 184, 189, 195, 203,
    204, 206, 211, 212, 216, 230, 234,
    265, 274, 284, 295, 351, 371, 374,
    381, 383, 400, 403, 407, 408, 411,
    416, 427, 434, 440, 452, 456
Spanish-American War, 1, 13, 89, 90, 95,
    106, 117, 127, 128, 164, 165, 171,
    182, 199, 203, 204, 207, 230, 231,
    233, 266, 267, 278, 352, 361, 364,
    365, 367, 371, 372, 373, 375, 379,
    381, 382, 393, 400, 402, 417, 418,
    419, 435, 436, 438, 441, 442, 443,
    448
Spofford, William K., 245, 265, 309,
    351
Stallman, Robert W., 2, 4, 6, 10, 11, 12,
    14, 17, 18, 34, 35, 40, 49, 54, 58, 60,
    61, 64, 71, 80, 82, 83, 84, 85, 87, 88,
    94, 99, 101, 104, 107, 113, 115, 116,
    117, 118, 120, 122, 123, 124, 131,
    132, 137, 139, 140, 142, 144, 145,
    158, 159, 161, 163, 165, 166, 171,
    172, 174, 177, 178, 181, 182, 184,
    185, 186, 188, 189, 197, 198, 203,
    206, 208, 210, 211, 212, 216, 217,
    219, 221, 223, 230, 231, 232, 234,
    235, 237, 241, 243, 250, 253, 265,
    267, 274, 275, 280, 284, 286, 288,
    295, 296, 297, 298, 307, 310, 313,
    315, 328, 337, 351, 352, 354, 358,
    360, 362, 366, 371, 372, 373, 374,
    376, 379, 381, 389, 392, 393, 395,
    397, 399–400, 401, 402, 403, 408,
    411, 412–13, 416, 417, 418, 421–22,
    427, 437, 439, 440, 441, 442, 444,
    448, 452, 454, 455, 456
Stangé, Émile, 124
Stappenbeck, Herb, 301, 302, 351
Starrett, Vincent, 352, 360
Stein, William Bysshe, 46, 47, 59, 72, 74,
    80, 154, 158, 256, 265, 281, 284,
    325, 351
Stevens, Wallace, 322
Stevenson, Robert Louis, 14
Stewart, Cora Howorth (Crane's com-
    mon-law wife), 1, 6, 61, 62, 65, 81,
    85, 89, 100, 114, 138, 139, 172, 181,
    185, 190, 203, 207–08, 212, 231,
    234, 236, 238, 266, 297, 361, 367,
    392, 396, 400, 417, 441
Stewart, Donald William, 61
Stewart, Randall, 329, 351
Stokes, Frederick, 400, 436
Stone, Edward, 44, 59, 300, 301, 351
Strand Magazine, 371
Stronks, James B., 7, 10, 59, 83, 84, 87,
    88, 140, 142, 187, 189, 218, 219,
    386, 388, 391, 392, 410, 411
Sullivan, Harry Stack, 40
Swann, Charles, 24, 59, 119, 122, 423,
    424, 427, 444, 451, 452

Tennenbaum, Ruth Betsy, 260, 265
Tennyson, Alfred, Lord, 217, 219
Thomas, R., 300
Thrall, Charles H., 400–01
Three Friends, 171, 172, 372, 442
Tibbetts, A. M., 66, 80
Tillotson newspaper syndicate, 375, 436
Tolstoy, Leo, 14, 35, 101, 116, 122, 144,
    145, 239, 275, 377, 404, 413, 443
Trachtenberg, Alan, 134–35, 137
Treves, Frederick, 237
Trilling, Lionel, 334
Triton, 372
Twain, Mark (Samuel L. Clemens), 14,
    144, 178, 213, 217, 267, 268, 303

Van Der Beets, Richard, 49, 59
Vanouse, Donald, 21, 43, 59, 62, 80,
    358, 360
Velestino, Second Battle of, 100, 101,
    103
Vorpahl, Ben Merchant, 70, 76, 80,
    225–26, 228, 230, 293, 295

Walcutt, Charles Child, 25, 26, 59, 247–48, 265
Walhout, Clarence, 342–43, 351
Walker, John Brisben, 361
Warner, Michael D., 154, 158, 248–49, 255, 265
Warshaver, Gerald, 18, 59
Webster, H. T., 276, 284
Weimer, David, 124, 130, 137
Weinig, Sister Mary Anthony, 23, 59
Weintraub, Stanley, 235, 265
Weiss, Daniel, 40, 41, 59, 154–55, 158
Wells, H. G., 104, 105, 113, 158, 314, 351, 455, 456
Wertheim, Stanley, 10, 12, 59, 69, 80, 84, 88, 99, 113, 117–18, 123, 128, 137, 138, 142, 158, 163, 166, 167, 168, 170, 171, 177, 181, 184, 189, 195, 203, 204, 206, 211, 212, 216, 230, 234, 236, 265, 274, 284, 295, 351, 360, 371, 374, 381, 383, 403, 407, 408, 411, 416, 427, 434, 440, 445, 452, 456
West, Ray B., 34–35, 59
Westbrook, Max, 18, 31–32, 59, 130, 138, 176, 177, 261–62, 265, 301, 302, 320, 321, 334, 352, 410, 411
Westminster Gazette, 203
Whitman, Walt, 92

Wilkeson, Frank, 197, 276
Willard, Josiah, 125
Wilson, Christopher P., 355–56, 360
Wister, Owen, 67, 291, 367
Wolford, Chester L., 2, 4, 9, 10, 15, 18, 23–24, 27, 59, 63, 64, 68, 71, 80, 82, 84, 86, 87, 88, 92, 96–97, 99, 107, 113, 115, 117, 118, 119, 123, 131, 138, 139–40, 142, 169, 170, 175–76, 177, 178, 179, 180, 181, 183, 184, 193, 194, 195, 198, 200–01, 203, 205, 206, 209, 210, 211, 213, 214, 216, 219, 223, 230, 241, 244, 245, 246, 247, 254, 256, 258, 265, 270, 271, 274, 277, 278, 280, 281, 284, 287, 292, 295, 308, 309, 327, 352, 356, 357, 358, 360, 365–66, 368, 371, 373, 374, 379, 381, 387, 388, 390, 392, 395, 398, 399, 402, 403, 405, 406, 407, 410, 411, 414, 416, 418, 419–20, 425, 427, 433, 434, 438, 440, 449, 450, 452, 455, 456
Wolter, Jürgen, 50–51, 59
Wordsworth, William, 108
Wycherley, Alan, 33, 59

The Youth's Companion, 113, 114, 115

Zola, Emile, 125–26

Index of Crane's Works

Active Service, 357
"'And If He Wills, We Must Die,'" 1–4,
    183, 393, 394, 418, 419
"The Angel Child," 5–10, 164, 207,
    208, 209, 211–12, 213, 240, 396,
    397, 409
"A Battle in Greece," 100

"The Black Dog," 128, 309
The Black Riders and Other Poems,
    191, 236, 308, 310
"The Blue Hotel," 8, 10–59, 63, 64, 65,
    66, 73, 74, 86, 93, 103, 110, 140,
    149, 200–01, 223, 232, 240–41,
    268, 269, 270, 282, 288, 304,
    310–11, 340, 379, 413, 414, 415,
    421, 428, 433
"Brer Washington's Conversion," 186
"The Bride Comes to Yellow Sky," 15,
    19, 20, 42, 60–80, 149, 225, 242,
    268, 269, 270, 271, 272, 282, 293,
    311, 356–57, 413, 414, 415, 420,
    433

"The Carriage-Lamps," 81–84, 86, 139,
    185, 187, 213, 240, 409
"Charity, Thou Art a Lie," 191
"Chased by a Big Spanish Man-o'-War,"
    372
"The City Urchin and the Chaste
    Villagers," 82, 84–88, 139, 140,
    187, 190, 240, 385, 386, 409
"The Clan of No-Name," 89–99, 117,
    199, 278, 365, 402, 431, 438
"Coney Island's Fading Days," 309
"Crane at Velestino," 100
"The Cry of a Huckleberry Pudding,"
    128, 147

"A Dark Brown Dog," 103
"Death and the Child," 16, 94, 99–113,
    240, 368, 382–83, 419–20, 421,
    422, 448
"The Dogs of War," 100
"The Duel That was Not Fought," 145

"An Episode of War," 64, 113–23, 162,
    222, 236, 275, 365, 366, 420, 447
"An Experiment in Luxury," 126, 127, 129
"An Experiment in Misery," 92, 96,
    123–38, 312, 447

"The Fight," 82, 85, 86, 87, 138–42, 240,
    385, 386, 397
"The Filibustering Industry," 160
"The Fire-Tribe and the White-Face,"
    419
"The Five White Mice," 42, 73, 74, 118,
    143–58, 162, 173, 220, 222, 223,
    224, 225, 269, 287, 288, 289, 311,
    357, 390, 413, 447, 453, 454, 455
"Flanagan and His Short Filibustering
    Adventure," 118, 158–63, 304, 307,
    308, 447
"Four Men in a Cave," 447
"A Fragment of Velestino," 100, 446–47
"A Freight Car Incident," 63

George's Mother, 17–18, 95, 125, 143,
    221, 238, 242, 259, 312, 333, 363,
    377, 453
"Ghosts on the Jersey Coast," 299, 309
"The Ghostly Sphinx of Metedeconk,"
    299
"'God Rest Ye, Merry Gentlemen,'"
    164–66, 205, 232, 364, 373, 376,
    400

"A Great Mistake," 103
"A Grey Sleeve," 167–70, 198, 356, 404–05

"His New Mittens," 140, 171–77, 241, 385, 390, 391, 398, 409
"The Holler Tree," 277

"The Ideal and the Real," 186
"An Illusion in Red and White," 266, 412
"In Heaven," 191
"In the Depths of a Coal Mine," 309
"In the First Land Fight Four of Our Men Are Killed," 231, 442
"An Indiana Campaign," 91, 177–81, 278, 431

"Joys of Seaside Life," 354

"The Kicking Twelfth," 1, 2, 3, 4, 181–84, 199, 393, 394, 418–19
"The Knife," 81, 185–89, 240, 254

Last Words, 1, 114, 181, 392, 417
"A Little Pilgrim," 189–95, 217, 240, 330, 386
"The Little Regiment," 16, 91, 115, 195–203, 277, 365
"The Little Regiment" and Other Episodes of the American Civil War, 3, 91, 114, 115, 117, 167, 169, 177, 179, 180, 183, 195, 274, 275, 277, 278–79, 282, 363–64, 394, 403, 404, 419, 427, 431
"The Lone Charge of William B. Perkins," 165, 203–06, 278, 364
"The Loss of an Arm" (alternate title for "An Episode of War"), 114
"The Lover and the Tell-Tale," 7, 207–211, 240, 385, 390, 396, 397
"Lynx-Hunting," 5, 7, 82–83, 86, 139, 211–16, 240, 409

Maggie: A Girl of the Streets, 17, 19, 20, 66, 93, 95, 125–26, 127, 140, 172, 173, 221, 236, 238, 240, 241, 242, 250, 259, 312, 314, 333, 340, 357, 363, 377, 390–91, 409, 410
"Making An Orator," 191, 216–19, 240
"The Making of the 307th" (alternate title for "Virtue in War"), 375, 435, 436

"A Man Adrift on a Slim Spar," 91, 312–13, 330
"A Man and Some Others," 15, 19, 64, 92, 96, 144, 146, 148, 151, 220–30, 269, 287, 288, 289, 293, 311, 312, 357, 358, 413, 415
"A Man by the Name of Mud," 145
"A Man Feared," 18, 63
"A Man Said to the Universe," 309
"Manacled," 266, 412
"Marines Signaling Under Fire at Guantánamo," 90, 165, 230–34, 373, 400, 402, 442
"Memoirs of a Private," 362
"The Men in the Storm," 124, 127, 312
"The Merry-Go-Round" (alternate title for "The Pace of Youth"), 352
"The Mesmeric Mountain," 18
"Midnight Sketches," 123
"The Monster," 8, 9, 18, 60, 65, 66, 74, 86, 93, 117, 140, 171, 175, 179–80, 186, 209, 214, 222, 234–65, 304, 339, 379, 390, 391, 397, 405, 409, 410, 420–21, 439
"The Monster" and Other Stories, 11, 171, 234, 266, 385, 412
"Moonlight on the Snow," 15, 19, 62–63, 64, 228, 266–74, 412, 413
"A Mystery of Heroism," 64, 91, 94, 105, 117, 168, 173, 179, 199, 205, 222, 274–84, 365, 366, 378, 390, 431, 448

"Narrow Escape of the Three Friends," 442

"An Ominous Baby," 103
"On the Boardwalk," 354
"One Dash—Horses," 63, 64, 144, 146, 148, 149, 222, 223, 224, 225, 269, 285–95, 311, 357, 366, 413, 420
"The Open Boat," 16–17, 19, 93, 103, 106, 110, 117, 132, 146–47, 149, 158, 159, 161, 162, 194, 223, 225, 232, 236, 238, 257, 288, 290, 296–352, 358, 405, 421, 433
"The Open Boat" and Other Stories, 60, 99, 123, 143, 158, 220, 285, 296, 352, 453
"The Open Boat" and Other Tales of Adventure, 60, 99, 143, 158, 220, 285, 296, 453

"The Pace of Youth," 20, 64, 65, 146, 168, 169, 222, 288, 309, 352–60

"The Price of the Harness," 91, 92, 106, 117, 128, 146–47, 165, 199, 205, 361–71, 378, 401, 402, 438

"The Private's Story," 362, 443

The Red Badge of Courage, 3, 17, 19, 20, 27, 64, 66, 93, 94, 95, 100–01, 102–03, 104, 106, 114, 115, 116, 117, 118, 121, 127, 146, 151, 167–68, 169, 173, 178, 180, 183, 184, 196, 197, 198, 199, 200, 204, 213, 214, 222, 232, 238, 242, 257, 259, 269, 274, 275, 276, 277, 278–79, 281, 282, 291, 292, 300, 302, 309, 310, 314, 324, 333, 339, 340, 345, 357, 363–64, 366, 367, 368, 394, 404, 405, 408, 419, 421, 428, 429, 430, 431, 432, 433, 446–47, 448

"The Red Badge of Courage Was His Wig-Wag Flag," 90, 231, 442

"Regulars Get No Glory," 362, 376

"The Reluctant Voyagers," 300, 308, 309

"The Revenge of the *Adolphus,*" 165, 232, 371–74, 400

"The Second Generation," 91, 165, 199, 365, 374–81, 402, 435–36, 437–38

"The Serjeant's Private Mad-house," 381–83

"Shame," 187, 240, 384–88, 397

"'Showin' Off,'" 173–74, 209, 240, 385, 388–92, 397

"The Shrapnel of Their Friends," 1, 2, 3, 4, 182–83, 392–95, 418, 419

"Six Years Afloat," 299

"Small Glowing Pebbles," 309

"The Snake," 420

"Stephen Crane at Velestino," 100, 101

"Stephen Crane Tells of War's Horrors," 446

"Stephen Crane's Own Story," 160, 162, 296, 297, 298, 299, 304, 305, 306–07, 316

"Stephen Crane's Pen Picture of C. H. Thrall," 400

"Stephen Crane's Vivid Story of the Battle of San Juan," 362, 442

"The Stove," 6, 7, 187, 209, 240, 395–399, 408

"Sullivan County Bears," 18

"A Texas Legend," 63

The Third Violet, 114, 168, 169, 196, 197, 314, 356

"This Majestic Lie," 399–403

"Three Miraculous Soldiers," 169, 198, 403–07

"To the Maiden," 309, 313

"The Trial, Execution, and Burial of Homer Phelps," 82, 86, 138, 139, 191, 240, 385, 397, 407–11

"Twelve O'Clock," 64, 266, 270, 400, 412–16

"Two or Three Angels," 192

"Uncle Jake and the Bell-Handle," 18

"The Upturned Face," 1, 2, 3, 64, 181, 183, 184, 242, 393, 394, 409, 417–27

"The Veteran," 15, 91, 92, 95, 96, 179, 213, 241, 269, 277, 278, 281, 304, 314, 366, 427–34

"Virtue in War," 91, 92, 199, 365–66, 374–75, 377–78, 402, 435–40

"War Memories," 47, 92, 102, 118, 127, 162, 232, 401–02, 418, 440–52

"West Pointer and Volunteer; Or, Virtue in War" (alternate title for "Virtue in War"), 375, 435

"When a People Reach the Top of a Hill," 313

Whilomville Stories, 5, 81, 84, 138, 185, 189, 207, 211, 216, 384, 388, 389, 395, 407

"The Wise Men," 143, 145, 151, 220, 287, 357, 453–56

"The Woof of Thin Red Threads" (alternate title for "The Price of the Harness"), 361

Wounds in the Rain, 3, 89, 91, 92, 96, 164, 165, 183, 203, 205, 230, 232, 233, 361, 363, 364, 365, 367, 371, 373, 374, 377, 381, 382, 394, 399, 419, 435, 436, 439, 440, 447, 448

"The Wreck of the *New Era,*" 299, 309